Redemption and Resistance

Redemption and Resistance

The Messianic Hopes of Jews and Christians
in Antiquity

Edited by

Markus Bockmuehl & James Carleton Paget

t&t clark

Published by T&T Clark
A Continuum imprint
The Tower Building, 11 York Road, London SE1 7NX
80 Maiden Lane, Suite 704, New York, NY 10038

www.continuumbooks.com

All rights reserved. No part of this publication may be reproduced or transmitted in any form or by any means, electronic or mechanical, including photocopying, recording or any information storage or retrieval system, without permission in writing from the publishers.

Copyright © Markus Bockmuehl & James Carleton Paget and contributors, 2009

First published in hardback, 2007

This edition published, 2009

British Library Cataloguing-in-Publication Data
A catalogue record for this book is available from the British Library

ISBN-10: 0-567-03044-X (paperback)
ISBN-13: 978-0-567-03044-3 (paperback)

Typeset by Free Range Book Design & Production Ltd
Printed on acid-free paper in Great Britain by the MPG Books Group, Bodmin and King's Lynn

Contents

List of Contributors	ix
List of Abbreviations	xiii
Preface – Raphael Loewe	xix
Introduction – *Markus Bockmuehl & James Carleton Paget*	xxi
PART I: ORIGINS OF JEWISH MESSIANIC EXPECTATION	1
Chapter 1. THE PERSIAN PERIOD – *Joachim Schaper*	3
Chapter 2. THE HASMONEAN PERIOD – *Jan Willem van Henten*	15
Chapter 3. THE HERODIAN PERIOD – *Sean Freyne*	29
Chapter 4. PLUTARCH'S LIFE OF NUMA: SOME OBSERVATIONS ON GRAECO-ROMAN 'MESSIANISM' – *Hans Dieter Betz*	44
PART II: THE NEW TESTAMENT	63
Chapter 5. RESISTANCE AND REDEMPTION IN THE JESUS TRADITION – *Markus Bockmuehl*	65
Chapter 6. MESSIANISM AND CHRISTOLOGY: MARK, MATTHEW, LUKE AND ACTS – *Graham Stanton*	78
Chapter 7. MESSIAH AND RESISTANCE IN THE GOSPEL AND EPISTLES OF JOHN – *Judith M. Lieu*	97
Chapter 8. THE CHRIST OF PAUL – *Andrew Chester*	109
Chapter 9. THE CATHOLIC EPISTLES AND HEBREWS – *David G. Horrell*	122
Chapter 10. THE APOCALYPSE – *Paul Spilsbury*	136
PART III: JEWISH AND CHRISTIAN MESSIANISM IN CONTACT AND CONTROVERSY	147
Chapter 11. MESSIANISM AND POLITICS IN THE LAND OF ISRAEL, 66–135 C.E. – *Martin Goodman*	149

Chapter 12. JEWS AND CHRISTIANS IN THE HOLY LAND, 135–325 C.E. – *Oskar Skarsaune*	158
Chapter 13. SYRIA AND MESOPOTAMIA: THE SHARED TERM *MALKA MSHIHA* – *Sebastian Brock*	171
Chapter 14. EGYPT – *James Carleton Paget*	183
Chapter 15. THE WEST AND NORTH AFRICA – *Wolfram Kinzig*	198
Chapter 16. MATERIAL REMAINS – *David Noy*	215
Chapter 17. THE RABBIS AND MESSIANISM – *Philip S. Alexander*	227
Chapter 18. MESSIANISM IN ANCIENT BIBLE TRANSLATIONS IN GREEK AND LATIN – *Alison Salvesen*	245
Chapter 19. MESSIANISM IN ANCIENT BIBLE TRANSLATIONS IN ARAMAIC AND SYRIAC – *Robert P. Gordon*	262
Chapter 20. JEWISH AND CHRISTIAN MESSIANIC HOPES IN PRE-ISLAMIC BYZANTIUM – *Nicholas de Lange*	274
Chapter 21. FALSE PROPHET, FALSE MESSIAH AND THE RELIGIOUS SCENE IN SEVENTH-CENTURY JERUSALEM – *Guy G. Stroumsa*	285
Appendix: William Horbury's Publications	297
Works Cited	303
Index of Ancient Sources	351
Index of Authors	371
Index of Subjects	379

DOCTISSIMO AC DILECTISSIMO
IUDAICAE NECNON CHRISTIANAE SPEI MAGISTRO

WILLIAM HORBURY

AMICI DISCIPULIQUE HOC FLORILEGIO
PIAM GRATIAM AGUNT
AD DIEM NATALEM SEXAGESIMUM QUINTUM

LIST OF CONTRIBUTORS

1. **Philip S. Alexander** is Professor of Post-Biblical Studies at the University of Manchester and Co-Director of its Centre for Jewish Studies. His published research on Judaism in the Second Temple and Talmudic periods ranges widely across the fields of ancient history and geography, biblical interpretation, mysticism, magic, the Dead Sea Scrolls and the Jewish background to Christian origins; recent works include *The Targum of Canticles*, The Aramaic Bible 17A (London: T&T Clark, 2003) and *Mystical Texts*, Companion to the Qumran Scrolls 7 (London: T & T Clark International, 2006).
2. **Hans Dieter Betz** is Shailer Mathews Professor of New Testament Studies (emeritus) at the University of Chicago. His research and writing involve the early Christian literature in its Hellenistic cultural and religious environment. Major publications include Hermeneia Commentaries on Galatians, 2 Corinthians 8 and 9, The Sermon on the Mount (Minneapolis: Fortress Press, 1979, 1985, 1995); *Gesammelte Aufsätze* I–IV (Tübingen: Mohr Siebeck, 1990–8); *The 'Mithras Liturgy'* (Tübingen: Mohr Siebeck, 2003).
3. **Markus Bockmuehl** is Professor of Biblical and Early Christian Studies at the University of St Andrews, and in 2007 will move to a similar chair at the University of Oxford. His publications include *The Epistle to the Philippians* (Peabody: Hendrickson, 1998); (ed.) *The Cambridge Companion to Jesus* (Cambridge: Cambridge University Press, 2001); and *Seeing the Word: Refocusing New Testament Study* (Grand Rapids: Baker Academic, 2006).
4. **Sebastian Brock** is an Emeritus Fellow of Wolfson College, Oxford, and formerly Reader in Syriac Studies in the University of Oxford. He is a Fellow of the British Academy and his publications include *The Luminous Eye: the Spiritual World Vision of St Ephrem* (Kalamazoo: Cistercian, 1992); *From Ephrem to Romanos* (Aldershot: Ashgate, 1999); and *Fire from Heaven* (Aldershot: Ashgate, 2006).
5. **James Carleton Paget** is a Senior Lecturer in New Testament Studies at the University of Cambridge and Fellow of Peterhouse. He is the author of *The Epistle of Barnabas: Outline and Background* (Tübingen: Mohr Siebeck, 1994), and of a number of articles on subjects connected with Christian origins.
6. **Andrew Chester** is Lecturer in New Testament Studies, and Fellow of Selwyn College, in the University of Cambridge. Among his publications is *Divine Revelation and Divine Titles in the Pentateuchal Targumim* (Tübingen: Mohr Siebeck, 1986).
7. **Nicholas de Lange** is Professor of Hebrew and Jewish Studies in the University of Cambridge and a Fellow of Wolfson College. He is a co-editor of the *Bulletin of Judaeo-Greek Studies*. Among his publications is *Greek Jewish Texts from the Cairo Genizah* (Tübingen: J. C. B. Mohr, 1996).

8. **Sean Freyne** is former Professor of Theology at Trinity College, Dublin, and currently Director of its Centre for Mediterranean and Near Eastern Studies at the College. He is a Fellow of Trinity College, a Member of the Royal Irish Academy and a Trustee of the Chester Beatty Library, Dublin. Among his recent publications are *Galilee And Gospel: Collected Essays* (Tübingen: Mohr Siebeck, 2000); *Texts, Contexts And Cultures: Essays On Biblical Topics* (Dublin: Veritas, 2002); *Jesus, a Jewish Galilean: A New Reading of the Jesus Story* (London: T&T Clark, 2004).
9. **Martin Goodman** is Professor of Jewish Studies in the University of Oxford. He is a Fellow of Wolfson College and also a Fellow of the Oxford Centre for Hebrew and Jewish Studies. He has published a number of books, including *Rome and Jerusalem: The Clash of Ancient Civilizations* (London: Penguin, 2007).
10. **Robert P. Gordon** is Regius Professor of Hebrew in the University of Cambridge, and Fellow of St Catharine's College, Cambridge. His publications include *Studies in the Targum to the Twelve Prophets: From Nahum to Malachi* (Leiden: Brill, 1994); *The Old Testament in Syriac according to the Peshitta Version: Chronicles* (Leiden: Brill, 1998); *Hebrew Bible and Ancient Versions* (Aldershot: Ashgate, 2006).
11. **David G. Horrell** is Reader in New Testament Studies at the University of Exeter. His publications include *The Social Ethos of the Corinthian Correspondence* (Edinburgh: T&T Clark, 1996); *The Epistles of Peter and Jude* (London: Epworth, 1998); and *Solidarity and Difference: A Contemporary Reading of Paul's Ethics* (London: T&T Clark, 2005).
12. **Wolfram Kinzig** is Professor of Church History (Patristics) at the Evangelical-Theological Seminary of the University of Bonn and Speaker (Director) of the 'Centre for Religion and Society' (ZERG) at the same university. His publications include *In Search of Asterius* (Göttingen: Vandenhoeck & Ruprecht, 1990); *Novitas Christiana* (Göttingen: Vandenhoeck & Ruprecht, 1994); and *Harnack, Marcion und das Judentum* (Leipzig: Evangelische Verlagsanstalt, 2004).
13. **Judith M. Lieu** is Professor of New Testament Studies at King's College London. Her publications include *Christian Identity in the Jewish and Graeco-Roman World* (Oxford: Oxford University Press, 2004) and *Neither Jew nor Greek: Constructing Early Christianity* (Edinburgh: T&T Clark, 2003); she has co-edited with J. W. Rogerson, *The Oxford Handbook of Biblical Studies* (Oxford: Oxford University Press, 2006), and with Charlotte Hempel, *Biblical Traditions in Transmission: Essays in Honour of Michael A. Knibb* (Leiden: Brill, 2006).
14. **Raphael Loewe** is Goldsmid Professor of Hebrew (Emeritus) at University College London. Among his many and wide-ranging academic publications are *The Jewish Midrashim and Patristic and Scholastic Exegesis of the Bible* (Berlin: Akademie-Verlag, 1957) and *Ibn Gabirol* (London: Halban, 1990). In the year 2000 the literary quality of his work on editions of the Rylands, Barcelona and Rothschild Haggadah was awarded Cambridge University's Seatonian Prize for the best English poem on a sacred subject.
15. **David Noy** teaches for the University of Wales Lampeter and the Open University. He is the author of *Jewish Inscriptions of Western Europe* volumes 1 & 2 (Cambridge: Cambridge University Press, 1993 & 1995) and *Foreigners at Rome* (London/ Swansea: Duckworth/Classical Press of Wales, 2000), and co-

author of *Inscriptiones Judaicae Orientis* volumes 1 & 3 (Tübingen: Mohr Siebeck, 2004).

16. **Alison Salvesen** is a University Research Lecturer at the Oriental Institute, University of Oxford, a Fellow in Jewish Bible Versions at the Oxford Centre for Hebrew and Jewish Studies, and Supernumerary Fellow, Mansfield College. Her publications include *Symmachus in the Pentateuch* (Manchester: Manchester University Press, 1991) and *I-II Samuel in the Syriac Version of Jacob of Edessa* (Leiden: Brill, 1999).

17. **Joachim Schaper** is Professor of Hebrew, Old Testament and Early Jewish Studies, and teaches at the University of Aberdeen. Among his recent publications are *Priester und Leviten im achämenidischen Juda* (Forschungen zum Alten Testament 31; Tübingen: Mohr Siebeck, 2000) and *'Wie der Hirsch lechzt nach frischem Wasser ...': Literarische, biblisch-theologische und religionsgeschichtliche Studien zu Psalm 42/43* (Biblisch-theologische Studien 63; Neukirchen-Vluyn: Neukirchener Verlag, 2004).

18. **Oskar Skarsaune** is Professor of Church History at MF Norwegian School of Theology (Det teologiske Menighetsfakultet, Oslo), a Fellow of The Norwegian Academy of Science and Letters, and a Fellow of The Royal Norwegian Society of Sciences and Letters. His publications include *The Proof from Prophecy: A Study of Justin Martyr's Proof-Text Tradition* (Brill: Leiden, 1987); *Incarnation: Myth or Fact?* (St Louis: Concordia Publishing House, 1991); *In the Shadow of the Temple: Jewish Influences on Early Christianity* (Downers Grove: InterVarsity Press, 2002); *We Have Found the Messiah: Jewish Believers in Jesus in Antiquity* (Jerusalem: Caspari Center, 2005).

19. **Paul Spilsbury** is Professor of New Testament at Canadian Theological Seminary in Calgary, Alberta. His publications include *The Image of the Jew in Flavius Josephus' Paraphrase of the Bible* (Tübingen: Mohr Siebeck, 1998); *The Throne, the Lamb and the Dragon: a Reader's Guide to the Book of Revelation* (Downers Grove: IVP, 2002); and *Flavius Josephus, Judean Antiquities 8–10: Translation and Commentary* (Leiden: Brill, 2005).

20. **Graham Stanton** is Lady Margaret's Professor of Divinity in the University of Cambridge, and a Fellow of Fitzwilliam College. His publications include *Jesus and Gospel* (Cambridge: Cambridge University Press, 2004); *The Gospels and Jesus*, Oxford Bible Series (Oxford: Oxford University Press, 2nd edition 2002); *A Gospel for a New People: Studies in Matthew* (Edinburgh: T&T Clark, 1992; Louisville: Westminster / John Knox, 1993).

21. **Guy G. Stroumsa** is Martin Buber Professor of Comparative Religion at the Hebrew University, where he was the founding Director of the Center for the Study of Christianity. Among his publications are *Barbarian Philosophy: the Religious Revolution of Early Christianity* (Tübingen: Mohr Siebeck, 1999) and *La fin du sacrifice: mutations religieuses de l'antiquité tardive* (Paris, 2005).

22. **Jan Willem van Henten** is Professor of New Testament, Early Christian and Hellenistic-Jewish Literature, and Head of the Department of Art, Religion and Culture at the University of Amsterdam. His publications include *The Maccabean Martyrs as Saviours of the Jewish People* (Leiden: Brill, 1997) and (with Friedrich Avemarie) *Martyrdom and Noble Death: Selected Texts from Graeco-Roman, Jewish, and Christian Antiquity* (London: Routledge, 2002).

Abbreviations

Biblical Abbreviations

Old Testament
Gen.	Genesis
Exod.	Exodus
Lev.	Leviticus
Num.	Numbers
Deut.	Deuteronomy
Judg.	Judges
1 Sam.	1 Samuel
1 Chr.	1 Chronicles
2 Chr.	2 Chronicles
Neh.	Nehemiah
Est.	Esther
Ps(s).	Psalm(s)
Prov.	Proverbs
Eccl.	Ecclesiastes
Song	Song of Songs
Isa.	Isaiah
Jer.	Jeremiah
Lam.	Lamentations
Ezek.	Ezekiel
Dan.	Daniel
Obad.	Obadiah
Mic.	Micah
Hab.	Habbakuk
Zeph.	Zephaniah
Hag.	Haggai
Zech.	Zechariah
Mal.	Malachi

New Testament
Mt.	Matthew
Mk	Mark
Lk.	Luke
Jn	John
Rom.	romans
1 Cor.	1 Corinthians
2 Cor.	2 Corinthians
Gal.	Galatians

Eph.	Ephesians
Phil.	Philippians
Col.	Colossians
1 Thess.	1 Thessalonians
2 Thess.	2 Thessalonians
1 Tim.	1 Timothy
2 Tim.	2 Timothy
Tit.	Titus
Phlm.	Philemon
Heb.	Hebrews
Jas	James
1 Pet.	1 Peter
2 Pet.	2 Peter
1 Jn	1 John
2 Jn	2 John
Rev.	Revelation

Abbreviations of all other ancient sources follow the *SBL Handbook of Style* (Peabody, MA: Henrickson, 1999).

Additional Abbreviations

AB	Anchor Bible
ABRL	Anchor Bible Reference Library
AGJU	Arbeiten zur Geschichte des antiken Judentums und des Urchristentums
AGLB	Aus der Geschichte der Latinischen Bibel
AnBib	Analecta biblica
ANRW	Hildegard Temporini and Wolfgang Haase (eds.), *Aufstieg und Niedergang der römischen Welt: Geschichte und Kultur Roms im Spiegel der neueren Forschung* (Berlin: W. de Gruyter, 1972–)
ANTZ	Arbeiten zur neutestamentlichen Theologie und Zeitgeschichte
ARW	*Archiv für Religionswissenschaft*
ATD	Das Alte Testament Deutsch
BARev	*Biblical Archaeology Review*
BBB	Bonner biblische Beiträge
BBET	Beiträge zur Biblischen Exegese und Theologie
BETL	Bibliotheca ephemeridum theologicarum lovaniensium
BEvT	Beiträge zur evangelischen Theologie
Bib	*Biblica*
BKAT	Biblischer Kommentar: Altes Testament
BNTC	Black's New Testament Commentaries
BO	*Bibliotheca orientalis*
BSO(A)S	*Bulletin of the School of Oriental (and African) Studies*

BZ	*Biblische Zeitschrift*
BZAW	Beihefte zur ZAW
BZNW	Beihefte zur ZNW
CBQ	*Catholic Biblical Quarterly*
CBQMS	*Catholic Biblical Quarterly*, Monograph Series
ConBOT	Coniectanea biblica, Old Testament
CP	Classical Philology
CPJ	*Corpus Payrorum Judaicarum*, eds V. A. Tcherikover, A. Fuks, M. Stern, 3 vols (Cambridge, MA: Harvard University Press, 1957–64)
CRINT	Compendia rerum iudaicarum ad Novum Testamentum
CSCO	Corpus scriptorum christianorum orientalium
DJD	Discoveries in the Judaean Desert
DNP	Der Neue Pauly
EJ	*Encyclopedia Judaica*
EKKNT	Evangelisch-Katholischer Kommentar zum Neuen Testament
ETL	*Ephemerides theologicae lovanienses*
FAT	Forschungen zum Alten Testament
FF	*Forschungen und Fortschritte*
FO	*Folia Orientalia*
FRLANT	Forschungen zur Religion und Literatur des Alten und Neuen Testaments
HAT	Handbuch zum Alten Testament
HDR	Harvard Dissertations in Religion
HKAT	Handkommentar zum Alten Testament
HKNT	Handkommentar zum Neuen Testament
HNT	Handbuch zum Neuen Testament
HTKNT	Herders theologischer Kommentar zum Neuen Testament
HTR	*Harvard Theological Review*
HUCA	*Hebrew Union College Annual*
ICC	International Critical Commentary
IEJ	*Israel Exploration Journal*
Int	*Interpretation*
ISBE	Geoffrey Bromiley (ed.), *The International Standard Bible Encyclopedia* (4 vols.; Grand Rapids: Eerdmans, rev. edn, 1979–88)
ITQ	*Irish Theological Quarterly*
JAAR	*Journal of the American Academy of Religion*
JAC	*Jahrbuch für Antike und Christentum*
JAOS	*Journal of the American Oriental Society*
JB	*Jerusalem Bible*
JBL	*Journal of Biblical Literature*
JECS	*Journal of Early Christian Studies*
JEH	*Journal of Ecclesiastical History*

JGRChrJ	*Journal of Greco-Roman Christianity and Judaism*
JIWE	*Jewish Inscriptions of Western Europe*, ed. D. Noy, 2 vols (Cambridge: Cambridge University Press, 1993–5)
JJS	*Journal of Jewish Studies*
JNES	*Journal of Near Eastern Studies*
JPOS	*Journal of the Palestine Oriental Society*
JQR	*Jewish Quarterly Review*
JR	*Journal of Religion*
JRS	*Journal of Roman Studies*
JSAI	*Jerusalem Studies in Arabic and Islam*
JSHJSup	*Journal for the Study of the Historical Jesus, Supplement Series*
JSJ	*Journal for the Study of Judaism in the Persian, Hellenistic and Roman Period*
JSNT	*Journal for the Study of the New Testament*
JSNTSup	*Journal for the Study of the New Testament, Supplement Series*
JSOT	*Journal for the Study of the Old Testament*
JSOTSup	*Journal for the Study of the Old Testament, Supplement Series*
JSP	*Journal for the Study of the Pseudepigrapha*
JSPSup	*Journal for the Study of the Pseudepigrapha, Supplement Series*
JTS	*Journal of Theological Studies*
KAT	Kommentar zum Alten Testament
MH	*Museum Helveticum*
Mus	*Le Muséum*
NovT	*Novum Testamentum*
NovTSup	*Novum Testamentum*, Supplements
NTAbh	Neutestamentliche Abhandlungen
NTD	Das Neue Testament Deutsch
NTOA	Novum Testamentum et orbis antiquus
NTS	*New Testament Studies*
OBO	Orbis Biblicus et Orientalis
OBT	Overtures to Biblical Theology
ParOr	*Parole de l'Orient*
PIBA	Proceedings of the Irish Biblical Association
PJ	*Palästina-Jahrbuch*
PL	J.-P. Migne (ed.), *Patrologia cursus completus Series prima [latina]* (221 vols.; Paris: J.-P. Migne, 1844–65)
PW	Pauly-Wissowa Realencyclopädie
RAC	*Reallexikon für Antike und Christentum*
RB	*Revue biblique*
REJ	*Revue des études juives*
RevQ	*Revue de Qumran*
RGG	*Religion in Geschichte und Gegenwart*

RHR	*Revue de l'histoire des religions*
RSR	*Recherches de science religieuse*
SACStudies	Studies in Antiquity and Christianity
SANT	Studien zum Alten und Neuen Testament
SBLMS	SBL Monograph Series
SBLRBS	SBL Resources for Biblical Study
SBLSCS	SBL Septuagint and Cognate Studies
SBS	Stuttgarter Bibelstudien
SBT	Studies in Biblical Theology
SC	Sources chrétiennes
ScrHier	*Scripta Hierosolymitana*
SemeiaSt	Semeia Studies
SJ	Studia judaica
SJLA	Studies in Judaism in Late Antiquity
SJT	*Scottish Journal of Theology*
SNT	Studien zum Neuen Testament
SNTSMS	Society for New Testament Studies Monograph Series
SP	*Sacra Pagina*
SPB	Studia Postbiblica
ST	*Studia theologica*
StPat	*Studia Patristica*
SUNT	Studien zur Umwelt des Neuen Testaments
TBei	*Theologische Beiträge*
TDNT	Gerhard Kittel and Gerhard Friedrich (eds.), *Theological Dictionary of the New Testament* (trans. Geoffrey W. Bromiley; 10 vols.; Grand Rapids: Eerdmans, 1964–)
TRE	*Theologische Realenzyklopädie*
TSAJ	Texte und Studien zum Antiken Judentum
TU	Texte und Untersuchungen
TynBul	*Tyndale Bulletin*
TZ	*Theologische Zeitschrift*
UCOP	University of Cambridge Oriental Studies
VC	*Vigiliae christianae*
VT	*Vetus Testamentum*
VTSup	*Vetus Testamentum*, Supplements
WBC	Word Biblical Commentary
WMANT	Wissenschaftliche Monographien zum Alten und Neuen Testament
WUNT	Wissenschaftliche Untersuchungen zum Neuen Testament
ZAW	*Zeitschrift für die alttestamentliche Wissenschaft*
ZDMG	*Zeitschrift der deutschen morgenländischen Gesellschaft*
ZKG	*Zeitschrift für Kirchengeschichte*
ZNW	*Zeitschrift für die neutestamentliche Wissenschaft*
ZTK	*Zeitschrift für Theologie und Kirche*

Preface

Raphael Loewe

It is a privilege of which I am deeply sensible to be invited to act as outrider to this volume, the distinction of which matches that of the scholar in whose honour it has been produced. A survey of the bibliography of William Horbury's publications, which it includes, reveals an ever-increasing width of his interest in Judaism, Christianity and the complexity of their interaction against the background of the late-antique and medieval history of the West.

The rigour in source-analysis and reconstruction of textual history displayed in his doctoral thesis, which concerned the *sefer toledot yeshu'*, was a harbinger of things to come, and it is a matter of satisfaction to me that he accepted my suggestion to take over the material regarding Jewish-Christian apologetics left unpublished by Samuel Krauss. It appeared in 1995 under both their names, Professor Horbury contributing (through his knowledge of church history) a dimension which would have eluded Krauss, despite his great scholarship. Through all William's work there shines a scrupulousness in the handling of evidence, be it linguistic, historical or literary, which while faithfully representing what the document under review contains is also sensitive to the presumptive attitudes, whether friendly or hostile, of those it addressed. No less enriching is his preparedness to look at source-material the potential value of which his predecessors had neglected. A good example is his study of suffering and messianism in the Hebrew liturgical poetry of Yose b. Yose (Horbury 1981). Such material calls for a niceness of judgement to recognize that rhetorical exaggeration, addressed to an internal, captive audience or readership, will not always correspond to the facts of social history. For this, as for much else, the world of scholarship owes him a debt of gratitude.

The theme of this volume is the interlinkage, in late antiquity, of messianism, redemption and resistance in the Jewish and Christian communities respectively. As contemporary events in the wider world remind us all too poignantly, that can be a heady mixture, with literally explosive potentialities. It is to the credit of some in the period concerned that, being aware of this, they implicitly advocated a policy of self-restraint. On the Jewish side, a fine example is provided by the Aramaic Targum of the Song of Songs (see Altmann 1966: 159–60). In this connection William's objectivity, combined with his appreciation of positive aspects in a religious system of which, though not his birthright, he has made himself master, can be an object-lesson to all. His scholarly standards are worthy of the Cambridge tradition which produced both Lightfoots, alongside whom he surely ranks. The University can well say, in words reminiscent of what the Talmud (*b. Sukkah* 53a) records from the celebrations in the temple of the water-libation festivities, *ashrey yaldutenu shello biyyesh et ziqnutenu* – our younger generation of scholars have done their elders proud.

Raphael Loewe

Introduction

Markus Bockmuehl & James Carleton Paget

Even if culturally jaded 'Old' Europeans may still regard eschatological or utopian hopes for communal and national regeneration as the relic of a bygone age, they are today bewilderingly alive and well in many parts of the world. They act as catalysts in political, cultural or religious tensions, sometimes in all of these at once. They find expression in tin-pot despots of Latin American or Central Asian republics, in militant imams of Wahhabi Islam, or in more classically Jewish and Christian forms exemplified in phenomena as diverse as an ultra-orthodox rabbi in Brooklyn or the apocalyptic scenarios characteristic of the *Left Behind* mentality of American fundamentalist subculture. Far from historically primitive or regressive, these are in fact deeply contemporary phenomena, 'post-modern' in the strict sense of that term. And yet they escape analysis unless one seeks to understand them in light of the classic formative texts and traditions of Jewish and Christian messianism.

Hope for the arrival of a definitive and divinely appointed redeemer figure, or for his return to finish the job, is in ancient Jewish and Christian sources invariably tied to discontent about the order of the world as it is: its enforcement of injustice and oppression, its seemingly unanswerable resentment or mockery of the biblical God and his people. It is highly apposite, therefore, to understand messianic hopes for *redemption* as closely related to convictions and practices of *resistance* to political or religious oppression, whether active or passive, whether 'internally' against competing messianisms of other Jews or other Christians, or 'externally' against pagan ideals.

The aim of the present volume is to offer such a contextual understanding of ancient Jewish and Christian convictions about redemption in the crossfire of resistance, on a plotline reaching from Old Testament origins via distinctive Jewish and Christian developments to the rise of Islam. While we are convinced it will repay reading from cover to cover as a meaningful survey, the organization of this book also facilitates the use of any given chapter as a specific starting point contextualized for the reader by the surrounding chapters.

Contributors were assigned specific chapter briefs within the book's overall outline, but the Editors deliberately did not prescribe a definition of the highly contested terms 'messianism', 'resistance' and 'redemption', inviting authors instead to let their usage reflect engagement with their respective texts. While this editorial decision undoubtedly makes a 'systematic' reading of ancient messianism harder to attain, it does have the advantage of leaving the results, however variegated, tied more closely to the contours of the respective ancient sources. (The important new synthesis of Fitzmyer 2007 unfortunately appeared too late to be considered here.) Several of the contributors pay careful attention to these definitional questions (including, for example, Philip Alexander on messianism and David Horrell on resistance).

The inspiration and occasion for this book are provided by the work of William Horbury, from whose teaching and publications over more than thirty-five years all the contributors have in different ways derived significant formative benefit. Among the scholarly themes he has championed are the prevalence and basic accord of Jewish messianic expectations; their extensive influence as well as transformation in the thought of the early Christians; points of contact and controversy between these groups and their beliefs, and the relationship between such messianism and contemporary Graeco-Roman ideologies of rulers and ruler cult. William Horbury is widely acclaimed as one of his generation's most learned writers on ancient Judaism and its relationship with early Christianity – the epitome of 'a scholar's scholar', as the *Scottish Journal of Theology* recently called him (Bakhos 2006). His many doctoral students, including this volume's editors and several of its other contributors, treasure a dedicated, indefatigable advisor whose knowledge of their dissertation topics, and photographic memory of the books they were reading and failing to read, invariably outstripped their own from the day of their arrival at Cambridge to the day of their departure.

Both in agreement with his scholarship and at times in respectful disagreement, the editors and contributors present this volume as a token of profound gratitude for William Horbury's unmatched Jewish and Christian scholarship, unfailingly conveyed with a graciousness and generosity that alone permit true learning and debate to flourish.

It remains for us to give a brief overview of how this book unfolds. The outline progresses through three fairly obvious stages, from the origins of Jewish messianic expectation via the Jesus Movement and the New Testament to the developing interaction, in contact and controversy, of Jewish and Christian messianisms, both with each other and with pagan outsiders.

Joachim Schaper opens Part I by examining the contested question of the aftermath of Davidic royal ideology in the post-exilic period. Beginning with the hopes for national renewal surrounding Zerubbabel and Joshua in the prophetic books of Zechariah and Haggai, Schaper draws on post-exilic portions of Isaiah and Micah as well as the redaction of the 'Messianic' Psalter (Pss. 2–89) to show the persistence of such hopes in diverse Judaean circles. He finds additional evidence in the contested question of Nehemiah's quasi-messianic status, in the Chronicler's development of Davidic motifs, and in the Greek Pentateuch. Both in the province of Yehud and in the Diaspora, Jewish messianic hopes developed out of inner-biblical interpretation.

Jan Willem van Henten moves the discussion on to the Hasmonean era, the only time in the Second Temple period when changed political circumstances allowed the formation of a successfully independent Jewish state. This took place in the crucible of Jewish identity facing severe external and internal challenges from Israel's newly reconfigured Hellenistic cultural context. Van Henten traces the development of diverse royal and priestly messianisms primarily in the Maccabean literature and at Qumran, concluding that both developments respond, directly or indirectly, to the Judaean crisis under Antiochus IV.

Introduction xxiii

In Chapter 3, Sean Freyne addresses the Herodian Period, beginning with the extraordinarily successful and yet religiously ambivalent reign of Herod the Great (37–4 B.C.E), who vigorously invested both in building the Jerusalem Temple and in promoting various centres of the imperial cult. Although himself never of more than doubtfully messianic significance, Herod evoked a series of popular reactions, in successive messianic claimants and movements that culminated in the great revolt against Rome. After the dominant militancy of the messianisms of Qumran and the *Psalms of Solomon*, some Jewish apocalyptic writings tended to develop a Messiah transformed into a transcendent figure who framed such hopes in terms of an end-time struggle of wider cosmic dimensions.

At the same time, as William Horbury has repeatedly stressed, these strands of Jewish messianism developed not only in the context of internal and external conflict, but also in lively relation with contemporary trends in Graeco-Roman hero and ruler cult. Hans Dieter Betz illustrates this point with a close reading of Plutarch's *Life of Numa Pompilius*, the second king of Rome who is for Plutarch vested with messianic significance extending to the discovery of his empty tomb and apotheosis.

In Part II of this volume we turn from Jewish and Graeco-Roman antecedents to the Jesus movement, where many of the same themes were taken up and in many cases transformed. In Chapter 5, Markus Bockmuehl approaches Jesus of Nazareth's messianism specifically through the question of how redemption and resistance cohere in his teaching and above all in his person – a question of considerable controversy in recent scholarly debate. Taking his cue from the subsequent Gospel tradition, Bockmuehl identifies a strongly recurrent theme of eschatologically motivated non-violent resistance to evil. Such resistance was comprehensively understood, and identified in both social and demonic terms, in individual or systemic idolatry, sexual immorality and the antisocial exploitation of capital or property.

In Chapter 6, Graham Stanton turns to the issue of messianism in the Synoptic Gospels. After highlighting the conceptual difficulties surrounding this question in the history of ancient as well as modern interpretation, Stanton examines the Synoptic traditions and appeals to analogies with some Qumran material in order to argue for a more messianic 'Q' than is usually entertained. This is harder to substantiate in Mark, but even his sparing use of χριστός is pointedly soteriological in nature. That theme is greatly enhanced in Matthew's critical emphasis on Jesus as Davidide and Son of God; it is also dramatically highlighted in Luke's infancy narratives, but much less prominent or distinctive in later chapters, although in Acts it resurfaces as a *theologoumenon* in Petrine and Pauline speeches before a Jewish audience. In all three writers the Christians' intrinsically Jewish messianic beliefs have become at the same time a point of discontinuity and resistance vis-à-vis both Jews and Romans.

Chapter 7 complements the Synoptic picture with Judith Lieu's contribution on the Fourth Gospel and the Johannine Letters. Moving centripetally from the Prologue and the statement of the Gospel's purpose in 20.30-31, she bypasses compositional hypotheses and finds the Messiah of John reconfigured above all as Son of God, and that sonship in terms of being sent by the One God – providing the touchstone for the Gospel's intense dialogue and dispute with Judaism about the nature of the Messiah. Yet even in this supposedly 'spiritual'

Gospel the royal dimension of messianism comes to the fore, as Jesus is tried as king rather than Messiah. A cognate (if less coherently articulated) concern for the link between the unity of God and the confession of Jesus as Messiah is identified in the Johannine Epistles.

Andrew Chester next addresses our question of how the Jewish language of messianism is appropriated in Paul's mission to the Gentiles. Hundreds of uses of the term χριστός appear at first sight to constitute abundant evidence for Jewish messianism, but are in this chapter found to have lost all titular significance or connection with the messianic vision of Jesus, and to function as no more than a proper name. Chester concludes that while the Apostle does believe the crucified Jesus to be the Messiah and does link this belief with eschatology, baptism and salvation (though not with political resistance), messianic ideas are neither adequate nor indeed central to his distinctive proclamation of the transformed heavenly Christ.

In Chapter 9, David Horrell focuses on messianic themes in James, Hebrews and 1 Peter. The Letter of James appears to underplay the role of messianism in its view of redemption, but strongly advocates resistance to the world. Hebrews focuses its rich notion of redemption in Christ's superior high priesthood and sacrifice, although instead of overt social critique and resistance 'strangers and exiles' are called to resist sin and remain confident in the face of suffering and persecution. Setting the hope of redemption in an imminent eschatological framework, 1 Peter draws on a rich variety of biblical and Jewish messianic traditions. James C. Scott's notion of 'hidden transcripts' shows messianic witness and allegiance as a mode of resistance subtly embedded in a domestic and public tapestry of respectful submission to authority.

In the final contribution to this section, Paul Spilsbury's Chapter 10 surveys the theme of messianic hope in Revelation. It is seen to deploy its apocalyptic drama in casting the χριστός as exalted Messiah – the Lamb and messianic king who is the supreme divine agent in heaven and on earth. His cosmic empire challenges that of Rome itself and prepares a certain future in which he rules the New Jerusalem as the city and throne of heaven on earth.

Following this study of Jewish and Christian messianisms in their formative period, Part III puts this analysis to work in a wide-ranging examination of the contact and controversy between them, from the end of the Second Temple period to the rise of Islam.

Martin Goodman opens the argument with a critical assessment of the role of Jewish messianic views in the Holy Land between the First (66–73) and Second (132–5) Revolts against Rome. Goodman opts to approach the question of messianic stimuli in the Jewish Revolts from the minimalist perspective of asking what evidence, if any, points to the messianic views in a few sporadic surviving documents being more widely shared among first-century Jews. He proposes that such views were indeed widespread, but rather more marginal as a force for political action than has sometimes been argued. While Goodman allows a messianic aspect to the Bar Kokhba revolt, he doubts that we can see such influence in the first revolt, not least because Josephus, our chief witness to such an interpretation, is not to be trusted. Messianic influence may have been confined to extreme circumstances and certain self-selected groups like early Christianity.

Introduction

In the sequel Chapter 12, Oskar Skarsaune presents the history of these messianic encounters in the Holy Land from Bar Kokhba to Constantine. Christian convictions about the Messiah during this period were articulated in good part in reaction first to Jewish messianic militancy and then to its decided rejection by the rabbis in the aftermath of Bar Kokhba's failure. Although Christian developments are inevitably marked by the increasing importance in the Holy Land of Gentile Christian churches with a more supersessionist relationship to Judaism, contact and polemic between patristic and rabbinic figures continued throughout the third century. The balance of redemption and resistance in such debates was irreversibly changed with the first Christian emperor.

If these developments undoubtedly complicated Jewish and Christian contacts and debate about messianic hopes, the underlying arguments did not go away. Chapters 13–15 explore the surviving evidence in three different geographic regions. Sebastian Brock begins by examining the rich exegetical tapestry that attests to the continued liveliness of these matters among Jews and Christians in Syria and Mesopotamia. Brock traces common exegetical traditions like the phrase 'king Messiah' derived from Genesis 49 in the Syriac and Aramaic versions of the Old Testament as well as in Aphrahat and Christian apocrypha. His conclusion is that despite the different development of these traditions, the shared apocalyptic outlook of Aramaic Jewish and Syriac Christian sources kept their common interest in them alive.

In Chapter 14 the focus turns to Jews and Christians in Egypt. James Carleton Paget begins with key messianic passages in the Septuagint, the Greek Bible of Alexandria. He proceeds from that basis to examine on the Jewish side a variety of later sources including Philo as well as the contrast between the third and the more nationalistic fifth book of the *Sibylline Oracles*, and on the Christian side the *Epistle of Barnabas* as well as subsequent allegorist and (sectarian) anti-allegorist writers. Participation in the Trajanic revolt suggests the possibility of more intense messianic convictions among Jews in Egypt than elsewhere in the Diaspora. Christian messianic interest continued sporadically into the third century, but with reduced evidence for contact and controversy with Jewish views.

Wolfram Kinzig next examines the role of 'realist' messianic eschatology in the western part of the Empire. After briefly looking at Western authors writing in Greek, the chapter places particular focus on the Latin Church Fathers. Although Christ is in most cases expected to return to exercise the Messiah's role in establishing an eschatological kingdom, it is also clear that his identity is that of a pre-existent, heavenly figure. This offsets Christian expectation from mainstream Jewish messianism, but is more in line with minority views such as those of 4 *Ezra*.

Moving on from the geographic survey, Chapter 16 asks about the relevance of material remains, more specifically within the visual culture of synagogue architecture. David Noy takes as his focus first the 'resistant', and possibly messianic, qualities of the synagogue murals at Dura Europos as these took shape in correlation and competition with pagan society and with the artistic images in the adjacent, more modest Christian church. Western illustrations include the synagogue of Ostia and especially the Jewish catacombs, whose eschatological symbolism also took shape both alongside and over against that of the Christian catacombs – with pagan craftsmanship and pagan themes also in evidence.

The contested question of what happened to Jewish messianism after the Jewish Revolts is explored by Philip Alexander. He argues that while there is considerable evidence in non-rabbinic sources including liturgical, mystical and late apocalyptic texts, the 'core' rabbinic sources are for the most part intentionally silent on this subject until there is a remarkable rekindling of 'realist' messianic interest among the rabbis in sources dating from 450–650. The popular views on messianism came to be appropriated yet also firmly shaped in line with rabbinic interests.

Two chapters on the ancient versions in Greek and Latin (18) and in Aramaic (19) bring together a variety of exegetical themes encountered in earlier chapters. Alison Salvesen offers a close study of messianic themes in the Septuagint and other Greek translations, as well as in Jerome's Vulgate. Neither Jewish nor Christian translators appear to have a systematically messianic agenda; and in the absence of fuller information about their context and setting, Salvesen urges cautious conclusions.

Deepening the textual and translational aspects of themes raised earlier in relation to Christian and Jewish messianic hopes in Syria, Robert Gordon finds in the Aramaic Targums a sustained interest in a human Messiah, but little evidence that anti-Christian polemic has affected translational preferences. This is confirmed in the Targumic handling of themes like Messianic Israel, the eschatological subjection of the nations, the Servant of Isaiah 53 and the Ephraimite Messiah defeated in battle – though the expression of such hopes is moral and spiritual rather than militant or activist. The Peshitta likewise minimizes messianic interpretations in favour of a relatively close rendition of the Hebrew.

Nicholas de Lange devotes the penultimate chapter to the Byzantine period up to the rise of Islam, with special focus on messianism as expressed in liturgy, hymns and apocalypses. For Judaism and Christianity in late antiquity, messianic hope remained 'embedded in their very muscles and sinews', even though political circumstances (including the Emperor Julian's attempt to rebuild the Temple) appear to have contributed surprisingly little to the ebb and flow of messianic fervour. For all their diversity, both Jews and Christians experienced a resurgence of such expectations around the year 500.

In the concluding chapter, Guy Stroumsa raises the question of competing messianisms in Jewish and Christian circles in seventh-century Jerusalem, at a time when Byzantium's weakness and the rise of Islam had rekindled Christian fears and Jewish hopes, and in the process reconfigured many older debates about true and false messiahs and prophets – especially in the contested interpretation of Mohammed. Stroumsa concludes that while one party's messianic hopes might constitute another's eschatological nightmare, both depended on thought patterns inherited from early Jewish messianic expectations.

Spanning nearly a millennium of hopes and aspirations in hugely diverse social, political and cultural circumstances, this volume could propose 'results' or 'conclusions' only at the cost of indefensible cliché and caricature. Part of our contribution, we believe, is precisely to document both the remarkable resilience and the frequently incommensurate diversity of messianic hopes throughout antiquity, regardless of how narrowly or broadly they may be defined. Similarly, the volatility and adaptability of concepts of 'resistance' and 'redemption' appropriately reflects the fact that such hopes were always highly contextual in their expression – as indeed our opening paragraph shows them to be today. Without claiming to provide answers, we hope at any rate to offer here an entrée to the ebb and flow of current scholarly debate that illuminates this multifaceted history of ancient messianism from several pertinent angles.

In respectful critical dialogue with William Horbury's scholarship, these essays reflect that ongoing debate about the prevalence and nature of ancient messianic hopes. Is this a story of widespread popular aspiration and continuity over time, or are we dealing instead with phenomena so disparate and episodic as to permit little or no historical comparison? Like the wider scholarly discussion of these matters, the contributors advocate different points on that spectrum of opinion. They are all united, however, in their affection and good wishes for their teacher William Horbury and his wife Katharine on the occasion of his 65th birthday.

Part I

Origins of Jewish Messianic Expectation

Chapter 1

THE PERSIAN PERIOD

Joachim Schaper

1. *Introductory Remarks*

'The silence of the postexilic prophets other than Haggai and Zechariah, then, is deafening. It is reminiscent of the famous Sherlock Holmes saying about "The curious incident of the dog that barked in the night". When Watson objected that it did not bark Holmes replied, "That is the curious incident".'[1] This is how a contemporary Old Testament scholar sums up his observations on the alleged absence of messianic thought from post-exilic prophecy. Later, the same writer states, this time indeed with regard to the whole of post-exilic Old Testament literature: 'In summary, then, we have to say how little influence the concept of a renewal of the Davidic line after the exile exercised in the extant postexilic biblical literature.'[2] This view is characteristic of much of contemporary scholarship on Old Testament messianism. The present essay attempts to show why it is untenable.

Although the term 'messianism' is not used consistently in modern scholarship and is notoriously hard to define, we shall make an attempt by understanding it to refer to 'the expectation of a coming pre-eminent ruler – coming, whether at the end, as strictly implied by the word "eschatology", or simply at some time in the future. The future in question is often conceived as very near, and consequently messianism here covers the treatment of a present leader in a messianic way'[3] – as we shall soon see with regard to the early Persian period.

The broadness of this definition takes into account that a religious phenomenon whose perception in modern scholarship is often dominated by the notion of a transcendent, heavenly messiah in fact has its roots in the everyday political life of ancient Israel. Messianism originally was a *political*, not a religious concept, one is tempted to say – although, of course, it is somewhat anachronistic to differentiate between the two with regard to an ancient society like that of pre-exilic Israel. Whereas it is useful to make the distinction analytically, the political and religious spheres were, in the actual life of ancient Israel, inseparable. It is therefore advisable to take W. Horbury's line and to follow Gressmann, as

---

1   Mason 1998: 350.
2   Mason 1998: 364.
3   Horbury 1998c: 7. It is a great honour and pleasure to have been given the opportunity to contribute this essay to a *Festschrift* dedicated to my teacher and friend William Horbury whose scholarship and personal example are so immensely important to me.

opposed to Mowinckel, in not distinguishing artificially between 'political' and 'eschatological' messianism.[4]

Given the above definition, it is hardly possible to deny the existence of messianism or at least incipient forms of messianism in the pre-exilic period. Given the constraints of the present format, I shall only be able to give a mere *outline* of the development of Jewish messianism in the Persian period. That outline will have to be preceded by a few words about the 'pre-history', or rather: early history, of Jewish messianism during the pre-exilic period, since it is impossible to understand the messianic tendencies of the Achaemenid era without understanding their roots.

2. The Early History of Messianism

Messianism is often perceived as a religious concept produced by the absence of kingship in Jewish history. This is misleading. Messianism is not so much an indicator that something is wanting in the religious make-up of Israel at a given time. It is, as we shall see, rather more deeply rooted in the pre-exilic Israelite cult and Israel's concept of kingship.[5]

As Gressmann and Mowinckel demonstrated,[6] it was through the royal psalms that messianic hope was inspired. The royal psalms found in the Psalter are one of the main sources for research into the early history of messianism. However, it is not just with a view to the pre-exilic roots of messianism in Israelite kingship ideology (to be discussed below) that they can and have to be consulted, but also with regard to the further development of messianism in the post-exilic period.[7] We shall see that psalms of central importance, like Psalm 2, are relevant to research into messianism in both the pre-exilic and the post-exilic periods because of the theological significance of the editing process that led up to the formation of the Psalter in the post-exilic period.

A. R. Johnson 'identified an element of messianic hope as always present when these psalms were addressed to the reigning monarch'.[8] However, pre-exilic Israelite ritual had messianic overtones at a yet more foundational level. Long before first the Israelite, then the Judaean monarchy came to their respective ends

---

4   Cf. Horbury 1998c: 6–7.
5   This point has been stressed by Horbury 1998c: 19, evaluating the research of Gressmann and Mowinckel: '... Gressmann and Mowinckel jointly showed that messianism must be treated not just as a reaction to bad times, but as an abiding element in the circle of ideas which surrounded Israelite kingship and reflected foreign culture, including that of Egypt with its high monarchical doctrines. Both scholars recognized a myth of the messiah formed under external influence; Gressmann's position in principle did more justice to this influence than Mowinckel's. ... Both also recognised the formidable force of the acclamation of God as king, and saw it, perhaps questionably, as a deterrent to development of the messianic theme.'
6   Cf. Gressmann 1929; Mowinckel 1922, 1956.
7   Cf. Janowski 2002: 101–2.
8   Horbury 1998c: 24, summing up central points in Gressmann 1929; Mowinckel 1922, 1956 and Johnson 1967. Also cf. other 'classic' studies of messianism, such as Dürr 1925; Staerk 1938; Klausner 1955; and Scholem 1971.

there had been an ideal of kingship which was deeply ingrained in the cultures of the Ancient Near East and which did not fail to unfold in Israel, too.[9] 'One should perhaps go one step further, and affirm, on the lines sketched by Bentzen, that the praises of the king will always have been messianic in character, irrespective of any hint of non-fulfilment, for in hymns of praise the present king becomes for the moment the godlike figure of the ideal king.'[10]

This is where the key to a full understanding of messianism is to be found: the concept of a messiah is in the last instance derived, via a particular understanding of human kingship, from Israel's notion of *divine* kingship. Conceptualizing the enthronement of the Davidic ruler as his 'birth' as the son of God (Pss. 2.7, 110.3),[11] pre-exilic Israel was able to conceive of its Davidic rulers as the *vicarii* of the God of Israel.[12] The king's earthly rule could be thought of as an analogy of, and even a participation in, divine rule.[13] Contrary to the claims made by Gunkel, Gressmann and Mowinckel, there was no contradiction between the divine kingdom and the earthly Davidic kingdom. In spite of their protestations to the contrary, Gressmann and Mowinckel seem to have sensed that, since 'they both admitted that, however inconsistently, pre-exilic Israelites had already hoped for a coming king manifesting the divine attributes ascribed to the earthly monarch in the royal psalms. This admission suggests that the seeming inconsistency between theocracy and messianism should be treated with caution, especially in view of the association in other cultures between king-like deities and monarchs here below.'[14] By the same token, it does not make sense to postulate an opposition between kingship ideology and messianism, as we shall soon see.

It is often thought that the history of messianism only started with the demise of the northern kingdom and Judah's loss of independence. This presupposes that messianism *replaced* an earlier kingship ideology once the monarchy had vanished (in the case of Israel) or been severely damaged (in Judah). However, the Israelite concept of messianism[15] did not replace the earlier kingship ideology centring on the Davidic line but was deeply rooted in it, and whereas in other nations the demise of monarchies led to a demise of their ideologies, the fall of the Israelite kingdom under the Assyrian onslaught instead resulted in a deepened and renewed understanding of Israelite kingship ideology – the result of which is the messianic thought informing passages like Isa. 7.10-17 and Isa. 9.5-6.[16]

---

9   Many have attempted to trace Israelite kingship ideology back to some 'foreign roots', variously Mesopotamian or Egyptian. One such attempt has recently been made by Koch 2002 where he claims, among other things, a direct dependence of Ps. 2.7-9 on Egyptian texts (pp. 11–15).
10   Horbury 1998c: 24.
11   On the pre-exilic origin of Psalms 2 and 110, cf. Day 2004, especially pp. 225–9.
12   Cf. Gese 1983: 130: 'Die Inthronisation war die Geburt zum Gottessohn, und die davidische Königsherrschaft vom Zion war das Vikariat des Königtums Gottes.' For a detailed exploration, cf. Gese 1984b: 121 and Gese 1984c: 137–9.
13   Cf. Gese 1983: 130.
14   Horbury 1998c: 18.
15   For a history of Israelite messianism, with special regard to the relation between its pre-exilic and its post-exilic manifestations, cf. Gese 1983, *passim*.
16   As pointed out by Gese 1984c: 139–45; cf. especially 139–40: 'Solche staatlichen Katastrophen haben überall sonst die Königsideologien beseitigt, im alttestamentlichen Bereich aber kam es zu einer seltsamen Vertiefung der Tradition.'

The end of the Judaean monarchy under the neo-Babylonian impact only deepened that perception of the future king further. Jer. 23.5-6//33.15-16 with its expectation of a 'righteous branch' and Ezek. 17.22-24 witness to the liveliness of messianic expectation in the exilic period.

3. Messianism in the Early Achaemenid Period

Let us now turn to the role of messianism in the Persian period, when Judah was under the rule of the Achaemenid dynasty, following the victory of the Achaemenid king, Cyrus II ('the Great'), over the neo-Babylonian empire in 538 B.C. With regard to messianism (or the lack thereof) in the Persian and Hellenistic periods, it has been claimed by some contemporary scholars that the time from the early fifth to the late second century was characterized by a 'messianological vacuum'.[17] Even many of those who acknowledge that Zerubbabel was the focus of messianic expectations go on to say that after his disappearance messianism was dormant among the Jewish people.

Let us explore the evidence. Given the constraints of this paper, in what follows I shall concentrate on royal messianism, while some attention will be given to other messianic concepts.

I shall start with the books of Haggai and Zechariah. The future of Judah and Jerusalem – known, in the time of Achaemenid domination, as the province Yehud – and its inhabitants is conceived of, in Hag. 2.20-23 and in Zech. 1.16-17; 8.3, as a 'period of redemption which is now at hand'.[18] Zerubbabel and Joshua are the central figures of this expectation, and it is in the book of Zechariah that we get the first glimpse of the concept of two messiahs, the one priestly, the other 'political'.[19] The 'political' messiah whom Zechariah expected, i.e. Zerubbabel, is possibly best understood as a figure of potential resistance against the new Achaemenid order: while he was the governor appointed by the Persians to run the Yehud province, he was also a Davidide[20] and thus an obvious focus of attention and hope to all those who were expecting a restoration of Davidic rule. Right at the end of the book of Haggai, and thus in a most prominent position, the following oracle is found:

20 And the word of the LORD came to Haggai a second time on the twenty-fourth day of the month:

---

17   Horbury 1998c: 37, referring to Frost 1952: 66–7 and Collins 1995: 31–8, 40.
18   Wanke 1984: 168.
19   It does not seem quite right to call the non-priestly messiah a 'secular' messiah, as Wanke 1984: 169 does. However, Wanke's general conclusion is correct. On the concept of two messiahs, cf. Gese 1983: 134–5: '... beide Seiten gehören zusammen, und erst beide Seiten stellen den ganzen Messias dar, so wie in der Vision Sach 4,3 die beiden Ölbäume rechts und links vom göttlichen Leuchter in ihrer symmetrischen Entsprechung eine höhere Einheit bilden.'
20   Being the 'son of Shealtiel', he was a Davidide; cf. 1 Chr. 3.19 (LXX reading). On the problems generated by the genealogy, cf. Japhet 1993: 94–102, especially 100. Even if we follow the MT reading of 1 Chr. 3.19 and read 'Pedaiah' (i.e., Shealtiel's brother) and compare the claim in Haggai that *Shealtiel* was Zerubbabel's father, it follows that 'in either case, however, ... Jehoiachin would be Zerubbabel's grandfather' (Horbury 1998c: 177 n.17).

The Persian Period

21 Speak to Zerubbabel the governor of Judah: I am going to shake the heavens and the earth.
22 And I will overturn the thrones of kingdoms and destroy the might of the kingdoms of the nations. I will overturn chariots and their drivers. Horses and their riders shall fall, each by the sword of his fellow.
23 On that day – declares the LORD of Hosts – I will take you, O my servant Zerubbabel son of Shealtiel – declares the LORD – and make you as a signet; for I have chosen you – declares the LORD of Hosts.[21]

It has been pointed out that certain characteristics of messianic language are missing from the passage,[22] and 'the hopes clustering round Zerubbabel, attested in Haggai and Zechariah, have been interpreted as something less than messianic; the relevant oracles would then simply express divine ratification of a Persian governor'.[23] However, the wording of the oracles certainly fits into the general mould of messianic oracles found elsewhere in the Hebrew Bible. Indeed, the expectations documented in Zech. 4.1-14 and especially the oracle declaring Zerubbabel a 'signet' are quite explicitly worded, so that even the very cautious among present-day exegetes have to concede that it is distinctly possible that Zerubbabel was seen as the Messiah.[24] Also – and this has been much neglected in scholarship – YHWH's making Zerubbabel a 'signet' or 'seal' (Hag. 2.23: חותם) indicates the full identification of the deity with its representative.[25] According to traditional Israelite kingship ideology, such an identification could only be brought about by the accession of the new king: 'You are My son, I have fathered you this day' (JPS Tanakh). It seems to me that the image of the signet indicates just that: YHWH's total identification with his Davidic servant and expected future king.

Furthermore, 'Hag. 2. 23 on the signet seems to echo Jer. 22. 24, an oracle concerning Jehoiachin. Moreover, Haggai's messianism is bound up in other ways with the pre-exilic Jerusalem court tradition (...). Similarly, the title "branch" given to Zerubbabel in Zech. 3. 8; 6. 12 echoes Jer. 23. 5-6, "I will raise up to David a righteous branch", cf. Jer. 33. 15-16.'[26] This was a messianic expectation of a highly disruptive political nature which was never fulfilled – Zerubbabel disappeared from the scene of history without trace.[27]

The hope invested in the person of Zerubbabel is a 'classic' case of messianic expectation, not just because of the aspects of it we have just discussed but also because of its being a result of both restorative and utopian tendencies within early Second Temple Judaism. G. Scholem famously pointed out, with regard to

---

21   Translation from JPS Tanakh.
22   Cf. Wolff 1991: 84–5.
23   Horbury 1998c: 43, summing up a common misconception.
24   Cf. the overall conclusion in Wolff 1991: 85.
25   The owner is perceived as being in some way *present* in the seal. On the nature of seals, signets and related insignia, cf. Koschaker 1942. On the significance of seals especially, cf. Schaper 2004: 72–5. On the significance of the signet, cf. now also Kessler 2006 (*non vidi*).
26   Horbury 1998c: 177 n.17. The statement about Haggai's messianism takes up Mason 1982: 143.
27   The details cannot be reconstructed; cf. Stern 1984: 72.

a later period, that – given the three major cultural and religious 'tendencies' in rabbinic Judaism: the conservative, the restorative and the utopian – the 'messianic idea' is the result of a confluence of restorative and utopian concepts:[28]

> Both tendencies are deeply intertwined and yet at the same time of a contradictory nature; the Messianic idea crystallizes only out of the two of them together. Neither is entirely absent in the historical and ideological manifestations of Messianism. Only the proportion between them is subject to the widest fluctuations. ... Sometimes the one tendency appears with maximal emphasis while the other is reduced to a minimum, but we never find a 'pure case' of exclusive influence or crystallization of one of these tendencies. The reason for this is clear: even the restorative force has a utopian factor, and in utopianism restorative factors are at work.[29]

This was very much the case long before the birth of rabbinic Judaism, and the hopes of redemption focusing on Zerubbabel are our first clear-cut example. Here, the restorative aspect was the desire for a re-establishment of the Davidic dynasty. The utopian element, however, was the expectation of an upheaval of world-historical dimensions that is so clearly expressed in the oracle we discussed. One is tempted to interpret messianism as a whole, along the lines suggested by Scholem, as a 'theory of catastrophe',[30] and the transition from prophecy to apocalypticism in the early post-exilic period – which becomes visible, for the first time, in the cycle of visions in Zechariah[31] – ties in with Scholem's overall concept. 'The depth of Scholem's insight should not, however, preclude recognition of messianic hope as belonging to a biblically-focused exegetical tradition.'[32] The exegetical tradition provided the 'instruments' which enabled the supporters of Zerubbabel to formulate their hope and their claims. These 'instruments' were readily available, and we shall see that they were in use all the way through the Persian period.

There are numerous other eschatological texts in the Twelve Prophets, with some of the most important being Mic. 4–5,[33] Mal. 2.17-3.5 and Mal. 3.13-21. Some of them are messianic,[34] and Mic. 4.8 is especially pertinent:

> And you, O tower of the flock, hill of the daughter of Zion, to you shall it come, the former dominion shall come, the kingdom of the daughter of Jerusalem.[35]

The significance of messianism takes us beyond single books to larger literary units. Messianic expectations – or at least, more generally: eschatological concepts

---

28 Scholem here takes up the insight into the correspondence between *Urzeit* and *Endzeit* arrived at in earlier exegetical scholarship, especially by members of the *Religionsgeschichtliche Schule*; cf. generally Hamacher 1999.
29 Scholem 1971: 3–4.
30 Scholem 1971: 7.
31 Gese 1984a.
32 Horbury 2003b: 12.
33 Cf. Wanke 1984 *passim*, especially 177–80.
34 On the use of the terms 'messianism/messianic' and 'eschatology/eschatological', cf. Schaper 1995: 26–30.
35 Translation taken from the RSV.

– seem to have played an important role in the formation of the Twelve Prophets. The redactional processes that produced the Dodekapropheton spanned several centuries and came to an end only in the late Achaemenid period.[36] One of the scarlet threads that run through the Twelve is the concept of the Day of Yahweh, and various concepts of messianic figures and their reigns – concepts of exilic and post-exilic origin – figure prominently in the final text of the Dodekapropheton (Mic. 4.8; 5.1-3; 5.4-5; Hag. 2.20-23; Zech. 4.1-14; Mal. 3.13-21). This implies, first, that the importance of pre-exilic messianic concepts was not diminished in the Persian period and, second, that new messianic concepts were being added.

The reconstruction of the redaction history of the book of Isaiah, like that of the redaction history of the Twelve Prophets, provides insights into the history of eschatology and messianism in the (pre-exilic and) post-exilic period(s). Its literary growth reflects the development of messianism from the era of the actual prophet Isaiah up to the time of the final redaction of the book. The expectation of a messiah as expressed in Isaiah 7 – a text from 'the late pre-exilic or early exilic period'[37] which may be inspired by 'a tradition which stretches back to the time of the prophet'[38] – is so important not least because of its 'obvious allusion to the Zion tradition as attested especially in Ps 46.7 and 11 ... and Mic 3.11, with which, of course, the royal dynasty was closely associated (see especially 2 Sam 23.5)'.[39] At the same time, there was a 'relative freedom ... towards the earlier Davidic tradition' which provided the basis for the 'various salvific figures which might be read out of [Isa] 40-55' who 'were drawn together in the one figure of 61.1-3'.[40] A messianic theme permeates the whole of the book of Isaiah, a theme which, in the book's successive formative stages, underwent a number of transformations.[41]

4. *Messianism in the Middle Achaemenid Period*

The importance of messianic thought in Judah in this period especially has often been drawn into question. However, there are, as we shall soon see, a number of indications in the literature of the time that it played a significant role in the religious life of the Judahite population. Some of them are quite subtle and therefore tend to be overlooked. Generally speaking, it is not surprising that reference to messianic expectation should only have been made with great

---

36 Cf., among others, Nogalski 1993a, 1993b and Schart 1998.
37 Williamson 1998: 103.
38 Williamson 1998: 205.
39 Williamson 1998: 108.
40 Williamson 1998: 205.
41 This is essentially the central thesis of Williamson 1998, although he does not explicitly call the overarching theme 'messianic'. As Williamson points out, '[i]t has been usual in the past to concentrate attention upon the identity of the character who is variously presented as king, servant or Messiah', whereas he prefers to concentrate on 'the role which needs to be performed' and 'the outworking of that role in a variety of different contexts', i.e., as king, messiah and servant (Williamson 1998: 206). In a wider sense, however, all the results of the 'outworking of that role' are messianic.

caution in those days, since the Achaemenid overlords cannot have been particularly favourably disposed towards such views. This is why it is more difficult, for the biblical exegete, to find traces of messianic concepts in Persian period texts: not because they are non-existent, but because they have consciously been given a low profile.

It is one of the more intriguing observations in recent Psalms research that the history of the composition of the Psalter can provide us with valuable insights into the history of Israelite religion. This yields some interesting results with regard to the development of messianism in the period in question. F.-L. Hossfeld and E. Zenger have demonstrated, in their commentaries on the Psalms,[42] and Zenger has shown, especially in a recent article devoted specifically to the role of messianism in the formation of the Psalter,[43] that the collection of psalms extending from Ps. 2 to Ps. 89 – itself the result of the combination of two earlier collections (Pss. 3–41 and Pss. 42–89*, respectively, with Ps. 2 prefixed when both were combined) – originally existed independently and was assembled in the post-exilic period (we shall address the problem of dating soon). Zenger correctly assumes Pss. 2 and 89 to have originated in the *pre*-exilic period and thinks that they were 'strategically' positioned by the editor of the 'Messianic Psalter' (Pss. 2–89).[44]

Zenger estimates that the collection Pss. 2–89* was put together in the early Hellenistic period. His assumption is based entirely on his perception of the collection as 'utopian', as opposed to 'restorationist'.[45] In my view, the 'utopian' character of the 'messianic Psalter' 2–89* does not support such a late date. In itself, it proves nothing. Rather, for the purpose of dating the collection Pss. 2–89*, we should try to see the 'messianic Psalter', one of the predecessors of the actual Psalter in the Hebrew Bible, in the overall context of the literary formation of the Psalter and of the history of its translation into Greek in the first half of the second century B.C.[46] Seen in this context, it seems unlikely that the

---

42   Hossfeld and Zenger 2000; Hossfeld and Zenger 1993.
43   Zenger 2002.
44   Zenger gives the following reason for calling it 'messianic': 'Die Bezeichnung "messianisch" für den Psalter Ps 2-89* inspiriert sich zunächst am Begriff des משיח, der pointiert gleich an seinem Anfang in Ps 2,2 und dann ebenso in Ps 89,52 dezidiert an seinem Abschluß (vor der Doxologie 89,53) steht. Der Begriff ist beide male mit dem auf JHWH bezogenen Suffix verbunden und macht so deutlich, daß der Gesalbte als Mandatar JHWHs agieren soll. Und in beiden Psalmen wird der Gesalbte nicht in königlicher Funktion für *sein* Volk, sondern im Blick auf die ganze Völkerwelt präsentiert. So steht in diesen Psalmen vom Salbungsthema her zwar das mit David verbundene Königsbild im Hintergrund, aber dieses wird – nicht zuletzt durch Aufnahme von prophetischer Eschatologie – so universalisiert und dynamisiert, daß es das "historische" Davidbild zugleich transzendiert. Der Gesalbte Davids dieser beiden Rahmenpsalmen des Teilpsalters 2-89* ist die Figuration einer erhofften Zukunft, in der weltweit die in einem idealen Königsreich gegebenen Größen Gerechtigkeit und Barmherzigkeit, Lebensfülle und Frieden (vgl. Ps 72) Realität werden – und zwar als Gaben JHWHs. Dabei soll der von JHWH erwählte "Gesalbte" eine wichtige Mittlerrolle einnehmen.' This is another indication of the fact that kingship ideology and messianism were not mutually exclusive. Rather, in the history of Israelite religion, the latter is deeply rooted in the former.
45   Cf. Zenger 2002: 89.
46   For the date of the Greek Psalter, cf. the discussion in Schaper 1995: 34–45.

'Messianic Psalter' should have been put together only in the early Hellenistic period. The mid-Achaemenid period seems a much more defensible estimate, given the rather cautious and veiled manner in which it expresses the messianic hope. This estimate ties in with W. Horbury's general observation that '[t]his earlier part of the Second-Temple period, from Cyrus to Alexander, can be described as the great epoch of editing which made the Hebrew Bible into what may be called a messianic document. It was also … an age of concentration on royal and potentially messianic themes, especially in the portraits of Moses, Joshua, David and the kings in the Hexateuch and Chronicles.'[47] The 'messianic Psalter' reconstructed by Hossfeld and Zenger is another example of the messianic focus of much of Persian era biblical literature production and editing.

In the middle Achaemenid period, the person of Nehemiah seems to have been a focus for messianic expectations. Neh. 6.7 repeats an allegation made against Nehemiah: 'You have also set up prophets in Jerusalem to proclaim about you, "There is a king in Judah!"'.[48] This has been interpreted as an indication of the existence of a messianic movement centring around Nehemiah.[49] M. Smith tried to brush this aside with the remark that 'some of his admirers … may have been so foolish as to see in him the Messiah'.[50] The explanation offered to refute the theory about Nehemiah as the expected Messiah was that 'there is no evidence that messianic expectations played a major role in party divisions in Jerusalem between 515 and 201'.[51] However, we have already been able to show that this is not the case – certainly not in the early and middle Achaemenid periods.[52] And even M. Smith has to concede that '[e]ven if Kellermann's interpretation were correct, this episode would be evidence only of the aberration of a few fanatics. There is no evidence that Nehemiah shared their opinions.'[53] That is precisely not the point. The *existence of messianic expectations* is what the discussion about the history of 'messianism' in the Persian and Hellenistic periods – or any era, for that matter – centres on, not the attitude of the person who is thought to be the Messiah. To use a contemporary analogy: We shall never know whether R. Menachem Mendel Schneerson thought of himself as the Messiah – what we do know is that a messianic movement was and is focused on him.

5. Messianism in the Late Achaemenid Period

One of the main sources for an enquiry into messianic beliefs in the late Achaemenid era in the province of Yehud is the book of Chronicles. Most likely

---

47 Horbury 1998c: 42.
48 Translation taken from the JPS Tanakh.
49 Kellermann 1967: 179–82.
50 Smith 1987: 101.
51 Smith 1987: 198 n.37.
52 Cf. above, sections 3 and 4. The stance taken in the book of Haggai, to name one example, is an example of a messianic expectation which, to use Smith's formulation, 'played a major role in party divisions in Jerusalem'.
53 Smith 1987: 197 n.37.

it was written only after Ezra-Nehemiah, towards the very end of the Persian period.[54]

Some scholars have identified the completion of the temple and the institution of the cult as being the focus of the book[55] and are convinced that it does not display any traces of messianic concepts. Rather, they think that, given the fall of Judah and Jerusalem under the Babylonian onslaught, the demise of the monarchy, the exile and the return, the centrally important objective was the restitution of the cult. It has thus been suggested that Chronicles stresses the importance of the cult at the expense of the Davidic line and its potential significance in the ideological situation of the post-exilic period. W. Riley assumes that 'the temple can be termed a sign of the covenant with the people in the Chronicler's work'.[56] He understands the Chronicler to have dealt with the demise of the monarchy by 'concentrating on the cultic vocation which the ancient ideology attributed to kings' and placing 'the dynastic promise into the larger context of the Temple as the major effect of the Davidic covenant'.[57] Thus, while generally acknowledging the importance of the monarchy to the author of Chronicles, he denies that the book is in any way informed by messianic concepts.

There are several problems with this kind of argument. What was, one wonders, the ultimate political and religious purpose of the Chronicler's literary activity? The supposed centrality of temple theology to the Chronicler's ideology and the view that it was that ideology which enticed the Chronicler to propagate the Davidic house – rather than the other way round – fail to make sense of the overall narrative of the book. On general considerations, the Persian domination of Yehud is unlikely to have completely extinguished the yearning for a restitution of the Davidic line to (some kind of) power. This general assumption is supported, it seems to the present author, by the fact that, according to the Chronicler's concept, the conditions for the eternal establishment of the Davidic dynasty had been met by Solomon (cf. 1 Chr. 28.7, 2 Chr. 1.9-10; 9.22).[58] There was thus reason to believe, according to the logic of the Chronicler's argument, that the Davidic monarchy would be re-instituted. The promise uttered in 1 Chr. 17.14 is of particular significance here. Pre-conceived concepts of a supposed Ancient Near Eastern pattern of kingship only serve to distract the exegete from the fact that Chronicles has an unequivocal *concept of the eternity of the Davidic line*. 1 Chr. 3.19-24 traces the Davidic line all the way through the exile and beyond.[59]

The importance not just of the Davidic line but of the messianic notion of the 'ruler from Judah' is also obvious from 1 Chr. 5.2, 'interpreting the genealogy in 1 Chr. 2.3-15 and the oracle in Gen. 49.10', and from 1 Chr. 14.2, 'echoing

---

54 Following S. Japhet and H. G. M. Williamson, I regard Ezra-Nehemiah and Chronicles as separate works. For a discussion of the problem cf. Schaper 2000: 49–67.
55 Cf., among others, Riley 1993.
56 Riley 1993: 198.
57 Riley 1993: 201.
58 Cf. Williamson 1977, 1983. As Horbury 1998c: 177 n.24 puts it, Williamson 'prefers to avoid the word "messianic" (which might imply expectation of one unique eschatological monarch), but understands the Chronicler to expect the re-emergence of a ruling Davidic household in post-exilic Judah'.
59 Cf. Japhet 1993: 100–2.

Balaam's oracle in Num. 24. 7'.[60] The time-honoured concept of earthly Davidic rule as an analogy of and even a participation in, the rule of the divine kingdom[61] is reaffirmed and reinforced by such highly significant passages as 1 Chr. 28.5 and 29.23 (where the divine throne is called the מלכות יהוה כסא). It may well be an understatement to say that 'the Chronicler is best understood not only as royalist, but also tinged with messianism'.[62]

Although Riley overlooks the significance of messianism in the book of Chronicles he is certainly right in stressing the importance the Chronicler assigns to the temple cult. It is very important, however, to perceive the temple cult as stressed by the Chronicler in the overall context of his book. 'An antecedent of the dual messianism of the Qumran texts has indeed been discerned with some justice in the stress on the temple as well as the kingdom found in Chronicles', as W. Horbury points out with regard to a thesis put forward by W. Schniedewind.[63] However, it is indeed the case that the 'dual emphasis is outweighed ... by the persistent assertion in Chronicles of "the kingdom of the Lord in the hand of the sons of David". Chronicles is thereby also one of the sources which contributed to the prevalence of a single messianic figure, despite the popularity of the dual constitution.'[64] The messianism the Chronicler propagated is another example of the Davidic type, which was the prevalent one among a variety of similar beliefs and concentrated on a single messianic leader expected to emerge from the house of David.

Another indicator of significant messianic fervour in the late Persian period is the Greek Pentateuch. It carries a number of messianic interpretations of the Hebrew original which did not come out of the blue in the early Hellenistic period, at the time when the Pentateuch was translated in Alexandria. Rather, they are anchored in the messianic expectation that had been alive all the way through the Achaemenid period,[65] a period during which Judah had been under '[t]he overwhelming external impact of Persian rulers styled in Aramaic "king of kings" (Ezra 7.12)', which was 'accompanied internally, as the books of Chronicles also attest, by lively remembrance of "our [Israelite] kings and our priests" (Ezra 9,7, in a prayer-formula also found at greater length in Neh. 9,32; 34, Bar. 1,16)'.[66]

---

60 Horbury 1998c: 45.
61 Cf. above.
62 Horbury 1998c: 45.
63 Horbury 1998c: 45, with reference to Schniedewind 1994: 71–8.
64 Horbury 1998c: 45.
65 Horbury 2003b: 63: 'The Apocrypha, although in many cases they exemplify silence on messianism and a theocentric concentration on divine deliverance, do not encourage the view that there was a "messianological vacuum" in the late Persian and early Greek period. This notion is in any case implicitly questioned by the messianism of the LXX Pentateuch, but it is also questioned by the traces of messianic biblical interpretation in Ecclesiasticus and 1 Maccabees.'
66 Horbury 2006b.

6. Conclusion

Contrary to the claims of many scholars, a lively messianic expectation characterized (the beliefs of at least a significant proportion of the adherents of) the YHWH religion throughout the Persian era – not just during the immediate post-exilic period. What has been described as 'perhaps the major insight of the second half of the twentieth century in the study of ancient messianism, namely a regained recognition that messianic hope belongs to the stream of interpretative tradition which accompanies the Jewish scriptures throughout antiquity',[67] has been further affirmed by the above exploration. Already in the Persian period, Jews in the land of Israel and in the Diaspora who held messianic beliefs expressed such beliefs with the help of exegetical 'tools' that were time-honoured and readily available. The 'stream of interpretative tradition' in which they had their being had started long before the ancient versions of the Hebrew Scriptures came into existence.[68] It can be described as an 'inner-biblical'[69] interpretative tradition that was ultimately rooted in pre-exilic kingship ideology. *Urzeit* and *Endzeit* were expected to correspond, restorative and utopian forces joined together to give birth to a hope that has proved very resilient.

---

67 Horbury, 2003b, p. 5.
68 Horbury, 2003b, pp. 5–11 ('Messianic Hope in Ancient Biblical Interpretation') concentrates on messianic biblical interpretation from the time of the Greek Pentateuch onwards. However, this messianic interpretative tradition already informs the Hebrew Scriptures themselves – it started out as an '*inner*-biblical' interpretative tradition.
69 On the notion of 'inner-biblical interpretation', cf. Fishbane 1985; Carson and Williamson 1988; and Zakovitch 1992.

Chapter 2

The Hasmonean Period

Jan Willem van Henten

Introduction

How should we define pre-Christian messiahs from the Hasmonean period and how flexible should our model of messiahs be? Should one begin with the oldest passages in which the root *mem-shin-heth* 'anoint' occurs, from which the title Messiah derives? Or should one start at the other side of the spectrum, and take the Christian Messiah as a point of departure and, as a consequence, include a divine origin and a violent death, beneficial to others?

Whatever definition one chooses in a discussion of pre-Christian messiahs, there is always a subjective element in that choice, as is apparent from a beautiful passage in Amos Oz' recent autobiographical book *Tales of Love and Darkness*. The passage concerns a brief encounter of the young Amos Oz with his uncle, Professor Joseph Klausner. He is well known among biblical scholars because of his book about Jesus, written in the 1920s.[1] Professor Klausner teaches his nephew, and indirectly his nephew's readers, the following lesson during a conversation about skin cream:

> Do you know, my dear, the huge difference between the 'redeemer' in Gentile languages and our messiah? The messiah is simply someone who has been anointed with oil; every priest or king in the Bible is a messiah, and the Hebrew word 'messiah' is a thoroughly prosaic and everyday word, closely related to the word for face cream – unlike in the Gentile languages, where the messiah is called Redeemer and Savior? Or are you still too young to understand this lesson?

Whether this mildly ironic passage correctly represents Professor Klausner's viewpoint is irrelevant here, the example illustrates nicely that a discussion of pre-Christian messianism depends very much on the concept of the messiah one has in mind. The mini-lecture focuses on the well-established anointment ritual for leaders in the Hebrew Bible, mostly for priests and kings as representatives of God. Post-biblical passages like the Qumran documents still refer to this ritual (1QM ix 8).[2] Professor Klausner's point implies a principal difference in

---

1 Oz 2005: 61; Klausner 1925.
2 Notation of Qumran passages: Roman numerals indicate columns and Arabic numerals lines and fragments in the following order: fragment, column, line. 4Q375 i 9 refers to an anointed priest upon whose head the oil of anointing has been poured. See also 4Q376 1 i 1.

16   *Redemption and Resistance*

perspective between Jews and non-Jews and their various languages. One particular messiah as God's Redeemer does not fit his model, because messiahs are simply 'anointed ones', i.e., all persons with an office as leader, whether political, priestly or prophetical. As a consequence, messiahs execute their office simply in 'this world'.

This view obviously excludes many Qumran passages that are considered highly relevant by others, because they deal with 'messianic' figures, who play an important role in God's end-time scenario. Evidently, phrases with משיח 'anointed one' do occur in the Scrolls, although it is debated whether they are used absolutely as a title for '*the* Messiah' or 'the Lord's Messiah' as in New Testament passages or later Jewish writings.[3] In order to forgo the danger that a fixed and narrow definition may lead to the exclusion of relevant passages, I will use an open model of messianism that allows for various articulations and multiple messiahs. I will focus on passages with phrases related to the root משה 'anoint'. However, I will also go beyond them by discussing texts about royal and priestly authoritative figures, whether human or angelic, who fulfil God's mission in the future. I will concentrate my discussion on the role of these redeemer figures, so that readers can relate this to their own model of messianism.[4] I will start my discussion by dealing briefly with three issues that have often been associated with messianism in the Hasmonean period.

1. *The Context of Messianism in the Hasmonean Period*

Judaism in Palestine changed considerably in the Hellenistic period, starting with Alexander the Great (356–23 B.C.E.). Martin Hengel, the emeritus Tübingen professor of New Testament and famous for his *Judaism and Hellenism*,[5] argues that these transformations resulted in a new form of Jewish religion in the land of Israel. This in turn formed the matrix for the Jesus movement: 'If we want to clear up the beginnings of Christianity, we have to investigate first the impact of "Hellenistic civilization" in these regions'.[6] Although Hengel's argument has raised serious criticism (below), others scholars have argued that at least the messianic views in the second century B.C.E., expressed especially in the Qumran documents, are closely connected with the foundation of a Hellenistic-Jewish state by the Hasmoneans in the second half of this century. Some scholars consider the diversity of Qumran messianism a strongly critical response to the Hasmonean integration of the offices of high priest and ruler (below).[7] A discussion of

---

3   This point has been emphasized by M. de Jonge, e.g. in de Jonge 1991: 110.
4   Fitzmyer 1993a: 172–3 argues for a restriction to passages with phrases of משיח. Other discussions of definitions: Collins 1995: 11–12; Oegema 1998a: 26. Horbury 1998c: 64–108 argues for a broad focus and includes the ruler cult, angelic deliverers as well as spiritual messiahs in his discussion of pre-Christian messianism.
5   Hengel 1988, 1989a.
6   Hengel 2001: 8; also pp. 10, 12–13, 29.
7   E.g. H. Stegemann 1993: 286–7; Collins 1995: 49, 52–3, 56, 94, 195; Oegema 1998b; Evans 2000: 538.

messianism in the Hasmonean period, therefore, requires a contextual introduction that pays attention to:

1) the Judaism and Hellenism debate
2) the foundation of the Hasmonean dynasty preceded by the Maccabaean revolt
3) the ideology of the Hasmonean rulers.

Here, only brief discussions can be devoted to these three topics, and readers should keep in mind that individual scholarly opinions are far more elaborate than my brief and selective sketch.

a. The Judaism and Hellenism Debate

Although other scholars had already discussed the nexus of Judaism and Hellenism, Martin Hengel's magnum opus triggered an enormous debate because of his far-reaching conclusions.[8] For Hengel the interaction between Judaism and Hellenism provided the cultural-religious context for Christian messianism. Hengel stands in the tradition of Johann Gustav Droysen, a nineteenth-century German ancient historian, who characterized Hellenism as a melting-pot of Greek *and* Oriental cultures and practices.[9] Other scholars, however, have distinguished Hellenism from Hellenization. In their view Hellenism is the cultural milieu of the Hellenistic period – and sometimes also the Roman era – which includes the outcome of Hellenization.[10] Several scholars consider this Hellenization to have been a largely mono-directional process of Graecization, starting with a switch to the Greek language.[11]

Although the extent to which Greek practices impacted on Palestine is assessed quite differently,[12] there is unmistakable evidence of the incorporation of Greek conventions in Judaea in the second century B.C.E. Several prominent Jews have Greek names, and two burial monuments conspicuous by their Hellenized style have been found, west and east of Jerusalem. Both graves probably belonged to a priestly family. Although there are Hebrew or Aramaic inscriptions on both buildings, the monuments were clearly built with Hellenistic features including columns in Doric style.[13] This evidence indicates that at least part of the Jerusalem priesthood was receptive to Greek architectural conventions. At the same time, Jewish cultural practices also share significant conventions with cultures of neighbouring peoples, which are partly articulated as a response to

---

8   Good surveys and references: Levine 1998: 3–32; Collins 2001.
9   Droysen 1877–8; Hengel 1988: 2–5.
10 Préaux 1978; Bichler 1983.
11 The word Hellenization derives from ἑλληνίζω, 'speak or write correct Greek', Aristotle, *Rhet.* 3.5.1 (1407a 19). In Acts 6.1 the word ἑλληνιστής, 'Hellenist', refers to Jews who speak Greek. See, for a careful assessment of the use of Greek in ancient Jewish inscriptions from Palestine, van der Horst 2001, who calculates that slightly more than 53 per cent of the inscriptions are in Greek (157).
12 For a radical argument of a minimal impact of Greek culture on the Jews in their homeland see Feldman 1977, 1986.
13 The Bnei Hezir tomb and Jason's tomb, Levine 1998: 41–2.

Greek culture, which paradoxically confirms the process of accommodation: one beats the enemy by adopting its own weapons.[14] This process of cultural opposition and accommodation becomes apparent in one of the primary sources about the Maccabaean revolt, 2 Maccabees (*ca.* 125 B.C.E.).

2 Maccabees uses the Greek noun ἑλληνισμός, 'Hellenism', disapprovingly for the introduction of Greek customs and a Greek way of life as part of the Maccabaean revolt's prehistory.[15] 2 Maccabees describes in detail how the Hellenization of the Jews reached a dramatic peak at the beginning of the rule of the Seleucid king, Antiochus IV (175–164 B.C.E.). The problems started when the high priest Onias III was replaced by a certain Jason, a member of his own family. Jason took possession of the high priesthood by offering a high sum to the king. He ensured Greek forms of education by founding a gymnasium and ephebate, which presupposes that the king had already acknowledged Jerusalem as a *polis*, a Greek city. Jason's registration of the Jerusalemites as citizens of Antioch (2 Macc. 4.9, 12, 19) implies his enlisting of subdivisions of the citizens of the *polis* Jerusalem.[16] As a result of Jason's policy the priests neglected their sacrificial service and spent their time in the wrestling arena. The epitomist of 2 Maccabees considers this a terrible betrayal of Jewish practices and sighs: 'So Hellenism reached a high point with the introduction of foreign customs through the boundless wickedness of the impious Jason, no true high priest' (2 Macc. 4.13). Next Menelaus acquired the high priesthood by outbidding Jason. He even surpassed, in the epitomist's view, his predecessor's wickedness, and the struggle between Jason and Menelaus triggered the first invasion of Antiochus IV in Jerusalem, which caused eighty thousand victims within three days (2 Macc. 5.14). Guided by Menelaus, Antiochus also robbed the Temple of the holy vessels and eighteen hundred talents (169 B.C.E.; 2 Macc. 5.15-16, 21). Antiochus' second intervention in 167 B.C.E. led to the total abolition of the Jewish way of life, the enforcement of Greek practices and the desecration of the Jerusalem Temple. The Temple became dedicated to Zeus Olympius (2 Macc. 6.1-11).[17]

b. *The Maccabaean Revolt and the Foundation of the Hasmonean Dynasty*

1 Maccabees, another primary source, contemporaneous with 2 Maccabees, presents a very different picture of the so-called Maccabaean crisis. It puts almost all the blame on Antiochus IV, although it briefly confirms the foundation of a gymnasium, by anonymous persons who formed a pact with the Gentiles (1 Macc. 1.11-15).[18] 1 Maccabees most probably derives from circles within the

---

14   See especially Momigliano 1975.
15   The appropriate Jewish practices are indicated by the catchword Ἰουδαϊσμός 'Judaism' (2 Macc. 2.21; 8.1; 14.38). Further discussion in van Henten 1997.
16   Ameling 2003: 105–12.
17   Gera 1998: 141–61. Concise discussion: Collins 2001: 42–52.
18   The oldest source, the book of Daniel, suggests that part of the Jewish people did not remain faithful to God's covenant (11.30, 32), and also hints in very negative but veiled language at the king's adaptation of the Temple cult (7.25-26; 11.28-39).

Hasmonean court in Jerusalem. Its composition confirms the focus on Antiochus as evil king and depicts the revolt of Mattathias and his five sons, the Maccabaean brothers, as a progressing liberation from Antiochus' tyranny. Three phases of aggression by Antiochus IV are described. They correspond with three cycles of liberation and restoration by the Maccabees, which all culminate in a new festival of commemoration:

1. A) abolition of Jewish religious practice, desecration of the Temple, and introduction of the king's religion (1.41-64)
   B) re-dedication of the Temple (3.1–4.55)
   C) Chanukka festival (4.56-59)

2. A) plundering of the Temple (1.20-28)
   B) rescue from Nicanor's threat concerning the Temple (5.1–7.47)
   C) Day of Nicanor (7.48-49)

3. A) occupation of Jerusalem, foundation of the Gentile Citadel (*Akra*; 1.29-40)
   B) capture of the Citadel (8.1–13.50)
   C) festival of commemoration (13.51-52).

The Maccabaean revolt starts, according to 1 Maccabees, with Mattathias' refusal to participate in the local sacrifice commanded by the king (1 Macc. 2.15-27). The location is telling, the Maccabaean family belonged to the aristocracy of Modein, a town on the northwest border of Judaea. The Maccabees were priests by descent, belonging to the clan of Joarib. Josephus mentions Hasmon as their ancestor, from which the Hasmonean family name derives.[19] 1 Maccabees describes three generations of the Hasmonean dynasty, 1) Mattathias, 2) his five sons, Judas Maccabaeus, Jonathan and Simon being the most prominent, and 3) Simon's only remaining son. 1 Maccabees was probably composed during John Hyrcanus' reign (134–104 B.C.E.).[20] Two observations counter the pro-Hasmonean presentation of the facts in 1 Maccabees. A close reading of 1 and 2 Maccabees implies that the Hasmonean rule must have emerged, in fact, during a process of multiple reciprocal relationships with the Seleucid overlords.[21] Even when Simon and, afterwards, his son John Hyrcanus were sitting firmly in the saddle, there must have been considerable opposition against the Hasmonaeans within Jewish society. This can be deduced from sources such as 2 Maccabees and the Qumran documents, which suggest that non-Hasmonean priestly circles strongly opposed the Hasmonean combination of priestly and political leadership.

c. The Hasmonean Ideology of Kingship and Priesthood

The key document about the Hasmonean ideology of rulership is the honorary decree for Simon and his sons in 1 Macc. 14.25-49. Simon the Hasmonean is not

---

19 1 Macc 2.1. Joarib is mentioned as one of the twenty-four priestly clans in 1 Chr. 24.7 (cf. 9.10). Hasmon: Josephus, *Ant.* 12.265.
20 Detailed discussion of the Hasmonean rulers: Schürer 1973–87: 1.125–218.
21 Gruen 1998: 1–40.

yet called a king, but 1 Maccabees presents his power in the ideological framework of Hellenistic kings.[22] Representatives of the Jewish people probably did compose an honorary decree for Simon (140 B.C.E.), but the Hasmonean court clique has no doubt adapted the document 'in house' in its present form.[23] The ruler ideology presented in 1 Maccabees is, therefore, self-legitimation by the Hasmonean elite.

1 Macc. 14.25-49 reconfirms Simon's position as the Jews' political and military leader as well as the high priest (14.35, 38, 41-2). It depicts him as an autocratic ruler, who not only finances but also personifies the Jewish state. The decision to make Simon the political leader *and* high priest for ever, or at least, 'until a true prophet should appear' (14.41) suggests that the Hasmonaeans were the obvious rulers of the Jewish theocratic state. The combination of both offices was a radical change, although another high priest, Simon, the son of Onias, had practically achieved a similar theocratic leadership about sixty years earlier, according to Ben Sira's description (Sir 50.1-24). This Simon from the high priestly family of the Oniads took care of the protection of the Temple as well as the city of Jerusalem (Sir 50.1-4) and his leadership is legitimated as hereditary like the Davidic kingship (45.23-26). Simon in his function of high priest is highly praised in poetic terms as the sublime mediator between God and the Jewish people (50.5-21).

The reference to the true prophet in 1 Macc. 14.41 (cf. 4.46 and 9.27) is frequently interpreted in connection with the assumption that there were no further prophetic revelations after Malachi (early fifth century B.C.E.). 1 Macc. 14.41 can, however, also be read as a veiled claim by a Hasmonean ruler, perhaps Simon's son John Hyrcanus, that he would not only be the Jews' political and priestly leader, but also take over the prophetic leadership. Other sources may support such a reading.[24] A third interpretation of 1 Macc 4.46 and 14.41 is even possible, because the passages can also hint at the postponement of prophetic performance until the eschaton. In that case the prophet referred to would be the eschatological prophet who heralds God's day of judgement, as is, for example, exemplified in a prophecy by Malachi: 'Look, I will send you the prophet Elijah before the great and terrible day of the Lord comes' (Mal. 4.5).[25]

The Hasmonean ideology of a combined political and priestly leadership was not based on the family's descent from King David or a high priestly clan. The claim of hereditary leadership was based on successful deeds and analogy. The decree lists Simon's glorious deeds in detail with a focus upon his military actions (14.32-40):

---

22   For a discussion of the contributions of Hellenistic kingship traditions, especially those related to the ruler cult, to Jewish messianism, see Horbury 1998c: 68–77; 127–8 and 146–8. Josephus (*J.W.* 1.70; *Ant.* 13.301) reports that Aristoboulus I (104–103 B.C.E.) put on the royal diadem. Strabo, 16.2.40, states that Alexander Jannaeus (103–76 B.C.E.) was the first Hasmonean king; cf. Mendels 1992b: 55–79.
23   Van Henten 2001: 116–45.
24   Josephus, *Ant.* 13.282–3, 300; for rabbinic passages, cf. Schürer 1973–87: 1.210, 215.
25   See, for example, Bartlett 1973: 65; Zimmermann 1998: 412 n.339. This reading does not work well, however, with 1 Maccabees' focus upon the present in this world.

- protection of the Jerusalem Temple (14.31-2, 36; cf. 14.29)
- triumph over the people's enemies (14.31-2; cf. 14.29)
- fortification of various cities as well as the liberated Citadel (14.33-4, 36-7)
- creation of a stable and peaceful situation (14.36).

1 Macc. 14.35-36 explicitly states that the Jews made Simon their leader and high priest 'in recognition of *all that he had done*' and because 'his leadership was crowned with success'.[26] The latter phrase not only repeats similar statements about Judas Maccabaeus' deeds (1 Macc. 2.47; 3.4-8; cf. 16.2-3), but also associates the Hasmonaeans with the charismatic leadership of the Judges 'in whose hands deliverance was'.[27]

The description of the beginning of the Maccabaean revolt (1 Macc. 2.15-28) constructs an analogy between Mattathias and Phinehas the priest, who ended God's wrath about the Israelites' idolatry at Baal Peor by killing one of the godless and adulterous Israelites. God rewarded Phinehas with a covenant of perpetual priesthood (Num. 25; cf. 1 Macc. 2.15-27, 54, 57; 14.41). Another analogy highlights the Maccabaean brothers as heirs of David, again on the basis of their deeds. Mattathias' final words to his sons connects their mission to the models of Phinehas and David, as well as to the eternal covenants that God granted them both: 'Phinehas, our father, never flagged in his zeal, and his was the covenant of everlasting priesthood' ... 'David was a man of loyalty, and he was granted the throne of an everlasting kingdom' (1 Macc. 2.54, 57).[28] Thus, Mattathias' last words and the decree for Simon and his sons both suggest that the Hasmonaeans were the Jews' obvious rulers because they were successful and acted in line with the leadership of famous political and priestly leaders like David and Phinehas.

2. *Qumran Messianism*

Both the origin of the Qumran library and the identification of the Qumran group have been hotly debated, especially since Norman Golb's argument as presented in several studies from the 1980s onward. He claims that the ruins at Wadi Qumran on the Northwest shore of the Dead Sea were a former fortress and that the manuscripts found in the caves nearby have nothing to do with this fortress. Instead, they derive from various libraries in Jerusalem carried to safety during the war against Rome in 66–70 C.E. The majority opinion nevertheless remains that the ruins at Qumran once belonged to a group that had withdrawn itself from the mainstream of Jewish society and was either identical with the Essenes, a Jewish group described by Pliny, Josephus and Philo, or the group evolved out of these Essenes. An important argument in favour of this view is that the information provided by the 'Qumranites' about themselves in the scrolls closely

---

26 Translations of biblical passages are from the *New English Bible*.
27 1 Macc. 4.25; 5.62; Judg. 2.18; 3.9; 6.36-37; 15.18.
28 Judas Maccabaeus alludes to David's fight with Goliath in a prayer before a battle (1 Macc. 4.30). See also 1 Macc. 3.3-4.

matches the descriptions of the Essenes in Greek sources.[29] The Essenes formed a strongly hierarchical community with priestly leaders and a strict ritual way of life, based on a solar calendar of 364 days instead of the usual lunar calendar with 354 days. The Qumran scrolls document that the ideas of this group included a developed angelology, a conception of an eschatological Temple, a deterministic worldview, and last but not least, priestly and royal messiahs.[30]

Qumran messianism is unique, because it comprises, in a time frame of about 200 years, various figures and roles, various titles that sometimes overlap, and, at least in most passages, a time framework focusing upon the eschaton. Several passages concern messianic re-interpretations of biblical passages, especially of Gen. 49.10, Num. 24.17 and Isa. 11.1-6.[31] The diversity of Qumran messianism is already apparent from passages with the word משיח.[32] The most prominent Qumran messiah is probably the Messiah of Israel, who is mentioned in the Rule of the congregation (1QSa=1QS28a, from the second half of the first century B.C.E. (see also copies or closely related texts in 4Q255–264). This document focuses on the end of time (i 1) and deals, among other things, with rules for meetings of the community council. These meetings include a meal 'when [God] begets [reading יוליד] the Messiah with them'. This passage alludes to Psalm 2, a much-quoted royal psalm that refers to God's Anointed (v. 2). Psalm 2.7 reads: 'You are my son; today I have begotten you (ילדתיך)'. The passage clearly states that this messiah shall enter *after* the chief priest of the congregation of Israel. The messiah only blesses the community and stretches out his hands to the bread after the chief priest has taken from the first-fruit of the bread and the new wine (ii 12–21). Thus, this passage describes the coming of the messiah in the context of the end of times scenario and his participation in a community meal. He is clearly second in rank, after the priestly leader. In the light of the double messiahs elsewhere in the scrolls (below) we may safely assume that the chief priest too was considered to be a messianic figure.[33]

The running commentary on Genesis in 4Q252 (also called 4Q Patriarchal Blessings or 4Q Pesher Genesis, 30 B.C.E. – 70 C.E.) also mentions a political messiah. It comments upon Gen. 49.10, the section of Jacob's blessing of his sons that has been frequently interpreted in a messianic framework: 'The scepter shall not depart from Judah, nor the ruler's staff from between his feet'. The commentary reads: 'For the staff (המחקק) is the covenant of royalty ... until the

---

29   This view basically rests on the geographical location of the Essenes in the area of Qumran as stated by Pliny the Elder (*Natural History* 5.73) and the close correspondences in practices and beliefs between Essenes and Qumranites. For a counter-opinion see Beall 1988, and for a survey VanderKam 1994: 71–98.
30   See further García Martínez 1988; Magness 2002.
31   See Salvesen, this volume: 246–8 and 253.
32   In line with Hebrew Bible/Old Testament passages, the scrolls also refer to anointed human persons, especially prophets, without messianic connotations: CD ii 12–13. Also CD v 21–vi 1 (parallels: 4Q267 3 ii 17; 6Q15 3 4); 1QM xi 7–8; 4Q270 9 ii 14; 4Q287 10 13; 4Q521 8 9, and perhaps 4Q381 15 7). 4Q377 2 ii 5 calls Moses as a prophet 'God's Anointed one', Zimmermann 1998: 340. Anointed priests: 4Q375 i 9; 4Q376 i 1–2.
33   See also 4Q285 5 4–5. 4Q Florilegium (=4Q174) 1–3 i 11–12 and CD vii 18–20 (MS A).

Messiah of righteousness comes, the Branch of David' (4Q252 v 3–4).[34] A fragment of 4Q458 refers to someone 'anointed with the oil of kingship', perhaps a king, perhaps a royal messiah, but there is not enough preserved of the context to make sense of this passage.[35]

A priestly or prophetic messianic figure shimmers through in 11Q Melchizedek (11Q13, first century B.C.E.), a document that interprets several biblical passages, including Leviticus 25 about the Jubilee Year. The text's main figure is Melchizedek, a heavenly high priest and saviour of the righteous at the end of times. He acts as judge on the Day of Atonement at the time of God's final judgement, when Belial, the leader of the evil forces, and the spirits of his lot will be defeated. In column 2, in connection with the 'day of peace' within the Jubilee Year (ii 2, 15), the text focuses upon 'the messenger (מבשר) of good' who announces salvation as indicated in Isa. 52.7: '[How] beautiful on (the) mountains are the feet of the heral[d who pro]claims peace, the he[rald of good …' (ii 15–16). It is far from certain that this messenger should be identified with Melchizedek, but the messenger may be a messianic figure, because he is also associated with the 'Anointed of the spirit (משיח הרוח) as Daniel said' (ii 18). This must allude to the Anointed princes of Dan. 9.25-26, the only anointed figures mentioned in the book of Daniel.[36] This passage in Daniel focuses on Jerusalem's sanctuary, which implies that the Anointed princes are priestly figures. The second column of 11Q Melchizedek, however, builds on Isa. 61.1 and re-interprets Daniel's anointed ones as one messianic figure related to the future.[37] The function of this eschatological messiah of the spirit is focused upon prophecy and authoritative instruction.[38] He announces the rule of Melchizedek and proclaims salvation and comfort to the mourners of Zion.[39]

The political and priestly messiahs have sometimes been combined at Qumran. With slight variations in the Hebrew, several passages in the Damascus Document (dating perhaps from the beginning of the first century B.C.E.)[40] briefly refer to the arrival of 'the Messiah of Aaron and Israel' (CD xii 23–xiii 1; xiv 19; xix

---

34   Translations of Qumran passages are, with slight alterations, from García Martínez and Tigchelaar 1996.

35   Cf. 4Q215a 1 ii 10, which perhaps refers to 'the throne of the Anointed one', depending on the completion of a lacuna.

36   Contrary to the majority opinion Horbury 1998c: 8–9, 33–4 and 84–6, interprets the priestly princes of Dan. 9.25-26, as well as the Son of Man of Dan. 7, as messianic figures. Cf. the self-glorification or exaltation hymn in 4Q491 fragment 11, in which the speaker claims to be counted among the angelic beings (אלים). This heavenly mediator is not identified by the text, but several scholars argue that he is a (priestly) messianic figure. Detailed discussion and references can be found in Collins 1995: 113–53; Zimmermann 1998: 285–311.

37   While de Jonge 1991: 30 rejects this passage as a reference to a messianic figure, Horbury 1998c: 81, 86–108 and 120–4, seems to identify this 'messiah of the spirit' with Melchizedek. He argues for a widespread tradition of pre-existent and angelic spiritual messiahs.

38   Some scholars read in 1Q30 1 2 'the holy Messiah' instead of 'the holy spirit', but the text is too fragmentary to make sense of.

39   Zimmermann 1998: 412. 4Q521 2 ii also re-interprets Isaiah 61 after referring to a messiah to whom the heavens and the earth will listen.

40   The Damascus Document has been transmitted in two medieval copies from the Cairo Genizah (CD-A and CD-B) as well as in fragments from cave 4 at Qumran (4Q265–273).

10–11; xx 1).[41] This arrival is obviously a crucial caesura in history. Of these passages CD xix 10–11 most clearly sets this arrival in an eschatological context, because it connects the coming of the Messiah of Aaron and Israel with the final judgement and the consequent punishment of the wicked:

> These [i.e. those faithful to God] shall escape in the age of the visitation; but those that remain shall be delivered up to the sword when there comes the Messiah of Aaron and Israel. As happened in the age of the visitation of the first one, as said by Ezekiel ... (quotation of Ezek 9.4).

CD xii 23–xiii 1 (paralleled in 4Q266 10 i 12) sets this arrival in the 'time of wickedness'. The Community Rule (*ca.* 100 B.C.E.) also refers to this arrival (1 QS ix), but explicitly uses the plural 'The Messiahs of Aaron and Israel' next to 'the Prophet', which may imply that the Damascus Document also refers to two messiahs, one Davidic and one priestly.[42] 1QS ix 9–11, dealing with transgressions of community members, reads:

> They [the members] should not depart from any counsel of the law in order to walk (10) in complete stubbornness of their heart, but instead shall be ruled by the first directives which the men of the Community began to be taught (11) *until the Prophet comes, and the Messiahs of Aaron and Israel.*

The passage indicates a major change for the community in the future, when these three leaders arrive.

1QS ix 9–11 may be based on the messianic re-interpretation of a cluster of biblical passages as found in the Testimonia document from Qumran (4Q175, early first century B.C.E.).[43] This text focuses on God's promise to bring a prophet as his mouthpiece, in Deut. 18.18: 'I will raise up for them a prophet like you from among their brethren'. It also quotes a passage from Balaam's oracle (Num. 24.15-17) and one from the blessing of Levi (Deut. 33.8-11). Although 4Q175 lacks an explicit messianic reference, it does show that the combination of the three separate figures mentioned in 1QS ix (above) is not accidental. If we can combine both documents, 1QS's prophet may be the prophet promised in Deuteronomy 18, the Messiah of Israel the Davidic messiah announced by Balaam (Num. 24.17) and the Messiah of Aaron a priestly messiah indicated in Levi's blessing (Deut. 33.8-11). Unfortunately 1QS ix does not elaborate the role of these figures.

If one goes beyond explicit references to a משיח, the picture of royal messianic figures becomes more articulate. Three titles may refer to Davidic messiahs: the 'Branch of David' (צמח דויד), the 'Prince (נשיא) of the congregation',[44] as well as 'the Sceptre' (deriving from Num. 24.17). 4Q252 mentions two of these

---

41   CD xii 23–xiii 1, xiv 19 and xix 10–11 mention the 'Messiah of Aaron and Israel' and CD xx 1 the 'Messiah from Aaron and from Israel'.
42   Against Abegg 1995. See Collins 1995: 74–101.
43   Collins 1995: 74.
44   This title probably derives from Ezek. 34.24; 37.25. For elaborate discussion of the political messiah see Zimmermann 1998: 46–229.

titles next to a reference to the Messiah (above). Passages about the 'Branch of David' and the 'Prince of the congregation' suggest that the royal messiah in Qumran is the eschatological warrior who smites the wicked, executes judgement, restores David's kingdom, and founds the era of peace and justice at the end of times. This Davidic messiah, sometimes also called the 'Stump of Jesse', is clearly a military leader. He fights the final battle against the 'Kittim'. The name 'Kittim' derives from Kition, a city on the island of Cyprus.[45] It is frequently a code name for Gentile enemies of the faithful of Israel. If the scrolls refer to actual enemies with this name, it usually concerns the Romans. A fragmentary text related to the War Scroll (1QM), 4Q285 (*ca.* 30 B.C.E. – early first century C.E.), concerns the battle of the Davidic messiah against the Kittim, if fragments 4 and 5 are read together. Fragment 5 quotes from Isaiah 11, the famous text about the ideal Davidic king, announced as a shoot coming from the stump of Jesse and a branch growing from his roots. This fragment has caused quite a stir. Line 4 can be read as a reference to the violent death of the Davidic messiah: 'they will put to death the Prince of the congregation, the Bran[ch of David].' Most scholars, however, suggest that the more probable reading of this line is that the Prince of the congregation is the subject of the verb 'kill'.[46] In that case the Branch fights the Kittim, while the priests take charge of the disposal of the slain to avoid the defilement of the land. This fits in with the role of the shoot from the stump of Jesse, as announced in Isa. 11.4: 'he shall kill the wicked with the breath of his lips'. The object of the killing by the Branch, indicated with a singular suffix, is not made explicit. The context (fragment 4) suggests the Kittim as the Branch's opponents, so that their leader, perhaps, is the Branch's victim.

The Isaiah Pesher, which probably dates after Pompey's intervention in Jerusalem (63 B.C.E.), offers a long quotation from the beginning of Isa. 11 (11.1-5). The Pesher's interpretation focuses on the shoot of David and describes the role of this messiah at the end of time as follows (4QpIsa^a=4Q161 8–10 iii 18–22):

> [The interpretation of the word concerns the shoot] of David, which will sprout [in the final days, since] (19) [with the breath of his lips he will execute] his enemies and God will support him with [the spirit of] courage... (21) ... He will rule over all the peoples and Magog (22) [...] his sword will judge all the peoples ...[47]

The continuation of this passage (lines 22–9) suggests that the Branch will submit to the instruction of the priests. 4Q541 (sometimes called 4Q Aaronic A or 4Q Testament of Levi^d), dating from the end of the second century B.C.E. or

---

45 It sometimes refers to persons from the South of Cyprus (Isa. 23.1, 12; Ezek. 27.6), *HALAT* vol. 2, p. 480.

46 Further discussion in Bockmuehl 1992.

47 The Prince of the congregation is the beneficiary of a messianic blessing in 1QSb v 21–29 that builds on Isa. 11.4 and associates him with a young bull with horns of iron, a lion (cf. Gen. 49.9-10) as well as the Sceptre of Balaam's oracle (Num. 24.17). Similarly CD vii 18–21 (MS A). Num. 24.17-19 is quoted without interpretation in 4Q175 9–13 and 1QM xi 5–7. 4Q252 v 1 connects the Branch of David with the Sceptre of Judah of Gen. 49.10, to whom has been given the covenant of royalty for everlasting generations. 1Q28b v 27 briefly alludes to Num. 24.17.

somewhat later, describes the activities of a priestly leader who will appear in the final days. No title is given, but his acts would fit in with those of a priestly messiah. The text presupposes the restoration of the Jerusalem Temple, because it briefly mentions an atonement ritual: 'he will atone for the children of his generation' (4Q541 Fragment 9). The passage connects this figure with instruction and indicates a strongly beneficial role for all members of his people:

> ... and he will be sent to all the children of (3) his people. His word is like the word of heaven, and his teaching, according to the will of God. His eternal sun will shine (4) and his fire will burn in all the ends of the earth. Then, darkness will vanish (5) from the earth, and gloom from the globe (lines 3–6).

The response to the priestly leader's appearance does not match his beneficial work. The remaining part of the fragment prophesies that he will experience strong opposition through abundant lies, deceit and violence, because people will go astray in his time (lines 6–7).

The Qumran community's expectation of two messiahs acting simultaneously, a priestly as well as a Davidic messiah, may have been triggered by the Hasmonean combination of the political and priestly leadership (above), but several Hebrew Bible passages also support this view, especially Balaam's fourth oracle that conceives a Star as well as a Sceptre figure (Num. 24.15-17).[48] One version of the Damascus Document (Manuscript A) clearly builds on Balaam's oracle and projects two messiahs. This passage differs at first glance from the tandem of the royal and priestly messiahs, because it combines a Davidic messiah (Balaam's Sceptre) with a Star figure interpreted as an instructor who explains the Law. Both will come to Damascus, which may be a veiled reference to the community's place of exile. CD vii first identifies the 'Star' and then 'the Sceptre':

> And the star is the Interpreter of the Law, (19) who will come to Damascus, as is written [Num. 24.17]: 'A star moves out of Jacob, and a sceptre arises (20) out of Israel'. The sceptre is the Prince of the whole congregation and when he rises he will destroy (21) all the children of Seth. (CD vii 18–21)[49]

The Davidic messiah clearly operates as a military commander at the end of times, but the instructor needs clarification. Because he will come in the future, he has to be distinguished from the Teacher of Righteousness, the deceased leader of the community. Unfortunately CD vii (as well as vi) does not provide specific information about this Interpreter of the Law. Some scholars argue that he is a prophet, perhaps Elijah returning at the end of days.[50] The most plausible solution is, however, to interpret CD vii in line with other scrolls about two messiahs and take the instructor as the priestly messiah.[51] The Aaronic passage

---

48 Evans 2000: 539 also points to the anointment of Solomon and his high priest Zadok (1 Chr. 29.22) and the two branches of the olive tree in Zech. 4.12.
49 Cf. CD vi 7–11 and 4Q174, below. Also 4Q161 7–10 iii 15–22; 4Q285 5 4.
50 E.g. van der Woude 1957: 55.
51 The Levi blessing in Deut. 33.8-11, taken up in 4QTestimonia (above), also includes a reference to teaching (Deut. 33.10); cf. Brooke 1985: 204.

discussed above (4Q541 Fragment 9) supports this reading. It also presents the priestly messiah as an instructor. Thus, the Interpreter of the Law of CD vii may be identical with the Messiah of Aaron, the eschatological High Priest messiah.

A rather mysterious apocalyptic document in Aramaic, sometimes called 4Q Pseudo-Daniel^d or 4Q Son of God (=4Q246, *ca.* 100 B.C.E.), uses two synonymous titles, 'Son of God' and 'Son of the Most High' (ii 1), for a figure who has been identified in many different ways: a historical or future king, the people of God, the Antichrist, an angelic figure like Michael, Melchizedek, or the Prince of Light, or a messiah.[52] The two titles are given to this figure by an anonymous group, which will rule for several years over the earth and crush everything (lines 2–3). Perhaps this group should be identified with the People of God mentioned in line 4 in connection with the establishment of the eternal kingdom and eternal peace: 'Until the people of God arises and makes everything rest from the sword. (5) His kingdom will be an eternal kingdom, and all his paths in truth and upright[ness]' (lines 4–5). Lines 7–8 announce that all the cities will pay him homage, 'He is a great God among the gods'. The crux of this passage is whether we can take it as a unit that describes one coherent event in history. If so, the 'Son of God and Son of the Most High' figure may be the royal messiah, who establishes the eternal kingdom of peace. Yet, the manuscript has a blank at the beginning of line 4, which seems to go along with a transition in the content, because the rise of God's people heralds the new era. The eternal kingdom is, therefore, established by somebody other than the 'Son of God'.[53] In that case 'His kingdom' (line 4) could be interpreted as God's kingdom, which would be very much in line with eschatological expectations in the Hebrew Bible. It would also make the phrase 'He is a great God among the gods [probably angelic beings]' less problematic. In fact, there is just one Qumran passage about a 'Son of God' figure that is unambiguously messianic: 4Q174 (late first century B.C.E.). This anthology seems to have been composed as a commentary of Psalms 1 and 2. It combines quotations of various Hebrew Bible passages with explanations of those passages, including Levi's blessing in Deut. 33.8-11 (see above). It also builds on Nathan's oracle for David (2 Sam. 7.14). It connects God's promise about David's offspring with the Branch of David:

> ... 'I [God] will raise up your seed after you [David] and establish the throne of his kingdom (11) [for ev]er. I [God] will be a father to him and he will be a son to me.' [2 Sam. 7.13-14] This (refers to the) Branch of David, who will arise with the Interpreter of the law who (12) [will rise up] in Zi[on in] the last days ... (4Q174 1–3 i 10–12)

This passage again depicts the coming of the duo messiahs, the Branch of David and the priestly messiah identified with the Interpreter of the law (see above). The new element in 4Q174 is that the Branch of David is also associated with the 'Son of God' through the quotation of 2 Sam. 7. This can hardly be a coincidence, since

---

52   Zimmermann 1998: 128–70.
53   Cf. Collins 1995: 159 and Zimmermann 1998: 146–51.

the continuation of the passage quotes a section from another famous 'Son of God' text, Psalm 2 (above). 4Q174 interprets Ps. 2.1 as a prophecy about a conspiracy of the rulers of the nations against God and his Anointed one (lines 18–19).

3. Conclusion

The Maccabaean revolt and the establishment of the Hasmonean state are both responses to a severe crisis within Judaean society during Antiochus IV's rule. The primary sources perceive this crisis very differently. No doubt, Qumran messianism also developed through interaction with a response to a severe crisis. This time the Hasmoneans, with their claim of a hereditary and combined political and priestly leadership, were perceived as the main villains. The resistance of the Qumran community to their wicked opponents was, however, transposed from the present to a universal battle during the messianic era.

How are we to assess Qumran messianism if we look back to Professor Klausner's mini-lecture? Qumran messiahs go far beyond the anointed leaders of Israel in the Hebrew Bible. There are close correspondences to Christian messianism, including the notion of a messiah begotten by God and the association of the Davidic messiah with the Son of God. Yet, in comparison to the New Testament, Qumran messianism does not entail a fixed messiah figure, or a fixed title. The messianic passages are not very elaborate, but this does not necessarily imply that Qumran messianism did not amount to much. William Horbury objected to such a minimalist conclusion with the argument that Qumran messianism, and, as a matter of fact, messianism in the entire Hellenistic period, was not very developed exactly because it was well known and therefore self-evident.[54]

Several Qumran documents mention two simultaneous future messiahs (e.g. 1QS ix, 4Q175, 1QSa ii, CD vii and 4Q174). The political messiah, indicated by various names, is of Davidic descent. He functions as a military leader in the battle against the godless at the end of times and is Israel's ruler in the subsequent kingdom of peace. Although he figures more prominently in the texts, he is clearly subordinate to the priestly messiah (1QSa ii). The priestly messiah blesses the community (1QSa ii) and executes a ritual of atonement (4Q541), but his main function seems to be instruction and interpretation of the Law on behalf of God (4Q541, CD vii).

---

54 See Horbury 1998c, esp. 36–63.

Chapter 3

The Herodian Period

Sean Freyne

Virtually all recent studies of Jewish messianism are agreed that no standard notion of *the* messiah had been developed in the Second Temple period. Indeed it is somewhat of a surprise to discover that in the literature of the period the notion of the messiah is often absent when one might have expected otherwise. This fact bears out the oft-repeated statement of Sigmund Mowinckel that 'an eschatology without a messiah is conceivable, but not a messiah without a future hope.'[1] In this essay I propose to investigate the extent to which different messianic ideas were expressed in the Herodian period. Inevitably, the reign of Herod the Great as king of the Jews (40–4 B.C.E.) sets the tone for the whole subsequent period, at least until the First Revolt, since the aggressive Romanization of the country under his watch was continued subsequently, if not as spectacularly, by the later Herodians. Thus, the following exploration is developed in two stages. The first step is to examine some aspects of Herod's multifaceted legacy, paying special attention to the manner in which his vigorous promotion of Augustan rule impacted on Jewish identity concerns. This discussion will hopefully provide the proper context for examining the various ways in which the messianic idea was subsequently developed as one element in the counter-propaganda that Judaean religious beliefs generated.

1. *Herodian Rule, Roman Ideology and Messianic Claims*

Herod clearly accepted the rules of client kingship once he had been declared king of the Jews by the Roman senate in 40 B.C.E.[2] His Idumean pedigree was an advantage, especially since the young Hasmonean pretender-king, Antigonos, had in fact invited the Parthians to invade Palestine, and he had widespread popular support among the Judaean population. As reported by Josephus, Herod's meeting subsequently with Octavian, which took place on the island of Rhodes shortly after Octavian's victory over Antony at the battle of Actium in 31 B.C.E., is highly informative in terms of what was at stake for both men (*Ant.* 15.187–201). Herod, we are told, left aside his diadem, acknowledged that he had supported Antony and pledged himself to serve Rome in whatever capacity Octavian might see fit. The future emperor for his part appreciated Herod's

---

1   Mowinckel 1956: 8.
2   Paltiel 1991.

usefulness in terms of gaining full control of the territories that had been under Antony's command, availing himself of Herod's material support and show of loyalty in his subsequent journeys to Syria and Egypt.

Herod's relationship with Octavian and his dependency on the latter's patronage inevitably meant that the effects of his long reign on Judaean society were very different from those of his Hasmonean predecessors. These latter had succeeded in establishing an autonomous kingdom in Judaea for the first time since the Babylonian exile. Admittedly, they too had adopted such aspects of Hellenism as Greek language and names, Hellenistic forms of diplomacy, employment of mercenaries in their armies and the adoption of the Greek forms of court titulature.[3] Yet, in the establishment of a Jewish state they had extended its borders, re-appropriating traditional territories, banishing or forcibly converting non-Jews living in these lands (1 Macc. 15.33; *Ant.* 13.318). Despite this achievement, it is significant that none of the court propagandists, including Josephus, ever made messianic claims in regard to their diplomatic and military successes. Their achievements are deemed to be heroic by the standards of the Judges of old. Thus, the author of 1 Maccabees describes their seed as those 'to whom had been granted the deliverance of Israel through their agency' (1 Macc. 5.62).[4]

The speculation concerning the 'messiahs of Aaron and Israel' (1QS 9,11) that is found not only in the Qumran literature, but also in various writings from the Hasmonean period (*Jubilees* and *Testaments of Levi* and *Judah* in particular) can plausibly be linked to the dissension that we encounter during the period due to the appropriation of the high-priesthood by the regime.[5] This issue surfaced for the first time in the sources in the reign of John Hyrcanus when the Pharisees emerge as the party of opposition asking him to give up the priesthood and be content with 'ruling (*archein*) the people' (*Ant.* 13.288–300). It was, however, during the reign of his son, Alexander Jannaeus, who had also now formally adopted the title king that the quarrel with the pious Jews came to a head. During the Feast of Tabernacles his right to offer sacrifice was challenged, leading to wholesale slaughter (*Ant.* 13.372–4). Clearly, both episodes point to priesthood rather than kingship as the more important issue for religious Jews at that juncture.

However, by the end of the period it was the notion of kingship that had become more prominent, as the *Psalms of Solomon* clearly indicate, a collection that is also generally attributed to Pharisaic circles. The opening verses of *Pss. Sol.* 17 in particular are a thinly veiled allusion to the adoption of the title 'king' by those who had no right according to the promise, since this title belongs to God himself, (*Kyrie, su autos basileus hemon eis aiona*). Yet, for the psalmist this axiom did not negate the fact that the kingship had been entrusted to the Davidic house only. Those who had seized the monarchy 'by force' are described as sinners, who in their arrogant boasting 'had despoiled the throne of David' (*Pss. Sol.* 17.1-6). The Psalm goes on to refer to 'a man alien to our race', through whom God had overthrown them and destroyed their descendants from the earth (v. 7). This figure is generally taken to be Pompey, whose intervention in Judaean

---

3   McGing 1995, especially 63–6.
4   Goldstein 1987; Collins 1987.
5   For a discussion cf. Collins 1995: 74–5; and see van Henten, this volume: 23–7.

affairs in 63 B.C.E. had reduced Hasmonean rule to that of an ethnarchy. It could be plausibly argued, however, that it was Herod who is intended, since it was he who eventually put an end to the line, with the defeat of Antigonos and the murder of his own sons by Mariamme some time later.[6]

Irrespective of whether it is Pompey or Herod who should be seen as God's agent in putting an end to these usurpers of the throne of David, it is significant that the man described as 'alien to our race' is not designated God's 'anointed', as was the foreign ruler, Cyrus, earlier (Isa. 43.1). Instead Psalm 17 goes on to develop a very different profile for the expected anointed one, a description to which we shall return later. If the Hasmoneans could not develop a Davidic lineage, Herod, as an Idumean, certainly was in no position to do so. He had to rely on another authority to endorse his kingship, namely, that of Roman patronage. Nor did he make the mistake of appropriating the high-priesthood, though he clearly recognized the political potential of the office by ensuring that non-Judaeans would hold it, and only at his behest. It could be that in appointing Babylonians and Alexandrians to the post Herod was pointing to his role as 'king of the Jews', a title which he, at least, seems to have understood to include Jews in the Diaspora as well as in the homeland.

It was this international aspect that made his rule so different from that of the Hasmoneans. They indeed developed diplomatic ties with other peoples, most notably the Spartans. For a client king, however, Herod was a genuine player on the international scene to an unprecedented extent. The Hasmoneans may have described themselves as 'Philhellenes', but Herod was a genuine Hellenizer. He saw his role as extending the scope of the Greek way of life as filtered through Roman, or better, Augustan policy in the East. The list of his achievements in this regard is impressive: urban, Hippodamian-style layout of cities; monumental buildings and other architectural embellishments; support for Greek games at home and abroad, most notably those at Olympus; benefactions to foreign cities including Athens; propagation of the imperial cult of Roma and Augustus; the use of pagan images on his coins; the maintenance of a court in Hellenistic style. In these and other respects Herod was thoroughly imbued with the contemporary *Zeitgeist*, reflecting his family background as Hellenized, not Judaized, Idumeans.[7]

This presentation of Herod as a pan-Hellenist needs to be balanced with his attitudes to Judaism, even if one cannot agree with Peter Richardson's attempt to see him as genuinely Jewish in terms of his beliefs and commitments. Doron Mendels speaks instead of Herod's 'schizophrenia' insofar as he sought to placate his Jewish subjects, while at the same time having little interest in respecting Jewish religious sensibilities when his own political agenda demanded otherwise. The understanding of the episode of the Golden Eagle over the temple gate is an excellent example of the differing points of view with regard to Herod's sensitivity or otherwise towards his Jewish subjects (*Ant.* 17.149–67). While it is usually seen as a provocative act to place a recognized Roman emblem over the

---

6 For a recent discussion of the collection in terms of dating and provenance cf. Nickelsburg 2005: 238–47. Cf. also Atkinson 1996.
7 McGing 1995: 66–8; Kokkinos 1998: 94–139.

ceremonial entry to the temple, Richardson seeks to diminish its impact. He suggests ways in which it either was not seen by the majority of those entering from the city via 'Wilson's Arch', where he supposes the emblem to have been placed, and not on the main gate, as is often supposed, or because Jews generally had come to accept the representation of living creatures.[8] But this explanation does not take account of the fact that the eagle was above all a *Roman* symbol, suggesting conquest and superiority.[9] In all probability there were varying views of the incident at the time. Josephus suggests as much by naming the teachers, Judas and Matthias, who were responsible for instigating the removal and destruction of the emblem, which they deemed to have been against the law, whereas the Jewish officials, whom Herod summoned to his court in Jericho, sought to dissociate themselves from the whole affair. Herod, for his part, is represented as decorating the temple in ways that far surpassed anything that the Hasmoneans had accomplished.

The discussion by William Horbury of Herod's Jewish allegiances is characteristically learned and suggestive. He takes account of the fact that the rabbinic writings remember Herod's temple appreciatively (*b. B. Bat.* 3b–4a; *b. Sukkah* 51b). This tradition among the Babylonian sages, which follows closely the outline of Josephus' account, suggests to Horbury that there was a strand of thinking emanating from Nicolas of Damascus or Josephus, which was prepared to praise Herod for the building, despite the otherwise negative treatment of him as a tyrant.[10] According to Horbury, the act of rebuilding the temple may have meant that Herod was seen as 'touched by the aura of messianism' in some Jewish eyes.[11] Further support for this claim comes from the rather enigmatic reference by the first-century C.E. Roman satirist, Persius, to 'Herod's Days' (5.179–84) – a reference which Horbury interprets as an allusion to a festival observed by Roman Jews, possibly recalling accession days of various Herodian princes. In the case of Herod the Great this coincided with his ceremonial dedication of the temple, as reported by Josephus (*Ant.* 15.421–3).

Thus, in response to the efforts of the last of the Hasmoneans to discredit him as a foreigner, and, therefore, in breach of the law of the king (Deut. 17.15), Herod sought by various means to establish his credentials as king of the Jews. In addition to claiming descent from Babylonian Jews (*Ant.* 14.9) and making benefactions both in Jerusalem and the Diaspora, his major act as king of the Jews was the rebuilding of the temple in accordance with the original Solomonic dimensions. This was completed in 18 months and with due observance of the purity laws and the continuation of the sacrifices (*Ant.* 15.388–90).

Central to Horbury's claim is the fact that the building of a new temple seems to have been associated in some circles with the Messiah, and could be seen as

---

8   Richardson 1999, especially 15–18; Mendels 1992b: 209–42, here 214.
9   The image of an eagle is also found on one of Herod's coins, and its precise significance is variously understood. Thus Meshorer 2001: 68 suggests that the eagle was a symbol of holiness according to Deut. 32.31; Ezek. 1.10; 17.7. The ambivalence of such symbols suggests the need for a broader perspective in determining the particular intention in their use.
10   Horbury 1991.
11   Horbury 1991: 122. A similar suggestion has been put forward by Schalit 1969: 471–4.

the work of a Jewish king independently of Davidic origins. (Zech. 6.12, LXX; *1 En.* 53.6). At the same time, he also recognizes that aspects of Herod's rule, including his interest in the temple, reflect traits of Hellenistic kingship. Thus, he concludes that Herod's kingship was 'thoroughly Augustan and thoroughly Jewish'.[12] There may well be an overlap between Jewish expectation of the Messiah and Hellenistic kingship, since both had antecedents in earlier Near Eastern ideas of the king as a divine figure.[13] Indeed some Jews who may have favoured Herod over his Hasmonean rivals, might well have been tempted to exploit such overlaps between Augustan rhetoric and Jewish messianic hopes. However, to attribute a genuine messianic status to Herod's kingship, as he himself, or for that matter the majority of his Jewish subjects, might have envisaged, would seem to be going beyond the overall thrust of his reign.[14]

Herod's vigorous promotion of the imperial cult of Roma and Augustus at Caesarea, Sebaste and Banias, is difficult to square with notions of Jewish messianic beliefs in any strict sense. The extent to which the messianic idea might have been exploited by others during his reign must remain a moot point in the absence of any clear indications, other than the Matthean infancy narratives, which are highly developed theological accounts of a much later period. Certainly, the upsurge of discontent in all regions of the realm after Herod's death, to be discussed further below, which has been described as a form of popular messianism, points to widespread discontent. Was this due to social or religious factors, including messianic pretensions? The fact that the Hasmoneans do not appear to have regarded it as feasible to claim a messianic underpinning for their use of royal titles suggests that it would have been extremely unlikely for the Herodians to have done so either.

In evaluating Josephus' account of Herod's reign one has to take account of his favouring of priestly aristocratic, rather than kingly, rule, as the better form of government.[15] Yet, despite this overall purpose in his writing of the *Antiquities of the Jews*, it seems clear that he is fascinated by the figure of Herod, even if he is dependent on Nicholas for much of his account, whom he accuses of partiality with regard to Herod (*Ant.* 16.183–7). Thus, the speech put on Herod's lips as he announces the rebuilding project is quite significant. In addition to the evocation of Solomon's memory as the builder of the original temple as well the failure of the returnees from Babylon to rebuild it in accordance with its proper dimensions, the speech also has clear echoes of Augustan claims, as these are expressed in the *Res Gestae Divi Augusti*: now is the appropriate time for such an enterprise since the world is at peace and the prosperity of the Jewish nation has been achieved (*Ant.* 15.382–8). While Josephus may here be seeking to represent the historical situation in accordance with his source, one would have to enquire also about the significance of this rhetoric for his own situation as a

---

12 Horbury 1991: 112–13, 147.
13 See in particular the essays of Rajak 1996 and Gruen 1996.
14 Rocca 2006 is an attempt to read the account of the Davidic Messiah in *Pss. Sol.* 17.23-51 in terms of Herod's career, but the effort is somewhat forced and unconvincing.
15 Mason 2003.

Jewish apologist in Rome at the time of writing. What better way to goad his Flavian patrons into a sense of regret at the destruction of 'so famous a city' (as the Roman historian, Tacitus, describes Jerusalem, *Hist.* 5, 2), than to remind his readers that the building of the temple, now in ruins, was the direct result of the Augustan peace?

It seems more plausible, therefore, to look for clearer indications as to Herod's real stance with regard to the Jewish heritage by taking a broader view of his reign. In this regard the wishes expressed by Jewish leaders in Rome on his death, echoing sentiments expressed earlier to Pompey, namely, that kingship should be abolished entirely, is surely highly indicative (*Ant.* 17.299–303; cf. *Ant.* 14.40–1). It is much more likely, therefore, that the building of the temple, as well as his other deeds of benefaction, should be judged within the larger context of his overall objectives as a client king with pretensions to Hellenistic values. Even today the Herodian features of the Temple Mount bear clear signs of belonging to the Augustan architectural *koine* of the East: a high mound, an extended *temenos* or sacred precinct, surrounded by *stoa* with entrances from various directions, and a *naos* or sanctuary at the centre were typical.[16] It has been suggested that Alexandria with its *Kaisareion* was the centre where this style was developed.[17] Interestingly, Philo of Alexandria can describe the honours heaped on Augustus everywhere as follows: 'Besides all this (the many blessings accruing from the establishment of sole rule) the whole habitable world voted him honours equal to those of the Olympian gods. In cities old and new, they build temples, *propylaea*, sacred precincts and colonnades for him' (*Legat.* 149–51). Thus, all Herod's building projects, including that on the Temple Mount, participate in this general 'language' of acclamation of Augustus that was being expressed throughout the Roman East. Soon temples in similar architectural style were appearing in Petra, Heliopolis, Palmyra and the Dekapolis, for example, so that Herod's building programme in Judaea was a pioneering trendsetter for others who wished to honour Augustus in typical oriental fashion.[18]

In developing older temples into centres of the Imperial cult of Roma and Augustus, it was important not to offend older deities or their shrines. As Paul Zanker has noted, the Greeks, no less than the Judaeans, needed reassurance on that score.[19] When building from scratch at Caesarea Maritima, Banias or Sebaste, Herod was operating with an architectural *carte blanche*, so to speak. But Jerusalem was different and Herod was well aware of this. As mentioned already, the reconstruction of the *naos* to match the Solomonic original took place quickly (a year and a half according to *Ant.* 15.421) and with proper respect for the purity laws. It was in the extension of the sacred precincts and the building of the *stoa* that Herod was able to express architecturally his Hellenizing and Romanizing intentions more freely.

In particular it has been suggested that the enlarged outer courtyard had been constructed in such a way that it could function as a profane civic centre, similar

16 Levine 1981, especially 64.
17 Foerster 1976.
18 Roller 1998: 255–6.
19 Zanker 1988: 298.

to a Roman agora. Such an arrangement would certainly be in contravention of what was envisaged in such documents as the Temple Scroll where the outer court is deemed to participate in the holiness of the whole complex and was not open for impure Israelites and Gentiles. The prohibition of Gentiles from passing beyond a certain point under pain of death, one archaeological exemplar of which has been found, is a clear indication that the regulations of the outer court of the Herodian complex were much less strict than those laid down in the Essene document, which itself was based on Ezekiel's plan of the restored temple.[20] This situation of limited Gentile access to the Herodian temple could conceivably have been based on hopes of an eschatological assembly of the nations together with Israel, as envisaged in 'The Animal Apocalypse' (*1 En.* 90.28-35). However, it is much more likely that Herod's plans were inspired by the Augustan images of the age of renewal, given the scale and style of the overall architectural ensemble, and the current propaganda concerning Roman rule and its benefits.

While attempts to link Herod and his reign to the messianic idea by means of his temple reconstruction must be judged unwarranted, there is a sense in which his reign did have serious messianic repercussions. John Collins has proposed a helpful schema for understanding the political implications of various apocalyptic scenarios within the literature of the period as follows: (i) the triumphalism of imperial power regarded as the fulfilment of history; (ii) the deferred eschatology of those, such as Josephus, who hoped for an eventual utopia, but who were content with the existing status quo; (iii) the revolutionary expectation of an imminent and radical change.[21] The 'rhetoric of empire' as expressed by the Roman poets, Virgil and Horace, and enthusiastically endorsed by Herod's monumental buildings, fits well into the first of Collins' categories.

Herod's Judaean subjects were unlikely to be convinced, however. For the vast majority their Golden Age would be ushered in by a king in the Davidic line, not a foreign overlord. The very incongruity for many between official claims and the lived reality inevitably aroused feelings of resentment and hostility not only against those who were celebrating the triumph of the present, but also against those co-religionists who were prepared to tolerate such blasphemous claims in order to gain some personal benefits. It was left to the more radical groups, who had called for the abolition of kingship as espoused by Hasmoneans and Herodians alike, to develop alternative scenarios and strategies based on their own traditions, in which the figure(s) of messiah(s) would have an important role to play. In this respect the *Psalms of Solomon*, especially Psalm 17, represent at once a critique of Hasmonean kingship and a programme for post-Herodian hopes for a future when the kingship of Yahweh would finally reassert itself. Experiments in kingship that were based either on Hellenistic models or Rome's toleration of client kings had proved just as illusory as far as Israel's deeper aspirations were concerned as had Israelite and Judaean kingship of the pre-exilic period. Then the experience of domination by the Assyrian and Babylonian empires was the catalyst for a rethinking of Yahweh's kingship. The issue in the first century was whether or not an adequate understanding of Israel's mission

20   Yarbro Collins 2001, especially 54f.
21   Collins 2002.

and destiny could be retrieved that would both withstand the allurements of a new imperial power from the west for its Judaean retainers, and what, if any role the figure of a messiah might have to play in such a rethink.

2. Messianic Manifestations and Themes

The argument thus far is that Herodian rule, insofar as it expressed the propaganda of an Augustan Golden Age, had given rise to conditions for radical alternatives to emerge within a Judaean context. It was further suggested that the most likely circles in which such dissension might occur were those in which that rule was found to be both socially oppressive and religiously compromising. It now remains to examine the available evidence, both actual and literary, for messianic hopes in the period from the death of Herod to the aftermath of the first revolt, assessing in particular the extent to which the effects of his reign had been the catalyst in developing counter-images of the expected messianic kingdom.

(i) Messianic Claimants and Prophets

The fragmentation of Judaean society in the wake of Herod's reign is a constant theme of Josephus' narrative. On the eve of the first revolt no fewer than five different factions are listed, each vying for control in the conduct of the revolt, in addition to those others such as the Pharisees and Sadducees, who were opposed to it to begin with (*J.W.* 7.262–70).[22] One of the difficulties in assessing the situation accurately is Josephus' terminology in describing the rebels. Labels such as *lestai, neoi, poneroi, stasiastai* and the like, descriptions which betray his own bias against the revolutionaries, also occur in other Graeco-Roman writers describing situations of social unrest elsewhere.[23] Thus, the disturbances that occurred in all three regions of the country – Galilee, Perea and Idumea – shortly after the death of Herod, are summed up as acts of brigandage (*Ant.* 17.285). Hence, a general impression is given that the whole country was in revolt and that similar conditions prevailed in all the regions, even though on closer inspection there are significant differences.

In Galilee Judas the son of Hezechias is said to 'desire kingly rule'. Gathering a bunch of disaffected Galileans he stormed the royal arsenal, seized property and plundered the region (*Ant.* 17.271f.; *J.W.* 2.56). This action is not dissimilar to that which occurred later in 66 C.E., when some Galileans aided the radical party in Tiberias in sacking the Herodian palace and carrying off precious goods (*Life* 66). In neither instance is there any suggestion of messianic claims being made, and the actions of Judas and his followers could scarcely be seen in this light. Elsewhere I have argued that this Judas represented the remnants of Hasmonean opposition to Herod in Galilee, a suggestion dismissed by Richard Horsley in favour of his theory that all three episodes should be seen as examples of popular

22 Rhoads 1976: 94–149.
23 Mendels 1992a, especially 262–4.

messianic uprisings based on ideas of kingship among the peasants.[24] However, no useful purpose is served by labelling every claim to kingship in a Judaean context as messianic, especially since, as previously noted, even those Hasmoneans who adopted the title 'king', did not make any messianic claims in doing so.

The situation is somewhat different in the case of the other two episodes – Simon in Perea and Athronges in Idumea, both of whom are said 'to have put on the diadem', whereas Judas merely 'desired kingship' (*Ant.*), or 'attacked those who desired power' (*J.W.*). In addition both are acclaimed as king by their followers, and in the case of Athronges, his four brothers too had armed bands and supported his efforts. Several aspects of their description have biblical precedents from the period of the Judges. Thus, Simon, though a slave of Herod, is said to have had outstanding physical strength as well as good looks, recalling the image of the 'strong man' (*gibbor*) whom God had chosen to protect Israel in times of danger (Judg. 6.12; Ps. 89.19; Isa. 9.6; Zech. 9.13; 10.7). Athronges on the other hand was not distinguished by ancestry, possessions or character. Yet his description as a mere shepherd recalls the young David who was ignored by his father Jesse, when Saul came to anoint one of his sons as king (1 Sam. 16). Significantly also, both campaigns are directed against Herodian palaces and elites in the respective regions, and both were put down firmly by the Romans.[25]

What of Horsley's idea that all three episodes are examples of popular, as distinct from an elite form of messianism?[26] In the case of Simon and Athronges the allusions to the biblical stories of Judges and 1 Samuel could lend support to the suggestion, especially since it is on stories such as these that Horsley relies for his notions of popular kingship. However, his rather rigid categorization of elite and popular ideas are based on modern sociological models rather than on any clear class distinction in the accounts. In fact, support for the three pretenders does not seem to be popular in any general sense, but is based rather on various local 'strong men' and their thirst for power by displacing the Herodian elites. The biblical echoes may be nothing more than Josephus' stylistic colouring of the episodes because of lack of details, while he was at least familiar from his own experience with the nature of popular unrest in Galilee. Furthermore there is no mention of anointing of either Simon or Athronges, a feature one might expect in a royal messianic setting. In fact, as Mendels notes, several features of the accounts can be just as easily explained in terms of various stories of pseudo-kings in the Hellenistic historians.[27]

Once these various manifestations, whether prompted by messianic hopes or otherwise, had been dealt with by Varus, the Roman legate of Syria, there are no similar episodes until the eve of the first revolt. However, the intervening period was marked by various other forms of protest, not based on physical violence, but with a strong symbolic impact. Some 10 years after these events, a *sophistes* and founder of the Fourth Philosophy, Judas the Galilean, appealed

---

24   Freyne 1998: 213–16; Horsley 1995: 60–1.
25   Hengel 1989b: 290–3.
26   Horsley 1984; see Bockmuehl, this volume: 66–8 and 72–3.
27   Mendels 1992a: 262 n. 5.

to his co-religionists 'to call no man Lord except God', a call that has been described by G. Theissen as a manifesto of 'radical theocracy' that was opposed to the very notion of earthly kings.[28] Arguably, the anti-monarchic tradition, dating back to the time of Saul and David, had never been fully extinguished in Israel. As noted already, the response to the failure of kingship at the time of the Babylonian exile was to develop the notion of the kingship of Yahweh in various royal psalms as well as in Isaiah 40–55. It is no surprise, therefore, that after two experiments in Hellenistic kingship, those of the Hasmoneans and Herodians, there was a popular movement against any form of kingship (*Ant.* 14.41; 17.304). Judas' call, therefore, was merely an affirmation of this position.

This *theo*logical, as distinct from messianic understanding of Israel's redemption from oppressive regimes puts the emphasis on divine rather than human agency. It is from this perspective that the actions of the so-called sign-prophets mentioned by Josephus should be understood. While he carefully avoids any apocalyptic colouring of their exploits, naming them 'impostors and deceivers', they clearly operated within such a world-view.[29] The actions of Theudas (*Ant.* 20.97–8), the 'Egyptian prophet' (*Ant.* 20.168–72) and the unnamed false prophet operating during the siege of 70 C.E. (*J.W.* 6.285–7) have one thing in common, it would seem, namely, reliance on symbolic gestures and signs, intended to awaken the memory of God's saving acts in the past and affirming the possibility of their repetition in the present.

Horsley distinguishes between these examples and the 'oracular prophets' such as John the Baptist and Jesus son of Hananiah, who is depicted as a prophet of doom just prior to the revolt (*J.W.* 6.300–10). The sign-prophets recall the desert and conquest traditions relating to Yahweh's mighty deeds, whereas the oracular prophets are to be seen against the background of such writing prophets as Isaiah, Amos and Jeremiah, yet they both share the theocratic rather than the messianic model of redemption. True, John the Baptist is represented in the New Testament as awaiting a 'coming one' (Mt. 11.2/Lk. 7.20), but it is not clear how far this is the result of an early Christian interpretation of the career of Jesus as messianic and the beginning of the downgrading of John that is further developed in the Fourth Gospel. Certainly, John's own position, based on his baptism of repentance, would suggest an expectation of imminent divine judgement rather than a messianic era, free of foreign rule. Yet, according to Josephus, John's preaching of justice for all aroused Antipas' fears about a popular rising (*Ant.* 18.116–19), further underlining the continuation of the social discontent stemming from Herod's reign.

It is also worth considering the short reign of Agrippa I as a possible catalyst for messianic speculation in Judaea, especially in the light of Horbury's proposal, discussed earlier. Agrippa's appointment by Gaius in 41 C.E. as king over all the territories ruled by his grandfather, Herod the Great, removed temporarily at least Roman provincial rule from Judaea, to be followed subsequently by the imposition of direct rule once again over the whole Jewish territory, following Agrippa's demise in 44 C.E. Josephus represents Agrippa as a pious king when

---

28 Theissen 1992a, especially 104–9.
29 Horsley and Hanson 1985: 160–72.

contrasting him with his grandfather (*Ant.* 19.328–34), despite his generally negative view of the Herodians. A similar image occurs in the Mishnah, where his humility in reading from the law of the king and his observance of the regulations concerning the presentation of the first-fruits are acknowledged (*m. Soṭah* 7:8; *Bik.* 3:4). Agrippa also played an important mediating role with Rome on behalf of the Jews, first, in averting a major crisis when Gaius ordered that a statue of himself be erected in the Jerusalem temple (*Ant.* 18.294–7), and again in exhorting Claudius to safeguard the rights of the Alexandrian Jews (*Ant.* 19.278–91). If any of the Herodians was likely to be endowed with a messianic aura, one might have imagined that it would have been Agrippa, in the light of such a profile, yet there is no evidence of any such idealization of his character. Rather, his change of fortune from prisoner (under Tiberius) to king, provides Josephus with an excellent example of how God rewards the just and punishes the wicked. When the threat of profanation of the temple was at its highest, the people did not appeal to Agrippa as a saviour figure of messianic proportions, but rather engaged in a civic protest by refusing to sow the crops (*Ant.* 18.273–8).

One final manifestation of the royal messianic ideology, other than those to be found in the Gospels and which are subject to a separate treatment, occurred on the eve of the great revolt. A certain Menahem is reported to have stormed Herod's fortress at Masada, armed his followers and advanced on Jerusalem 'like a king', there to take charge of the siege of the royal (Herodian) palace as leader of the *sicarii*. Later he is said to have gone up in state to the temple to worship, 'arrayed in royal robes' (*J.W.* 2.433f.; 444). Josephus claims that he was the son of Judas the Galilean, the founder of the Fourth Philosophy, who had been described as a *sophistes*. On the basis of this rather slender and somewhat improbable piece of evidence, Horsley argues that Menahem's messianic role was that of teacher, not military ruler, the only representative of a messiah figure, stemming from the 'literate elite' in contrast to the alleged 'popular' manifestations already discussed.[30] However, there is nothing in Josephus' account to support this contention and Menahem's brief career is described in militaristic not didactic terms. Josephus has little time for him because of his attack on the priestly defenders of the temple, calling him an 'unbearable tyrant', a clear example of his usual disapproving rhetoric of such rebels. For purposes of this survey, it is sufficient to note that Menahem is another example of the long opposition to Herodian rule and those who were seen as its representatives throughout the first century C.E.[31] The coins of the first revolt where the idea of 'freedom of Zion' recurs as a leitmotif are a clear indication of the deep-felt religio-political ambitions of the rebels, not just during the first revolt but also in that of Bar Kokhba later, when the warlike messianic figure surfaces once again.[32]

---

30   Horsley 1985b; see Goodman, this volume: 153.
31   Hengel 1989b: 76–144 and 358–66 sees Menahem as the last of a dynasty with a militant messianic ideology dating back to Judas the Galilean. However, Judas' philosophy was theocratic rather than messianic.
32   Hengel 1989b: 116–22.

(ii) Conceptions of the Messiah in the Herodian Period

Josephus alludes to the high level of speculation on the eve of the revolt, based on 'an ambiguous oracle found in their sacred books that someone from their race would rule the world' (*J.W.* 6.312). The discovery of the Dead Sea Scrolls and the re-engagement of modern scholars with the Apocrypha and Pseudepigrapha have opened windows on various aspects of this 'exegetical' activity of the period. Dating texts precisely, especially in the case of the writings from the Qumran library, is not easy, yet it is possible to claim that on palaeographic grounds some texts do belong to the Herodian period, and therefore, presumably reflect the discussions and concerns of some circles at least of the time. In this regard the New Testament writings are valuable witnesses also that the issue of messiahs was a very live one in the first century C.E.

(a) The Qumran Scrolls: A Militant Messiah
In line with the argument of this paper, it is appropriate to focus on the evidence for Davidic messianism, even though both priestly and prophetic figures are also represented in the surviving texts, most notably of all 4Q521, the so-called 'messianic apocalypse' which describes the work of an eschatological prophet.[33] Collins concludes his study of a number of passages, mainly from Cave Four, by highlighting two aspects of particular importance: the Davidic messiah is one who will smite the nations, slay the wicked and restore the Davidic dynasty, and secondly, he is a messiah of justice who will usher in an era of peace and harmony.[34] Such a picture is quite close to that of *Pss. Sol.* 17, a fact that has also been highlighted by Atkinson, whose investigation deals with virtually the same Qumran fragments, but with an explicit focus on the reception of the Psalm in the Herodian period. His conclusion is that 'the common pre-Christian expectation of a Davidic messiah is of a violent warrior who would function as a righteous counterpart to the Herodian monarch.'[35]

Both scholars point to the importance of Isa. 11.2-4 and Psalm 2 for the later portrayals. Thus, *Pss. Sol.* 17, 21f. speaks of the future Davidic king's task as smashing the 'arrogance of sinners like a potter's jar', shattering all their substance 'with an iron rod', and destroying the unlawful nations with 'the word of his mouth'. This latter expression comes from the LXX translation of MT 'rod of his mouth', and 'rod of iron' echoes Ps. 2.9, a royal enthronement psalm. As Atkinson notes, 'the author of *Pss. Sol.* 17 has transformed Isaiah's verbal weapons into a literal sword, "the iron rod."'[36] It is difficult to agree with Charlesworth and others that this is a reference to a non-violent messiah, even if this Psalm and *Pss. Sol.* 18 also suggest other aspects of the messiah's reign, such as the establishment of truth and righteousness, the restoration of the tribes and a role as a teacher of truth.[37]

---

33   Zimmermann 1998 is the most detailed and up-to-date investigation of all the evidence, especially 343–89 on 4Q521; see Stanton, this volume: 81–2.
34   Collins 1995: 56–68, here p. 67.
35   Atkinson 1999: 460.
36   Atkinson 1999: 444.
37   Charlesworth 2001, especially 31–2.

This type of scriptural elaboration in the context of what was perceived to have been an unjust and illicit rule, is also to be found in the scroll fragments studied by both Collins and Atkinson. Thus, 4QpIsa (4Q161) 8–10.iii.11–22 speaks of an end-time battle against Gog and Magog in which the Kittim (Romans) will be defeated by 'the branch of David', a theme which is also found in a Herodian period fragment from what appears to be an expanded J.W. Scroll (4Q285). Yet another text, the so-called 'Aramaic Son of God text' (4Q246), speaks of a son of God and son of the Most High, who, after a period of oppression and wars, plays a role in the divine renewal to follow when peace is restored and all the cities will pay homage. In the envisaged restoration it is not entirely clear whether it is the people of God as a whole or, more probably, the individual introduced at the outset as 'the son of God', who enacts the final subjugation of the nations. In doing so 'he makes war' because 'the Great God will be his strength'.[38] If this messianic interpretation of the text is accepted, then the pattern of this fragmentary apocalypse (which appears to have been based on Dan. 7) is similar to that of *Pss. Sol.* 17: after the end-time destruction of the enemy nations, a new era of universal peace will be established. Because of its close relationship with Daniel, the text is probably to be dated earlier than the Herodian period, yet the emphasis on putting an end to the sword and the realization of a universal peace would certainly have resonated in the context of Augustan propaganda. The close structural, verbal and thematic parallelism with the Lukan infancy narrative (Lk. 1.32-33; 2.14, 35) suggest that, irrespective of the original date of this apocalypse, its sentiments could continue to have resonance throughout the first century C.E.[39]

(b) Apocalyptic and the Transformation of the Messiah

A well-established feature of apocalyptic literature is the manner in which previous writing is re-worked in new situations for the purpose of conveying a similar message of judgement on the ungodly and deliverance of the righteous. This phenomenon is also attested in the first-century C.E. apocalyptic literature. Since it is impossible to assign this corpus of writing to any particular group in the manner of the Qumran material, it seems more appropriate to distinguish between the pre- and post-revolt situations in order to decipher particular emphases and concerns of the times.

From the pre-revolt period, *The Testament of Moses*, a work that originally was addressed to the crisis generated by Antiochus Epiphanes, was revised to include events associated with the Hasmoneans and Herodians in particular (chs 6–7). The defiling of the priesthood and the oppression of the poor are singled out as events that will usher in God's judgement on the wicked leading to the vindication of the righteous. No role is attributed to a messianic intermediary in this end-time scenario, and there is no reference to the alleged messianic claimants who appeared on the death of Herod. Instead, God's kingdom will appear throughout the whole creation (10.1).[40] The *Similitudes of Enoch*, a first-century

---

38   For a detailed discussion of this intriguing and important text cf. Collins 1995: 155–72, especially 162–7.
39   Zimmermann 1998: 128–70, especially 159 and 168–9.
40   Nickelsburg 2005: 247–8. Cf. Yarbro Collins 1976b who sees the reference to the 'wings of an eagle' in 10.8 as an allusion to the incident of the Golden Eagle erected by Herod.

reworking of earlier parts of the Enochic corpus, also reflects a situation of oppression of the poor by godless kings, and can, therefore, be plausibly associated with the effects of Herodian rule (*1 En.* 46.5-8).[41] However, in this work there is an intermediary figure designated variously as 'the righteous one', 'the chosen one', 'the anointed one' and 'the Son of Man' (*1 En.* 48.6-7; 49.2-4). This figure is a composite of Daniel 7, (Son of Man), Isaiah 11 and Psalm 2 (royal ideology), Isaiah 40–55, (the servant of Yahweh), thus prefiguring various New Testament combinations of the same figures. The identity of this heavenly figure is hidden, but revealed to the chosen ones who know that he will pronounce the judgement on the wicked (*1 En.* 48.6-7; 61.13; 62.7).[42]

This re-imaging of the messiah figure from Davidic warrior to heavenly judge and vindicator of the righteous is highly significant in the context of the growing social anomie following Herod's death (*Ant.* 17.285). As with the varied responses of the Maccabeans and the *maskilim* to the crisis of Antiochus Epiphanes, two centuries later Jewish resistance to Roman imperialism was split between the freedom fighters and those who were awaiting God's imminent vindication, it would seem. Should Pseudo-Philo's *Biblical Antiquities* be dated with Mendels to the pre-revolt period, it would provide further confirmation of this critical stance to political messianism, insofar as no special emphasis is put on the hopes of a Davidic messiah by an author who is also clearly opposed to kingship.[43]

This work might equally be dated to the post-revolt context, however, sharing the negative perspective on messiahs and kingship of Josephus' writings from the same period. On the other hand, two apocalyptic works that are definitely to be dated to post-70, show an ambivalent attitude towards the messiah. They both combine aspects of the militant figure with an other-worldly, pre-existent dimension, as they explore the theological implications of the disaster that had befallen the nation and the hope of future redemption.[44] Thus, *Fourth Ezra* envisages a kingdom set up on earth that will last for 400 years, in the establishment of which a pre-existent messiah will play a role (7.28f.). In the Eagle vision of the same work, which is clearly directed against Roman rule (12.32-4; cf. 11.37–12.1), the lion who passes the sentence of judgement on the eagle is identified with the messiah, the descendant of David, whom the Most High has kept until the end of days. However, the earlier idea of an interim kingdom is missing. In the vision of 'the man arising from the sea' (ch. 13) the man is described in extremely warlike terms, but in the subsequent interpretation of the vision this militaristic language is softened and understood as deliverance for the just in the end-time cosmic struggle.[45] *Syrian Baruch* shares many of these descriptions of the messiah's role in the end-time struggle, including the ideas of pre-existence and a temporary messianic kingdom (40.1-3). His advent is set in the context of a highly apocalyptic setting, drawing on the usual biblical images

41 Nickelsburg 2005: 248–56.
42 Nickelsburg 1987, especially 58–62.
43 Mendels 1992a.
44 Nickelsburg 2005: 270–85.
45 Stone 1987.

of the end-time cosmic struggle. Yet the idea of restoration of Israel in the land has not been abandoned (ch. 29).

Concluding Reflection

This survey of messianic manifestations and musings in the context of the Herodian period and its effects, suggests that while a militant note is certainly the dominant one, other ideas about the messiah and his role can be seen to have surfaced in the period also. The lead-up to the revolt and its aftermath would appear to have been a time of particular concern as to how the hopes of Israel could be realized, and what if any role a redeemer figure might play in the end-time scenarios. The fact that apocalyptic speculation was one of several responses to the failure of the revolt shows that while a definite shift of emphasis is discernible, the notion of the militant and nationalistic messiah was not entirely extinguished. Indeed that strand of thinking was to continue in the Targumic tradition, despite the known reluctance of rabbinic Judaism to engage with the notion in traditional terms.[46] The career of Jesus of Nazareth is the subject of a separate discussion in this collection, yet in the more general context of Herodian-period politics it is possible to discern similar issues at play in the Gospel traditions also. In this regard the representation of messianic hopes and their realization in the career of Jesus provide another interesting window on the debates of the period and the different configurations of the messiah that were possible and current.[47]

---

46 Levey 1974; Neusner 1984.
47 Collins 1996; Freyne 2001.

Chapter 4

PLUTARCH'S LIFE OF NUMA:
SOME OBSERVATIONS ON GRAECO-ROMAN 'MESSIANISM'

Hans Dieter Betz[1]

In his major work on messianism William Horbury states the fundamental questions in this way: 'How did the Old Testament come to offer so much material which could be interpreted messianically in the Septuagint, the Targums, the Qumran texts and rabbinic literature? How did early Christian christology, as represented in the New Testament, come to be so deeply imbued with messianic terms and concepts?'[2] Sensing the tendency to underestimate 'the significance of messianic hope within the scripture and tradition' of Second Temple Judaism, which characterizes much of present scholarship, he shows by an impressive display of literary evidence from Haggai to Josephus that what is called messianism took shape in this long period, in order then to be adapted by early Christology. Horbury also recognizes that the rise of Jewish and Christian messianism coincides with developments in Greek and Roman ruler-cult. In a brief section he sketches three important aspects: its capacity for integration with ancestral religion; its use of extravagant prayer and praise to push aside suspicion of impiety, especially in the face of the deification of Augustus and his successors; and its unintended incitement of opposition and resistance, which led to alternative forms of messianism, among them early Christianity.[3] These insights are fruitful and could be supported by another vast canvas of sources testifying especially to Roman imperial messianism.[4] In the following I wish to call attention to one case of Graeco-Roman messianism, Plutarch's *Life of Numa Pompilius*. Of course, Plutarch does not use the term 'messianism', which was derived by modern scholars from the christological title ὁ Μεσσίας[5] and applied to movements fostered by eschatological expectations.[6] In the Graeco-Roman world, the correlate to messianism

---

1   The following essay is intended to celebrate and honour my colleague and friend William Horbury who I hope will find my observations stimulating. Because of the constraints of space I am offering some suggestions selected from a more detailed study presently in preparation.
2   Horbury 1998c: 2; see also Horbury 2003b.
3   Horbury 2003b: 68–77: 'Ruler-cult and messianism.'
4   Brief references to Horace, Ovid and Virgil indicate Horbury's awareness of what is waiting to be worked out in full (Horbury 2003b: 89–90, 346–8). Recently published secondary sources have collected much of the evidence and bibliographies; see Belayche 2001; Cancik and Hitzl 2003.
5   Occurring only twice in the New Testament: John 1.41: εὑρήκαμεν τὸν Μεσσίαν ὅ ἐστιν μεθερμηνευόμενον χριστός. Cf. 4.25. See BDAG, s.v. Μεσσίας, Χριστός.
6   See Kippenberg 1990 with further bibliography.

is the expectation of the return of the ideal king with the Golden Age.[7] Plutarch's *Numa* is informative and intriguing when viewed from this perspective, which so far, probably because of the complexities, has not been tried. Space does not allow a full discussion of what needs to be said about the literary genre of the individual *Life* and the collection of *Lives*, the nature of the sources, the history of tradition of the figure of Numa, and the function of the Numa traditions in the Imperial Age.

In the following pages a few aspects of Numa's 'messianism', which are of special interest for New Testament scholarship, will be examined. While it is agreed that the early Christian messianism develops in the wider context of Hellenistic and Roman ruler-cult, methodological problems arise when that context is brought to bear on the interpretation of specific texts and issues. The fact is that both Plutarch's writings and the early Christian literature have no knowledge of each other. Both, however, originate under Roman domination, and struggle to come to terms, each in their own way, with the ideology and the rituals of ruler-cult, the outcome of which are their 'messianic' responses. As will be shown, when concrete texts are read in the light of each other, which involves comparison, they begin to show details that may have escaped readers before. One distinction, however, needs to be kept in mind from the beginning. The name of *Numa* stands for Plutarch's biographical work carrying the title NOMAS,[8] not the problems concerning the historical Numa. Before leaving that topic entirely, it at least bears noting that the problems concerning the historical Numa are similar in some respects to those of the historical Jesus. There is the same stark contrast between the dearth of established evidence about the historical origins and the wealth of what we call later tradition. Plutarch's work stands at the end of more than six centuries of tradition, while the Gospels contain perhaps six decades of tradition.

What does that tradition say about Numa? It is unanimous that Numa Pompilius was the second king of Rome, succeeding its founder Romulus and ruling *ca.* 715–673, or 709–667 B.C.E.[9] A Sabine, son of the noble Pompon, from Cures, a small town of Etruscan character, he acquired legendary fame as a man of wisdom and virtue, a leader of great charismatic powers, a philosopher, a religious, political and legal reformer, miracle-worker and companion of deities.

1. Numa's *Messianic Ideology*

Plutarch states Numa's messianic ideas at various places throughout his work, but they are summarized impressively in connection with the establishment of the temple of Janus in the Roman Forum (chs 19–20).[10] Showing awareness of

---

7   On the concept, see Gatz 1967 with further bibliography.
8   The text edition used is by Ziegler 1969–73; unless noted otherwise, the English translation follows Perrin 1914. For Plutarch's biographical writings, see Ziegler 1964: 257–77 (reprinted from PW 21 (1951) 636–962); on Numa, see part IV, 262–5; Glaser 1936; still valuable is Schwegler 1853: 1.1.523–37, 1.2.539–68. For modern studies and bibliography, see Momigliano 1993; Scardigli 1995; Duff 1999.
9   All data share mythical uncertainty. See Glaser 1936: 1242–4.
10 See also *Fort. Rom.* 9, p. 322A–C.

Euhemerist theory, he leaves open whether the archaic Janus was originally a δαίμων or a βασιλεύς (19.6). He sees a link between Janus and the two kings Numa and Augustus Caesar. Moreover, the double-faced divine image is represented by, so-to-say, a double-faced shrine because of its double door (δίθυρος), called 'gates of war'. Ritually, the gate stays open during times of war and is closed during times of peace. It was rare to see the door closed, since Rome was embroiled in wars external and internal most of the time.[11] Reportedly, the door was closed during two long periods in history, the years of Numa's reign and the reign of Augustus Caesar after the defeat of Mark Antony at Actium (31 B.C.E.). Both periods of peace were preceded by wars: Numa succeeded the bellicose Romulus, and Augustus put an end to the disastrous Civil Wars raging between 90 and 31 B.C.E. Most importantly, Numa's reign of 43 years saw not a single day when the door of the Janus temple was open (20.2). The sequence of Janus, Numa and Augustus symbolizes one of Plutarch's most cherished ideas, the political programme of re-educating the Roman people which Numa had designed at the outset of his kingship. The completion of this programme during Numa's lifetime had set the standards of good kingship, and it became the model for Roman renewal under Augustus as well as under Trajan, the emperor in office (98–117 C.E.) during the time when Plutarch worked out his *Parallel Lives*. Thus, Numa's programme as sketched in the work unsurprisingly coincided with Plutarch's own political aims. His encomiastic praise of Numa's reign calls upon the imagery of what was known as the Golden Age:

> For not only was the Roman people softened and charmed by the righteousness and mildness of their king, but also the cities round about, as if some cooling breeze or salubrious wind were wafted upon them from Rome, began to experience a change of temper, and all of them were filled with longing desire to have good government, to be at peace, to till the earth, to rear their children in quiet, and to worship the gods. Festivals and feasts, hospitalities and friendly converse between people who visited one another promiscuously and without fear, – these prevailed throughout Italy, while honour and justice flowed into all hearts from the wisdom of Numa, as from a fountain, and the calm serenity of his spirit diffused itself abroad … For there is no record either of war, or faction, or political revolution while Numa was king. Nay more, nor hatred or jealousy was felt towards his person, nor did ambition lead men to plot and conspire against his throne. On the contrary, either fear of the gods, who seemed to have him in their especial care, or reverence for his virtue, or a marvellous felicity, which in his days kept life free from the taint of every vice … (20.3–6)

In short, Numa was a living example and model of an ideal ruler, just as Plato had envisaged, when he said that 'human ills would only then cease and disappear when, by some divine felicity, the power of a king should be united in one person with the insight of a philosopher, thereby establishing virtue in control and mastery over vice' (20.7). This statement leads up to a beatitude adapted from Plato's: 'Blessed', indeed, is such a philosopher-king 'in himself, and blessed, too, are those who hear the words of wisdom issuing from his lips.'[12]

---

11 A picture of the shrine, with doors closed, is found on a coin of Nero. See Nash 1961: 1.502–3; E. Torstorici, in Steinby 1993–2000: 3.92–3.
12 20.7: 'Μακάριος μὲν γὰρ αὐτὸς' ὁ σώφρων ὡς ἀληθῶς, μακάριοι δ' οἱ συνήκοοι τῶν ἐκ τοῦ σωφρονοῦντος στόματος ἰόντων λόγων.' Cf. Plato, *Leg.* 4, p. 711e: … μακαρίως μὲν αὐτὸς ζῇ, μακάριοι

Moreover, cautiously, Plutarch offers Numa's ideal kingship as a challenging example to the later Roman emperor cult. During his lifetime Numa is not deified, but he remains a human king of exemplary wisdom, virtue and devotion to the deity. His reign is regarded as a divine gift granted by Good Tyche (5.1; 6.1). Ennobled by his close love association (θεῖος γάμος) with the Nymph Egeria (4.1–2), the world of divine wisdom and power is at his disposal.

A manifestation, and, indeed, an incarnation of virtue, Numa sets the example for the people to follow: 'For possibly there is no need of any compulsion or menace in dealing with the multitude, but when they see with their own eyes a conspicuous and shining example [παράδειγμα] of virtue in the life of their ruler, they will of their own accord walk in wisdom's ways, and unite with him in conforming themselves to a blameless and blessed life of friendship and mutual concord, attended by righteousness and temperance.' Plutarch concludes the section with an almost hymnic praise of life in such a realm: 'Such a life is the noblest end of all government, and he is most a king who can inculcate such a life and such a disposition in his subjects. This, then, as it appears, Numa was preeminent in discerning' (20.8).[13] These words sum up the message going out from Plutarch, prominent member of the Academy in Athens and highest-ranking priest of Apollo at Delphi.

2. The Concept of Numa's Kingship

When Plutarch describes Numa's kingship, he does so in his characteristic way of mixing a good deal of scepticism with a greater degree of trust in divine providence. For him, Numa's journey to Rome, coming from a modest origin and going into a contentious and confusing situation, had all the marks of destiny. Moreover, the very notion of kingship itself underwent reconceptualization. That is why, instead of beginning with him, Plutarch first places Numa opposite his forerunner and antitype, Romulus, the original founder of Rome. This pairing of Romulus and Numa invites comparison with the figure of the militant King David and peaceful Messiah Jesus as 'son of David'. Also, contrasting Numa with Romulus is not unlike the Messiah Jesus, figuring in contrast to the Herodian kings, installed by the Roman overlords. In both instances genealogies as well as portents and signs collaborate in situations of political turmoil and bring about what the divine will had ordained.[14]

Plutarch follows the tradition by beginning (2.1–3) with the famous legend of Romulus' sudden 'disappearance' in the clouds of a violent thunderstorm. This is said to have happened 37 years after the founding of Rome, when Romulus officiated in public sacrifices outside the city in the Goat's Marsh. With the full senate and the people being present, all were terrified, fled and dispersed, only

---

δὲ οἱ ξυνήκοοι τῶν ἐκ τοῦ σωφρονοῦντος στόματος ἰόντων λόγων. On Plato's idea of the philosopher-king see *Resp.* 5, p. 473d; 6, pp. 487e, 499b, 501e; *Leg.* 4, pp. 711d, 712a, 713e.

13   The paragraph has a close parallel in Plutarch, *Fort. Rom.* 9, pp. 321A–322B, according to Ziegler 1964: 83–5 [III.1.a] written before *Numa*.

14   Concerning Jesus, this is the aim of the so-called nativity stories in Mt. 1–2//Lk. 1–2.

to discover that Romulus had vanished. However, when rumours began to circulate suspecting that alienated patricians had secretly done away with Romulus, those same people were eager to arrange for his deification. One of them, by the name of Proculus, swore that the fully armoured Romulus had appeared to him in a vision, declaring 'that he was not dead but blessed with a better lot', his new divine name being Quirinus (2.3; cf. 3.4).[15] While relating these common features of ascension stories, Plutarch leaves no doubt that he regards them as fabrications (cf. 1.4; 2.1–2).

Soon new political disturbance and squabble (ταραχή καὶ στάσις) about the question of succession filled the city, with parties strongly opposing each other. Distrustful, the people suspected that the senate was planning for a so-called *interregnum* (μεσοβασιλεία), so that they could in fact establish an oligarchic regime (ὀλιγαρχία) of their own and keep permanent control (2.4–3.1). The parties, therefore, demanded the immediate nomination of a new rightfully chosen king. The senate yielded to their will and followed the agreed protocol. Since after the co-regent Tatius' death Romulus had ruled as a monarch (*Rom.* 23.2–4; *Num.* 2.5), the new king was to be nominated by the other section of the people, the Sabines. This conformed to the agreement according to which each tribe should in turn nominate a candidate from the other side. It so happened that both sides of the senate agreed in choosing Numa Pompilius. Thus, in fact, he was the people's choice because all knew him as a man of proven virtue and great wisdom.[16] He was married to the former co-regent Tatius' only daughter, Tatia, but the couple had not settled in Rome in Tatius' palace on the hill called Quirinalis, but had stayed in Numa's modest home town of Cures. The interplay between the names Cures, Quirinus and Quirinalis can only have been understood as a divine sign of approval (3.2–3).

In 3.4–7, Plutarch inserts a biographical sketch of Numa, treating the questions of his name (ὁ Νομᾶς), his city (πόλις) and family's genealogy. He was the son of the noble Pomponius, from a good family, and the date of his birth on April 21 fortuitously coincided with the same date as Rome's foundation by Romulus (3.4). The reasons for Numa's choice were his character and moral conduct, because they were so very different from Romulus'. 'By natural temperament he was inclined to the practice of every virtue, and he had refined himself still more by education, endurance of hardships, and philosophy' (3.5; my trans.). Through his discipline he had subdued in himself not only 'the infamous passions of the soul, but also that violence and rapacity which are in such high repute among Barbarians, believing that true bravery (ἀνδρεία) consists in the subjugation of one's passions by reason' (3.5). His virtues, in other words, looked like those of archaic Rome as well as Greek philosophy: abstinence from luxury and extrav-

---

15 It should be noted that the resurrection and ascension of Jesus also involves a change of name from Jesus of Nazareth to Jesus Christ or Christ Jesus, whereby the original title Χριστός, presumably rendering Μεσσίας, becomes part of his name.

16 A similar picture is presented in the Gospels: Jesus as a wise and righteous figure has, at least at first, the common people on his side, while the Jewish authorities collaborate with the Romans to maintain their own power positions. In the eyes of the Jewish people the Herodians are not the people's choice, but are imposed by Rome, and considered corrupt and lacking legitimacy as Jews.

agance, integrity as a judge and counsellor, cherishing privacy and simplicity, and most importantly 'the service of the gods, and the rational contemplation of their nature and power' (3.6; see also *Comp. Lyc. Num.* 1.1–7). No wonder, therefore, that he had a great name and fame (ὄνομα μέγα καὶ δόξα), and that was also why Tatius had given him his only daughter Tatia as his wife. This period of his life came to an end when in the thirteenth year of marriage Tatia died (3.7).

In deep distress Numa left Cures and for some time wandered about in the countryside, desiring to find new meaning in his life. He made his home in inspiring groves of the gods, sacred meadows and desolate places (4.1). While this looks like an almost natural depression on the part of Numa (cf. 4.1), the comparable story in Mk 1.12-13 par. about Jesus' 40 days in the Judaean desert seems strangely unmotivated. Both Mt. (4.1-11) and Lk. (4.1-13) expand Mark by versions of Jesus' temptation by Satan. Plutarch, on the other side, inserts the legend (λόγος) of the nymph Egeria.[17] Accordingly, on his wanderings Numa met and befriended Egeria who took care of him and who ultimately became his lover and wife (4.1–8; 21.1–2). She not only made him a happy man again but became his source of divine strength and revelation until his death (4.2). Since this story obviously strains human credulity,[18] Plutarch inserts apologetic reflections and a whole series of parallels from mythology telling of sexual union between goddesses and humans. His own Platonizing explanation allows that such relationships could perhaps be imagined as instances of divine philanthropy.[19] Conceivably, it could be the desire of a deity who is φιλάνθρωπος to seek association with humans of unimpaired goodness. Yet, Plutarch must admit: 'But that an immortal god should take carnal pleasure in a mortal body and its beauty, this, surely, is hard to believe' (4.3). At any rate, the authority of mythical traditions stands behind it, as is shown by examples in a longer excursus (4.4–8).

Why, in the first place, was the Egeria legend told about Numa? If, presumably, Numa told it himself, Plutarch interprets it as an instance of clever pragmatism employed by great leaders of the people.[20] Overcoming difficult stubbornness which great leaders like Lycurgus and Numa had to face, they attempted to educate unruly and brutish populations by deception for their own betterment. They were justified when 'they pretended to get a sanction from the god, which sanction was the salvation of the very ones against whom it was contrived' (4.8). In other words, Numa's wisdom was, far from naive, a shrewd *pia fraus* to achieve goals of political pedagogy.

---

17   The Egeria legend was famous before Plutarch. Her home was a rivulet of Lake Nemi and the old temple of Diana there. She also had a shrine in Rome in the grove of the Camenae on the slope of the Aventine. See Altheim 1930: 127–36; Latte 1960: 169–71; Graf 1997.

18   Cf. also the strange account in Mk 1.13 of Jesus in the desert being together with the animals and served by angels. Not surprisingly, the verse is ignored or rewritten as the Temptation narratives (Mt. 4.1-11; Lk. 4.1-13).

19   Cf. Lk. 1.34-35, where the angel announces to Mary that she will conceive a son by the Holy Spirit; Luke circumscribes the sexual issue with delicate ambiguity: δύναμις ὑψίστου ἐπισκιάσει σοι.

20   Plutarch attributes such pragmatism to Pythagoras (8.2–6), but it is in line with Plato as well (see his justification for the 'noble lie', *Resp.* 3, pp. 389b–c; 414b–c; cf. Critias, *Sisyphus* Fragment 25; Polybius 6.56.7; Cicero, *Leg.* 3.10.23–15.34; Livy 1.19.4–5). See also Glaser 1936: 1248.

Turning from the excursus on Egeria back to the story of Numa's accession to kingship, Plutarch describes at length the protocol of his appointment. It begins with a bipartisan embassy sent by the senate to Cures offering Numa the kingship (5.1–5). Numa declines the offer and justifies it in a well-composed speech. Actually, Plutarch uses this occasion to insert a contest of two speeches, one by Numa and the other by his father Pompon and Marcius; both speeches of course reflect Plutarch's own ideas. In his speech Numa outlines the philosopher's preference for an unpretentious and private life away from politics and dedicated to contemplation. As Romulus' experiences have shown him, kingship involves a heavy burden of constant insecurity, intrigues, hypocritical accusations, betrayal, probably violent death, and at death fabricated deification.[21] By contrast, Numa wants to preserve his independence as a human being devoted to philosophy. Regarding the legacy of Romulus, he insists he lacks all the competences required for serving as king of Rome (5.2–5). The Romans are in fact looking for a different kind of king, a powerful military leader like Romulus had been.[22] 'I should therefore become a laughing-stock if I sought to serve the gods, and taught men to honour justice and hate violence and war, in a city which desires a leader of its armies rather than a king' (5.5).

This statement raises the intriguing question of the difference between a king and a military commander. For Plutarch's Numa, of course (like Plato's ideal ruler), legitimacy as king can only be claimed by a philosopher, while all other so-called kings are no more than military generals.

It appears that similar reflections are debated in the Gospels when they point to the people's confusion between Jesus as messianic redeemer and as military leader in the struggle against the Roman occupiers. This confusion is shown to breed suspicion with the Roman governor, hostility among the Jewish authorities, false hopes among the population and even among the disciples. As the passion narratives emphasize, the false hopes turn into the scoffing of the disillusioned and the carnivalesque mockery of the soldiers (Mk 14.65; 15.16-20 par.), not to mention the utter incomprehension of the disciples. The old information contained in the Emmaus story (Lk. 24.21) sums it up: 'But we had hoped that he is the one to redeem Israel.' The same misunderstanding motivates Jesus' rebuke of Peter in Mk 8.27-33 par.: 'Get behind me, Satan, for you do not think in God's terms but in human terms.'[23] The combined misunderstanding by them all about Jesus' role and aims leads, finally, to his crucifixion and death, the truth of which is first disclosed by the military officer under the cross: 'Truly, this man was a son of God.'[24]

---

21   Notably, Plutarch treats the *consecratio* as a standard topic; see the basic study by Bickerman 1929. As could be expected, Proculus, one of the delegates sent to Numa, is the very one who swore the oath of having seen the vision of Romulus rising to heaven (cf. 2.3; *Rom.* 28.1–3; Livy 1.16.5–8).
22   The great examples of such leaders in Roman history are Camillus, Marius, Pompey, Sulla and, of course, Julius Caesar; see Plutarch's other *Lives* on these heroes.
23   For the refusal of kingship, see also Mt. 4.8-10; Lk. 4.5-8; Jn 6.15; Acts 1.6-8.
24   Mk 15.39: ἀληθῶς οὗτος ὁ ἄνθρωπος υἱὸς θεοῦ ἦν. The statement should be taken, first, in its pagan meaning. It took a military man to recognize that Jesus is not a failed insurrectionist.

Going back to Numa: The Roman delegates do not give up easily, but offer serious reasons why Numa is indeed their right choice (6.1). They are pleading that if they return to Rome without his consent, revolt and civil war (στάσις καὶ πόλεμος ἐμφύλιος) are unavoidable, because there is no other candidate who could unite the factions. At that point, when the delegates had withdrawn, also his father Pompon and another relative, Marcius, put pressure on Numa, arguing that he should 'accept such a great and divine gift' (δέχεσθαι μέγα καὶ θεῖον δῶρον). Praising Numa for his virtuous life, they point to the fact that if he fails his obligation, he lets his great abilities concerning justice and righteousness (δικαιοσύνη) lie idle and dormant. Theologically and ethically they have a point: having such powerful gifts places the sage under obligation to engage in noble actions, so as to further the service to the gods as well as moving the people toward a life of piety and morality. The people may still love Tatius and honour Romulus, but it may also be true that after all their wars and victories the Romans 'long for a gentle leader and friend of justice who will lead them toward lawful order and peace' (6.3). Even if the people behave uncontrollably and are crazy for war, it would be a salvation for them to be ruled by a righteous king who through his own good example would gradually change their ways for the better (6.2–3). The implication is that only this sort of leader can truly be a king of his people because he can accomplish what no military commander can.

If these challenges had not yet moved Numa to change his mind, auspicious signs and the ardent pleading by the citizens of Cures did, 'begging him to go and take up the kingship for the sake of the community and cohesion among the citizens' (6.4; my trans.). In other words, military prowess can defend a city from external enemies, but the true king's task is to save the people as well from their own internal self-destruction.

One cannot read these passages of Plutarch without recalling the deliberations in the Gospels about the nature of kingship. Indeed, it is at this point that the figure of Numa comes close to that of Jesus the Messiah. For the Gospels Jesus is the Messiah because he is the true king, that is, the pivotal saviour figure in the kingdom of God.[25] By contrast, the Herodian kings are held in low esteem and lack divine authority. Pivotal is the figure of Pilate, the Roman governor, who represents the emperor. Thus the Roman emperors are not to be confused with kings. Julius Caesar came as close as any of the Roman leaders to accepting the diadem and title *rex*, but ancient authors and modern scholars are divided whether there is evidence that he crossed the institutional line.[26] Shortly before his assassination, the Roman senate had heaped excessive honours on Caesar and made him *dictator perpetuus*, but that was as far as he wanted things to go. The question remains: What did Caesar's ambivalent conduct indicate? Did the assassination have the aim of preventing Caesar from ending the Republic by

---

25 This is pointed out by Matthew (2.2-3), Mark (15.32), Luke (2.11; Acts 5.31; 13.23), and John (4.42), naming Jesus by the attribute σωτήρ.

26 See, especially, Plutarch, *Caes.*, 57–61; 67.4. He distinguishes between Caesar's ambivalent behaviour and his resistance against accepting the diadem and the title *rex*. For the modern debates, see Gesche 1968, 1976: 154–79; Weinstock 1971; the important essays reprinted in Wlosok 1978; Fishwick 1987: 56–72; Christ 1994: 99–101.

accepting Roman kingship? Or did Caesar himself have doubts about taking up the role of Romulus? Did he want to test the popular sentiment by dressing in royal garb, yet refusing officially the diadem and title *rex*? At any rate, he died not as king but as *dictator*. Peculiar also is Plutarch's notion that during his life Caesar was possessed and guided by a 'great daimon' (μέγας δαίμων) who after his death turned into a vengeful ghost persecuting his murderers until their demise. How this notion can be reconciled with Caesar's deification, arranged by his heir Octavianus, is another open question. Should we expect that Caesar's ascension to the gods put an end to his vengeful ghost?[27] As far as kingship is concerned, Augustus preferred the constitutionally new titles of σεβαστός, *augustus* and *princeps*, and, likewise, later emperors did not call themselves kings. This shows the difference in rank between emperor and king, even when the emperors were inspired by the Greek ideal of good kingship.

Held against this background, therefore, Pilate's inscription on Jesus' cross expresses several meanings. In all likelihood, the *titulus crucis* is historical, even if it is awkward and the exact wording varies in the accounts. It declares with annoying boldness that Jesus is, or was, the *true* king of the Jews.[28] That is why his crown of thorns is the only appropriate way to honour the true king.[29] Despite proliferating golden crowns among Hellenistic rulers, under Roman domination kingship had become the role of provincial potentates. When the place of Alexander the Great was claimed by Roman emperors, there could no longer be kings like him.[30] Thus, the only true king was God, and his realm was the heavenly kingdom, the βασιλεία τοῦ θεοῦ or βασιλεία τῶν οὐρανῶν. This is also why in the great interrogation by Pilate (John 18–19) Jesus remains tantalizingly evasive. When asked, 'Are you *the* king of the Jews?' (18.33), he lets Pilate give the answer: 'You say that I am (*a*) king.' Pilate asks whether Jesus claims to be a worldly king, but Jesus changes the meaning from 'the' to 'a' king implying that the true and messianic king belongs to a realm not of this world (18.36-37). Pilate has it right, therefore, when he finally lets the writing on the cross stand, declaring Jesus to be 'the king of the Jews' (v. 39; cf. 19.3, 14-22). For Pilate this may be sarcastic denunciation, but for the reader of the Gospel it is proclamation: Jesus is the true messianic king of the Jews.

3. *Numa's Inauguration*

To return to Numa, finally his father's reasoning persuaded him to accept the kingship of Rome, and the following chapter 7 contains a detailed description

---

27   Cf. the New Testament post-resurrection stories in which there is some fear on the part of the apostles that the appearing Jesus is his vengeful ghost. That fear is laid to rest by Jesus' greetings (for 'fear' see Mk 16.8; for the greeting Mt. 28.5, 10; Lk. 24.37-40; Jn 20.19-23, 26).
28   Cf. Mk 15.26: ὁ βασιλεὺς τῶν Ἰουδαίων; Mt. 27.37; Lk. 23.38; Jn 19.19-22.
29   See Mk 15.17; Jn 19.5: ἀκάνθινος στέφανος; cf. Mt. 27.29; Jn 19.2.
30   Thus, the New Testament does not call the emperor βασιλεύς but Καῖσαρ; for the dilemma of the high priests, see their reply to Pilate (Jn 19.15): οὐκ ἔχομεν βασιλέα εἰ μὴ Καίσαρα.

of the steps leading toward his installation. After sacrificing to the gods, he sets out for Rome, presumably on foot without pomp and circumstance. Senate and people meet him on his way and provide him with a jubilant entrance into the city. Traditionally, this entrance into the city is the great moment for any king, but Numa does not enter in a victory parade like later rulers did.[31] There is no parade with horses, chariots, troops, and shining armour. He enters as it befits the philosopher-king, on foot and unarmed, but in the joyous company of the people: 'as if the city were receiving, not a king, but a kingdom' (7.1). In contrast, *Rom.* 26.1-2 describes Romulus' later royal extravagances: 'For he dressed in a scarlet tunic, and wore over it a toga bordered with purple, and sat on a recumbent throne when he gave audience.'[32] The scenario brings to mind the account of Jesus' entrance into Jerusalem (Mk 11.1-10 par.; Jn 12.12-15). This entrance makes a mockery of a royal triumph, but it befits the Messiah that Jesus rides on a donkey (cf. Zech. 9.5) and is accompanied by his disciples, while the common people greet him jubilantly.[33]

Upon entering Rome, first, sacrifices are brought in the temples (7.1),[34] followed by the unanimous election by the citizens in the Forum. Plutarch underscores that the Roman king is elected, and not by one or the other political party or tribe, and not even by the senate, but by the whole citizenry. Even this election by the people, however, does not suffice by itself. Therefore, when the royal insignia (τὰ βασιλικά) are brought to Numa, he requests a pause because the kingdom has first to be established to him by divine will. He takes the augurs and priests with him, and together they ascend to the Capitol. There, at the proper place, the chief of the augurs turns the veiled head of Numa to the south, and while standing behind him and laying his right hand on his head he prays aloud and looks around the horizon for birds or other signs sent by the gods (7.2). All the while the large crowd in the Forum stands waiting in incredible silence, until finally auspicious birds (ὄρνιθες ἀγαθοί) appear and fly toward the scene on the right.[35] This is the awaited confirmation by the divine will, so that now Numa puts on the royal robe and goes down to the Forum, where the people are assembled and present him with a rousing welcome as the most pious man beloved by the gods (7.3). Notably, there is no anointing of the king.

---

31   The beginnings of the Roman triumphal procession is described in Plutarch's *Rom.* 16.5-6: Romulus began the processions on foot and carried a trophy on his right shoulder. Horse-drawn chariots came in use only later. According to *Rom.* 16.8, Plutarch himself saw in Rome images of him bearing the trophy, showing him walking barefoot (τοῦ δὲ Ῥωμύλου τὰς εἰκόνας ὁρᾶν ἔστιν ἐν Ῥώμῃ τὰς τροπαιοφόρους πεζὰς ἁπάσας). Evidently, such images were a topos. For the evidence, see Sehlmeyer 1999.

32   Dionysius of Halicarnassus 2.34 gives a full decription of a triumphal procession in what Plutarch says (*Rom.* 16.8) was the later style: 'Romulus himself came last in the procession, clad in a purple robe and wearing a crown of laurel upon his head, and, that he might maintain the royal dignity, he rode in a chariot drawn by four horses.' On the Roman parade, see the material in Alföldi 1980: 88–100; 101–11.

33   Notably, the people welcome him as bringer of the kingdom of David: εὐλογημένη ἡ ἐρχομένη βασιλεία τοῦ πατρὸς ἡμῶν Δαυίδ (Mk 11.10a).

34   Cf. Mk 11.11: When Jesus enters Jerusalem, his first visit is to the Temple. He does so not for sightseeing but for performing the appropriate rituals, whatever they might have been.

35   For Romulus' inaugural sign of the 12 vultures flying over the Palatine, see Plutarch, *Rom.* 9.4-5 (cf. Ennius, *Ann.* 72–91; Livy 1.7.1; Suetonius, *Aug.* 95). Does Plutarch know of

This inauguration throws light also on a familiar Gospel scene, the baptism of Jesus by John the Baptist (Mk 1.9-11 par.). There are of course no augurs (μάντεις), but in their place there is the prophet (προφήτης), and there is the sudden appearance of a bird, the dove (περιστερά), representing the Holy Spirit. Flying down toward him (εἰς αὐτόν),[36] the dove designates him as the one whom the heavenly voice identifies: σὺ εἶ ὁ υἱός μου ὁ ἀγαπητός, ἐν σοὶ εὐδόκησα. It appears that an earlier story of Jesus' baptism has been expanded to become his inauguration as Messiah. The difference is that, while the baptism is performed by the prophet John, the inauguration is the work of the dove representing the divine spirit.

As to inauguration, there are two peculiarities in both instances. First, there is no mentioning of an anointing, contrary to what should be expected and was practised in the Near East and Israel,[37] even in the case of King David.[38] In the inauguration of the 'son of David', however, there is no ritual of anointing.[39] Not even his title of Messiah (the 'Anointed')[40] has any ritual background. Second, there is no mention of Numa as being seated on a throne. The important act being his 'inauguration', there is no 'enthronement', a practice that came only later.[41] Likewise, according to the Synoptic accounts Jesus the Messiah is not enthroned on earth; the promise which the angel makes in Luke is to be fulfilled in heaven.[42]

In Plutarch's view, Numa has instituted nothing less than the proper protocol for the elections of Roman kings (8.1):[43] The candidate was nominated by the senate in accordance with popular preference, offering the kingship by a bipartisan delegation from the senate to the candidate of choice, acceptance (or decline) of the offer by the future king, peaceful entrance into the city, acclamation by the people, sacrifices in the great temples, formal election by the citizens in the Forum, ratification by divine election carried out by augurs and priests on the Capitol (inauguration), transfer of the royal robes and insignia, descent into

---

the augury concerning Lucius Tarquinius Priscus, about which Livy 1.34 and Cicero, *Leg.* 1.1.4 report? The story is said to have originated with the ambitious wife of Tarquinius, Tanaquil, who reported that during their approach to Rome an eagle flew down and snatched up Tarquinius' cap, circled around giving out loud cries, and then came down again and put the cap back on his head. Taking this preposterous prodigy to forecast his future greatness, this immigrant, son of the notorious Corinthian Demaretus, later became king of Rome.

36   Mk 1.10. The ambiguous preposition εἰς is changed in the other versions of the story (cf. Mt. 3.16; Lk. 3.22; Jn 1.33: ἐπ' αὐτόν).

37   For passages and background see Mettinger 1976; Kutsch 1963; Karrer 1991: 95–213, 267–93, 377–405; Waschke 2001.

38   See 2 Sam. 2.4, 7; 3.39; 5.3; etc., and the essay by Kutsch 1979.

39   As if it was missing, some traditions interpreted the descent of the Holy Spirit figuratively as Jesus' anointing with the Spirit (Lk. 4.18; Acts 4.27; 10.38; Heb. 1.9; cf. 2 Cor. 1.21). Notably, the μυρίζεις of the woman at Bethany (Mk 14.3-9 par.) is taken to anticipate Jesus' funerary ritual.

40   In Jn 1.41; 4.25, the title ὁ Μεσσίας is explained as ὁ Χριστός, not as 'the anointed'.

41   Cf. *Rom.* 26.2, where a throne is first attributed to later extravagances at Romulus' audiences: ἐν θρόνῳ ἀνακλίτῳ καθήμενος ἐχρημάτιζεν.

42   Lk. 1.32: καὶ δώσει αὐτῷ κύριος ὁ θεὸς τὸν θρόνον Δαυὶδ τοῦ πατρὸς αὐτοῦ. Cf. Lk. 22.30; Mk 10.37, 40; Mt. 19.28; 25.31; Rev. 1.4 etc.

43   See Mommsen 1887: 2.3–17; Siber 1952: 15–31.

the Forum, and triumphal reception by the citizenry as the most pious and beloved of the gods (7.1–3). Anointing and enthronement were not part of the rituals.[44]

4. Persuasion by Miracles

Beyond these initial acts, however, how did the Roman people receive Numa's entire reform programme of παιδαγωγία πρὸς τὸ θεῖον, laid out in chapters 8–20? Plutarch raises this question realizing that the previously barbarian Romans would not have accepted such far-reaching innovations, unless they were persuaded by some extraordinary means (15.1).[45] According to him, it was Numa's superhuman power (δύναμις), assisted by the gods, that so overwhelmed the city by amazement that they accepted all sorts of myths and legends, however awkward the ἀτοπία of it all, and they thought nothing Numa willed to be beyond belief and impossible (15.1). If this ἀτοπία is Plutarch's response to Numa's exploits with the divine, it has an interesting analogy in early Christian experiences with the preaching of the gospel. Paul's experiences of resistance were manifold, but he summarizes them in the expressions of σκάνδαλον τοῦ σταυροῦ and μωρία τοῦ κηρύγματος, which he regards as an integral element of faith (Rom. 16.17; 1 Cor. 1.21-24; Gal. 5.11). A controversial subject is also the assessment of miracle-stories in the Gospels and Acts. On the one hand, they testify to Jesus' divine δύναμις and ἐξουσία during his lifetime, and after his resurrection through the apostles; on the other hand, mere credulity on the part of converts hinders rather than creates genuine Christian faith.

To document Numa's supreme standing in the community Plutarch reports on three popular miracle-stories (15.2–6).[46] The first of these legends tells about a miraculous feeding (15.2), for which Numa had invited a good number of citizens to come to his table. First he served them quite ordinary food on simple dishes. When the people had begun with this rather miserly meal, Numa surprised them by announcing that the goddess (Egeria), his consort, had come to visit him, and, instantly, the house was transformed and filled with precious beakers, and the tables were overloaded with exquisite foods and splendid dishes. In a similar

---

44   On this point see Karrer 1991: 113, 134–5, 137–47. When Herod was appointed as King of Judaea, it was done in Rome according to legal protocol by the Roman senate acting on the proposal of Mark Antony and Octavian, together with the following sacrifice on the Capitol and a banquet sponsored by Antony (Josephus, *Ant.* 14.381–9; *J.W.* 1.282–5).

45   There is similarity here to Romulus' spectacular triumphal procession (*Rom.* 16.4–8). Cf. also the wording of Cotta's defence of the foundations of Roman religion in Cicero, *Nat. d.* 3.5 (ed. A. S. Pease, 2.982–6); see also 1.44 (ed. Pease, 1.298).

46   Clearly, these stories originated in the oral tradition. This explains why different versions circulated and were written down. The first two stories are told also in Dionysius of Halicarnassus 2.60.5–7, albeit in versions different from Plutarch. Livy (1.19.5) briefly mentions such miracles as inventions deemed necessary for overcoming disbelief regarding Egeria, but he prefers not to report them. The second miracle-story can be traced to Valerius Antias (1st century B.C.E). Since Plutarch cites Valerius Antias in ch. 22.4, he may also be cited here. The third story is attested by Plutarch alone. Notably, the oral versions continue to be modified even in the written accounts, since all authors make sure their own interests are brought to expression.

way, the Synoptic feeding miracles juxtapose what seem to the disciples to be insufficient provisions with the experience of divine abundance.[47]

The second legend is said to supersede the first in ἀτοπία and demonstrates Numa's own magical powers: a conversation he had with Jupiter himself (15.3–6). To begin with, Numa was able to capture two satyr-like *daimones*, Picus and Faunus, who roamed around on the Aventine hill which at the time was outside the city, uninhabited and abounding in springs and shady groves. Picus and Faunus belong to the tricksters, not unlike the Idaean Dactyls of the Greeks, and they were known for their magical potions and lore. Numa, the greater magician, overpowered and captured them, when they came to their preferred spring, by lacing the water with wine and honey. When they were caught and they tried to escape by changing into terrifying appearances, Numa held them tight. Offering a deal, they prophesied about things to come and gave him a charm (καθαρμός) against thunder and lightning, which the story says is still practised, by using onions, hair and sprats.

The third legend, which is another version of the second, has it that through the *daimones*' magic, Jupiter himself was brought down from heaven, angry but willing to grant Numa an oracular exchange about the right ingredients of the charm. Because Egeria had taught him how to proceed in the consultation, Jupiter consented to reveal the charm, and he returned to heaven a gracious god (ἵλεω). This is why the place of the interview was called Ilicium.

Plutarch himself judges such legends to be ridiculous fables, but he reports them nonetheless because they show the popular credulity toward religion customary at the time (15.6). That Numa himself shared this credulity is shown by the concluding episode. 'Yet Numa himself, as they say, held fast to such great hopes in the deity that once, when a message was brought to him that enemies were approaching, he smiled and said: "But I am sacrificing."' (15.6, my trans.).

Numa's response is ambiguous. Does the story allude to the 'disappearance' of Romulus which happened while he was performing the official sacrifices? (*Rom.* 27.3). If so, it may imply Numa's hope for his transferral to the gods, too. Or is Plutarch's interpretation right, according to which, instead of panicking and blowing the trumpets of war, the philosopher's peace (εἰρήνη) during his sacrifice and prayer was symbolic of the Romans' 43 years of quietly training and gathering strength (*Fort. Rom.* 9, pp. 321F–322A)? Or should the sacrifice secure the support of the gods against a military onslaught (cf. 7.1)?

In comparison, for all the reporting of miracle-stories by the Gospels, they also treat them with ambiguity, in part as expressions of popular credulity, in part as genuine beginnings of belief, but they do not simply identify faith in miracles with genuine faith in Christ and God. Jesus' passion and crucifixion drives the point home by showing that his ultimate faith remains obedience to God's will, not reliance on his power to extricate himself by a final miraculous act. Above all, this is demonstrated by the episode in the Garden of Gethsemane (Mk 14.32-42 par.).

---

47   See the miracle-stories of the Feeding of the 5000 in Mk 6.32-44; Mt. 14.13-21; Jn 6.1-13; and the Feeding of the 4000 in Mk 8.1-10; Mt. 15.32-39.

5. Numa's Death, Burial and Rediscovery of his Tomb

With respect to messianism, especially illuminating are the events concerning Numa's end. In chapter 21 Plutarch returns to Numa's biographical data, beginning with his family (21.1–3), his death (21.4), his funeral and burial (22.1–4), and the spectacular rediscovery of his tomb (22.5).

Rather elaborate is the account of Numa's death, funeral procession and burial, followed by the rediscovery of his tomb in 181 B.C.E. It is based on carefully selected sources, which themselves are based on different strands of tradition.[48] Several sections can be recognized, but these do not necessarily constitute verbatim excerpts; some may be Plutarch's elaborations informed by oral traditions.

(a) The first account cites L. Calpurnius Piso as a source:

... Numa died, not a speedy nor a sudden death, but wasting away gradually from old age and a mild disorder, as Piso writes. He was something over 80 years old when he died. His funeral was as enviable as his life. The [neighbouring] peoples which were allies and friends were assembled for the rites with public offerings and crowns; the senators carried his bier; the priests of the gods together served as his escorts; and the rest of the people, mixed with women and children, followed with wailing and lamentation, not as though they were attending the funeral of an aged king, but as though each one of them was burying some dearest relation missed in the prime of life. (21.4–22.1; transl. modified)[49]

Numa's death and burial should be seen in contrast to Romulus'. Numa dies in old age, of natural causes, and in peace, just as he had lived. Romulus, however, 'disappeared' under violent and mysterious circumstances, followed by confusion and suspicion;[50] of course, since he had vanished without a trace of his body and clothing,[51] there could not have been a funeral.[52]

(b) In addition, no tradition tells of Numa's dramatic apotheosis. The reason may be that he was a holy man during his whole life, a sage and philosopher, righteous king and lawgiver, prophet and miracle-worker, living as a spiritual

---

48 Plutarch's account is longer and more detailed than the one in Dionysius of Halicarnassus 2.76.6; cf. also Polybius 6.53.1–54.1; Cicero, *Leg.* 2.22.55–7, 68. Peter 1865: 171 suggests Varro as the possible source. However, Plutarch may simply draw on other literary examples of large funeral processions, or even on his own witnessing of such processions. On funerary rituals, see Toynbee 1996.

49 Carrying this further, Ovid speaks of Numa's consort (*coniunx*), Egeria's, great sorrow. Her tears streaming incessantly, she in the end finds mercy with Diana who turns her into a spring in Diana's grove in Aricia (*Metam.* 15.487–551). Egeria then becomes Ovid's own source of poetic inspiration, for which he often drinks from her spring (*Fast.* 3.273–6). See Buchheit 1993, especially 81–2.

50 *Rom.* 27.3–4. Plutarch mentions the general uncertainty (ἀσάφεια, ὑποψία, διαβολή) among the people, suspecting that he might have been murdered, a situation resembling the end of Aeneas, as reported as early as Cato's *Origines*; probably, Cato depends on Fabius Pictor, for which see Schröder 1971: 126–31.

51 See *Rom.* 27.5: οὔτε μέρος ὤφθη σώματος οὔτε λείψανον ἐσθῆτος. Cf. Numa's empty tomb (*Numa* 22.5): ὤφθη καὶ μέρος οὐδὲν οὐδὲ λείψανον ἔχουσα τοῦ σώματος.

52 Cf. *Rom.* 27.3–29.7, with Plutarch's collection of parallels; *Numa* 2.1–3 is comparatively brief.

leader of men and a close companion of divinity. If so, what then was Numa's post-mortem existence? Plutarch defers his own explanation until after bringing in another tradition.[53] This information seems to come from a different source, either one of the Hellenistic Pseudo-Pythagorica[54] or oral information he picked up in conversations with his Pythagorean friends, perhaps even in Rome. Dealing with Numa's peculiar rejection of burial by cremation,[55] its legendary character is indicated by the phrase 'as it is said' (ὡς λέγεται):

> They did not burn his body, because, as it is said, he forbade it; but they made two stone coffins and buried them under the Janiculum. One of these held his body, and the other the sacred books which he had written out with his own hand, as the Greek lawgivers their tablets. But since, while he was still living, he had taught the priests the written contents of the books, and had inculcated in their hearts the scope and meaning of them all, he commanded that they should be buried with his body, convinced that such mysteries ought not to be entrusted to the care of lifeless documents. (22.2)

(c) Plutarch enriches his account by an excursus about the peculiar practices of the Pythagoreans concerning writing:

> This is the reason, we are told, why the Pythagoreans also do not entrust their precepts in writing, but implant the memory and the practice of them in living disciples worthy to receive them. And when their treatment of the abstruse and mysterious processes of geometry had been divulged to a certain unworthy person, they said the gods threatened to punish such lawlessness and impiety with some signal and widespread calamity. (22.3–4)

Notably, these are legendary *topoi* concerning Pythagoras' distrust of writings and the rules of silence.[56] Like most writers Plutarch does not clearly distinguish between the historical Pythagoras and later Pythagorean traditions. His own position remains ambiguous: 'Therefore we may well be indulgent with those who are eager to prove, on the basis of so many resemblances between them, that Numa was acquainted with Pythagoras' (22.4).

(d) Specific details concerning the rediscovery of the tomb on the Janiculum,[57] with the coffins and their contents, are introduced from Valerius Antias (22.4–5, trans. modified):

---

53   Cf. the different view of Dionysius of Halicarnassus 2.76.5: 'He lived to a very advanced age without any impairment of his faculties and without suffering any blow at Fortune's hands; and he died the easiest of all deaths, being withered by age, the genius who had been allotted to him from his birth having continued to the same favour to him till he disappeared from among men.' This account of Numa's 'disappearance' (ἠφανίσθη) out of his tomb seems to imply his post-mortem apotheosis.

54   See Burkert 1961, especially 238–46; Riedweg 2002: 157–67.

55   Notably, the issue of cremation is not mentioned either by Dionysius of Halicarnassus 2.76.6 or by Cicero, *Leg.* 2.56. The reason why Numa forbade his cremation may be that he followed Etruscan practice, or more likely Pythagorean usage, or both. See Nock 1972, especially 288–92.

56   Cf. on the name Tacita *Numa* 8.6. Similarly, Lycurgus did not put his laws into writing either; see *Lyc.* 13.1–3.

57   The tomb is attested since L. Cassius Hemina (*ca.* 150 B.C.E); see also Pliny, *Nat.* 13.84–6. For the location, see P. Liverani in Steinby 1993–2000: 4.292.

Antias, however, writes that there were twelve hierophantic books, and twelve others containing Greek philosophy, which were placed together in the coffin. And about four hundred years afterwards, when Publius Cornelius and Marcus Baebius were consuls, heavy rains fell, and the torrent of water tore away the earth and exposed the coffins. When their lids had fallen off, one coffin was seen to be entirely empty, without any relic whatever of the body, but in the other the writings were found. These Petilius, who was then praetor, is said to have read, and then brought to the senate, declaring that, in his opinion, it was not legitimate or holy that the writings should be made available to the public. The books were therefore carried to the comitium and burned.

Plutarch's story of the rediscovery of the tomb is one among several different versions,[58] their relationship to one another being the subject of ongoing discussions.[59] According to him, the rediscovery in the year 181 B.C.E. was nothing less than a natural miracle. Torrential rains had caused a kind of landslide and laid bare the two coffins, with their lids having fallen off.

One of the coffins was completely empty and did not show either bone fragments or remains of cloth. This could only be seen as evidence of the so-called 'empty tomb', indicating that the bodily remains of Numa had mysteriously vanished. Other such tales of empty tombs would suggest that he had been elevated in body to the realm of the gods. The other coffin held twenty-four books, twelve of them turned out to be 'hierophantic' and twelve to be Greek philosophy. The number twelve and the two categories clearly fulfilled the expectations of the Italian Pythagoreans. For them Numa was a revered hierophant and mystagogue, so that the first set of his books would have contained secret rituals and other teachings which thus far were made orally known only to approved initiates. The second set included books of Greek philosophy and thus constituted indisputable evidence that Numa's philosophy was Greek and present in Rome from the beginning, and that it had laid the ground for Roman institutions of religion and state.[60]

The importance of the findings was recognized at once, and the books were given to the then praetor Petilius. After reading them, he presented them to the senate, along with his recommendation that it would be illegitimate and sacrilegious to make the writings known to the public. This suggests that by taking them into his tomb Numa wanted to preclude his esoteric writings being exposed to the public, and that violating his last will would be a ritual offence and not in the public interest. The senate agreed, and the books were publicly burned in the Comitium.

Plutarch seems to have used Antias' account selectively, at least in comparison with Livy, whose longer version reflects various suspicions regarding the political

---

58 Discoveries of books from tombs constitute an ancient topic by itself, for which see Speyer 1970: 43–124.
59 For detailed analyses and comparisons of the sources, together with further secondary literature, see Rosen 1985; Willi 1998.
60 Important is what Plutarch does not say: that the coffins were both inscribed in Latin and Greek with Numa's name, that seven books in Latin contained the pontifical laws (*ius pontificum*), and the other seven in Greek the *disciplina sapientiae*. Cf. Valerius Antias according to Livy 40.29.3–14. These versions seem to be intended to fend off anticipated critical questions.

content of the books and their undesirable consequences for the situation in Rome at the time. Only five years earlier Rome had endured the infamous Bacchanalia scandal of 186 B.C.E., and fears of political and religious conspiracies were widespread. On the other hand, it has been argued by some that the entire rediscovery of Numa's tomb was an orchestrated fraud to serve political goals. At any rate, the burning of the books set a precedent for future actions of this kind, by which the authorities would get rid of politically 'dangerous books'.[61]

Whatever the doubtful accounts, the discovery of an empty tomb connects Numa and Christ, but at the same time the differences are just as instructive. In both cases, the empty tomb witnesses to the post-mortem existence of those buried. Their bodily resurrection is a matter of inference from the emptiness of the tomb, but the significance of their post-mortem existence varied greatly. There are no extant graves or remains that could function in an ongoing hero-cult: both graves have essentially vanished, even though at a later time grave monuments were 're-invented'. In the case of Jesus, competing claims to authenticity connect Jesus' tomb in Mk 16.1-8 (par.) to the Church of the Holy Sepulchre or the so-called Garden Tomb in Jerusalem; in the case of Numa, Renaissance iconography shows a monument somehow tied to the Villa Lante on the Gianicolo.[62] Evidently, the emptiness of the tombs had the effect of impeding a local hero-cult while opening up other forms of post-mortem reappearance and new chapters in the history of messianism.

6. Conclusion

What are we to make of this reading of Plutarch's *Numa* and the New Testament in the context of Graeco-Roman messianism? Having to confine our reading to a few examples means that the number of points of contact could be increased significantly. Since both bodies of texts are not aware of each other, these points of contact do not consist of intertextual references. Another explanation is, therefore, that both textual bodies refer to the wider context of Graeco-Roman ruler-cult and its literary manifestations of messianism. In this wider context the literary genre of biographies of religio-political founder figures has assumed greater significance, probably since Aristoxenos of Tarentum (4th century B.C.E.), a former student of Aristotle who joined the Pythagoreans in Southern Italy. Centuries later, through intermediate sources, this biographical tradition reaches Plutarch, for whom the figure of Numa as philosopher-king becomes a paradigm of the good ruler in the Roman Imperial Era after Domitian (51–96 C.E.). As chief-priest at Delphi, which at that time was the centre of Greek religion, Plutarch was honoured as an official representative vis-à-vis Rome. In this situation the writing of the *Lives* becomes paramount in importance. Trying to exercise whatever influence he has, Plutarch cautiously recommends Numa the philosopher-king as a model for the Flavian emperors. On the other side, Hellenistic Judaism also has to confront ruler-cult and in so doing develops

---

61 See Speyer 1981: 51–80.
62 For the material, see Lilius 1981, especially 1.156–62; vol. 2, figs 6–10 and tavola 52–3.

messianism in its various forms. Early Christianity originates in the middle of these confrontations and shares in them, until it goes its own way with its messianic faith in Jesus Christ. When Christianity expands into the Gentile world, the fundamental antagonism emerges between the central figure of Christ and the Roman ruler-cult. In this context we also see the sudden appearance of biographies of Jesus, first the Gospel of Mark, and then the reworkings by Matthew, Luke and John. Although the origin of the genre 'gospel' is still unexplained, its appearance was obviously welcomed. Especially the author of Luke/Acts realizes the need for a biography of Jesus to introduce the first history of Christianity, the book of Acts. All four Gospels, like the rest of the New Testament, present Jesus the Messiah as the contrast figure to the Roman rulers. In this regard, the Gospels as biographical narratives begin to function in a way parallel to Plutarch's *Life of Numa*. The points of contact between Plutarch's biography and the New Testament, foremost but not exclusively the Gospels, have their origin in reference to the overarching struggles against the ruler-cult and its expectations and demands. Without being specific about the details it can be stated that Christian messianism in the New Testament aims at combating the figure of the deified Roman emperor. The New Testament has two other objectives analogous to Plutarch: one is the reconciliation between Greek and Roman Christians, and the other the creation of a history of primitive Christianity by adding together four biographies of Jesus the Messiah, somewhat similar to Plutarch whose four biographies of the pairs Theseus/Romulus and Lycurgus/Numa describe the contributions of non-Greeks and Greeks to the origins of Rome.

Part II

The New Testament

Chapter 5

Resistance and Redemption in the Jesus Tradition

Markus Bockmuehl

Was Jesus messianic? And if so, what sort of Messiah was he? That pair of historical questions remains vital to the Jesus tradition's understanding of redemption and resistance. The present chapter will examine our theme primarily in relation to the latter of these twin questions: if Jesus was indeed perceived, by others and perhaps by himself, to be the (or a) divinely anointed prophetic or royal end-time Messiah, does not this necessarily evoke the question of how then concretely this Messiah went about saving all that is lost and righting all that is wrong?

The Revolution of Jesus

The theme of resistance in the messianism of Jesus has tended to find its most colourful exponents among those who envisage him as a political rebel – a leader or fomenter of insurrection, agitating, or at least implicitly aiding and abetting, revolution against Rome and Jewish authorities collaborating with the occupying power. Drawing their stimulus from hints in the Gospels and echoes in ancient anti-Christian polemic, such views have periodically surfaced in scholarship since their first modern restatement by Hermann Samuel Reimarus (1694–1768); over the past century, prominent exponents have included Robert Eisler, Joel Carmichael, S. G. F. Brandon, Hyam Maccoby, Robert Eisenman and others.[1] These, in other respects diverse, accounts share the view that while Jesus himself may or may not have been personally engaged in violent pursuit of Jewish independence from Rome and its collaborators, what he did say and do gave plenty of implicit encouragement to those who were. Among the Twelve, Simon 'the Zealot', Judas Iscariot and even Simon *Bariona* were thought to provide evidence of significant militant sympathies in the Jesus movement.[2] Similarly, some scholars believed that Josephus' accounts of Judas the Galilean and of the

---

[1] Reimarus 1772 (ET Reimarus 1970); Eisler 1929 (ET Eisler 1931); Carmichael 1963; Brandon 1957, 1967, 1968; Maccoby 1973 (cf. Maccoby 2003: 9 and *passim*); Eisenman 1996, 1997. Bammel 1984a offers an extensive historical survey of 'political' Jesus interpretation to *ca*. 1980. See also Hagner 1984 and Vogler 1988: 40–8 on Eisler, Carmichael and Maccoby in the context of other Jewish interpreters of Jesus.

[2] Theissen and Merz 1998: 459–60 (cf. Theissen 2004: 203) suggests that whatever ὁ [καλούμενος] ζηλωτής means (Lk. 6.15; Acts 1.13), it does single Simon out among the disciples as an exception. For *Bariona* see also Bockmuehl 2004: 62–9.

role subsequently played by the towns of Gischala and Gamla at the beginning of the Jewish War (A.D. 66–7) were indicative of the general socio-political character of Galilee as a hotbed of popular discontent.

Theories of straightforward militant insurrection soon began to be found wanting in the wake of criticisms by Oscar Cullmann (1970), Martin Hengel (1971, 1973) and others. To be sure, the umbilical cord of militancy was sometimes severed on logically and historically dubious grounds, such as that Josephus' silence about 'Zealots' prior to the 60s of the first century demonstrates the non-existence of any militants with whom Jesus might have sympathized.

For reasons both good and bad, then, this 'revolutionary' Jesus soon gave way to a plethora of more moderate interpretations of Jesus, allied with new social-science approaches and neo-Marxian socio-economic analysis among scholars trained in the 1960s. An increasingly important corollary was the interpretation of Jesus in contemporary Christian political theology, including not only the influential pacifist work of John Howard Yoder (1972) but also Latin American (and other) forms of 'liberation theology' that were linked with the study of Jesus in writers like Juan Luis Segundo (1985, 1988). Within New Testament scholarship proper, in addition to Gerd Theissen and others, it is perhaps above all Richard A. Horsley who has advanced the interpretation of Jesus as a subversive activist linked most closely to Jewish movements of social protest and anti-imperial insurrection.[3]

Prolifically engaged throughout the 1970s and 1980s, this debate received a certain renewed focus by the publication in English of Martin Hengel's magisterial dissertation (Hengel 1961, 1989b), to which the work of Richard Horsley continues to serve as a powerful counterpoint. Is the social context of first-century Jewish protest best understood in terms of a 'Jewish freedom movement' fired by deeply held theological and eschatological convictions, or is the more accurate framework a quasi-Marxian account of egalitarian protest and resistance against institutionalized repression and injustice, within which ideological or religious means serve socio-economic ends? Hengel's view is that:

> In Zealotism and early Christianity, two eschatological messianic movements were firmly opposed to each other. Despite certain external parallels, the contrast between them was irreconcilable. The expectation of Jesus as the Son of Man who was to come again and as the judge of the world was bound to contradict all the hopes of the Zealots, which were directed towards such warlike messianic pretenders as Menahem or Simon bar Giora. (Hengel 1989b: 301–2)

For all its complexities, the 'Jewish freedom movement' between A.D. 6 and 70 was in Hengel's view a widespread and coherent phenomenon marked by 'a certain unified ideological foundation' that combined radical Pharisaic piety and praxis with an eschatologically driven commitment to unrestricted zeal in achieving its aim of a Jewish theocracy.[4] While Jesus did touch on certain Zealot

---

3   Horsley 1993, 2003; Horsley and Hanson 1999. Cf. e.g. Theissen 1978, 1991, 1992b, 2004, also Hanson and Oakman 1998: 125–8; Moxnes 1988, 2003; Myers 1988; Wink 1992, 2003. Horrell 1997 critically compares Horsley's and Theissen's conflicting notions of leadership and views of subsistence.
4   Hengel 1989b: 404, 377–8 and *passim*.

Resistance and Redemption in the Jesus Tradition

ideas and was indeed turned over to the Romans on the false allegation of being a Zealot messianic pretender, his proclamation in substance 'represented the real overcoming of the Zealots' attempt to bring about God's rule on earth by violence' – a stance endorsed by the 'anti-political tendency' of the Fourth Gospel.[5]

Hengel's account has come under sustained attack for its supposedly homogenizing depiction of pre-70 Judaism and insufficiently nuanced awareness of Jesus' social setting. Among Hengel's fiercest critics has been Richard A. Horsley, who employs a social-science approach to stress the complex (and largely, but not necessarily non-violent) nature of social protest at this time. Far from contrasting a pacifist and 'non-resistant' Jesus movement with a violent Jewish resistance, Horsley is certain that no violent 'Zealots' existed before the winter of A.D. 67–8, and there is 'simply no evidence for an organized movement of violent resistance that agitated for armed revolt from 6 to 66 C.E.' (Horsley 1993: x–xi).

In place of this, Horsley posits for first-century Palestine a social order of considerable tension and diversity, in which a 'spiral of violence' worked its way from institutionalized injustice ('structural violence') to largely non-violent protest and resistance (but including endemic social bandits and brigands, champions of the oppressed who 'constitute at most a moderate protest against an established order').[6] This resistance was met by the Roman and high priestly establishment's response of formal repression and persecution. Open revolt was only the final stage – possibly, but not necessarily, violent; and during the late Second Temple period and its aftermath, the three examples Horsley identifies are the insurrections of 4 B.C., A.D. 66–73 and 132–5. It is *within*, rather than against this context, he argues, that Jesus and his movement must be read. The purpose of Jesus was to enact a radical condemnation of Roman imperial order and the social renewal of Israel's peasant villages through 'covenantal communities' that explicitly represented his strongly anti-imperial alternative to Rome (Horsley 2003, *passim*).

Contrary to the pacifist or purely eschatological Jesus posited by some, this Jesus is in the first instance a socio-political rather than an eschatological agent, like a Jeremiah more than like a utopian Messiah. Like Hengel, Horsley addresses these complex matters in a number of different ways. Overall, however, it is clear that for him the role of eschatological divine agency has been (not eliminated, but) subsumed within his account of Jesus as emphatically wedded to an activist agenda. 'The issue for Jesus' contemporaries was apparently less one of theological ideas or eschatological expectations ... than one of concrete social-historical phenomena' (Horsley 1985a: 435). This polarity is put a little less starkly elsewhere, but Horsley's vision remains as distinctive for what it denies as for what it (often quite reasonably) affirms. In keeping with much recent Q

---

5   Hengel 1989b: 378–9. Even if 'anti-political' were an appropriate characterization of the Fourth Gospel (but Jn 18.20, 23, 33-38; 19.12, 15 etc. beg that question), this could hardly be said to make Jesus 'anti-messianic', *pace* Williams 2000: 101–2 (who also takes this to lend succour to 'a contemporary critique of the *ersatz* messianism of the modern state of Israel'). Theissen 2004: 204–6 too describes the Jesus movement as 'anti-political'; but this is for him distinct from 'unpolitical', since in fact it empowers political effectiveness in a violent society.

6   Horsley 1993: 38; 23–49 *passim*. For further discussion of Horsley, see Freyne, this volume: 37–9.

scholarship, he downplays the significance of future-eschatological texts like the 'synoptic apocalypse' of Mark 13 parr. Instead, he affirms:

> It is difficult to think of Jesus' sayings that envisage an 'all-transforming' action in God's ruling. ... Jesus' sayings portray not an 'all-transforming act' but a number of respects in which social relations (political-economic-religious) will be or are being transformed. Thus also Jesus' preaching of the kingdom of God does not refer to an 'act' in the sense of one particular event ... (Horsley 1993: 168–9)

Horsley and Hengel are of course just two single reference points on a map densely congested with other important scholarly contributions; but for present purposes they do serve as convenient and highly influential markers of mutually exclusive poles of interpretation on this matter.

A Debate Past Its 'Sell-By' Date?

How then might one adjudicate this argument? Our purpose here cannot be to reheat the somewhat dated leftovers of that controversy about Jesus' militant sympathies, an issue that remains unresolved, if perhaps also sustained in a somewhat tetchy and uneasy truce, between the governing interpretative frameworks of socio-economic and religious ideology. Whether readily or reluctantly, some of the heirs and successors of the leading antagonists in the older debate would now acknowledge the validity of the other side's questions; and notions of resistance are becoming more sophisticated.[7]

Suffice it to say that straightforwardly militant or quietist interpretations of Jesus are rendered equally implausible by the effects his ministry evoked among friends as well as enemies. It is telling to note the lack of a concerted Roman response, first to Jesus himself and then most certainly among the circle of his followers. If the New Testament evidence is even approximately reliable, such organized persecution as Christians did experience prior to the fire of Rome in A.D. 64 was predominantly at the hands of Jewish or pro-Jewish officials rather than Roman ones, in Palestine particularly at times when a Roman power vacuum more easily permitted the settling of old scores.[8] Official pagan repression, where it occasionally emerges (e.g. in Philippi or Thessalonica[9]), seems never to relate to any charge of insurrection, whether or not linked with Jesus. Of the leading twelve disciples, only Peter and Andrew are said to have suffered their master's fate on a Roman cross, and that

---

7   Theissen 2004 represents one recent example of such nuanced analysis. Forms of resistance before and below the threshold of formal confrontation have also been influentially explored by Scott 1985, 1990 and applied to the New Testament by Horsley 2004 (especially his own contributions to that volume); cf. Horrell, this volume: 122–3, 126–7, 134.
8   Examples appear to include the martyrdoms of Stephen and James the Son of Zebedee as well as another possible persecution in A.D. 48 (cf. Bockmuehl 2001); the first and especially the second Jewish war against Rome may be additional examples (cf. Horbury 1998a).
9   Persecution of Macedonian Christians is intimated in 2 Cor. 8.1f.; Phil. 1.28-30; 1 Thess. 1.6; 3.3; 2 Thess. 1.4; 1 Thess. 2.14 shows it to emanate from pagans, unlike in Palestine. See also Hardin 2006 on Acts 17.1-10.

not until many years later. None of this is what we should expect if Jesus or his followers had, either in fact or at least in popular perception, engaged in systematic anti-Roman agitation.[10]

Conversely, however, any historically plausible reconstruction must indeed be able to account convincingly for his death at Roman hands. There is something prima facie self-evident about this point, as Hyam Maccoby (then advocating a strongly insurrectionist thesis) put it almost 35 years ago:

> There is no need to doubt that Jesus often spoke to the people on purely religious and moral topics, like any other Pharisee teacher, but if he had confined himself to these topics he would never have ended his life on a Roman cross.[11]

A historically credible Jesus, in other words, must be 'crucifiable'.[12] While there may be pre-Roman precedent for a Jewish high priest disposing of Pharisaic opponents by crucifixion,[13] what is most telling in the case of Jesus is the Roman *titulus*. There is in principle a plausible narrative sequence from the one who rides into Jerusalem to the royal acclaim of his followers to his crucifixion as 'king of the Jews'.[14] That phrase, although subject ever since antiquity to a wide variety of pro- and anti-Christian polemic, expresses in any case the *Roman* capital crime – *laesa maiestas* or *perduellio*, perhaps.

At the same time, there is good reason to wonder if indeed that Roman indictment really represented a duly constituted *formal* charge – rather than the more likely informality of the perfunctory pseudo-legal stamp of convenience, designed to nip in the bud a breach of the Roman peace.[15] Jewish opposition, by contrast, whether from Sadducees or others, is much more likely to have been confined to the charge as expressed in parts of the passion narrative and echoed in later polemic in rabbinic literature. The Talmud, for example, famously regards not only Jesus but his 'five' (*sic*) disciples as deserving of death – not for insurrection but for deception and sorcery.[16]

---

10 The pre-Christian Paul may well have been closer to such a position of theologically Pharisaic Jewish militant nationalism, sympathetic perhaps to the messianism of the *Psalms of Solomon* 17 (see e.g. Hengel and Deines 1991; Taylor 1998; cf. Theissen 2004: 203 n.249). In Corinth, Gallio's judgement as reported in Acts 18.14-16 treats Christianity as in the first instance an inner-Jewish problem. That changed a decade later under Nero, but not at first systematically – aside from periodic harassment of Christians, Trajan's correspondence with Pliny is arguably the first systematic Roman reflection on how to deal with Christianity as a threat to public order.
11 Maccoby 1973: 129. Cf. Maccoby 2003: 8, 73, 136–7, though the greater concern of this later book is to show Jesus as a Pharisaic Hasid.
12 So rightly McKnight 1999: 9, although this point is surely tempered by the ease with which 800 Pharisees were found 'crucifiable' by Alexander Jannaeus *ca.* 86 B.C., or for that matter 6,000 of Spartacus' followers by Crassus along the Appian Way in 71 B.C.
13 Josephus, *Ant.* 13.380–3; *J.W.* 1.97–8; cf. 4QpNahum (4Q169) 3+4.i.7–8.
14 It is arguably Luke who presents this link most clearly (19.38; 23.2-4, 37-38), but it is in fact strongly implicit in all four Gospels.
15 See e.g. Theissen and Merz 1998: 457–9; also Bammel 1984b. Riedo-Emmenegger 2005 studies the Jesus movement from the pragmatic perspective of comparable provocations against the *Pax Romana*, noting that its survival is distinctly unusual.
16 B. *Sanh.* 43a. See already Lk. 23.2 διαστρέφοντα τὸ ἔθνος ἡμῶν; also Mk 3.22. The five disciples, Mattai, Nakai, Nezer, Buni and Todah may include Matthew, Nicodemus and Thaddaeus: cf. Bockmuehl 2004: 56 n.5.

This is also a point memorably made in William Horbury's work on the contest between ancient Jewish and Christian messianic hopes. He demonstrates the early existence and persistence of narrative traditions hostile to the person of Jesus, and employed by pagan critics like Fronto, Sassanius Hierocles and Celsus (at least in relation to the disciples) as well as in Jewish polemics echoed in the Tosefta, both Talmuds and especially the *Toledot Yeshu* tradition (on which see esp. Horbury 1970). Horbury argues persuasively that from its earliest appearances in both settings this tradition served an aetiological polemic, providing 'the crime of the crucified ... to fit the punishment'.[17] In Jewish eyes that crime was, understandably, the Deuteronomic one of sorcery and false prophecy; but in pagan sources Jesus' felony took a more recognizably Roman form. For Jews, resistance to Rome might be tactically disagreeable but certainly not a capital crime; for Romans, sorcery and false prophecy might be culturally contemptible but hardly merited crucifixion. Far from providing a plausible backdrop against which to debunk the New Testament's supposedly tendentious view of a pacifist Jesus, Jesus' engagement in robbery or insurrection would have implied the sorts of 'habitual acts of violence' that would at once render nonsensical the New Testament's diverse claims about Jesus' patience, humility and self-denial.[18] In that sense the shape of Christology necessarily subverts the assertion of a militant Jesus.

Redemption or Resistance – A Case of Irreconcilable Differences?

To recognize the implausibility of the more extreme theories, however, is still to leave a continuing scholarly debate little advanced as to substance. Why should the theme of resistance in the ministry of Jesus have proved, for the past three generations, quite so intractably resistant to scholarly consensus? Of course the issue was periodically studied and debated between Reimarus and Eisler. But since the 1930s, it would be impossible to assert of even a single decade of scholarship the sort of Tacitean *sub Tiberio quies* that Ernst Bammel's learned survey was able to affirm for the general tenor of what preceded: 'There the matter rested for most of the nineteenth century.'[19]

What, therefore, might account for the extent to which after all these years the production of contemporary scholarly heat still far outstrips the shedding of generally acknowledged first-century historical light? Two obvious answers to that question may at once be acknowledged, but hardly exhaust the issue.

First and most obviously, the last quarter-century's seemingly boundless hyperactivity in new and renewed 'historical Jesus' debates makes the revival of a subset of questions surrounding the 'revolutionary' Jesus less surprising. There is a thriving business even in third-order surveys and taxonomies, with abundant

---

17 Horbury 1998b: 172; cf. 166 and *passim*. A succinct summary also appears in Horbury 1999: 29–30.
18 Horbury 1998b: 172, citing C. K. Barrett and G. N. Stanton. Cf. Sweet 1984: 9 for the analogous christological point that constructing a militant Jesus requires 'discounting those aspects of the traditional picture of him which give most reason for seeking his support'.
19 Bammel 1984a: 13; cf. Tacitus, *Ann.* 5.9.

reviews of surveys of studies of 'the historical Jesus'. Is our question likely to 'rest' even for a decade?

Second, however, to acknowledge this state of affairs is perhaps merely to dodge the question by relativizing it on a larger canvas – which, one suspects, is itself a function of wider and partly inscrutable cultural trends in which we are all enmeshed. The fact that this debate seems more protracted and inconclusive in today's 'postmodern' context than in nineteenth-century Germany is perhaps also unsurprising. At a time when New Testament scholarship in many areas lacks consensus about basic criteria of what makes for good or bad argument,[20] perhaps the phenomenon of profuse debate without agreement even on supposed 'essentials' is itself indicative of a wider cultural loss of nerve that follows the demise of long-held critical and credal paradigms.

In an engaging survey of Christian scholarship on the Zealots, Daniel R. Schwartz 1992 argued that the later twentieth-century rediscovery of the 'political' Jesus, whether in the guise of Zealot militancy or (latterly) of socio-economic protest, was in part driven by less than strictly historical concerns. He suggested that, in the aftermath of the churches' quietism during the mid-century Shoah, Christian scholars felt a peculiar burden to find a Jesus more credibly engaged with the fate of his people. Adopting what is always the critic's safest course of action, Schwartz volunteers no constructive historical proposal of his own. It is certainly true that the social location of scholarship is of particular pertinence when discussing that of Jesus. Nevertheless, a number of scholars, including several members of the North American Jesus Seminar, would advocate a socially radical Jesus without being overly interested in his Jewishness. In practice, the absence of substantive engagement arguably renders Schwartz's study entertaining rather than illuminating for the problem of how messianism and resistance were in fact related for Jesus of Nazareth.

All of which, to be sure, is still to describe the problem rather than to answer it. What accounts for the seeming inability to move the discussion forward? One characteristically postmodern explanation is that the study of history can only ever be the study of the historians themselves: the most responsible thing to do with the Quest for the historical Jesus is to abandon it in favour of the Quest for the Questers – or in other words, for the *contemporary* Jesus.[21] But that sort of capitulation to a reductionism of power politics is today beginning to sound tired and inadequate even to seasoned readers of postmodernity. However successfully diversely vested interpretations of the past can be constructed and deconstructed, the past itself cannot: as Aristotle points out, history remains what Alcibiades did and suffered.[22]

---

20   So rightly Williams 2003: 218; cf. Bockmuehl 2006: 30–9 and *passim*.
21   So explicitly Arnal 2005b: 75–7; similarly Arnal 2005a on the concern for Jesus' 'Jewishness'.
22   *Poetics* 2.6, 1451b11; cf. Evans 1997: 103–28.

Three Suggestions for Future Debate

Space does not here permit the formulation of a solution to this problem, let alone a survey of the relevant texts and traditions documenting either Jesus' messianism or indeed his political stance. In the remainder of this essay, however, I would like instead to develop the modest proposal that future discussion of our topic stands to gain, at least in clarity, by attending to three factors that have not always been given their due in the debate. They pertain respectively to methodology, to the messianic *function* of resistance within the Jesus tradition, and to the way this focuses messianic eschatology on the *person* of the Messiah.

1. First, then, a suggestion about method. It may be that, far from being able to locate a methodologically superior Archimedean point from which to arbitrate between conflicting approaches like those of Hengel and Horsley, the answer to the critical issue of Jesus' resistance depends on more than merely historical-critical questions. In such debates, which might indeed profitably consider the origins of Jewish militant movements or, for example, the social character of the 'historical Galilee' that underlies the Gospel narratives, one might rightly expect to see progress based on new evidence or better methods.[23] To a greater degree than is sometimes acknowledged, however, the more properly basic disputes rest more often on *metacritical* decisions about the heuristic place one assigns to certain contested presuppositions – decisions that will in turn reflect something of our own scholarship's social and religious setting. This raises doubts about the customary scholarly quest for decisive resolution on the basis of more sophisticated methodological firepower. Two of these metacritical decisions may be worth highlighting in brief as illustrative examples (and not necessarily as the most important).

a. In the current debate, a good deal of the disagreement relates to the relative role (governing or ancillary) assigned to contemporary approaches of *social theory and cultural anthropology*, but also conversely to the methodological recognition and analytical validity of *religious convictions* as a central motivation for the ministry of Jesus. There is no denying that genuine interpretative and historical gains have been achieved by socio-cultural interrogation of first-century Palestine's literary and material remains. At what point, however, does the usefulness of our methods become apparent rather than real, because they do more to flatter contemporary cultural preferences than to confront us with those of our text? Dale Allison 2000: 148–9 shrewdly highlights one important aspect of this problem in his seminal essay on recent 'secular' Jesus scholarship:

> The earliest extant interpretations of the Jesus tradition are all thoroughly religious. This is because the first interpreters were all consumed by thoughts about God, miracles, and eschatology or the afterlife. One good explanation of this circumstance is that Jesus

---

[23] Sean Freyne 1998, 2000, 2004 and Mark Chancey 2005; Chancey 2002 has done much to situate Jesus more securely in the social and religious setting of Galilee, in the process debunking once popular notions of a Galilee determined either by religious militancy or on the other hand by Hellenizing rejection of Judaean religious taboos.

himself was just such a person, a deeply religious personality who interpreted everything in terms of an unseen world, and that he and the traditions about him attracted like-minded others. We might accordingly do well to ask ourselves to what extent our competence to find Jesus requires an 'ability to appreciate a distinctly religious personality,' and to what extent our growing secularity may sometimes constrict that ability.

The conflict between theological and 'cultural studies' approaches to Jesus seems an apposite example to consider under this heading.

b. *Theories of Synoptic Gospel origins* play a remarkably significant role in determining the overall place of resistance in Jesus' ministry. Horsley holds to a position in which Jesus' urgent and imminent message of social reform is nonetheless rooted in a clearly 'apocalyptic' milieu;[24] but his commitment to a relatively mainstream form of the 'Q' hypothesis as indicative of the shape of the earliest sayings tradition nevertheless leads him to downplay the futurist or transcendental eschatology of texts like the Synoptic apocalypse (Mark 13 parr.). Although retaining the theme of judgement in such passages as indicative of Jesus' political concern with injustice, Horsley 1993: 168–9 explicitly denies the authenticity of texts that might envisage specific divine 'acts' or 'particular events' in the eschaton. (Scholars like John Dominic Crossan, Robert W. Funk and others, who consider Jesus accessible only in the hypothetically earliest, de-eschatologized redactional layers of 'Q' and *Thomas*, go further in this same direction and consider all 'apocalyptic' or eschatological material as secondary adulteration of the radical and sapiential egalitarianism of the original Jesus movement.) Matters soon look quite different on the basis of a Synoptic theory like Hengel's, which has emerged more clearly only in recent years. Dispensing with Q, he argues for the sequence of the Gospels as Mark, Luke and Matthew (while other, more numerous 'Q sceptics' have put Matthew before Luke).[25] Similarly, for others who on various internal and external grounds would date at least parts of the Synoptic apocalypse tradition to around A.D. 40,[26] the place of apocalyptic eschatology is also bound to loom rather larger in any understanding of Jesus' messianism.

2. In relation to the Gospel tradition's actual use of the theme of resistance, it ought to become a point of departure for future debate that *the themes of non-violent resistance and messianic redemption are for the ministry of Jesus two sides of the same coin*. Human resistance is a function of divine redemption, rather than vice versa; but each is unintelligible without the other, and neither is adequately described in *exclusively* social or theological terms. Virtually *all* known Jewish groups were in some theological (and at least to that extent political) sense opposed to Rome; and despite his repudiation of violence Jesus was presumably no exception.

At the same time, explicit resistance in the Gospel tradition is narratively focused less on Rome or its Herodian puppet underlings than on the teaching and

---

24   E.g. Horsley 1993: 157–60, 172–7 and *passim*.
25   See esp. Hengel 2000. Contrast Goodacre 2002, who develops the more popular Mark-Matthew-Luke hypothesis of Austin Farrer and Michael Goulder.
26   So e.g. Theissen 1991: 151–65; cf. e.g. Crossley 2004.

the 'politics of holiness' of mainly Galilean Pharisees (of whom, all the same, Jesus was one); on the corrupt power plays of Judaean Sadducees (and in that perhaps limited sense on the Temple they controlled); and to a lesser extent on scribes and Herodians.[27]

Beyond these identifiable *human* opponents, however, the Jesus tradition frequently signals and exemplifies resistance to other forms of oppression, whether personal or structural, 'natural' or demonic in origin. Illustrations abound: healings, exorcisms and epiphanic ('nature') miracles speak to this point as powerfully as does the Sermon on the Mount's insistent ethic of poverty, transparency and pacifism, or on the other hand the parables' social commentary on absentee landlords or the disenfranchised subsistence lifestyle of day labourers and widows.

Pace Horsley 2003 and other 'anti-imperial' interpretations, Jesus' record specifically in relation to *Rome* is a good deal more ambiguous and open to continuing debate and disagreement. His teaching and praxis of a strikingly generous non-violence towards Roman authority, whether in the Sermon on the Mount (e.g. Mt. 5.41, 44-45) or in the encounter with the centurion at Capernaum (Mt. 8.5-13 par.), in the principle of 'giving to Caesar (only) what is Caesar's' (Mk 12.17 parr.) or in the passion narrative (e.g. Mk 15.1-4 parr.), may for all its undoubted 'radicalness' entail a critical toleration and respect even for Gentile governing authorities. This form of tacit non-co-operation thus falls not only below the threshold of armed conflict as Horsley describes it, but in fact its tactic of critically generous *co-operation* arguably lies outside even what James C. Scott describes as the weapons of peasant 'resistance without protest': 'footdragging, dissimulation, false-compliance, pilfering, feigned ignorance, slander, arson, sabotage'.[28] For all its undoubted dissenting or subversive potential, to commend the full complement of taxes along with the voluntary second mile may in this respect be more compatible with Pauline and rabbinic counsel than is sometimes assumed.[29] But what is crystal clear is that in the Gospels neither political activism nor religious eschatology is meaningful in isolation: the Jesus tradition in all four Gospels has a habit of deconstructing the one in terms of the other. Thus, seemingly clear socio-political questions about Pilate's bloodbath of pilgrims or the controversial Temple Tax may suddenly turn out to pose deeply moral and *theological* challenges: 'unless you repent, you will all perish as they did' – 'but then the children are free'.[30] Conversely, those seeking

---

27 See e.g. Borg 1998: 43–65, although his focus on Jesus' resistance to Pharisaic 'holiness politics' (pp. 88–134) tends to sweep under the carpet Jesus' own halakhic notion of divine holiness and purity as infectious, in the interest of a starkly opposed (but vaguely defined) principle of 'compassion'. Aside from its exegetical difficulties, an explicit 'substitution' of compassion for holiness (Borg 1998: 135–55) suggests Marcionite and supersessionist implications. Cf. e.g. Borg 1994.

28 For these classic formulations see Scott 1987; Scott 1986: 6; cf. Scott 1990 and see the studies represented in Horsley 2004.

29 Mt. 5.41; Mt. 22.15-22 par. Mk 12.13-17, Lk. 20.21-26. Cf. e.g. Rom. 13.1-8; *m. 'Abot* 3.2.

30 Lk. 13.3; Mt. 17.25-26 (on which see Horbury 1984). Wright 1996: 248–51 rightly notes that in Jesus' context repentance is an eschatological and political act of turning to the God of Israel and away from violence and exploitation.

assurance in the scenario of an apocalyptic ticket to heaven are famously confronted with the threat of damnation for those whose 'ticket' does not entail tangible *social engagement* for the poor and outcast.³¹ As is paradigmatically encapsulated in key texts like the Lord's Prayer, the will of God – that is, the sanctification of the Name and the coming of God's kingdom – takes the concrete shape of his people's daily material sustenance, the forgiveness of their sins in the context of human reconciliation, and their deliverance out of the ordeal of the Evil One.³² The ministry of Jesus demonstrates that God's name is honoured and the kingdom comes 'by the finger of God' in Israel's deliverance from material and spiritual oppression; it is this that causes Satan's fall.³³

3. Finally, a point about the nature of biblical eschatology as expounded in the Jesus tradition's peculiar concentration of its messianic hope on the person of the Messiah. In the relationship of human resistance to a hope for redemption, we are often dealing with concerns that tend in modern political philosophies to be regarded as self-evidently contradictory. But even if one grants that the Jesus tradition affirms a transcendental and at times imminent eschatology, the co-existence of such beliefs with a longer-term perspective on discipleship should *not* be assumed to be a mainly compensatory phenomenon – due (for example) to the subsequent imposition of an apocalyptic eschatology alien to Jesus, or on the other hand to the failure of such eschatology.

The ability *to hold together prophetic urgency with patience and indeed postponement* is deeply intrinsic to the biblical and Jewish apocalyptic milieux among whom Jesus operated. On the one hand, he predicted the destruction of the Temple and envisaged other cataclysmic events before the impending arrival of the heavenly Son of Man. In the wake of Albert Schweitzer, that 'coming of the Kingdom with power' within a generation (Mk 9.1 par.; 13.30; cf. Mt. 10.23) has suggested to many interpreters either a failed activist agenda, or a failed eschatology, or both. To avoid either of these conclusions, scholars have in the past had resort to the transfiguration, the resurrection, or (perhaps most plausibly) to Pentecost. Passages like Jn 21.21-23 and 2 Pet. 3.4 suggest that such predictions did not indeed materialize in the way at least some of Jesus' listeners understood them.

It is, however, at least equally striking that this problem appears not to have worried most early Christians unduly, despite occasional hints in passages like those just cited. If one is not to regard this relative nonchalance as a case of exceptionally adept self-delusion, the reasons for it must be sought elsewhere – perhaps indeed in a seemingly contradictory thread in the Jesus tradition itself. The Synoptic Jesus buttresses his calls for constant watchfulness with the strangely ambivalent insistence that 'the day or the hour' is known neither to his disciples nor even to

---

31   E.g. Mt. 25.31-46; Lk. 16.19-31, etc.
32   I.e. 'do not let us succumb to the Trial': cf. 11QPs^a (11Q5=Ps 155) 24.10 וְאַל תְּבִיאֵנִי; *b.Ber.* 60b יְהִי רָצוֹן מִלְּפָנֶיךָ אֱלֹהֵי ה׳ שֶׁתַּשְׁכִּיבֵנִי לְשָׁלוֹם וְתֵן חֶלְקִי בְּתוֹרָתֶךָ; בְּקֻשּׁוֹת מִמֶּנִּי וְתַרְגִּילֵנִי לִידֵי מִצְוָה וְאַל תַּרְגִּילֵנִי לִידֵי עֲבֵירָה וְאַל תְּבִיאֵנִי לִידֵי חֵטְא וְלֹא לִידֵי עָוֹן וְלֹא לִידֵי נִסָּיוֹן). See also Jeremias 1976: 104–6.
33   Cf. Luke 10.18. N. T. Wright critically annotates Borg's interpretation of Jesus as a 'spirit person' who, for all his social concern, held a 'mystical' rather than redemptive eschatology (in Borg 1998: xix–xxiv).

himself (Mk 13.32 par.) – a statement whose surprising christological implications must constitute a good claim to authenticity. Despite the urgent flavour of its language about the coming events, in substance it remains remarkably restrained and (aside from the Temple's destruction) short on datable specifics. What is more, an explicitly *longer-term* perspective features even in the very same context of the Synoptic apocalypse (Mk 13.26f. par.): wars, persecutions, apostasy, false Messiahs etc. are all scheduled before the end – not to mention extensive Palestinian and worldwide evangelism (Mt. 10.23; Mk 14.9; cf. Lk. 21.7-9 par.).

Scholars will disagree about the extent to which such features may betray more about the evangelists' contexts than about that of Jesus. But it is entirely commonplace in Jewish apocalyptic texts to affirm that the end is at once near and urgent and yet contingent upon various preliminary developments that may sometimes have the effect of postponing it. Similarly co-existent concerns for urgent eschatology and pragmatic 'good citizenship' occur even in the earliest Christian literature (e.g. 1 Thess. 4.15–5.10 bracketed by 4.11-12; 5.11-24; cf. 2 Thess. 2.1-6).

Re-appropriation and re-adaptation of prophetic promises had always been a staple of Jewish religion, indeed a positive theological asset rather than a liability. Just as Isaiah's word of prophecy undergoes an *aggiornamento* without detriment to its divine author's trustworthiness (e.g. Isa. 16.13-14), so Jeremiah's prediction of 70 years of exile (25.11-12; 29.10) is re-interpreted in Dan. 9.24-27 as 490 years, while *4 Ezra* 12 in turn revises Daniel's vision of the fourth kingdom (2.40; 7.23) to apply to Rome. The Dead Sea commentator on Habakkuk saw no hermeneutical difficulty in affirming that the true meaning of prophecy, hidden from the prophets themselves, was revealed to the Teacher of Righteousness, while rabbinic Judaism readily absorbed the revered Rabbi Akiba's tragic identification of Simon Bar Koseba as the Messiah.[34] For all these cases, the *relecture* of earlier appropriations of prophecy invariably *reaffirms* the foundational faith in God's promises.

In the ministry of Jesus, likewise, an eschatology of God's definitive redemption stands in no conflict with the charge to cast out demons and 'bring in the poor, the crippled, the blind and the lame' (Mk 3.15 parr.; Lk. 14.21). Indeed the articulation of social protest by a patiently critical modus vivendi within unjust social orders finds an anchor in a transcendent eschatology that involves the coming of the Son of Man, to judge and to rule. This is partly a matter of distinguishing the eschatological part from the whole, and proximate from final aims (or, to borrow from Dietrich Bonhoeffer, distinguishing the penultimate from the ultimate commitments in the task of *Wegbereitung*, 'preparing the way').[35] But it also relates to the untroubled co-existence in Jewish and Christian texts of an unshakeable trust in God's redemptive action with a socially and politically concrete commitment to those whom God redeems.[36]

---

34   1QpHab 7.1-8; *y. Ta'an.* 4.8, 24a; *Lam. R.* 2.4. Bauckham 1980 similarly elaborates on the function of delay in other rabbinic, apocalyptic and New Testament texts on eschatology.
35   Bonhoeffer 1949: 75–92 (ET Bonhoeffer 1965: 120–43).
36   Cf. now Beavis 2006, who argues for ancient utopianism's moderating effect on political activism.

Resistance and Redemption in the Jesus Tradition 77

Most importantly, perhaps, the mediation of seemingly 'irreconcilable differences' between human resistance and messianic redemption lies in the Gospel tradition's insistence that they find their point of coherence in the person of Jesus himself. For all four evangelists and their known sources, the actions and teachings of Jesus cry out at every turn to be understood as *making present* in his person the divine agency of the final redemption. Whether resisting satanic slander in the desert by the power of the divine word or declaring Isaiah's messianic healer and evangelist of the poor present in his person, whether as the one who binds the strong man and plunders his house or drives out the demons by the finger of God, whether as eschatological Davidide or as mysteriously suffering and transcendent Son of Man: both the evangelists and what can be known of Jesus of Nazareth unmistakably point to the coherence of *his own messianism*, concretely resistant and eschatologically resilient, in the question of his own messianic presence and identity. As the New Testament writers affirm without exception, this resistance and resilience finds its definitive focus in the Jesus whose identity and presence as Messianic Son were found to be confirmed 'with power' by the resurrection (e.g. Acts 2.36; Rom. 1.3-4).

Conclusion

We have seen that the correlation of redemption and resistance in the ministry of Jesus must to some extent be understood in the light of the footprint he left on history. The evidence certainly points to an eschatologically motivated non-violent resistance to evil – be it individual or communal, moral or political, demonic or structural. The early Church of the first two or three centuries repeatedly raises (from St Paul to the Apologists and others) a number of distinctive social positions derivable from emphases that first surface in the Jesus tradition, including the treatment of socially and religiously disenfranchised groups like the poor and the enslaved, the dying and the unborn, widows and children. We find firm and unwavering resistance to practices related to individual or systemic idolatry, sexual immorality and the antisocial exploitation of capital or property. Resistance, then, for Jesus as indeed for both Jewish and the subsequent 'footprint' of early Christian messianism, is intrinsically part of Redemption. And it is resistance to evil comprehensively understood: not just external but internal; not just personal but social and political; not just 'natural' but demonic. By the same token, this *Wirkungsgeschichte* of messianic resistance to evil does not readily fit the programme of an anti-imperial agitator for large-scale political change and social reconstitution. On that point we find ourselves returning to William Horbury's incisive reminder about the historical significance of Jesus' aftermath: while the historical study of Jesus undoubtedly helps shed light on early Christology, the converse is at least equally true.

Chapter 6

MESSIANISM AND CHRISTOLOGY:
MARK, MATTHEW, LUKE AND ACTS

Graham Stanton

To what extent were convictions about the significance of Jesus *shaped* by the messianic expectations of *some* of his earliest followers? How and when were aspects of Jewish messianism *transformed* into early Christology? How prominent were debate and dispute on this issue between followers of Jesus and their opponents? My brief in this chapter is to tackle these questions with special reference to three New Testament writers: Mark, Matthew and Luke. Given the complexity of the issues and the evidence, even that narrower focus is a tall order.

In spite of well over a century of lively scholarly discussion, and the availability of a mountain of new or re-assessed evidence, the relationship between messianism and Christology is now even more problematic than it was 120 years ago. In 1886 V. H. Stanton claimed that his book was 'the first attempt either in England or on the Continent to examine systematically and thoroughly the historical relations of Christian Messianic beliefs to Jewish, and to appreciate their significance ...'[1] Again and again he anticipates current discussion. He is alert to the possibility that Christian views may have been affected by *Jewish* developments, even though he gives prominence to the more usual view that there was considerable Christian *transformation* of Jewish conceptions of the Messiah.[2] He repeatedly shows how central interpretation of Scripture was to debate and dispute. A. Edersheim's claim that some Septuagint passages appear to give a specifically messianic turn is brushed aside: 'We cannot, however, rely upon the text of the LXX as we now possess it for information respecting purely Jewish opinion.'[3]

By comparison with current discussion, the primary sources on which V. H. Stanton drew were limited and heavily weighted towards rabbinic writings. Nonetheless it is still rewarding to keep an eye on his agenda, for he was grappling with issues which cry out for even more scholarly attention following the ready availability of the Dead Sea Scrolls.

It is arguable that Stanton's book was not in fact the first to grapple with the relationship between messianism and Christology. If we allow a little scholarly licence, Justin Martyr's *Dialogue with Trypho,* written *ca.* A.D. 160 has a good claim to that accolade.

---

1   Stanton 1886.
2   Stanton 1886: 2.
3   Stanton 1886: 114.

In his initial challenge to Justin, Trypho the Jew insists that Christian claims concerning the Messiah are misleading and mistaken: 'You Christians ... have *formed* (or even *"remoulded"*) for yourselves a Christ for whom you are blindly giving up your lives' (*Dial.* 8.4; χριστὸν ἑαυτοῖς τινα ἀναπλάσσετε). In reply, Justin quotes chunks of Scripture back at Trypho, insisting that Christians are interpreting Scripture aright.

If we take the view that in this passage Justin is putting his own opinions into Trypho's mouth, this is a plausible, striking concession from the Christian philosopher-teacher. Justin is accepting that Christians are *shaping* a Messiah for themselves, a Messiah somewhat at odds with Jewish expectations. Christians are doing that on the basis of Scripture, and thus Justin concedes that there is a gulf between Jews and Christians concerning messianism and Christology.

The verbs used by V. H. Stanton and by translators of Justin Martyr's Greek, 'formed', 'transformed', 're-moulded', 'shaped' are all attempts to gloss ἀναπλάσσετε, a *hapax* in the New Testament, but used by Hellenistic writers with the sense, 'to form anew'. Melito uses the verb of a potter who reshapes a vessel he has spoiled, while Barnabas draws on ἀναπλάσσω to speak of a person's 'spiritual transformation'.[4] The semantic field is broad, but at its heart continuity and discontinuity are held together.

The questions posed at the outset of this chapter touch raw nerves in Jewish-Christian relationships. They also bring to the fore considerable confusion among scholars and translators (and even teachers and preachers) concerning the use of the terms 'Messiah' and 'Christ'. Is it appropriate to follow the NRSV and REB and translate χριστός by 'Messiah' where pre-Christian 'messianism' is prominent, and by 'Christ' where a christological title or a 'surname' for Jesus is being used? Why do the NRSV translators use 'Messiah' to introduce and to conclude Matthew's genealogy (Mt. 1.1, 16, 17 and 18) ? The REB translators, on the other hand, muddy matters by translating Matthew's first and fourth uses of Ἰησοῦ Χριστός as 'Jesus *Christ*', while Χριστός is translated as 'Messiah' in verses 16 and 17. By indicating that 'Messiah' and 'Christ' are synonymous terms, are the REB translators seeking to reflect first-century readers' views or to assist today's readers?

Definitions and delimitation of sources could run and run, so I must make do with a mere sketch. I take 'messianism' to refer to the expectation of a divinely anointed royal Davidic person who will fulfil Scripture and inaugurate a new age. I shall assume without discussion that the *Psalms of Solomon* 17 and 18 are an explicit expression of messianism from the first century B.C., and that *4 Ezra* and the *Similitudes of Enoch* include passages which pre-date Christian modification or transformation of messianism.

The Dead Sea Scrolls contain a rich vein of traditions, even though they are difficult to mine. Traditions in 4Q521 and 4Q246 overlap in part with *Psalms of Solomon* 17 and *4 Ezra*.[5] Nor must passages within New Testament writings be neglected; Mt. 2.4; Lk. 1.69; 2.26; and 3.15, for example, contain some of our most important evidence of first-century Jewish messianic views.

---

4   See BDAG for details and references.
5   See Abegg and Evans 1998; also Brooke 1998.

In short, as far as first-century messianism is concerned, I shall be taking a *via media* through the minefield. I shall not assume that Jewish views were so diverse and diffuse that we can only talk about 'messianisms'. Nor shall I adopt a revisionist position and assume that most first-century Jews held strikingly similar views concerning a coming Davidic Messiah.[6]

1. *Q traditions*

Χριστός/Messiah is not found in Q traditions shared by Matthew and Luke. That has led some scholars to claim that Q traditions were transmitted by early followers of Jesus who made no messianic claims about him, and who confessed Jesus merely as Wisdom's envoy (or saw him in some other role as an intermediary) rather than as Christ crucified.

However, too much should not be made of the absence of Χριστός from Q. Christopher Tuckett wisely insists it would be rather bold to deduce from the non-use of the term in Q that the idea of Jesus' 'messiahship' was actually problematic for the Q Christians: Q's non-use of the term may be purely coincidental.[7]

What is surprising is the extent of traditions in Q which are compatible with messianic convictions.[8] Several Q traditions refer to God's fulfilment in the present of eschatological hopes set out in Scripture.[9] In some cases there is a clear hint that this eschatological fulfilment is taking place through the 'kingly' actions and the words of Jesus himself. For example, Jesus links his exorcisms to his claim that God's kingly rule is breaking into the present era. 'If it is by the finger of God that I cast out the demons, then the kingdom of God has come to you' (Mt. 12.28 = Lk. 11.20).

The implied comparison between the preaching of Jesus, Solomon and Jonah is striking: 'Something (neuter) greater than Solomon is here ... Something (neuter) greater than Jonah is here' (Mt. 12.41-42 = Lk. 11.31-32). Although the focus is on the preaching of Jesus, the person of Jesus is accorded greater authority than wise King Solomon or the prophet Jonah. So who is this Jesus? If 'messianic' is used in a loose sense, then this passage may well have evoked messianic hopes for some.

Similarly, Mt. 13.16-17 = Lk. 10.23-24. Jesus says to his disciples: 'Blessed are the eyes that see what you see! For I tell you that many *prophets and kings* desired to see what you see, but did not see it, and to hear what you hear, but did not hear it.' The fulfilment of eschatological hopes is linked implicitly both to the actions and to the words of Jesus, but the status of Jesus himself is left open.

Two Q traditions, however, are much more explicit than the passages just referred to. The temptation of Jesus, with the devil's twofold challenge, 'If you are the Son of God' (Mt. 4.1-11 = Lk. 4.1-13), was almost certainly preceded by Q's account of the baptism of Jesus.[10] The temptation narratives indicate a prior

---

6   See Neusner *et al.* 1987; also Schürer 1973–87: 2.488–549 (§29 'Messianism').
7   Tuckett 1996: 214.
8   See especially Meadors 1999; also Dahl 1991: 397.
9   Stanton 1973.
10   Stanton 1973: 35. See now the revised edition of U. Luz's commentary: Luz 2002: 210 and 223 n.23.

appointment as God's Son and also Jesus' reception of the Spirit. In the first two temptations the authority of Jesus as God's Son is challenged: 'If you are the Son of God …' We now have evidence from 4Q246 and 4Q174 that 'Son of God' was interpreted in some Jewish circles with messianic significance. In the former passage we read, with reference to a king: ' "Son of God" he shall be called, and they will name him "Son of the Most High".' In the exposition of 2 Sam. 7.14 in 4Q174 the promise of the Lord that the throne of the Branch of David's kingdom will be established for ever is followed by an assurance: 'I [will be] his father and he shall be my son.'[11] So the devil's jibe, 'If you are the Son of God' may well reflect resistance to messianic claims.

In the reply of Jesus to John the Baptist's enquiry, the wording of Mt. 11.2-6 and the parallel passage in Lk. 7.19, 22-23 is almost identical. The list of the actions of Jesus comes to a climax with 'the dead are raised to life, the poor are brought good news'. With the exception of 'lepers are cleansed', the items in the list are all allusions to phrases in Isa. 29.18; 35.5-6; and 61.1-2. If we were writing out that list, we might be inclined to place 'the dead are raised to life' as the dramatic conclusion. However the list unexpectedly reaches its climax with the clear allusion to Isa. 61.1, 'the poor are brought good news'. Jesus is claiming that both his actions and his proclamation of God's good news are fulfilment of scriptural promises.

One of the fragments of the so-called Messianic Apocalypse discovered in Cave 4 at Qumran and known as 4Q521 provides a significant parallel and sheds fresh light on the interpretation of this Q passage.[12]

Frag. 2 col. II
1 [for the heav]ens and the earth will listen to his anointed one,. … *11* And the Lord will perform marvellous acts such as have not existed, just as he sa[id] *12* [for] he will heal the badly wounded and will make the dead live, he will proclaim good news to the poor *13* and […] … […] he will lead the […] and enrich the hungry. *14* […] and all […]

Once again phrases from Isaiah are woven together. In line 12 we find an astonishing parallel with the reply of Jesus to John in the Q tradition. 'He will heal the wounded, give life to the dead and preach good news to the poor.' The order is identical: in both passages proclamation of good news to the poor forms the climax of the list of actions to be carried out by God. In both passages allusion to the fulfilment of Isa. 61.1 is unmistakable.

This fragment of 4Q521 opens with an almost certain reference to the Messiah, 'his anointed one'. In the lines which follow it is *God* who cares for the various needy groups, and raises the dead. God does not usually 'preach good news'; this is the task of his herald, messenger, or prophet.[13] So the herald or messenger referred to in this fragment is the Messiah: Isa. 61.1 is interpreted messianically.

---

11   Collins 1995: 154–64.
12   The translation is taken from García Martínez and Tigchelaar 1997–8: 2.1045.
13   Collins 1995: 116–23. For discussion of more recent literature and support for the view taken here, see Collins 1998, esp. 112–16; Evans 1999: 585–8.

There is further support for this interpretation in another Qumran fragment. In lines 15 and 16 of 11Q13 (known earlier as 11QMelchizedek) Isa. 52.7 is quoted in full. The herald of good tidings of Isa. 52.7 is closely linked with Isa. 61.1 and is identified as '*the* anointed one', the Messiah.[14]

So we now have clear evidence that before the time of Jesus, Isa. 61.1 with its reference to the anointed prophet being sent to preach good news to the poor, was understood to refer to a *messianic prophet*. It is highly likely that when Jesus referred to his own actions and words in terms of this passage (and the related passages in Deutero-Isaiah), he was making an indirect messianic claim. He was not merely a prophet proclaiming God's good news, he was himself part of the good news.

Note how this Q tradition concludes. 'Blessed are those who take no offence at me.' That saying clearly implies that there were those who did take offence at the actions and words of Jesus. We know from both Christian and Jewish sources that Jesus was seen in his own lifetime to be a false prophet who led Israel astray, a magician whose healings and exorcisms were the result of collaboration with the prince of demons.[15] So this passage raises the question of the relationship of Jesus to God. Was Jesus a messianic prophet fulfilling Isaiah 61 and proclaiming God's good news to the poor? Or was he a false prophet leading Israel astray? Jesus' proclamation of God's good news, his gospelling if you like, was in competition and dialogue with an alternative story. 'Redemption' met with 'resistance'.

I am not claiming that royal, Davidic themes are prominent among the Q traditions. However, some of those traditions are not out of kilter with messianic claims. In two such passages resistance to such claims lurks in the background.

2. Mark

Whereas Matthew and Luke use their extended birth narratives to spell out the significance of Jesus as the promised Davidic Messiah, Mark gives us only a single line of introduction which in some manuscripts has one word alongside 'Jesus': he is 'Christ / Messiah'.[16] So in this opening line does 'Christ' function as no more than a 'surname' for Jesus, as it so often is for Paul? By no means!

The opening verses of Mark do not take us very far in our quest. The affirmation of the voice from heaven that Jesus is 'Son of God', and the opening summary of the proclamation of Jesus in terms of God's kingly rule are both set in the context of the fulfilment of Scripture. While it may be appropriate to describe that context as 'messianic', Jesus is not portrayed explicitly as the royal Davidic Messiah either in Mk 1.1, or in the chapters which follow.

In order to defend the view that Mark's reference to 'Christ' in his opening line reflects his own (and his readers') understanding of the profound significance of

---

14   For text and translation, with recent bibliography, see García Martínez and Tigchelaar 1997–8: 2.1206–9. For earlier discussion and bibliography see Stanton 1973.
15   See Stanton 2004: 127–47.
16   The longer reading, with 'Son of God' as an exepegetic comment on 'Christ' may well be original.

Jesus as Χριστός, I shall turn to the evangelist's final comment on the messiahship of Jesus, for it is even more revealing than either Peter's so-called confession of Jesus' messiahship at Caesarea Philippi (Mk 8.29), or the positive response of Jesus to the high priest's question, 'Are you the Messiah, the Son of the Blessed One?' (Mk 14.62). For it allows two themes to interpret one another: 'Kingship' and 'Messiahship'.

In Mark's passion narrative, Jesus is mocked three times in his final hours. Roman soldiers hail him as 'King of the Jews' (15.18), as do passers-by and the two bandits crucified with Jesus (15.27 and 32). The phrase 'King of the Jews' is used five times in this context (15.2, 9, 12, 18, 26), followed by the synonymous 'King of Israel' on the lips of the chief priests and the scribes (15.32). The sixfold repetition of this death knell heightens the dramatic atmosphere. But there is more than dramatic tension at stake in the final words attributed in this Gospel to the religious leaders. 'He saved others; he cannot save himself. Let the Messiah, the King of Israel, come down from the cross now, so that we may see and believe' (15.31-32).

These words are packed with dramatic irony. In his study of Mark's use of irony, Jerry Camery-Hoggatt offers a sophisticated exposition of the ways irony functions, though curiously he has next to nothing to say about the verse I shall focus on in a moment. He notes that irony forces the reader to decision; it divides listeners into 'insiders' and 'outsiders' and thus aids in group-boundary definition. In Mark irony may even be parabolic.[17] Precisely! The final words of the religious leaders fill the death knell phrase, 'King of Israel', with soteriological comment: 'He saved others; he cannot save himself.' 'Let him come down from the cross now, so that *we may see and believe.*'

Morna Hooker refers to the 'supreme irony' in the words attributed to the Jewish leaders, for if Jesus is to save others, he cannot save himself.[18] Morna Hooker's further astute comments on Mk 15.31-32 are all soteriological. Alas, along with most exegetes, she misses the importance of the jibe for Mark's *Christology*. This is the final comment by a religious leader on the significance of Jesus: Jesus is the Messiah, the King of Israel. It is counterbalanced by the Roman centurion's confession: 'Truly this man was God's Son' (Mark 15.39).

The religious leaders are unwitting mouthpieces for the evangelist's own stance. They have no way of knowing that for Mark himself, and for his readers and listeners, their designation of Jesus as 'Messiah, King of the Jews' is exactly right. Donald Juel correctly noted that in Mark's passion narrative Jesus' enemies, whether Jewish or Roman, do not understand in what sense the words they speak are true. Contrary to their intentions and beyond their ability to understand, they speak the truth. 'The irony in the story is pronounced, but it only works if Jesus is the Christ.'[19]

As is well known, the evangelist uses Χριστός sparingly. In the light of his decision to focus his story on the crucified Messiah, there can be no doubt that in his opening line (1.1) 'Messiah' is more than a surname. It is part of the

---

17   Camery-Hoggatt 1992: 4–5.
18   Hooker 1991: 374.
19   Juel 1992: 453.

evangelist's way of setting up the tension between what he himself and his readers confess concerning Jesus, and the struggles of the characters in the story to understand the significance of Jesus. As for the Messianic Secret, Robert Fowler astutely notes that 'inasmuch as the readers know from the very beginning that Jesus is the Christ, the Son of God, there is never any question of a Messianic Secret *for the reader of the gospel.*'[20]

This is the christological conviction that undergirds Mark's Gospel. So for Mark the evangelist, Jesus is the crucified Messiah. This understanding of the significance of Jesus both opens and closes Mark's Gospel: it is his first and his last comment on the messiahship of Jesus in Mk 1.1 and 15.31-32.

3. Matthew

The opening line of Matthew's Gospel makes a bold assertion about the significance of Jesus: he is the Messiah, the son of David, the son of Abraham. Whereas Mark and Luke use the title 'son of David' for Jesus only four times, Matthew uses it ten times. In five passages the evangelist adds 'Son of David' to his sources (9.27; 12.23; 15.22; 21.9, 15). Why is the title 'Son of David' of particular interest to the evangelist? Before I tackle that teasing question, I shall underline briefly the extent to which the 'messiahship' of Jesus dominates Matthew's thinking and even the structure of his Gospel.

Matthew's reference in 1.1 to Jesus Christ as 'son of David', 'son of Abraham', provides the framework for the genealogy which follows. The genealogy is divided into three groups of fourteen names: from Abraham to David, from David to the Babylonian exile, and from the exile to 'the Christ' (Mt. 1.17). The number fourteen seems to have been chosen deliberately in order to underline the Davidic descent of Jesus, for the Hebrew form of 'David' has a numerical value of fourteen.

The genealogy concludes with Joseph, who is a son of David. He is not the father of Jesus, but Jesus is 'ingrafted' into David's line through his conception by the Holy Spirit (Mt. 1.20). 'Joseph can acknowledge Jesus by naming him, and that makes him "son of David"; the Holy Spirit has to act and God has to designate Jesus through revelation to make him "Son of God".'[21]

The first theological theme Matthew associates with Jesus the Messiah, the son of David, is as the one who will save his people from their sins (Mt. 1.21). The son whom Mary will bear will be 'Son of God', even though that title is not used explicitly in 1.18-25. Van Egmond correctly notes that 'this notion of the Davidic Messiah as "son of God" is now well attested at Qumran in such texts as 4Q369 and 4Q174.'[22]

Even though Messiah Jesus is only a baby, Matthew sketches a 'clash of kings' with telling subtlety and irony. When King Herod hears of the homage the wise men wish to pay to King Jesus, 'he was frightened, and all Jerusalem with him'

---

20 Fowler 1981: 159. I owe the reference to Camery-Hoggatt 1992: 93.
21 Brown 1993: 135. See also pp. 50–1.
22 Van Egmond 2006, esp. 50–1.

(2.3). So King Herod enlists the assistance of the wise men in his search for the child Jesus. Once again 'redemption' is met with 'resistance'.

Near the climax of his story Matthew emphasizes the turmoil caused by Jesus in Jerusalem by making a series of redactional changes to Mk 11.1-11 at Mt. 21.1-11. From the evangelist's point of view, the entry of Jesus into Jerusalem is 'messianic'; it is in fulfilment of Scripture:

Tell the daughter of Zion,
Look, your king is coming to you,
Humble, and mounted on a donkey …

The crowds … were shouting, Hosanna to the Son of David … When Jesus entered Jerusalem, '*the whole city was in turmoil*' (Mt. 21.10) just as it had been when the wise men reached Jerusalem to pay homage to the king of the Jews (Mt. 2.2-3). Matthew opens and closes his story by emphasizing the significance of Jesus as the Davidic Messiah whose redemptive coming is welcomed by a few, but resisted by many.[23]

The structure of Matthew's Gospel is strongly influenced by Mark's Gospel. But in the opening main section in chapters 5 to 9 Matthew reshapes Mark radically in order to present Jesus as 'Messiah of Word' in the Sermon on the Mount (Mt. 5–7) and as 'Messiah of Deed' in chapters 8–9. And just in case the reader misses the latter point, the evangelist underlines it at Mt. 11.2 with a redactional comment: John hears in prison 'what *the Messiah* was doing', a reference to the actions of Jesus recorded in Mt. 8–9.

In short, the evangelist extends and underlines 'messianic' themes in his sources, often linking them closely with his portrayal of Jesus as 'Son of God'. This juxtaposition of Son of God and Messiah is hardly distinctively Matthean, however, for it is also found in Mk 14.61 and Lk. 22.67, 70.

Resistance to Jesus the Son of David

In four redactional passages acknowledgement of Jesus as the 'Son of David' by participants in Matthew's story provokes hostility from the Jewish leaders. Since no other major christological theme in Matthew elicits such sustained opposition from the Jewish leaders, our suspicions are roused: are the 'Son of David' passages intended by the evangelist to be a response to critics in his own day? Although the christological disputes in Matthew's Gospel are neither as intense nor as sustained as they are in John's Gospel, they are an important and often overlooked feature.

Matthew expands Mark's three references to the title 'Son of David' to nine: 1.1; 9.27; 12.23; 15.22; 20.30, 31 (= Mk 10.47, 48); 21.9, 15; 22.42 (= Mk 12.35; the title Son of David is implied). Why does Matthew open his Gospel with a reference to Jesus as 'Son of David' and then proceed to add redactionally further references in contexts which are broadly Marcan (9.27; 12.23; 15.22;

---

23   Cf. Beaton 2002: 4–5, who notes that in Mt. 12.18-21 the evangelist uses his quotation of Isa. 42.1-4 to present Jesus as the enigmatic Davidic Messiah who is surrounded by increasing hostility evidenced in his interactions with various people and groups in Mt. 11–13.

21.9, 15)? As several writers have noted, Matthew connects the 'Son of David' title with the healing ministry of Jesus, but that observation hardly accounts for the evangelist's strong emphasis on this particular christological theme.[24]

Most scholars have overlooked the fact that in addition to the healing motif, another theme is equally prominent in the 'Son of David' passages which come from the evangelist's own hand. In four such passages (Mt. 2.3; 9.27-28; 12.23; 21.9,15) acknowledgement of Jesus as the 'Son of David' by participants in Matthew's story provokes hostility from the Jewish leaders.[25] These four passages all come at critical points in the evangelist's presentation of one of his major themes: the conflict between Jesus and the Jewish leaders.[26] Matthew insists vigorously that Jesus is the Son of David, even though he is aware that some of his readers will soon learn that this claim is unacceptable to their Jewish rivals.

Why does the evangelist stress so strongly in four redactional passages that Jesus is the Son of David?[27] Why is acknowledgement of Jesus as 'Son of David' so vigorously opposed by the Jewish religious leaders? And why does Matthew set out so carefully this fourfold pattern of positive response by some and rejection by the Jewish leaders?

We are in contact with claims and counter-claims being made at the time Matthew wrote. The evangelist is well aware that his readers and listeners will face fierce opposition to their claims that Jesus was indeed the Davidic Messiah. Matthew insists that this claim is part of the very essence of Christian convictions about the significance of Jesus. But at the same time in several redactional passages he sets out a portrait of the Davidic Messiah which differs from many current expectations. The one born 'king of the Jews' is the child Jesus, the Davidic Messiah (2.2-6); in accordance with prophecy Jesus heals every disease and infirmity (8.17); Jesus is the one who is 'meek and lowly in heart' (11.29), the chosen Servant of God (12.17-21), 'the humble king' (21.5). All these passages bear the redactional stamp of the evangelist himself. They convey a quite distinctive portrait of Jesus, every facet of which is embedded in Scripture.

Matthew is deeply indebted to messianic themes in his sources. He has developed many of them, but on the whole he is a conservative redactor. Like his predecessors, he insists that the messiahship of Jesus is firmly anchored in Scripture. His most creative step is to extend considerably Mark's use of 'Son of David'. I have claimed that in some of these passages we overhear dialogue and dispute between the evangelist and some of his critics who resist aspects of Matthew's transformation of messianism and its application to Jesus.

---

24 So, for example, Burger 1972: 72–106; Gibbs 1964; Kingsbury 1976; Duling 1978; Luz 1991.
25 A notable exception is Verseput 1987; he does not discuss the reasons for this link.
26 See Kingsbury 1987. He fails to note that confession of Jesus as 'Son of David' provokes hostility from the Jewish leaders.
27 For exegetical discussion of the four passages, see Stanton 1992: 180–5.

4. Luke and Acts

In both Matthew's and Luke's infancy narratives Jesus is portrayed as the Davidic Messiah promised by Scripture. Although there are significant similarities, there is no question of direct literary dependence. Luke's emphasis on the Davidic messiahship of Jesus in his opening chapters is not sustained strongly later in his Gospel, though, as we shall see, it is prominent in two speeches in Acts.

The annunciation to Mary: Luke 1.32-33, 2 Sam. 7.9-16 and 4Q174

Luke's account of the annunciation of Gabriel to Mary (Lk. 1.26-38) is the first christological statement in Luke's Gospel – and thus particularly important. Mary is told that the son she will bear will be 'great and will be called Son of the most High', and he will be given by God 'the throne of his ancestor David'; 'he will reign over the house of Jacob forever and of his kingdom there will be no end' (1.32-33).

The similarity of the phraseology to parts of 2 Sam. 7.9-16 has often been noted.[28] Even more important for our present purposes are lines 10–13 of 4Q174:

> 10 [And] YHWH [de]clares to you that *2 Sam 7.12-14* 'he will build you a house. I will raise up your seed after you and establish the throne of his kingdom *11* [for ev]er. I will be a father to him and he will be a son to me.' This (refers to the) 'branch of David', who will arise with the Interpreter of the law who *12* [will rise up] in Zi[on in] the [l]ast days, as it is written: *Amos 9.11* 'I will raise up the hut of David which has fallen.' This (refers to) 'the hut of David which has fal[len]', w]ho will arise to save Israel.

Luke (or his source) and 4Q174 both interpret 2 Sam. 7 messianically. Raymond Brown's comment is fully justified: 'there is nothing distinctively Christian in vss. 32-33 of Luke, except that the expected Davidic Messiah has been identified with Jesus.'[29]

In Lk. 1.35 the angel responds to Mary's poignant, 'How can this be, since I am a virgin?' with the affirmation: 'the Holy Spirit will come upon you, and the power of the Most High will overshadow you; therefore the child to be born will be called holy; he will be called Son of God.' The angel's words recall Isa. 11.1-2, with its reference to the eschatological coming of the Spirit upon a branch from the stock of Jesse. Gabriel's final 'christological' comment in v. 35 repeats the opening claim in v. 32a that Jesus will be called 'Son of God', thus echoing 2 Sam. 7.14 *for a second time*. The link between 'Son of God' and the Davidic Messiah could hardly have been made more strongly or more clearly. As we shall see, this is not the last time this link is forged in Luke's two volumes.

Zechariah's prophecy: a horn of salvation for us ... the dawn from on high (Luke 1.68-79)

Davidic Messiahship is central in Zechariah's prophecy, the Benedictus, spoken while he was filled with the Holy Spirit (1.68-79). Some scholars have argued that

---

28 Strauss 1995: 88–9 helpfully sets out side by side Lk. 1.32-33 and the similar phrases in 2 Sam. 7.9-16 and Ps. 89.26-36.
29 Brown 1993: 311.

all these verses, usually set out as a poem or hymn in modern translations, were composed by Luke himself, while others have insisted that most of this passage was a purely Jewish, pre-Lucan composition.

A third view also has strong support: this passage was composed or redacted by Jewish Christians who shared with their fellow Jews hopes of messianic and Davidic deliverance 'from our enemies, out of the hands of all who hate us' (v. 71). The verbs in the opening two verses imply that those hopes had already been fulfilled with the coming of Jesus.

The Old Testament, Qumran and early Jewish parallels are extensive and striking.[30] One parallel will suffice here. The Fifteenth Benediction of the *Shemoneh Esreh* (which may well stem from the first century) includes words which echo Lk. 1.69:

> Let the shoot of David (Your servant) speedily spring up and raise his horn in Your salvation ...
> May you be blessed, O Lord, who lets the horn of salvation flourish.
>
> Luke 1.69: (the Lord God of Israel) has raised up a horn of salvation for us[31]
> In the house of his servant David.

In this verse, as in verses 68 and 70-71, Jewish hopes of political and national deliverance are prominent. Mark L. Strauss has correctly noted that in these verses 'Luke continues to define the role of the coming Davidic king in language reminiscent of the political and national deliverance of the Old Testament and Judaism.'[32]

In verses 76-77 Zechariah prophesies that John, who will be called 'prophet of the Most High' will give 'knowledge of salvation to his people' (1.76-77) and promises that 'the dawn (ἀνατολή) from on high will break upon us' (1.78). The meaning of ἀνατολή has been much discussed. Does the noun refer to the rising of a '*shoot*' or '*branch*', a term often used of the messianic king? If so, 4Q174 11–12 (quoted above) is again relevant. If this is the meaning of ἀνατολή, the finale of the Benedictus forms an inclusio with its opening theme, the Davidic Messiah as the 'horn of salvation' (v. 69).

However an equally strong case can be made for taking ἀνατολή as the rising of the dawn's *light* from on high. On this reading, the next clause (v. 79) is epexegetical: the ἀνατολή 'will give light to those who sit in darkness', recalling Isa. 9.2, 6-7 and Num. 24.17 where light imagery is used to refer to the coming of the Davidic king.

Perhaps both 'the rising of light' and 'branch' or 'shoot' are in mind. *T. Jud.* 24.1-6 (whether Jewish or Christian) links the motifs of rising light and the Davidic shoot or branch:

> And after these things a star will arise to you from Jacob in peace. And a man shall arise from my seed like the sun of righteousness ... . This is the branch (βλαστός) of God Most High.

---

30 They are set out by Brown 1993: 386–9.
31 NRSV translates 'a mighty saviour for us', while REB has 'a strong deliverer'.
32 Strauss 1995: 101.

In either case, there is a clear messianic reference to Jesus.[33]

A Davidic Saviour, Christ the Lord (Luke 2.11)

In his account of the birth of the Messiah (Lk. 2.1-20) Luke notes that Joseph took Mary to Bethlehem, the city of David, for the birth of her son, 'because he (Joseph) was descended from the house and family of David'. The significance of this double reference to the Davidic background of the birth of Jesus becomes clear in the words of the angel to the shepherds in 2.11:

> To you is born this day in the city of David a Saviour, who is the Messiah, the Lord (χριστὸς κύριος).

Luke sets all three titles in a Davidic context. 'Saviour' refers to God at Lk. 1.47 and to Jesus at Acts 5.31 and 13.23, all in broadly messianic settings. The noun 'salvation' in Lk. 1.69, 71 is used similarly with reference to God's fulfilment of Scripture through Jesus. In spite of these anticipations, Luke's reference to Jesus as 'Saviour' is striking, for, to quote Raymond Brown, 'it is cast in the format of an imperial proclamation, as part of Luke's gentle propaganda that Jesus, not Augustus, was the Savior and source of peace whose birthday marked the beginning of time (i.e. the eschatological "this day").'[34] Brown wrote these words as far back as 1977, wisely emphasizing that the imperial setting is only secondary to the messianic setting.

Luke makes a similar point in Paul's speech in Pisidian Antioch: 'Of David's posterity God has brought to Israel a Saviour, Jesus, as he promised' (Acts 13.23). Given that the imperial cult was prominent in Antioch, there is a sub-text to the Davidic, messianic themes in this speech, as in the annunciation of the angel at Lk. 2.11: Jesus, not the emperor or any other person or god, was Saviour, God's provision of salvation.[35] I shall return to this point below.

Χριστός is often said to be Luke's most important christological title, so it is a surprise to find that his first use of it in his two volumes is baffling.[36] Why does Luke use the double title, Χριστός κύριος? The double title is unexpected, though there is a parallel in *Pss. Sol.* 17.32.

I do not think we need to resort to textual emendation or to the poorly supported variant. Elsewhere Luke juxtaposes awkwardly two titles, and so here. In Acts 2.36 Luke writes that God has made Jesus both Lord and Christ. When Jesus is taken before Pilate in Lk. 23.2, he is said to have claimed to be 'the Messiah, a king'. The seriousness of the allegation is underlined with an explanatory gloss for Pilate (and for many of Luke's readers): Messiah implies kingship. Hence in the double title Χριστός κυρίος in 2.11, κυρίος should be read

---

33 Simon Gathercole 2005 has recently revived the view that ἀνατολή refers not only to a Davidic Messiah, but also to *a heavenly, pre-existent* figure. Gathercole notes that his theory fits well with William Horbury's suggestion of the 'superhuman' nature of the Messiah: see pp. 473–4, 479, 487, with reference to Horbury 1998c: 86–108.
34 Brown 1993: 424.
35 Stanton 2004: 45–6.
36 See, for example, Fitzmyer 1981–5: 1.197.

as Luke's explanation of Χριστός for non-Jewish readers. Once Luke has made this key point in 2.11, he has no need to labour it.

Redemption and resistance (Luke 2.25-38)

In the lengthy account of the presentation in the Temple (2.25-38) Luke states once again that Jesus is the promised Davidic Messiah, and adds two fresh points. Simeon is portrayed as looking for 'the consolation *of Israel*' (2.25). The very next verse explains that this hope is to be equated with the coming of the Lord's Messiah. The phrase used a few verses later to sum up Anna's expectation, 'the redemption *of Israel*' (2.38), is surely synonymous.

Luke then notes for the first time that the messianic salvation promised *for Gentiles* has been fulfilled (2.30-32). For my present purposes a further fresh note is even more striking. Simeon's blessing is accompanied by these blunt words to Mary: 'This child is destined for the falling and rising of many in Israel, and to be a sign that will be opposed' (2.34 NRSV). I take 'falling and rising *in Israel*' to refer to the two responses Jesus will ultimately elicit among his own people, a point which will become prominent in Acts.

In Jewish expectation the messianic king often faces opposition and war from the Gentile nations, but here it is 'many *in Israel*' who will fall, and who stand in opposition to the 'sign'.[37] As in Matthew, the promised redemption meets resistance.

Luke's insistence that Jesus is the promised Davidic Messiah permeates the infancy narratives. Unlike Matthew, Luke does not cite Scripture explicitly, but his portrayal of Jesus in rich and varied poetic images is set against the colourful backdrop of pastiches of Scripture, especially Isaiah.

Luke 3–24

Luke does not neglect messianic themes in the remainder of his Gospel, but in comparison with his opening chapters, they are rarely prominent. More often than not, Luke is content to re-phrase or clarify a Marcan messianic tradition. In the paragraphs which follow only the most striking passages will be mentioned.

In the middle of his summary of the proclamation of John the Baptist (Lk. 3.3-18) Luke springs a surprise. John's prophetic, radical ethical preaching has led people to ask whether perhaps John might be the Messiah (Lk. 3.15). Once again Luke shows his awareness of a general messianic expectation on the part of many. From the context it is clear that the evangelist has in mind royal Davidic themes, even if in fact 'the crowds' addressed by John had more varied expectations. John's implicit denial that he is the Messiah is found only here in the Synoptic tradition.

Does Luke present the baptism of Jesus as a *messianic anointing* (Lk. 3.21-32)? The evangelist is less clear than we might suppose, and more terse than we might wish. Even if we adopt the traditional version of the voice from heaven with its allusion to Ps. 2.7, 'You are my Son' (rather than the so-called Western reading), this is not *necessarily* a messianic anointing.

---

[37] Strauss 1995: 120.

Messianism and Christology

In spite of Luke's interest in the verb χρίω elsewhere, he does not use it here with reference to the Spirit, as we might have expected. For that use, we have to wait until Jesus refers to his baptism by means of his citation of Isa. 61.1 in the synagogue scene in Nazareth (Lk. 4.18), and in the summary given to Cornelius by Peter (Acts 10.36-43). But although those passages refer to the anointing of the Spirit, they do not refer explicitly to a *messianic* anointing.

Luke's fullest comment on the baptism of Jesus as a messianic anointing is part of the prayer of Peter and John in Acts 4.24-9 with its citation of Psalm 2: '"Why did the Gentiles rage? ... The kings of the earth took their stand against the Lord and against his Messiah"... For in this city, in fact, both Herod and Pilate ... gathered together against your holy servant Jesus, *whom you anointed*'. Resistance to the Lord's Messiah is prominent in the foreground, but from Luke's perspective God's anointing of Jesus at his baptism forms the backdrop: 'You are my Son.'

Luke's interpretation of Ps. 2.7 in Davidic messianic terms in Acts 13.33 provides further evidence that Luke intends his somewhat minimalist account of the baptism of Jesus with its allusion to Ps. 2.7 to be a messianic anointing.

Many scholars have shared Bultmann's view that the baptism of Jesus is his consecration as Messiah. This is, strictly speaking, incorrect, for the voice from heaven, 'You are my Son', doesn't necessarily need to be understood in terms of messiahship.[38] However, we have seen from several other passages in Luke-Acts that Luke does interpret the baptism of Jesus as a Davidic messianic anointing, even if this is the only place in the New Testament where Ps. 2.7 is applied to an event other than resurrection.

Luke's account of the visit of Jesus to his synagogue at Nazareth should be interpreted similarly. Jesus reads part of Isaiah 61 from the scroll and claims that God's promised anointing of him with the Spirit has now been fulfilled, and that he (Jesus) has brought good news to the poor. Although we now have evidence from 4Q521 and 11Q13 that Isa. 61.1ff. was interpreted messianically at the time of Jesus,[39] this was a *possible* but not a *necessary* reading of this passage.

Since there is no explicit reference to the Davidic royal Messiah in Lk. 4.16-30, it is possible that Luke intends to portray Jesus as a prophet or even as a messianic prophet rather than as the Davidic Messiah. Possible, but unlikely. For in his pointed redaction of Mark just a few verses later in Lk. 4.41, Luke not only emphasizes that 'Son of God' and 'Messiah' are synonymous titles,[40] but that they are appropriate responses to Jesus on the part of the exorcized demons. And from previous passages it is clear that Luke has in mind royal, Davidic messiahship.

In the later chapters of the Gospel the evangelist continues to clarify and modify references to the messiahship of Jesus found in his sources, especially Mark. Although the later passages are all of interest, they add little to the general picture sketched in the preceding paragraphs.

---

38 So too Fitzmyer 1981–5: 1.480, 485.
39 See Stanton 2004: 16–17.
40 See also Acts 9.20-22.

In Luke 24, however, two significant points call for comment. On the road to Emmaus, Cleopas and his companion refer to their hope that Jesus of Nazareth 'was to be the liberator of Israel' (Lk. 24.21).[41] This view is repeated in Jerusalem in the apostles' question to the Risen Lord: 'Is this not the time at which you are to restore sovereignty to Israel?' (Acts 1.6). The phraseology differs, but the line of thought is similar. To these passages Lk. 1.68 (Benedictus); 2.38 (Anna); and 21.28 (end-times), must be added. Here a major point is being made. First-century messianic expectation includes the hope that Israel will be redeemed, that she will be delivered from Roman occupation, that 'the kingdom' will be restored to her. There are plenty of Old Testament, early Jewish, and Qumran parallels.[42] But from Luke's perspective this element of messianic expectation has to be *transformed* radically or abandoned. In the light of the gift of the Spirit, Luke clearly understands God's eschatological plans to be 'universal rather than nationalist'.[43]

Conversation on the road to Emmaus includes a second topic of direct relevance to the present discussion. The Risen Lord rebukes Cleopas and his companion for their failure to believe 'all that the prophets have said. Was not the Messiah bound to suffer in this way before entering upon his glory?' (Lk. 24.26, and similarly 24.46). The sufferings of the Messiah are referred to again at Acts 3.18 (Peter), Acts 17.3 (Paul in the synagogue at Thessalonica), and Acts 26.23 (Paul to Agrippa).

This time the reverse process has taken place. It is not a question of a strand of Jewish messianic expectation being transformed by followers of Jesus – as with the 'deliverance of Israel' passages. Here we have a distinctively Christian conviction being linked *de novo* to 'messianism', for we have no early Jewish evidence for a suffering Messiah. Now the move is not *from* messianism *to* Christology, but in the reverse direction. And 'a suffering Messiah' is not merely a Lucan theologoumenon. Paul recognizes that proclamation of a crucified Christ 'is an offence to Jews' (1 Cor. 1.23) and quotes an early tradition: 'Christ died for our sins' (1 Cor. 15.3). Even if Paul usually used Χριστός as a (sur)name for Jesus, as a learned Jew he was well aware of its links with messianism.

Peter's Day of Pentecost Speech: Acts 2.14-36

Several passages from Acts have already been referred to in the comments above on Luke's Gospel. They confirm that Davidic messianic themes are prominent in Acts as well as in Luke's Gospel. However in Acts Luke's focus shifts. Peter's Day of Pentecost speech in Jerusalem, and Paul's speech in the synagogue in Pisidian Antioch are set-piece speeches. They are intended to show the readers of Acts the content and method of Christian proclamation to be used in Luke's own day.

Like the other speeches in Acts, Peter's Pentecost speech is thoroughly Lucan in its present final form, though it almost certainly draws on earlier pre-Lucan traditions. The speech opens with citation of Joel 3.1-5 in 2.14-21. Here God's

---

41 Fitzmyer 1981–5: 1.1564: 'delivering Israel from Roman occupation, a hope alive among Palestinian Jews of the time ... and echoed in *Pss. Sol.* 9.1'.
42 They are set out conveniently by Brown 1993: 386–9.
43 Barrett 1994–8: 1.76–7.

pouring out of his Spirit 'in the last days' is linked to eschatological themes, to general messianic expectations. At v. 22 there is an abrupt change to royal Davidic themes as the heart of christological proclamation; this section concludes with the declaration that God has made 'this same Jesus, whom you crucified, both Lord and Messiah' (Acts 2.36).

Peter develops his defence of the resurrection and exaltation of Jesus via his reading of Ps. 16.8-11 (LXX 15.8-11). The patriarch David spoke as a prophet with foreknowledge of the resurrection of the Messiah (v. 31). God had sworn to David that one of his own direct descendants should sit on his throne. The fulfilment of a royal Davidic psalm in the death and resurrection of Jesus the Messiah is set out vigorously.

The final verses of Peter's speech develop what may seem to us to be a quaint line of argument: Ps. 110.1 with its reference to exaltation to God's right hand is cited. Since it was not David who ascended to heaven, David (speaking as a prophet, v. 30) must have been speaking of another, Jesus, the one exalted to God's right hand. Through his exaltation Jesus has been vindicated and enthroned as the Davidic Messiah.

Paul's Speech in Pisidian Antioch: Acts 13.16-41

Paul's speech in the synagogue at Pisidian Antioch is Luke's first and only example of Paul's proclamation in a synagogue setting. The structure and content are broadly similar to Peter's Day of Pentecost speech. This is no coincidence, for one of Luke's purposes in Acts is to show that Peter and Paul are theological twins.

Luke introduces Paul as a preacher in a memorable way. Immediately after his baptism Paul proclaimed Jesus publicly in the synagogues in Damascus, declaring him to be the Son of God (Acts 9.20). Undaunted by opposition, Paul confounded the Jews of Damascus 'with his cogent proofs that Jesus was the Messiah'. 'Son of God' and 'Messiah' form an inclusio in this pericope (Acts 9.19b-22), and are almost synonymous terms here. The 'cogent proofs' are from the Scriptures, as the earlier chapters have shown. The reader will not be surprised to learn that proclamation of the messiahship of Jesus led to intense opposition and the hatching of a plot. This narrative in Acts 9.19b-25 is Luke's 'template' for all his later references to Paul's preaching in diaspora synagogues.

Following his escape from Damascus, and then Jerusalem, Paul moves off stage to make room for Peter. When Paul returns to centre stage, Luke uses his 'template' as the basis of his elaborate account of Paul's proclamation of Jesus as Messiah in the synagogue in Pisidian Antioch (Acts 13.13-52).

Luke takes pains over his description of Paul's audience: 'men of Israel, and you others who worship God' (Acts 13.16, 26). In the narrative that follows, they become 'many Jews and Gentile worshippers' (v. 43). Paul's first christological comment to this 'mixed' audience is that Jesus is a descendant of King David. In fulfilment of God's promise, Jesus is a *saviour* brought to Israel (Acts 13.22-23). Paul and his companions are the people to whom the message of *salvation* has been sent. The Davidic Messiah's coming is for the redemption and salvation of Israel. Luke's readers know that this is in accord with the angel's announcement at the birth of Jesus (Lk. 2.11; cf. also Acts 5.11): 'to you is born this day in the city of David a Saviour, who is the Messiah the Lord.'

Given the care Luke takes in his description of the synagogue audience, there may be some significance in his choice of *saviour* and *salvation*. The royal Messiah of David's line is clearly in mind, and there are deep biblical roots. But there may be a subtext for those 'God-worshippers' and Gentiles who heard or read this speech. Is it a coincidence that 'saviour' and 'salvation' were prominent in the language of the imperial cult, and that the imperial cult was prominent in the Roman colony of Antioch?[44]

In the final section of this speech, the resurrection of Jesus is declared to be the fulfilment of God's promise 'in the second Psalm': 'You are my son; this day I have begotten you' (Acts 13.32-33). C. K. Barrett notes that here Jesus is the messianic Son of God and refers to *Pss. Sol.* 17.23f. 'Ps. 2 is a royal and hence a messianic Psalm; when the king accedes to the throne he is adopted into the divine family. Jesus is both the Son of David (cf. Rom. 1.3) and Son of God; these are complementary, not contradictory expressions.'[45]

As earlier in Damascus, so in Pisidian Antioch. Paul's preaching in the synagogues drew a mixed response: acceptance on the part of some, fierce resistance on the part of others. Luke's references to Paul's preaching in synagogue settings follow the same pattern. Proclamation focused on Jesus as the promised Messiah and on Paul's interpretation of scriptural passages. Debate ensued. There was a mixed response and on occasion Paul and his companions were hounded out of town.

Luke's accounts of what happened in the synagogues in Iconium (14.1), Thessalonica (17.1-3), Beroea (17.10), Athens (17.16-17), Corinth (18.4-6), and Ephesus (18.19) are terse. Luke does not need to repeat either the content of Paul's preaching or the response it received. The reader knows that Paul based his claims concerning the messiahship of Jesus on Scripture.

The rare variations from the pattern stand out. The necessity for the Messiah to suffer is underlined in the synagogue in Thessalonica (17.3; cf. 26.23 in front of Agrippa). And Luke notes several times over that Paul's proclamation of Jesus as Messiah was not confined to Jews: in some audiences there were God-worshippers and Gentiles.

One question calls for further comment, especially given the role it has played in theological discussion. In Luke's view, when did Jesus become the Messiah sent by God? At his baptism, his resurrection, his ascension, at Pentecost, his exaltation, or his parousia?[46] Strauss insists that Luke presents Jesus' messiahship as achieved in various stages. From his birth he is the Messiah-designate. At his baptism he is anointed by the Spirit and empowered for his messianic task. 'Only at his exaltation-enthronement, however, is Jesus installed in the full authority as reigning Christ and Lord.'[47]

This is by no means an unusual conclusion. However it rests on the assumption that Luke intended his two writings to be read as one work. The literary and

---

44   Stanton 2004: 45–6.
45   Barrett 1994–8: 1.646.
46   J. A. T. Robinson's view that Jesus was predestined to become the Messiah when in the future he is sent as such has not won support. For discussion, see Barrett 1994–8: 1.190, 202–7.
47   Strauss 1995: 144–5.

theological unity of Luke's two writings are now taken for granted by most scholars. But Kavin Rowe and Andrew Gregory have recently reminded us that Luke's Gospel and Acts circulated separately in the early church: we have little or no evidence that they were read as two volumes of one work.[48] If we take seriously the possibility that Luke may have intended both his Gospel and Acts to be intelligible on their own, there is a corollary for our present question.[49] The exaltation of Jesus as Messiah and Lord is prominent in Acts, but with only a couple of possible exceptions (Lk. 9.31, 51, and 24.51 [s.v.l.]), conspicuous by its absence in Luke's Gospel.

Now there may be an easy explanation: Luke's purposes in his Gospel may not have required reference to the exaltation-enthronement of Jesus as Messiah. However it is also possible that Luke was less interested in christological precision than we usually suppose. Or perhaps his own views developed between the writing of his Gospel and Acts.

Several scholars have insisted that Χριστός is the most important christological title in Luke's writings. Some have gone a step further and rejected claims that Luke downplays Χριστός in favour of κύριος.[50] I do not think that Luke is interested in issues of precedence, but there can be no doubt that one of his primary aims in both his writings is to stress that Jesus is the promised Davidic Messiah.

5. Conclusions

In the opening pages of this chapter I referred to the cluster of verbs used by ancient and by modern writers to spell out the relationship between 'messianism' and 'Christology'. No single verb in the semantic field with 'transformation' at its heart adequately sums up the views of Mark, Matthew and Luke, for the three evangelists differ in their emphases. Nonetheless they share convictions concerning the messiahship of Jesus. They all insist that there is a measure of *discontinuity* between first-century Jewish messianism and their own views concerning Jesus the Messiah. But they all underline *continuity* by insisting that the messiahship of Jesus is the fulfilment of scriptural hopes and expectations.

The early post-Easter decades witnessed steadily increasing engagement with the questions raised at the outset of this chapter. One can trace a trajectory from the Q traditions which are messianic only in a broad sense, to Mark's Gospel, and then to Matthew's and Luke's more extensive engagement with messianism and Christology. In Peter's Day of Pentecost speech (Acts 2.14-36) and in Paul's speech in Pisidian Antioch (Acts 13.16-41) we are in some respects well on the way to Justin's *Dialogue* with his Jewish opponent Trypho. Justin and Trypho are at odds over the interpretation of scriptural passages alleged to refer to the Messiah, and these issues dominate their agenda.

---

48 Rowe 2005.
49 Hence the sub-heading for this section is 'Luke and Acts', not the more usual 'Luke-Acts'.
50 Tuckett 2001b, esp. 149–61, p. 161 n.104.

But a conclusion along these lines has to be qualified. The crucifixion of Jesus forced his followers to accept that their claims concerning 'Messiah crucified' were at odds with first-century messianic expectations. Here there was radical discontinuity right at the outset, as there was over rejection of messianic traditions which held out hopes of military success against the Romans.

At several points we have noted resistance to the ways followers of Jesus were interpreting messiahship. The words of Jesus, 'Blessed are those who take no offence at me' (Mt. 11.6 = Lk. 7.23) follow his implicit claim to messiahship. The threefold mocking of the crucified Jesus as 'King of the Jews' (Mk 15.18, 27, 32) at the climax of Mark's story reflects resistance to Christian claims. Resistance is more overt and more extensive in Matthew's and Luke's Gospels. Luke's repeated references in Acts to the mixed response to Christian proclamation probably reflects in part the experience of preachers in Luke's own day.

Although we have discussed only some of the strands of earliest Christianity, a set of fascinating issues has emerged. Followers of Jesus, whether Jews or Gentiles, insisted on the importance of his messiahship as the fulfilment of scriptural promises. This was one way 'church' emphasized her continuity with Israel. That claim was regularly juxtaposed with the conviction that God's promised age of redemption, a new creation, had broken in with the sending of Messiah King Jesus, great David's greater Son.

Chapter 7

MESSIAH AND RESISTANCE IN THE GOSPEL AND EPISTLES OF JOHN

Judith M. Lieu

What is the relationship between the prologue of the Fourth Gospel and its avowed purpose, between Jn 1.1, 14, 'In the beginning was the word, and the word was with God, and the word was God ... and the word became flesh', and Jn 20.30-31, '... but these things are written so that you might believe that Jesus is the Christ [Messiah] the son of God, and so that through believing you might have life in his name'? A polarization of these passages might be represented by the contrasting positions of older scholarship: C. H. Dodd, espousing the Hellenistic milieu and ethos of the Gospel, argued that the author 'develops his doctrine of the person of Christ in categories which are substantially independent of the Jewish messianic idea';[1] by contrast, W. C. van Unnik claimed that 'His book was ... a mission-book which sought to win. For this purpose, to make clear that Jesus is the Messiah, he worked over the material he received' (van Unnik 1973: 62).[2] Dodd's position was swiftly overtaken by the recognition of the diversity of first-century Jewishness, in the diaspora as well as in Israel-Palestine, while the argument that John has a primary missionary purpose has not been found persuasive.[3]

This issue at stake is not only a question of whether in 20.31 the subjunctive verb, 'you might believe', should be read as an aorist (ingressive) or as a present (continuous), nor whether the confession is 'that Jesus is the Christ/ Messiah' or 'that the Christ/ Messiah is Jesus', although both of these are important.[4] On a textual level the explanation of the Aramaic *Messias* and its meaning (1.41; 4.25) is distinctive to this Gospel, and the term *'Christ'* plays an important role (18x), both as a point of conflict and as a key confession (e.g. 1.20, 41; 7.26-27, 31, 41-42; 9.22; 11.27). Yet this has to be balanced with the yet more frequent 'son (of God)', as already in 20.31, as well as with the *logos* of the prologue. Next, how is the Gospel as a whole to be read, including both the narrative sections and the discourses with their focus on Jesus' self-revelation and on the conflict as to his true identity? Beyond this, although inseparable from it, what life

---

1   Dodd 1953: 361; cf. p. 9, John wrote in a Hellenistic city such as Ephesus for 'non-Christians who are concerned about eternal life and the way to it'.
2   See also Robinson 1962.
3   See already Barrett 1975([= the 1967 Franz Delitzsch lectures, published in 1970]): 1–19.
4   NA^{27} reads with caution (i.e. πιστεύ[σ]ητε) the aorist despite the support for the present from P^{66} ℵ* B. The debate as to subject and predicate in the confession turns on the significance of the anarthrous proper name 'Jesus' and articular 'Christ' and 'son', alongside the order of the words (see also below, pp. 99 and 106). For a recent discussion and defence of 'Jesus' as predicate and of a missionary purpose as compatible with the present subjunctive see Carson 2005.

setting is to be envisaged for the Gospel (and, in the final part of this chapter, for the Epistles) within which these conflicts are being re-positioned? Finally (in this list, but not in importance nor necessarily in logic), does the Johannine presentation of Jesus stand in unbroken continuity with contemporary Jewish messianism (as well as with the earliest confession of Jesus as Messiah), or would it have been 'perceived as radically non-Jewish' and as 'altogether different ... from the "messianology" of the first Christians' (Horbury 1998c: 151 and 118)? William Horbury has argued vigorously against the latter alternative and for the former; more recently he has distinguished his position from one that would ascribe 'New Testament christology to association of Christ with the God of Israel'.[5] Given the promiscuity with which terms such as 'messianic' are sometimes used, Horbury's careful positioning-by-contrast here will serve as a lodestone in the following exploration of these different yet interlocking levels of interpretation, so as to avoid straying too freely into the broader field of Johannine Christology.

Source and Composition

One approach to the problem posed on the textual level as described earlier is via theories as to the sources of the Gospel, most popularly the hypothesis of an earlier 'Signs Gospel' (SG).[6] The identification of this earlier, mainly narrative, source, with its own characteristic presentation of Jesus, is often accompanied by a reconstruction of the stages in the history of (what was to become) 'the Johannine community'. According to this view the confession of Jesus as *Messiah* belongs to the earliest stage, its antiquity being authenticated by the archaic '*messias*' (1.41); the goal, preserved in 20.30-31, of the SG, or perhaps of an earlier 'Signs Source' (SQ) which lacked a passion account, was to persuade Jews in the local context that Jesus was the Messiah on the basis of what he *did* (the 'signs'). This Gospel can as easily be called 'Jewish' as 'Christian' for as yet it is unaware of subsequent conflicts, or of potential ones over the place of the law or of the Gentiles (Fortna 1989: 205–16). This theory supposes that miracles could be offered as proof of messiahship; it has, therefore, to face the challenge of the absence of a clear association of miracles with the Messiah in Jewish sources (de Jonge 1977: 131). Is John (e.g. 7.31) to supply the missing evidence; or are we to see a broadening of 'messianic' to include ideas associated with an expected prophet or Moses (comparing the 'signs prophets' of Josephus); or is it that the SG only reflects a connection already made in earlier ('Christian') tradition between *Jesus'* miracles and his messiahship?[7] A certain circularity may

---

5 Horbury 2003b: 13 with reference to the work of R. Bauckham; he anticipates this argument in Horbury 1998c: 112–19.
6 Widely argued or assumed; see Fortna 1989 with reference to his own and others' earlier work.
7 On the prophet-like-Moses, see below, p. 101. For a thorough and nuanced discussion, see Ashton 1991: 238–79; also Painter 1991: 15: 'All of this suggests that, even if there was no tradition concerning signs to be worked by the Messiah, a tradition of notable signs would be useful in dialogue with the synagogue.' Suggestions of the influence of a 'divine man' typology are unsupported and unpersuasive.

seem unavoidable, for our choices here are not independent of a prior decision as to the definition of 'messianic' and of the positioning of John among the unstable (at this period) categories, 'Jewish' and 'Christian'.

This model, that the Gospel retains the evidence of stages in the development of a Christology, has been widely followed without necessarily subscription to the literary hypothesis of a SG. Invariably this is tied to the notion of a 'Johannine community' with a continuous history of belief and experience, one that starts with a widely shared belief in Jesus as Messiah.[8] Whether we are exposing the archaeology of the community or of the Gospel itself, the story drives forward along a trajectory of increasingly distinctive belief and experience. So, for example, Robert Fortna argues, 'But mere faith in Jesus' messiahship had been proved inadequate ... once Christianity was torn loose from its Jewish moorings – as it had for 4E's time and community – belief in Jesus' status, belief merely **that [he] is the Christ**, is not enough. It must lead – in a way partly comparable to but now also distinct from the whole Jewish mystery of salvation – to **life in [Jesus'] name.**'[9] While this comment implies that a break with the synagogue was the cause of a development beyond a 'simple messianic faith', others would argue that only prior developments in christological reflection could explain the intensifying animosity that is already reflected in John 7 (vv. 13, 30), despite this chapter's debates about the Messiah (vv. 26, 31, 41-42). The task then becomes to trace and to explain these developments, usually in terms of other concepts or influences, whose origins have then to be identified.[10] In either case there are two questions to be answered: first, whether the confession of Jesus as the Christ=Messiah is, in the Fourth Gospel, only a relic of the past, as implied by Fortna, or whether it still plays a focal role in any understanding of him; second, are these developments essentially incremental and continuous – internally and/or with Jewish conceptions – or is there a fundamental discontinuity as we move towards the Fourth Gospel in its 'final form'?

In practice answers to these questions rarely sit neatly into one or other alternative. Still adopting the 'archaeological' mode while attentive to the specific nuances and precise definitions of the contextual sources, John Ashton (1991: 279) argues:

> [T]he Gospel ... remains faithful to its source in its insistence that Jesus fulfils in every respect the eschatological expectations of the Jews. For all the mysteriousness and otherness of his person, he is set firmly in the context of a living tradition. He is *not* utterly unintelligible and remote; the area of his intelligibility is limited and defined in the lapidary formula drawn from one of the most ancient of Christian confessions: 'Jesus is the Messiah'.

---

8   This is so widespread among scholars otherwise adopting very different perspectives as hardly to need referencing: see Painter 1991: 40–63; Loader 1992: 17–18, 213–18.
9   Fortna 1989: 203–4 with reference to Jn 20.31b, which he identifies as an addition by the evangelist.
10 Ashton 1991: 279–336. Ashton, in company with others (e.g. de Jonge 1977: 56–8), persuasively includes the application to Jesus of the expectation of the prophet promised by Moses, and of the identification of and death penalty for the false prophet (Deut. 13.1-5; 18.18-20), as reflected in Jn 7.14-19a and elsewhere; however, only by an overly loose use of 'messianism' could this be further explored here.

By contrast, John Painter, who also traces through and behind the Gospel a number of stages in christological understanding and in relations with 'the synagogue', justifies the title of his study, 'the Quest for the Messiah':

> [T]he finished Gospel allows for a number of levels of perception so that Jesus is understood as the fulfilment of various messianic conceptions. Ultimately the evangelist is intent to show that, whatever the conceptual starting-point of the quest for the Messiah, it finds its fulfilment in Jesus. This means that the conception is finally clarified by the reality of Jesus revealed in this Gospel.[11]

The Christ of John

Yet is it possible to describe how John understands the affirmations of and the debates surrounding Jesus as the Christ/Messiah without being committed to appeals to hypothesized sources or history? What do they mean for the reader of the Gospel? This means how do they sit alongside not only the prologue's pre-existent *logos* (cf. also 8.58), but also the pervasive language of sonship, of 'being sent', 'from above' (6.38-40; 8.15-18 etc.), the distinctive 'son of man' sayings on Jesus' own mouth (1.51; 9.35 etc.), the 'I am' sayings both with and without a predicate (8.12, 58 etc.), and even such claims as 'I and the father are one' or Thomas's acclamation, 'my Lord and my God' (10.30; 20.28)? In his discussion of the origins of the 'cult of Christ' William Horbury has argued that each of these can be sourced within a 'spirit messianism' current in Jewish thought of the period that can be demonstrated from other texts.[12] Certainly he has persuasively demonstrated that speculations regarding the nature and unity of the one God need not be the primary inspiration or starting point of Johannine Christology;[13] there is now wide agreement that the Johannine conception does arise out of earlier patterns of thought that can be plotted. Yet the scattered referencing of parallels and potential hardly addresses the unifying thrust of the presentation of Jesus in John. For this reason few would challenge the assertion that John has redefined 'Messiah', and, indeed, each of the designations he uses, and most would agree that 'Jesus' kingship and his prophetic mission are both redefined in terms of the unique relation between Son and Father' (de Jonge 1977: 51–2). Admittedly, the counter-argument could be made that 'son of God' was already a messianic title (cf. 4Q246) (Collins 1993), but this does not really address John's distinctive and fundamental understanding of that relationship in terms of intimacy and of sending (3.35). To put it somewhat trenchantly: in John 'this Messiah is in a quite precise sense without any real analogy the Son of God' (Thyen 2005: 126).

---

11   Painter 1991: 14–15; cf. p. 244 on John 6, 'The development represents another stage in the evangelist's quest for the Messiah, now a Messiah who brings life through giving up his own life.'
12   Horbury 1998c: 140–51; 'the Johannine and Pauline conceptions can be interpreted as variations on a spirit-christology which continued and developed a spirit-messianism, and against a background of ruler-cult which influenced both Jewish and Christian developments' (p. 151).
13   *Contra* Boyarin 2001.

The implications and inspiration for this decisive move can then be sought in a number of different directions. Drawing on the insights of theories of a literary or historical development behind the Gospel, a fundamental question must be whether the many controversies also have a location outside the literary or narrative world of the text, and consequently how to identify the role of conflict in the articulation of Johannine thought. If, for example, 'the Jews' represent those against whom the Johannine community had to defend themselves in practice or in imagination, then there might be presupposed at least some common ground, whether in messianic expectation or regarding the grounds on which claims could be fought. Yet even where current expectation appears to be under debate, as over the origin and activities of the Messiah (7.27, 31, 41-42, [52: the prophet]), commentators will disagree both as to how firmly the views presented can be identified in Jewish sources, and whether the intention is to offer an explicit or implicit proof.[14] Other disputes, such as those implied by 3.13; 5.17-18; or 10.31-39, are not easily labelled 'messianic'. Many would agree that other motifs, most notably that of the Moses-like prophet (ch. 6), are present and perhaps even more influential in Johannine thought.[15] Moreover, in the first part of the Gospel, Jesus' preferred designation appears to be 'son of man', although this title is not the subject of debate in the narrative.[16]

One solution that seeks to maintain a 'messianic debate' with contemporary Judaism while acknowledging the variety of Johannine Christology is offered by James McGrath: he argues that all of the elements in John's Christology can be paralleled to some extent in earlier Christian thought, including those that go beyond the messianic, such as sonship, wisdom and divine agency models. John's own distinctive beliefs arise from the attempt by what itself can still be called a form of Jewish Christianity to defend and legitimate these pre-Johannine christological views – 'the Messiahship of Jesus as understood by many, if not indeed most or all, early Christians' – in debate with 'the local synagogue' (McGrath 2001: 145, 232). It is because the common denominator in all of these, including the Moses-like prophet, is whether Jesus is God's appointed agent, that the author can continue to use the confession of Jesus as the Messiah or Christ as the central reference point, even if 'messiahship' has to be redefined to 'do justice to who the Messiah in fact turned out to be'.[17] Moreover, that confession and the dangers surrounding it (9.22) are still to be located in the anxieties surrounding messianism after 70 C.E.[18] This makes a useful contribution in suggesting how John's thought can be seen in terms of 'messianism', even if some

---

14 See below, pp. 102–4.
15 Meeks 1967; such hopes are eschatological but to call them messianic would be to denude that term of specificity (see above n. 10). Meeks also locates this motif in a polemical context (p. 318), although he may trace it more widely than is warranted, and it is not evident that it is given priority over a Davidic messianic conception (p. 21).
16 Except at 12.34 (see below); to what extent 'son of man' was combined with 'Messiah' in Jewish thought is debated (cf. Collins 1993b: 80–2), but John's distinctive employment of it excludes it from a discussion of messianism.
17 McGrath 2001: 194 (and compare Painter at n. 11 above).
18 McGrath 2001: 77–8; McGrath follows a somewhat traditional understanding of post-70 Judaism here.

will feel that the category has been stretched to breaking point. Yet, in so far as it depends on setting John in a linear development from Paul and Matthew, presuppositions about what lies prior to the written Gospel are, as with but in a different way to the SG hypothesis, again being used to explain what lies within it, not only the explicitly polemical material but even the non-polemical prologue, whose prime position surely makes it something of an interpretative key.

There is much that suggests a rather more complex picture and set of strategies than this harmonious view of John and his sources. It is widely recognized that the dispute over the Messiah's origin in Bethlehem, and Jesus' failing in this respect (7.42), might resonate ironically not only for those familiar with accounts of his birth absent from John (Matthew and Luke), but more fundamentally for readers of the Gospel who by now know the importance of Jesus' true origin 'from above' or 'with the father'. The same extends to the disputes about origin in 7.27 and 52.[19] In 1.41-51 recognition of Jesus, which starts from 'the Messiah', pushes forward to Jesus' self-designation as 'son of man' (cf. 9.35), whereas in 12.34 the crowd's prior knowledge about the Messiah renders them incapable of understanding that same self-designation.[20] All this, and the refusal actually to engage with these messianic debates (also 7.31), suggests that the categories offered are being dismissed as at best inadequate and at most wrongly directed. Such an attack might be directed not only against contemporary (or prior) Jewish thought, but also against other patterns of Christian thought that did find probative value in Jesus' miracles or birth.[21] Further, even the objections of Jesus' interlocutors are couched in Johannine language (7.27 πόθεν, 31 σημεῖα; 12.34 μένειν): they give only a veiled glimpse of 'real' debates for they are there to serve the Johannine agenda.

This Johannine agenda brings us back to the (re-)definition of Christ as son of God (11.27), and of sonship in terms of being sent.[22] It does seem likely that the primary influences for this lie outside what may properly be called messianism, although not necessarily outside Jewish traditions, and the same perhaps may be said of the resultant structure.[23] Subsequent history has demonstrated that further questions are posed by the Johannine model, not least as to the seriousness with which the physical humanity is taken of one whose true origin is 'from above'. Some would see such conflicts as already reflected in the Gospel, although it is not obvious that they are addressed by John's use of Christ.[24]

---

19   On this, and what follows, see de Jonge 1977: 77–102.
20   Horbury 2003b: 129–30 misses the Johannine irony when he takes this as evidence for the incorporation of 'son of man' into Jewish messianic thought.
21   Some have seen a specific polemic against a Davidic messianism (Anderson 1996: 178, and also n. 15 above), but this seems overstated (cf. the retention of 12.12-16); more ambivalent is a possible distancing from a miracle-based messianism/Christology, although this need not have been present at an earlier stage of the community (so the SG hypothesis).
22   Cf. 1.17 and 17.3 where 'Jesus Christ' (only here in the Gospel) is contextually closely related to the God who sent him.
23   See, for example, Ashton 1991: 292–373; Loader 1992.
24   Contrast Schnelle 1992: 135–9, who understands Jn 20.31-32 in the light of an anti-docetic reading of 1 John (see below) as emphasizing the identity between Jesus and the Christ.

Messiah and Resistance in the Gospel and Epistles of John 103

To a greater or lesser extent each of these attempts to understand John's messianism relies on extra-textual constructions, whereas an important trend in recent scholarship seeks to interpret the Gospels as coherent and self-explicating within their 'final form'. Adopting this perspective, H. Thyen argues that already in 1.34 (and anticipated in 1.14) we become aware that this Messiah is in a precise way without analogy 'Son of God', but what this means can only unfold within the Gospel itself; it reaches a climax, not a let-down, in 20.30-31, because its unique (μονογενής, 3.16) character becomes apparent only 'in the light of Easter morning'. Within this framework possible sources of the concept or distinctions between ontological, moral or functional categories of sonship become irrelevant.[25] The pointed appeal to the Hebraic form '*messias*' at 4.25 (by a Samaritan!) as well as at 1.41 is not an archaism or a relic but a deliberate demonstration 'that salvation is from the Jews' (4.22), and, despite the significant influence of the deuteronomic prophet on the Gospel, it is only the predicate 'Christ' which is taken up and redefined.[26] However, for the reader, Jesus' revelatory 'I am' in 4.26, an *inclusio* with v. 10, redefines the woman's confession of him as Messiah (vv. 25, 29), just as the debates of chapter 7 direct the reader beyond Jesus' birth in Bethlehem to his true origin (Thyen 2005: 264–9, 409–10).[27] Hence, the anticipation of exclusion from the synagogue (9.22) can only be predicated on interpreting 'Christ/Messiah' through 'son of God', and 'son of God' through the one who from the beginning was God: it expresses the Johannine confession (in play with Lk. 6.22), not any actual formulation by Jewish authorities.[28]

Thyen's approach provides a consistent synchronic reading of the Gospel and also illustrates well the ambiguities of applying to it the categories of (even a 'Christian') 'messianism'.[29] As already noted in relation to the SG hypothesis, particularly important is the question of continuity, a question that may be answered differently on the linguistic, historical and theological levels. U. Wilckens (2003: 133) is surely right to see a 'hiatus' between the use even of such terms as prophet, Messiah, or son of God in the Old Testament and in John, and this remains largely true even if we introduce other Jewish and early Christian sources into the gap. For Thyen, not only is 'salvation from the Jews', but the mother of Jesus represents 'the messianic people of Israel' whom the (=all) Christians to whom the Gospel speaks must welcome (19.26-27) (Thyen 2005: 739); at the same time, acknowledging that Jesus' claim 'the father has sent me'

---

25 Thyen 2005: 126, 773–6. Thyen does engage with debates concerning possible backgrounds, and draws on them, but he does not find in any of these *the key* to the Johannine understanding: see, for example, pp. 407–9.
26 Thyen 2005: 264, 417 (against Meeks 1967).
27 See above p. 102.
28 Thyen 2005: 310, 470 etc. The man's 'exclusion' follows his confession of Jesus not as Messiah (absent from this chapter except at 9.22) but as 'from God' (9.33-34). Fundamental to Thyen's reading is a degree of intertextuality with the Synoptic Gospels.
29 Moloney 1998 also offers a literary reading with some similar insights, although his conclusion is yet more radical: 'A belief that reaches beyond all human, historical, and cultural conditioning accepts that Jesus is the long-awaited Christ, but only insofar as he has come from God and returns to God …' (pp. 543–4 on 20.30-31).

is 'the language of *myth*', he asserts that it is 'the language of a myth that has broken through the experience of transcendence of the monotheistic religion of revelation' (Thyen 2005: 126–7). Even if Johannine messianic thought is not inspired by the question of God, it is necessarily driven to confront it.

Kingship and Resistance in John

William Horbury (2003b: 20) has sought to show how messianism should be contextualized not only alongside 'revolution and social upheaval' but also 'in religion and in the conflict of political theories'. So understood there is far more to be found in John under this heading than might be expected. Scholars interested in the historical traditions the Gospel might enshrine saw in 6.14 not only evidence of the charged atmosphere of first-century Galilee (or Judaism), but a turning point in Jesus' ministry as he deliberately rejected the path of revolutionary messianism that could have been implicit in the Feeding of the Five Thousand if seen as a deliberate evocation of the miracles of the Exodus and Conquest, such as might have been re-enacted in the wilderness by other would-be revolutionary leaders (Dodd 1963: 212–17). The Festivals of Passover (2.13; 6.4; 11.55) and Dedication (10.22) could carry echoes of hopes of freedom, confirmed perhaps by the Sanhedrin's fear of revolution and destruction at the hands of the Romans (11.47-53). A Roman cohort is involved in Jesus' arrest, and one of his disciples reacts with violence (18.3, 10). Jesus' ministry is overshadowed by attempts to kill him (5.18; 7.1, 30, 32; 8.37, 40; 10.31; 12.10), and he anticipates violence against his followers in the future (16.2). We may see in the warnings against thieves and hirelings (10.7-13) awareness of the tumultuous years leading to the Jewish revolt. All this demonstrates that the Gospel narrative is played out against a backcloth deeply resonant with social upheaval.

This should not be relegated to the historical context of Jesus' ministry or to earlier tradition, as if these no longer belonged to John's world. Such a view results from (or in) a fixation on its overworked description as 'the spiritual Gospel', or on the prevalence of 'eternal life' rather than 'the kingdom of God' as that which Jesus offers and proclaims.[30] It may also be a response to the recognition in John of the features of a sectarian mentality, epitomized by the claim that neither Jesus nor his future followers truly belong to the world (17.16).[31] On the contrary, a sectarian stance towards society could itself belong to 'the conflict of political theories' and come under the rubric of resistance. This is particularly true where John's theology is seen as an aggressive claim for superiority, a revolt against and a denunciation of the world, rather than as one of defensive alienation: 'a group in radical tension with its neighbours ... The strategy is not that of drawing the wagons into a circle so much as that of relentless criticism and attack'.[32] However, rather than explore this further, we shall focus on those aspects that are closer to the broad question of messianism and resistance.

30   On the various ways in which the epithet 'the spiritual Gospel' might be understood see Lieu 2005.
31   The classic articulation is that of Meeks 1972, taken up and developed by many others since.
32   Neyrey 1988: 205. Neyrey adopts a history-of-the-community layering of the Gospel and sees this response as belonging to the final stage.

It is through the theme of kingship that we come closest to 'religion and ... political theories' in John.[33] Jesus' withdrawal lest 'they make him king' (6.14) is echoed by the cry of 'the Jews' to Pilate, 'Everyone who makes himself king opposes Caesar', shortly to be followed by, 'We have no king but Caesar' (19.12, 15). Most see here a *de facto* denial of God as king, although another intertext might be offered by the followers of Judas the Galilean who recognized 'God as their only leader and master' (Josephus, *Ant.* 18.23). However, it is the universal proclamation of the crucified Jesus as 'King of the Jews', although based on tradition, which receives pointed and ironical attention (19.19-21).[34] These events are preceded by an extended conversation between Pilate and Jesus about kingship and about authority (18.33-38; 19.10-11), set within the by now familiar framework of Jesus' true origin (18.36-37; 19.9, 11).[35] Jesus does not *make* himself king for he *is* king; his kingship is also 'not of this world' but that does not render it spiritual or unworldly. Its structures and strategies may be different, but such a difference offers a profound and thoroughly political challenge to existing power. For John, who, as we have seen, emphasized the political dimension of the events leading to Jesus' death, that power was not an abstract concept but irreducibly the Roman Empire:

> There is here a clear refusal to acknowledge the authority of Rome, as a power limited to this world, over those who by believing in Jesus have become children of God and so gained the ascendancy over this world ... Even Jesus' transcendence of the category of kingship is thus not 'apolitical'...[36]

Even if in 16.2 the future persecution anticipated seems to come from a Jewish corner, the attention paid to Jesus' Roman trial, in sharp contrast to the Synoptics, suggests that John knows that the ultimate conflict of loyalty will come with regard to the absolute claims of Caesar. In this light the Samaritans' recognition of Jesus as 'saviour of the world' (4.42) is not (only) a claim to the universality of the Gospel but a counter-claim to imperial adulation. Both the implied debate and the solution can only be understood within the broad framework also inhabited by Jewish debates about resistance and loyalty.

In John, Jesus is not tried or crucified as Messiah/Christ, again in contrast to the Synoptics where this is central to the Jewish trial. He is accused before Pilate also of *making* himself son of God (19.7), but we have seen that in John this epithet goes beyond a traditional messianic sense. The paired charges take us back to Nathanael's confession, 'You are the son of God, you are the king of Israel' (1.49). The probable allusion here to Zeph. 3.15, 'The king of Israel, the LORD, is in your midst, you will no longer see evil things', means that these cannot be taken merely as synonyms of 'Messiah' (v. 41).[37] Similarly, at the entry into

---

33   On this theme and what follows see Meeks 1967, especially 61–99.
34   Hence the importance of retaining the translation 'the Jews' at vv. 12, 14.
35   A number of studies have shown how the careful structuring of the trial draws particular attention to this theme: see Moloney 1998: 492–501 with references to earlier literature.
36   Rensberger 1989: 87–106, quotation from p. 98 with reference to Jn 19.11.
37   *Contra* Horbury 1998c: 142–3 (although on p. 38 he recognizes Zeph. 3.14-20 as one of the passages that look to God alone as king and saviour), and Moloney 1998: 56. Meeks

Jerusalem, John adds to the traditional quotation of Ps. 118.25-26 the same phrase from Zeph. 3.15, 'even the king of Israel' (12.14).[38] If Jesus is king of Israel, an epithet proper to God, then the rejection of any king but Caesar by the high priests, as well as Jesus' own account before Pilate of his kingship, become yet more confrontational. The precise nuances of John's differentiation between 'King of Israel' and 'King of the Jews' are not easy to discern;[39] yet the divine referentiality of the former grounds resistance and final confidence in the absolute claim of God.

Christ in the Epistles of John

At the heart of the conflict reflected in 1 John is the confession, Ἰησοῦς ἔστιν ὁ Χριστός (2.22; 5.1), or Ἰησοῦς ἐστιν υἱὸς τοῦ θεοῦ (4.15). The two appear to be synonyms and recall the way that the Gospel puts them in immediate apposition (Jn 20.31), a step the Epistles never take, even if it is implicit in the equivalence of denial of '(Jesus as) Christ' with denial of the son (1 Jn 2.22). There are two significant questions in the interpretation of this confession: first, the identification of subject and predicate, that 'the *Christos* [whom we know about] is Jesus' or that 'Jesus [whom we know about] is the *Christos*'; second, whether χριστός is to be translated against a Jewish background as 'Messiah', or whether it has acquired a distinctive meaning best rendered by 'Christ'.[40]

Where the second alternative in each case is adopted, the 'secessionists' (cf. 1 Jn 2.18) are usually reconstructed as holding a pattern of thought that identified the 'divine' component as 'the Christ' and that perhaps was, at the least, ambivalent about its complete union with, or embodiment in, Jesus: this is a form of docetism, and is often found more explicitly presupposed by the singular emphasis on coming in the flesh (1 Jn 4.2; 2 Jn 7), and by the obscure 1 Jn 5.6.[41] Generally, this view presupposes that 1 John is later than the Gospel and that the position adopted by the secessionists is in some way related to an (over-)interpretation of the high Christology reflected in the latter; thus, the equivalence of 'Christ' and 'son of God' is derivative from the steps we have traced in John.[42] Conversely, the author's

---

1967: 89 does not recognize the Zephaniah allusion and sees a deliberate ambiguity as to whether 'king of Israel' is the equivalent of 'Christ'. The allusion is strengthened by the echo of Zeph. 3.13 in Jesus' description of Nathanael (1.47), 'The remnant of Israel shall not do injustice or speak folly, and there shall not be found in their mouth a word of guile'. Thyen 2005: 142–3, who also notes the only other divine use of 'king of Israel', in Isa. 44.6, 'Thus says God, the king of Israel, who rescues them', sees this as another instance of John's explication of the Messiah as the 'son of God without analogy'.

38 Mark is more overtly messianic, adding 'blessed be the coming kingdom of our father David' (Mk 11.10), while Luke also glosses 'the coming one' with 'king'. The opening words of Zech. 9.9 quoted in Jn 12.15, 'Rejoice greatly (John, 'Do not fear'), daughter of Zion' are also found in Zeph. 3.14.

39 It is not obvious that 'Israel' is claimed by the new community of faith; see 1.31.

40 See Griffith 2002: 166–79, who argues for 'the Messiah is Jesus'. See also n. 4 above.

41 See Brown 1982: 50–79, 352–3.

42 Unusually Schnelle 1992: 47–70 places the Epistles first and assumes that 'opponents ... denied ... the soteriological identity between earthly Jesus and the heavenly Christ' (p. 62), but does not fully explain the origins of this 'heavenly Christ' concept.

concern is to stress the soteriological significance and necessity of the human experience and death of Jesus. A more precise articulation of this position continues to exercise interpreters, but since it would hardly fall under even a 'Christian' messianism, it need not be pursued here.

The difficulty with this position is the extent to which it relies on imaginatively filling the gaps. To some extent this difficulty is met by the minority alternative position that the contested confession is indeed its most natural reading, that Jesus is the promised Messiah. This presupposes a context where some former members were denying that fundamental belief, perhaps under pressure to 'return to the synagogue' (Griffith 2002: 174–91). If the letter adds anything to that basic belief, it is an emphasis on the death of Jesus as Messiah in order to deal with sin (2.2; 4.10). This interpretation takes seriously the extent to which ideas and formulations in 1 John can be paralleled in other Second Temple Jewish sources. An epithet such as 'the righteous one' (1 Jn 2.1) can be seen as a 'primitive messianic title' (cf. Acts 3.14; 7.52). The idea of an eschatological opponent of God or of God's envoy is also rooted in Jewish sources even if the label 'antichrist' appears to be a new formulation (1 Jn 2.18).[43] However, the weakness of this reconstruction is its restriction of 'the son of God' to a traditional messianic category; as in the Gospel, this does not do full justice to the letter's emphasis on the reciprocity between father and son, into which the believer is incorporated.[44]

A mediating position recognizes the 'Christian' lens through which the conflict is being understood. This starts from the enigmatic conclusion to the letter, 'keep yourself from idols' (5.21), understanding it as warning against capitulation in the face of imperial persecution (E. Stegemann 1985). The core confession to be held on to expresses the Christian, not a Roman, perspective, but the context might well be Jewish believers now faced with the choice between solidarity with the synagogue or with the community founded on faith in Jesus as Messiah. The weakness again of this view is its difficulty in giving an account of the structure and themes of the letter as a whole. Although the letter frames an antithesis to 'the world' as stark as the Gospel, the actual contours of that world are hidden; the warning against 'everything that is in the world' and the certainty of its transience (2.15-17) suggests an isolationist mentality, but we cannot tell how that was expressed, and there is no challenge to social or political power structures.

The allusiveness of 1 John's language means that a final consensus as to its meaning is unlikely to be achieved. However, while it is not certain that 1 John presupposes the steps taken in the Gospel in the redefinition of 'Christ' in terms of sonship, it does reflect a similar process, perhaps less coherently presented.[45] On these grounds the suggestion that, as in the Gospel, the significance of the confession of Jesus for the understanding of (the unity of) God is at stake is

---

43 See Horbury 2003b: 330–43, although the argument that 'antichrist' is a pre-Christian term (p. 333) goes beyond the evidence.

44 Strecker 1996: 232–6 understands 1 Jn 4.2 in an anti-docetic sense but finds in 2 John 7 the expectation of a future messianic reign; 2 John is too brief to sustain this.

45 This could be because it is assumed or has yet to be fully explicated; the relationship between the two writings remains an open question.

attractive.[46] The warning against idols, a formulation that presupposes Jewish categories, would then make ironic sense, if conflict over faithful worship of the one God were at stake. Albeit by a different route, we are returned to William Horbury's insistence on the importance of 'messianism and monotheism'.[47]

---

46   See Wilckens 2003: 91–6 who leaves open whether the opponents are 'returning to the synagogue' or caught in an internal schism.

47   This essay is offered to William Horbury in deep respect for his scholarship and gratitude for his collegiality.

Chapter 8

THE CHRIST OF PAUL

Andrew Chester

1. Introduction

The main focus of this chapter is the extent to which Paul reflects a specific messianic hope in his writings, with special reference to the use of χριστός. This question has to be set in the context of Jewish messianic hope of the first century and around. Jewish messianism, however, is not a homogeneous phenomenon; nor is there any agreement on the definition of a 'messiah'. It is not possible to discuss that whole issue here. Instead I simply note that the brief, working definition that I will use is that a messiah is 'the agent of final divine deliverance'; this definition corresponds closely to a prevalent approach in recent discussion.[1] It has of course been argued that a text can only be defined as 'messianic' if the specific term 'messiah' is found in it.[2] Equally, it has been maintained, especially in relation to the Hebrew Bible, that the messiah should be understood as a 'future royal ruler'.[3] These definitions, however, are either too limited or too broad to do justice to the main ways in which messianic hope manifests itself in Judaism in both literary and other forms by the first century C.E. In relation to my working definition, Paul obviously sees Christ as the means by which final divine deliverance is brought about; indeed, it should not be doubted that Paul sees Jesus as the fulfilment of Jewish messianic hope. Yet what emerges from the evidence of his letters, and will become clear in this chapter, is that his main focus is not on Jesus as messiah; nor do messianic categories play a prominent part in his theology.

2. Paul's Use of Χριστός

Paul's use of χριστός, then, presents us with a paradox. It is found much more frequently in his writings than anywhere else in the New Testament,[4] and vastly more than 'messiah' in any Jewish text. We could therefore expect his letters to

---

1   Thus e.g. Collins 1995: 11–14; Neusner, in Neusner *et al.* 1987: ix–xiv; Oegema 1998a: 23–7; Barton 1998: 373–4.
2   So for example de Jonge 1966: 132–3; Charlesworth, in Charlesworth 1992: 4.
3   This is a position represented by e.g. Horbury 1998c: 6–7; Joyce 1998: 326–7.
4   *ca.* 270 times in the seven generally accepted genuine Pauline letters.

be a major source of information for Jewish messianism. In fact, however, if we had only Paul's writings, we would be able to say next to nothing about messianism. What we find is that χριστός is used almost entirely as a proper name, not a title, in Paul.[5] Clearly Paul inherits a tradition where Jesus is seen as the fulfilment of Jewish messianic hope, and hence has the designation 'messiah', but is probably already used as a name (cf. Acts 11.26), and not, primarily at least, as a title. Paul takes it for granted that Jesus is the true Jewish messiah, but that is not at all the main focus of his writings and theology.

The mode of Paul's usage also reflects the fact that χριστός is not now being used as a title. Thus we might expect that (as in Jewish usage generally) the use of the definite article would mark out a reference to the messiah.[6] In the vast majority of cases where Paul uses ὁ χριστός, however, no messianic reference is evident (and the use of the article can often be explained on specifically grammatical grounds), while at least one or two uses of χριστός without the article have some possible messianic significance.[7] Thus 'messiah' is not distinguished linguistically by Paul with any clarity. Nor does χριστός used in combination with other christological terms (Ἰησοῦς χριστός, χριστός Ἰησοῦς, κύριος Ἰησοῦς χριστός, χριστός Ἰησοῦς ὁ κύριος ἡμῶν) suggest specific messianic reference.[8] This undifferentiated usage is evident from Paul's earliest writings (as, for example, 1 Thessalonians) onwards.[9] Equally, he never says Jesus is the Christ, or speaks of 'Jesus the Christ' (Ἰησοῦς ὁ χριστός);[10] nor does he use characteristic Jewish expressions with a genitive (such as 'Israel', 'God' or 'Lord') following χριστός.

The fact that χριστός is used in these ways, along with the interpretation of this evidence by Kramer, Dahl and others, has indeed been used to argue the case that Paul did not understand Jesus as the messiah, or the climax of the history of God's dealings with Israel.[11] That, however, is an altogether implausible position. The fact that Paul uses χριστός almost entirely as a proper name, not a title, carries no implication whatever that Paul does not understand Jesus as the messiah, or

---

5   Cf. e.g. Torrey 1937; Kramer 1966: 203–14; Dahl 1974, 1991: 15–25; Grundmann 1974: 540–2; Hengel 1983; de Jonge 1986: 321–4; Fredriksen 1988: 55–6; Aune 1992: 405–6; Schnelle 2005: 247–8.

6   This is simply asserted to be the case by Conzelmann 1955: 65. See, however, Kramer 1966: 206–12, who carefully differentiates and explains Paul's usage with the article. So also Kramer, 212–13, shows Conzelmann's further assertion (1955: 65), that χριστός, as subject of a sentence, has titular significance, to be similarly without foundation.

7   Dahl 1974: 39 (with note 174), sees the idea of Jesus' messiahship as potentially present in 1 Cor. 10.4; 15.22; 2 Cor. 5.10; 11.2-3; Eph. 1.10, 12, 20; 5.14; Phil. 1.15, 17; 3.7 (all with the article, in addition to the clear messianic reference at Rom. 9.5), and at Rom. 15.7; 1 Cor. 1.23; Gal. 3.16 (all without). In the majority of these, however, it seems to me difficult to find any real messianic sense. On the absence of the article with χριστός at 1 Cor. 15.3, cf. e.g. Jeremias 1966, 1969.

8   Cf. further on this point Kramer 1966: 203–6 (cf. also 141–7, 151–6, 179–81).

9   Cf. Hengel 1983: 66.

10 The textual variant at 1 Cor. 3.11 is clearly secondary; cf. further Dahl 1974: 37.

11 Thus e.g. Gaston 1987: 6–7, 33, 113–14. So he says, for example (p. 7): 'Jesus is then for Paul not the Messiah. He is neither the climax of the history of Israel nor the fulfilment of the covenant …'. Cf. also Gager 2000: 59–60, 142, 146.

that the term itself is devoid of any significance.[12] On the contrary, it would make no sense for Paul to use the term χριστός at all if he did not take for granted Jesus' messianic status. In fact, then, at least as far as Paul's use of Χριστός Ἰησοῦς is concerned, it is better to understand it as a titular name, where χριστός is the *cognomen* (with Ἰησοῦς as the *nomen*), but with the overtone of a title always there.[13] Certainly χριστός very quickly becomes simply a name, but that does not mean that the significance of the title is simply abandoned.

There are indeed a few passages where Paul may use χριστός with some specific messianic implication or point of reference.[14] This is clearly so at Rom. 9.5, in the list of the privileges his fellow Jews have been given, culminating in the messiah, or Christ. It is also central to 1 Cor. 15.23-28, where Christ hands over the (messianic) kingdom to God as part of the final events. A clear case can also be made for messianic implications within Rom. 15.7-12, with the portrayal of Christ as a servant to the circumcised (v. 8), and the citation of Isa. 11.10, including the designation 'the root of Jesse' (v. 12). This is also probable at 2 Cor. 5.10, attributing to Christ a role in the final judgement, as in Jewish traditions of the messiah. Possibly Gal. 3.16 should be understood as having at least messianic overtones, with Christ being portrayed as the fulfilment of the scriptural promises (specifically to Abraham). Only at 1 Cor. 15.23-28, however, is the portrayal of Christ as messiah, and the use of Jewish messianic tradition, at all significant for Paul's argument. This passage represents, along with Rom. 1.3-4, the most developed messianic passage in the whole Pauline corpus; but is most plausibly understood as Paul moving the messianic expectation to a transcendent level, away from any specific realization on earth.[15] Equally, at Rom. 1.3-4, Paul clearly portrays Jesus as the Davidic messiah (probably using a tradition he has inherited). The emphasis, however, is not on Jesus as messiah, but on his exalted post-resurrection status as Son of God and κύριος.[16]

---

12 For emphasis on this point, cf. e.g. Dahl 1974: 37–47; 1991: 15–25; Grundmann 1974: 540–55; Hengel 1995: 1–7; Rowland 1998: 486–9; Dunn 1998: 198–9; Schnelle 2005: 247–8.

13 On this cf. Schnelle 2005: 247–8.

14 Cf. further Kramer 1966: 203–14; Dahl 1974; de Jonge 1986: 321–4; de Jonge 1988: 114; Hengel 1995: 1–7.

15 Cf. MacRae 1987: 172.

16 Cf. MacRae 1987: 171–2, who rightly notes that divine sonship is not an exclusive property of the messiah in biblical tradition; cf. also Dahl 1974: 40, 43–4. It can be added that 'Son of God' is scarcely found denoting the messiah in subsequent Jewish tradition, apart from a few instances (not all of them certain by any means) in the Qumran texts: thus 4Q369; possibly 4Q538; perhaps 4Q246; while 4Q174 cites 2 Sam. 7.11-14 in what is probably a sequence of messianic texts. The interpretation of Rom. 1.3-4 has been much debated; for an indication of the range of views, cf. e.g. Dunn 1988: 1.5–6, 11–16. Wright 2002: 416–19 (cf. Wright 2003: 242–5, 568, 572) understands 'Son of God' in 1.4 as having primarily a messianic sense, with 1.3-5 as a whole showing Christ to be the 'royal and powerful "Son of God" to whom the world owes loyal allegiance'. Eskola 2001: 217–50 argues that 1.3-4 contain no contrast in their portrayal of Jesus, but depict the heavenly enthronement (on the pattern of merkabah mysticism) of the exalted Christ as Davidic messiah. Neither Wright nor Eskola, however, establishes a convincing case.

Hence, I would wish to argue, the number of specifically messianic references in Paul is very limited, and so also is their significance. Indeed, even these passages can be read without an understanding of χριστός as messiah, yet still make complete sense,[17] and that is true of Paul's use of χριστός more generally. Paul is of course aware that χριστός has the basic sense of 'anointed one', denoting the messiah (as he shows at e.g. 2 Cor. 1.21),[18] but he is not concerned with this as a theme in his letters. Thus although Paul presupposes that Jesus is the Davidic messiah promised in Scripture (and taken up in subsequent Jewish tradition), he never sets out to prove this, or to make use of the obvious messianic passages from the Hebrew Bible.[19] Nor indeed does he use in this way those passages from the Hebrew Bible that are developed distinctively within the New Testament to show that Jesus is the messiah. Thus he lays no real emphasis either on Christ being the messiah, or on the specifically messianic implications of his use of χριστός.

3. Χριστός and Messianism in Paul: Themes at Issue

3.1 Χριστός as an Appellative

Although the position I have outlined in section 2 represents the majority view in scholarly discussion, it is important to note that there are alternative interpretations of Paul's use of χριστός, and hence of his messianism more generally. Thus, first, it has been argued that χριστός in some cases has to be understood as an appellative.[20] Specifically, it is argued that the form χριστός Ἰησοῦς, as an inversion of Ἰησοῦς χριστός, is problematic, since Graeco-Roman double names have a fixed form that does not admit of inversion. In fact, then, χριστός must originally have been an appositional appellative, and retains this sense.[21] From this, Karrer then argues that the appellative use more generally, with χριστός on its own, is the earliest layer of tradition in Paul, and underlies its subsequent development. It is found especially in the χριστός ἀπέθανεν formula in Rom. 5.6, 8; 1 Cor. 15.3, where it has the specific sense 'anointed is the one who died'.[22] The further point of Karrer's argument is that χριστός derives its basic significance not from Jewish (royal) messianic tradition, or the (no longer practised) anointing of kings or priests, but from the practice of cultic anointing.[23] Thus the Holy of Holies was itself probably known as 'the anointed' (τὸν χριστόν),[24] and it was

---

17   Cf. de Jonge 1988: 14.
18   Thus at 2 Cor. 1.21, Paul juxtaposes χριστός with the verb χρίειν; notably, however, Paul makes this 'anointing' refer (in contrast to the New Testament generally) not to Jesus but to the Christian community; cf. Hengel 1983: 67–8.
19   Cf. Hengel 1983: 67.
20   Cf. Karrer 1991: 48–89, 368–73; McCasland 1946.
21   Cf. McCasland 1946.
22   Cf. Karrer 1991: 48–92, 368–73, 406.
23   Cf. Karrer 1991: 95–213.
24   Karrer 1991: 406.

The Christ of Paul

here, as nowhere else, that God was near and effective. It was this that Jesus fulfilled, in his unparalleled closeness to God; hence the appellative χριστός could now be used of him.

Karrer's argument overall, although philologically sophisticated, is problematic,[25] and fails to do justice to the evidence for Jewish messianic expectation. Yet the specific argument for χριστός, in χριστός Ἰησοῦς, as an appositional appellative, is also not compelling. It would be more plausible if the form Ἰησοῦς ὁ χριστός were found, but in any case, the Roman usage of double names was more variable than McCasland and Karrer suggest.[26] Paul is certainly aware that 'Jesus' is the actual proper name, as also that χριστός was originally an appellative. Hence he never uses the form κύριος χριστός (as distinct from κύριος Ἰησοῦς and κύριος Ἰησοῦς χριστός), but he can readily use *both* χριστός and Ἰησοῦς as proper names, and does not retain an appellative sense for χριστός.[27]

3.2 Χριστός *as a Title*

Second, it has been variously argued that Paul uses χριστός mainly as a title, not a proper name. Thus, more than fifty years ago, Bornkamm[28] set out the view that it is used first and foremost as a title, with specific function; its occasional use as a proper name provides no basis for seeing it as meaningless and replaced by κύριος. This position has been developed further and in distinctive ways more recently. So, for example, Hays[29] has used Rom. 15.3-9 as a basis for his argument that the importance for Paul (at least as a presupposition for his theology) of understanding Jesus as the Davidic messiah has been considerably underestimated in New Testament scholarship, and correspondingly, the view that χριστός for Paul is a name, not a title, is seriously misleading. Thus he argues that in citing Ps. 69.9 at v. 3, and Ps. 18.49 at v. 9, Paul is taking up a christological reading of the Psalms, with the Psalms of Lament understood as Prayers of the Messiah. This interpretation of the Psalms of Lament, he argues, can be traced back to the very earliest level of New Testament tradition, and may indeed reflect an innovation already within Judaism. This idea of the messiah praying these psalms only makes sense if the messiah is indeed seen as representatively embodying the fate of the whole people of Israel, so in the Christian interpretation from the start it is Jesus who carries the fate of Israel. Clearly the Christian proclamation of a crucified messiah involved a radical transformation of Jewish messianic hope, but this oxymoronic concept again had its hermeneutical basis in the idea of the messiah praying these psalms.

This view has been taken still further by Wright,[30] who understands, and translates, χριστός as 'the Messiah' throughout. Messiahship, he argues, remained a central concept for Paul, and was not simply set aside or transcended; that is

---

25 For criticism of Karrer, cf. e.g. Zeller 1993: 156–9; Stuhlmacher 1993: 151–4; Niebuhr 1993: 343–5.
26 Cf. Zeller 1993: 158–9; cf. also Hengel 1983: 66–8.
27 Cf. Kramer 1966: 214; Dahl 1974: 38; Hengel 1983: 68–73.
28 Bornkamm 1952: 40; see also Cullmann 1963: 134. Cf. further Sänger 1994: 224–44.
29 Hays 2005: 101–18.
30 Wright 1991: 41–55; Wright 2003: 393–8, 553–83.

immediately obvious from his usage of 'the Messiah' (ὁ χριστός: e.g. Rom. 9.5; 15.3, 7) and Son of God. One main aspect of the significance of this is incorporative, as is clear, in different ways, from, for example, his use of ἐν χριστῷ and εἰς χριστόν.[31] Hence what is true of Christ is true of his people. The conviction that Jesus is indeed the messiah, Wright claims, represents the initial primary meaning of Paul's 'Damascus Road' experience.[32] But if Jesus has thus been vindicated as messiah, then it follows that he is to be seen as Israel's true representative. And if he is the messiah, then it also follows that he, not Caesar, is the world's true Lord (as his use of κύριος also demonstrates). This theme is clearly implied by the classic biblical portrayals of the messiah, above all Pss. 2, 72, 89; Isa. 11, 42 (49); Dan. 7. For Paul, therefore, the present time is the kingdom of the messiah, who is already ruling the world as its rightful Lord. The future kingdom will come when Christ, as the messiah, completes this work and hands over the kingdom to God (1 Cor. 15.23-28; cf. Eph. 5.5). Here the royal messianic emphasis is explicit, with Jesus putting all enemies under his feet. Paul, along with other early Christians, redefines the Jewish kingdom-of-God framework, but does not spiritualize it. He sees the great turnaround of the eras as having already begun: Jesus as messiah is the first-fruits of the resurrection, with the messiah's people following later.

This attempt to show that Paul's primary focus is on Jesus as *messiah*, however, seems exaggerated.[33] Even if Hays' argument were found convincing otherwise, it is not clear that he has shown that Paul himself lays emphasis on Jesus as messiah or Son of David. The sheer quantity of usage of χριστός in itself proves nothing; what matters is the way (and contexts) in which it is used, and these suggest hardly anything specifically messianic. This also is a basic problem for the arguments of Bornkamm and, especially, Wright. Thus it needs to be demonstrated that Paul is using χριστός throughout as a title, and with genuinely messianic emphasis. It is question-begging to see Paul's use of ἐν Χριστῷ and εἰς Χριστόν, and the theme of incorporation, as fundamentally messianic in emphasis, as also to claim that Jesus, as the messiah, is therefore 'Israel's true representative', and 'the world's true Lord'. Nor is this the primary emphasis of the texts he cites from the Hebrew Bible (Pss. 2, 72, 89; Isa. 11, 49; Dan. 7). In any case, however, these are precisely the texts that Paul does *not* use; they are conspicuous only by their absence. The sole exception is Rom. 15.12; but the main emphasis in Rom. 15.7-12 is on the divine sphere of salvation now being extended to include Gentiles.[34] The point is not that Christ now rules over them, or over the world; that is not the focus here at all. Nor is it clear in what real sense the expectation of the (messianic) *kingdom* is worked out by Paul, or made at all prominent in his thought.[35] He certainly portrays Christ handing over the messianic kingdom

---

31   Wright 1991: 45–55, 174.
32   Wright 2003: 393–5, 563–70.
33   Wright's basic argument is taken over by e.g. Schreiner 2001: 75–7. Hurtado 2003: 98–101 argues that χριστός functions virtually as a name in Paul's writings, but at the same time has messianic force throughout, both for Paul and also for those he addresses.
34   *Pace* Wright 2003: 266–7, 394.
35   For his fullest discussion of 1 Cor. 15.20-28, cf. Wright 2003: 333–8.

to God, at the eschatological denouement, so that it can be superseded by the divine kingdom, but we can gather little about Paul's specific understanding of this messianic kingdom: neither his use of 'kingdom' otherwise, nor his 'messianic' understanding more generally, address this issue in any real sense. Phil. 2.9-11 can certainly be seen as portraying Christ as sharing in divine rule, but the focus there is not χριστός but the exalted κύριος. The limits of Paul's messianic perspective have, then, to be recognized and respected.

3.3 The Cult of Christ and Angelic Messianism in Paul

Third, an altogether distinctive understanding of Paul's messianism has come from William Horbury himself.[36] Thus he argues that Jewish messianism was a sustained, continuous phenomenon, with strong inner coherence and homogeneity, from at least the eighth century B.C.E. down into and beyond the New Testament period.[37] One important aspect of this messianism, which Horbury believes to have been seriously underrated, is where the messiah has supernatural or angelic attributes.[38] He finds this attested widely in the LXX, as well as Targums and rabbinic texts, and *Pss. Sol.* 17.23, 47, and 1QSa, along with *4 Ezra* 12.32; 14.52; *1 En.* 39, 46, 48, and *Sib. Or.* 5.414–15. It too thus represents a long-established and continuous tradition, but altogether compatible with the fully human messiah of Jewish tradition otherwise. Jewish messianism, by the first century (and indeed well before), also needs to be set in relation to the prevalent Greek and Roman ruler-cult. Certainly this encountered Jewish opposition, but it also elicited imitation, especially in the exceptional homage and honour given to Jewish leaders and messianic figures, and the glorious terms in which they are depicted.

All this, Horbury argues, is of immediate significance for the New Testament, including Paul.[39] Christ is honoured by hymns and acclamations (e.g. Rom. 10.9; 1 Cor. 12.3; Phil. 2.6-11), and these, along with invoking and confessing his name, and being baptized 'into Christ Jesus' and eating 'the Lord's Supper' (all in Paul), point unmistakably to a cult of Christ as one element in early Christian worship. This cult of Christ is itself best understood as being deeply rooted in Jewish messianism, and specifically the expectation of an angel-like or 'spiritual' messiah. That is, it was through messianism rather than directly that angelology impinged on nascent Christology. Correspondingly, praises offered to Christ draw on Jewish royal and messianic praise. The main christological titles that Paul (as the New Testament more generally) uses also show vividly the impact of Jewish messianism on the cult of Christ. Thus χριστός itself is important: it is used to

---

36 Horbury 1998c, 2003b: 1–19, 35–64. As (I think) William Horbury's first research student, I could wish that I were discussing one of the topics where I am in complete agreement with him. The fact that I can differ is, however, itself a tribute to him. None of his students can remotely match the depth and breadth of his learning; but he has always encouraged us to examine the evidence and come to our own conclusions.

37 Horbury 1998c: 5–108; Horbury 2003b: 35–64 (= Day [ed.] 1998, 402–33); Horbury 2005.

38 Horbury 1998c: 83–108; Horbury 2003b: 53–64; Horbury 2005: 17–23.

39 Horbury 1998c: 109–52.

show the messiah specifically receiving homage (Rom. 15.7-12; Phil. 2.5-11), as well as, implicitly, in relation to deliverance and conquest (Gal. 1.4; 5.1). At Rom. 1.3-4, using 'Son of God', Jesus' messianic descent according to the flesh is contrasted with his messianic divine power, and that is the point also at Rom. 9.5, using the (probable) title θεός. So also Paul's emphasis on κύριος reflects the high and worshipful status of the messianic king, as does his use of σωτήρ (e.g. Phil. 3.20), a title redolent of the ruler-cult, but also of Jewish messianism.

Clearly this argument as a whole is not only erudite and fascinating, but is also more nuanced and less sweeping than for example that of Wright. Among the questions that would need to be raised in this case are whether there is as much continuity and coherence in Jewish messianism overall as is implied here; whether angelic or spiritual messianism is as clear and prominent a phenomenon as is claimed; and whether χριστός is the main point of emphasis at both 2 Cor. 4.4-5 and Phil. 2.5-11.

4. *Paul's Understanding of* Χριστός *and Messianism: The Evidence of Acts*

The argument for χριστός as (primarily) a title in Paul might look significantly stronger if the Paul (and especially his proclamation in synagogues) that Acts presents corresponded to what Paul says in his letters. Thus, for example, immediately following his 'Damascus Road' experience, he proclaims that Jesus is 'the Son of God' and 'the Messiah' (ὁ χριστός: 9.20, 22), and again (17.3; 18.5) that Jesus is 'the Messiah' (ὁ χριστός), as also that the Messiah must suffer (e.g. 17.3; 26.23). Similarly he portrays Jesus as a Saviour, and the fulfilment of God's promises to David (13.22-23), as also at 13.32-37, where he applies Ps. 2.7 to Jesus, while at 17.7 Paul and Silas are accused of saying that 'there is another king, Jesus'.

The problem with all this is, first, knowing whether Paul said any of it. The speeches in Acts are differentiated more according to the specific setting than the speaker,[40] and Paul is presented as proclaiming basically the same message as Peter and the early Christians as a whole. Thus there is overlap here, for example, with some of what Peter says, while the assertion that the messiah is Jesus (9.22; 17.3; 18.5) is also what Apollos says at 18.28, and may appear to be a stereotyped usage, while 9.20 has been seen as reproducing a 'confessional formula'.[41] The charge against Paul in 17.7 seems striking, but again it comes very close to the accusation brought against Jesus in Lk. 23.2. Hence it is very difficult to tell whether any of this distinctively represents Paul. Certainly it is entirely plausible that Paul in his basic preaching, especially in the synagogue, proclaimed Jesus as messiah. Whether he did so as Acts describes, we cannot know. In his letters, at least, the acclamation we find is 'Jesus is Lord', not 'Jesus is Messiah' (Rom. 10.9; 1 Cor. 12.3; at Phil. 2.11, it is 'Jesus Christ is Lord'). In any case, the second problem here is that in Acts the messianic emphasis is very clear, in exactly the

---

40   Cf. Barrett 1994–8: 1.623.
41   Thus e.g. Stählin 1962: 141.

way that in Paul it is not. Equally, Acts uses (in Paul's speeches as well as those of Peter) some of the Old Testament texts that are important for showing (on Wright's terms) the messiah to be 'the world's true Lord', along with other Old Testament texts to demonstrate Jesus' messianic status (thus e.g. 13.33-35). This again is precisely what Paul in his letters does not do. We have, then, to be very careful in evaluating this evidence, and beware of too easily reading it into our understanding of Paul's messianic perspective.

5. *The Political Dimension of Paul's Messianism*

The main distinctive interpretation of both χριστός and of Paul's messianism by Wright points to a political cutting-edge to Paul's whole perspective. This is indeed an emphasis that has been more widely represented in recent New Testament scholarship.[42] Thus Wright argues that Paul's messianism (in conjunction with his conviction about the resurrection of Christ) shows unmistakably that Jesus is the true Lord of the world, in contrast to Caesar and in spite of all appearances (e.g. Rom. 1.3-5; 15.12; 1 Cor. 15.20-28; Phil. 2.6-11; 3.19-21; 1 Thess. 4.15, 17; 5.3), with Phil. 2 and 1 Thess. 4, 5, along with Rom. 1.16-17, also echoing and parodying imperial ideology and imperial cult.[43] Horbury makes much less of this, but there are obvious political implications in his portrayal of Christ as an exalted messianic king, given acclamation and worship, and titles (Saviour, God, Lord) that belong fully within the ruler-cult.[44] The contrast with Caesar and clear political challenge in the passages Wright cites seem far from evident, however. Further, he draws attention to this political dimension in the New Testament more widely, as for example in Revelation.[45] Yet the differences between Paul and Revelation are considerable here. It is not simply a matter of the usual contrast between what Paul says in Romans 13, and the portrayal of the Roman state and its power in Revelation 13 and 17, significant though that is. The subversive critique of Roman ideology and oppression, and the contrast drawn throughout with both God and Christ, pervade the whole of Revelation, while the hope for the kingdom is fulfilled very specifically: the saints will reign with Christ in the new Jerusalem (5.9-10; 20.6; 22.5). All this is precisely what we do not find in Paul (including 1 Corinthians 15), in relation to Christ and the (messianic) kingdom. And as far as echoing, and potential parody, of imperial ideology is concerned, it would seem that the portrayal in the Pastorals (1 Tim. 6.14; 2 Tim. 1.10; 4.1, 8; Tit. 2.13), of the ἐπιφάνεια, kingdom and judgement

---

42   Thus as far as Paul is concerned, as well as Wright's own discussion of the theme, this kind of argument is represented, for example, in several of the essays in Horsley 1997, 2000 and by Crossan and Reed 2004. In Oakes 2001, it is related specifically to Phil. 2.9-11. It is very difficult indeed, however, to show a real challenge to Rome or political thrust in Paul's writings; much more so than these and other studies of the topic make it appear.

43   Wright 2003: 394–5, 563–70.

44   Horbury 1998c: 109–19, 144–52.

45   Wright 2003: 568. On Revelation, see especially Rowland 1993; Bauckham 1993a, esp. 338–452; Bauckham 1993b. For a discussion of the messianism of Revelation, see Spilsbury, this volume: 136–46.

of Christ, as κύριος, θεός and σωτήρ,[46] is much more plausible than, for example, 1 Thess. 4.15-17; 5.3. But an argument for the Pastorals as presenting us with political confrontation would hardly seem plausible. A genuinely political dimension to Paul's understanding of χριστός and messianism is, then, much less obvious than Wright and others would have us believe.

6. Paul and Jesus' Messianic Vision

A further issue that needs to be raised is whether Paul stands in real continuity with the main focus of Jesus' messianic role and message. Although I cannot address here the complex questions involved, it seems clear to me that Paul knew at least something of Jesus' life and teaching.[47] Yet what is lacking in Paul is anything that corresponds to the sharp thrust and cutting-edge of Jesus' message of the kingdom, of those who belong in it and the theme of radical reversal.[48] He portrays Jesus handing over the messianic kingdom to God; and it is possible that in his depiction of cosmic transformation (Rom. 8.18-25), and the emphasis on all cosmic powers and forces as subject to Christ, he might imply the transformation of the present world and human society. But this all lacks any specificity, and there is nothing of the transformation of people's lives and desperate condition in the way that this belongs integrally to Jesus' messianic role in the inaugurating of the kingdom. Despite Paul's constant use of χριστός, then, it is difficult to find anything that really corresponds to Jesus' own messianic vision.

7. Paul's Messianic Perspective

7.1 The Messianic Age and Eschatology

It seems easier, therefore, to say what Paul's understanding of χριστός and messianism does not entail than what it does. That does not mean, however, that it was a matter of indifference to Paul that Jesus was the messiah, even though it was not at all his main point of focus.[49] It is precisely because he believes the

---

46   For careful assessment of this, cf. Marshall and Towner 1999: 287, with reference to further discussion.

47   On this cf. e.g. Stuhlmacher 1983, 1989; Wedderburn 1989; Thompson 1991; Dunn 1994.

48   Wenham 1995: 34–103 argues for a close correlation between what Jesus and Paul say about the kingdom, but there is very little specifically related to the kingdom in his discussion of Paul.

49   The view attributed to Hengel by Wright 2003: 555, that 'the entire fabric of Paul's messianic belief ... is an illusion', is completely misleading. Hengel makes it absolutely clear that he sees Paul's messianic belief as anything but illusory; thus e.g. Hengel 1983: 70–7; Hengel 1995: 1–7. Kramer, certainly, occasionally gives the impression that χριστός in Paul's letters is devoid of significance (e.g. Kramer 1966: 43, 213). But his point (rightly or wrongly) is that this is *not* Paul's own understanding, but how Gentile Christians would inevitably understand χριστός. Overall (Kramer 1966: 19–44, 133–50, 203–14) he attributes considerably more to Paul's own

The Christ of Paul

messiah has come that he sees the final age as now set in motion. Hence his entire outlook now is eschatological, and this perspective pervades the whole of his thought and theology.[50] It is on this basis that he believes that the climax of the final events, and of the whole divine plan and purpose, will follow in the very near future. This directs and gives intense urgency to all Paul's preaching and mission. It is indeed the very fact that the eschatological age is now set in motion that allows Paul to see the promises and prophecies of Scripture as fulfilled in Christ, even though he does not bring the standard messianic prophecies into his argument;[51] hence also Scripture can be applied directly to the Christian community. All this is made completely clear in 1 Cor. 10.1-11, but the basic perspective again runs right through Paul's writings. So also Paul can portray Christ sitting in final judgement (2 Cor. 5.10), as the messiah does in some Jewish messianic traditions; but he relates the Parousia primarily to Jesus as exalted κύριος, not χριστός.[52]

7.2 The Death of Christ, Salvation and Baptism

A further aspect of Paul's eschatological perspective, that derives from his understanding that the messianic age is now under way, is that the death and resurrection of Christ represent the decisive act of God, the event that marks the turn of the ages. Paul has clearly inherited a very strong tradition that Christ had died, been buried, and been raised up by God. It is also integral to this early tradition that Christ died 'for us'.[53] It is this that represents the very heart of Paul's gospel for this new, eschatological age. Therefore he can speak of 'Christ crucified' and of 'the cross of Christ'. Hence also baptism, as the fundamental point of initiation into the eschatological Christian community, is baptism 'into Christ' and into the death of Christ.[54] It is this that determines all else in the new age that is already under way. Hence Paul can speak of the Christian community as 'the body of Christ' and, correspondingly, of the individual as being 'in Christ' (ἐν Χριστῷ).[55] To say this does not of course exhaust the significance of either of these themes in Paul,[56] but it at least alerts us to their primary point of reference.

---

perspective. So also Dahl 1974: 37–47; Dahl 1991: 15–25, while emphasizing that χριστός is a proper name virtually throughout Paul' writings, gives a very nuanced account of its significance, as does Schreiber 2000: 405–20, although he exaggerates the titular use of χριστός. Cf. also Grundmann 1974: 540–55; Dunn 1998: 198–9; Rowland 1998: 486–9; Schnelle 2005: 47–8.

50   Cf. Beker 1980; Schreiber 2000: 406–18; Hengel 1983: 70–1.
51   Cf. Hengel 1983: 71–2.
52   Thus e.g. 1 Thess. 4.15-17; 2 Thess. 2.2. Schreiber 2000: 413–4, argues, especially in relation to Phil. 3.20-21, for the royal messianic connotations of the Parousia in Paul. But the real focus, with the phrase 'the Lord Jesus Christ' is, as at 1 Thess. 5.23, on κύριος. The use of μαραναθα at 1 Cor. 16.22 suggests that this point of focus goes back very early; cf. Hengel 1983: 66. Phil. 1.10; 2.16 (cf. 1.6) has 'the day of Christ'.
53   Cf. Kramer 1966: 19–44; de Jonge 1986: 321–4; Hengel 1995: 2–3.
54   Cf. further Kramer 1966: 28, 64, 137, 200.
55   Cf. Kramer 1966: 136–8, 141–6; Grundmann 1974: 547–52.
56   For more detailed treatment, and reference to further discussion, cf. Moule 1977: 47–89; Neugebauer 1958.

7.3 Christ, Baptism and Ethical Perspective

Because baptism is not only into the death of Christ, but also involves being united with his resurrection, it therefore means entering into a new life.[57] That is, baptism marks the radical point of transition, of moving from the old life, characterized by sin, law and death, to the new life brought in by Christ's death and resurrection. Hence it has potentially profound ethical consequences, and these are set at least partly in terms of Christ.[58] So also, because the Spirit (itself a sign of the eschatological age now brought into being through Christ) is received at baptism, and characterizes and enables this new way of life, Christ and Spirit can also be bound up integrally together by Paul. Again, in the final, messianic age now set in motion, the law as it has been now no longer regulates the way of life lived in relation to God; hence Paul can speak of Christ as 'the end of the law', and also of 'the law of Christ'. Yet to set these themes primarily in relation to Christ is already to begin to exceed the limits of the evidence. Beyond a quite narrow range of reference, Paul does not use 'Christ' in an altogether distinctive or consistent way; that is so, indeed, with the ecclesiological and ethical themes that I have just touched on. Paul's usage of χριστός is not bland and insignificant, but it does not allow us to construct a consistent set of themes that he relates only to Christ.

7.4 Paul's Vision of Christ

At the very least, however, Paul's primary emphasis in relation to Christ represents something utterly remarkable. For Paul had found the early Christian proclamation of the crucified messiah completely abhorrent; it was indeed this that had led him to persecute the early Christian movement. Yet his extraordinary 'Damascus road' experience had then compelled him to accept that Jesus had actually been vindicated by God, and that therefore the claim that Jesus was the messiah had also been vindicated. Hence it became an underlying conviction for Paul that this person, Jesus, who had appeared to him, was the fulfilment of Jewish messianic hope. It is precisely this that gives rise to the unprecedently large number of instances of χριστός in Paul, and it is this that had convinced him that the messianic age was already under way. Following his vision, he knew that Jesus was the messiah, and as a Jew he of course had an understanding of the nature and significance of messianic identity. Yet, in his writings at least, he lays no emphasis on Jesus as messiah, and makes very little of messianic tradition more generally. That, as I have stressed, is the paradox of Paul's usage.

The reason for this lies in what is specific to Jesus, and to Paul's vision of him. That is, Paul sees Jesus as fulfilling Jewish messianic hope and bringing final deliverance; but he sees him as doing so in a different way and on a different level to anything within Jewish messianic tradition. That is one reason why he does not

---

57   Cf. Schreiber 2000: 408–9.
58   Kramer 1966: 138–40, sees the passages where χριστός is set in relation to exhortation as deriving directly from the theme of Christ dying for us (Rom. 14.15; 1 Cor. 8.11-12); it is this that determines all conduct towards one another; cf. also Rom. 15.7-12; 2 Cor. 10.1.

set messianic categories as such centrally. There is, however, a further dimension to this. In his original vision that has convinced him that Jesus is vindicated as messiah (and probably in further visions as well: cf. 2 Cor. 12.1), Paul has also seen Jesus set alongside God in the heavenly world and embodying in himself the divine glory.[59] Messianic categories are not able to do justice to this,[60] and Paul finds himself forced to speak of Christ as having, for example, the form and image of God, to convey the way that he knows, from his visionary experience, that Jesus has been transformed.[61] Hence also Paul is drawn into using κύριος, to depict the extraordinarily exalted, indeed divine, form that Jesus now has.

Paul, therefore, sees Jesus as fulfilling Jewish messianic hope and bringing final divine deliverance; but he also sees him as transcending the limits of that messianic expectation. He sees him, that is, as the messiah, but he also sees him as more than the messiah. Hence it is that he both uses χριστός for Jesus throughout, yet at the same time attributes very little indeed of specific messianic significance to it. Χριστός, then, points to something of the importance that Jesus has for Paul. Yet, ironically, within Paul's Christology χριστός is the least distinctive of the main terms he uses. Indeed, the christological titles themselves do not capture Paul's most distinctive emphasis. What he proclaims is the crucified Jesus, now transformed to take on a heavenly body of glory. As such he mediates the divine and human worlds as no one else has or can.

---

59   Cf. Segal 1990: 34–71; Segal 1992b; Newman 1992: 164–212; Kim 2002: 165–213.
60   Here, as I have indicated above (3.3), I have to differ from William Horbury.
61   Thus I would see the closest analogy here to be those figures who, in various traditions, are transformed, on entering the heavenly world, to take on angelic – or, indeed, more than angelic – appearance. On these traditions, cf. Himmelfarb 1993. But it is this transformation, and not any messianic identity or lack of it, that is the crucial point.

Chapter 9

THE CATHOLIC EPISTLES AND HEBREWS

David G. Horrell

The Catholic Epistles, despite being grouped and named as such since at least the fourth century (Eusebius, *Hist. eccl.* 3.23.25) and appearing along with Acts in the textual tradition as the *Apostolos*, do not constitute a collection of texts with a distinctive and closely shared theological perspective. Add to this much-neglected collection the letter to the Hebrews, often attributed to Paul in the early tradition (e.g. Clement of Alexandria in Eusebius's *Hist. eccl.* 6.14.2–4) but now never seriously argued to be his, and we have a group of texts which, while sharing internally and with other early Christian texts some common theological convictions, encompasses considerable variety. It would therefore seem appropriate to consider each text's individual perspective, rather than offer a synthetic treatment.

In order to make my task manageable in the available space, I shall focus on three examples from this group of letters: James, Hebrews and 1 Peter. (The Johannine Epistles are considered along with the Gospel of John in Chapter 7.) I shall take as my key questions the following: What is the character of the messianism evident in this text? What notion and means of redemption is envisaged, and how is this related to the text's messianism? And in what ways, if at all, does this particular type of messianism represent a form of resistance?

For our general understanding of what constitutes messianism we may follow William Horbury's broad definition: 'the expectation of a coming pre-eminent ruler', including 'the treatment of a present ruler in a messianic way' (Horbury 1998c: 7). The term Messiah, 'in its etymological sense', denotes 'God's eschatological Anointed One, the Messiah' (Charlesworth 1992: 4). I should also make clear that in this essay my primary aim is to outline the contours of the specifically 'Christian' messianism set out in James, Hebrews and 1 Peter, rather than to determine whether this depiction of Jesus does or does not derive from an existing facet of Jewish messianic belief.

Redemption may be understood in a broad sense to refer to the means by which those in some kind of negative situation – whether of suffering, oppression or their own wickedness – may be rescued from that situation by some other (person/divinity, etc.), and more specifically, and etymologically, as the act of purchasing back, or freeing by payment of ransom.

My understanding of what constitutes resistance, and the forms it may take, is primarily shaped by the work of James C. Scott, especially his already classic *Domination and the Arts of Resistance* (Scott 1990).[1] Building on his earlier work

---

1   For recent applications of Scott's work to New Testament studies, see Horsley 2004.

on peasants in Malaysia (Scott 1985), but casting his net much more widely, Scott insists that we must not restrict our definition of resistance to the open and physical forms of rebellion that are comparatively rare, of generally short duration, and usually quashed by superior force. Scott's interest is in the many and diverse ways in which subordinates express and practise their resistance to oppression. One such mode of resistance is through what Scott calls hidden transcripts, modes of discourse generally kept hidden from the public stage, where the official, sanctioned transcript dominates. Such a 'hidden' transcript may be expressed when the oppressed meet away from the gaze of their oppressors, as in the visions of reversal and judgement expressed in African-American slave religion, visions, of course, often directly indebted to biblical language and imagery. Other modes of resistance may appear on the public stage, but in ways which (generally) avoid direct and personal confrontation: anonymous rumours and gossip, euphemisms, ambiguous gestures and 'accidental' acts of insubordination, and so on.

The Letter of James

The letter of James is notoriously *non*-messianic, at least in terms of explicit references to the Anointed One, ὁ Χριστός, which appear only in 1.1 and 2.1. There is no good reason to doubt that James is a Christian text, despite some earlier suggestions to this effect,[2] but the letter's focus hardly falls on the Messiah.

Nevertheless, the relevant material in James, explicit and implicit, does allow us to sketch something of the content of its Christian messianism. In the opening address, describing the letter as addressed to the twelve tribes in the Diaspora, James[3] describes himself as θεοῦ καὶ κυρίου Ἰησοῦ Χριστοῦ δοῦλος (1.1). Here Jesus is acclaimed, as in Paul and elsewhere in the New Testament, as Lord and Messiah.[4] These are acclamations of Jesus that reach back to the earliest layers of early Christian tradition (cf. Mk 8.29; 14.61-62; 1 Cor. 16.22; Rev. 22.20).[5]

The reference in 2.1 is more intriguing, in at least two respects. First, it is unclear whether the πίστις Ἰησοῦ here should be taken as an objective genitive ('faith in our Lord Jesus Christ') or a subjective genitive ('the faith of …'). Luke Timothy Johnson (1995: 220) argues cogently for the latter: elsewhere in the letter faith is clearly directed to God (2.19, 23), and echoes of Jesus' teaching in the declarations in 2.5 (cf. Lk. 6.20) and 2.8 (cf. Mk 12.31, citing Lev. 19.18) suggest that

---

2   See Johnson 1995: 48 nn. 139, 151, and Ropes 1916: 32–3, for discussion and dismissal of the arguments of F. Spitta and L. Massebieau that 1.1 and 2.1 are interpolations into a Jewish letter. Johnson shows how these theories fit into a late-nineteenth-century tendency to dismiss James as 'the least Christian book of the New Testament' (Johnson 1995: 150–1, quoting Adolf Jülicher).

3   The letter's authenticity is also much debated, but I shall not enter that argument here.

4   It is possible that θεοῦ also refers to Christ – 'slave of Jesus Christ, God and Lord' – but this seems highly unlikely here (so Ropes 1916: 117; Laws 1980: 46; Johnson 1995: 168; but cf. 2 Pet. 1.1; Tit. 2.13).

5   Whether Jesus regarded himself as the Messiah is of course open to debate, but that the early Christians rapidly made this identification of him is clear.

the idea here is likely to be that the ἀδελφοί share (ἔχετε) the (Torah-based) faith practised and announced by Jesus.

Second, it is difficult to know how to take the reference to glory at the end of the verse. Among the various possibilities[6] two are particularly worthy of consideration: one suggestion is that the intention is to refer to 'our glorious Lord' or 'Lord of glory' – despite the 'extraordinary separation' (Johnson 1995: 220) between κύριος and δόξα – with 'glory' probably a way of referring to Christ's resurrected state.[7] The separation between κύριος and δόξα is indeed a difficulty here. A second, attractive possibility, therefore, is to take δόξα as in apposition to what precedes, and thus as a description of Jesus as 'the glory'.[8] The Hebrew Bible refers frequently to God's glory (כבד יהוה/δόξα κυρίου), and in some texts this 'glory' refers specifically to the manifestation of God's presence (Exod. 33.18–34.8; cf. 2 Macc. 2.8), sometimes apparently in human-like form (Ezek. 1.26-28).[9] This seems to have fostered the development of a 'glory Christology' in Paul (see Newman 1992; Segal 1992: 334). Although an absolute christological use of δόξα would be striking for the New Testament[10] it seems at least plausible that the writer of James would thus identify the Messiah.

The double reference to the παρουσία τοῦ κυρίου in 5.7-8 is most likely, given its frequent use in early Christian texts, a reference to the coming (again) of Christ (cf. 1 Cor. 15.23; 1 Thess. 2.19; 2 Pet. 1.16; 3.4; 1 Jn 2.28, etc.), which the author sees as near (ἤγγικεν; cf. Mk 1.15 par.; Rom. 13.12; 1 Pet. 4.7, etc.). His messianism is thus, as is that of early Christianity generally, characterized by an imminent eschatological hope.

There are other texts in James which may indicate something of the form and content of the author's messianic beliefs, but it is less than certain that the references are specifically messianic. It is possible that the καλὸν ὄνομα by which believers are named, and which is the cause of hostility, is the name of Christ (2.7). It is also possible that 5.6 provides another messianic 'title', describing Jesus as ὁ δίκαιος.[11] Most commentators take this rather as a general reference to the righteous (poor) who are persecuted by the rich;[12] but it may be that a specifi-

---

6   See e.g. Dibelius and Greeven 1976: 127–8; Laws 1980: 94–5; Adamson 1976: 102–3, for the range of suggestions.
7   So Johnson 1995: 221, citing Lk. 24.26; Acts 22.11; Jn 17.5; 1 Cor. 2.8; 15.43; 2 Cor. 4.6; Phil. 2.11; 3.21; Col. 1.11; Heb. 2.7 and 1 Pet. 1.11 as instances where δόξα serves 'as shorthand for the resurrection'. The grammatical awkwardness here probably explains the omission of τῆς δόξης in some later MSS and their transposition to follow πίστις ('faith in the glory of our Lord ...') in a few others.
8   For arguments to this effect, see Laws 1980: 94–7; Adamson 1976: 103–4 (who argues for the transposition of ἡμῶν to read 'our glory': this seems to me an unnecessary move). On the 'genitive in simple apposition' see Wallace 1996: 94–100.
9   For a concise overview, see Fossum 1999; and specifically on the Septuagintal background, Brockington 1955.
10 Comparable references to Christ as the glory might be found in Acts 7.55 (if the καί is read epexegetically) and 1 Pet. 4.14 (which could be rendered: the spirit of the glory and of God), though neither of these is secure. For other relevant New Testament references, see Fossum 1999: 351–2. Cf., later, Justin, Dial. 61.2: δόξα κυρίου ... καλεῖται.
11 Cf. 1 En. 53.6: 'the Righteous and Elect One ...'.
12 E.g. Laws 1980: 205–6; Dibelius and Greeven 1976: 239; Johnson 1995: 304; Davids 1982: 179–80. Not only is the referent of δίκαιος uncertain, but so also is the sense of the final

cally christological reference was intended and/or heard, given other clearly messianic uses of the term in the New Testament (Acts 3.14; 7.52; 22.14).[13] The murdered Messiah may be seen as the exemplary δίκαιος, without the category being restricted to that single figure; his suffering followers, like the suffering righteous of former times (e.g. Ps. 37; Wis. 2.10–3.8) follow in the steps of *the* suffering δίκαιος.

More generally, James is notable for its focus on wisdom (1.5; 3.13-18), such that the whole letter has been described as the 'wisdom of James' (Bauckham 1999). Richard Bauckham argues that the kind of wisdom set out by James has close parallels with the wisdom taught by Jesus: '[t]he wisdom of Jesus functions for James as the focus and principle guiding his appropriation of other Jewish traditions. His wisdom is the Jewish wisdom of a faithful disciple of Jesus the Jewish sage' (Bauckham 1999: 108; see pp. 93–108; Bauckham 2004). There is no indication that this focus on wisdom reflects a wisdom Christology, as, for example, in Col. 1.15-20. But James's depiction of 'the wisdom that comes down from above' (3.15, 17) does at least hint that, as perhaps with δόξα in 2.1, the author might have been willing to see the Messiah as the embodiment of divine σοφία.

If the letter of James gives little explicit information as to the form of messianism the author held, it gives even less insight into his notion of redemption. It is clear enough that the letter regards its addressees as suffering trials and temptation (1.2-4, 12; 2.6-7; 5.13), and as needing to avoid and escape from wickedness and sin (1.21; 5.15-20). Their trials are intended to produce endurance (1.3-4), a quality appropriate for those who have hope for their salvation (5.7-11). This eschatological hope – that those who humble themselves before God will be exalted (4.10) – is focused on the imminent παρουσία τοῦ κυρίου (5.7-8). But, in contrast to the letter to the Hebrews, to which we turn next, there is no indication as to how the Messiah, or specifically his death (and resurrection), might play some redemptive role. Forgiveness of sins is evidently the Lord's prerogative (5.14-15); but the means to forgiveness of sins, insofar as it is discussed at all, is mutual confession and prayer in the community (5.16) and specifically – assuming the implicit link between sickness and sin – anointing and prayer on the part of the elders (5.14-15). It is the power of prayer that is stressed here (5.16-18). Salvation is clearly seen as a result of accepting the gospel, the 'implanted word (λόγος)'[14] that has 'the power to save' (1.21), but how and with what role for the Messiah remains unstated. Indeed, as is often noted, the heart of the religion James calls for is defined in practical, ethical terms (1.27), and it is this faith-evident-in-works that saves (so 2.14). James's concise definition of true religion (θρησκεία) in 1.27 thus contrasts with the christologically focused creed in 1 Tim. 3.16. This observation should by no means be taken

---

phrase of the verse. Does it refer to the non-resistance of the δίκαιος against his murderers or should it perhaps be taken as a question – 'Does he not oppose you?' – with either the δίκαιος (Davids 1982: 180) or God (Johnson 1995: 305) as the implied subject?

13   Cf. also Luke 23.47, which Peter Doble 1996 plausibly argues to be another instance of Luke's δίκαιος-Christology. Other descriptions of Christ as δίκαιος are not clearly titular: 1 Pet. 3.18; 1 Jn 2.1, 29; 3.7.

14   This can hardly be a christological reference (cf. also 1.18), but almost certainly refers to the gospel (so Johnson 1995: 202). But cf. the comments of Reumann 1999: 130–1.

as an implicit criticism of James, a fate the letter has suffered too often due to its negative judgement by a (Protestant) Christianity centred upon Pauline doctrines. Recent work, calling attention to the importance of the ethical focus of James, has indeed gone some way to correcting that injustice and highlighting the theological importance of James's radical ethics (see e.g. Maynard-Reid 1987; Chester and Martin 1994; Bauckham 1999).

Just as James's messianism is not clearly linked with the letter's evident hope of redemption, nor is it explicitly connected with the forms of resistance the letter expresses. To say that is already to imply that the letter *does* express resistance, as indeed it does, but this is not grounded in the letter's messianism – unless we see in 5.6 a reference to Christ as the paradigmatic and non-violent victim of the rich and powerful, a theme we will see in some respects in 1 Peter.

The letter of James expresses resistance to the world in general, seeing a clear and sharp distinction between friendship with God and with the world (1.27; 4.4-5), and resistance to the rich and powerful in particular. The letter insists that God has chosen the poor and not the rich to inherit the kingdom (2.5) and candidly labels the rich as oppressors (2.6). James does not give us any more precise indication about who it is to whom resistance is directed. In encouraging the readers of the letter – implicitly at least, grouped on the side of the poor – to wait patiently for their promised salvation (5.7-11), the author exclaims a vituperative woe upon the rich, drawing upon the language and imagery of the prophetic tradition (e.g., Isa. 3.14-15; Amos 2.6-8; Zeph. 1.11-15; Mal. 3.5) to detail vividly the miserable reversal-of-fortunes that awaits the rich, whose wealth is amassed at the expense of the poor (5.1-6; cf. Lk. 6.20-25; 1 *En.* 94.6–99.16).[15] Such an outburst forms a fine example of what Scott (1990) terms the hidden transcript, the discourse of the oppressed which is generally – for pragmatic reasons of survival – hidden from the oppressors' view. In public settings, where the powerful call the shots – in court (2.6) or with one's employer (5.4) – due deference, however insincere, is usually the sensible strategy. Yet when the oppressed have opportunity and means to communicate with one another, away from the gaze of the powerful, they articulate their own vision of the world and the future. 'Symbolic inversions' (Scott 1990: 166–72) are one form this envisioning often takes. Vivid and violent depictions of the fate of the rich, anticipations of a reversal of fortunes, find frequent expression in slave religion and folk tales, popular songs and carnival dramas, as Scott so well shows. And of course, in some of these instances, such as among the slaves of the American South, biblical imagery and language provides resources for resistant transcripts. Such expressions of the dreams of the oppressed should not be dismissed as merely the opiate of the masses (Marx) or as safety valves that actually ensure the stable continuation of the system. Rather, as Scott persuasively argues, they are dangerous and potentially disruptive of the established power relations, precisely because, by articulating a different version of reality, they call into question the inevitability and rectitude of 'the way things are'. Especially powerful are those moments when the hidden transcript is expressed openly in the full gaze of the dominant, whether such expressions are quickly silenced by rapid and violent reaction or whether they foster further overt expression and action, such as to renegotiate the structures and

---

15   Cf. further Crossley 2006: 75–96.

patterns of social relationships (see Scott 1990: 202–27). The inclusion in the Christian canon of texts such as James – along with Luke's Gospel, the book of Revelation, and so on – has ensured that such potentially explosive expressions of open hostility to the rich and powerful, with all their destabilizing possibilities, cannot altogether be ignored, though their force has frequently been softened through various forms of spiritualizing or psychologizing exegesis.

The Letter to the Hebrews

If the letter of James offers only minimal glimpses into the form of Christian messianism held by the author, the letter to the Hebrews contains an *embarras de richesses*. This anonymous letter, the authorship of which is likely to remain unknown and even the genre of which is uncertain, constitutes the richest and most sustained expression of christological belief in the New Testament. It is also one of the New Testament texts most thoroughly infused with Old Testament quotations and images, many of which are explicitly used to express convictions about the nature and achievements of Jesus the Messiah.

The richness of the letter's messianism is anticipated *in nuce* in the opening four verses, which constitute one complex sentence: the Son, greater than both prophets and angels, the heir of all things (κληρονόμος πάντων) and the one through whom 'the ages' (τοὺς αἰῶνας) were made, is the radiance of God's glory (ἀπαύγασμα τῆς δόξης – literally 'the radiance of the glory'; cf. on Jas 2.1 above) and the exact representation of God's very being (χαρακτὴρ τῆς ὑποστάσεως αὐτοῦ). He 'sustains all things by his powerful word' and, having 'made purification for sins ... sat down at the right hand of the Majesty on high' (v. 3, NRSV). One could spend a whole essay (and more!) discussing the words of this opening sentence, full as they are with both scriptural imagery (e.g., wisdom as the agent of creation [Prov. 8.22-31; Sir. 24.1-9]; the appearance of God's glory) and points of contact with other New Testament expressions of high Christology (e.g., Jn 1.1-18; Phil. 2.6-11; Col. 1.15-20; cf. Barrett 1999: 114–15). Indeed, many of the themes of the opening verses are expanded in the chapters that follow. It is interesting to note, however, that the specific designation Messiah, Χριστός, first appears only in Heb 3.6 and thereafter, sometimes with the definite article – implying *the* Messiah (e.g. 3.14; 5.5; 9.14, 28; 11.26) – but not always (3.6; 9.11, 24; 10.10; 13.8, 21). For the writer to the Hebrews, the primary designation of Jesus' identity is as 'the Son', though this is evidently a facet of his appointment as Messiah, as 5.5, with its quotation of Ps. 2.7, makes clear (cf. also 1.5).

The first point the author develops, using a catena of Old Testament quotations (mostly from the Psalms) to do so, is the Son's superiority to angels (1.5-14). Whether the author is polemically insisting on this point, against those whose reverence for angelic figures is deemed too high (cf. Col. 2.18; Manson 1962: 252–8), or is rather asserting the superior status of Jesus while sharing with his readers a positive regard for the angels is uncertain.[16] A second major point

---

16 Lindars 1991: 37–8 and Hurtado 2003: 499 both conclude that polemic is unlikely here.

concerns the humanity of the Messiah, his sharing 'flesh and blood' (2.14), and its redemptive significance: only by becoming like his ἀδελφοί (2.17) could he know their temptations and thus help them (4.15–5.4) and only so could he truly function as their high priest before God, obtaining forgiveness for their sins (εἰς τὸ ἱλάσκεσθαι τὰς ἁμαρτίας τοῦ λαοῦ, 2.17).[17] The depiction of Jesus Messiah as a priestly character, specifically as high priest, is a prominent aspect of Hebrews' messianism, though this is not to the exclusion of royal images, as (*inter alia*) the quotations of Ps. 2.7 (1.5, 5.5), Ps. 44.7-8 LXX (1.8), and 2 Sam. 7.14 (1.5) indicate.

After comparing Jesus with Moses, and again stressing the superiority of Jesus (3.1-6), the author indeed develops this important theme of Jesus as high priest. Particularly striking is his conviction that Jesus is a priest not in the Aaronic line, but rather in 'the order of Melchizedek' (5.6). The initial stimulus for this striking and unusual identification – nowhere else in the New Testament outside Hebrews 5–7 is Melchizedek mentioned – almost certainly came from Ps. 110, the first verse of which was very widely used as a messianic text in early Christianity (see Hengel 1995: 119–225). As Larry Hurtado suggests, the author of Hebrews probably 'took Psalm 110 as a whole to be referring to Jesus, and sought to emphasize the particular christological meaning of 110:4' (Hurtado 2003: 501). This led him to Gen. 14.17-20, the only other biblical text to mention Melchizedek, and to a messianic interpretation of this passage too (7.1-10). The silence of the Genesis text as to Melchizedek's parentage, for example, gives the author scope to pronounce him 'without father or mother or genealogy', with neither beginning nor end, like the Son of God, a priest forever (7.3). The other key point from the Genesis text is the tithe that Abraham paid to Melchizedek, which for the author of Hebrews demonstrates 'the innate inferiority of Abraham to Melchizedek' and indeed 'the superiority of the Melchizedek-type priesthood over the Levitical priesthood', since Levi effectively also 'paid tithes to Melchizedek' (Tuckett 2001a: 99), being 'still in the loins of his ancestor [Abraham]' when Abraham met Melchizedek (7.10).[18]

A text from Qumran, 11QMelchizedek, shows that the author of Hebrews was not alone in finding some special significance in the figure of Melchizedek; he is here depicted as 'a heavenly redemption figure' (Fitzmyer 1997: 267), and an agent of judgement, even as the *Elohim* of Ps. 82.1 (11QMelch 9–10). It seems unlikely that the two texts are directly related, however; rather they indicate distinct currents in what may have been a wider stream of Jewish (and Christian) reflection.[19]

The superiority of Christ's priesthood, with its once-for-all perfect sacrifice, compared with the Levitical priesthood and its repeated sacrifices, is the dominant

---

17   It is debated whether ἱλάσκεσθαι conveys here a sense of propitiation (cf. ESV) or of expiation or atonement (cf. NRSV, NIV). Cf. Lane 1991: 66 (who favours propitiation); Attridge 1989: 96 n. 192 (who favours expiation).

18   The author's reference to the tithe in 7.5, which appears to suggest knowledge of post-biblical Jewish priestly tradition, is one of the pieces of evidence William Horbury 2003a picks up to suggest that the writer to the Hebrews knew and was influenced by post-biblical developments of the idea of Pentateuchal theocracy in (probably) Palestinian Judaism, rather than by sectarian or visionary strands of first-century Judaism.

19   See Kobelski 1981: 127–9; Lindars 1991: 72–7; Fitzmyer 1997: 221–67; Hurtado 2003: 501. Cf. also Philo *Leg.* 3.79; *2 En.* 71.32-33; 72.1-7.

theme of the following chapters. Indeed, the contrast is explicitly depicted as one between a new, better covenant and an old, faulty one now rendered obsolete, πεπαλαίωκεν (7.18-19; 8.6-13; 9.11-15; see Haber 2005). The kind of 'dualism' evident here in Hebrews, not least in the contrasts drawn between earthly patterns (ὑποδείγματα) and heavenly things (9.23), between the law with its repeated sacrifices as the earthly shadow (σκιά) and the true form itself (αὐτὴν τὴν εἰκόνα, 10.1), has often been seen as an indication of Platonic, or more directly Philonic, influence. At the very least, however, the author's 'dualism' is horizontal as well as vertical, eschatological as well as eternal, such that the 'former' things point forward to, and are fulfilled and consummated in, the new covenant made possible by Christ (cf. Barrett 1999: 122–5; Hurst 1990: 13–17). Moreover, as L. D. Hurst (1990) has shown, direct influence from Platonic or Philonic thought is by no means demonstrable, and a more plausible view may be to see the author of Hebrews as developing Old Testament thought along lines influenced by certain strands of early Christian thought (Acts 7; Paul) and Jewish apocalyptic.

Central to this section (9.1–10.18) is the comparison between the repeated sacrifices of the old covenant and the once-for-all sacrifice of Christ, a comparison drawn by depicting Christ's sacrifice and high-priestly actions in terms of the ritual of the Day of Atonement (cf. Lev. 16; *m. Yoma*):[20] public sacrifice (cf. 10.10; 13.12); the entry of the priest, with blood, into the Holy Place (9.2-5, 12, 24-26; 10.19-20); intercession and atonement made by the high priest (2.17; 4.14–5.10); return of the priest to the waiting people (9.28). The author insists that the repeated sacrifices of the old covenant can never *really* deal with sin, can never 'make perfect' (τελειῶσαι) those who worship (10.1-2), while Jesus' perfect and unrepeatable sacrifice achieves precisely that (10.10). It is interesting to notice that the author does not shrink from an implication of this striking claim: if anyone deliberately sins *after* such a sanctification, no further sacrifice for sins remains, but only 'a fearful expectation of judgment' (10.26, ESV). Similarly, the author insists that repentance for apostates is impossible (6.4-6). (Despite this author's apparent optimism, Christians were not, of course, made perfect, and the Church had soon to face precisely the issues of post-baptismal sin and the return of apostates.)

It should already be clear from the above that redemption is central to the letter to the Hebrews, and, indeed, is inseparable from its messianism, since the letter focuses so heavily on the Messiah's function as both priest and atoning sacrifice, his once-for-all achievement of forgiveness for God's people. This redemption has been obtained by the shedding of blood, the offering of a perfect sacrifice. The Messiah's humanity means that he can be sympathetic and understanding towards human frailty, such that those who seek salvation should 'draw near with confidence' (4.16). As the parallels with the Day of Atonement suggest, participation in the assembled company of worshippers is, if implicitly, fundamental to sharing in this redemption. More specifically, faith is seen as crucial to this drawing near (10.22, 39), as it is to living in the way to which God calls his people (11.1ff.). Faith belongs alongside hope and love (10.22-24), an echo of the

---

20 For this comparison set out in brief, see Barrett 1999: 124–5. It is interesting, as Barrett notes (p. 127 n. 28), that the author makes nothing of the scapegoat idea.

famous Pauline triad (1 Cor. 13.13) but also – since love is closely linked with good works (10.24) – an echo of James's insistence that faith without works is dead.

But does the messianism of the letter to the Hebrews, and the pattern of redemption it includes, in any sense sustain a mode of resistance? Unlike the letter of James, here there is no open hostility towards the oppressive rich, no vision of a coming reversal when the poor will be lifted up and the rich punished. There is, however, a sense that the people of God live in an awkward and tense relationship with the world: they are 'strangers and exiles on the earth' (11.13; cf. 1 Pet. 1.1, 17; 2.11), a wandering people looking towards their heavenly country (11.16).[21] This world is a place of sin, not yet subject to the Son's rule (2.8; 11.7). Indeed, it is clear that the followers of the Messiah to whom the letter is addressed have suffered hostility from the world, and can expect to do so in the future (10.32ff.; 12.3-4). In this, they are experiencing a similar fate to that suffered by the 'great cloud of witnesses' (12.1), the exemplars of faith who suffered at the world's hands (11.1-40, esp. 32-38). Most of all, they are following the Son himself, 'who endured from sinners such hostility' (12.3), though they have not yet had to follow him to the point of death (12.4). The 'struggle against sin' (12.4) is a struggle against hostility in the world, as the parallel with 12.3 makes clear. Unlike in James, where again the addressees endure suffering, here the Messiah explicitly represents a path for his followers to tread, of enduring the shame of suffering for the prize that lies ahead (12.2). He is a pioneer, the first of many sons (2.10-18; cf. Rom. 8.29). This imagery, which we find again in 1 Peter, is important to the letter insofar as it presents the Messiah as a sympathetic fellow-sufferer in order to encourage his followers to faithfulness despite their suffering. And the author's exhortation to his readers to hold firmly to their original confidence (3.14; cf. 3.6; 4.16; 10.35) is also a call to perservere in their way of life, resisting pressures to turn away.

In some ways, therefore, the letter does sustain a pattern of life and belief which we may define as one of resistance. What the letter does not define more precisely is the identity of those who are resisted, though the parallel drawn between those 'sinners' who opposed the Son and the opposition faced by his followers might suggest that 'the rulers of this age' are at least included here (cf. 1 Cor. 2.8). As in 1 Peter, where we get somewhat more clues as to the focus for resistance, it is the readers' commitment to their Messiah and to the God of their Messiah that generates hostility from the world; it is this that *makes* them strangers and exiles.[22] This living-at-odds with the world, and with the dominant powers in that world, may thus be seen as a mode of resistance, a refusal to conform even when physical coercion is threatened.

---

21   The image of the wandering people of God was famously seen by Ernst Käsemann 1984 (1939) as the central theme of Hebrews.
22   *Pace* Elliott 1981, who argues that the addressees of 1 Peter already had the actual socio-political status of πάροικοι. Cf. further Feldmeier 1992; Seland 2005: 39–78.

The First Letter of Peter

Like the letter to the Hebrews (and like Romans), 1 Peter contains more Old Testament quotations than most of the New Testament writings. A number of these quotations are clearly read by the author, 'Peter',[23] as messianic, and thus both inform and reflect the letter's Christology. The letter's focus is not as heavily christological as is Hebrews', but it does present a rich range of messianic images, not least since it draws together a wide range of early Christian teachings (see Horrell 2002).

As William Schutter (1989: 100–23) and Paul Achtemeier (1999: 144–7) have pointed out, a key statement about the author's approach to reading the Scriptures, a 'hermeneutical key', is outlined in 1.10-12, the closing verses of the letter's introductory thanksgiving. The subject of the prophets' enquiry – that is, the Jewish prophets of the Hebrew Bible, not Christian prophets (*pace* Selwyn 1952: 134) – was the 'salvation' revealed in the last days (cf. 1.5). Moreover, the spirit of Christ was present among them (ἐν αὐτοῖς; cf. 1 Cor. 10.4), showing the sufferings and the glory that lay ahead for the Messiah. Given this explicitly Christian-messianic view of scriptural prophecy, it is no surprise that the author found in Isaiah's suffering servant (Isa. 52.13–53.12) a depiction of the sufferings of Christ (2.21-25), saw messianic significance in a collection of 'stone' texts (2.4-8), and, indeed, 'has, in a way singular among Christian canonical writings, appropriated without remainder the language of Israel for the church' (Achtemeier 1999: 142; cf. Achtemeier 1996: 67–73).

One obvious focus of attention is the three messianic passages identified long ago by Hans Windisch as *Christuslieder*: 1.18-21, 2.21-25 and 3.18-22 (Windisch 1930: 65, 70). Building on Windisch's observation, Rudolf Bultmann (1967=1947) reconstructed the author's *Vorlagen*, arguing that a single christological credal confession (*Bekenntnis*) underlay 1.20 and 3.18-19, 22, while a separate hymn (*Lied*) was adapted in 2.21-24. Bultmann's attempts to separate out fragments of tradition from the author's own contributions are, as he partly acknowledges, somewhat speculative, relying on distinctions between what is poetic and prosaic, and on assumptions as to how symmetrical and rhythmic an original creed or song would be. Nonetheless, the observation that these passages contain traditional material seems well founded, and their content per se makes them important sources of the author's (and his predecessors' and contemporaries') messianic convictions.

The first such text, 1.18-21, begins with a statement about the readers' redemption (ἐλυτρώθητε). Their purchase – for this is the metaphor of redemption here – has been made not with silver or gold, but 'with the precious blood of Christ, like that of a flawless and faultless lamb' (1.19).[24] John Elliott (2000: 374) notes the similarities of language here with Heb. 9.12-14: both texts, without any direct dependence, use the language and imagery of Israel's sacrificial cult (cf.

---

23 Debate continues concerning the authorship of this letter, with a range of possibilities: that Peter wrote it; that Silvanus (5.12) acted as secretary and wrote it, with or without Peter's direct guidance; that a Petrine circle produced it; or that it is pseudonymous.

24 Cf. Elliott 2000: 354, 375, for the translation 'flawless and faultless'.

Exod. 24.3-8) to depict the redemptive achievements of the Messiah. The opening of 1 Peter has already made brief reference to another such image: the sprinkling of blood (1.2; cf. Exod. 24.8; Num. 19.4).

According to Bultmann's analysis (Bultmann 1967: 294), the credal material proper is contained in v. 20, where two well-known christological motifs are found: that of the Messiah's being 'foreordained (προεγνωσμένου) before the foundation of the world' (cf. Jn 17.24; with echoes of the Wisdom tradition, e.g., Prov. 8.23; Sir. 24.9) and 'made manifest (φανερωθέντος) in these last times' (cf. Rom. 16.26; Col. 1.26; 1 Tim. 3.16; 2 Tim. 1.10). These ideas are also paralleled in Jewish texts that suggest belief in the pre-existence of the Messiah, hidden before his coming, or return.[25] For Bultmann (1967: 295), v. 20 provided the beginning of the credal tradition that then continued in 3.18, though the following verse (1.21) also contains material central to early Christian faith: that God raised the Messiah from death and glorified him (cf. Acts 2.36; Rom. 1.4; Phil. 2.9-11, etc.).

If a key point in 1.18-21 is the notion of the Messiah's pre-existence, or at least, his pre-creation conception in the divine purpose,[26] then the second traditional section, 2.21-25, focuses on the sufferings of Christ, presenting him as a model for discipleship, specifically for slaves suffering under wicked masters (2.18-21). As Achtemeier (1999: 147) notes, the Isaianic suffering servant material (52.13–53.12, esp. 53.3-12) is here clearly and explicitly used messianically, compared with its surprisingly restricted use elsewhere in the New Testament (Achtemeier notes Mt. 8.17; Mk 10.45; Lk. 22.37; Acts 8.32-33; Rom. 4.25a: 'The fullest citation is Acts 8.32-33, and while it is understood to refer to Jesus, it receives no further explication. When Luke does come to describe the Passion, he ignores the Isaianic material').[27] Isaiah's language is drawn on to depict the Messiah's sufferings as redemptive: he bears his people's sins in his own body on the cross; his wounds bring healing to others. As with Hebrews, though depicted here in distinctive ways, the model of redemption is sacrificial and vicarious. We may note some contrast of emphasis here, compared to the generally more participatory model which seems to dominate Paul's thought, with its theme of suffering and dying *with* Christ, though images of sacrificial atonement are also used.[28] But 1 Peter and Hebrews are also clear, as is Paul, that the suffering of Christ marks a way for his disciples to follow.

In arriving at 3.18-22, the third of the credal christological sections, we arrive at probably the most enigmatic text in 1 Peter, and among the more enigmatic in the New Testament, the details of which, especially in vv. 19-21, cannot concern us here.[29] We find the gist of previous christological sections recapitu-

---

25 See *2 Bar.* 30.1; *Pss. Sol.* 18.5; *1 En.* 46.1-4; 48.2-6; 62.7; *4 Ezra* 7.28-29; 12.31-34; 13.26. The relevance of some of these texts depends on the conclusion that the Son of Man in *1 Enoch* is identified with the Messiah; see further Charlesworth 1992: 29–30; VanderKam 1992.

26 Windisch 1930: 57 comments: 'Natürlich ist Christus auch persönlich präexistent gedacht (φανερωθέντος)'.

27 Achtemeier 1999: 147. Peter Doble 2006 has recently suggested that the Psalms are more likely Luke's source for the idea of a Davidide who suffers 'according to the Scriptures'. On the subject of Isaiah 53 in the New Testament, see further Bellinger and Farmer 1998.

28 Cf., on Paul, Sanders 1977: 467–8; Hooker 1990: 26–41.

29 Achtemeier 1996: 240 describes it as 'the most difficult passage in the entire letter', though Norbert Brox 1979: 196 regards 4.6 as 'noch dunkler'.

lated (he suffered once for sins, the righteous for the unrighteous), before we move to the depiction of Christ's 'journey' in the Spirit. William Dalton 1989 has made a convincing case that the journey here is not a 'descent into hell' in the days between death and resurrection, but rather a post-resurrection journey of ascent, as the risen and vindicated Christ ascends to his place at God's right hand. On this journey, Christ made announcement (κηρύσσω, not εὐαγγελίζω) of his victory to the imprisoned spirits – the wicked angels of Gen. 6.1-4 (cf. *1 En.* 6-16), so Dalton again convincingly argues – and now sits at God's right hand, with 'angels, authorities, and powers made subject to him' (3.22, NRSV). This description of the Messiah's triumph, as Bultmann (1967: 290) notes, parallels other early Christian depictions (1 Cor. 15.25-28; Eph. 1.10; Phil. 2.9-11; 3.21; Col. 2.15) – though Bultmann, with a now outdated notion of Gnosticism's influence on New Testament texts, sees this cosmic depiction of Christ's work of redemption as a 'charakteristisch gnostische Auffassung'. Its focus on the vindication and enthronement of the Messiah places it in logical connection with 1.18-21 and 2.21-25, since the three texts in order highlight Christ's pre-existence and incarnation (1.20), his suffering and death (2.21-25), and his glorious vindication (3.22; cf. Horrell 1998: 69).

What this leaves out of the picture is 2.4-10, aptly described by Richard Bauckham (1988: 310) as 'a particularly complex and studied piece of exegesis'. There are two key themes in this section: Jesus as the precious and elect stone, and the church as the elect and holy people of God (see also Elliott 1966). Both themes are introduced in vv. 4-5, two verses which serve to summarize and encapsulate the substance of the midrashic material in vv. 6-10, where the Old Testament texts are cited and interpreted. Three texts cited in vv. 6-8 are linked together by the catchword λίθος: Isa. 28.16; Ps. 118.22; Isa. 8.14. The author of 1 Peter is hardly being innovative in reading these texts messianically; they are already cited as messianic texts elsewhere in the New Testament (Mk 12.10-11 and par.; Rom. 9.32-33; cf. Acts 4.11).[30] Nonetheless, in drawing the three texts together – uniquely in the New Testament – and weaving them into this rich exposition of christological and ecclesiological identity, the author of 1 Peter makes a significant contribution to the development and expression of Christian messianism.

In this brief sketch of some of the key messianic texts in 1 Peter we have already seen something of the images of redemption which the author uses. The readers of the epistle have been purchased by the precious blood of Christ. They have been purchased from what the author denotes as their futile ways – one indication that the addressees are probably (mostly) Gentiles (1.14, 18; 4.2-4) – in order that they might attain salvation on the last day, which is coming soon (1.5-9). This sure and certain hope of redemption, again set in an imminent eschatological framework, is the basis for hope and joy, despite suffering.

Indeed, as with James and Hebrews, it is clear that the letter's addressees are suffering; this theme is especially evident in 1 Peter. To what extent the nature and causes of suffering are the same across all three texts is harder to discern,

---

30 There are also some parallels in the use of such imagery to express eschatological expectations about the community at Qumran (see e.g. 1QS 8.4-8, with clear allusion to Isa. 28.16; 4QpIs[d]; Elliott 1966: 26–33; Best 1969).

not least since the provenance and date of James in particular are uncertain. Sporadic and informal hostility against Christians, sometimes involving Jews, sometimes not, is evidently prevalent from the earliest days (e.g. Acts 8.1-3; 2 Cor. 11.23-25; 1 Thess. 1.6; 2.14; Rev. 2.13), and Roman magistrates sometimes became involved (Acts 16.16-40; 17.5-9; 18.12-17). The situation for the addressees of Hebrews is apparently one in which martyrdom is not yet (or currently) a reality (Heb. 12.4). The situation depicted by 1 Peter, I would argue (see Horrell, forthcoming), is one in which suffering arises not only from general and informal public hostility but also from the Roman judgement of Christianity as essentially seditious and criminal; a judgement, probably dating from Nero's time,[31] which could lead, when the process of personal accusation brought Christians before the courts, to punishment and execution (1 Pet. 4.16; Pliny *Ep.* 10.96–7).

But how does the author of 1 Peter urge Christians to respond to this suffering, and can the letter be seen in any sense as promoting resistance? The contrasting arguments and ensuing debate of David Balch (1981, 1986) and John Elliott (1981, 1986) illustrate the difficulties here. While Balch sees the letter, and specifically its household code (2.11–3.12), as promoting a strategy of assimilation to society, in order to lessen hostility and criticism, Elliott insists that the letter reflects and reinforces the distinct identity of members of a 'conversionist sect', and thus deliberately resists and opposes pressures to conform. In assessing the letter's stance on conformity and resistance, we must first acknowledge that, unlike in James or Hebrews, there is material in 1 Peter that draws on the Pauline tradition in urging believers to respectful submission to authority in the spheres of both empire and household (1 Pet. 2.13, 18, 3.1; cf. Rom. 13.1-7; Col. 3.18–4.1, etc.). As feminist critics have forcefully shown, such teaching is at least in danger of ideologically legitimating the suffering of the weak, of abused wives and beaten slaves, suggesting that their Christ-like duty is uncomplaining loyalty, even to their abusers (see esp. Corley 1995).

At the same time, and bearing Scott's work in mind, an assessment of the letter's message in its original historical setting can discern that, in calling for quiet submission and outward conformity, it represents a strategy for survival in a hostile world (Carter 2004: 31–3) and a means by which certain forms of 'witness' can be sustained (cf. 2.12; 3.1, 15, etc.). Scott's work in particular should warn us against seeing rebellion and resistance only in texts and communities that are blatantly and overtly opposed to the established powers in the world. More usual, but no less forms of resistance, are modes of communication and action that subtly and changeably weave resistance into what is in various other respects a discourse of conformity and obedience. Indeed, the conformity 1 Peter urges does not 'go all the way' (*pace* Carter 2004); rather, it encourages its readers to retain precisely that confession on which hostility is focused: their allegiance to the Messiah, Χριστός, which leads to their public labelling and punishment as Χριστιανοί (4.16). This loyalty to Christ entails alienation from the world, and just as the hostility and persecution aims to persuade Christians to abandon this

---

31   Cf. de Ste. Croix 1963: 8; Frend 2000: 821, 835; Giovannini 1996.

loyalty – cursing Christ and offering sacrifice to the Roman gods and the emperor are, after all, sufficient to ensure pardon (Pliny, *Ep.* 96.5–7; 97.2) – so the letter seeks to sustain and reinforce resistance to this pressure to conform, even and particularly when it leads to suffering and death. In Scott's terms, we have here a form of resistance that is not only covert, but has been uncovered and brought into the public sphere. The official 'transcript' presented by the empire requires a level of obeisance to the emperor and the Roman gods which Christians are not prepared to give; their guilt is indicated positively by the resistant confession *Christianus sum*, and negatively by a refusal to offer sacrifice to the gods and the emperor. What probably remains 'hidden', at least much of the time, is the fuller discourse and worldview which sustains such resistance, of which we have seen glimpses in all three of our selected letters: that a time is coming soon when God – or specifically his Messiah – will come in judgement, to deal decisively with the wicked and to bring salvation to those who have suffered patiently.[32]

---

[32] I am very grateful to James Crossley and Francesca Stavrakopoulou, as well as to the Editors, for their comments on an earlier draft of this essay.

Chapter 10

THE APOCALYPSE

Paul Spilsbury

The book of Revelation gives powerful and poignant expression to the hopes and fears of Christians living in the cities of Asia (Rev. 1.4, 11) in the declining years of the first century.[1] The book is pervaded by an air of doom (e.g. 2.2, 10, 13, 19; 3.3, 10, 19; 6.9, 11; 7.14–17; 12.11; 13.10; 14.12; 18.24; 20.4), and while it is difficult to assess the nature of references to suffering and martyrdom,[2] it seems clear that the anticipation of such is a key datum of John's outlook and mindset.[3] As Thompson has shown, 'John *encourages* his audience to see themselves in conflict with society; such conflict is part of his vision of the world' (Thompson 1990: 174, emphasis original). There is little doubt that John interpreted the source of the troubles he foresaw as stemming ultimately from the cosmic and primordial hostility of Satan (Yarbro Collins 1976a) and, further, that the primary manifestation of this hostility in the historical sphere was the imperial and religious institutions of Rome as they were experienced in the urban centres of Asia Minor (Thompson 1990: 174). The dragon, the enemy of the messiah and of the followers of the Lamb, is identified as 'that ancient serpent, who is called the Devil and Satan, the deceiver of the whole world' (Rev. 12.9). In the process of making war against 'those who keep the commandments of God and hold the testimony of Jesus' (Rev. 12.17), the dragon appears to summon from the sea and from the earth two beasts who are to work in unholy tandem to fulfil the dragon's hostile designs against the saints. The first beast, from the sea, is described in terms powerfully reminiscent of the four beasts of Daniel 7, including the blasphemous 'little horn' (Dan. 7.8) whose hubris is eventually condemned before the throne of the Ancient of Days (Dan. 7.9-11). As in Daniel (7.17), the beast in the Apocalypse stands for a human kingdom granted rule over the earth for a set period of time, though now it is clear that Rome is in view.[4] A similar application of Daniel's vision to Rome

---

1 For discussions of dating and provenance of the book of Revelation, see Aune 1997–8: 1.lvi–lxx; Court 1979: 125–38; Sweet 1979: 21–7; Thompson 1990: 13–15; and Yarbro Collins 1984: 58–64, among others.
2 On whether, and in what sense, references to crisis in apocalyptic literature reflect historical circumstances, see the discussion in Thompson 1990: 25–34.
3 A. Yarbro Collins has written on the notion of 'perceived crisis' as a way of understanding John's mindset. Only those in John's social setting who shared his point of view would have experienced a sense of crisis akin to his (Yarbro Collins 1984: 165). See also Hurtado 2003: 594.
4 John was by no means alone in identifying the fourth beast of Daniel with Rome. For a convenient summary of ancient interpretations of the four kingdoms, see J. J. Collins 1993a: 166–70.

is found in John's contemporary, Flavius Josephus, who speaks of empire (ἡ ἀρχή) being passed from one nation to another and currently resting over Rome (*J. W.* 5.367).[5] Unlike Josephus, who saw divine legitimacy in Rome's rise to power, John saw the beast's rule as diabolical (Rev. 13.4) and a dire threat to followers of the messiah, for 'it was allowed to make war on the saints and to conquer them' (Rev. 13.7).[6] Alongside this beast the second one, arising out of the earth (Rev. 13.11), is referred to as 'the false prophet' (Rev. 16.13; 19.20; 20.10). Already in chapter 13 one of its primary characteristics is its ability to deceive the inhabitants of earth (Rev. 13.14). The historical point of reference for this beast would seem to be the priesthood of the imperial cult (Aune 1997–8: 2.756; Thompson 1990: 164),[7] whose role, as John sees it, is to 'make the earth and its inhabitants worship the first beast' (Rev. 13.12). It causes ordinary people to regard the first beast in such a way that 'any deviation or counter-attraction is regarded as strange, antisocial and to be repudiated' (Rowland 1997: 184). It also has the power to require people to be branded with a mark, with dire economic consequences for those who demurred. Here John may have been alluding to trade guilds, with their religious basis for membership (Hemer 1986: 108–9; Aune 1997–8: 2.768), but even more than that, he saw the mark of the beast as an evil parody of the seal of the living God (Rev. 7.2-3) with which the servants of the living God are sealed (O'Donovan 1996: 154).

Messiah in the Apocalypse

It is in this conflicted atmosphere that John puts forward his powerful construction of Jesus the messiah. In a world riven by cosmic conflict God's anointed must necessarily be cast in terms suitable to the task. Accordingly, John's portrayal of the messiah is both rich and complex not only for the way that it weaves together 'mythic' and 'historic' realities along with intertextual allusions from a wide range of sources, but also for the quality of religious experience that it draws upon. John claims to have been 'in the spirit' (Rev. 1.10; cf. 4.2; 17.3; 21.10) when he saw and heard the things that are recorded in this book, and the work's most sublime visions of heavenly worship evoke the liturgical rhythms of the community of faith.[8] John's vision calls on his readers to see what cannot be

---

5   On the importance of the book of Daniel for Josephus' understanding of history, see Mason 1994 and Spilsbury 2003. Josephus read Daniel in such a way as to give legitimacy to Roman power. A similar attitude to ruling authorities may be discerned in Wis. 6.1-3; Rom. 13.1-7; and 1 Pet. 2.13-17.
6   A similar reading of Daniel may be discerned at Qumran, on which see Brooke 1991.
7   On the strength of the imperial cult in Asia Minor in general, and in the seven churches of the Apocalypse in particular, see Friesen 2001: 25–103; Price 1984; Thompson 1990: 158–64. Price, followed by Thompson, argues that for Christians it was sacrificing in general, whether to the emperor or the traditional gods, that was the issue, not necessarily (or even primarily) sacrificing to the emperor. On the extent to which Christian affirmations about Christ were formulated in opposition to the imperial cult, see Horbury 1998c: 68–77.
8   On the impact of John's religious experience and the context of worship, see Barker 2000: 62–4; Friesen 2001: 194–209; and Vanni 1999. On the importance of early Christian religious experience more generally, see Hurtado 2003.

138 Redemption and Resistance

seen. He calls on them to listen to the words of the Spirit. Despite our remove from John's ecstasy and the sense that this sometimes gives of being at arm's length from his meaning, there remain numerous possible lines of approach that might be taken in our attempt to begin to understand the Apocalypse. In the study that follows I have chosen to focus on the word χριστός as a 'way in' to the labyrinth of Revelation's world of signification. I do this not at all because the subject of messiah is thereby exhausted, but because it is perhaps as effective a way as any other to the very heart of the matter. In John's usage the term appears three times as a personal name (1.1, 2, 5), and four times (11.15; 12.10; 20.4, 6) as a title, for a total of seven uses. Given the obvious importance of this number for John as a symbol of completeness or perfection (Sweet 1979: 14–15), it would be remiss of us to focus on the titular usages alone. As we shall see, John's use of the term χριστός provides cohesiveness and balance to the portrayal of the messiah in the Apocalypse.[9]

Revelation 1.1-2

In the opening sentence, where 'Christ' twice occurs as a proper name, the messiah is presented as a *mediator of divine mysteries*. The 'revelation' to which the book's title refers is given to him so that he might make it known to his servants.[10] The sequence of communication that starts with God and passes through Jesus Christ and 'his angel' to the seer (Carrell 1997: 112; Bauckham 1993a: 243–66) is alluded to again in chapter 10 when a 'mighty angel' hands a scroll to John.[11] Echoes of Ezekiel 1–3 invite readers to see Revelation 10 as a continuation of chapter 5 so that the scroll that was described as 'sealed with seven seals' (an innovation derived partly from the book of Daniel)[12] in chapter 5 is open in the hand of the angel in chapter 10 (Rev. 10.2, 8), and ready to be given to John. Also in chapter 5, John had described how the Lamb 'went and took the scroll from the right hand of the one who was seated on the throne', and broke its seals (chapter 6, 8.1).

The closing statements of the book are also relevant to this discussion. Here both the angel and Jesus make reference to their role in the process of revelation.[13] In 22.6 the angel states: 'These words are trustworthy and true, for the Lord, the God of the spirits of the prophets, has sent his angel to show his servants what must soon take place.' The phrase δεῖξαι τοῖς δούλοις αὐτοῦ ἃ δεῖ γενέσθαι ἐν τάχει,[14] is an echo of the opening sentence of the Apocalypse, where it is ascribed

---

9   For the use of the term χριστός as a title and as a name, see Horbury 1998c and Hurtado 2003.
10 I take 'of Jesus Christ' in the phrase ἀποκάλυψις Ἰησοῦ Χριστοῦ to be a subjective genitive on the basis of the subsequent phrase 'which God gave to him'. See Aune 1997–8.
11 Bauckham 1993a: 243–57 follows Mazzaferri 1989 in arguing that the 'little scroll' of Rev. 10.2 is to be identified with the sealed scroll in Rev. 5.1. Aune's arguments against this thesis do not seem convincing (Aune 1997–8).
12 See Dan. 8.26; 12.4 in which the divine revelation is sealed up for the time of the end.
13 On the 'revealing angel' in the book of Revelation, see further Carrell 1997.
14 Cf. Rev. 4.1, '... I will show you what must take place after this'.

to Jesus Christ. In the present context, though, no reference is made to the role of the messiah in the mediation of the divine message.[15] Indeed, in all six of the other occurrences of the verb δείκνυμι, 'to show', in the book (Rev. 4.1[16]; 17.1; 21.9, 10; 22.1, 8) an angel is the subject of the action. However, in Rev. 22.16 Christ himself states, 'It is I, Jesus, who sent *my* angel to you with this testimony for the churches' (emphasis added). In this passage Christ is not so much the mediator of the message as its source. Also, the reference to 'my angel' is distinctive, and an indication of the close association in the Apocalypse between Christ and God, for in Rev. 22.6, which we have just cited, we are told that it was 'the Lord, the God of the spirits of the prophets' who sent 'his angel' to communicate with John. Further, the reference to the seven churches harks back to the opening verse of the book in which we are told that Jesus has made known the divine message by sending 'his angel' to his servant John.[17]

This ambiguity regarding whose angel it was suggests at the very least a close association in John's mind between Christ and God. Further, the phrase 'my angel' emphasizes the subordination of the angel to Christ (Carrell 1997: 121; cf. Heb. 1.5-14; 2.5-9). This point is also implied in the vision of the exalted Christ in 1.12-20 in which he is depicted holding the angels of the seven churches in his right hand (20), and later directing John to write to each of them. The oracles to the seven churches that follow, in chapters 2 and 3, are thus represented as the direct words of Christ – a move that 'indicates a profound inclusion of Jesus within the sphere of action otherwise restricted to God' (Hurtado 2003: 591; see also Vanni 1999: 615). It would seem, therefore, that John has made a special effort to delineate the relative status of Christ and the angel in the mediation of the divine message. While it is apparent that they share certain functions, and can sometimes be spoken of in the same terms,[18] there remains a qualitative difference between the two that is made still clearer in the twin passages (Rev. 19.10; 22.8-9) in which John foolishly attempts to worship his angelic interpreter but is prevented from doing so.[19] This prohibition is in striking contrast to the worship of the Lamb in chapter 5 (Rev. 5.11-14) and the inclusion of the Lamb on the throne of God in chapter 22 (Rev. 22.3; cf. 21.22).[20]

---

15   On this point, see Stuckenbruck 1995.
16   There is some question about the identity of the voice in 4.1 that summons John through the open door into heaven, on which, see Aune 1997–8 and Carrell 1997.
17   The subject of the verb σημαίνειν 'to make known', could be either God or Jesus Christ, but it is most likely that 'Jesus Christ' is intended (Aune 1997–8). In Rev. 12.7 Michael is also said to have angels, and together they war against the dragon and his angels (12.7, 9).
18   On the angelomorphic aspects of the Christology of the Apocalypse, see Carrell 1997 and Stuckenbruck 1995. On the connection between angel-Christology and messianism more generally, see Horbury 1998c: 119–27.
19   Bauckham 1993a: 118–49 has shown that angelic refusal of veneration is a recurring theme in Second Temple and early Christian literature. On this theme see also Stuckenbruck 1995: 75–103.
20   On these passages, see Bauckham 1993a: 133–40; also Stuckenbruck 1995: 245–61 and Hurtado 2003: 590–4.

Revelation 1.4-5a

The next reference to 'Christ' is in the epistolary greeting, where John conveys to his readers grace from God, from 'the seven spirits who are before his throne', and from 'Jesus Christ' (Rev. 1.4-5). Leaving aside the difficult reference to the seven spirits,[21] we have in the association of Christ with God as *a source of divine grace* a formulation already familiar to us from other documents in the New Testament (Rom. 1.7; 1 Cor. 1.3; 2 Cor. 1.2; Eph. 1.2; Phil. 1.2; 1 Tim. 1.2; Tit. 1.4; Phlm. 1.3; 2 Jn 3; see also 2 Pet. 1.2). John goes further, though, by adding a series of laudatory epithets to the name of Jesus that become important thematically later in the Apocalypse: Christ is 'the faithful witness' (ὁ μάρτυς ὁ πιστός), the 'firstborn from the dead' (ὁ πρωτότοκος τῶν νεκρῶν), and the 'ruler of the kings of the earth' (ὁ ἄρχων τῶν βασιλέων τῆς γῆς) (Rev. 1.5). Each of these titles echoes and transforms phrases in Ps. 89 [LXX 88], a messianic psalm (cf. Ps. 89.20, 38 [LXX 88.21, 39]) that, in turn, echoes Nathan's oracle to David (2 Sam. 7).

The theme of *faithful witness* is particularly rich and complex in John's vision (Dehandschutter 1980; Bauckham 1993b: 72–3; Bredin 2003: 159–171; Sweet 1981), and we will touch on only a few aspects here. In 3.14 the exalted Christ addressing the church in Laodicea identifies himself as 'the Amen, the faithful and true witness, the origin of God's creation'. 'Amen' is an allusion to Isa. 65.16 where it is a title for God (באלהי אמן, LXX τὸν θεὸν τὸν ἀληθινόν, NRSV 'the God of faithfulness') who stands as the guarantor of every oath or blessing in the land. Significantly, אמן is rendered throughout the LXX by both πιστός and ἀληθινός, both of which terms are used here by John, thus indicating that he intends the terms as a translation and interpretation of the Hebrew word (Aune 1997–8: 1.37). John evidently also took the term ναί, 'indeed', as a functional equivalent for ἀμήν as is indicated by their use together at the end of 1.7 (Aune 1997–8: 1.56). In Rev. 22.20 Jesus is identified as 'the one who testifies to these things' (ὁ μαρτυρῶν ταῦτα), followed by an oath beginning with ναί, and a response prefaced with ἀμήν. John has therefore assimilated God's role of guarantor of truth to Christ (Carrell 1997: 126–7). It is Christ who attests to the trustworthiness of the revelation (de Jonge 1980). It is important to note, further, that those who associate themselves with the messiah in the book of Revelation are said to be those who hold the testimony of Jesus (μαρτυρία Ἰησοῦ, Rev. 12.17; 19.10; cf. 1.9; 20.4). The messiah's testimony becomes theirs so that in chapter 11 two witnesses with characteristics of Moses and Elijah symbolize all those who follow Christ in resisting the lies, idolatry and corruption of evil forces in the world (Sweet 1981: 105–6). And, in the end, they shed their blood 'in the great city that is prophetically called Sodom and Egypt, where also their Lord was crucified' (Rev. 11.8). Thus to bear the witness of Jesus is to share his fate (Hays 1996: 179).

The second title ascribed to Christ in Rev. 1.5, ὁ πρωτότοκος, identifies Christ as *the pre-eminent one*, who, like the firstborn son in a family enjoyed primacy

---

21 The identity of the seven spirits has been argued for variously by Bauckham 1993a: 162–6; Aune 1997–8: 1.33–6; Horbury 1998c: 120–2; and Massyngberde Ford 1975: 19–20, among others.

of status and succession. It is probably in this sense that John applies to Jesus the term ἡ ἀρχὴ τῆς κτίσεως, 'the beginning of creation' in Rev. 3.14. Already in Col. 1.15 we have the identification of Christ as 'the firstborn of all creation' (πρωτότοκος πάσης κτίσεως). Aune suggests that the circulation of Colossians in the same region to which the Apocalypse was sent may account for this christological tradition in Revelation (Aune 1997–8: 1.38). This possibility would seem to be strengthened by the reference in Col. 1.18 to Christ as 'the beginning, the firstborn from the dead' (ἀρχή, πρωτότοκος ἐκ τῶν νεκρῶν), which provides an intertextual link between Rev. 3.14 and 1.5, where the messiah is also called firstborn 'from the dead'.

The identification of Christ as the resurrected one is carried forward at Rev. 1.18 where the glorious figure describes himself as 'the living one', and continues, 'I was dead, and see, I am alive forever and ever'. This last phrase echoes descriptions of God elsewhere in the Apocalypse (Rev. 4.9, 19; 10.6; 15.7). More than this, the close association with the notion of 'witness' with that of life from the dead in this context implies that 'witness' is already beginning to take on the sense of 'martyrdom' in John's understanding (Bredin 2003: 163).

The third title of Christ in 1.5, 'ruler of the kings of the earth', occurs only here in the Apocalypse, but is echoed in the phrase 'king of kings' (βασιλεὺς βασιλέων) used of the Lamb at Rev. 17.14, and of the rider on the white horse at 19.16. In both of these instances the title is combined with the similar title 'Lord of lords' (κύριος κυρίων), and is used in the context of the final battle between the messiah and the forces of the beast, themselves referred to as 'the kings of the whole world' (Rev. 16.14), or 'the kings of the earth' (Rev. 19.19). A related reference to the rule of the messiah is found in Rev. 12.5 where the son of the woman clothed in the sun is said to be destined 'to rule [or 'shepherd', ποιμαίνειν] all the nations with a rod of iron'. Here is a clear allusion to Ps. 2.9, which was already interpreted messianically in *Pss. Sol.* 17.23-24.[22] In Rev. 12.5 the emphasis is on the future since John adds to his source the word μέλλει, 'is about to', indicating the imminence and inevitability of the messiah's rule. The precise nature of that rule, however, is made clear only as the full implications of the image of the Lamb are assimilated, as we shall see.

Revelation 1.5b-6

Rev. 1.5b-6 is a doxology, *ascribing glory and eternal dominion* to the messiah.[23] Elsewhere in the New Testament, doxologies are typically directed to God,[24] though later in Revelation a doxology is addressed to God and to the Lamb (Rev. 5.13). In 1.5b-6 the doxology is addressed to Christ alone (cf. 2 Tim. 4.18; 2 Pet.

---

22 Further allusions to Psalm 2 may be present at 2.18, 26-28; 11.15, 18; 12.10; 14.1; 16.14, 16; 19.15, on which see Bauckham 1993b: 69–70.
23 On doxologies in early Christian and Jewish literature, see the discussion in Aune 1997–8: 1.43–6.
24 Rom. 9.5 may be punctuated in such a way as to make it a doxology to Christ. On this passage see further Dunn 1988: 535–6 and Fitzmyer 1993b: 548–9, among others.

3.18) suggesting that John and his churches practised the worship of Jesus in a form usually reserved for the one true God alone.[25]

Something else that is distinctive about this doxology is its inclusion of a brief narrative of salvation history in the form of two compound statements identifying the messiah as *the agent of redemption* in the world. In the first of these statements Christ is praised as the one 'who loved us and freed us from our sins by his blood' (ἐν τῷ αἵματι αὐτοῦ), and in the second he is said to have 'made us to be a kingdom, priests serving his God and Father' (cf. Gal. 2.20; Eph. 5.2). John's statement that the messiah 'freed us' (λύσαντι) is unique in the New Testament (Aune 1997–8: 1.47; Carnegie 1982: 250). However, other statements associated with the Lamb later in Revelation are functional equivalents: in 5.9 the heavenly worship sings, 'You are worthy ... for you were slaughtered and by your blood (ἐν τῷ αἵματί σου) you ransomed (ἠγόρασας) for God saints from every tribe and language and people and nation'. In Rev. 14.4 the Lamb's followers are referred to as those who have been 'redeemed (ἠγοράσθησαν) from humankind as first-fruits of God and the Lamb', while in 7.14 they are said to have 'washed their robes and made them white in the blood of the Lamb' (ἐν τῷ αἵματι τοῦ ἀρνίου). These statements emphasize the sacrificial aspect of the image of the Lamb in the Apocalypse (Guthrie 1994: 400), and in particular its association with the biblical story of the Passover and the Exodus from Egypt.[26] Indeed, the biblical story of the escape from Egypt, the passage through the Red Sea, and the flight into the wilderness provides the framework for the narrative of salvation in Revelation (Bauckham 1993b: 70–2). John effectively presents salvation as an escape from hostile powers that continue to pursue those associated with the Lamb (see Rev. 12.13-17). The current status of the 'ransomed' is nourishment in the wilderness, and the goal of salvation is the holy city still awaiting in the eschatological future.

Numerous other echoes of the Exodus story resound throughout the book of Revelation (e.g. Rev. 2.14; 9.3-6; 11.8; 12.14; 15.3; 16. 2, 4, 10-13, 17-21), not the least of which is the second statement of the doxology in which the messiah is said to have 'made us to be a kingdom, priests serving his God and Father' (cf. 1.6; Exod. 19.6). Taken together these allusions create a literary atmosphere that seems to invite readers to interpret the events of the Apocalypse and of their own experience in the light of the Exodus. However, the association of the Lamb with the paschal lamb does not preclude other associations of the image. In 6.15-16 the people of the earth[27] appeal to the mountains and the rocks to fall on them and to hide them from 'the face of the one seated on the throne and from the wrath of the Lamb'.[28] The paradoxical juxtaposition of 'wrath' and 'Lamb' points to a reinterpretation of the working of divine judgement in the world, not

---

25 For differing construals of this phenomenon, see Bauckham 1993b: 118–49 and Hurtado 2003: 590–4.

26 However, note that in Rev. 1.13 Christ's appearance implies that he is himself a high priest, i.e. the one who offers the sacrifice (Vanni 1999: 613).

27 The seven categories of persons referred to in 6.15 indicate that the wrath of the Lamb applies to all of humanity (Vanni 1999: 607).

28 On a similar emphasis on the messiah as judge at Qumran, see the discussion in Horbury 1998c: 59–63.

through violent revenge, but through the suffering witness of Jesus (Bredin 2003: 195). Nevertheless, the association with wrath continues in 14.10 when those who had worshipped the beast are destined to be 'tormented with fire and sulphur in the presence of the holy angels and in the presence of the Lamb'. Then in 17.14 the kings of the earth wage war against the Lamb, but the outcome of the battle is that 'the Lamb will conquer them, for he is the Lord of lords and the King of kings'. The Lamb in this scene is identical with the rider on the white horse[29] in chapter 19 from whose mouth comes a sharp sword 'with which to strike down the nations', (19.15) and who will 'tread the wine press of the fury of the wrath of God the almighty' (cf. Rev. 14.19-20). These images suggest that the Lamb cannot be separated from themes of divine wrath, or eschatological victory over the forces of evil,[30] but Bredin has shown that even here traditional motifs of divine violence have been transformed by the eirenic power of Jesus' sacrificial death, for the rider overcomes not by brute force but by the power of righteousness, faithfulness and truth (Bredin 2003: 203–5). Bauckham and Hart suggest that violent images of holy war be taken as 'imaginative expressions' of the hope that God will eventually remove all evil from the world (Bauckham and Hart 1999: 140). In another context Bauckham argues that the unveiling of the slaughtered Lamb in chapter 5 as the one worthy to open the scroll profoundly reinterprets and modifies the traditional presentation of the messiah as a violent figure (Bauckham 1993a: 179–85). Also, those who associate themselves with the messiah in the book of Revelation are called, not to militarism (see Rev. 13.10b 'if you kill with the sword, with the sword you must be killed'), but to self-sacrifice in imitation of Jesus. It is no coincidence that just as the Lamb had been 'slaughtered' (Rev. 5.6, 9, 12; 13.8), so too the martyrs are described this way in 6.9 where the sacrificial aspect of their deaths is implied by their location 'under the altar' (see also Rev. 7.14; 11.7). Further, insofar as the followers of the messiah share in his victory, they do so through their own suffering witness, as is indicated most clearly in Rev. 12.11, where they are proclaimed to have overcome the dragon 'by the blood of the Lamb and the word of their testimony for they did not cling to their life even in the face of death'.

Revelation 11.15 and 12.10

The next two references to the messiah in the book of Revelation belong together in that they both take the titular form τοῦ Χριστοῦ αὐτοῦ, 'his messiah', evoking Old Testament passages about God's anointed ones, the kings of Israel (e.g. 1 Sam. 12.3; Pss. 2.2; 18.51; 20.7; 28.8; 83.10; 89.39, 52; 132.10, 17). Both passages (Rev. 11.15; 12.10-12; cf. 7.10) in which this phrase occurs in Revelation are victory songs (Yarbro Collins 1976; Jörns 1971: 110–20). In 11.15 heavenly voices respond to the blowing of the seventh trumpet by proclaiming: 'The kingdom of the world has become the kingdom of our Lord and of his Messiah,

---

29 On the identity of the rider, see Bredin 2003: 200–16 and Carrell 1997: 196–219.
30 Other aspects of the Lamb's identity and function are indicated by its seven eyes and seven horns (Rev. 5.6), on which see e.g. Caird 1966: 75.

and he will reign forever and ever'. The singular verb βασιλεύσει,[31] 'he will reign', instead of a verb in the plural, raises the possibility that the phrase 'and his messiah' is an interpolation (Aune 1997–8: 2.639). However, similarly anomalous grammar occurs elsewhere in the Apocalypse (e.g. Rev. 22.3-4), and may be an indication that John thought of God and Christ together as a unity (Bauckham 1993b: 60–1; Carrell 1997: 114–15, 120). Bauckham states, further, that '[John] places Christ on the divine side of the distinction between God and creation, but he wishes to avoid ways of speaking which sound to him as polytheistic' (Bauckham 1993b: 61). It is possible, therefore, that in 11.15, too, John intentionally groups the messiah together with God in the statement 'he will reign forever and ever'. If that is so, this passage should be viewed together with those other places in the Apocalypse in which John depicts the worship of the messiah along with God (e.g. Rev. 1.5b-6; 5.8-14). It should also be noted that the motif of reigning corresponds to the royal connotations of the phrase 'his messiah' noted above. It seems clear, therefore, that John intended his readers to understand that the messiah is *a kingly figure* whose reign, which is at the same time the reign of God (de Jonge 1980: 270), will have no end. More than that, the messiah is presented as the bringer of the eschatological kingdom – the one who will establish the kingdom of God in the world.

The second use of the phrase τοῦ Χριστοῦ αὐτοῦ occurs in Rev. 12.10 in what is a heavenly proclamation of victory, this time in response to the expulsion from heaven of the dragon and its angels. The celestial voice shouts: 'Now have come the salvation and the power and the kingdom of our God and the authority of his Messiah, for the accuser of our comrades has been thrown down'. Here again is a reference to the arrival of the kingdom of God, linked this time with the distinctive phrase, 'the authority (ἡ ἐξουσία) of his Messiah', which is used only here in the Apocalypse. In 2.26 the risen Christ promises: 'To everyone who conquers and continues to do my works to the end, I will give authority over the nations; to rule them with an iron rod as when clay pots are shattered' (see also Rev. 2.28; 11.3, 6). The allusion to Ps. 2.8-9 in this statement is significant because elsewhere in Revelation echoes from this psalm apply to Christ himself (19.15).[32] In contrast to these references, in chapter 13 the dragon gives to the beast 'his throne and great authority', (Rev. 13.2) and the people of the world worship the dragon 'for he had given his authority to the beast' (Rev. 13.4; cf. 13.5, 7, 12; 17.12, 13). Messianic and diabolical authority are thus opposed to each other as rival forms of power in the world.[33] Yet, whereas the beast's authority is based on brute force, intimidation and exploitation of the peoples of the earth, the authority of the messiah is founded on the shed blood of the slaughtered lamb.

---

31   Strictly speaking the syntax of this sentence requires that ἡ βασιλεία, 'the kingdom', be taken as the subject of the verb βασιλεύσει (Aune 1997–8: 2.639). De Jonge 1980: 269–70 takes the subject to be 'God'. Vanni 1999: 608–11 argues that John's strained grammar is an indication of the ineffability of his mystical experience (cf. 2 Cor. 12.4).

32   Messianic interpretations of the psalm are also attested in *Pss. Sol.* 17.23-24; 1QSa 2.11–22; Acts 13.33; Heb. 1.5; 5.5; Justin *Dial.* 61.6; 88.8; 122.6.

33   On this point, see further Friesen 2001: 194–209. Horbury 1998c: 74–7 has shown that in this regard John's view is not unlike that of other Jewish responses to the imperial cult imposed in an absolute or oppressive way.

Revelation 20.4-6

The last two uses of χριστός occur in close proximity to each other in Revelation 20.4-6, in which John describes his vision of the millennial reign of the messiah and the resurrected martyrs. In both instances the term appears with the definite article, without modifiers. The first of these instances states that those who had refused to worship the beast or to be branded with its mark 'came to life and reigned with the messiah a thousand years' (Rev. 20.4, NRSV modified). After pronouncing a blessing on those thus raised from the dead, the text continues: 'Over these the second death has no power, but they will be priests of God and of the messiah, and they will reign with him a thousand years' (Rev. 20.6, NRSV modified). The reference to reigning priests in this passage evokes the promises of Exod. 19.6 (cf. Isa. 61.6) already alluded to in Rev. 1.6. What is distinctive here is the notion that the blessed martyrs will be priests not only of God, *but of the messiah as well*. Although the notion of priests *of* the messiah is not repeated elsewhere in Revelation, in the final vision of the book, the new Jerusalem is said to have no temple, 'for its temple is the Lord God the Almighty and the Lamb' (Rev. 21.22; see also v. 23). John's emphasis on the unmediated presence of God (Bauckham 1993b: 140–3) in the new Jerusalem may be at the heart of his depiction of the followers of the messiah as both his and God's priests. No priestly class is now needed to broker access to God's/the Lamb's presence. However, since God's/the Lamb's servants are said to 'see his face', and further that 'his name will be written on his forehead' (Rev. 22.4), they may in some sense be said to be high priests (Schüssler Fiorenza 1972: 388). Indeed, all who enter the city are 'priests who worship him and kings who reign with him' (Bauckham 1993b: 142). As Hurtado has noted, such language promotes both the intimate link between Jesus and God, and 'a corresponding devotional practice that reveres Jesus along with God' (Hurtado 2003: 594).

Conclusion

In a historical context characterized not only as impending crisis but, perhaps even more significantly, as the outworking of cosmic conflict between the One on the throne and the dragon, John presents to his readers a multi-layered and deeply textured picture of the messiah. It is a portrayal that resounds with echoes of the biblical tradition, the mythic stories of the Ancient Near East, and the political realities of the Roman province of Asia at the end of the first century. Using the literary power of apocalyptic, John presents the worshipping community with a messiah who has been transfigured. Here is a glorious divine personage in whose hands lie the destinies not only of the Christian churches for whom John functions as prophet, but of the world itself. The erstwhile teller of parables is now the revealer of divine mysteries and the guardian and guarantor of the true vision of God. The exorcist's skirmishes with the demonic once engaged round the Galilean countryside are now writ large on the canvas of the cosmos. Ancient hopes of a David-like king, the conqueror of armies and dispenser of divine judgement, have been both retained and transformed. As the agent of divine redemption the messiah is both king of kings and the slaughtered Lamb whose example stands as a challenge to all who would be identified with him to 'follow him wherever he goes' (cf. Rev. 14.4) – even into suffering and martyrdom, for it is only thus that any may hope to share in his victory over the forces of chaos and evil in the world. Thus, we see that Revelation's view of salvation is essentially eschatological because victory over the dragon, while affected in this life through suffering witness, is not realized till after the resurrection. It is only in the new heaven and new earth that the dragon's influence is finally removed. Ultimately the messiah is himself the subject of all Christian hopes, for when the saints enter the New Jerusalem they find there the throne of God and of the Lamb (Rev. 22.3), and that the Lamb's presence and his light (Rev. 21.23) are indistinguishable from God's.

Part III

Jewish and Christian Messianism in Contact and Controversy

Chapter 11

Messianism and Politics in the Land of Israel, 66–135 C.E.

Martin Goodman

At least one Jew in the land of Israel hoped quite explicitly in the late first century C.E. for a messiah to redeem Israel in the last days:

> Whereas you saw a man come up from the midst of the sea: the same is he whom God the Highest has kept a great season, which by his own self shall deliver his creature ... Behold, the days come, when the most High will begin to deliver them that are upon the earth ... And one shall undertake to fight against another, one city against another ... And the time shall be when these things shall come to pass, and the signs shall happen which I showed you before, and then shall my Son be declared, whom you saw as a man ascending. And when all the people hear his voice, every man shall in their own land leave the battle one against another ... But he shall stand upon the top of Mount Zion ... And this my Son shall rebuke the wicked inventions of those nations ...[1]

The author of this text, the apocalypse of *4 Ezra*, seems to have believed that the eschaton was now arrived. He was writing, probably in Hebrew, in the eighties or nineties of the first century C.E. in the immediate aftermath of the destruction of the Temple in 70.[2] This chapter will ask how many Jews in Judaea shared his beliefs about the imminent arrival of the messiah, and what impact such beliefs had on the political actions which led Judaean Jews into two disastrous wars against Rome, in 66–70 C.E. and 132–5 C.E.

Of the scholars who have argued that messianic ideas had a major influence on Jewish behaviour in this period, William Horbury has been among the most persuasive and learned.[3] It is certainly possible to argue, as he and others have done, that messianic ideas were so pervasive that it is legitimate to expect them to have played a part in fomenting Jewish rebellion, and that the fact that we can now in most cases reconstruct only a few elements of the specific messianic hopes that led to action – the naming of individuals as kings, irrational behaviour which suggests expectation of an imminent end to history, or other facets of the full narrative of the messianic age that can be put together by combining a large number of ancient sources – is only a result of the haphazard preservation of ancient evidence or, in some cases, the deliberate suppression by ancient Jewish authors of information about messianic expectation which they believed might prejudice the ability of Jews to live peacefully in a Gentile world.

1   *4 Ezra* 13.25-6, 29, 31-3, 35, 37.
2   On the date and original language of *4 Ezra*, see Nickelsburg 1981: 287–94; the dating of *2 Baruch*, which contains a number of messianic references, is less certain.
3   See especially Horbury 1998c.

But what I shall present here in tribute to William's scholarship is an alternative, minimalist view, in the hope that by establishing a minimum foundation of near-certainty on this topic, I may help to illuminate possible more maximalist interpretations. I shall attempt to distinguish the evidence for the availability of messianic ideas to Jews – that is, the fact that such ideas are attested in ancient sources – from the evidence that such ideas were adopted by anyone more than the writer of the document which survives, bearing in mind that each was preserved by a specific group in antiquity only because it was believed to be of religious importance. Secondly, and more difficult, I shall try to assess how central such beliefs were in the religious lives of the Jews who adopted them, attempting to strike a balance between the extreme view, sometimes adopted by Jacob Neusner, that what a text discusses constitutes its 'Judaism', so that the Mishnah is 'Judaism without Messiah',[4] and the contrary assumption that messianic hope, once present, *must* play a central role in religious and political life[5] – a view hard to sustain in the light of later Jewish history, in which messianic expectation has often been little more than a vague protestation of hope, in contrast to periods, such as the time of Shabbetai Zvi, when huge numbers of Jews were enthused by messianic fervour.[6] Finally, I shall investigate the evidence that any of these ideas had an impact on the political behaviour of Judaean Jews. In keeping with the minimalist approach, I shall concentrate only on those texts which refer to a messianic figure of some kind, leaving to one side evidence of more general concerns about the last days: that Jews were capable of eschatological speculation which had little to say about a messiah is evident from the apparent lack of reference to a messianic leader in the extensive depiction of the final battles in the War Scroll from Qumran.[7]

Even for a minimalist, there are prima facie reasons to believe that messianism played a central role in the political conflicts in Judaea in 66–70 and 132–5. Writing in the decade after the war of 66–70 had ended, Josephus, who had participated in the war both on the Jewish and on the Roman side, claimed that the Jews had been particularly led astray by 'an ambiguous oracle, found in their sacred texts' that a ruler would come from Judaea to rule the world.[8] And a text in the Jerusalem Talmud records that Rabbi Akiba, who lived through and suffered in, the revolt of 132–5, declared that the leader of the revolt, Shimon bar Kosiba, was the messiah.[9] In the light of such evidence, it might seem reasonable to put the onus on those who wish to argue against messianism as a cause of both revolts to prove their case.

That many Jews before 70 C.E. speculated in a great number of different ways about the nature of the messiah and the last days has been amply confirmed by the variety of messianic ideas found in the Dead Sea Scrolls, and there is no reason to posit a change in this variety after 70: some Jews doubtless abandoned

---

4 Neusner 1987.
5 See Gager 1998, on the messianic reflex.
6 Scholem 1973.
7 Collins 1995; Brooke 1998.
8 Josephus, *J.W.* 6.312–15.
9 *y. Ta'an.* 4.8, 24a.

Messianism and Politics in the Land of Israel, 66–135 C.E.   151

Judaism altogether as a result of the disaster, but in general it is an error to imagine that many instantly jettisoned their religious philosophies, and it is particularly unlikely that any Jew will have felt less strongly after 70 about the coming of a messiah, which one might expect to be more eagerly anticipated in the aftermath of defeat rather than less.[10] But in assessing the prevalence of continued speculation we are at the mercy of the later religious traditions which preserved all the extant Jewish literary material composed between 66 and 135. Most surviving Jewish writings from these years, such as *4 Ezra* and the works of Josephus, were preserved by Christians, whose own specific messianic concerns inevitably encouraged an interest in such texts.[11] By contrast, the rabbinic movement in the first two centuries C.E. preserved almost no traces of messianic speculation, so that (as we have seen) the Mishnah has been described as 'Judaism without Messiah',[12] but it is very uncertain how many Judaean Jews had contact with rabbinic circles even by the end of the second century, let alone before 135,[13] and the genre of halakhic compilations such as Mishnah and Tosefta did not encourage inclusion of theological ideas (although it may be more significant that in the extant manuscripts of the tannaitic midrashim on Exodus, Leviticus, Numbers and Deuteronomy no messianic interpretation is found of some of the biblical texts which were understood as messianic in other Jewish texts).[14] In principle it would be best to use contemporary documents as a check on the influence of these later traditions, but the contracts and other private documents found in the Judaean Desert caves, which provide much insight into Jewish law and custom in the period, reveal nothing about messianic hopes.[15]

Discerning the significance of speculation about the messiah is in any case difficult. Extensive speculation may have reflected either an urgent need to achieve clarity about the imminent last days or a general, more intellectual lack of certainty about a historical process whose outlines were generally accepted but whose details were shrouded in mystery. So, for instance, the lack of evidence for speculation by rabbinic Jews in this period may have been caused not by a lack of interest in the subject but by a consensus within the rabbinic movement about what the messiah would be like. By contrast, discerning the impact of messianic beliefs on behaviour in the Judaean revolts should in theory be more straightforward, since it was a characteristic of the Graeco-Roman historiographical tradition through which the narratives of these events are known to try to explain the political and military actions they described.

What, then, is the evidence that messianic hope encouraged Judaean Jews to rebel against Rome in 66–70 C.E.? It will be best to start with the 'ambiguous oracle' cited by Josephus: 'what especially incited them [the Jews] to the war was an ambiguous oracle, similarly found in their sacred writings, that at that time one from

---

10   On continuity after 70 C.E., see Goodman 1994.
11   See Green 1987.
12   See above n. 4.
13   Goodman 1983; Cohen 1999.
14   Note, for instance, the lack of any interpretation in *Sifre* to Numbers of the key messianic text in Num. 24.16-19.
15   On these texts, see Cotton 1998.

their country would rule the inhabited world. This they understood as referring to them, and many of the wise went astray in the interpretation of it, but in fact the oracle signified the hegemony of Vespasian, who was proclaimed emperor in Judaea.'[16] Josephus introduced this oracle into his history as a way of reassuring his readers that 'God cares for men' and had provided signs to enable his people – the Jews – to escape destruction, so that the calamity which had befallen them was due to their own folly.[17] The first oracle he cites was one which predicted that the city and the sanctuary would be taken when the Temple became four-square;[18] the messianic oracle was the second and, so Josephus wrote, more significant – although the alleged basis of this oracle in the writings of the Jews was left as unclear as that of the warning not to make the Temple square, for which the scriptural warrant is wholly obscure.[19]

The importance of this messianic oracle in Josephus' view as an encouragement to the rebels is not in doubt, but there are good reasons to suspect exaggeration. The 'correct' interpretation of the oracle which he provided in this passage was of immense importance both for Vespasian, as evidence of divine approval of his remarkable seizure of supreme power in the Roman world despite his lowly origins, and for Josephus, whose release from captivity in 69 C.E. was owed directly to his alleged prophetic revelation two years before that Vespasian would become emperor.[20] This prophecy was much used by the Flavian dynasty in its search for respectability in the Roman world. Suetonius wrote in the early second century how Vespasian had consulted the oracle of 'the god of Carmel in Judaea', receiving the encouraging message that 'whatever he planned or wished, however great it might be, would come to pass', and that 'one of his high-born prisoners, Josephus by name, as he was being put in chains, declared most confidently that he would soon be released by the same man, who would then, however, be emperor';[21] Suetonius had just previously told his readers how 'there had spread over all the east an old and established belief that it was fated at that time for men coming from Judaea to control affairs (*rerum potirentur*)', and that 'the people of Judaea, failing to recognize that this prediction referred to the Roman emperor, took it to themselves and hence rebelled.'[22] Suetonius' contemporary Tacitus had used identical language to refer to the belief 'contained in the ancient writings of the priests' that at that time the East would become strong and 'men coming from Judaea would control affairs': 'This ambiguous prophecy had in reality pointed to Vespasian and Titus, but the common people, as is the way of human ambition, interpreted these great destinies in their favour, and could not be turned to the truth even in adversity'.[23]

16   Josephus, *J.W.* 6.312–13.
17   Josephus, *J.W.* 6.310.
18   Josephus, *J.W.* 6.311.
19   Either Num. 24.17 or Dan. 7.13 may have been the biblical source text to which Josephus referred, but since he failed to make this clear, and since there appears to have been no biblical source for the prohibition to make the temple square, the same may be true of the messianic oracle.
20   Josephus, *J.W.* 6.399–407.
21   Suetonius, *Vesp.* 5.6.
22   Suetonius, *Vesp.* 4.5.
23   Tacitus, *Hist.* 5.13.2.

Messianism and Politics in the Land of Israel, 66–135 C.E.

Josephus' motives for stressing the messianic oracle are thus clear enough, so it is all the more striking that he did not refer to the 'incorrect' interpretation of the oracle by the rebels either in his narrative of the events leading up to the outbreak of the revolt or in the conduct of the war itself.[24] Mentions of messianism are so absent from this detailed history that some have even suggested that Josephus tried to disguise the extent of Jewish messianic hopes from his Roman readers,[25] a rather implausible notion in light of the prominence he allotted to the 'ambiguous oracle' in the passage just cited. Josephus wrote a great deal about 'pseudo-prophets', 'deceivers', and would-be kings, but nothing about 'pseudo-messiahs'.[26]

Such reticence is particularly striking in Josephus' rather full description of two leaders of rebellion who might quite plausibly have presented themselves as messianic figures: Menahem son of Judas (leader of the *sicarii* in Jerusalem in 66 C.E.) and Simon bar Gioras (commander-in-chief of the Jewish forces in the last phase of the siege of Jerusalem).

In the summer of 66 C.E., with the revolt well under way, 'a certain Menahem, son [descendant?] of Judas called Galilaean – a very clever sophist who at one time, under Quirinius, had upbraided the Jews for recognizing the Romans as masters when they already had God', looted weapons from Masada and returned to Jerusalem with a bodyguard 'like a king', becoming the leader of the revolution, until his success made him an 'insufferable tyrant' and the rival forces which had controlled Jerusalem before his arrival attacked him in the Temple 'where he had gone up in state to pay his devotions, dressed in royal robes and attended by his armed zealots'.[27] Menahem's self-aggrandizement and royal pretensions despite his humble origins has suggested to some historians that he saw his leadership as messianic. But Josephus, who despised him, accused him only of a naked desire for power, and it is hard to see why he would not have included in his polemic some reference to his messianic delusions if they were believed to have been part of his self-presentation.[28]

The political career of Simon bar Gioras began soon after that of Menahem but came to a head between 68 and 70, when he proved such an effective military leader that he became the acknowledged commander of all the groups defending Jerusalem once the siege of the city started in earnest in the spring of 70. His clear devotion to national independence contrasted with the more equivocal political stance of the provisional government which had formed in October 66 and which he helped to depose, but it was not until after the Temple had been destroyed that he arrogated to himself an image of supernatural authority. As the ruins burned he hid in the tunnels beneath until, forced by hunger, and unable to excavate a route to safety, he emerged dressed in white tunics with a purple mantle buckled over them. Josephus asserted that this clothing was intended to cheat the Romans by astonishing them, and that at first

---

24 Goodman 1987: 89–93.
25 Hengel 1989b.
26 For the evidence, but with a messianic interpretation, see Horsley and Hanson 1985.
27 Josephus, *J.W.* 2.433–4, 442–4.
28 Price 1992: 232. For a discussion of Menahem, see Freyne, this volume: 39.

the soldiers who saw him were indeed struck with amazement, but that the effect was only temporary and in due course he was sent off to Rome for execution as part of the celebrations of the triumph over Judaea; but Josephus is hardly reliable as a guide to Simon's motivation, and it is worth asking why (as Josephus stressed) he 'willingly exposed himself to punishment' unless he thought that he was somehow specially protected by divine power at this time of calamity.[29]

Certainly there were some who thought that God could only have allowed his people to suffer so much if the end of the world was close. Once the Temple was on fire a mixed multitude of six thousand took refuge on a portico of the outer court, misled by a 'false prophet' who had told the people of the city that the signs of their deliverance would be given to them there: not one of them survived.[30] Josephus noted that many prophets were suborned at this stage of the war by the rebel leaders to delude the people to await help from God, in order to discourage desertion,[31] although he had noted previously that the Zealots had 'scoffed at the oracles of the prophets as if they were idle fables'.[32] How long the fervour which had prompted the martyrdom of six thousand in the burning Temple continued among survivors is impossible to know. Their main hope was presumably a more practical wish that the Temple would be rebuilt, as it had been after its earlier destruction by the Babylonians. There was nothing eschatological about such a hope, which was entirely realistic, if only the Romans would allow it: the assertion by Josephus in *Against Apion*, a work written at least a quarter of a century after 70, that the Temple was the main place where Jews worshipped their God, was quite practical when priests like him were available to serve and the site of the sanctuary stood empty of other buildings.[33]

In fact evidence is negligible that messianic hope had any political effect in Judaea over the sixty years between 70 and 130, as the region came under much closer Roman military control. According to the second-century Christian historian Hegisippus, cited by Eusebius in the fourth century, Vespasian, Domitian and Trajan all hunted down Jews of Davidic descent and executed them in order to wipe out the royal line on which the Jews had set their hopes.[34] These stories are unrecorded by any other source and may simply represent an apologetic emphasis on the Davidic status of Jesus, since the persecution was alleged to have affected relations of Jesus in Galilee,[35] but it would not be wholly surprising if the Flavian dynasty which put such store on its 'correct' reading of the messianic oracle made a show of demonstrating the 'incorrectness' of the readings customary among those Jews who still believed that one of them would rule the world. On the other hand Roman apprehensions in Judaea and Galilee were not apparently acute, since there is little evidence of any drastic clampdown

---

29 Josephus, *J.W.* 7.29–33.
30 Josephus, *J.W.* 6.283–5.
31 Josephus, *J.W.* 6.283–5.
32 Josephus, *J.W.* 4.385.
33 See Josephus *C. Ap.* 2.193; Goodman 2004: 25.
34 Eusebius *Hist. eccl.* 3.12, 19–20, 32. For recent comment on this passage see Horbury 2006a: 70–1.
35 So Schürer 1973–87: 1.528.

in Judaea in 115–7, when the uprisings in Cyprus and Cyrene were led by individuals, variously named as Lukuas, Andreas and Artemion, whose motivation has been characterized by William Horbury as messianic for strong reasons, not least the suddenness of the outbreak, its savagery, the tenacity of the rebels, the destruction of pagan shrines, and the apparent aim of the rebels to return from exile to the holy land.[36]

The messianism even of these rebels in the diaspora can only be conjectured, however plausibly, but one group in this period was defined by its devotion to a messiah, and that, of course, was the Church. According to Acts, composed some time in the late first or early second century C.E., followers of the new movement were first called 'Christians' in Antioch well before 70,[37] and the term was the standard terminology both for Tacitus and Pliny in the first decades of the second century and for their rather older contemporary Josephus,[38] although *Christianos* as a self-designation is still rare in this period.[39] Ignatius exhorting his brethren in Magnesia that they too should not merely be called but should actually be 'Christians' seems to presuppose the term as one generally used by outsiders.[40] Whether *Christianos* was always connected as a name with *Christos* is uncertain – Ignatius never made any such link[41] – and, given the use of *Christos* as an epithet without clear reference to any messianic concept already in the letters of Paul, it would be rash to think of all Christians as messianists in a Jewish sense. On the other hand, that some Christians remained in the land of Israel between 70 and 135 C.E. is certain, and William Horbury has argued persuasively that for those steeped in Jewish traditions of the time it was possible to consider the cult of Christ as a direct offshoot of one variety of Jewish messianism.[42]

About the revolt which broke out in Judaea in 132 C.E. the amount of evidence is far less full than for the war of 66 to 70, simply because no one like Josephus wrote about it (or, if they did, their writing is now lost), so it is not significant in itself that no ancient writer alleged messianic fervour as a cause of the war. Of the testimony that does survive, that of Dio, who asserted that the immediate trigger of the uprising was the foundation of Aelia Capitolina, a Roman colony, on the site of Jerusalem, is probably to be preferred to the traditions that the war was a response to an imperial ban on circumcision.[43] The ideology of the Jewish leaders, including Shimon Bar Kosiba himself as expressed in the extant letters found in the Judaean Desert and in the formal documents for leasing state land in En Gedi produced by his regime, was practical, military and efficient.[44] As Peter Schäfer has

---

36 Horbury 1996. See Carleton Paget, this volume: 189–91.
37 Acts 11.26.
38 Tacitus *Ann.* 15.44; Pliny *Ep.* 10.96; Josephus, *Ant.* 18.64 (on the assumption that at least the final sentence of the Testimonium Flavianum found in the manuscripts of Josephus' works was indeed written originally by him).
39 Lieu 2004, ch. 8.
40 Ignatius, *Magn.* 4.4.
41 Lieu 2004: 251.
42 See especially Horbury 1998c.
43 Cassius Dio 69.12.1 (Aelia Capitolina); *SHA Hadrianus* 14.2 (ban on circumcision).
44 Schäfer 1981: 74–7.

pointed out, no tradition claims that a messiah could not have just these qualities, along with the exceptional strength and determination ascribed to Bar Kosiba in later rabbinic tradition,[45] but none of the contemporary evidence – the documents and the coins – unequivocally suggests eschatological fervour, even if the coin legends 'for the redemption of Israel' and the use of stars as symbols might be understood that way.[46] Rather, Bar Kosiba and his followers emerge from the letters as pious Jews who wished to keep the Sabbath and the festivals and who were devoted above all to the Temple, which is depicted in a great variety of types on many of the coins.[47] In contrast to many of those who led uprisings in the first century by portraying themselves as kings, Bar Kosiba proclaimed himself *Nasi Yisrael*, 'Prince of Israel', and stressed on the coins also the authority of a certain *Eleazer haCohen*, 'Eleazer the Priest',[48] about whom no traditions survive either in the rabbinic or the Christian stories about Bar Kosiba, so that it is tempting to see his function in the regime simply as representative of the priests and the Temple, for whose restoration, it can reasonably be assumed, the rebels believed themselves to be fighting.[49]

What, then, to make of the later tradition that Rabbi Akiba, who lived at the time of the war, pronounced Bar Kosiba to be the messiah: 'R. Shimon b. Yohai taught: "My teacher Akiba used to expound the verse 'A star shall step forth from Jacob' (Num. 24.17) as 'Kozba steps forth from Jacob'. When R. Akiba saw Bar Kozba, he exclaimed: 'This one is the King Messiah'. R. Yohanan b. Torta said to him: 'Akiba, grass will grow between your jaws and still the son of David will not have come".'[50] These sayings are preserved only in the Jerusalem Talmud, which was redacted at the earliest in the fourth century, but Peter Schäfer has argued persuasively that both R. Akiba's declaration and its repudiation by the otherwise unknown Yohanan b. Torta should be dated much earlier, probably to the time of the war itself.[51] Certainly Christians such as Justin Martyr already knew within a decade or so of the end of the rebellion that Bar Kosiba had been known as 'Bar Kochba' ('son of a star'), which must surely be linked to the claim of Akiba that he was the star who, according to Numbers, will 'step forth from Jacob'.[52]

What, then, can be concluded from this minimalist survey of the impact of messianism on the history of Judaea between 66 and 135 C.E.? Perhaps only this: it is clear that messianic beliefs permeated Jewish society in this period as they had done throughout late Second Temple times, but uncertainty about the nature of the messianic age may have prevented hopes for a messiah providing

---

45 Schäfer 2003: 17–18.
46 Mildenberg and Mottahedeh 1984.
47 Meshorer 2001, plates 64–6, 69.
48 Mildenberg and Mottahedeh 1984: 29, 64–5.
49 Schäfer 2003: 20.
50 *y. Ta'an.* 4: 8, 63d.
51 Schäfer 2003: 2–5.
52 Num. 24.17, Justin Martyr, *1 Apol.* 31–6 refers to Bar Kosiba as 'Barchochebas', although the explicit link between this name and a star found in Euseb. *Hist. eccl.* 4.6.2 is not attested in Justin's writings. For further possible evidence of a messianic interpretation of the leader of the revolt, see the *Apocalypse of Peter* and Bauckham's discussion of it in Bauckham 1998b.

the driving force for political action except in the most extreme circumstances and among self-selected groups, such as the Messianists who constituted the early Church. It is prudent to stress the caution of Yohanan b. Torta as much as the enthusiasm of Akiba: 'Grass will grow between your jaws and still the son of David will not have come.'[53]

---

53 So Rajak 2002: 165, noting that 'the Talmudic story [about Akiba] also exposes the scathing response of another rabbi'. For further discussion of Rabbinic attitudes to Messianism, see Alexander, this volume: 227–44.

Chapter 12

JEWS AND CHRISTIANS IN THE HOLY LAND, 135–325 C.E.

Oskar Skarsaune

There is hardly any topic of significance within the field of Jewish-Christian relations during the first centuries that William Horbury has not illuminated by taking a fresh look at the sources and reading them in new ways. This is also true about the theme of this essay. I therefore offer the following pages more as a supplement than an alternative to Horbury's own pertinent contributions.[1] I hardly need to add that the following essay makes no claim to completeness.

1. *Introduction*

I shall begin by briefly outlining the geographical, historical and demographical frameworks that are of importance in understanding the theological developments among Jews and Christians in the Land of Israel of this period.[2]

By far the most important factor was the loss of the Jewish centre, Jerusalem. According to quite solid evidence in Christian writers, Hadrian barred Jews from entering his new colonial city, Aelia Capitolina, erected on the ruins of Jerusalem.[3] Jerusalem had been the centre of authority and the seat of Jewish leadership prior to the first Jewish war. After 70 this seat moved to Jamnia, but the removal was probably conceived of as only temporary. After the Bar Kokhba war most Jews would have realized that the loss of Jerusalem was long term. One had to adjust to it. From now on, the Jewish loss of Jerusalem becomes a standing trope in Christian anti-Jewish polemic, as seen, for example, in Justin.

Not only was Jerusalem emptied of its Jews, there soon followed a general migration of Jews from the territory of Judaea into Galilee. In Aelia we now find Gentiles, the Roman army and its officers, and all the people necessary to sustain the infrastructure.[4] Apart from Aelia, there were well-established Gentile population segments in the large coastal cities, Caesarea in particular, and also in some of the larger Hellenized cities inland, like Scythopolis. The Jewish leadership, on the other hand, seems to have shunned the big Romanized cities.

---

1   See, e.g., Horbury 1998d: 127–61; Horbury 2003b: 275–88.
2   In what follows I am much indebted to the excellent reviews of the period by Cohen 1992 and Gafni 1992.
3   Justin, *1 Apol.* 47; *Dial.* 16.2; 40.2; 92.2. On Eusebius, *Hist. eccl.* 4.6.2–4, see below, p. 163.
4   See Eliav 2003.

They took part in the general drift of Jews towards Galilee, but in the beginning they established their academies in small villages, like Ussha, not in Sepphoris or Tiberias.

In terms of Jews and Christians, the above description of the main scenes of Jews and Gentiles is valid for Jews and Gentile Christians as well. But Christians came in two categories: those of Jewish and those of Gentile origin. The geographical location of the two types of Christians was not the same. The Jewish believers in Jesus were living among other Jews, mainly in rural Galilee. The Gentile believers were living among other Gentiles in the Hellenistic-Roman cities, Aelia and Caesarea being the most prominent ones. Close fellowship between Gentile and Jewish believers would normally be rare; in Aelia it was impossible, due to Hadrian's decree. This situation of almost complete segregation of Gentile and Jewish Christians probably lasted throughout the period covered by this essay. This segregation is attested as late as in the fourth century by Epiphanius, himself a native of the Land of Israel. He says that in the cities of Tiberias, Sepphoris, Nazareth and Capernaum 'neither Greek nor Samaritan nor Christian is in their [the Jews'] midst', and 'the [Jewish] inhabitants guard lest there be a resident Gentile'.[5] However, some Christian communities in Caesarea and other large cities with a 'mixed' population may have had a mixed membership of Jewish and Gentile believers. This is indicated for Caesarea in the third century.[6]

In Aelia itself the Gentile Christians were *supplanting* their Jewish predecessors. One could say, perhaps, that the theology nowadays called *supersessionism* was dramatized in very concrete terms during the first years of Aelia. A Jewish community of believers in Jesus was literally substituted by a Gentile Christian community.

In the third century one observes an increasing *urbanization* of rabbinic leadership. Judah the Prince resided in Sepphoris and Beit Shearim. Some time later the permanent seat of the Patriarch was Tiberias. Apart from Sepphoris and Tiberias, other leading rabbis are associated with Caesarea. In Caesarea we have a setting for more direct and more frequent encounters between leading Jewish sages and Gentile Christians than would have been the case earlier.[7] On the other hand, when named rabbis of the late second and the third centuries are said to have controversies with *minim* in Sepphoris, Tiberias and Capernaum,[8] these *minim* base their arguments on the *Hebrew* text of the Bible, trying in particular to wrest a 'two divine powers' theology out of plurals in verbs and other linguistic subtleties in the biblical text.[9] There can hardly be any doubt that these *minim* were Jewish, and that some of them were believers in Jesus.[10] There is also little doubt that these *minim* in their outward appearance were indistinguishable from other Jews.

5   *Pan.*, 30.11.9–10; translation according to Koch 1976: 135.
6   When Origen preached in the community at Caesarea on Sunday, some of his Christian listeners had visited the synagogue on Saturday, *Hom. Lev.* 5.8 (GCS 6, p. 349). See the comment in de Lange 1976: 86.
7   See Bietenhard 1974 and especially Raban and Holum 1996: 381–547 (parts 8 and 9); and further bibliography below, notes 42 and 43.
8   Büchler 1912.
9   Segal 1977.
10   See Segal 1977 *passim*, and also Alexander 2007.

Let me add some further remarks on the changes that took place at the turn from the second to the third century. Most important of these changes was a new pattern of Jewish leadership. In Sepphoris, Judah 'The Prince' established a new position as Jewish 'patriarch', recognized by the Romans.[11] The same man was the editor of the Mishnah. In both respects the career of Judah the Prince marked a watershed in Jewish history in the land of Israel. Before Judah, the circles of rabbinic *haverim* were never able to rid themselves completely of the fact that they were a sect. The great majority of the people, derogatorily named *amme-ha-arez* by the rabbis, ignored their strict rulings on purity and tithing. After Judah, and with the Roman recognition that he and his successors earned, the long battle for rabbinic hegemony gained new momentum. But many years would still pass before this hegemony was anything like complete.[12]

In the following, I shall restrict myself mainly to the land of Israel west of the Jordan, but for both periods the Transjordan area was an important hinterland, especially the Decapolis area with Basanitis and Gaulanitis.

2. Jewish and Christian Messianism in the Aftermath of Bar Kokhba

Whether Bar Kokhba himself had messianic aspirations or not, there is hardly any doubt that he was seen as fulfilling the role of the Messiah by many of his contemporaries[13] – even by some leading rabbis, first among whom was no less a figure than Akiba.[14] But this flourishing of messianic fervour was to be the last for a very long time.[15] Leading rabbis concluded that the way of militant messianism was not the right one for Israel. It had proved destructive in 66–70 C.E.; it had done so in 115–17 C.E.,[16] and now the third revolt had ended in complete disaster. The way for Israel was now to leave messianic redemption to God and to focus on the sanctification of the people. Sanctification came through observance of the commandments which set Israel apart and made it a holy people: rules of purity, especially concerning food and drink, rules of sanctifying time and space, rules of sanctifying the human body and its natural functions, marital life, etc. In short, leading rabbis focused their attention on those aspects

---

11   On Judah and the Patriarchate, see the groundbreaking study of Jacobs 1995.
12   Seth Schwartz has convincingly argued that the rabbis remained marginal for a much longer period than has been thought. See Schwartz 2001, esp. 101–76; also the response of Millar 2006.
13   For a recent discussion, see Bauckham 1998a: 187–90. See Goodman, this volume: 155–7.
14   I am not convinced by the attempt of P. Schäfer to remove Akiba from the well-known passage in *y. Ta'an.* 4.8, in which Akiba is said to have proclaimed Bar Kokhba as the Star of Num. 24.17. Schäfer's argument is based on rather complicated and speculative redactional criticism of the passage. I fail to understand why later rabbis should attribute a great mistake concerning Bar Kokhba to one of their greatest heroes, if in fact he did not make it. See Schäfer 2003.
15   In saying this, I have in mind the attitudes of Jewish religious leaders. Popular messianism on ground level could well be a different matter. For the possibility of a flourishing of messianic expectations during the Roman campaign against the Parthians in 197, see Horbury 2003b: 285–8.
16   On this uprising, see now the magisterial study by Horbury 1996.

of the Jewish heritage which some decades later found their expression in the Mishnah.[17] Explicit messianism is almost absent in the Mishnah.[18] It is, as a whole, little concerned with what God has done, is now doing, and shall do in the eschaton. Instead, the Mishnah is intensely concerned with preserving and developing the knowledge of what human beings should do to sanctify themselves. Since the Temple is at the centre of holiness according to the Torah, the Mishnah meticulously preserves the traditions about exactly how things were done in the Temple. But whether this knowledge would be of relevance some day in a rebuilt Temple is a question the Mishnah consciously ignores. Should God rebuild Jerusalem and the sanctuary 'speedily, in our days'[19] – fine, the how-to-do manual for the Temple service is there, in the Mishnah. Should God tarry – the necessary knowledge is laid down in the Mishnah in any case.

We are poorly informed as to how the rabbis as well as the ordinary *amme-ha-aretz* digested the failure of Bar Kokhba as a messianic figure. The dominant motif in later rabbinic traditions about him is that he was a *liar* and a *false* Messiah. As is well known, his cognomen Kosiba from the village of his origin was transformed into Kokhba (Aramaic for star) by himself or his supporters. But his opponents changed it, instead, to Bar Koziba, '*Son of the Lie*'. Other rabbis may have taken a more positive view of his career, even after his failure. It is difficult to prove, but it remains a fascinating possibility that the portrait of the Messiah of Ephraim who fights for Israel but ends being killed, thus preparing the way for the Messiah of David, may be an attempt to invest the fate of Bar Kokhba with some meaning.[20] If so, not every rabbi automatically denounced Bar Kokhba after his failure.

But it seems that another strategy was popular with some rabbis. In order to defuse the militant activism latent in several traditional messianic prophecies of Scripture, they chose to 'historicize' these prophecies. The biblical texts did not speak of a future Messiah, but of the historic king contemporary with each text. Psalm 72 did not speak of a future Messiah, but about its alleged author, Solomon. Psalm 110, the great anthem of the Liberator of Jerusalem, was spoken with reference to Hezekiah, not a future Messiah.[21]

In the following, I will argue that Christians in the land of Israel, Christians who experienced the Bar Kokhba war and its aftermath at close range, were very much in contact with these developments within Jewish messianism. They responded to

---

17   Neusner 1981.
18   Neusner 1987. There are references to the 'days of the Messiah' at *m. Ber.* 1.5 and the 'footsteps of the Messiah' at *m. Soṭah* 9.15. On these and other passages where the term 'anointed' occurs, see Neusner 1987: 270–5.
19   As is said in the fourteenth benediction of the Amidah.
20   For this interpretation, see Heinemann 1975.
21   In rabbinic literature this understanding of the messianic prophecies is only attested for in the third century, *b. Sanh.* 94a: Isa. 9.5 and 9.6 refer to Hezekiah. According to *b. Sanh.* 99a, Rabbi Hillel [third cent.] said: 'There shall be no Messiah for Israel, because they have already enjoyed him in the days of Hezekiah.' In Justin, however, this exegesis is explicitly attributed to the Jewish teachers of Justin's time. They say Ps. 110 refers to Hezekiah (*Dial.* 32.6–33.2; 83.1-4), Ps. 72 refers to Solomon (*Dial.* 34); Ps. 24 refers to Solomon or Hezekiah (*Dial.* 36; 85); Isa. 7.14/8.4 refers to Hezekiah (*Dial.* 67.1). On this see Alexander, this volume: 227–44.

the fervent flourishing of messianism during the successful years of Bar Kokhba, but they also responded to the 'historicizing' of Jewish messianism after the war.

a. The True Messiah: Jesus or Bar Kokhba?

For those among the Jews who held Jesus to be the true Messiah of Israel, the few years of the Bar Kokhba war were probably a very difficult period. For one thing, Justin claims that Bar Kokhba persecuted believers in Jesus quite violently (*1 Apol.* 31.6). On a theological level, however, it could have been even more challenging for believers in Jesus to uphold Jesus' claim to be the Messiah, as long as Bar Kokhba appeared to accomplish successfully the messianic task not accomplished by Jesus: liberating Israel.

I believe the answer to this challenge is clearly to be heard in extant Christian sources.

1. *The Apocalypse of Peter*

Richard Bauckham has argued that this writing was written by a Jewish believer in Jesus in the land of Israel during the Bar Kokhba war.[22] The author of the writing seems to belong to those Jewish believers in Jesus who were persecuted by Bar Kokhba because they would not recognize his messianic role. At the time of writing the author believed that they had not yet seen the climax of the persecution. In other words, the book was written before the defeat of Bar Kokhba. Bauckham's main argument is the way the author uses material from the Synoptic apocalypse in Matthew 24. Whereas Mt. 24 talks about *several* false Messiahs *and false prophets*, in the *Apocalypse of Peter* this is narrowed down to *one false Messiah* only. The author is narrowly focused on the one false Messiah who will precede the parousia of Jesus. The meaning of the parable of the sprouting fig tree, according to the *Apocalypse of Peter*, is different from that implied in Mt. 24. The parable is now said to refer to a persecution of the righteous ones within Israel by the false Messiah. 'But this deceiver is not the Messiah. And when they reject him, he will kill with the sword and there shall be many martyrs. Then shall the boughs of the fig tree, i.e. the house of Israel, sprout, and there shall be many martyrs by his hand: they shall be killed and become martyrs.'[23] Evidently, the persecution and martyrdoms have already begun, but are not ended. And the false Messiah is not yet exposed as such. He is a real threat to the faithful in Israel. They may be tempted to join him.

2. *Aristo of Pella's* Controversy between Jason and Papiscus

The next Christian writer to comment on Bar Kokhba is Aristo of Pella, probably in his lost *Controversy between Jason and Papiscus*.[24] Aristo, as his cognomen indicates, was based in Pella in the Decapolis, the town to which all or some of the Jerusalem community allegedly fled before the Jewish war of 66–70. He wrote in Greek, but seems to have had some competence in Hebrew and Aramaic. Since the hero of his book, Jason, is portrayed as a Jewish believer in Jesus, and since

---

22   See Bauckham 1998a, 1998b.
23   *Apoc. Pet.* 2; transl. according to Hennecke 1973: 2.669.
24   On what little is known about him and his writing, see Goodspeed 1966: 99–100.

Jews and Christians in the Holy Land, 135–325 C.E.

Aristo seems to have been knowledgeable in the two native Jewish languages, it is likely he was of Jewish origin himself. Aristo is said by Eusebius to have reported the following:

> The commander of the Jews at that time was a man named Bar Kokhba, which means a star. He was nothing but an assassin (*phonikos*) and a robber (*lēstrikos anēr*); nevertheless he used his name to impress his servile followers with the belief that he was in truth a luminary (*phōstēr*) come down from heaven to shine upon (*epilampsai*) their evil plight.

The report continues by saying that after Bar Kokhba's defeat at Beithar, 'the whole nation was wholly prohibited from setting foot upon the country round about Jerusalem, by the decree and ordinances of a law of Hadrian, which forbade them even from afar to gaze on the soil inherited from their fathers. Such is the account given by Aristo of Pella.'[25]

It is uncertain how much of this report is a paraphrase of Aristo, and how much is Eusebius' additions from other sources. But the minimum that has to be attributed to Aristo is the information on the Hadrianic decree. Very likely some strokes in the portrait of Bar Kokhba and the remarks on the meaning of his name also come from Aristo. In Eusebius' text the name Bar Kokhba is said to mean *astera*, and Bar Kokhba is said to have bragged about being a heavenly *light* come to *enlighten* Israel in its sufferings. It is uncertain whether Bar Kokhba made much of his cognomen's connotations of enlightenment. There is no doubt, however, that Eusebius' (probably Aristo's) description of him makes excellent sense as a conscious counterfeit of traditional Christian descriptions of Jesus as the Messiah. According to these, Jesus was the bright Star of Num. 24.17 (Rev. 22.16); coming from on high (Lk. 1.78), enlightening those who sat in darkness (Lk. 1.79; Mt. 4.16 = Isa. 9.2). But he did it by 'the way of peace' (Lk. 1.79), not by sword as a bandit (*lēstēs*, Mt. 26.55). As Eusebius (Aristo?) saw things, it was the exact opposite with Bar Kokhba. He claimed to be a light from on high, but in reality he was an *anēr phonikos kai lēstrikos*. By his reliance on the sword and by killing people, he dragged Israel with him into disaster and destruction.

Messianic testimonies in Justin Martyr

Justin spent the early years of his life in his native town of Flavia Neapolis (now Nablus) in Samaria. If he was converted to faith in Jesus while still living at Nablus is uncertain, but *Dial.* 2.6 easily bears that interpretation. Whether Justin was still in Samaria during the Bar Kokhba war, or had already embarked on that odyssey which finally brought him to Rome, is also uncertain. Be that as it may – it is beyond any reasonable doubt that in his so-called *First Apology* as well as in his *Dialogue with Trypho* Justin has incorporated much material coming from a source at home in the land of Israel and datable to the years immediately after the Bar Kokhba war. In this material the Bar Kokhba war is still a fresh experience, and the questions raised by Bar Kokhba's bid for Messiahship are vital to the theologians speaking through Justin's material.[26]

---

25 Eusebius, *Hist. eccl.* 4.6.2–4; transl. according to Lawlor and Oulton 1927: 1.107–8.
26 For brevity's sake, I here only refer to my analysis of this material in Skarsaune 1987: 228–34.

Some of the modified biblical texts used by Justin (but not created by him) have a markedly anti-Bar Kokhba tendency.

Justin's proof from Scripture in the *First Apology* opens with Gen. 49.10-11 and an *expanded* version of Num. 24.17, Bar Kokhba's scriptural slogan (*1 Apol.* 32). These two testimonies were the most important messianic proof-texts *in the Torah* according to Jewish messianic expectations around the beginning of the Common Era.[27] In *Targum Onqelos* they are the only two texts of the Torah taken to refer to the Messiah. The significance of this is strengthened by the observation that when Justin quotes Gen. 49.10 directly from his Christian testimony source, the textform of the passage agrees with the Targum against the Septuagint text.

In Gen. 49.10 Justin's text in the quote highlights the fact that the Messiah is to be 'the expectation of the nations'. Bar Kokhba never was that. Bar Kokhba's favourite Scripture, Num. 24.17, is severely modified and expanded in Justin:

1 *Apol.* 32.12:
(a) A star shall rise out of Jacob,   (Num. 24.17)
(b) and a flower shall spring *from the root of Jesse*,   (Isa. 11.1)
(c) and in his arm *shall nations trust*.   (Isa. 51.5)

In this modified version the biblical quote makes two polemical points: (1) the Messiah is *from David*, and (2) he is a saviour not for Israel only, but for *all nations*. Bar Kokhba was neither.

To conclude: The material here surveyed testifies to an intense engagement with Jewish messianism in its most concrete form, actualized by Bar Kokhba's apparently successful liberation of Israel. In its dealing with the concrete facts of Israel's political fate, this Christian engagement with the historical dimensions of messianism goes far beyond anything found in the New Testament.

b. The Messiah – Only Human or also Divine?

What has just been said needs to be balanced by other evidence which indicates a moving away from the concreteness of messianism here documented. I indicated above that some rabbis in the wake of the catastrophe of Bar Kokhba's defeat may have 'historicized' messianic prophecies in order to defuse their activist potential. This exegetical strategy was then also used to counter Christian exegesis of the same prophecies. When, for example, believers in Jesus quoted Psalm 72 as a prophecy fulfilled by Jesus in his present universal and superhuman messianic reign, Jewish exegetes would counter that this Psalm was not about the Messiah at all, but was rather a description of Solomon's historic reign. In their turn, Christian exegetes retorted that the Messiah of this and similar texts clearly was depicted as performing superhuman feats, and could therefore not be human only.[28] They would bolster this by pointing out that the Messiah was the same Son of God *through whom* God created the world (according to Gen. 1.1), and to whom God said 'let *us* make

---

27 See Skarsaune 1987: 260–6; Horbury 1998c: 50–1 and 92–5; and Collins 1995: 61–7.
28 See Justin's arguments to this effect in the references given in note 21 above.

humankind in *our* image …' (in Gen. 1.26). They would further point out that in Gen. 19.24 this divine Son of God was clearly in evidence as 'the Lord' speaking with Abraham on earth, while the other 'Lord' in heaven, raining sulphur and fire on Sodom and Gomorrah, had to be the Father.[29]

I believe a good case can be made for the view that the first Christian writer to launch this line of argument was Aristo of Pella in his *Controversy between Jason and Papiscus*.[30] What is certain is that this argument is broadly developed in Justin's *Dialogue* (not in his *Apology*). Justin certainly did not invent this line of argument on his own, and there is striking rabbinic evidence that such arguments played a role in debates among Jewish believers and leading rabbis in the Land of Israel in the 140s or 150s, prior to Justin's writing of the *Dialogue*. In *b. Sanh*. 38b, a certain *min* argues a duality of Lords from Gen. 19.24, exactly like Justin. 'A certain fuller said, "Leave him [the *min*] to me, I will answer him: It is written, And Lamech said to his wives, Ada and Zillah, hear my voice, ye wives of Lamech [Gen. 4.23]; but he should have said 'my wives!' But such is the scriptural idiom – so here too [Gen. 19.24], it is the scriptural idiom."'[31] The fuller adds that he has this argument from 'a public discourse of Rabbi Meir'. This passage suggests that Meir, mainly active in the Galilee of the first couple of decades after 135, was already familiar with the argument we have found in Justin (and surmised was contained in Aristo's *Jason and Papiscus*). This is clear evidence of the time and the region in which this line of argument originated. Meir's argument, and also the arguments attributed to the *minim* in the Talmudic context, are all based on the *Hebrew* text of the Bible (not the Greek). Accordingly the *minim* are Galilaean Jews, just like their rabbinic opponents, and some of them probably were Jewish believers in Jesus, arguing for his divinity.

3. *Further echoes of contact and controversy in Galilee*

The development away from messianic activism and into other modes of controversy is also to be seen in other texts. The Jewish believers of Galilee seem to have left a literary trace of their thinking in five fragments preserved by Jerome, commenting on texts from the book of Isaiah.[32] Jerome says he has these fragments from the Nazoreans of Syrian Berea. The contents of the fragments clearly speak for an origin in Galilee in the latter part of the second century, or early in the third. The main points of these fragments are (1) a criticism of rabbinic leaders, from Hillel and Shammai to Akiba and Meir, for having rejected Jesus as the Messiah, and (2) for having substituted the *light* of Jesus' teaching with the *darkness* of their own *deuterōsis*. The latter term is probably a wooden

---

29   See Justin's *Dial*. 55–62. Exactly the same argument recurs in the fifth- and sixth-century dialogues of *Timothy and Aquila*, *Athanasius and Zacchaeus*, and *Simon and Theophilus*, but apparently independent of Justin's *Dialogue*. See Lahey 2001.

30   See Skarsaune 1987: 234–42, for Justin's dependence on the *Controversy*; and Lahey 2001 for the same theory concerning the three later dialogues.

31   Translation according to Epstein 1935: 246.

32   All the five fragments occur in Jerome's commentary on Isaiah. Latin texts and English translations conveniently presented in Klijn and Reinink 1973: 220–5. For discussion of the fragments, see Schmidtke 1911: 108–26; Klijn 1972; Pritz 1988: 57–70; Kinzig 2007.

Greek translation of the Hebrew term *Mishnah*. The fragments also call the rabbis *deuterōtai*, again a wooden translation of Aramaic *tannaim*.

In these fragments one gets a picture of Jewish believers in the Galilee of the late second or early third century who vigorously oppose the emerging Mishnah of the rabbis. Their way of doing this recalls the similar polemic against *deuterōsis* in the Syriac *Didascalia Apostolorum* (only some decades later). Elisheva Fonrobert has aptly called this writing 'a Mishnah for the disciples of Jesus'.[33] In other words, Jesus is here the Messiah who has given his disciples the right *halakah*; that of the rabbis is only darkness.

4. Emerging Gentile Christianity in the Land of Israel

Whereas Jewish believers and rabbis shared the same geographical scene, Galilee, Gentile Christians had Aelia as their new centre. From Eusebius' *Ecclesiastical History* one may piece together a list of 23 Gentile bishops of Jerusalem, beginning with the first one after the Bar Kokhba war, Marcus, and ending with the last one 'before the persecution', Hermon. One of the bishops who stands out from this list of mere names is Narcissus. He served as bishop in two rounds, probably on both sides of the year 200 C.E. In an interesting study of Narcissus[34] O. Irsai interprets the portrait of him as a conscious attempt by the Gentile Christian community of Jerusalem to cast him as a worthy successor of the Apostolic and Jewish-Christian leaders of the 'Mother community'. He sees this as an effective counter-offensive against the bid for hegemony, at Jerusalem's cost, by the Montanists of Asia Minor and the powerful bishop of Rome, Victor. Be that as it may, there is hardly any reason to doubt Irsai's main point: Narcissus was portrayed as a worthy bishop of the Mother community of Jerusalem. The radical discontinuity of 135 was made to appear insignificant.

Basically the same supersessionism is to be observed in Justin.[35] No wonder – he may have received some of his most important theological source material from the newly established Gentile Christian community in Jerusalem. For Justin, the Church of the Gentiles has replaced the Jewish people as the true Israel. But Justin disagrees with Christians who exclude Jewish believers in Jesus from this new Israel, if these believers maintain a Jewish lifestyle. In this question it was the Christians with whom Justin disagreed who were destined to become the winners, not Justin.

Perhaps one may find a more explicitly positive attitude towards the Jewish elements of the early Jerusalem community in Justin's younger contemporary, Hegesippus.[36] He may have had his origin in Aelia, or at least in the land of Israel,

---

33 Fonrobert 2001.
34 Irsai 1993.
35 For substantiation of this paragraph, see Skarsaune 1987: 326–53.
36 There is no recent full-scale monograph on Hegesippus, and no standard edition of his fragments. For lack of this, there is the very useful study and edition of the fragments by Lawlor 1912. The fragments most relevant in our context are found in Eusebius, *Hist. eccl.* 2.23.3–19; 3.11–12, 20.1–6, 32.

and there is no compelling reason to dispute Eusebius' contention that he was of Jewish origin.[37] What matters in our context, however, is the fact that Hegesippus, writing in the 190s, made the first Jewish leaders of the Jerusalem community – the relatives of Jesus – the very icons of orthodoxy, providing him with the yardstick with which to measure the orthodoxy of other communities from Jerusalem to Rome.[38] It should be considered beyond doubt that in so doing, Hegesippus could draw on a rich source of pre-Bar Kokhba narratives about James, Symeon and other early leaders. These he put to good use towards the end of the second century, propagating the early Jerusalem Church as the mother of orthodoxy.

Another writer who also draws on early Jewish Christian traditions from the land of Israel is Julius Africanus, himself born in Aelia, in his later life acting as a kind of ambassador (in Rome) for the city of Emmaus.[39] Africanus displays considerable Jewish learning. In his *Chronicle* he is clearly dependent upon Jewish models. In his *Letter to Aristides* he renders Jewish-Christian traditions about the relatives of Jesus and their way of harmonizing the different pedigrees of Jesus in Matthew and Luke. This harmonization is what interests Africanus, but it seems likely that the main interest of the traditions he quotes was something else: a very learned engagement with the problems concerning the Davidic descent of Jesus, the illegitimacy of the Herodian dynasty, and the possibility that Jesus was of Davidic as well as of priestly origin.[40] Africanus is not as forthcoming as Hegesippus when it comes to making the Jerusalem community the yardstick of orthodoxy, but his background is very similar to Hegesippus'.

5. Messianism in the Third Century: Origen meets the Rabbis

We turn to Origen in Caesarea in the 230s and 240s. Here we see a Gentile Christian encountering Jewish scholars, debating with them but also seeking information from them on problems of text and interpretation of the biblical books. In the third century, Caesarea emerged as an important centre of leading rabbis, establishing academies of great influence. At the head of this development we find rabbis like Bar Kappara and Hoshaya, older contemporaries of Origen.[41] The great luminary of Tiberias, Rabbi Yohanan, often visited Caesarea, and there are indications of direct interchanges between him and Origen.[42] Maybe the last of the great Caesareans, Rabbi Abbahu, also found it relevant to respond to Origen.[43]

---

37 The arguments of Telfer 1960 to the contrary are far from convincing.
38 See especially his comments in *Hist. eccl.* 4.22.1–7.
39 The modern monograph which most intensively discusses Africanus' Jewish background and learning is Viellefond 1970: 13–70. See also Habas-Rubin 1994. It is doubtful whether Africanus himself was Jewish.
40 See in particular Bauckham 1990: 315–73, esp. 355–63.
41 See de Lange 1976: 27–8.
42 See Kimelman 1980: 567–95.
43 Levine 1975.

A distinguished series of pioneering studies have shown beyond doubt that Origen is right when he claims that some of his exegeses were obtained from Jewish sages whom he interrogated in person. They have also demonstrated that Origen conducts a debate with Jewish sages in many places where he does not say so explicitly.[44] Even more intriguing, many rabbinic texts are better understood when they are read as conscious counter-polemic against interpretations of the same texts launched by Origen. While this may be seen as a continuation of the rather intense Jewish/Christian debate and exchange in the second-century land of Israel, the contents of Origen's debates with the Jewish sages belong to an entirely different world of thought. This is most easily seen in Origen's choice of which book in the Bible he makes the basis for much of his debate with the rabbis. It is the Song of Songs. One looks in vain for quotes from this book in all recorded debates between Jews and Christians prior to Origen.[45] On the Jewish side the allegorical exegesis of the Song goes back at least to Akiba. But the third century was apparently the heyday of Jewish allegorization of the Song, and some of these allegoric interpretations appear to be targeted especially at Origen's Christian interpretation.

Origen's interpretation of the Song is christological, of course, but the difference with regard to earlier Christology is that Origen's Christ is little concerned with contemporary historical events. The Christ that Origen finds portrayed in the Song's bridegroom is the divine revealer of God's essence and will. And what the rabbis find in those specific texts which Origen applies to Christ, is the *halakah of the sages*, not the Messiah. Origen and his rabbinic opponents agree that Israel of old was nourished by the words of the Law and the Prophets, but now, for Origen this nourishment is surpassed by that given by Christ, whereas for the rabbis it is surpassed (!) by that given in the Mishnah.[46] The debate is not about a Christian Messiah saving Israel and the nations from servitude to Satan, versus a Jewish Messiah liberating Israel. The debate now is about the divine *logos* enlightening God's people – is *he* Christ or is *it* the halakah of the Sages?

The rabbis of the third century did not entirely shy away from traditional messianism, but when the Messiah makes an appearance in third-century rabbinic literature, after being virtually absent in the Mishnah, he has been 'rabbinized'.[47] He is now a Messiah on rabbinical terms. This development was prepared by the inverse phenomenon of the 'messianization' of Judah the Prince and his successors. Judah was said to be of David's seed through Hillel, and the classic

---

44   In addition to the studies by Bietenhard, de Lange and Kimelman mentioned in the preceding notes, see the following: Bacher 1890; Marmorstein 1920; Bardy 1925; Baer 1961: 98–116; Urbach 1971; Brooks 1988; Blowers 1988.

45   The one apparent exception is Origen's older contemporary Hippolytus of Rome, who wrote a commentary on Song 1.1–3.8 in which he made the bride of the Song a model for Mary Magdalene or the Church in a hermeneutically not very consistent way. He may have responded to Jewish exegesis of the Song, e.g. the allegorical interpretation advanced by Akiba, but he was not directly involved in intensive Jewish/Christian debate like Origen.

46   For several *midrashim* to this effect, developed from specific sayings in the Song, and attributed to Rabbi Yohanan or his pupils and colleagues, see Kimelman 1980: 578–82.

47   See in particular Neusner 1987; Alexander, this volume: 227–44.

messianic prophecy of the Torah, Gen. 49.10, was applied to him. He was now the sceptre and the ruler's staff that should not depart from Judah until the final consummation in a rabbi-like Messiah.[48]

It is striking to see to what extent Origen's rabbinic partners in the discussion answer his christological exegesis by an entirely non-messianic understanding of the same texts. For example, Rabbi Yohanan and his colleagues took Ps. 110 to refer to *Abraham*, not the Messiah. According to A. Altmann, at this time 'Abraham assumes the role which Christian theology assigned to Jesus'.[49]

In line with this, it may also have been at this period that the rabbis elaborated a fully developed Akedah theology, making Isaac the perfect victim for Israel's sin, and making Abraham's willingness to sacrifice him the perfect sacrifice. In *Talmud Yerushalmi* and several *midrashim*, the following exchange between Abraham and God is ascribed to Rabbi Yohanan: 'Abraham says to God, "When you said to me that I should bring my son Isaac as sacrifice, I could have protested and said, 'You promised me seed through him!' But I obeyed your will. So now it is right on your part, when Isaac's offspring is in need because of their sins and there is no one to intercede for them, that you yourself intercede." "The Lord will see," [Gen. 22.14]: You will see and remember the binding of their ancestor Isaac, and will therefore be full of mercy towards them.'[50]

The Akedah motif is certainly older in Jewish thought than this third-century version.[51] But it seems that Jewish as well as Christian developments of the motif are not unrelated to each other. Rather the contrary – it makes good sense to see the motif develop through mutual responses to what was going on in the other camp.[52]

In all of this, we observe in the third century a markedly different atmosphere compared with the fervent eschatological-historical messianism of the second century, during and immediately after the Bar Kokhba war. And this change of atmosphere is the same on both sides. If any proof of ongoing 'contact and controversy' is asked for, this is it.

6. Epilogue: The Significance of Constantine

The period following the Bar Kokhba war, and especially the third century, was a time of political calm for the Jews of the Land of Israel. As a rule, the Jewish

---

48 On the application of Gen. 49.10 and Davidic ancestry to Judah the Prince, see Jacobs 1995: 212–24, esp. pp. 218–21, with reference to *b. Hor.* 11b; *b. Sanh.* 5a, and *Gen. Rab.* 97.10. In the Targums the ruler's staff is regularly taken to signify the Sages as a collective. See Skarsaune 1987: 262–4.
49 Altmann 1968: 251.
50 My free paraphrase of passages like *y. Ta'an.* 2.4, *Lev. Rab.* 29.9, *Gen. Rab.* 56.10. See Str-B 3.242.
51 See, e.g., Vermes 1973: 193–227; Kessler 2004.
52 Otherwise it is difficult to understand the Jewish version which allows Isaac actually to be killed and burnt to ashes, and then resurrected from the dead, or which allows him *three* years in Paradise to recover from his wounds. 'The amoraic traditions of the death and ashes of Isaac and his subsequent resurrection can be reasonably understood as an attempt to enrich Judaism with a figure that was as colorful as the one known to Christian exegesis' (Segal 1996: 114).

Patriarch was on good terms with the imperial authorities and enjoyed certain privileges. It was the Gentile Christians who made themselves conspicuous and therefore vulnerable, claiming the Jewish privileges of exemption from the imperial cult without being Jewish. In a memorable study, Saul Lieberman made the point that when rabbis speak about 'the righteous among the Gentiles', they may have been inspired to do so by what they observed during the Diocletian persecution.[53] Some Egyptian Christians were brought to Lydda, there to stand trial and be executed. Eusebius describes how the attending Jews of the city were amazed to hear these Egyptian Christians tell their biblical names, and confess faith in the God of Israel and his Messiah in face of torture and death (*Mart. Pal.*, 8.1).

With Constantine, the scales tipped in the other direction. There was no immediate recalling of the Jewish Patriarch's privileges or authority, but they were counterbalanced by similar privileges given to prominent bishops. Perhaps most striking is the life story of Joseph of Tiberias, recounted so vividly by Epiphanius.[54] Starting as an assistant to the Jewish Patriarch of Tiberias, Joseph ended by becoming a Nicene Christian and being endowed with the status of *comes* and considerable funds by the emperor himself. It was a sign of the times. The rabbis gradually transferred main authority to the schools of Babylon. During the fourth and fifth centuries they completed the *gemara* surrounding the Mishnah. Christians became content with regarding the emperor as the earthly representative of the heavenly King Messiah, Jesus the Christ. Instead of intensely looking forward to messianic fulfilment on earth, they looked up to heaven in a kind of more static cosmos. But neither in Judaism nor in Christianity was messianism of an earlier brand extinct for good.

53 Lieberman 1939–44.
54 Epiphanius, *Pan.*, 30.4–12. See Pritz 1985; Thornton 1990; Goranson 1999; Stemberger 2000: 71–81.

Chapter 13

Syria and Mesopotamia:
the Shared Term *malka mshiḥa*

Sebastian Brock

The early history of the Aramaic-speaking Christian communities is shrouded in darkness, and it was only when they found their voice, as it were, with the adoption of the Edessene dialect of Aramaic as their literary language, that we can begin to trace something of their history. This dialect, which is generally known today as 'Syriac', would certainly still have been comprehensible to speakers of Palestinian Aramaic in the early centuries C.E., and although the Gospels reached Syriac by way of Greek, a number of direct links between early Syriac-speaking Christianity and Palestinian Aramaic can nevertheless be discerned in certain texts, some of which will be mentioned below.

The fact that it was the Aramaic dialect of Edessa (modern Şanliurfa, in south-east Turkey) which came to be adopted as the literary dialect of Aramaic-speaking Christianity indicates that Edessa must have played a particularly important role in the early history of Syriac Christianity. Unfortunately the evidence for the nature of the early Christian community in Edessa is conflicting: on the one hand, there are pointers to a Greek, and Gentile, origin of Edessene Christianity to be found in the earliest Syriac Christian work written in Edessa, the *Book of the Laws of the Countries*, associated with Bardaisan (d. 222), which breathes the air of the Greek intellectual world, and in the fact that the earliest Syriac translation of the Gospels is made from Greek; on the other hand, Edessa's own foundation story, already known to Eusebius in his *Ecclesiastical History* (1.13), and then found in a much expanded form in the early fifth-century Syriac narrative entitled *The Teaching of Addai the Apostle*, attributes the conversion of King Abgar to the preaching of the apostle Addai, who is sent from Palestine by Thomas, after the ascension of Christ; also pointing in the direction of Palestine is the fact that the Syriac Old Testament is translated from Hebrew, and not from Greek.

Modern scholars have been divided over their interpretation of this conflicting evidence. The abundance of anachronistic elements in *The Teaching of Addai* has led some to reject its evidence altogether,[1] while others[2] have tried to isolate a historical core. One possible way of resolving the question of the background to the Christian mission to Edessa, Gentile and Greek or Jewish and Aramaic, is to

---

1   Thus Drijvers 1992, 1996 and in his various earlier publications, following W. Bauer.
2   E.g. Barnard 1968, following F. C. Burkitt. For a recent survey, see ter Haar Romeny 2005.

suppose that Christianity reached Edessa by two different paths, the more educated classes by way of Greek from Antioch, and the lower classes by way of Aramaic, more directly, from Palestine. The question of the historical origins is not of direct concern here, but what is of relevance is the fact that early Syriac writings have preserved a number of Jewish features that are not to be found in Greek Christian literature;[3] quite a number of these can be specifically linked with Jewish Palestinian Aramaic.

In the light of recent studies, most notably Michael Weitzman's *The Syriac Version of the Old Testament,* it is clear that the Hebrew Bible must have been translated into Edessene Aramaic/Syriac at some time during the second century C.E., perhaps over the course of several decades.[4] Whether this was the work of Jews or of Christians (or done partly by Jews and partly by Christians, or indeed, by Jews who had become Christians) remains uncertain. If the whole or part was the work of Christians, then these Christians must have come from a Jewish background, for otherwise their extensive knowledge of Hebrew (and certain Jewish exegetical traditions) would be inexplicable; if, on the other hand, it was the work of Jews, the fact that their translation (and not one made from Greek) was taken over as the standard Old Testament, still indicates that there must have been close links between the emerging Christian community and its roots in Judaism. Furthermore, the presence in early Syriac literature of a number of non-biblical traditions and phraseology of Jewish origin points in the same direction.

Two features, both of which specifically provide links between Syriac and Palestinian Jewish Aramaic, may be singled out here. Then, to these two a third such link, provided by the phrase *malka mshiha*, 'King Messiah', will be added, and it is this particular phrase which will constitute the central theme of the present chapter.

One of the features of the Targum tradition in general is a desire on the part of the translators to bring out the transcendence of God. This was achieved by adopting various 'distancing mechanisms', one of which was to render 'the Lord was seen by …' by 'the Lord was revealed to'. In the Official Pentateuch Targum tradition of Onqelos, the form this took was straightforward, *'itgli l-*, 'revealed to', but in the Palestinian Targum tradition represented by codex Neofiti, one finds *'itgli 'al*, 'was revealed *over*' in all twenty-one occurrences. Turning to the Syriac Peshitta it is remarkable that this version follows the wording of Neofiti in twelve instances, whereas only in five does it translate the Hebrew literally. What is even more striking is the considerable number of places in early Syriac literature where *'etgli 'al* (the Syriac equivalent) is introduced in connection with biblical passages where neither Neofiti, nor the Peshitta, have it, whereas sometimes there is a Jewish Palestinian Aramaic counterpart that can be identified.[5] The only reasonable explanation for this phenomenon is to suppose that this phraseology was inherited by nascent Syriac Christianity from the same sort of Palestinian Jewish milieu that produced the Palestinian Targum.

---

3   Some examples can be found in Brock 1979.
4   Weitzman 1999; see also Brock 1998.
5   See further Brock 1995.

The second feature to which attention is drawn here concerns the distinctive rendering in the Syriac Gospels of two key passages, Lk. 1.35 and Jn 1.14. In the Greek original two different Greek verbs are used: in Luke, Mary is informed by the angel that 'the Holy Spirit will come and the Power of the Most High will *overshadow* (ἐπισκιάσει) you', whereas in John we have 'the Word became flesh and *dwelt* (ἐσκήνωσεν) in/among us'. Both Greek verbs could readily have been translated literally into Syriac, but surprisingly all the Syriac versions provide a single verb, *aggen*, which is by no means an obvious choice, and for which there is no really satisfactory English equivalent, though perhaps 'tabernacle' might be used. Although the verb *aggen* does indeed occur a number of times in the Peshitta Old Testament, in passages such as Isa. 31.5 ('Thus the Lord Almighty will *aggen* over Jerusalem'), none of these passages suggest any explanation for the choice of the verb in these two Gospel verses. In order to find a satisfactory rationale behind the choice one has to turn to the Palestinian Targum tradition in Exod. 12. The meaning of the Hebrew verb *pasaḥ*, which occurs a number of times in this chapter, was already in antiquity a matter of dispute, and several different interpretations are recorded; among these is that of the Palestinian Targum tradition, where Neofiti regularly employs the Aramaic verb *aggen*.[6]

In order to discover why the original Syriac translator of these two Gospel passages chose this particular verb one needs to turn to Ephrem's *Commentary on Exodus*, where he comments (XII.2–3):

> The (passover) lamb is a symbol of our Lord who came to the womb on the tenth of Nisan. For, on the tenth of the seventh month (i.e. Tishri), when Zechariah was told about the birth of John,[7] up to the tenth of the first month (i.e. Nisan), when the announcement was made to Mary by the angel, constitute six months. That was why the angel said to her 'This is the sixth month for her who had been called barren' (Luke 1.36). On the tenth, therefore, when the (passover) lamb was confined (Exod. 12.3), our Lord was conceived, and on the fourteenth, when it was slaughtered, he whom the lamb symbolized was crucified.[8]

In the light of this passage, it seems very probable that it was a desire to bring out this typological parallel that led the translator to adopt this particular verb, whose presence in the Palestinian Targum of Exodus 12 he must have been aware of.

A third such distinctive link between Syriac Christianity and Palestinian Judaism turns out to be provided by the phrase *malka mshiḥa*, 'King Messiah'. Although the concept of the royal Messiah is widespread and has been widely discussed, comparatively little attention has been paid to this particular phrase. In origin the phrase will have started out with the second word either as an adjective, or as a substantive in apposition, thus either 'the anointed king', or 'the

---

6 For details see Brock 1982.
7 This is based on the assumption (first found in the *Protogospel of James*) that Zacharias was High Priest and that the occasion was the Day of Atonement.
8 Similarly in his *Hymns on the Nativity*, 5.14. The 10th Nisan as the day of the Annunciation/conception was widespread in early Syriac literature.

king, the anointed one'; since in Late Aramaic usage *malka* follows, rather than precedes, the name, in Syriac Christian usage *mshiha* should be taken as standing in apposition, 'the King, Christ', and this will properly apply also to the Jewish usage, i.e. 'the King, the Messiah', rather than 'King Messiah' (as it is conventionally rendered).[9] Below, in order to bring out the commonality between Jewish and Syriac Christian usage I simply transliterate.[10]

It comes as a matter of surprise to discover that the precise phrase *malka mshiha* is far from common: it is not found in any Jewish text of the Hellenistic period, and it is largely absent from mainstream rabbinic literature; it does, however, feature not infrequently in the Palestinian Targum tradition (but never in the Babylonian),[11] in the Palestinian Talmud and Midrashim,[12] and in poetry;[13] from the seventh century onwards it also appears in some Jewish apocalyptic texts.[14] What would appear on the surface to be the earliest occurrence of the phrase is a famous passage in *y. Ta'an.* 4.8 (commenting on Num. 24.17) where we are told that 'When Rabbi Akiba saw Bar Kozba, he exclaimed "This is *malka mshiha*!"'. This of course would take us back to the Bar Kokhba rebellion of 132–5 if the attribution of these words to R. Akiba were correct; serious doubt, however, has been cast on this by Peter Schäfer,[15] and so we are left without any clear evidence for the date at which usage of the term *malka mshiha* originated.

In the Palestinian Pentateuch Targum tradition *malka mshiha* features in the following places in Neofiti: Gen. 3.15; 49.10, 11; Num. 11.26; 24.7, to which the Fragmentary Targum adds Exod. 12.42, and *Pseudo-Jonathan* Gen. 35.21; Exod. 40.9; Num. 23.21; 24.17, 20, 24; Deut. 25.19 and 30.4. Several of these are of course important messianic passages for Christian writers, but (as will be seen) the occurrences of *malka mshiha* in Syriac writers are only associated with one of these passages, Gen. 49 (and, at that, to the previous verse, 49.9).

A good example of the Jewish apocalyptic texts of the seventh century is to be found in the *Prayer of R. Simeon b. Yohai*; this text, while commenting on Dan. 2, tells how the 'fourth king' loves silver and gold, makes coins of brass and hides them under the Euphrates together with silver and gold, where 'they are stored for the King Messiah, as it is said, "And I will give you the treasures of darkness …"'(Isa. 45.3). A little later the author quotes 2 Chr. 10.19, 'So Israel rebelled against the House of David, unto this day', with the comment ' "unto this day"

---

9 This was pointed out long ago by (among others) Str-B, commenting on Lk. 23.2 (1924: II, 263); the same point is made more recently by Schreiber (2000: 440 n. 140). This equally applies to Syriac (e.g. the *Teaching of Addai* regularly has *Abgar malka*).
10 In most of the translations (where available) of the relevant Syriac texts the link with Jewish tradition is obscured.
11 See Levey 1974; Pérez Fernández 1981: 142 and *passim*. The nearest that *Targum Onqelos* and *Jonathan* ever get to the title is at Num. 24.7, where 'king' and 'messiah' are in parallelism, and 2 Sam. 23.3, (David said) 'He (*sc.* God) decided to appoint for me a king, he is the Messiah, who is destined to arise and rule in the fear of the Lord'.
12 E.g. *y. Ta'an.* 4.8, *y. Ber.* 2.4 (discussed by Goldberg 1979: 10–17); *Gen. Rab.* 97 (ed. Albeck, 1212–13); *Lam. Rab.* 1.16; *Pesiq. Rab.* 36; *Pirqe R. El.* 3.5; 8.4; 11.3; 32.1; *Midrash Tehillim* 21.1–2; 72.6; 87.6; 93.3; 104.5 etc.
13 Yahalom and Sokoloff 1999: 278.
14 See especially Alexander 1998.
15 Schäfer 1981: 168–9; Schäfer 2003: 2–4.

means unto the day the King Messiah will come'. At the eschaton it will be the King Messiah who fights against the armies of Armilus.[16] A Greek Christian text from the reign of Heraclius provides a firm dating for the emergence of these apocalyptic features. In the *Doctrina Iacobi nuper baptizati*[17] we are told (V.6) that 'Some of the Jews were saying that in Tiberias our priest of the Jews saw a great revelation in a vision, which was saying to him that after eight years the Anointed One, the King of Israel, the Christ, is coming and he will be born of a virgin and raise up the nation of the Jews'. Elsewhere in this text (I.5, III.9, IV.3, V.1–2, 4–5, 16) reference is made to 'Hermolaos', clearly the same figure as Armilus who probably occurs in a poem by Qillir that evidently belongs to the same period.[18] Eventually, from the tenth century onwards, these apocalyptic traditions about the King Messiah get taken up into mainstream Jewish tradition by such authoritative figures as Sa'adya[19] in the tenth century and Maimonides in the twelfth.[20]

In the Greek New Testament, although Jesus is described as 'King of the Jews' on a number of occasions (notably in the inscription on the cross, Mt. 27.37, Mk 15.26, Lk. 23.38, Jn 19.19), the combination βασιλεὺς χριστός never occurs; the closest approximation is to be found in the reverse order of words, in Lk. 23.2, where the crowd accuse Jesus before Pilate, saying 'we have found this man perverting our nation, and forbidding us to give tribute to Caesar, and saying that he himself is Christ, a king' (λέγοντα αὐτὸν χριστὸν βασιλέα εἶναι). Although there is no variant in the Greek manuscripts recorded here, in both Old Syriac manuscripts and in the Peshitta we find 'and he says of himself that he is King Messiah (*malka mshiḥa*)'.[21] In passing it might be observed that, given the difficulty of dating the Jewish texts, the Old Syriac, usually dated to the late second or early third century C.E., is almost certainly the oldest extant witness to the term *malka mshiḥa*.[22] While the kingship of Christ is a theme which is frequently touched on in Greek Patristic literature, it would appear that the combination

---

16 See Lewis 1976: 314–20.

17 For this work, whose *terminus ante quem* is 646/7, see especially Dagron and Déroche 1991, with a re-edition of the work (for the date: p. 247).

18 Fleischer 1984–5: 415, where he restores line 39 as [*'rml*]*yws* (the spelling *-yws* is also found in the *Nevu'ot Daniel*, for which see DiTommaso 2005: 184–5). In the influential *Christian Apocalypse of Pseudo-Methodius* (IX.4, ed. Reinink, CSCO 540–1) from the end of the seventh century *'rml'ws*, clearly the same name, turns up as the king of the Romans who marries Byzantia, daughter of Kushyat (in the genealogy devised to provide an eschatological exegesis of Ps. 68.31, 'Kush will surrender to kud'. The early Greek and Latin translations of this apocalypse (ed. Aerts and Kortekaas, CSCO 569) specifically identify 'Armelaos' as Romulus. Did Hermelaos start out as some sort of code name for Heraclius, regarded as a negative figure in contemporary Jewish texts, but later taken up as a positive figure in *Ps. Methodius*? A comparative study of these late apocalyptic traditions common to Jewish and Christian sources would be instructive: clearly some interaction is taking place.

19 In ch. 8 of his *Book of Beliefs and Opinions*, for which see Alexander 1998.

20 *Mishneh Torah*, XIV.11.1: 'King Messiah will arise and restore the Kingdom of David to its former dominion. He will build up the Sanctuary and gather together the outcasts of Israel (Ps. 147.2)', cited in Horbury 2003b: 304.

21 The Harklean revision restores the Greek word order (as one would expect).

22 Although Justin knows the title βασιλεύς (cf. *Dial.* 86.3) the combination βασιλεύς χριστός never occurs in the Apostolic Fathers.

βασιλεὺς χριστός (in that order) is only very rarely found, and at that, in rather marginal places, such as in a Manichaean prayer from the Dakhleh oasis[23] and a liturgical fragment of the seventh century.[24] By contrast, Syriac literature proves to be far more productive of examples, but before turning to this, attention might be drawn to a passage in the *Pseudo-Clementine Recognitions* (I.45.3): in the course of a list of terms for 'king' in different societies (e.g. *apud Romanos Caesar, apud Aegyptios Pharao*) the author goes on: *ita apud Iudaeos Christus communi nomine rex appelatur*.[25]

The Syriac author who makes the most use of the title *malka mshiha* happens to be the earliest major Syriac writer whose works survive, Aphrahat, writing within the Persian Empire in the second quarter of the fourth century. In the course of his 23 'Demonstrations' he uses the title *malka mshiha* no less than fifteen times. While he uses various other titles involving 'king', such as *malka d-ʿalme*, 'king of the worlds/ages' (XIV.15), they never feature more than a few times each, thus making the frequency of *malka mshiha* all the more striking. To go through all the passages would be out of place here, and only a few will be quoted by way of illustration.

Demonstration IV.6 describes the various symbols (lit. mysteries, *raze*) of Christ that are connected with the patriarch Jacob. Among them is an allusion to the wording of Jacob's Blessing in Gen. 49.9:

Judah, the lion's whelp, was in his (*sc.* Jacob's) loins, in whom was hidden *malka mshiha*.

Interest in the ancestry of the Messiah is of course common in both Jewish and Christian texts, but a specific reference to *malka mshiha* is rare; in Aphrahat another one is to be found in *Demonstration* XXIII.16:

From the offspring of Ruth was born the family of the House of David; from their seed was born *malka mshiha*.

For this one can find a good parallel in the *Tg. Ruth* 3.15, where among the righteous who will descend from Ruth is *malka mshiha*.[26]

Whereas in *Demonstration* IV.6, Aphrahat refers to *malka mshiha* in connection with Gen. 49.9, in the Palestinian Targum tradition *malka mshiha* features in the following verses, where, for example, Neofiti has for verse 10:[27]

---

23   Jenkins 1995: 250 (line 35); the context (lines 33–6) reads προσ(κυνῶ καὶ δοξάζω) τὸν τῆς μεγαλειότητος ἔγγονον, τὸν φωτεινὸν νοῦν βασιλέα χρ(ιστὸν) τὸν ἐκ τῶν ἐξωτέρων αἰώνων ἐληλυθότα ...
24   Wessely, in PO 18 (1924), 438.
25   This corresponds to p. 27, line 34, in de Lagarde's edition of the Syriac translation.
26   A desire on the part of Gentile women such as Ruth and Tamar to become ancestors of the Messiah is another shared feature between Jewish and early Syriac literature: for a highly imaginative treatment of Tamar from this perspective, see Brock 2002.
27   Pérez Fernández 1981: 123 describes Gen. 49.10 as 'el texto fundamental del mesianismo'. For a discussion of this passage, see Skarsaune, this volume: 164; and Salvesen, this volume: 246–7.

Kings shall not cease from among those of the House of Judah ... until *malka mshiḥa* comes, to whom royalty/the kingdom (*malkuta*) belongs and to whom all kingdoms will submit.

Although many Syriac writers, including Aphrahat (II.6, XIV.1, XIX.11; cp V.10) quote this verse with the addition of '(to whom) the kingdom belongs',[28] none, it would seem, ever introduces the term *malka mshiḥa* here. This difference is significant in that it strongly suggests that, while our extant Jewish and Syriac Christian texts share common Palestinian roots, each has developed its inheritance in a different way.

On several occasions Aphrahat introduces *malka mshiḥa* in connection with passages in Daniel. In *Demonstration* XIX.9–10 he twice quotes Dan. 9.25 in the course of extended quotations from that chapter: whereas the Peshitta renders *mashiaḥ nagid* in verse 25 by *mshiḥa malka*, on both occasions Aphrahat alters the word order to *malka mshiḥa*.[29] The same passage is referred to indirectly in *Demonstration* XXIII.46:

After the return, Israel resided in Jerusalem for 70 weeks, just as Daniel prophesied. These weeks are 490 years. After the killing of *malka mshiḥa* Jerusalem was laid ruin, not to be inhabited again, and up to the completion of what is decreed it has remained in desolation. [ch. IX.8]

In *Demonstration* V.14 Aphrahat introduces *malka mshiḥa* in connection with Dan. 2:

He showed that 'in the days of those kings who will rise up in the kingdom, the God of heaven will raise up a kingdom which will never be destroyed or pass away (Dan. 2.44)' – which is the kingdom of *malka mshiḥa*, which will remove the fourth kingdom.

In the same section he quotes Dan. 2.34, with its reference to 'the stone not hewn by human hands', and goes on to comment:

The stone which smote the image and broke it to pieces and by which the whole earth was filled is the kingdom of *malka mshiḥa* who will make an end to the kingdom of this world and he will rule for ever and ever.

Later Syriac writers were to take the stone as referring to Christ himself, rather than his kingdom.

---

28   For an amazingly extensive collection of materials on the exegesis of this verse, see Posnanski 1904. The appearance of the addition of *malkuta* in Syriac writers as well as in *Targum Onqelos* is duly noted by Horbury 2003b: 55 n.44; that it does not belong to the original Peshitta was shown by Jansma 1973. As Jansma indicated (and likewise, Vööbus before him) many Syriac writers attest the addition; although 'King' is occasionally also added (e.g. Jacob of Serugh, *Prose Homilies*, ed. F. Rilliet, PO 43:4 (1986), 80/81), I have never found 'King Messiah' here in any Syriac sources.
29   On the second occasion one of the two manuscripts has restored the word order of the Peshitta.

Aphrahat refers to *malka mshiha* in connection with one further biblical passage, Isa. 65.8-9. The entire final *Demonstration* has the title 'On the Cluster (*tutitha*; *sc.* of Blessing)', referring to these verses, but in section 13 he specifies that 'The whole "bunch (*sgola*)" is the people of Israel and the blessing that was in its midst is *malka mshiha*'.

A further significant context in which Aphrahat uses the title *malka mshiha* is to be found in *Demonstration* XXII.4, where he associates it with the descent of Christ to the underworld:

> But when the dead saw light in the darkness, they raised up their heads from the imprisonment of death, looked out and beheld the radiance of *malka mshiha*.

In contrast to Aphrahat, with his rather frequent references to *malka mshiha*,[30] the other great Syriac author of the fourth century, Ephrem (d. 373), has only a single reference. In the *Hymns on Virginity* 6.6 he writes:

> The olive tree is like John: a symbol of his Lord he proclaimed beforehand.
> *Malka mshiha* shone forth and came: the olive tree went out to meet its Lord.

In this cluster of poems Ephrem is providing a whole set of variations on the word play *meshha – mshiha*, '(olive) oil – Christ/anointed one', and so it is likely that Ephrem will have uppermost in his mind the sense 'anointed king'.[31]

Although Ephrem transmits quite a number of exegetical traditions of Jewish origin, scholars in general 'feel' he is certainly not as close to the Jewish roots of Syriac Christianity as Aphrahat is. The same applies to another early Syriac work, the *Book of Steps*, probably dating from the end of the fourth century. Here too we encounter a single reference. In VI.2 the anonymous author states that when one has become truly humble, 'then *malka mshiha* will say, "Behold, this person is now as perfect as on the day I fashioned him"'; whereupon the gates of heaven will be opened for him.

It is in a group of texts of Edessene provenance from the first half of the fifth century that we next encounter the term *malka mshiha* in Syriac. Towards the end of the *Teaching of Addai the Apostle*, we are told that the clergy ordained by Addai's successor, Aggai, put into practice what they preached, and when people saw this, 'many were converted by them and were confessing *malka mshiha*, and praising God' (p. 51). This is the only occurrence in the *Teaching of Addai*, but in a text which must emanate from the same milieu in Edessa, the (highly legendary) *Acts of Sharbel*, *malka mshiha* occurs no less than six times. Thus, for example, in the course of the address by Barsamya, bishop of Edessa, to the pagan high priest Sharbel, we find a reference to Abgar the 'Black' who, according to the *Teaching of Addai*, was converted by Addai:

---

30   Other passages are I.4, IX.8 and XIV.30, 40.
31   The phrase also occurs in the *Response to Hymns on the Unleavened Bread* 6: 'To you, Lord, be praise, O *malka mshiha*, for by your blood your holy Church was saved'; the *Responses*, however, are sometimes secondary. It is also to be found in nos 67 and 71 of the *Necrosima*, attributed to Ephrem in vol. VI of the eighteenth-century Roman edition of his works.

Syria and Mesopotamia

King Abgar, the ancestor of the present (king) Abgar who worships idols along with you, was also believing in *malka mshiha*, the Son of him whom you call 'Lord of all the gods'.[32]

Later on (p. 51), when Sharbel is converted and arraigned before the court, he tells the judge:

Far be it from me that I should say that there are gods, powers, fates and horoscopes; rather, I confess the one God who made heaven, earth, the seas and all that is in them, and in the Son who is from him, *malka mshiha*.

And a little further on (p. 51), alluding to Mt. 10.32 (and parallels), he states:

Death on behalf of this cause is true life for those who acknowledge *malka mshiha*, and he too will acknowledge them in the presence of his glorious Father.

The term also features once each in two other Edessene martyr acts,[33] and occasionally in other Syriac prose literature of the fifth century.[34] It would thus appear that during the course of the fifth century the term dropped out of use. Certainly the great poets of the fifth and sixth century no longer seem to have any particular interest in the title, though Narsai does employ it on occasion, but usually without giving it any particular context; a single exception to this is to be found in Narsai's *Homily* XXXIII (ed. Mingana, II, p. 161):

Another (prophet, *sc*. Zechariah) cries out 'Listen, daughter of the peoples, instead of the daughter of Sion, for behold *malka mshiha* is coming'.[35]

There appear to be no occurrences in any of Isaac of Antioch's verse homilies that have been published so far, and the only example I have come across in the extensive corpus of Jacob of Serugh's verse homilies is in two passages, in one of which it is only as a variant reading.

In Jacob's *memra* (verse homily) on Peter, John, Paul and the conversion of Antioch,[36] a young boy who died and was brought back to life again by Paul describes his death experience and at one point (lines 690–1) states:

---

32   Cureton 1864: 43; all the other passages speak of 'confessing *malka mshiha*' (pp. 42, 45, 49, 51 *bis*).

33   *Martyrdom of Barsamya* (Cureton 1864: 68, line 7), *Martyrdom of Habbib* (ed. Burkitt), section 36.

34   E.g. *Martyrdom of Cyriacus* (ed. Pigulevskaya, *Revue de l'Orient Chrétien* 26 (1927/8), p. 334; Departure of Mary (ed. Lewis, *Apocrypha Syriaca* (Studia Sinaitica XI, 1902), p. 157.

35   Other passages in Narsai (ed. Mingana) are: I, 280 (*Hom*. 17; though this homily is slightly later than Narsai): 'Where *malka mshiha* is sitting at the right hand, do not occupy yourselves with empty thoughts about earthly things'; I, 354 (*Hom*. 21): (the priest) 'gives the Bread, and says "The Body of *malka mshiha*"'; II, 127 (*Hom*. 30): 'In this manner the venerable sign of the crucifixion carries, with the sight of it, the great image of *malka mshiha*'.

36   Edited by Thomas, 1978. The text is included in the extra vol. 6 of the Gorgias Press reprint of P. Bedjan's five volumes of Jacob's verse homilies (2006).

I saw the chariot upon which *malka mshiha* was sitting, with the Watchers and Angels worshipping before him with trembling.

The other passage occurs in a *memra* on the Virgin Mary where the printed text[37] has:

When the great King set his face to come to our country
He resided in the purest shrine of all the universe (*sc.* Mary), since it so pleased him.

One of the fragmentary Syriac manuscripts[38] at Deir al-Surian, in Egypt, happens to include this passage, but with the reading *malka mshiha*, instead of 'great King (*malka rabba*)'. Since (as will be seen) *malka mshiha* becomes quite common again in the liturgical texts, its is possible that its presence in this liturgical MS is due to the scribe's familiarity with the title.

One sixth-century Syriac author who does introduce the term at least on one occasion is Daniel of Salah, in his extensive *Commentary on the Psalms*:[39] it is particularly intriguing that it features in his commentary on Psalm 72, which is one of the seven places in the Targum to Psalms where *malka mshiha* features.

In view of the use of *malka mshiha* in Jewish apocalyptic literature of the seventh century it is remarkable that this term also features in a Syriac apocalyptic text which probably belongs to the same period. In the recently published Syriac Apocalypse of Daniel[40] we find the following passage (chs 29–30), coming near the beginning of the description of the final denouement.

(29) Then the God of gods, Lord of lords and King of kings, Adonai Sebaoth, the Lord Almighty will be fully seen over Sion, and he will establish the cherub of the sanctuary over Sion and the throne of righteousness over the mountains of Jerusalem. The < >[41] of *malka mshiha* from heaven will be seen on earth; radiant seraphs will be standing before him, and glorious angels will be ministering before him. He will cause his Shekhinta to reside on the mountains of Jerusalem, and he will tabernacle over her (*sc.* Jerusalem) and sanctify her; in the shadow of his wings he will protect her and he will cause to shine out over her the radiance of his countenance, while his right hand, mighty in its strength, will overshadow her.
(30) Then the advent of *malka mshiha* will take place in great glory, for his name exists before the sun, and his rule and kingdom exist before the moon ...[42]

---

37 Ed. P. Bedjan, at the end of Bedjan 1902: 620.
38 Fragment 8 in the *Catalogue of Syriac Manuscripts*, in the course of preparation; this is a single folio deriving from the same manuscript as the *Homiliary* now in the British Library, Add. 12165, which is dated 1015. (I am most grateful to Bishop Mattaos and the Librarian, Fr Bigoul, for permission to cite this evidence.)
39 An edition of this important work is currently being prepared by D. G. K. Taylor. In the meantime I have used a recent manuscript copy of the text.
40 Henze 2001.
41 The text is lacking a subject, and a feminine noun must have been lost.
42 My translation; Henze (p. 103) misleadingly renders 'Christ the King' both times, thus obscuring the interest of the term. For the pre-existence of the King Messiah, see *Midrash Tehillim* 93.3.

Although the Syriac Apocalypse of Daniel has certain features in common with other Syriac apocalyptic texts of the seventh century, the term *malka mshiha* is absent from the two most important of them, the anonymous poem on Alexander the Great, from the reign of Heraclius, and the *Apocalypse of Pseudo-Methodius*, of *ca.* 692, and appears not to feature in any of the various other texts either.

It has already been noted earlier that the term King Messiah eventually came to be incorporated into mainstream Jewish tradition. In some ways the same thing could be said in connection with the Syriac tradition, for it is in the liturgical texts, both East and West Syriac, that one can find fairly plentiful examples where *malka mshiha* features. The fact that it turns up in both the Maronite and Syrian Orthodox Weekday Office is an indication of its general familiarity; thus, for example, on Sunday Matins (*Sapro*) in the Maronite rite a verse text has '*malko mshiho* makes straight his path to the mount of Jebus, which is Jerusalem: he fixes his cross on the grave of Adam', and on Wednesday Matins in the Syrian Orthodox we find 'O *malka mshiha*, at the gate of your compassion I knock at every moment, asking compassion and mercy from your rich treasure'. A second occurrence at the same service has reference to the departed: 'O *malka mshiha* our Saviour, make memorial for the departed … cause them to rejoice in your Bridal Chamber'.[43]

It is, however, in the Festal Hymnaries of both the East and West Syriac liturgical traditions that the term is most frequently encountered,[44] and in these it is noticeable that it tends to feature most frequently at particular points in the liturgical year. Not surprisingly one of these is the Nativity, where we find examples such as the following:

(a) East Syriac liturgical tradition (Church of the East):
Hudra I, 558: 'Glorious is your Nativity, O King who has shone forth from David, for at it peace and harmony has come about between the assemblies above and those below; at it great hope has come, and salvation for all the peoples. Praise to you, O *malka mshiha*; have mercy on us'.
Hudra I, 559: 'O resplendent womb (*sc.* of Mary) which has prepared all kinds of joys for the race of mortals, since *malka mshiha* has shone forth[45] for us from you in a wonder …'.

(b) West Syriac liturgical tradition (Syrian Orthodox):
Fenqitho II, 238a = 253b: 'At the Nativity of *malka mshiha* the Watchers flew down to Bethlehem …'.
Fenqitho II, 465b: 'On this day *malka mshiha* has been born from the Virgin Mary, the Lord, Lord of all'.

---

43   The term also features in some of the Syrian Orthodox burial services. The eschatological 'Bridal Chamber' turns up remarkably frequently in Syriac liturgical texts; for it, see Brock 2005.
44   The examples are taken from the three-volume edition of the East Syrian *Hudra* by T. Darmo (Trissur, 1960–2), and the seven-volume edition of the West Syrian *Fenqitho* (Mosul, 1886–96). I have noticed approximately twenty occurrences in each of the volumes of the *Hudra* and *Fenqitho*.
45   The verb *dnah* is rather frequently used in connection with *malka mshiha*: e.g. *Fenqitho* II, 234a, III, 84a, 385b.

This last text is of interest in the light of *Lamentations Rabbah* 1.51, where, in response to the question 'What is the name of *malka mshiha*?', R. Abba b. Kahana said 'His name is "the Lord"' (based on Jer. 23.6, 'In his days Judah will be saved, and Israel will dwell securely. And this is the name by which he shall be called: "The Lord is our righteousness"').

In a number of passages *malka mshiha* is used where mention is made of revelation and liberation. Thus, for example, in the East Syriac *Hudra* at Epiphany: I, 646: 'At his revelation *malka mshiha* liberated creation and delivered it from error'. Here one might compare *Targum Pseudo-Jonathan* at Exod. 40.9, where *malka mshiha* 'is destined to redeem Israel at the end of days', or the *Targum to Lamentations* 4.22 where the Congregation of Sion 'will be delivered by the hands of *malka mshiha* and Elijah the High Priest'.

Elsewhere in the *Fenqitho* Old Testament prophets and John the Baptist are described as foretelling the future coming of *malka mshiha*. Thus, on the Sunday of Enkainia 'Isaiah summoned and gave the good news to the Church concerning the light of *malka mshiha* who is coming and will give her joy' (*Fenqitho* II, 41a), while at the commemoration of John the Baptist (Jan. 7th), he is described as 'proclaiming and crying out "Behold, there will come after me *malka mshiha*"' (*Fenqitho* III, 293b).

Finally, reference to *malka mshiha* can also be in a purely eschatological context, as in the following: 'Then the glorious throne of judgement is set up; the Just Judge takes his seat upon it and the *malka mshiha* is revealed. The angels come forth in haste as all the peoples, nations, races and generations stand in crowds there in trepidation' (*Fenqitho* III, 202b).

There can be little doubt that the Syriac use of the term *malka mshiha* had its origin in the Jewish Palestinian Aramaic milieu out of which the Palestinian Targums also emerged, thus providing yet another clear example of the influence of the Jewish roots of at least one strand of early Syriac Christianity. In all likelihood it was Gen. 49.9-11 which provided the common exegetical starting point for both Jewish and Syriac Christian tradition. It is, furthermore, remarkable that the Old Syriac Gospels would seem to provide the earliest roughly datable evidence for the emergence of the term; in any case they give us the *terminus ante quem* for the borrowing. Although the two exegetical traditions, Christian Syriac and Jewish, reflect a few common elements as far as the association of *malka mshiha* with specific passages is concerned , it is clear that for the most part each developed in its own way, and for the most part separately. It seems very possible, however, that shared apocalyptic concerns, in the face of the upheavals of the seventh century that affected both communities, brought the term to the forefront again, and this in turn led to a resurgence of interest in the term on the Syriac side which resulted in its surprisingly frequent use in the liturgical texts, while on the Jewish side, it led to the eventual incorporation of the term into the mainstream of medieval Jewish tradition.[46]

---

46. For further discussion of Messianism in the Targums, see Gordon, this volume: 262–73.

Chapter 14

EGYPT

James Carleton Paget

Introduction

Origen reports that Celsus, himself possibly an Alexandrian, described the dispute between Jews and Christians in Plato's terms as no more than 'a battle about the shadow of an ass' (*Cels.* 3.1 and Plato, *Phaedrus* 260C). The content of this 'battle', Celsus stated, was Christ or the messiah. '(T)hey both believe', he continues, 'that by divine inspiration a certain saviour was prophesied to be coming to dwell among mankind; but they do not agree as to whether the one prophesied has come or not.'[1] What precisely they believed and the extent to which their beliefs coincided, has been a major concern of William Horbury's research.[2] In articles and books on the subject he has emphasized what he sees as the considerable extent to which Jewish messianic beliefs influenced Christian ones, a view which forms part of a larger thesis about the ongoing contact between Jews and Christians in antiquity.[3] The applicability of Horbury's convergence thesis to the Jewish and Christian material of Egypt is not easy to determine. This is mainly because our sources, though richer for Egypt than many other parts of the Roman Empire, do not teem with messianic references. Moreover, for a variety of reasons, Christian and Jewish sources rarely emerge from the same chronological period, making comparison more difficult.

It is the aim of this essay to re-examine the material from Egypt pertinent to messianism, here understood to refer to a coming pre-eminent ruler, associated either with a pre-existent or human figure, often in an eschatological or millennial setting, and not necessarily termed 'messiah';[4] to see to what extent something coherent and self-contained emerges from it; to determine how much such material relates to issues of resistance; and to look again at the ways in which Jewish and Christian ideas about the messiah converged.

---

1   For a discussion of this passage and the view that it should not be taken literally see Lona 2005: 178–9.
2   I am delighted to contribute to a volume in honour of William Horbury. Over many years, as undergraduate, graduate and colleague, I have benefited immeasurably from his immense learning and friendship.
3   Reflected in Horbury 1998c and Horbury 2003b.
4   For difficulties connected with the term see Green 1987; and for an equivalent definition see Horbury 1998c: 6–7.

1. Messianism among Jews in Egypt

An account of messianism in Egypt should begin with the Septuagint. Egypt constitutes the home of initial efforts to translate the Hebrew Bible into Greek, in particular the Pentateuch. The date of the earliest translation, of the Pentateuch, remains a matter of dispute but a consensus seems to have gathered around a time in the late third/early second century. William Horbury, in particular, has drawn attention to passages in the Septuagint whose rendition into Greek seems to be motivated by messianic presuppositions. Especially important in this respect are three pentateuchal passages, Gen. 49.9-10, Num. 24.7 and 17, and Deut. 33.4-5.[5] They come from oracles associated with Jacob, Balaam and Moses respectively and appear at significant moments in the text. Most important, especially from the perspective of its subsequent interpretation, were the two verses in Num. 24, which seem to envisage a future ruler, referred to both as a man and a star who will rule over an empire. *Sib. Or.* 3 and 5, Philo and the Targumim all support this messianic view of the passage.[6] But assessing the importance of these passages as witness to late-third-century Egyptian messianism is difficult.[7] Their subsequent interpretation should be distinguished from what they actually say.[8]

Mention of the Septuagint brings to mind the obvious importance that the Old Testament ascribes to Egypt and its place in Israel's future. In this context we might in particular note Isa. 19.20 and 25 (cf. Jer. 46), in which the bright future of Israel is bound up with the punishment of Egypt, and where in Isa. 19.20, a deliverer for the Jews originates in that country. Egypt's significance, at least from an eschatological perspective, is heightened, because of its association with the events of the Exodus.[9]

Sib. Or. 3 is generally held to have been written in Egypt. Support for this position is found in the double reference to Egypt in 156–61 in which it appears as a second world empire after the Macedonians, the sympathetic references to a seventh king of Egypt (see 193, 318 and 608), and the presence of material apparently reliant upon the Egyptian *Potter's Oracle*.[10] While none of these arguments clinches the matter, Egypt on balance still seems the best suggestion.[11]

---

5   Horbury 1998c: 50–1. LXX Gen. 49.9-10 seems to have messianic overtones in its rendition of MT 'gone up' by ἀναβαίνω, here recalling the use of the same verb in the messianic Isa. 11.1; and in its translation by 'ruler' and 'governor' of MT's 'sceptre' and 'staff'. LXX Num. 24.7 famously renders 'Water shall flow from his buckets' with 'There shall come forth a man from his seed'; LXX Num. 24.17 renders MT 'sceptre' as 'man', again with an apparently messianic meaning (on the messianic connotations of 'man' see Horbury 2003b: 144–51). LXX Deut. 33.4-5 states that 'they shall have a ruler in the beloved' here rendering a verb in the past in the MT by the future; and replaces MT 'nation' by 'nations' rendering the messianic aspect a bit stronger. For a more cautious study of the LXX of these passages, see Salvesen in this volume.

6   See Hengel 1996: 338.

7   Horbury 1998c: 48 quotes Frankel's extravagant judgement, arising from the LXX of the above passages, that messianism was more developed in Alexandria than Judaea in the third century.

8   For a sceptical discussion, see Oegema 1994: 44–8; and Salvesen, this volume: 246–8.

9   See Horbury 1996: 298–301.

10   See Collins 1983: 355–6.

11   For arguments in favour of an Asian provenance, see Buitenwerf 2003: 130–3. For an Egyptian interest in Asia, see Frankfurter 1996: 147 and 165.

Dating the work is problematic, if only because it consists of oracles emanating from different periods. Most scholars settle upon a rolling period of 180 to 130 B.C.E.[12] Two of these contain possibly messianic passages, although nowhere is the word messiah explicitly mentioned. In the first (286–7) the seer states that the God of heaven will send a king and will judge each man in blood and the gleam of fire. Here the context might imply a reference to Cyrus who will rebuild the temple,[13] and 'if the passage has any bearing on the eschatology of the sibyl, it suggests that the final restoration of the Jews will also be mediated by a gentile king.'[14] The passage may operate on a second, messianic level. In this case, the king could either be a non-Jewish (for instance Egyptian) 'messianic' deliverer, as with Cyrus, or a Jewish messiah proper. The second reference occurs at 652–6. Here it is stated that 'then God will send a king from the sun who will give every land respite from the evil war, killing some and imposing pledges of loyalty on others. Nor will he do all these things by himself, but in obedience to the excellent decree of the great God.' Much of the debate over this passage has centred on the extent to which the 'king' can be taken to refer to an Egyptian monarch (here parallels with the author of the Egyptian *Potter's Oracle*'s reference to a king who 'comes from the sun as a bestower of blessings' are made), probably the seventh king, already alluded to above, and often thought to be Philometor (180–45 B.C.E.).[15] On this reading 'Egyptian royal ideology serves the purpose of Jewish messianic hope and eschatological deliverance',[16] and the author is seen to look to the political power of Egypt to free Judaea from Seleucid rule.[17] But such an identification of the Jewish messiah with an Egyptian monarch can seem forced. In 601–18 the seventh king is depicted as defeated by the monarch from Asia.[18] Moreover, we could render ἀπ' ἡλίου as 'from the east', here viewing it as a contraction of ἐξ ἀνατολῶν ἡλίου, and possibly as a reference to a Cyrus-like monarch, an observation which would render the parallel with *The Potter's Oracle* unsound.[19] But also the general tone of *Sib. Or. 3* is antagonistic to the culture in which the author resides, an observation which is supported by, amongst other things, a strong criticism of the Greeks and Macedonians (171–4, 381–3, 545–9),[20] and threats against Egypt and Alexandria

---

12   See Collins 1974: 28–32; Collins 1983: 354–5.
13   This seems likely as the whole passage (265–94) is a kind of retrospective prophecy of the Babylonian exile.
14   Collins 1987: 99.
15   Frankfurter 1996: 144 argues that such use of indigenous Egyptian tradition is evidenced elsewhere in Jewish Egyptian writings. See, for instance, the *Testament of Abraham* where extensive use is made of Egyptian afterlife mythology.
16   Chester 1991: 35. Gruen 1998: 277–8 agrees that Egyptian royal terminology is being used but denies that it contains any clues about the identity of the Egyptian monarch concerned. First, he notes that Egyptian monarchs never identified themselves by numbers; and second that the number seven should be taken to have a kind of mystical quality, 'not the denotation of royal stature'.
17   Collins 1987: 99.
18   Gruen 1998: 274–5.
19   See Isa. 41.2, 25; and Buitenwerf 2003: 273.
20   Gruen 1998: 287–90 argues that the author is more eirenic towards the Greeks, in particular highlighting the fact that he calls for the Greeks to convert (545–72; 624–34).

(348–9, 611–15). In such a setting 'it is hard to see how these Sibylline authors could be considered supporters of the Ptolemaic ideology.'[21] Such a thesis sees the messianism of *Sib. Or.* 3 as compatible with a revival of nationalistic sentiment,[22] further evidenced in the author's accentuated interest in the land, the law and the temple,[23] all possibly stimulated by the Maccabean revolt.[24]

For the period following the writing of the *Sib. Or.* 3, we lack much evidence for messianic belief. *3 Maccabees*, militant in tone, and highly nationalistic in sentiment, never refers to a messianic figure. The *Exagoge* of Ezekiel the Tragedian, although concerned with the future redemption of Israel,[25] and portraying Moses in a kingly manner (36–41; 68–89), also has no messianic references. And the *Wisdom of Solomon*, although keen to attack rulers and to herald the time of the righteous' vindication and wisdom's actions on behalf of Israel, is similarly non-messianic.

It is with Philo that evidence for messianic belief re-emerges, although this has been differently assessed. Wolfson[26] and Goodenough[27] famously argued that something like a conventional nationalistic messianism could be discerned within his works. Citing the passage from *Praem.* 79–172 in which Philo presents what looks like a conventional eschatological scenario (reunion of exiles, the prosperity of the land, peace among men and beasts and the ruin of Israel's enemies), Wolfson argued that the solution found by Philo for the Jewish problem of his time was the revival of the old prophetic promises of the ultimate disappearance of the diaspora, something which would involve the activities of the messiah (here in particular citing *Praem.* 95). Others have argued for the presence of an almost allegorized messianism in Philo.[28] In one strategy messianic terminology is applied to the Logos. In this context one might point to the passage in *Conf.* 62–3 where Philo quotes the messianic LXX Zech. 6.12[29] which reads: 'Behold a man who is the rising'. In the subsequent interpretation he associates the man with the son who follows the ways of his father and shaped the different kinds, looking at the archetypal patterns, a clear reference to the Logos.[30] In another strategy, messianic-like scenarios are denationalized. An example of this is present at *Praem.* where what looks like the dramatic reversal of Jewish

---

Barclay 1996: 222 noting that this only takes place when the Greeks have abandoned idolatry, sees it 'as the correlate of a cultural antagonism which recognizes no value in the religious practice of non-Jews'.

21 Barclay 1996: 223 contrasts the tone of *Sib. Or.* 3 with that of *The Letter of Aristeas*, with its strong endorsement of Ptolemaic kingship.

22 See passages predicting ultimate vindication of the Jews at 211–17, 282–94, 573–600, 669–731, 767–808.

23 See esp. 218–64; 573–600.

24 See Momigliano 1975.

25 *Exagoge* 106–7 and the reference to 'my gifts'; and Horbury 2003b: 65–82.

26 Wolfson 1947: 407.

27 Goodenough 1938: 25. On the difference between the two scholars, see Collins 2000: 134–5.

28 De Savignac 1959; Hecht 1987.

29 On the messianic associations of this passage see Horbury 2003b: 145, and relevant bibliography.

30 Hecht 1987: 150. See also *Virt.* 75; *Mos.* 2.44 and 288; *Opif.* 89–91.

fortunes is dependent upon Jewish repentance [164], where the eschatological battle is seen in terms of a victory of ethics over the enemy, and where, by extension, Philo is not interested in contrasting the Jews with the Gentiles but the virtuous with the wicked [94; see also 162]; and where the messianic figure mentioned in Num. 24.7 and clearly alluded to in *Praem.* 95, does battle with some fanatics 'whose lust for war defies restraint or remonstrance'.[31]

While those who argue that Philo consciously sought to denude biblical texts of their nationalistic-messianic content have a point, they can appear on occasion to overplay their card. So, for instance, Philo goes one better than the more cautious Josephus (*Ant.* 4.115–16) in at least referring to Balaam's oracle in Num. 24.7, and while it is possible to see his interpretation of it in *Praem.* as strongly ethical, that is less clearly the case in *Mos.* 1.290 where the passage is quoted without allegorizing comment.[32] Moreover, it is wrong to denude Philo's work of any eschatological thrust for he does read the blessings and curses of Deuteronomy 28 and Leviticus 26 as predictions of a definitive eschatological upheaval;[33] and there is in any case in *Praem.* a complex interweaving of ethical and more nationalistic language (see 162f.), something which we find in strongly messianic texts like the *Psalms of Solomon* (see 17.26, 32, 37).

Some would take Philo's references to messianic texts and his interest in issues of national redemption (however conceived) to point to the importance of such views in the Alexandria, and by extension, Egypt, of his day. As Collins has written, 'The fact that he (Philo) still finds some place for national eschatology indicates that messianic beliefs must have been widespread in his time …'[34] Hecht argues that if it is right to see Philo as consciously denuding messianic passages of their nationalist content, and this at a tumultuous time in the history of the Alexandrian community,[35] then this could imply the presence of a number of messianically oriented Jews in Alexandria.[36]

Verification of such a conclusion is impossible. An attempt to mirror-read Philo's reinterpretation of well-known messianic passages seems unconvincing, not least because his rereading, if that is what it is, seems strangely lacking in polemic, an important point when one considers that on many occasions he is explicit that his interpretations of biblical passages are ripostes against alternative, unsatisfactory ones. Moreover, we hear of no messianically oriented disturbances in Egypt until the Trajanic revolt of 115–17. True, Josephus reports that an Egyptian false prophet appeared in Judaea *ca.* 52–60 C.E. and quickly gathered to himself a large following (*J.W.* 2.261–3; *Ant.* 20.169–272), a fact which might 'hint uncertainly at the contemporary importance of messianism in Egypt …'.[37] And we do hear of distur-

---

31   Collins 2000: 135–6; Hecht 1987: 154–7, esp. 155, who argues that 'the particularism gives way to a general vision of the Golden Age.'
32   See Oegema 1994: 116 and 121, who argues that Philo's thought on this passage, under the influence of the changed political circumstances of the post-Flaccus era, has changed from the militaristic view of the passage in *Mos.* 1 to the more ethical interpretation in *Praem.*
33   Collins 2000: 137.
34   Collins 2000: 137.
35   On this see Mélèze-Modrzejewski 1997: 161–83.
36   Hecht 1987: 160–2. He realizes that it is difficult to date the relevant treatises and maintains that his thesis stands whether we date them before or after the governorship of Flaccus.
37   Horbury 1996: 296. See also Frankfurter 1996: 145–6, here citing the story as evidence

bances in Egypt connected with the first Jewish revolt, in particular at the end of it when in 73 some sicarii, fleeing from Judaea, entered Alexandria and tried 'to induce many of their hosts to assert their independence, to look upon the Romans as no better than themselves and to esteem God as their Lord'.[38] But it is difficult to deduce that much of importance from the Egyptian; and in relation to the incident involving the sicarii, we should note that Josephus asserts that the assembly was able to persuade the people to desist from following them and to hand them over to the Romans. Moreover, it is important to note that the Egyptian Jews did not join in the first revolt that was itself possibly inspired by messianic longings.

The oracles contained within *Sib. Or.* 5 are thought to span a period running from about 80 to 130 C.E.[39] While there are parallels between this collection and the contents of *Sib. Or.* 3, in significant areas its tone and emphases are different. It is considerably harsher in the manner in which it attacks non-Jews, in particular the Romans and Egyptians.[40] Its endorsement of the Jewish people is uncritical:[41] they are envisaged as 'the divine and heavenly race of the blessed Jews' (5.249) whose triumph in an Egypt rid of its gods and the unclean foot of Greeks seems inevitable. Like *Sib. Or.* 3, in its vision of the future it attributes an important place to Judaea,[42] and in particular the temple (418–33), although at one point the temple is envisaged as being rebuilt in Egypt (492–511). These strongly nationalistic sentiments are expressed against the background of a violent and militaristic end-time scenario which will be marked by the arrival of an antichrist figure in the form of Nero redivivus, who emerges from the east and is seen both as a symbol of Rome's wickedness and an instrument of her punishment.[43]

Less prominent than the antichrist is a messianic-like figure described in possibly four passages (in none of these is he called the messiah). In 5.414–27, in the most detailed description appearing after a harshly judgemental discussion of the destruction of the temple in Jerusalem, we are presented with a blessed man who comes from the expanses of heaven holding a sceptre in his hand which God has given him. After destroying the wicked and removing every city from its foundation with fire, he goes on to establish the holy city and its temple with a brightness exceeding the sun, the moon and the stars (420f.),[44] rid of all immoral activity (429–31). In this oracle we can discern the influence of Daniel 7[45] as we can in the oracle at 258–60. This shows signs of Christian redaction but is held

of Jewish prophets 'spilling over' into Palestine, perhaps wielding Exodus imagery as an extension of their Egyptian provenance.
 38   Josephus, *J.W.* 7.410–11.
 39   See Collins 1974: 73–9; and Barclay 1996: 225 and 450–1, for further bibliography.
 40   For the attack on the Romans see 162–78. For attacks upon the Egyptians see 75–85, 276–80, 351–60, 403–5 and 484–91. See Hengel 1996: 329–30.
 41   See 238–85. Hengel 1996 notes the complete absence of any criticism of the Jewish people, something that is at least hinted at in *Sib. Or.* 3.
 42   See 250–1 and Hengel 1996: 332 n. 71.
 43   See 93–110, 137–54, 214–27, 361–85.
 44   See Isa. 60.1-3, 19-20.
 45   See Horbury 2003b: 143, drawing attention to the fact that the author refers to a blessed man from the heavens (414) in the time of the saints (432).

by a majority of scholars, at least in part, to be of Jewish origin.[46] The messiah is again viewed as a man from heaven (here from the sky) and portrayed as the 'best of the Hebrews' who causes the sun to stand and speaks with fair speech and holy lips. Again the context in which this much briefer passage is set envisages the future in a paradisal reconstituted holy land with Jerusalem and its temple at the centre of things. The two other passages have often been taken to have less claim to being called messianic. The first of these, found at 108–9, simply speaks of a certain king sent from God who will destroy all the great kings and noble men; and the second (158–61) of a star who will destroy the whole earth including Rome, described as Babylon. This oracle, with its allusion to Num. 24.17, has a greater claim to being messianic, and to envisaging a heavenly messiah.

Whether these oracles, including or excluding 258–60, witness to a unified conception of the messiah, is unclear. Chester has explicitly denied unity, differentiating between 414f. and 256f., and 108–9 and 158–60 respectively, noting that the latter are brief, enigmatic and negative in their emphasis, while the former 'are much fuller and clearer, containing not only the theme of judgment but also positive emphasis on the nature of the messianic age ... and especially the place of the Jews, land, Jerusalem and temple ...'.[47] Horbury, on the other hand, has emphasized their unity, seeing them as complementary, and arguing implicitly for their general endorsement of a pre-existent, heavenly messiah.[48] The matter is difficult to decide. It is not clear that any of the oracles contradict each other, even if some are more detailed in what they assert than others. Moreover, the brevity of 108–9 makes it impossible to say whether it endorses a pre-existent understanding of the messiah or not. What is more important to observe is that in the descriptions of the messiah(s) we find in *Sib. Or.* 5 there is a greater emphasis on the nationalistic and militaristic/judgemental aspect of the figure (see the use of Dan. 7) than was the case in *Sib. Or.* 3 where the thought has been entertained by some that the messiah might be an Egyptian king. Such a possibility for a work as flagrantly nationalistic as *Sib. Or.* 5 is out of the question.[49]

Why Jews in Cyrenaica, Cyprus and Egypt (and possibly Mesopotamia) revolted against Rome towards the end of Trajan's principate, remains 'notoriously obscure',[50] not least because our sources have nothing to say on the subject.[51] On one reading, it was a reaction to the revolt of Jews in Mesopotamia, but such a view depends upon dating the outbreak of the revolt after the events in Mesopotamia and this seems unlikely.[52] Others have emphasized ethnic

---

46 See Chester 1992: 241 for a defence of its Jewish origin, especially on the grounds that it fits the context in which it is found and that the term 'man' appears elsewhere in the first century as a designation for the messiah; and Horbury 1998c: 103 and 192 n.139, for the view that the whole oracle is an interpolation.
47 Chester 1992: 243.
48 Horbury 1998c: 103. See also Oegema 1994: 226.
49 Oegema 1994: 226–7.
50 Barnes 1989: 145.
51 See especially Eusebius *Hist. eccl.* 4.2.1–5; and Cassius Dio 58.32. For a helpful presentation of all relevant sources see Pucci Ben Zeev 2005.
52 See Barnes 1989. For a refutation of Barnes see Horbury 1996: 284–95.

tensions, in particular tensions with Greeks,[53] social difficulties, growing discontent at the failure of the Romans to rebuild the temple[54] or the ongoing decline of the Jews' political status in Egypt.[55] But while some of the above must have been contributory, none can account for all aspects of this 'tumultus judaicus'.[56] Perhaps more is accounted for, some have claimed, if we assert its messianic origins.[57] In such an interpretation direct evidence for a messiah figure is found in Eusebius' mention of a kingly figure, Loukuas, who, he claims, led the Cyrenian Jews and later on the combined Cyrenian and Egyptian forces;[58] and in the reference in the *Acta Pauli et Antonini*, dated to 119 or 120, but referring to events possibly in the direct aftermath of the revolt,[59] to a Jewish king led out by the Greeks and lampooned by them in a mock procession. The claim that this is a reference to Loukuas who was captured by the Romans and exposed to ridicule in Alexandria is speculative[60] but the passage possibly gives evidence of an association of the revolt with a king. Other proof of messianic origin is found in the implied suddenness with which the revolt broke out,[61] its violent character,[62] in the rebels' strongly anti-idolatrous character, seen in particular in the destruction of religious buildings,[63] which may have led to the description of them as 'ἀνόσιοι' or impious.[64] The possibility that the revolt appeared to be heading eastward toward Palestine, and more specifically, Jerusalem, has also been seen as another factor supporting messianic origins.[65]

---

53   Applebaum 1979: 335 n. 445, and his own reservations about such a view. *CPJ* 439 implies some tension between Jews and Greeks but this seems to precede the revolt.
54   Goodman 2004: 26.
55   Mélèze-Modrzejewski 1997: 205.
56   This description is found on inscriptions from the Caesareum in Cyrene which mention parts of buildings or buildings pulled down by the Jewish rebels.
57   See Fuks 1961; Tcherikover 1963; Applebaum 1979; Hengel 1996; Frankfurter 1992, 1996; Horbury 1996.
58   *Hist. eccl.* 4.1.2. Dio 58.32 mentions a certain Andreas and some have been tempted to assimilate him to Loukuas. See Fuks 1961: 103 n.74; and Applebaum 1979: 259.
59   Musurillo 1954: 183–4.
60   Fuks 1961: 103.
61   Hengel 1996: 337–9.
62   See Cassius Dio 58.32, possibly confirmed by *CPJ* 437.
63   Note the destruction of the temples of Apollo, of Hecate, and of Artemis in Cyrene, and in Alexandria of the Serapeum and Nemesion. See Applebaum 1979: 259–60, 274–6, and 316–7.
64   See *CPJ* 438 where it is stated that 'villagers massed against the impious (ἀνοσίους) Jews'. Fuks 1961: 104 argues that the term refers to the iconoclasm of the Jews and implies that 'they waged war not only against the pagans but against their gods.' For the possibility that the religious character of the war was reciprocated on the Egyptian side, in particular by local priests, see Frankfurter 1992.
65   Applebaum 1979: 336–7 supports this view, highlighting the movement of the Cyrenian Jews into Egypt, the struggle for the Delta junction at Memphis and the activities in Cyprus. Horbury 1996: 298–9, while not supporting Applebaum's thesis, does point to the importance in certain Jewish texts, including Jewish prayer, of the theme of the return from exile and of the presence in some Septuagintal texts of Egypt in lists of Jewish communities presented as returning from exile. See especially LXX Isa. 11.11-16 where a highway will be made across the Delta and the Egyptian sea, not for the Assyrians, as in the MT, but for 'my people left in Egypt'.

Such an interpretation of the causes of the revolt has its difficulties and none of the points necessarily implies a messianic cause.[66] What makes it cogent is the convergence between some of the emphases identified in *Sib. Or.* 5 and aspects of the revolt itself. An extreme and hostile nationalism allied to a messianic figure with strongly militaristic aims, whose eyes may have been set on occupying Jerusalem and Palestine, chimes in with the concerns of *Sib. Or.* 5, as outlined above.[67] Indeed in the mysterious figure of Loukuas we might gain a clear view of what messianism looks like in its natural state – violent, nationalistic and destructive, good grounds to explain why such a figure may only have rarely been witnessed in the ancient history of the Jews.

2. Christian Messianism in Egypt

The origins in Egypt of the messianic movement, later to be known as Christianity, are not easy to determine.[68] Most scholars agree that it began within the Jewish community and was probably started by missionaries from Palestine. For whatever reason there is no information about the impact that the earliest Christians had upon the Egyptian Jewish community. The claim that Claudius' statement to the Jews in his letter to the Alexandrians (P. Lond. 1912, dated to 38 C.E.) that they ought not 'to bring in or invite Jews coming from Syria or Egypt …' is the first known allusion to Christians in Egypt, and gives evidence of early disturbances caused by them, remains a conjecture with few supporters, even if it is based upon believable premisses.[69]

Christian reaction to the Trajanic revolt is not known. Certainly if it possessed messianic elements, then on the basis of what is known about the Bar Kochba revolt,[70] a rift between the rebels and their Jesus-worshipping fellow Jews seems likely, although we should not discount the possibility that some Christians joined the revolt, or found themselves caught up in its general violence. The view that its result was the demise of Christian Judaism in Egypt and the rise of Gentile Christianity, and a concomitant break with the Jewish community, itself in an almost completely annihilated state, could be seen as overplayed, especially in its suggestion that continuities between the Judaism of pre-117 and the Christianity of post-117 did not exist.[71]

---

66   On objections see Horbury 1996: 297–8.
67   Hengel 1996 exploits this convergence. See Frankfurter 1998: 145, who notes the convergence between the massing of Jewish forces in Memphis (*CPJ* 439) and the curses on that city at *Sib. Or.* 5.60–92 and 179–86.
68   On this see Pearson and Goehring 1986 and Pearson 2006: 336–7.
69   For this thesis see Mélèze-Modrzejewski 1997: 229. It is easy to imagine that the arrival of Christian missionaries in the city would have caused a disturbance, particularly at the frenzied time at which Claudius wrote his letter, just as they were to do in Antioch and Rome, for example. But verisimilitude is one thing, proof another. Frankfurter 1998: 145 uses this letter to support his view that the outer regions of Egypt were hotbeds of insurgency.
70   See Justin, *1 Apol.* 31. See also Skarsaune, this volume: 160–5.
71   See Mélèze-Modrzejewski 1997: 228, and for a view favouring some continuity, see Pearson 2003.

In this context it is worth examining the probably Alexandrian[72] *Epistle of Barnabas*. Its date is uncertain but the majority of scholars place it after 117, although a date before is possible.[73] Whatever the date, it is interesting to note that the epistle shows a number of features in common with *Sib. Or.* 5 and other Jewish apocalypses. The text posits the return of Christ (4.3; 7.9; 15.4), and in its strongly eschatological tone, displays a strikingly anti-Roman aspect. In 4.3-5, here interpreting Dan. 7, and displaying similarities with *Sib. Or.* 5.403-33 and *4 Ezra* 11–13, the author expects the imminent fall of Rome, to be followed by the messianic reign of the saints when the beloved comes to his inheritance (4.3). This anti-Roman character is also possibly present at 12.9 where the Son of God is seen to uproot Amalek (Exod. 17.14)[74] and again in the reference to the 'enemies' at 16.4.[75] *Barnabas* shows an interest in related messianic themes. So, for instance, in 6.8-19 he engages in an interpretation of the words of Exod. 33.1, 3 about entering into the land flowing with milk and honey, and at 16.5 he presents what he takes to be the proper understanding of the eschatological temple, here citing Dan. 9.24-27 (see also 6.15). Both of these passages constitute christological/spiritualized reinterpretations of hopes associated with the land and the temple, hopes which featured so importantly in *Sib. Or.* 3 and 5. But such reinterpretation gives evidence of dependence upon Jewish messianic aspirations, indicated in the fact that the author feels the need to express his hopes using such symbols, and in the possibility that this reinterpretation could be taken to imply the presence in *Barnabas*' community of those who were tempted to follow the hopes of a nationalistic Jewish author like the writer of *Sib. Or.* 5. This possibility is enhanced if we accept the view that *Barnabas* was written at a time full of Jewish expectation stimulated by the thought that the temple might be rebuilt;[76] and that there are other signs that *Barnabas*' addressees were being attracted to aspects of non-Christian Judaism.[77]

Barnabas could be seen to display some continuities with Jewish messianic hope and to support the thesis of Jewish origins for early Christianity in Egypt and the ongoing importance of Jewish influence even after the Trajanic revolt, dependent, of course, upon one's dating of the text. Such continuity, at least in terms of messianic ideas, is less easy to demonstrate for the following period. Jewish literature dries up, and the Jewish community recovered only slowly from the devastation of the revolt.[78] Our Christian sources are dominated by a series of Gnostic

---

72   See Carleton Paget 1994: 30–45. For a Syrian provenance see Hvalvik 1996: 41.
73   For a Hadrianic date, see Hvalvik 1996: 17–27 and Prostmeier 1999: 14–19. For an earlier date, in the principate of Nerva, see Carleton Paget 1994: 9–30.
74   The evidence for seeing Amalek as Rome is presented by Horbury 1998d: 146–7.
75   This should probably be taken as a reference to the Romans who are rebuilding the temple.
76   Some scholars take 16.3-4 to refer to a mooted rebuilding of the temple either in Nerva's or Hadrian's principate.
77   See especially 3.6 and 4.6b, although the reading of the latter verse is disputed.
78   For the view that the Jews of Egypt almost disappeared see Mélèze-Modrzejewski 1997: 227–30. Haas 1997: 103–4, accepts that the Jewish community was 'dealt a severe blow' by the revolt but thinks that traces of life can be espied in the pamphlets making up the *Acta Alexandrinorum*. Cf. esp. *Acta Pauli et Antonini*.

writers, including Basilides and Valentinus, and then products of the school of the elusive Pantaenus, Clement and Origen, all of whom in the main tend to evince a distaste for an eschatologically oriented messianism, and this in spite of the fact that some of their sources clearly held to such opinions.[79] Origen indirectly gives evidence of millennarian interpretations, especially in his harsh comments about Christians who interpret Revelation literally. At *Princ.* 2.11.2 he criticizes those whom he describes as 'disciples of the mere word' who 'consider that the promises of the future are to be looked for in the form of pleasure and bodily luxury ... and picture for themselves the earthly city of Jerusalem about to be rebuilt with precious stones ...', clearly alluding to Rev. 21.10-21. Origen tells us nothing about the messianic beliefs of those to whom he alludes.[80] But given that they are literalist interpreters of Revelation, one must assume that they maintained a view of Christ's return and a messianism which bore some relationship to what we have noted in *Barnabas*.[81]

One incident from the middle of the third century indicates ongoing interest in messianic-like speculation on the part of some Egyptian Christians. Eusebius records in *Hist. eccl.* 7.24.1–25.7 that the Bishop of Alexandria and follower of Origen, Dionysius, wrote two treatises entitled *On Promises* in refutation of the teaching of an Egyptian Bishop, Nepos.[82] The latter had written a book entitled *Against the Allegorists* in which he had argued for a literalist exegesis of Revelation from which arose the view 'that the kingdom of Christ will be on earth' (24.4). Dionysius' *On Promises* contained an attack upon Nepos' work in which, amongst other things, Dionysius describes how he came to the nome of Arsinoe where the 'doctrine', as he calls it, had been present for some time and had caused schisms and defections of whole churches. Dionysius called together the whole community and urged them to discuss the issue publicly. This led the leaders to bring forth Nepos' book which was refuted in such a way by Dionysius that the community and its leaders, in particular, the major leader, Coracion, described as 'the leader and introducer of this teaching' (*Hist. eccl.* 7.24.6), came over to him.

The movement in rural Egypt, described by Dionysius, seems to have received its support from a predominantly peasant population.[83] The popularity of

---

79   Relevant sources in this context would be *Barnabas*, *Apocalypse of Peter*, Justin and Irenaeus. For possible signs of veneration of Christ as a king in Clement, here in the hymn at *Paidagogos* 3.12, see Horbury 2003b: 278. In the curious work known as the *Prophetic Eclogues*, there may be some muted signs of messianism. See especially the interpretation of Psalm 19.
80   For the possibility that he might be referring to millenarians like Irenaeus see Simonetti 1975: 46.
81   It is interesting that in at least two places in his *Contra Celsum* Origen appears to endorse a two-advents view for Jesus, the first being his earthly life ending in his resurrection, and the second being his return in glory (see 1.56 and 2.29). But we should probably regard this Origenist nod to messianism, present in *Barnabas* and Tertullian, as an opportunistic rebuttal of a Jewish argument against Jesus (his coming did not comport with Jewish expectations of a glorious messiah) rather than as a reflection of sincerely held convictions.
82   Helpful analysis is found in Simonetti 1975 and Frankfurter 1993: 270–8. See also de Lange, p. 278, below.
83   See *Hist. eccl.* 7.24.6 where Eusebius implies that it was a movement mainly found in villages. The incident can be seen as a battle between town (Alexandria) and country.

millennialist ideas amongst this social group may be explicable by reference to the difficult economic and social circumstances of third-century Egypt.[84] It seems that Nepos gave intellectual support to the movement by writing down ideas which originally had been communicated orally to a largely illiterate audience, and his presence may imply that the movement, although predominantly agrarian and poor, boasted supporters from more educated circles.[85] The debate takes on a hermeneutical character, although it is clear that Dionysius is principally concerned with the conclusions drawn from the interpretations of the movement's leaders, not straightforwardly the method of interpretation. In this respect it is relevant that he refers to it as a doctrine or teaching (*Hist. eccl.* 7.24.9), and he attempts to undermine the authority of Revelation (*Hist. eccl.* 7.24.8–25.27). The fact that the whole incident had led to schisms and defections is significant. When Origen described the views of those millennialists known to him, he spoke about them critically but did not imply that they were heretics.[86] How this schism manifested itself is not clear, although it seems to have been initiated by the millennialists themselves. The fact of its existence points to the fervour with which opinions on both sides were held (the Origenist Dionysius' account, possibly falsely, makes us think of a gentlemanly tiff which was easily resolved by argument). As with the passage in *De Princ.*, the reader is not given a detailed description of the beliefs of the group, although we should assume a messianic component based upon the claim that 'the kingdom of Christ will be on earth' (*Hist. eccl.* 7.24.4).

An insight into the kind of atmosphere out of which the movement associated with Coracion and Nepos emerged comes from *The Apocalypse of Elijah*. This text, which has a complex transmission history, has been taken by some to have a Jewish Vorlage, although its most recent detailed expositor disagrees with this.[87] The text is taken up with themes of an apocalyptic nature, including the actions and defeat of the antichrist, the sufferings of the end-time and the establishment of the millennium. A messianic figure is also mentioned. At 3.2 a person is described who will come in the manner of a covey of doves with a crown of doves surrounding him. He will walk upon heaven's vault with the sign of the cross leading him. 'The whole world will behold him like the sun which shines from the eastern horizon to the western.' In another passage, here interrupting a detailed account of the wicked actions of the antichrist, the messianic figure, described as Christ, will pity those who are his own and send out a large number of angels and those with the sign of Christ on their head will be taken up into heaven (5.2-4). Right at the end of the piece (5.36-39), at the execution of the antichrist, and here recalling Revelation 21, 'Christ the king and all his saints will come forth from heaven. He will burn the earth and spend a thousand years upon it. Because the world has been contaminated with sinners, he will create a new heaven and earth, and rule with the saints.' These presentations hint at a possibly

---

84 See Frankfurter 1993: 247–78.
85 Frankfurter 1993: 272–4.
86 Simonetti 1975: 50–1, notes this point but sees the whole incident as of more general significance, constituting an attack upon the spiritualist exegesis of the Origenist school.
87 See Frankfurter 1993 opposing Wintermute 1983 and others.

richer messianic tradition, a point which is supported by noting the detailed character of the description of the antichrist,[88] in some ways a greater focus of the author's attention, and the possibly messianic-like descriptions of Enoch and Elijah.[89]

There is a temptation to connect *The Apocalypse of Elijah* and the group around Nepos and Coracion. Both emerge from approximately the same period of time in rural Egypt, and entertained millennial beliefs influenced by Revelation (in the case of *The Apocalypse of Elijah* we should assume the influence of other texts as well). Frankfurter resists this temptation, preferring to argue that at this period of Egyptian history, which was marked by rebellion, and when Christianity in the Chora at least only grew sporadically, it would be better to take the two as representing 'a type of religious situation that occurred often around Egypt in the third century …'.[90]

However we conceive the relationship between the Dionysius text and *The Apocalypse of Elijah*, what do they tell us about the development of messianism in Egypt? On one reading they could be taken to represent an ongoing trail of millennialism, going back beyond the Trajanic revolt, and of Jewish provenance. *The Apocalypse of Elijah* is a text that has so much in common with Judaism that the suggestion has been made, as was noted, that it betrays a Jewish Vorlage; and the millennial interpretation associated with Coracion and Nepos were described by Dionysius as 'rather Jewish', though such a description may have more to do with a growing view that millennialism was Judaizing than a sense that its content bore a close relationship to actual Jewish concerns. Frankfurter, who sees some continuities between what he terms the prophetic, millennialist activities of pre-117 Egyptian Jews and later Christian apocalyptic traditions, argues that the heightened eschatological tone of the group around Coracion and Nepos and *The Apocalypse of Elijah*, arose in particularly straitened social and political circumstances associated with third-century Egypt. Such a view could imply that the millennialism described above was not a part of an ongoing tradition stretching back some way, and this in spite of Dionysius' claim that 'the doctrine had long been prevalent' (*Hist. eccl.* 7.24.6).

3. Conclusions

The story of messianism and resistance amongst Jews and Christians in Egypt is constructed out of fragments of information. In one narrative which ends with the Trajanic revolt, the view is taken that in increasingly trying political circumstances, particularly those following the Roman conquest of Egypt, many Jews (but by no means all) began to look towards some messianically inspired redemption from Roman rule. In such a view a contrast is drawn between, on the one hand, the messianic, but only mildly nationalistic, *Sib. Or.* 3, and the

---

88 See 3.5 where the work of the antichrist is clearly aligned with that of Christ. On this see Frankfurter 1993: 112–25.
89 See Oegema 1994: 256–7.
90 Frankfurter 1993: 278.

similarly messianic but much more rebarbatively nationalistic *Sib. Or.* 5. In this reconstruction emphasis is also placed upon the possibility that refugee sicarii who entered Egypt at the end of the first revolt continued to cause ferment and contributed both to a growing messianic expectation and a developing sense of resistance to Roman rule especially amongst the poorer element of the population, a development which, in the aftermath of the first Jewish revolt, seems understandable.[91] In all of this, Egyptian Jews are seen to be closer to Palestinian Jewry than to Jews elsewhere in the Diaspora including Asia where, in spite of evidence of apocalyptic writings, there was never any serious sign of resistance to Roman rule or of messianic movements. There are lots of 'gaps' in such a narrative which runs counter to another view of Egyptian, especially Alexandrian, Judaism, which sees it, sometimes uncritically, as the homestead of Jewish efforts at integration with the prevailing culture taken to be exemplified in an Aristoboulos or Philo, rather than the learned rant of the authors of *Sib. Or.* 5. And it is very difficult to construct from it a detailed or unified account of Jewish messianism as it supposedly developed.

The Christian evidence is even more fragmentary. Jews who held Jesus of Nazareth to be the messiah and entered Alexandria at the time they probably did (the 30s C.E.) might have been expected to have left their mark but we hear nothing of them for some time. The first Christian source which is probably Egyptian, the *Epistle of Barnabas*, shows clear signs of continuity with Jewish messianic ideas and related millennial hopes; and here, too, we witness signs of resistance to Romans but in a setting where Jewish literal interpretation of the law is harshly condemned and Jewish nationalistic promises are interpreted in a broadly christocentric manner. Tracing the messianic/millennialist tendencies evidenced in *Barnabas* into a later era is more difficult. *Barnabas* remained a popular text in Egypt (its place in the Sinaitic Codex is evidence of as much) and Origen, in his opposition to millennialists, hints at their presence within the community. Clearer evidence of their subsequent presence emerges from the mid-third century in the groups gathered around Nepos and Coracion, and the author of *The Apocalypse of Elijah*. Both boast a strong interest in Revelation and, in the case of the latter, an explicit interest in messianism. To what extent they were dependent upon a Jewish interpretative tradition is difficult to discern: the Jewish Vorlage of *The Apocalypse of Elijah* has not been established and the description of Nepos' interpretation of Revelation as 'ἰουδαϊκότερον' has more to do with a growing sense that Jewishness was equivalent to brash millennialism. That neither of these sources nor many earlier ones, save *Barnabas*, witness to evidence of an ongoing argument between Jews and Christians about the nature of messianism, as presented by Celsus,[92] may have something to do with the limited presence of Jews in Egypt in the period following the Trajanic revolt rather than with a belief that Jews and Christians no longer argued about this matter.

---

91   This can perhaps be overplayed. Both *Sib. Or.* 3 and 5 were probably written by people educated enough to have composed Homeric pentameters. For the view that after 66 C.E. there was a radicalization of the Jewish upper classes in Egypt and Cyrenaica, see Kerkeslager 2006: 58.

92   If Celsus is an Alexandrian, then his reference to a Jew who appeared to say things which directly contradicted Christian messianic assertions (see especially *Cels.* 1.28 and 32), would be directly relevant to our discussion.

Finally, and with an eye to later developments, we should note the degree to which texts boasting an apocalyptic, and on occasion, messianic, content, become the preserve of some sectarian groups like the Melitians, and subsequently of Egyptian monks, although the grounds for keeping and copying such works may not straightforwardly have been connected with their millennial or messianic content.[93]

---

[93] For a list of such texts preserved by Egyptian monks see Frankfurter 1998: 186–7 and his preceding and following discussion about their use and appeal.

Chapter 15

THE WEST AND NORTH AFRICA

Wolfram Kinzig

In patristic research the term 'messianism' has so far played only a minor role.[1] It is principally through William Horbury's interdisciplinary research that patristic scholars have been faced with the question as to whether there is a continuity between the Jewish expectation of a messianic figure and eschatological concepts found in the early Church.[2] Since among students of the Church Fathers the term is not very familiar, it appears useful to ask by way of introduction what we are actually looking for when we speak of Christian messianism in the west.

In the later books of the Old Testament and in ancient Judaism the messiah was principally seen as a political figure whose primary task was the restoration of Israel. In Qumran two messiahs, a king and a priest, were expected at the end of times. There were regularly those who claimed to fulfil these roles. As is well known, the Bar Kokhba revolt of 132–5 C.E. had strong messianic overtones, and there are many other examples.[3]

In Christianity there appears to be no immediate relation between messianism and (political) resistance. Thus we have very few apocalyptic texts from the third century, although this was the period of the fiercest Christian persecutions.[4] Some nurtured the hope that Christ would return as a warrior king and would conquer the forces of evil operating in this world. But this did not lead to political action. In most minds the Church, the 'true Israel', had replaced Israel as a religious or political entity, and the home of the *ecclesia* was not on earth, but in heaven. In particular, if I am not mistaken, the combination of two messiahs (priest and king) is nowhere found.

---

1   In recent encyclopedias such as the *Theologische Realenzyklopädie* or the *Lexikon für Theologie und Kirche* (third edn) one finds, therefore, under the entry 'Messias' or 'Messianismus' or 'Messianische Bewegungen' no treatment of the question as regards the early Church. In the new article on 'Messias/Messianismus' in the fourth edition of the *Religion in Geschichte und Gegenwart* Astrid Reuter mentions the early Church only in passing (cf. Reuter in Auffarth *et al.* 2002: 1153–4). Cf., however, the relevant entries in Desroche 1969 which remain superficial and Stegemann 1993a: 84–6. As regards the history of the term cf. also Biller and Dierse 1980. In what follows I shall refrain from quoting all relevant works in order to keep the footnotes to a minimum. A rich bibliography is found in Daley 1991 (repr. 2003).
2   Cf. esp. Horbury 1998c, 1998d, 1999, 2003b.
3   In the introduction to his *Messianism among Jews and Christians* Horbury gives a *status quaestionis* with rich bibliography (Horbury 2003b: 1–31).
4   Cf. Schwarte 1978: 265.

Moreover, Christians were hardly inclined to identify real people with Christ. In ancient Christianity no figure of any historical significance is known who claimed to be Jesus Christ having returned from heaven.[5] This may seem surprising, but it is perhaps explained by the fact that the Christian expectation of the eschatological return of Christ was always combined with the idea of a cosmological drama of major proportions. Hence it was very difficult for someone to pretend to be Christ unless this pretence was accompanied by some major cosmic upheaval. In fact, Hippolytus of Rome riles against a group which had sought Christ in the desert 'like at the time of the prophet Elisa the sons of the prophets who spent three days in the mountains searching Elijah who had been lifted up to heaven' (cf. 2 Kings 2). Hippolytus adds that the Lord will appear as judge of the entire world and, one might add, this will be an event immediately obvious to everyone.[6]

However, this does not mean that the Christians were not perceived by outsiders as a messianic movement in a political sense. There is the famous passage in which the Roman historian Suetonius mentions a certain *Chrestus* whose instigations led to continuous tumults among the Jews in Rome and, finally, in 49 C.E. to the publication of an edict by the emperor Claudius expelling the Jewish community from the capital.[7] The passage is a notorious *crux* in the history of primitive Christianity, since given the awkward spelling of the name it is unclear whether the remark refers to Christ at all or whether we are not dealing here with some inner-Jewish dispute.[8]

In mainstream Christian eschatology the political role of the Jewish messiah was not altogether denied, but it was not ascribed to Jesus Christ, but rather to his opponent who was now depicted as a Jewish king who was a kind of negative mirror-image of Christ and was, therefore, called 'Antichrist'. Since the end of the second century he was expected to precede Christ's return and was quickly ascribed demonic features and often identified with the devil himself.[9]

To the extent that Christ was not expected to play a political role after his return to earth, there was no Christian messianism. However, it appears that Jewish messianism was not restricted to a political understanding. There was a strand of Jewish thought in which the messiah was promoted to the status of a heavenly redeemer, a 'Son of Man', who would 'judge the secret things' (*1 En.* 49.4).[10] Furthermore, the Christians insisted that Jesus incarnate was none other than the 'Christ', the messiah who had been foretold by the prophets and who would

---

5   Cf., however, Sulpicius Severus, *Vita Martini* 24 who mentions reports of men pretending to be Elijah or Christ or John the Baptist.
6   *Comm. Dan.* 2.18.4.
7   Suetonius, *Claudius* 25.4: 'Iudaeos impulsore Chresto assidue tumultuantes Roma expulit (*sc.* Claudius).' The edict is also mentioned in Acts 18.2.
8   The latter interpretation has been strongly advocated by Slingerland 1997, but cf. Orosius., *Hist.* 7.6.16–17. who clearly refers the passage to Christ. The misspelling occurred often; cf. below p. 205 and n. 48.
9   For this idea cf. e.g. Lorein 2003; Horbury 2003b: 329–49; Badilita 2005 (with full bibliography); Hughes 2005 (*non vidi*).
10   This is time and again emphasized by Horbury in his writings; cf. e.g. Horbury 2003b: 12–19.

return at the end of days to judge the living and the dead. In this respect, there obviously *was* a Christian messianism, although not as it was understood by the majority of the Jews.

The study of Christian messianism is further complicated by the fact that there is a certain confusion surrounding the term 'messianism' in historical research outside biblical and Jewish studies. Sometimes messianism is equated with 'millenarianism',[11] in particular where messianism is primarily seen as a movement with political ambitions.[12] However, as will be shown below, in the early Church there were messianic expectations and concepts which did not necessarily include belief in a thousand-year-reign of the messiah preceding the final judgement.

In answering the question of continuity between Jewish and Christian messianism it is, therefore, better generally to look for Christian individuals or groups who had a 'realist' expectation of the messiah, i.e. who were interested in an active role of the messiah within the final events. For the purpose of this article, therefore, I understand by Christian messianism *a view which expects the advent of a royal figure here on earth within the context of a cosmic drama leading to the end or to the re-establishment of the world. This figure saves the righteous and punishes the wicked.*

In this wider sense most Christian groups were messianic, since they expected the return of Jesus Christ whom they identified with the messiah announced by the prophets and expected by the Jews. There are some exceptions. Occasionally, by his ascent to heaven Christ appears to have fulfilled his task. In the *Shepherd of Hermas* Christ is presented as dwelling in heaven receiving the righteous who will sit at the Lord's right hand. Christ here plays no active role at all at the end of times.[13] Authors like Cyprian may have a very strong sense of eschatology, and yet Christ's role in this respect is only mentioned in passing.[14]

On the whole, however, in most western authors, Christ is ascribed a specific role within the cosmic drama which marks the end of times, but there is a certain confusion as to what that role would be. Most Latin Fathers agree that Jesus Christ bears divine features. Sometimes it is even difficult to say whether the figure expected is Christ or God himself, since he is simply called 'Lord'.[15] But they were unclear what Christ would actually do at the end of times. Expectations moved between two extremes. On the one hand there were those who advocated a philosemitic form of eschatology in which Christ was expected to restore Israel and to rebuild Jerusalem and the temple here on earth (as opposed to Jerusalem descending from heaven with no temple such as promised

---

11   Cf. e.g. Strauß *et al.* 1992: 635 (Burridge); cf. also Chester 1991, 1992.
12   Cf. e.g. the classical and widely discussed study by Cohn 1957 which in the subtitle of its second edition (Cohn 1961) clearly indicated this context: *Revolutionary Messianism in Medieval and Reformation Europe and its Bearing on Modern Totalitarian Movements*. In addition, Desroche 1969.
13   Cf. Hermas, *Sim.* 5.3.3; 9.24.4; *Vis.* 3.1.9–2.3. Cf. also Grillmeier 1990: 147.
14   Cf. e.g. *Ep.* 8; 9.2; 51.18, 29; Cyprian, *Laps.* 17; *Fort.* 12–13, etc.
15   Cf. e.g. *1 Clement* quoting Mal. 3.1. The coming 'kingdom of Christ' is mentioned in 50.3. In the *Passio Perpetuae* 11–12, in a vision of the things to come, a divine figure is seen sitting on a throne, being both old and young; his precise identity is not revealed.

in Rev. 21–2.). The Gentiles would then be included in some form in this eschatological kingdom of Israel. Glimpses of these groups can be discovered in the writings of Justin Martyr and Tertullian,[16] but they were not confined to the west. In the east Cerinthus and later Apollinarios of Laodicea appear to have held such views. The latter was rigorously denounced by his own pupil Jerome and both, Cerinthus and Apollinarios, were condemned as heretics, although by different people for different reasons.[17]

On the other hand some tried to sever the ties to Judaism altogether. Arguing against philosemitic eschatologies like those just mentioned, Marcion, who worked in Rome before being expelled from the Roman congregation in 144 C.E., distinguished between two Christs. The first belonged to the Jewish creator God and was prophesied in the Old Testament, whereas the other, that of the Christians, was the revealer of the loving God. Here the Christian belief in Christ's saving work was altogether removed from Jewish messianic expectation. The Jewish messiah was seen as a heroic warrior who was expected to restore the earthly kingdom of the Jews. His rule, however, would not be eternal, but terminated upon the arrival of Jesus Christ for the final judgement.[18]

Marcion's views were quickly refuted. The early Christians were aware of the fact that the work of Christ could only be fully understood against the background of the Old Testament, but they interpreted it differently from the Jews. There is fairly universal agreement that in Christ incarnate the Davidic messiah announced to the Jews by the prophets had arrived. This is also true for theologians writing in the west. Prophecies such as Gen. 49.10 ('The sceptre shall not depart from Judah, nor the ruler's staff from between his feet, until he comes to whom it belongs; and to him shall be the obedience of his peoples') were fulfilled by the coming of Christ. The end of political independence as a result of Roman occupation and the destruction of Jerusalem and the Temple in 70 C.E. meant that the 'sceptre' and the 'staff' had been handed over to the messianic king.[19] The present time, therefore, had to be seen in an eschatological perspective. However, the messiah had not come in the glorious manner expected by the Jews, but, rather, humbly, and his incarnation had, at first sight, ended in defeat. Over against Jewish criticism the Fathers took some trouble to establish the prophecies for this appearance of Christ from the Scriptures.[20]

The Christians were faced with yet another problem, because the messiah as foretold in the Scriptures had not brought about a state on earth which was in any way comparable to the paradise with Jerusalem as its centre whose reestablishment the books of Isaiah (esp. 56–66), Ezekiel (esp. 40–48) and other prophets had promised for the end of times. Not only that, Christ had simply

---

16 Cf. Kinzig 1998: 69–77.
17 Cf. Kinzig 1998, 2003; Markschies 1998, 2004; Hill 2000; Newman 2001; Vianès-Abou Samra 2004.
18 As regards the details of Marcion's doctrine cf. Harnack 1924: 117, 137–41, 289–91.
19 Cf. e.g. Justin, *1 Apol.* 32.3–4; 54.5; *Dial.* 11.4; 52; 120.3–6.
20 This is true for most western theologians. For the distinction between two advents of Christ, one in humility, the other in glory cf. the references given by Adolf von Harnack in Hahn and Hahn 1897: 386 and Durst 1987: 225–6.

disappeared, an event which was described by early Christians as an ascension to heaven along the lines of Elijah's ascension in the Old Testament (cf. 2 Kings 2) or of Greek and Roman heroes such as Herakles or Romulus.[21] What followed Christ's ascension was in the mind of many a drama with various acts. Some thought he would descend to the underworld to redeem those who had died before him.[22] Christ would then come to sit at the right hand of God the Father[23] where he would receive the martyrs who went from their cruel deaths straight to heaven in order to form a kind of heavenly senate together with the apostles.[24] From heaven he would come to judge mankind. This forensic activity was often embedded in an extensive apocalyptic scenario. The most important proof-texts for the design of this scenario were found in both the Old and the New Testaments. Apart from those mentioned above they were prophecies from Daniel (esp. ch. 7), the Apocalypse in the Gospel of Matthew (chs. 24–5) and the Revelation of John (esp. chs. 20–22). Sometimes a final act was added on the basis of 1 Cor. 15.24-28: Christ would deliver his kingdom to God the Father and would then himself be subjected to the Father 'that God may be everything to every one'.[25] It is only Christ's activity as eschatological king and judge which can be considered messianic in the sense defined above. It became part of the *regula fidei* and later of the creed.[26] Ideas about what would happen in the intermediate period between Christ's resurrection and his return were, on the whole, not homogeneous and derived from various sources, both Jewish and pagan. We have to keep this in mind when we now deal with ideas about Christ's return itself.

In many respects the tone for subsequent discussions in the west was set by the early theologians still writing in Greek, such as Justin Martyr and Hippolytus. Justin (who is dealt with in chapter 12) is the first western author who clearly advocated a biblically grounded messianism with post-millennialist features.[27] It is significant that his eschatology is developed in the context of anti-Jewish discourse. This is no single occurrence: in an early Latin book of biblical testimonies (*Testimonia*), probably stemming from the pen of Cyprian, we find among the various headings under which the quotations are grouped titles such as: 'That Jesus Christ will come as a judge' (2.28), 'That he will reign as king forever' (2.29) and 'That he himself is both judge and king' (2.30). Books such

---

21   For details, cf. Strecker 1962; Bertram 1966; Lohfink 1971; Segal 1980; Weiser and Pöhlmann 1986; Colpe 1991; Colpe *et al.* 1996a; Colpe *et al.* 1996b; Colpe and Habermehl 1996; Fiedrowicz 2000: 265–7.
22   For the *descensus ad inferos* cf. Vogels 1976; Grillmeier 1978; Koch 1986; Colpe 1996.
23   As regards this motif cf. Bertram 1966: 38–9; Markschies 2000: 1–69; Eskola 2001.
24   Cf. Koep 1952: 120–3. Hill 2001 sees a relationship between the assumption of a subterranean intermediate state and the expectation of a millennium, whereas those who opposed chiliasm or were indefinite on the issue expected an immediate entry into heaven for the righteous at death. In my view, the evidence does not support such neat distinctions.
25   As regards the exegesis of 1 Cor. 15.24-28 cf. Schendel 1971.
26   A full list of references (compiled by Harnack) is found in Hahn and Hahn 1897: 385–6.
27   English-speaking scholars frequently distinguish between pre- and post-millennialism depending on whether Christ is expected to come *before* or *after* the millennium; cf. e.g. Richard Bauckham in: Böcher *et al.* 1981: 739. It continues to play a prominent role amongst Christian evangelicals in the United States (who tend to reject a post-millennial eschatology).

as the *Testimonies* were destined to be used in discussion with Jews in order to establish the messiahship of Jesus.[28]

Strangely enough, there is little in Irenaeus that is pertinent to our topic.[29] After Justin it is Hippolytus of Rome (†235) who gives the most vivid picture of Christ's role in the eschatological drama. The context is biblical exegesis.[30] In his *Commentary on Daniel* Hippolytus makes a clear distinction between this world and Christ's future kingdom from heaven. When the four beasts foretold in Dan. 7.17-18 are suppressed, the 'earthly state' will be replaced by the 'heavenly' rule of saints which will be indestructible and eternal. Christ who has received from God all power and might[31] will come with the powers and the armies of angels in order to judge the world, to overturn the Antichrist and all earthly kingdoms and to hand over power to the saints; by contrast, the wicked will be burnt in an unquenchable fire.[32] Whereas Christ first had come as an ordinary man, he will now come as judge of the entire world. Then he had come to save man, now he will punish the sinners.[33] Christ is the heavenly priest who at his first coming had purified those who believed in him and forgiven them their sins. The faults of those, however, who did not believe in him were sealed and became indelible until the final judgement.[34] This judgement is preceded by a general resurrection.[35]

Whereas in those western authors who wrote in Greek the term *messias* is absent, it is occasionally discussed in the Latin Fathers.[36] It was familiar to Latin-speaking Christians through the Bible, being mentioned in Jn 1.41 and 4.25 both in the Old Latin versions[37] and in the Vulgate. In Jn 1.41 it is said that *Christus* is the translation of *messias* whence in theory it would have been clear to every reader of the Bible that when Jesus Christ was invoked the epithet referred to the messiah. These verses are repeatedly quoted or alluded to in Latin sources.[38]

---

28   Cf. esp. 1.1–7 where it is emphasized that the Jews did not recognize Christ as the messiah.
29   Irenaeus, it is true, holds a pre-millennialist position in *Haer.* 5.31–6 (for the distinction cf. above n. 27), but apart from quoting prophecies from Scripture he has little to say about Christ's role in the millennium and thereafter. Christ appears here mainly to prepare and accustom the righteous to the kingdom of God (cf. esp. 5.35.1). It is unclear what, if any, role is attributed to Christ in the final judgement (cf. 5.35.2). Finally, after the coming of the heavenly Jerusalem, the Son will yield up his work to the Father (cf. 5.36.2 quoting 1 Cor. 15.27-8). On Irenaeus cf. also Daley 1991: 28–32.
30   Cf. also his treatise *De Christo et Antichristo*. In other writings Hippolytus is more reticent; for details cf. Daley 1991: 38–41.
31   Cf. 4.11.3; cf. 1 Cor. 15.27; Eph. 1.22; Heb. 2.8.
32   Cf. 4.10.2–3; 4.55; furthermore 4.11.
33   Cf. 4.18.6 and also 4.39.4–5.
34   Cf. 4.32.5–7 and also 4.37.
35   Cf. 4.39.7.
36   For some of the following references I am indebted to the articles 'christus' (by 'Mbr.') in: *TLL* 3 (1906–12) 1028–9 and 'Christus' (by Walther Schwering) in *TLL Onom.* 2 (1907) 409–16. For Augustine's usage cf. also Madec 1986–94: 870–2.
37   There are numerous references in the *Vetus Latina Database*.
38   Quotations of, or allusions to, Jn 1.41 are found in Tertullian, *Prax.* 21; Ambrose, *Exp. Ps. 118*, litt. 18, cap. 41; Gaudentius, *Tract.* 17.5; *Comm. Is.* 18.17 (on Isa. 65.22-25); Augustine, *Tract. Ev. Jo.* 7.13; *Enarrationes in Psalmos* 65.4 *sermo* 101.2; Jerome, *Faust.* 12.44.

At least among the savants it was also clear that *Christus* was no proper name,[39] but the Greek translation of Hebrew *mashiach* which meant 'the anointed' (Latin *unctus*). Lactantius, Jerome, Augustine and Eucherius are witnesses to this translation of the title.[40] But even where *messias* is not mentioned, it was repeatedly emphasized that *Christus* was equivalent to *unctus*[41]; in these cases it was often derived from *chrisma*.[42] The learned Lactantius and Jerome also give Aquila's alternative Greek translation *eleimménos*.[43] When discussing Hab. 3.13 Jerome claims that Aquila's and the *Quinta*'s translations are more faithful to the Hebrew *et-m^{e}shichecha* (Latin transcription: *eth messiach*) than the LXX and the other interpreters.[44] Moreover, it was known that *Christus* was a royal title, since the Israelite kings used to be anointed.[45]

However, not all Christians were as educated as their theological teachers and bishops. As will be seen, *Christus* was generally understood as a name rather than a title and, in any case, even if the early Christians, notably those of pagan descent, had Jn 1.41 in mind, this does not mean that they were aware of the Jewish concepts of messianism associated with that title.[46] There appear to have been Gnostic groups in the west which used the title of messiah in their initiation ceremonies, but apart from a rather mystifying account by Irenaeus nothing is known about these rituals.[47] Within the scope of this paper we must limit ourselves to those authors who offer more extensive discussions of the title *messias* and to asking how these relate to their eschatologies. These are Lactantius, Ambrose, Jerome and Augustine.

Lactantius (*ca*. 250–325) gives an extensive explanation when discussing the titles of Christ:

Quotations of, or allusions to, Jn 4.25 are found in Ambrose, *Isaac* 4.26; Ambrosiaster, *Comm. 1 Cor.* 9.21; *Quaest.* 2.51; Jerome, *Epist.* 108.13; 125.1; Augustine, *Tract. Ev. Jo.* 15.27, 28, 32; *De Diversis Quaestionibus LXXXIII* 64.8; Gregory of Elvira, *Tract.* 12.31.

39 Cf. esp. Tertullian, *Prax.* 28.

40 Cf. Lactantius, *Inst.* 4.7.4–8, cf. 4.13.9; Jerome, *Nom. hebr.* p. 66.17 (Lagarde); Augustine, *Enarrationes in Psalmos 130 sermo 3.13*; *Tract. Ev. Jo.* 7.13, 23; 15.27; Faustinus, *De Trinitate* 12.44; 15.9; *C. Litt. Petil.* 2.239; Eucherius, *Instructiones* 2.1.

41 Cf. e.g. Tertullian, *Nat.* 1.3; Hilary, *Trin.* 11.19; Ambrosiaster, *Quaest.* 1.49; Jerome, *Epist.* 65.13; *Optatus* 4.7.5; Faustinus, *De Trinitate* 39; Damasus, *Ep.* 9 (PL 13,374A); Maximinus, *Dissertatio contra Ambrosium* fol. 301r, l.12; Rufinus, *Symb.* 6; Augustine, *C. Iul.* 1.7.31 etc.

42 Ambrosiaster, *Comm. Rom.* 3.31; Rufinus, *Symb.* 6; Augustine, *Quaest. Hept.* 1.84; *Civ.* 16.38; 17.4; Prosper Aquitanus, *Liber sententiarum* 346; *Expositio psalmorum* 104.12-15. Cf. also Tertullian, *Apol.* 3.5; Ambrosiaster, *Comm. Gal.* 5.24; Augustine, *Civ.* 20.10 for the Christians' name being derived from *chrîsis/chrîsma*.

43 Cf. Lactantius, *Inst.*, 4.7.7; Jerome, *Comm. Isa.* 8.42 (on Isa. 27.13); *Comm. Zach.* 1.2; 3.12, 14; *Comm. Mal.* 3.1; 4.5–6. As regards *eleimménos* as a title for the messiah cf. Blanc 1975: 295–6; Schürer 1973–87: 2.517.

44 Jerome, *Comm. Abd.* 2.3.

45 Cf. Jerome, *Comm. Isa.* 12.21 (on Isa. 45.1-7; referring to Cyrus); *Optatus* 4.7.3; Faustinus, *De Trinitate* 39; Damasus *Ep.* 9 (PL 13.374A); Ambrosiaster, *Comm. Rom.* 3.31; *Quaest.* 1.49; Rufinus, *Symb.* 6; Augustine, *Civ.* 17.6 (referring to Saul); Nicetas of Remesiana, *Explanatio symboli* 3 (Burn p. 41.4); Prosper Aquitanus, *Expositio Psalmorum* 104.12–15 etc.

46 Cf. e.g. the incidental use of *messias* in Damasus, *Carmen* 50.3 (in a list of titles of Jesus); Prudentius, *Perist.* 10.16.

47 Cf. Irenaeus, *Haer.* 1.21.3 regarding the Marcosians who had spread to the Rhône Valley.

Christ is not a proper name, but a title of power and dominion; for by this the Jews were accustomed to call their kings. But the meaning of this name must be set forth on account of the error of the ignorant, who by the change of a letter are accustomed to call him Chrestus.[48]

Lactantius goes on to say that *Christus* is the Greek equivalent of Hebrew *mashiach* and that an alternative (i.e. Aquila's) Greek translation was *eleimménos* (which Lactantius disapproves of as being novel), that it means 'the anointed' (*unctum*) and that it refers to the Hebrew custom of anointing kings and priests. Finally, he explains that with regard to Christ this points not to 'this earthly kingdom, the time for receiving which has not yet arrived', but to 'his heavenly and eternal kingdom'.[49]

At the end of the same work Lactantius discusses Christ's kingdom in some detail (7.14–27).[50] Here he basically follows the sequence of events described in the book of Revelation. At his second coming Christ will appear as a warrior king surrounded by angels who will deliver those who have followed the Antichrist into the hands of the just, 'and they shall be slain from the third hour until the evening, and blood shall flow like a torrent'.[51] However, the Antichrist will escape and continue to wage war against Christ, before he will finally be overcome. This gruesome task having been completed, 'the dead will rise again, on whom the same king and God will pass judgment, to whom the supreme father will give the great power both of judging and of reigning'.[52] Yet only those will rise and be judged 'who have been exercised in the religion of God', whereas those who have not known God 'are already judged and condemned' (7.20.5; cf. Ps. 1.5). Both have to pass through a fire which, however, will only harm the wicked, whereas the righteous will remain untouched. Those who are found worthy will receive immortality whereas the others 'will not rise again, but will be hidden in the same darkness with the wicked, being destined to certain punishment'.[53]

Lactantius places the millennial reign after this judgement. Christ will rule for a thousand years with the righteous. His rule is set within the confines of the present world. For Lactantius expects there to be some who will not die, but will be presided over and judged by those raised from the dead.[54] The sacred city will then be planted in the middle of the earth where God himself will dwell together with the righteous.[55] Lactantius describes the bliss of the millennial reign in some detail without, however, specifically mentioning Christ again.[56] After the end of

---

48 The same was emphasized by Tertullian; cf. *Nat.* 1.3; *Apol.* 3.5. On the variation *Christus/Chrestus* in Latin cf. the article 'Chrestus' (by Walther Schwering), in *TLL Onom.* 2: 407–8 (with the supplement on p. 816).
49 Lactantius, *Inst.* 4.7.4–8; translation taken from www.newadvent.org/fathers/07014.htm (28/04/2006), altered.
50 In what follows English translations are taken from www.newadvent.org/fathers/07014.htm (20/05/2006).
51 *Inst.* 7.19.5.
52 *Inst.* 7.20.1.
53 *Inst.* 7.21.5–8.
54 Cf. *Inst.* 7.24.3.
55 *Inst.* 7.24.6.
56 *Inst.* 7.24.7–15. It is unclear whether the 'great king' who is venerated by all the nations and all kings (7.24.15) is Christ and not rather God himself.

the millennium (which in fact will last seven thousand years)[57] the prince of devils who had been bound by God will be loosed afresh and make war against the holy city, before being entirely destroyed by God's anger in a cataclysmic event. After a further seven years of peace and everlasting rest the world 'will be renewed by God, and the heavens will be folded together, and the earth will be changed'. The righteous will be transformed into angels and will serve God for ever. At the same time there will be a general resurrection after which the wicked will receive everlasting punishment.[58] Hence Christ, after having fulfilled his task as judge, is no longer mentioned by Lactantius and simply disappears from the narrative. This may be partly accounted for by the fact that for his eschatological scenario Lactantius not only draws on the biblical writings but in equal measure on pagan sources such as the *Sibylline Oracles*, Virgil's *Aeneid*, Book VI, his *Fourth Eclogue* and other works.

His wide knowledge of pagan authors notwithstanding, Lactantius is fairly typical of much of later Christian messianism in the west. There was broad agreement that the final series of events would, on the whole, follow the relevant biblical texts mentioned above with some discussion about the existence of a final millennium and the date of the coming of the Antichrist.

In the second half of the fourth century some Latin Fathers came under the influence of Greek speculation about the end of the world. Ambrose and Jerome had read Origen on the subject and faced now the serious difficulty that Origenist allegory was not altogether compatible with the more 'literal' approach favoured in the west. Both Ambrose's and Jerome's eschatologies vacillate between a traditional 'realist' position as suggested by apocalyptic passages in the Holy Scriptures and a 'spiritual interpretation' based on Origen and, to a certain extent, on Paul.

In his discussion of the term *messias* Ambrose (333/4–397) is fairly conventional. He emphasizes with implicit reference to Jn 4.19-26 that God is not worshipped in a particular place but rather in spirit and that the messiah expected by the Jews was none other than Christ:

> On this account also we know that this well can be taken in the mystical sense, because there the Samaritan woman – who is a guardian,[59] I mean a guardian of the heavenly precepts – drew the divine mysteries from that well, learning that God is spirit and is adored, not in a place but in spirit, and that Christ is the messiah and therefore that he who is until now awaited by the Jews has already come. Hearing these things, that woman, who manifests the beauty of the Church, learned and believed the sacraments of the law.[60]

Ambrose seems at first to be aware that the title *messias* is something specifically Jewish linking Christianity to Judaism. Yet from Ambrose's writings as a whole it becomes clear that Christ's return in the end must not be understood in a literal but rather in a figurative sense, just as his final judgement must not be taken too

---

57   *Inst.* 7.26.1.
58   *Inst.* 7.26.5–6.
59   Ambrose derives *Samaritana* from Hebrew *shamar* ('to guard').
60   Ambrose, *Isaac* 4.26; translation taken from McHugh 1972; altered. Cf. also Ambrosiaster, *Quaest.* 2.51.

literally. Christ sees into our hearts and thus knows our thoughts and deeds and has, therefore, no need to question us about them.[61] Therefore, the final resurrection does not necessarily comprise the body, but has strong spiritualizing overtones.[62] Likewise the punishments and rewards accorded by Christ are sometimes given an allegorical meaning.[63] In some passages Ambrose even appears to come close to the Origenist idea of a universal salvation.[64] However, Ambrose is not consistent in this. In other passages the eschatological events are described in a fairly traditional manner including Christ's final epiphany and judgement.[65] In any case, the process of spiritual purification does not end with the beatitude of the saved, but there is scope for further growth culminating in the final vision of God.[66] Although Ambrose does mention Christ's acting as a judge, there is, in fact, no longer a need for a second coming in any meaningful sense of the word, because Christ is perpetually present anyway.

Jerome (*ca.* 347–419) is another proponent of an Origenist theology in the west, although, as is well known, his Origenism is not without its qualifications. Jerome fairly consistently rejected a millenarian exegesis as it was suggested to him by both Victorinus of Pettau and his teacher Apollinarius.[67] Yet he did not espouse a clear-cut Origenist eschatology either. Rather, when dealing with the end of the world in his exegetical writings, he performs an odd balancing act between a more literal and a more spiritual understanding of the relevant passages in the Bible, fending off both an Origenistic view and an expectation which he terms 'Jewish' or 'Judaizing'. The details of his own position (which is, then, not very consistent) cannot be explained here.[68] When Jerome deals with *messias* as a term, he confines himself to remarks on its philological origin and meaning.[69] As far as Christ's second coming is concerned, John P. O'Connell has rightly remarked that 'Jerome's eschatology is very incomplete. For it is usually difficult, if not impossible, to determine whether the realism of his scriptural quotations is to be taken literally or figuratively.'[70] In some passages he seems to indicate that at the end of days he expects Christ to come in majesty in order to destroy Antichrist.[71] He will be accompanied by the angels, prophets and apostles.[72] There may be earthquakes accompanying this event. The purpose of his coming will be to judge the world. However, not all mankind will have to pass trial. Those who believe in Christ will not be judged, whereas those who do not

---

61 Cf. *Comm. Luc.* 10.49.
62 Cf. e.g. *Comm. Luc.* 10.49; *Ep.* 35.13; *Ob. Theo.* 29–32.
63 Cf. *Comm. Luc.* 7.204–6; *Comm. Pss.* 1.47–8, 54.
64 Cf. esp. *Comm. Pss.* 39.17; 118.20.29.
65 Cf. e.g. *Fid.* 2.119; *Comm. Pss.* 7.17; 20.11; 21.8–9; 118.3, 15-17; *Paen.* 1.22; *Nab.* 52; *Comm. Ps.* 36.26.
66 Cf. *Comm. Luc.* 5.61; *Bon. Mor.* 48.
67 Cf. above p. 201.
68 Cf. e.g. O'Connell 1948.
69 Cf. above p. 204 and n. 40.
70 O'Connell 1948: 32.
71 Cf. *Ep.* 121.11; *Comm. Agg.* 2.21–4; *Comm. Mt.* 4.24.27.
72 Cf. *Comm. Zach.* 3.14.6f.; cf. *Comm. Nah* 1.3.

believe will be damned straight away. Only those who believe and are overcome by sin will have to account for their deeds before Christ.[73]

The most extensive discussion of the title *messias* and his theological significance is found in the writings of Augustine (354–430). In his massive work against the Manichaean Faustus Augustine argues against Faustus' denial that the Prophets predicted Christ. It is obvious, Augustine says, that the Son of Man mentioned by Daniel is the saviour whom the Jews still expect, but who has already arrived in Christ. The truth of this statement is proven by historical events: the conversion of the Gentiles, the destruction of the Temple and with it the end of sacrifices:

> This was all clearly foretold by Daniel when he prophesied of the anointing of the Most Holy [cf. Dan. 9.24]. Now that all these things have taken place, we ask the Jews for the anointed Most Holy, and they have no answer to give. How could they argue with us not about the fact of Christ's coming, but only about (the date of) his advent, if they did not know him well from their own prophetical books? Why do they ask John whether he is Christ [cf. Lk. 3.15; Jn 1.19-20]? Why do they say to the Lord, 'How long will you make us to doubt? If you are the Christ, tell us plainly' [Jn 10.24]. Why do Peter and Andrew and Philip say to Nathanael, 'We have found the messiah, which is interpreted Christ' [Jn 1.41], but because this name was known to them from the prophecies of their Scriptures? In no other nation were the kings and priests anointed, and called Anointed or Christs. Nor could this symbolical anointing be discontinued till the coming of him who was thus prefigured. For among all their anointed ones the Jews looked for one who was to save them. But in the mysterious justice of God they were blinded; and thinking only of the power of the messiah, they did not understand his weakness, in which he died for us.[74]

Augustine clearly emphasizes the unity of the Old and New Testaments. The coming of Christ was foretold by the prophets, but the Jews refused to acknowledge him. Christ is the *Jewish* messiah, because in no other nation the kings are anointed and hence called Christ. The Jews are, however, unable to accept that Christ is this messianic king because of his passion and death on the cross.

In another passage of the same work Augustine points out that the Church has taken over many expressions from the Hebrew Bible like *adonai* or *amen*. The pagans do not understand these expressions and ridicule the Church who, however, is not to be intimidated. Augustine exclaims that, if the Church 'is charged with loving Emmanuel, she laughs at the ignorance of that person, and holds fast by the truth of this name. If she is charged with loving messiah, she scorns her powerless adversary and clings to her anointed teacher.'[75]

---

73 Cf. *Tract. Ps.* 1 (*Anecdota Maredsolana*, III/2, p. 78); *Comm. Eccl.* 12.13–14; *Comm. Mt.* 2.12.36; 2.20.23; *Comm. Isa.* 6.10 (on Isa. 13.6); 8.2 (24.1); 8.19 (26.9cd–10); 8.28 (26.19); 17.23 (62.10-12); 18.27 (66.15-16); 18.29 (66.18-19); *Comm. Am.* 2.7.4–6; *Comm. Nah.* 1.1; *Comm. Soph.* 1.10; 2.3f.; 3.1-7; *Comm. Zach.* 3.12, 11-14; *Comm. Mal.* 3.17–18; *Comm. Dan.* 2.7.9a-10; [4].12, 1-3; *Comm. Gal.* 3.6.5; *Jo. Hier.* 33ff.
74 Augustine, *Faust.* 12.44. Translation taken from www.newadvent.org/fathers/140612.htm(01/04/2006); altered.
75 Augustine, *Faust.* 15.9; Translation taken from www.newadvent.org/fathers/140615.htm(01/04/2006); altered.

Augustine here only alludes to the translation of *messias*. In his *Sermons on the Gospel of John* he is more specific. After quoting Jn 1.41 he continues by saying:

> *Messias* in Hebrew; Christ in Greek; in Latin 'anointed'. For he is called Christ after the anointing. *Chrîsma* is 'anointing' in Greek; Christ, therefore, is the anointed. He is peculiarly anointed, pre-eminently anointed; wherewith all Christians are anointed, he is pre-eminently anointed. Hear how he speaks in the Psalm: 'Wherefore God, your God, has anointed you with the oil of gladness above your fellows' [Ps. 44(45).8]. For all the holy ones are his fellows, but he in a peculiar sense is the Holy of Holies, peculiarly anointed, peculiarly Christ.[76]

Christ is not seen here primarily as the king, but rather as the 'Holy of Holies', God himself. The anointment appears to have given him a divine quality which in the baptismal anointment is transferred to all believers.[77] This divine anointment is prefigured in Jacob's anointing of the stone at Bethel (Gen. 28.18).[78]

In his work against the Donatist Petilian Augustine emphasizes the consequences this anointing has for the Church. Here his point of reference is Ps. 132(133): the Christians who cling to Christ and 'preach the truth without fear' will receive a spiritual sanctification.[79]

Occasionally, Augustine even mentions the Punic translation of *messias*. When commenting on Jn 4.25 he says:

> What is this? Just now she said: 'The Jews are contending for the temple, and we for this mountain [cf. Jn 4.20]; when he has come, he will despise the mountain and overthrow the temple; he will teach us all things that we may know how to worship in spirit and in truth.' She knew who could teach her, but she did not yet know him that was now teaching her. But now she was worthy to receive the manifestation of him. Now *messias* is 'anointed'; 'anointed' in Greek is Christ; in Hebrew *messias*; whence also in Punic *messe* means 'anoint!'. For the Hebrew, Punic and Syriac are cognate and neighbouring languages.[80]

Christ reveals himself to the Samaritan woman as the messiah whose cult will surpass the cult both of the Samaritans and the Jews.[81] This is part of a process which has begun with the patriarchs Abraham, Isaac and Jacob.[82]

---

76 Augustine, *Tract. Ev Jo.* 7.13. Translation taken from www.newadvent.org/fathers/1701007.htm(01/04/2006); altered.
77 Cf. also Augustine, *Enarrationes in Psalmos* 130 sermo 3.13.
78 Ibid. 23.
79 *C. Litt. Petil.* 2.239.
80 Augustine, *Tract. Ev. Jo.* 15.27. Translation taken from www.newadvent.org/fathers/1701015.htm(01/04/2006); altered. Cf. also *C. Litt. Petil.* 2.239. In *sermo* 101.2 Augustine appears to play with the assonance between *messis* (harvest), *messor* (harvester) and *messias*.
81 A similar interpretation is found in Augustine, *De Diversis Quaestionibus LXXXIII* 64.8.
82 Cf. ibid., 32.

It is not easy to see how these etymological and exegetical explanations of the significance of Christ as the messiah relate to Augustine's eschatology. As is well known, *De civitate dei* contains a long narrative of events at the end of times which successively reviews all relevant biblical texts (books 20–22).[83] But, taken together, not much is said about Christ.[84] The first resurrection is the resurrection of souls. This is no future event, but is happening in the present (20.6). Equally, the thousand years mentioned in Revelation do not refer to some imaginary seventh day (Sabbath), but to the time since Christ's first advent on earth, and it is unclear how many years have already passed (20.7). What is clear, though, is what future events are in store for us: the return and preaching of Elijah, the conversion of the Jews, the persecution of the Antichrist, the coming of Christ as judge, the resurrection of the dead, the separation of the righteous from the wicked, the final conflagration of the earth and the renewal of the world. It is only the precise sequence of these events that is unknown to us (20.30). Christ is the founder and king of the *civitas dei* which has begun with creation, is hidden in the visible Church and will finally, at the end of days, be fully revealed. It is the same Christ who was crucified and rose again from the dead, wherefore he will return in his servant-form (*forma servi*).[85] This is not only to safeguard the identity of the Christ of the second advent with that of the first, but also because 'it is not permitted to the wicked to see God'.[86] Then 'the form of a servant will pass away. For to this end he had manifested himself, that he might execute judgment. After the judgment, he shall go hence, will lead with him the body of which he is the head, and deliver the kingdom to God. Then will openly be seen that form of God which could not be seen by the wicked, to whose vision the form of a servant must be shown.'[87] Yet the decisive event for Augustine is not Christ's return, but his work as redeemer through his incarnation.

Ambrose, Jerome and Augustine were writing at a time when in the east there was a fierce debate about the trinity and Christology going on. One may wonder whether this had any impact on western eschatology. However, given the fact that not many Latin Fathers were familiar with this debate, the implications of such speculation for eschatology are not often drawn out in their writings. Hilary of Poitiers (*ca.* 315–367/8), in many respects a wanderer between the worlds, is a notable exception.[88] In his earlier works such as his *Commentary on Matthew* Hilary starts out by presenting a fairly traditional apocalyptic scenario. He expects the Antichrist to erect his kingdom in Jerusalem;[89] however, without giving a precise date when this will happen.[90] This will be followed by Christ's second coming. The saviour will arrive in Jerusalem, the place of his passion, in

---

83   The same is true for the passages dealing with the resurrection and the end in the *Enchiridion* (esp. chs. 111–13).
84   Cf. also the evidence from other works collected in Eger 1933: 41–59.
85   Cf. e.g. *Tract. Ev. Jo.* 40.4; cf. also *Enchir.* 111.3.
86   *Tract. Ev. Jo.* 19.16.
87   *Tract. Ev. Jo.* 19.18; translation taken from URL <http://www.ccel.org(24/05/2006); altered.
88   For Hilary's eschatology cf. esp. Durst 1987 with rich documentation.
89   Cf. *Comm. Mt.* 25.3.8; 26.2; 33.2.
90   Cf. *Comm. Mt.* 25.8.

a triumphant procession.[91] Christ's advent will be accompanied by cosmic turmoil which Hilary describes by following closely the apocalypse in Mt. 24.29-31.[92] There will be a general resurrection,[93] after which the universal judgement will take place.[94] Yet even in Hilary's early works there are spiritualizing features that go beyond the boundaries of tradition. The resurrection of the righteous will start a process of constructing the 'heavenly Zion' and will, therefore, transcend the confines of this world. Instead it is considered as a kind of 'marriage' of the human flesh with the Holy Spirit.[95] It is, therefore, a spiritual process rather than a 'real' one, the gradual realization of the kingdom of God in every believer.[96]

These 'spiritualist' inklings are reinforced in his work on the trinity. Here they are combined with christological considerations.[97] The eschatological process is completed when Christ 'hands over his kingdom to the Father' (cf. 1 Cor. 15.24-28).[98] This includes the righteous who are 'conformed to the glory of his body' and thus form the kingdom of God. Christ reigns in his glorious body until the authorities are abolished, death is conquered and his enemies are subdued. It is only then that Christ himself will be subjected to God. In this process Christ's human body which has already assumed the body of all mankind will be transformed into the Godhead so that God may be all in all. As a result Christ's becoming wholly God through the transfiguration of his human body entails our transformation into the perfect image of God.[99] As Brian Daley quite rightly remarks, this is 'the first appearance in a Latin writer's works of the emerging Greek soteriology and eschatology of "divinization"'.[100]

Generally speaking, Hilary's comparatively high level of theological sophistication regarding the relation between Christology and eschatology was not sustained by subsequent writers in the west. Instead, confronted with increasing political instability the Latin Fathers kept alive and even reinforced the conventional interest in the dramatic elements of the final events.[101] The end of the world fired the imagination of many writers, among them a new breed of Latin authors who devoted themselves to composing Christian poetry. Commodian, Prudentius (born 348 C.E.) and Orientius (fifth cent.) were in many respects typical of the *Zeitgeist*. In Commodian's *Carmen apologeticum* (date of composition unknown) the Lord will come in the very end. The bodies of the saints will be resurrected and immediately carried away by the clouds up towards the coming Christ (cf. 1 Thess. 4.17). Those who have nailed him to the cross will also come to life

---

91 Cf. *Comm. Mt.* 21.2; 25.8.
92 Cf. *Comm. Mt.* 26.1.
93 Cf. *Comm. Pss.* 55.7; 118.11.5 etc.
94 Cf. *Comm. Mt.* 10.16; *Comm. Pss.* 1.15–18; 57.7.
95 Cf. *Comm. Mt.* 27.4 and *Comm. Pss.* 68.31.
96 Cf. *Comm. Mt.* 27.4; *Comm. Pss.* 9.4; 148.8.
97 Michael Durst even speaks of the *Christozentrik* of Hilary's eschatology (Durst 1987: 316, 335).
98 Cf. Schendel 1971: 158–67.
99 For the details cf. the extensive discussion in *Trin.* 11.36–49.
100 Daley 1991: 96.
101 Cf. e.g. Kötting 1958; Luneau 1964; Schwarte 1966.

again, only to be sent back to the underworld straight away where they will burn in fire.[102] In Prudentius' works the cosmic events accompanying Christ's proclaiming judgement are described in some detail.[103] In the *Peristephanon* Prudentius paints a powerful picture of the martyrs' receiving Christ in order to intercede for their native cities and the pious Christians.[104] Orientius offers perhaps the gloomiest description of the final judgement.[105] Many homilists of the fourth and fifth centuries also use the threat of future punishment for moral exhortation.

To sum up, from the Latin texts we can glean a fairly homogeneous picture with regard to the final events and to Christ's action within these events.
  1. In the Latin fathers the Hebrew term *messias* is not entirely absent, but it is not often used and usually occurs in an exegetical context (referring to John 1 and 4).
  2. Christ is seen as the messiah predicted by the prophets, but this messiah, whom the Jews still expect, has already arrived.
  3. The messiah is no longer human, but a divine figure instead.
  4. The messiah's task usually is no longer the restoration of Israel; instead, after victory over the Antichrist, he rules together with the saints during the millennium and/or performs the final judgement and is the centre of the heavenly kingdom (which is often not clearly defined).
  5. The expectation of Christ's advent as king and judge is not necessarily dependent on the expectation of a millennial reign of the saints. His coming may precede the millennium, in which case Christ appears as a military leader overcoming the Antichrist and the forces of evil, but in other sources his coming is immediately followed by the final judgement without a millennial expectation being found.
  6. Whereas the majority of Latin authors represents a 'realist' tradition, a minority is influenced by eastern spiritualizing exegesis.
  6.1 The 'realist' tradition takes the biblical accounts of the final events 'literally' in the sense that it accords to them a close approximation between what is said and what will happen by reducing the metaphorical or allegorical content.[106]
  6.1.1 As regards the scope of this chapter there are basically three tasks assigned to Christ at the end of times. There is almost universal agreement that Christ will act as *judge* in the final judgement and will separate the righteous from the wicked. In addition, in some premillennial texts he is considered as the supreme *king* in the millennial rule of the saints. Also, when there is no millenarianism present, Christ is usually referred to as king, but these authors have often not a very clear idea as to the nature of his kingdom. Occasionally, Christ's *priestly* role is also mentioned.

---

102   C. *Apol.* 1041–59. However, Commodian is not consistent in describing Christ's role at the end of time; cf. *Inst.* 1.45 and 2.35 and Kinzig 1998: 81–6.
103   Cf. e.g. *Liber Cathemerinon* 9.106–14; 11.101–16.
104   Cf. *Liber Peristephanon* 4.9–60.
105   Cf. esp. *Commonitorium* 2.347–92 and Daley 1991: 162.
106   Irenaeus, for example, repeatedly insists that biblical prophecies about the end must not be allegorized; cf. *Haer.* 5.35.1–2.

6.1.2 Generally speaking, all authors closely follow the biblical texts. Only rarely pagan ideas about the world are integrated (e.g. in Lactantius) without, however, displacing the biblical basis.[107]

6.1.3 All three roles, Christ as king, as priest and as judge, are based upon Jewish descriptions of the messiah and are, therefore, perfectly compatible with certain strands of apocalyptic Judaism.

6.1.4 The only point on which the Latin Christian texts of the 'realist' type differ from most Jewish speculation about the messiah is in that they insist upon Christ's dual nature as God and man (or Son of God and Son of Man), but there are Jewish sources such as *4 Ezra* where the divine nature of the messiah is also mentioned.[108]

6.2 The 'spiritualizing' tradition tends to increase the metaphorical and allegorical content of the Bible. Here it is thought that the eschatological events or realities are of such a peculiar nature that they can only be described by drawing on images and metaphors. Whereas in the Greek east, ever since Origen, this tradition was predominant, in the Latin west only a few authors may be named in this respect, the most important ones being Hilary, Ambrose and Jerome. It is perhaps no coincidence that there is little coherence in their accounts of the end of the world. The theological cost of this kind of approach was substantial. If the resurrection, the final judgement and future bliss or damnation were spiritualized in this manner, there was basically neither room nor need for a messiah who is, as we have seen, by tradition essentially a worldly figure and a human being. Conversely, such an eschatology only 'worked' where there was a Christology emphasizing the divinity (and hence 'spiritual' nature) of Christ.

7. In western theological thought there appears to be little relation between reflections on the nature and the work of Christ and his role at the end of days, Hilary being a notable exception.[109] Christology comes into play when one asks what Christ has *already* brought to humankind, not what he will do in the future. In order to understand the reasons for this lack of theological cohesion in the minds of the Latin Fathers further studies are needed. Tentatively I suggest here (a) that in Latin literature christological reflections are found in doctrinal treatises, whereas eschatological considerations occur in apologetical and exegetical literature, and (b) that one has to keep in mind that the often quoted 'crisis of apocalypticism' in the third century was mainly an eastern phenomenon, whereas in the west apocalyptic thought persisted all through late antiquity and beyond. Greek theology attempted a synthesis between, on the one hand, philosophical speculation concerning the end of the cosmos and, on the other, biblical eschatology and – broadly speaking – combined the Platonic idea of an 'assim-

---

107 Philosophy comes into play especially when the Fathers attempt to describe the possibility and the process of resurrection, since the Scripture offers no plausible 'scientific' categories with which to understand this event. This is not considered here.

108 In this respect Stone 1990 (esp. 207–13 for the role of the messiah in *Fourth Ezra*); Chester 1992: 248–9; Kerner 1998; Lehnart 1999 and above n. 10.

109 This seems to be true not only for the western tradition. Browsing through Alois Grillmeier's magisterial study on the development of christological doctrine in the early Church one is baffled to see that in his index there are very few references to the return of Christ or eschatology; cf. Grillmeier 1990.

ilation to God' or divinization (*homoíosis theoû*) with Gen. 1.26-27. seeing the ultimate goal of man in the restoration of the divine likeness. In the west, however, where the interest in Greek philosophy was limited to small esoteric circles and many intellectuals were no longer able to read Plato in the original language, the books of Daniel and of Revelation became much more influential as regards eschatological speculation. Christ's return is embedded in an eschatological drama, whose apocalyptic imagery is repeated time and time again.

There are, then, continuities and discontinuities between Jewish and Christian messianic expectation in the west. In most authors Christ will return in the end to fulfil a traditional messianic role in erecting an eschatological rule. However, Christ is no earthly king, but rather a pre-existent, divine figure coming from heaven. Christian eschatology in the west in this respect appears to differ from mainstream Jewish expectations of the end, but it is in line with eschatologies such as those depicted in *4 Ezra*. Yet the identification of this messiah with the historical person of Jesus is peculiar to Christian messianism. It rests upon the biblical prophecies, but the converse is also true: these prophecies are read in the light of the coming of Christ.

Chapter 16

MATERIAL REMAINS

David Noy

The material remains left by Jews and Christians in the Graeco-Roman world can convey a fairly unambiguous message or one whose interpretation inspires much debate. An epitaph from a Jewish catacomb, decorated with Jewish symbols and commemorating someone with an exclusively Jewish name, leaves no doubt about the allegiance of the deceased, even if there may be room for argument about what the symbols meant to the people who used them. The foundations of a synagogue which was destroyed by fire and had a church built on top of it provide a basis for reconstructing the local balance of power at a particular time. On the other hand, a wall-painting of a biblical scene can be viewed differently according to whether it is found in a synagogue or a Christian catacomb, and can generate a variety of theories about what was in the minds of the people who commissioned it. This chapter will concentrate on two sites, Dura and Rome, in order to look at the changing balance in Jewish-Christian relations and at some possible expressions of messianic beliefs through paintings and symbols.

In 244/5 C.E. members of the Jewish community of Dura-Europos, a Mesopotamian city just within the eastern frontier of the Roman Empire, set up a number of inscriptions recording the renovation of their synagogue. The alterations, which presumably took place over a number of years, included the expansion of the building to incorporate adjacent properties, and the decoration of the walls of the main House of Assembly with a series of frescoes depicting events and images from the Bible and Jewish history. The circumstances of the synagogue's destruction, buried in the creation of a massive earthwork intended to protect the city from the Persian attack which came in 256, led to the survival of the paintings until their recovery by archaeologists in the 1930s. They may not have been unique in their own time, but their preservation has made them into a unique survival of third-century Jewish art.

All the walls of the House of Assembly appear to have been repainted at the same time, apart from one central area which was modified later. The execution of the work indicates that it was done by local artists who used the styles (e.g. of clothing)[1] with which they were familiar, adapted as far as possible to a Jewish environment. Hachlili 1998: 460 writes: 'The art at Dura is expressed in a wholly local manner and, at the same time, includes all the important Jewish features and symbols.' The artists are unlikely to have been Jews themselves, but

---

1   Goldman 1973 *passim*.

would have worked from models provided by their employers. This is significant because the artists would have used their habitual forms unless told otherwise – for example, if asked to depict a temple they would paint a Syrian one, and if asked to depict a musician-king they would paint Orpheus, even if what they painted was going to be interpreted very differently. Such depictions do not need to be given any meaning beyond the fact that the Jewish community apparently did not object.[2] The technical standard of the paintings may not be very high when compared to works of art from elsewhere in the Roman Empire, but it was certainly the best available at Dura. In a few places captions were painted in Greek to identify individual figures (Aaron, and Solomon and an officer[3]), and in other places such captions were added to the paintings later in Aramaic, although mostly in places where they seem rather superfluous because the scenes are readily identifiable. The captions are not biblical quotations. They are only found on the West Wall, and were probably deemed unnecessary elsewhere.[4] The Greek captions, which were presumably the work of the original painters, were perhaps copied unthinkingly from the models they were using.

The centre of the West Wall (i.e. the wall facing Jerusalem) has an aedicula for the Torah-shrine, above the arch of which a temple façade is depicted, flanked by a menorah (with lulab and ethrog) and the sacrifice of Isaac. The sacrifice takes the place normally occupied by the shofar when this full array of Jewish symbols became normal. The panel on the wall itself immediately above this was reworked and was not well preserved; it includes Jacob with his sons and grandsons, David as Orpheus playing the lyre to animals, and a seated monarch with his court (see further below). There are two panels to either side in which four male figures are depicted: one is certainly Moses with the Burning Bush (captioned very confusingly as 'Moses son of Levi').[5] The others are probably Moses again, Isaiah and Jeremiah,[6] although alternatives have been proposed for all of them (Joshua, Ezra, Joshua or Abraham). They are, at least, almost universally agreed to be biblical prophets. The whole surface of all four walls of the room appears to have been painted, with the paintings divided into three registers on each wall.

The messages intended to be conveyed by the paintings have been hotly debated.[7] Their clarity is not helped by the loss of about 40 per cent of the paintings, but the West Wall, which would have been the focus of attention for people during services, is well preserved, with only a small part of the upper register missing. Even if the paintings had all survived, however, it is very doubtful if there would have been any agreement about the intentions behind them. The following points are perhaps uncontentious:

1. The theme of Esther and Mordechai, taken from a book whose canonical status was uncertain, can hardly have been chosen accidentally by a community on the fringe of the Persian Empire, although whether the message was meant to be one of hostility to, or reconciliation with, Persia is unclear. Sabar 2000: 159 sees it as the Jews' thanks to

2 *Contra*, e.g., Goodenough 1988: 202.
3 Noy and Bloedhorn 2004: Syr102, 100.
4 Hachlili 1998: 134.
5 Noy and Bloedhorn 2004: Syr99.
6 Kessler 1987.

their Roman benefactors, arguing against the view of Levit-Tawil 1979 that it shows Jewish support for Shapur I. On either interpretation, the meaning was derived from the immediate situation of the Durene Jews, something which has perhaps encouraged some scholars to look for other 'immediate' meanings elsewhere in the paintings.
2. A series of Iranian inscriptions was added to the paintings in ca. 253.[8] Their exact nature is very unclear[9] but they seem to record the dates on which various people with Iranian names looked at the paintings, and occasionally to add comments about the content. They were added without defacing or spoiling the paintings, and in fact are invisible in most photographs. They show interest in and respect for the paintings from people outside the community of Jews at Dura. The early explorers of the catacombs at Rome such as Antonio Bosio left their names across some of the paintings they found,[10] perhaps in a similar spirit although in a rather more defacing way.
3. The choice of paintings above the aedicula for the Torah-shrine in the centre of the West Wall must have been seen as particularly significant. Abraham's sacrifice of Isaac, next to the menorah and other symbols, was the centrepiece which would have caught the eye when the scrolls were taken from the Torah-shrine. It was an 'affirmation of Jewish identity',[11] or an introduction to the whole programme of the paintings.[12] It may also have made a statement about Jewish sacrifice in a city where acts of sacrifice were depicted on the walls of pagan temples.[13] The depictions of the menorah are the earliest ones known in a synagogue context.[14]
4. The range of paintings shows the Jews as a group for whom events from the Bible could be represented in a narrative form as factual history, whatever other interpretations may have been added.
5. It is unknown how likely non-Jews were to see the inside of the synagogue, and how much of the paintings they would have understood if they did see them. The primary audience must have been committed Jews, but perhaps the city also had Godfearers who were interested in Judaism without making a full conversion.

One of the most debated topics is whether the whole range of paintings represents a carefully planned programme with a clear message or whether individual parts should be viewed separately. For example, Goodenough believes that there was a 'master hand' or even committee which planned the paintings,[15] while Hachlili argues strongly for the latter view.[16] It is of course possible that a whole programme of paintings was planned without a specific message beyond a celebration of Jewish history and a desire to make the synagogue into an impressive building. Inscriptions show that the foremost individual in the Jewish community was Samuel son of Yedaya, and this may explain why the figure of

7   See e.g. Gutmann 1973: 137–9 and Hachlili 1998: ch. 3 for summaries of many competing views.
8   Noy and Bloedhorn 2004: Syr111–25.
9   See Noy and Bloedhorn 2004 for a survey of theories which have been proposed.
10 See numerous illustrations in Pavia 2000.
11 Elsner 2001: 283.
12 Revel-Neher 2000: 61.
13 Millar 1993: 469.
14 Levine 2000b: 144.
15 Goodenough 1988: 192.
16 Hachlili 1998: 195; see also Elsner 2001: 281.

the prophet Samuel is so prominent in the fresco of Samuel anointing David.[17] Other such local factors which are now irrecoverable may have been similarly influential.

The synagogue has to be understood in the light of the existence of a Christian community at Dura. The house-church, which took its final form *ca.* 240, has a much more limited range of images: the Good Shepherd juxtaposed with Adam and Eve, David and Goliath (both figures have incised captions), some of Christ's miracles and (probably) the women at his tomb.[18] The women, shown in procession, may be intended to lead the viewer's eye towards the font.[19] The first two pictures have a clear symbolic function: the completion of the Old Testament by the New.[20] According to Hachlili 1998: 427–8, 'The episodes are depicted in a static, two-dimensional style, and are not rendered in the narrative programmatic cycles found in the synagogue.' The paintings were of a lower technical standard than those of the synagogue, individually and as a whole. It seems clear from comparison of the synagogue and house-church that the Jewish community was larger and had much greater resources than the Christian one. A graffito of 232/3[21] suggests that the Christian paintings may be earlier than the final phase of the synagogue, however. Nothing is known of the background of the Christian group at Dura: whether it began as a breakaway group of Jews, or among converted pagans. It is not possible to know if the Jews and Christians were in competition with each other in any sense, but if they were, the material evidence would suggest that the Jews were having the better of it. Kessler sees the synagogue paintings, with their themes of (as he reads them) divine protection for the Jews and messianic restoration, as a response to pressures from Christianity,[22] but such pressures are not what a comparison of the buildings and their paintings would indicate.

If the Jews were using the paintings in the synagogue as part of a theological debate, it seems more likely to have been with pagans than with Christians. Dura had a wide variety of native and imported pagan cults.[23] There is an illustration on the synagogue's West Wall of the episode in 1 Sam. 5 where the power of the Ark destroys the statue of the Philistines' god Dagon when it is brought into his temple. Elsner 2001: 282 comments that the paintings 'appear to present a visual meditation on temples – pagan and Jewish – and to make the case for one over the other in no uncertain terms'. Two divine images which have fallen from their pedestals and are lying on the ground before the Ark resemble the painting of Adonis in a nearby temple[24] – was this a message of Jewish triumph, or simply the natural way for the painter to depict a pagan god? Goodenough (1988: 225) goes so far as to say that 'the artist is telling us as clearly as if in words that

17 Noy and Bloedhorn 2004: Syr85–7; Wharton 1995: 44.
18 Kraeling 1967: pls. XVII–XXII.
19 Butcher 2003: 326.
20 Elsner 2001: 280.
21 Butcher 2003: 326.
22 Weitzmann and Kessler 1990: 177.
23 Millar 1993: 468.
24 Goodenough 1988: 223.

paganism is a mockery and empty shell'. Applebaum 1979: 322 believes that the scene, along with the Exodus frescoes, alludes to Mesopotamian participation in the Jewish revolt against Trajan (115–17 C.E.). Such a reference, like the possible messianic theme discussed below, would necessarily be very cryptic, but the link seems a tenuous one: it is not known if the Jews of third-century Dura were descended directly from the Mesopotamian population of Trajan's time; the rise of Shapur I had changed the political situation completely; and allusion to unsuccessful revolts in the past (unlike the glorification of the Maccabean revolt) does not seem to have been a Jewish practice. Nevertheless, it is likely that a non-Jewish viewer who did not know the biblical story on which the fresco was based would understand the scene as a general image of Jewish triumph.

The temple buildings in the paintings would have been familiar to people accustomed to the cityscape of Dura, and Goodenough (1988: 188) points out that they contain Greek or Persian details such as winged Victories in the acroteria and garlanded sacrificial animals. However, apart from the Philistine temple, they represent the Jerusalem Temple at various stages in its history.[25] Jewish viewers would have known that the Temple was also built on the site of the sacrifice of Isaac. Depiction of the Temple was important in a world where the actual building had been destroyed nearly two centuries ago – although we cannot tell if it would have been 'read' purely historically or also prospectively as something whose actual restoration could be expected. The latter view does not have to imply a messianic reading, since the emperor Julian attempted the restoration a century later, and it was already possible to see an emperor such as Alexander Severus as sympathetic to Judaism. It may also have boosted Jewish self-esteem to present their religion as a temple-orientated one in a city where, in the absence of a monumental forum area, temples were the most prominent buildings.

The Iranian inscriptions show that Persian visitors saw the synagogue as 'a local Jewish temple',[26] and the model of an introverted sacred space exclusive to cult members (rather than a public space open to all) was the norm in temple-building at Dura.[27] One inscription calls it 'this edifice of the God of the Gods of the Jews',[28] which suggests that it was categorized as a temple (although 'God of Gods' has a Jewish precedent in Ps. 136.2). The fact that the House of Assembly could only be reached through a complex series of corridors and rooms may have contributed to visitors experiencing a 'sense of revealed accessibility to Presence'.[29] There is one indication that the Jews themselves borrowed a local temple-building custom. Human bones were found buried under the sill and socket of the main doorway,[30] a practice known from pagan buildings at Dura but not something to be expected in a Jewish context where contact with the remains of the dead was normally avoided.

Goodenough (1988: 250) believes that 'the assembly room was made to look as much as possible like the inner sanctuaries of the great temples', with a

25 Renov 1970.
26 Fine 1997: 146.
27 Wharton 1995: 29.
28 Noy and Bloedhorn 2004: Syr113.
29 Wharton 1995: 31.
30 Kraeling 1956: 19.

portable Torah-shrine in its aedicula taking the place of the cult statue. Fine (1997: 145) argues that 'the synagogue Torah shrine and the Temple of Jerusalem bear an intimate relationship', especially as 'the shrine stands on the wall that is aligned with Jerusalem' (something which presumably only Jews would have appreciated). He also believes that viewers were encouraged to link the Ark of the Covenant and the Temple of the paintings with the actual Torah-shrine. Links were thus made both with nearby pagan temples and with the tradition of the Jewish Temple.

Another major area of debate is the question of whether, going beyond what Elsner (2001: 301) calls the 'resistant' nature of the paintings, a messianic theme can be found, based on a general understanding of the Ark's symbolism,[31] or on very close reading of individual scenes. Kessler (1987: 150–1), discussing the figure which he identifies as Isaiah, writes: 'The frescoist was trying to depict the common messianic topos according to which the advent of the redeemer is to be ushered in by an eternal day that dispels night.'[32] According to this view, Isaiah is to be read as prophesying the messianic age, and the central area above the aedicula depicts the messiah with representatives of the twelve tribes. The reworking of this area suggests to Goodenough (1988: 189) 'the development of an idea in the mind of the artist, or of the people in the synagogue who repeatedly asked for these modifications'. He does not give a messianic interpretation but other suggestions about how this area should be understood include a David/Messiah figure dressed as a Persian king[33] or a messianic banquet given by David in the Garden of Eden.[34] The messianic reading can be extended to the whole of the centre of the West Wall or the whole of Register B.[35]

The messianic interpretation summarized very briefly here[36] is a possible reading, as it is for much Jewish art in the Roman world, but one which cannot be proved and which is not part of the more obvious messages of the synagogue paintings. Of course, its potentially subversive nature means that some amount of disguise would be essential, and, even if such a meaning was expounded verbally to the local community, it might not be obvious to Jews from elsewhere. The paintings indicate a Jewish community which was proud of its heritage but also conscious of its position in a multicultural city, anxious to impress its own members and visitors with its artistic repertoire, and to allude to its past and future role in the world beyond Dura.

The Jewish community of Rome has left material evidence from the same period but in a different form: the catacombs which flourished from the late second to fourth centuries. No remains of synagogues have been found at Rome itself. The synagogue of Ostia has been thoroughly excavated, and was in existence from

---

31   Gutmann 1973: 138, citing Wischnitzer.
32   Cf. Isa. 60.1-20, and the detailed discussion of Sonne 1947.
33   Weitzmann and Kessler 1990: 164.
34   Hachlili 1998: 101, citing Kraeling.
35   Hachlili 1998: 180–1, citing Goldstein and Grabar.
36   Kessler gives one of the fullest of such interpretations: Weitzmann and Kessler 1990: Part II. See the criticism by Wharton 1995: 22.

the first century C.E., with major renovations in the second and fourth centuries.[37] There is no evidence of wall-paintings, but only the very lowest part of the walls is preserved for most of the building. The mosaics which have survived use only inanimate motifs (a chalice and a loaf) and geometric patterns. The building was adapted in the fourth century to create a free-standing, apse-shaped aedicula for the Torah-shrine, orientated, as earlier at Dura, so that the congregation looking towards it would be facing Jerusalem. On the corbels of the architraves facing the congregation, Jewish symbols were engraved in low relief: each corbel has a large menorah, flanked by lulab and etrog on the left and shofar on the right.[38] Thus the congregations at Ostia and Dura saw something very similar to each other as they faced Jerusalem: a range of symbols which had become fairly standard by the fourth century but in the third century was still moving from the partly narrative (the sacrifice of Isaac) to the purely symbolic.

There is a literary tradition that Ostia had a Christian community with a bishop by the mid-third century, and it certainly had a bishop by 313, as did Portus by 314.[39] Constantine built a basilica, remains of which have been identified 500 metres from the synagogue.[40] Part of the baths of Mithras was converted to a church, probably in the mid-fourth century.[41] A hall which was rebuilt in the fourth century has a depiction of Christ in *opus sectile* on the wall.[42] Thus there was a significant Christian presence in Ostia at the time of the synagogue's fourth-century renovation. There is no evidence for the relationship between the two communities, but it appears that both had command of significant resources.[43]

At Rome, the catacombs provide the only material remains for the study of the Jewish community. It seems likely that a catacomb was envisaged as a more exclusive area than a synagogue. Anecdotal evidence shows that non-Jews entered synagogues for various reasons,[44] and wall-paintings and other decorations were therefore potentially visible to people outside the community. The Jewish catacombs, on the other hand, were only likely to be visited by those who wished to commemorate the deceased, at the funeral and later – unlike the Christian catacombs which, where they contained martyrs' remains, gradually developed into locations for religious services and meals (*refrigeria*), and places of pilgrimage.[45] Such people need not be exclusively Jews, since intermarriage and conversion may have been of some significance, but it is probable that any messages to be found in the decoration of the catacombs were aimed at a more restricted audience than those of synagogues.

---

37   Runesson 2001: 31.
38   Runesson 2001: figs. 57–9.
39   Meiggs 1973: 390–1, 394.
40   Liber Pontificalis 1.183–4; Meiggs 1973: 396 n.1; Zetterholm 2001: 111; Brandt 2004: 10.
41   Meiggs 1973: 397.
42   Meiggs 1973: 588.
43   Zetterholm 2001: 112 treats the renovation of the synagogue as a reaction to the success of Christianity, but that is only one of the possible explanations.
44   E.g. John Chrysostom, *Adv. Jud.* 1.3.
45   Fiocchi Nicolai 2001: chs. 5–6.

A visitor to the Jewish catacombs would have been impressed less by the decoration of the walls than by the proliferation of Jewish symbols on the tombs: incised on marble plaques with epitaphs, painted on tiles and plaster covering the loculi, and depicted on gold-glasses fixed in the plaster. The commonest and most distinctive was the menorah, but it was also associated with the ethrog and lulab (as at Dura), as well as the shofar and Torah-shrine. These other symbols very rarely occur without a menorah. A declaration of the deceased's Jewishness was hardly necessary in an exclusive burial area, and there has been much speculation about what messages the symbols were intended to convey. Levine (2000b: 147) summarizes a range of theories: 'Most scholars attribute the emergence of the menorah as the central symbol in Jewish art to either newly emergent Jewish ideas or beliefs, or to certain socio-psychological needs felt at the time by individual Jews (in a burial context) or entire Jewish communities (in a synagogue context).' The sudden spread of the use of Jewish symbols from the third century C.E. indicates 'transition from basically representational art to art featuring symbols with multiple meanings'.[46] The wall-paintings of Dura can be seen as the beginning of this transition, with much representation and some symbolism, and the catacombs as a much more advanced development of the trend. Levine compares it to the inherently symbolic nature of much Christian art, with its use of the fish, chi-rho and cross, and notes that menoroth occur in a Jewish context exactly where crosses occur for Christians; in fact the chi-rho and menorah have been found together among graffiti in the cryptoporticus of the imperial residence of the Horti Sallustiani, presumably scratched by fellow-workers.[47] This suggests that the Jews who used the menorah and other symbols in the commemoration of their deceased were reacting to Christianity: the Christian use of symbols motivated a change in Jewish artistic practice. On this interpretation, any more specific meaning associated with the symbols, such as the messianic allusion proposed by some scholars, would be much less significant than the general statement of Jewish identity – the same function as the Temple and the sacrifice of Isaac had in the Dura wall-paintings, but with the advantage of being much easier to depict. The menorah would be 'read' initially not as part of the equipment of the past and future Temple, and not even as the object which was portrayed in Rome in a different form on the Arch of Titus,[48] but as a statement of membership of the Jewish community and difference from the Christians. The designations *Ioudaios* and *Hebraios* are rarely found in the catacombs, as they were superfluous in the context; the menorah and other symbols made a more immediately obvious statement of the same point.

There is one example from Rome of an attempt to depict the Temple: a gold-glass which was found in a Christian catacomb but is undoubtedly Jewish in view of the menoroth on it.[49] The centre is occupied by a temple with a menorah in

---

46   Levine 2000b: 149.
47   Levine 2000b: 151; Brandt 2004: 23.
48   It may still have been in Rome, if not destroyed in the fire at the Temple of Peace in 192 C.E. described by Cassius Dio, 73(72).24.1–2.
49   *JIWE* 2.588, with bibliography.

its pediment and two huts nearby. The most likely explanation is that this represents the Temple with *sukkoth* for the Feast of Tabernacles. It is labelled in Greek 'house of peace', an otherwise unknown designation for the Temple. The reason for the glass's use in a Christian context is unknown, and indicates a breakdown in the normally rigid separation of Christian and Jewish symbols in the catacombs.

In the Jewish catacombs, the wall-paintings seem to have been of secondary importance.[50] The significance of paintings is often difficult to interpret. A figure of a shepherd on the ceiling of the fourth-century underground tomb of Trebius Justus would be interpreted as the Good Shepherd in a Christian context, but found among scenes of work and idealized daily life, it seems only to allude to the owner's estate.[51] The Jewish catacombs have not left any trace of paintings of biblical scenes. Painted Rooms I and II at Vigna Randanini have geometric and animal motifs, but in the centres of the ceilings are figures of Victory crowning a youth, and Fortune. While there was some reuse of space elsewhere in the catacomb (with paintings which adorned the walls around earlier burials cut through for later burials), these paintings appear to be contemporary with the arcosolia in the walls, and according to Hachlili (1998: 276) 'most accept that these decorations were painted specifically for Jews'.[52] Painted Room IV has a menorah and possibly ethrogim.[53] At Villa Torlonia, more use was made of Jewish symbols, notably two menoroth flanking a Torah-shrine in the lunette of an arcosolium. Use was also made of standard decorations and motifs which are found in many other contexts – for example, marble incrustation, black lozenges, dolphins.[54] A sarcophagus from Vigna Randanini has a typical pagan repertoire of the four seasons and grape-treading cupids, but the *clipeus* contains a menorah rather than the portrait of the deceased which would normally be placed there.[55]

There were painters available at Rome who could illustrate biblical scenes, since a wide range is found in the Christian catacombs.[56] By the fourth century they were presumably able to make a living from work in the catacombs, but many Christian and Jewish sarcophagi and epitaphs on marble must have been commissioned from workshops which also worked for pagans: the menorah-sarcophagus is a good example of a standard item for pagan use given a final adaptation for a Jewish customer. In Christian catacomb art, Christ's miracles, particularly the raising of Lazarus and the loaves and fishes, were the favourite New Testament scenes. Symbolic motifs, particularly the Good Shepherd, were depicted. Among the Old Testament scenes, some of those used by the Jews at Dura are found, particularly the sacrifice of Isaac, but also Moses receiving the Law. Daniel in the lions' den, Jonah and Noah are also found in a number of different versions. Christ enthroned,

---

50 See Rutgers 1995: 73–7 for a general survey.
51 Pergola 1998: 70 notes that in the third century the image of a shepherd with a sheep on his shoulders was used indiscriminately by pagans and Christians.
52 Rutgers 1995:54 believes the two rooms were initially a separate hypogeum but is undecided about whether the original users were Jews.
53 Rutgers 1995: 74.
54 Rutgers 1995: 74–5.
55 Rutgers 1995: 79.
56 Nestori 1975 provides a catalogue.

presumably in judgement, is very rare, and it seems that the Bible, rather than any possible messianic future, was the main interest of those who commissioned the art. Depictions of the crucifixion are also very unusual;[57] one exception is the 'Passion Sarcophagus',[58] but even that does not depict the crucifixion itself.

Some of the difficulties of interpreting wall-paintings are illustrated by the Catacomb of via Dino Compagni, often referred to as the via Latina Catacomb. This small catacomb from the first half of the fourth century contains the burials of about 400 people in 325 tombs.[59] According to Ferrua's interpretation, there are four separate groups of paintings using either Christian or pagan themes, indicating a wealthy extended family with both converted and unconverted members.[60] The Christian themes come from the Old and New Testaments, and include both the familiar (the sacrifice of Isaac, in two different versions; the raising of Lazarus) and the unusual (Absalom hanged from the oak tree; Christ between Peter and Paul). The most important theme in the pagan paintings is the exploits of Hercules, including the death of Admetus. Some of the themes, such as Lazarus and Admetus, are clearly appropriate in a burial context, but most have no funerary connections. It seems unlikely that the paintings should be read as part of a pagan–Christian debate, although figures such as Moses, Jonah and Hercules *might* have a symbolic theological function. Their presumably peaceful co-existence in one catacomb suggests that they were not intended to be read as symbolizing the victory of one religious group over another, or the resistance of one group to another, as might have been the case if they were found separately.

Another small catacomb, that of Vibia on the via Appia, has a mixture of faith-groups: Christians, Mithraists and Sabazists.[61] Vibia herself is depicted in the lunette of her arcosolium, being led to judgement in a pagan underworld by a figure labelled *angelus bonus*. Christians at Rome were able to borrow from, and co-exist with, pagan art as Jews at Dura did.

As far as the evidence goes (and nothing is known about wall-paintings which may have existed at Monteverde), it seems that Jews and Christians did not use a shared repertoire in their catacomb paintings. The only human figures used by the Jews are ones which really come from the pagan world but in context had presumably lost all but decorative significance. It is impossible to say whether the absence of biblical paintings represents a strict interpretation of the second commandment or a feeling of having been pre-empted by the Christians. In a sense, the relationship was the reverse of that at Dura. There, the Jews were the more prosperous and secure community, and were able to commission elaborate paintings using the best available craftsmen and a mixture of local and Jewish iconography, while the Christians got a limited repertoire and poorer quality. At Rome, whatever the motivation, the effect has been to create in the archaeological record an impression that the Jews were 'making do', while the Christians could indulge in a full range of (sometimes) high-quality images.

57 Hertling and Kirschbaum 1960: 229.
58 Hertling and Kirschbaum 1960: pl. 39.
59 Ferrua 1991: 156.
60 Ferrua 1991: 158.
61 Fiocchi Nicolai 2001: 74; Pergola 1998: 90–1.

At Dura and Rome, Jewish and Christian spaces were almost adjacent to each other. In contrast, at Jerusalem the exclusion of Jews after the defeat of Bar-Kokhba[62] meant that the city was a *tabula rasa* for the christianizing efforts of the empress Helena and others in the fourth century. Instead of co-existing, Jews were allowed into the city only for ceremonial mourning on the 9th of Ab, a tradition which the Christian authorities eagerly took over from the pagans. Even when Jewish residents were officially allowed in Jerusalem in the fifth century, they can at first only have been a marginal presence in a city which was now central to Christianity, and on one occasion Jews praying on the Temple Mount were stoned by extremist monks.[63]

Elsewhere, competition between Jews and Christians usually began from the basis of a strong Jewish presence in a city, but in the fourth and especially fifth centuries there was only one possible winner if the competition turned into a serious struggle. Many synagogues were destroyed or converted into churches, and their Jewish communities might be scattered or converted too. Apamea in Syria is one example of the many places where a centrally placed synagogue was converted to a church in the early fifth century and there is no subsequent archaeological record of a Jewish community in the city.[64] The protection which the law offered to synagogues in theory was often unenforceable,[65] as was illustrated most clearly when Ambrose prevented the emperor Theodosius I from punishing the bishop of Callinicum for destroying the synagogue there.[66] However, archaeology shows that the law which prohibited the building or embellishment of synagogues[67] was not always enforced either. Foerster (1992: 304–14) gives some examples of synagogues in the Galilee which were built or refurbished in the fifth or sixth century. At Capernaum, the late-fourth- and early-fifth-century 'white synagogue' replaced an earlier building, and was in use until the seventh century.[68] The octagonal church which was built in the second half of the fifth century over the supposed House of Peter co-existed with the synagogue rather than replacing it.[69] Wharton (2000: 202) points out that the continued existence of a synagogue at Capernaum was important for Christian purposes because of its association with the activities of Jesus. However, in other places synagogues continued to exist and prosper in prominent locations without any apparent Christian theological justification; two well-known and much studied examples are Sardis and Sepphoris.[70]

The differences between Dura and Rome highlight the beginning of the process by which economic and political power switched from the Jews to the Christians. The destroyed and converted synagogues show its logical culmination, but the

---

62 Eusebius, *Hist. eccl.* 4.6.3.
63 Gaddis 2005: 189.
64 Noy and Sorek 2003: 20–2.
65 Codex Theodosianus 16.8.9 dated 393, 16.8.12, 16.8.20–1, 16.8.25–6 – the numerous repetitions of this law attest the failure to enforce it effectively. Gaddis 2005: 209.
66 Ambrose, *Ep.* 40; Gaddis 2005: 194–6.
67 Codex Theodosianus 16.8.25 (dated 423), 16.8.27; *Novella of Theodosius*, 3.3.
68 Loffreda 1985: 32–42.
69 Loffreda 1985: 51.
70 See e.g. Kroll 2001 and Levine and Weiss 2000 respectively.

synagogues which flourished into the seventh century prove that it was by no means universal. The remains of a synagogue which was deliberately destroyed in the fifth century or of one which was still being improved two hundred years later make a fairly clear statement about the position of the local Jewish community. Within a synagogue or catacomb, symbols and pictures are much harder to interpret, and there can never be agreement about all the messages conveyed – even supposing, as seems very unlikely, that all ancient viewers received the same messages. The possible messianic message of a wall-painting may have been as debatable to third-century Jews as to modern academics. Material remains show that Jewish art changed over time and varied according to place, in reaction to Christian iconography, in rivalry with pagan or Christian neighbours, but always with adaptation to local circumstances.

Chapter 17

THE RABBIS AND MESSIANISM

Philip S. Alexander

If you have a sapling in your hand, and someone says to you, 'Look, the Messiah has come!', first plant the sapling and then go out to greet him
('Abot de Rabbi Nathan B 31)

Questions of Method

Many classic studies of rabbinic messianism are characterized by a harmonizing approach to the evidence. Since messianism figures prominently in both pre- and post-Talmudic Judaism, it is assumed that it must have been central to rabbinic theology throughout the intervening Talmudic period as well, and so wherever in rabbinic texts we meet with messianic references, however brief, we can take them as alluding to the same age-old, universal 'messianic idea' of Judaism.[1] In the present essay I will challenge this synthetic, synchronic view, and offer in its place one that is more diachronic and nuanced. This revisionist perspective will be predicated, first, on a narrow definition of Rabbinism. For *rabbinic* messianic beliefs I will accept only the testimony of core *rabbinic* sources – the Mishnah, the Tosefta, the Talmuds and the Midrashim. Other Jewish sources from late antiquity containing messianism – the Amidah, the Targums, the *Piyyutim*, the Heikhalot literature, and the late Hebrew apocalypses – will be considered separately as non-rabbinic or quasi-rabbinic.[2] A key strategy will be to read these two bodies of evidence *against* each other. Second, I will treat the rabbinic sources diachronically. The dating of individual traditions within rabbinic literature is, of course, highly contentious, but for the purposes of the present broad-brush analysis it will suffice to take the date when the bulk of the document reached closure as the approximate date of any given tradition within it.

Messianism can be classified into two ideal types – the historical realist and the mystical. Historical realism depicts the messianic age as belonging to the end of

---

1   See Moore 1927–30: 2.323–96; Klausner 1955; Scholem 1971: 1–36; Urbach 1975: 649–90. Neusner 1984 was one of the first to demonstrate that a more diachronic analysis of the rabbinic evidence was possible, and that the rabbis' views changed significantly over time. For general introductions to Jewish messianism see Aescoly 1987; Patai 1988; Schäfer and Cohen 1998.

2   By 'quasi-rabbinic' I mean texts which, though not rabbinic in origin, have undergone extensive rabbinic redaction.

human history, as the outcome of mundane, geo-political events. The Messiah is a human king, and the kingdom he inaugurates an earthly kingdom. Within this realist category is an important subset of texts which, while basically subscribing to historical realism, suffuse it with large doses of supernaturalism and utopianism. Wonders, prodigies and miracles abound, which are missing from the more prosaically realist scenarios, and the differences between the messianic age and this age are exaggerated. This form of realism might be dubbed 'magical realism'.[3] By mystical messianism I mean that form of messianism, found often but not exclusively in the Jewish mystical tradition, which treats the messianic scenario essentially as a spiritual, cosmic process. Events on earth may be heard as noises off-stage, but the primary focus is on what is happening on a cosmic scale in the heavenly world. The Messiah is no longer a warrior who fights with sword and shield the flesh and blood enemies of Israel, but rather a spiritual hero, a sort of Gnostic redeemer, who mediates between heaven and earth, who takes up spiritual weapons against spiritual foes, and brings essentially a spiritual redemption.[4]

Non-Rabbinic Jewish Messianism in Late Antiquity

The Amidah (Eighteen Benedictions)

This major prayer, recited regularly in some form or other in synagogues throughout the Talmudic period, is deeply messianic in tone. In the old Palestinian version, preserved in the Cairo Genizah (Schürer 2: 455–63), six or seven of the benedictions (nos. 2, 7, 10, 11, 12, 14, 16; note also 5) contain either direct or oblique messianic allusions. They paint a messianic scenario. The Messiah is of David's line, and when he comes Jerusalem will be rebuilt (14). Israel's enemies, the 'insolent empire' will be uprooted and destroyed (12); the exiles will be gathered in (10), and the dead will be raised (2); the Temple service (16) and the judicial system (11) will be restored (Kimelman 1997).

This is the classic statement of prosaic messianic realism. The Messiah is a human king, though he acts as God's agent, and the events of the messianic age,

---

3   For a further subdivision of the realist type into gradualist ('post-millennial') and catastrophic ('pre-millennial') see below.
4   It is hard to say which of these two types is the earlier. At first sight it might seem easier to explain mystical messianism as a spiritualizing reinterpretation of realist messianism, designed, at least in part, to avoid the political dangers of realism, but mystical messianism has deep roots in the tradition and picks up strongly elements of the ideology of kingship in the Hebrew Bible and the Ancient Near East. 'There are striking similarities between some descriptions of the medieval Messiah and the more magical-mythical understanding of the king in the ancient period as expressed in some biblical texts. In certain cases, such as the view that the king is a channel for transmitting power to others, scholars' findings are astonishingly close to the mystical and mythical conceptions of the ideal type of Messiah in later Jewish texts' (Idel 1998: 39). It should certainly not be assumed, as Klausner 1955, Scholem 1971: 1–36 and others do (e.g. Buchanan 1978: i–ii), that realism is the default position, and that other views are a deviation from this norm. Idel 1998: 31 is justified in seeing this position as influenced, consciously or unconsciously, by modern political Zionism.

with the exception of the resurrection of the dead, are all natural events that take place on the everyday stage of human history. The messianic age involves neither more nor less than the restoration of the Davidic polity: what is envisaged is a thoroughly this-wordly political process. It is the very ordinariness of the process that makes the prayer so potentially politically subversive. Here were Jews praying fervently in public for the overthrow of the Roman empire and the restoration of their state. The prayer is, however, hardly a clarion call to arms. There is, on first reading, a stress throughout that it is *God* who will take the initiative (note especially benediction 7, 'See our affliction and defend our cause. Redeem us for your name's sake. Blessed are you, O Lord, who redeems Israel'). But deeper reflection discloses a certain ambivalence in this language, and it is not hard to think of ways that it could be reconciled with political activism. At the very least it is surely fair to say that the regular praying of this prayer would have kept alive among Jews nationalist longings and a hope for political independence.

That the Rabbis knew the Amidah is in no doubt: they refer to it regularly in their writings, and, indeed, there is a rabbinic tradition that benediction 12 was modified by them at the end of the first century C.E. to insert a 'cursing of the heretics' (*m. Ber.* 4:3; *y. Ber.* 2:4; *b. Ber.* 29a; 33a; *b. Meg.* 17b–18a: Horbury 1982). But it is not a rabbinic composition, a point which rabbinic sources themselves concede (*b. Meg.* 17b; *Sipre Deut.* 343). Though the forms in which we now have it must be post-70 C.E., since they refer to the destruction of the Temple, the core of the prayer probably originated before 70. Many of its benedictions, particularly the messianic ones, are curiously paralleled in Sir 51, a work dating to the second century B.C.E.[5]

The Targumim

The Targumim constitute a massive and diverse body of literature, which, taken as a whole, contains numerous messianic references. It is possible to detect a pattern in the distribution of the evidence. *Onqelos* to the Torah and *Jonathan* to the Prophets, the so-called 'official' Targumim, are much more sparing in their messianism than the Palestinian Targumim (*Neofiti* 1, *Fragment Targum*, Cairo Genizah Fragments) and *Pseudo-Jonathan* to the Torah, and the Targumim of the Writings. There is a crucial diachronic implication in this because *Onqelos* and *Jonathan* are basically older than the other Targumim. It seems, then, that, broadly speaking, the later the Targum the more messianism it is likely to contain. Certainly the fullest messianic references occur in the Targums of the Writings, which are unquestionably much later than *Onqelos*, *Jonathan* and the Palestinian Targums to the Torah.

The reticence of *Onqelos* and *Jonathan* about the Messiah cannot be explained simply in terms of their genre. *Onqelos* and *Jonathan* are generally literal, one-to-one versions, whereas the Palestinian Targums to the Pentateuch and the Targums to the Writings tend towards paraphrase. This certainly gives the latter

---

5   Interestingly this chapter is missing from the Greek version of Ben Sira. Perhaps its nationalism was out of keeping with the more universalist outlook of Hellenistic Judaism, or there were worries about publishing such subversive sentiments in the common tongue.

scope to introduce more circumstantial detail. But genre cannot be the whole story. It does not explain why the other Targums find *more* messianic allusions in Scripture. *Onqelos* introduces the Messiah in Gen. 49.10-12 and Num. 24.17-20, 23-24: it would have been very hard to avoid references here. But it does not find messianic allusions in other Pentateuchal verses where the Palestinian Targums and *Pseudo-Jonathan* find them.[6] The messianic reticence is even more obvious in *Jonathan* to the Prophets. Samson Levey summarizes the situation there thus: 'Very striking is the fact that J[onathan] abounds in eschatological material, so much so that there are not many chapters in the Latter Prophets, Ezekiel included, without an eschatological reference, and yet the Messianic references are so relatively few. J[onathan], like its counterpart O[nqelos] to the Pentateuch, is exceedingly sparing in its Messianism. Even Zech. 9.9 and Mal. 4.5 are not interpreted Messianically!' (Levey 1974: 102). And when we turn to the Targums of the Writings we find messianism introduced almost gratuitously and attached to verses which were not traditionally regarded as messianic, and where the messianic interpretation is far-fetched.[7]

The messianism that emerges from the Targumim, taken as a whole, even the later more paraphrastic versions, is broadly of the realist type that we found in the Amidah. However, more details of the end-time are disclosed. The wars of Gog and Magog, Armilus (the anti-Messiah), Elijah, the Messiah of Ephraim (who will precede Messiah son of David, and who will fall in battle against the eschatological enemies of Israel) are introduced. However, particularly in the later strata of the tradition, elements of magical realism creep in: the Messiah is sometimes cast as a larger-than-life, even supernatural figure. He will rule over the whole world and make the Torah the universal law. He will be endowed with the gift of prophecy and will intercede for sin. He will punish the wicked and consign them to Gehinnom. He will live forever, as will the righteous who will enjoy the divine glory in his presence (Levey 1974: 143).

As rabbinic tradition itself recognizes, the Targum goes back to the pre-70 period and did not originate with the Rabbis (*y. Meg.* 4.1). Its institutional base was the synagogue and the primary school (the *Beit Sefer*), not the *Beit Midrash* (P. S. Alexander 1999b). There is no doubt, however, that just as the Rabbis tried to regulate prayer in the synagogue and influence the content of the Amidah, so they tried to regulate both the content of the Targum and the way in which it was delivered in the synagogue, though with only limited success (*m. Meg.* 4:6, 9-10).

---

6   E.g., *Frg. Tg.* Gen. 3.15; 49.1; Exod. 12.42; Num. 11.26; 24.7; *Ps.-J.* Gen. 3.15; 35.21; 49.1; Exod. 17.16; 40.9-11; Num. 23.21; Deut. 25.19; 30.4-9.

7   Pss. 18.28-32; 21.1-8; 45.1-18; 61.7-9; 72.1-20; 80.15-18; 89.51-52; 132.11-18; Song 1.8, 17; 4.5; 7.4; 7.12-8.4; Ruth 1.1; 3.15; Lam. 2.22; 4.22; Eccl. 1.11; 7.24; Est. 1.1 (*Targum Sheni*); 1 Chr. 3.24. Levey 1974: 141 puts this point, somewhat oddly, thus: 'The Messianic interpretations [of the Targums to the Hagiographa] other than those in Psalms are not too important to the overall picture, because they are peripheral and Midrashic, instead of genuinely exegetical. … The Messianic exposition in Psalms adds little in the way of Messianic details, but it does demonstrate once more the tendency on the part of the Targum not to be too liberal in attributing Messianic intentions to the Bible.' This rather misses the point. The reticence of the Targums is not uniform: the older Targums are much more reticent than the younger. And it is precisely the non-exegetical basis of the messianic references in the Targums to the Writings – their gratuitousness – that indicates their lack of reticence.

The old 'official' Targums, *Onqelos* and *Jonathan* to the Prophets, show signs in places of that influence. Some of the late Targumim, such as *Targum Song of Songs* and *Targum Lamentations*, seem to have been composed in rabbinic circles, and are redolent of rabbinic doctrines and values.[8]

Piyyut *and the 'Mourners for Zion'*

Synagogue poetry (*piyyut*) is full of messianic references. Though most of the best known messianic *piyyutim* were composed long after the Talmudic period, there is good evidence that messianism had emerged as a powerful theme of the *payyetanim* already in late antiquity (Lewis 1974; Horbury 1981; Weinberger 1998: 21–72; Swartz and Yahalom 2004).[9] The messianism is often associated with compositions for the Ninth of Ab and adjacent sabbaths, the point in the liturgical year when some sort of messianic longing is well-nigh unavoidable. One of the earliest-known *payyetanim*, Qillir (6th/7th century) certainly wrote five, and possibly as many as forty laments (*qinot*), for the fall of Jerusalem and the Temple (Weinberger 1998: 61–3). Like the Targum, the setting for *piyyut* is the public worship of the synagogue, and there is no compelling evidence that the early *payyetanim*, Yose ben Yose, Yannai and Qillir belonged to the rabbinic movement. Indeed, there are indications that some of them were from priestly circles. They do, indeed, allude in many of their compositions to biblical *aggadot* which are found also in rabbinic sources, but it would be wrong simply to assume that they borrowed them from there. More likely both *piyyut* and midrash were drawing on common folklore. The *payyetanim*, like the Targumist, also display a notable independence of rabbinic midrash.[10]

It is possible that the *Qinot* of the early *payyetanim* were influenced by the liturgies of a shadowy group known as the Mourners for Zion (*'Abelei Tziyyon*, a phrase derived from Isa. 61.3), who may have done something to keep alive messianic longings in the Talmudic era. The Mourners for Zion devoted themselves to a life of prayer and penance for the destruction of the Temple. They seem to have emerged in the immediate aftermath of the destruction, and their theology, and even some of their early liturgies, may be preserved in *2 Baruch* and the *Paralipomena Ieremiae* (Bogaert 1969: 127–221). There are grounds for

---

8   See further below. On the Targumim more generally, see Gordon, this volume: 262–73.
9   Interestingly, the Israeli poet Ted Carmi treats the footsteps-of-the-Messiah pericope in *m. Soṭah* 9:15 as a poem (Carmi 1981: 190–1). Another messianic hymn is found in rabbinic literature at *Pesiqta deRab Kahana*, Supplement 6 (end): 'Blessed is the hour in which the Messiah was created!/ Blessed is the womb whence he came!/ Blessed is the generation whose eyes behold him!/ Blessed is the eye which has been given the privilege of seeing him/ whose lips open with blessing and peace,/ whose diction is pure delight,/ whose garments are glory and majesty,/ who is confident and serene in his speech/ the utterance of whose tongue is pardon and forgiveness,/whose supplication during his study of Torah is purity and holiness' (trans. Braude and Kapstein). On the *piyyutim*, see de Lange, this volume: 280–3.
10   The *payyetan* came to fulfil the role of *meturgeman* as well: 'The cantor-poet performed not only an aesthetic function in ornamenting the fixed prayers in the synagogue service but also a didactic role in interpreting Jewish legend and law. One of his responsibilities was to translate the reading from the Torah (*y. Meg* 4.1, 42d) into the vernacular. In this practice he often incurred the wrath of the rabbis, who faulted him for translating in a manner they perceived to be contrary to Jewish law' (Weinberger 1998: 29).

thinking that they may have continued throughout the Tannaitic and Amoraic periods (there is a clear allusion to them in *t. Soṭah* 15:10-15, in a tradition attributed to Rabbi Ishmael), right down to the Middle Ages. They reappear again in *Pisqas* 34, and 36–37 of *Pesiqta Rabbati* (Pisqa 36 reads like a manifesto of the movement), and possibly in Pisqa 26, which contains striking parallels to material found in *2 Baruch* 1–12 and 77 (Bogaert 1969: 222–41; Goldberg 1978). Their relationship to the Qaraite Mourners for Zion who from *ca.* 850 onwards established themselves in some numbers in Jerusalem is disputed. The profoundly messianic orientation of that community is abundantly clear from its extensive surviving literature. That it drew on some of the traditions of the pre-Qaraite Mourners for Zion is surely likely, and as a result it may be used cautiously to help us understand the theology, ideals and standpoint of the earlier movement, for which we have no direct evidence between the second century (*2 Baruch*) and possibly the sixth/seventh century C.E. (*Pesiqta Rabbati*). The Rabbis were clearly aware of the Mourners for Zion, but they were not a rabbinic movement. The crucial text in *t. Soṭah* 15:10-15 is, in fact, a sharp criticism of their extreme asceticism. The Qaraite Mourners for Zion, were of course, bitterly anti-rabbinic (Polliack 1997; Erder 2003, 2004; Frank 2004). And strong, anti-rabbinic sentiments are evident in *Pesiqta Rabbati* 34, 36–7, though, paradoxically, these mourning-for-Zion texts have been preserved within a broadly *rabbinic* collection of midrashim.

Heikhalot Literature

The Heikhalot literature also contains some interesting messianic traditions.[11] In Schäfer, *Synopse*, §§64–5 (= *3 Enoch* 45) Metatron shows to Rabbi Ishmael, inscribed on the celestial curtain (the *Pargod*), the whole history of humanity down to the last days, including the Messiah ben Joseph and the Messiah ben David, Gog and Magog and the eschatological wars. A rather more detailed eschatological scenario is found in Schäfer, *Synopse*, §§130–8 (= *'Aggadat Rabbi Yishmaʿel*, Even-Shmuel, *Midreshei Ge'ullah*, pp. 148–52), which emphasizes the importance of repentance in bringing the messianic age. Another scenario occurs at Schäfer, *Synopse*, §§140–5 (= *'Aggadat ha-Mashiah*, Even-Shmuel, *Midreshei Ge'ullah*, pp. 326–7), which also mentions the eschatological wars, as well as the resurrection of the dead and the rebuilding of Jerusalem. In Schäfer, *Synopse*, §§68–70 (= *3 Enoch* 48A) Metatron shows Ishmael the right hand of God in heaven waiting to redeem Israel: 'All the souls of the righteous who are worthy to see the joy of Jerusalem stand beside it, praising it and entreating it, saying three times every day, "Awake, awake! Clothe yourself in strength, arm of the Lord" (Isa. 51:9).' But God's mighty arm will only be revealed at the hour of deepest darkness and apostasy, and when it is, 'At once Israel shall be saved from among the gentiles and the Messiah shall appear to them and bring them up to Jerusalem with great joy. Moreover, the kingdom of Israel, gathered from the four quarters of the world, shall eat with the Messiah, and the gentiles shall eat with them.' Another intriguing messianic passage is the so-called David Apocalypse at Schäfer, *Synopse*, §§122–6 (= *Heikhalot Rabbati*, ed. Wertheimer chs 6–7; Even-

---

11   For a short introduction to the Heikhalot literature see P. S. Alexander 1983.

Shmuel, *Midreshei Ge'ullah*, pp. 8–10). Ishmael ascends to heaven and is shown the terrible tribulations stored up for Israel, a reference to the birth-pangs of the Messiah, but he is then shown 'deliverances and consolations', which include a vision of David's glory: 'And behold, David, King of Israel, was coming out first [from the heavenly Eden], and I saw all the kings of the house of David following him, each one with a crown on his head, but David's crown was brighter and more beautiful than all the others, and its radiance reached from one end of the world to the other. When David went up into the great *Beit Midrash*[12] that is in heaven, a fiery throne was prepared for him, the height of which was forty *parasangs*, double its length and breadth. When David came and sat by himself on his throne, facing the throne of his Maker, all the kings of the house of David sat before him, and all the kings of Israel stood behind him. Then David arose and uttered songs and praises such as no ear had ever heard before. When David began and said, "The Lord shall reign for ever" (Ps. 146.10), Metatron and the entire heavenly household responded, "Holy, holy, holy is the Lord of hosts" (Isa. 6.3).'

The messianic messages of the Heikhalot corpus are very mixed. The *'Aggadat Rabbi Yishmaʿel* and the *'Aggadat ha-Mashiah* are both presented basically from the standpoint of historical realism. *3 Enoch* 48A is an extreme case of magical realism, attention focusing on God's dramatic *deus-ex-machina* intervention at the end of history, with the Messiah playing only a bit-part in the final drama. The David Apocalypse is utterly different: it seems to envisage the messianic redemption as a process which takes place *totally* in heaven, and which has effectively already been completed! David goes up to the *heavenly* Jerusalem, not the earthly, and is enthroned there. There is no direct reference whatsoever to events on the terrestrial plane, or to the end of history. David is depicted as an exalted heavenly being, who leads the heavenly choirs in the performance of the celestial liturgy.

The lack of consistency in Heikhalot mysticism has probably something to do with the highly complex redaction-history of the traditions. It would be wrong to assume that everything in the great medieval Heikhalot manuscripts originated in the Heikhalot circles of late antiquity. The *'Aggadat Rabbi Yishmaʿel* and the *'Aggadat ha-Mashiah* may have been late additions, that originated elsewhere. It is the David Apocalypse that chimes best with the Heikhalot worldview. Heikhalot mysticism is overwhelmingly interested not in history but in heaven. The mystics' consolation seems to come from the knowledge that in heaven, the world that really matters, Israel's representatives occupy a position of privilege and power, which is the exact opposite of her oppressed and lowly status on earth (P. S. Alexander 1991). Messianism plays a very muted role in the major Heikhalot texts, and when it does occur, it tends to be spiritualized. What we have here is a foretaste of a development

---

12   The reading *Beit Midrash* is suspicious, though it is found in both Budapest 238 and New York 8128. The idea that there is a celestial *Beit Midrash* is well attested in rabbinic texts, as is David's role as a scholar (see below), but the functions he performs here are priestly rather than scholastic. *Beit Midrash* may be a deliberate rabbinic alteration of an original *Beit Miqdash* (temple). On the rabbinic idea that the eschatological *Beit Miqdash* will have essentially the characteristics of a *Beit Midrash*, see below. Even-Shmuel (Kaufman) 1954: 9 actually reads *Beit ha-Miqdash*, but this is probably one of his many silent, conjectural emendations, though in this case it is a good one.

that was to reach its climax in the later Qabbalah – messianism is seen fundamentally as a spiritual process that takes places in the upper world. It is this that is of primary importance, not historical and political events that may happen on earth (Idel 1998). The Heikhalot literature, in other words, offers, in terms of our classification, an early example of mystical messianism.

Heikhalot literature and ideas would not have had the reach nor the audience of the Amidah, the Targum, or even *Piyyut*, but its teachings were undoubtedly known in some shape or form to the Rabbis, as the concerned allusions to them in the Talmuds show (*m. Ḥag.* 2:1; *b. Ḥag.* 11b–16a, and parallels). The Heikhalot texts themselves affirm a link with rabbinic circles, by claiming as their heroes Rabbi Ishmael, Rabbi Akiba and Rabbi Nehunyah ben Haqanah, and it is possible that in the versions in which we now have them they were subjected to a rabbinizing redaction (P. S. Alexander 2006b). But their core ideas sit uneasily with rabbinic Judaism, and the circles which produced them were, at best, on the fringes of rabbinic society.

Late Hebrew Apocalyptic

Finally, we must mention late Hebrew apocalyptic. Under this rubric I include a substantial collection of Jewish apocalyptic writings dating roughly from the late sixth to the ninth centuries C.E. (Lewis 1976; Buchanan 1978; P. S. Alexander 1990; Himmelfarb 1990; Idel 2003; Reeves 2005). The most emblematic text of the collection is the *Book of Zerubbabel*, but also significant are the *Book of Elijah*, *The Secrets of Rabbi Shimʿon bar Yohai*, *The Prayer of Rabbi Shimʿon bar Yohai*, *The Signs of the Messiah* and *The Chapters of the Messiah*. The major texts are presented conveniently in Even-Shmuel's *Midreshei Ge'ullah*. In this literature messianism runs riot. We have vast, baroque scenarios of the end-time, in which miraculous and supernatural events are commonplace. There is much vivid detail about Gog and Magog and the messianic wars, in which Armilus and the Messiah of Ephraim play a leading role. Long lists of portents heralding the Messiah's advent are given. Elements such as the fantastic accounts of the eschatological messianic banquet, at which Leviathan, Behemoth and a fabulous bird known as Ziz Saddai are on the menu, recall the descriptions of the very material joys of paradise in Islamic literature. These texts are classic examples of what I have termed magical realism.

As we shall see there is a convergence between the late Hebrew apocalypses and late rabbinic messianism (many motifs and traditions are shared), and there are grounds for thinking that the apocalypses contributed to the definitive systematization of rabbinic messianism by Saʿadia Gaon early in the tenth century (*Book of Beliefs and Opinions*, Treatise 8), but there are problems with classifying them as straightforwardly rabbinic. Their authors and compilers, like the Heikhalot circles, belonged to the margins of the rabbinic world.

The Development of Rabbinic Messianism

It is against the background of this strong and persistent tradition of 'popular' messianism that we should read the classic rabbinic sources. A clear pattern emerges when we review these in chronological order. The earlier texts have much less to say about the Messiah than the later. There are few significant references to the Messiah in the Mishnah, the Tosefta and the Tannaitic Midrashim (*Mekilta deRabbi Yishmaʿel*, *Sifra* and *Sipre*). Such allusions as there are show that the compilers of these works are fully aware of the popular messianism found in the Amidah and the other non-rabbinic sources we have surveyed, but they have chosen not to say much about it. The messianic allusions are casual, and they play little part in the argument of the passages where they occur. By way of contrast, when we come to the later strata of the Talmuds, and in particular to the later midrashim, such as *Lamentations Rabbah*, *Song of Songs Rabbah*, and *Pesiqta deRab Kahana*, references are abundant and much more informative.

The paucity and insubstantiality of the earlier evidence cannot be explained either by assuming that messianic ideas were so widespread that the Rabbis did not need to refer to them in detail (in other words, they could take messianism for granted), or by assuming that the earlier texts are talking about other things, which left scant opportunity to talk about the end of the world. The broad agenda of the later texts is little different from the earlier, yet in the later messianism plays a more prominent role. And if belief in messianism could simply be taken as read why do the later texts start to craft so carefully a distinctively *rabbinic* doctrine of the Messiah? The lack of reference in the earlier texts looks intentional. The authors of those texts saw little role for messianism in their theology. For them the focus was on the present. Israel's redemption will come through the study of Torah and the scrupulous performance of the *mitzvot* here and now. Their teaching was not eschatologically orientated (P. S. Alexander 2001). They are not interested in history as a grand narrative of salvation stretching from the creation to the consummation. When they do introduce messianic motifs, they do not develop them. Or, at times, they seem pointedly to avoid naming the Messiah, and when opportunities present themselves in Scripture for messianic allusions, opportunities seized with both hands by latter *darshanim*, they decline to take them (see, e.g., *Sipra*, *Behuqotai* to Lev. 26).

A case in point is *m. Soṭah* 9:15, one of the few substantial messianic passages in the Mishnah, which ends with the famous dictum of Pinhas ben Ya'ir: 'Heedfulness leads to cleanliness, cleanliness leads to purity, purity leads to abstinence, abstinence leads to holiness, holiness leads to humility, humility leads to the fear of sin, the fear of sin leads to piety, piety leads to the holy spirit, the holy spirit leads to the resurrection of the dead, and the resurrection of the dead shall come through Elijah, blessed be his memory. Amen.' Three elements here of the classic messianic scenario are at once obvious – the return of prophecy (the holy spirit), the resurrection of the dead, and the eschatological role of Elijah – but interestingly the Messiah himself is not named in the saying, and the messianic goal is seen as the culmination of a process of religious self-discipline which leaves us wondering whether Pinhas is really thinking of a state that occurs only at the *eschaton*, or one that is substantially realizable in the life of the individual here and now. Certainly he makes clear that the messianic era will be brought about by individuals devoting themselves to rabbinic values, a point that sounds like a drumbeat through rabbinic messianism. Pinhas's dictum sits very uneasily with the one immediately preceding it, in which, following popular perceptions, we are told that the Messiah will come only when society has become utterly sinful, when it has reached a nadir of depravity and immorality. But here we are given a very practical programme for avoiding such a disastrous state of affairs. Read from the standpoint of the earlier pericope this could be seem as a recipe for ensuring that the Messiah will never come, yet it is advocated precisely as a way of ushering in the messianic era!

The essentially realized eschatology of the early rabbinic sources comes out in a variety of ways. Sometimes it is asserted explicitly. It is surely no accident that the exposition of Pinhas ben Ya'ir's dictum in *y. Šeqal* 3.3, an exposition which consists of finding biblical proof-texts for each element, and which pointedly ignores the eschatological potential of 'the holy spirit', ends by quoting a saying of Rabbi Meir: 'Whoever lives permanently in the Land of Israel, speaks the Holy Language, eats his produce in a state of purity, recites the *Shemaʿ* morning and evening – let him be given the good news that he [already] belongs to the world to come'.[13] There is surely here a rejection of utopianism and supernaturalism which mark some popular scenarios of the messianic era, and which has its roots in biblical prophecy. It was necessary to lower people's expectations about the messianic age, if they were going to be persuaded to see it as in any sense realizable here and now. Hence the sayings that play down the differences between this age and the age to come: the only difference, according to one tradition, is that Israel will enjoy then political independence (*b. Sanh*. 91b; cf. *b. Sanh*. 63a, 151b; *b. Pesaḥ*. 68a). The Messiah's role is limited: it is merely to gather in the exiles (*Gen. Rab*. 98.9). It is in this setting that we should place the statement that Hillel was of David's line (*Gen. Rab*. 98.8). The political purpose of this is obvious: it is intended to bolster the authority of the House of the Patriarch, who claimed descent from Hillel. But its theological implications should not be missed. What it suggests is: Don't look for a future ruler of the House of David. You are already living under a scion of his house. This is as good as it gets! The Exilarchs in Babylonia also asserted Davidic ancestry (*Gen. Rab*. 33:3; *y. Ketub*. 12.3; *y. Kil*. 9.3: Goodblatt 1994). It is hardly surprising that later tradition was to claim that the Messiah could not come till the rule of the Patriarchs and the Exilarchs had been terminated (*b. Sanh*. 38a). The message may be that so long as the Jewish people accept the Davidic pretensions of the Nasi' and the Resh Galuta the *true* Son of David can never come.

Corroboration that the Rabbis were ambivalent about popular messianism can be found in their attitude towards a number of festivals which potentially have messianic associations. The most noteworthy of these is the Ninth of Ab, which commemorated the destruction of the Temple. This inevitably had messianic overtones, because mourning for the loss of the Temple was bound up with longing for its restoration, an event linked to the messianic age. We have already noted that there seem to have been groups of Jews, the Mourners for Zion, who, throughout the Tannaitic and Amoraic periods, devoted themselves to extreme forms of penance for the destruction of the Temple. In the Mishnah the Ninth of Ab is treated as a minor fast (*m. Taʿan*. 4.6-7), and we have already noted an interesting tradition in *t. Soṭah* 15.10-15 in which a famous rabbi rebukes the Mourners for Zion for their excessive zeal.

---

13   This I take to be the force of the original. Note the echo of Isa. 52.7 in 'let him be given the good news'.

Rabbinic attitudes towards Hanukkah are also instructive. There seems to be little doubt that Hanukkah was observed as a popular festival throughout the Talmudic period, but it is cold-shouldered by the Rabbis, who are conspicuously ambivalent about the Hasmoneans (P. S. Alexander 1999a). The reasons for this are surely not hard to find. The celebration of the inauguration of the last independent Jewish state could easily stir up yearnings for liberation. The Rabbis' attitude towards Hanukkah contrasts sharply with their attitude towards Purim. There is a tractate on Purim in the Mishnah, *Massekhet Megillah*, but there is no corresponding *Massekhet Hanukkah*: Both festivals are similar, as liturgical cross-references from one to the other recognize: both are festivals of deliverance from Gentile tyranny. But there is one crucial difference. Purim celebrates deliverance in the Diaspora, whereas Hanukkah celebrates deliverance in the homeland, and the establishment of an independent Jewish state. It is almost inevitably bound up with messianism and militarism.

The third festival which tended to develop messianic overtones was Passover. The going out from Egypt was commonly seen as a foreshadowing of the going out from exile of the Jewish people at the inauguration of the messianic age. Unlike Hanukkah, Passover is a major Torah festival, and there is no way that the Rabbis could or would have wanted to ignore or downplay it. However, it is interesting to note how meagre are the references to the messianic exodus in the earliest rabbinic treatments of the festival and of the going out from Egypt (note its absence in *Sipre Deut.* 306–41 and *Mekilta Shirah*).

When we turn to the later rabbinic sources, the two Talmuds and the later Midrashim, we find the situation almost exactly reversed. They present a mirror image of the picture in the Mishnah, Tosefta and Tannaitic Midrashim. There was no immediate *volte face*. One can detect a growing interest in messianism in the fourth and early fifth centuries, but when we examine traditions from roughly 450 to 650 C.E. the reversal is complete. Messianic dicta become numerous, substantial and rich. There are detailed and deeply moving stories about the messianic age. The Rabbis develop a strong interest in the Ninth of Ab (*b. Giṭ.* 55a–58b; *Pesiq. Rab Kah* 16–22; *Lam. Rab. passim*),[14] and Passover becomes inextricably linked to the future exodus from the exile of Edom which will inaugurate the messianic age (*Pesiq. Rab Kah* 5 *passim*; *b. ʿAbod. Zar*; and see further below). They even begin to support the celebration of Hanukkah (*b. Šabb.* 21b; *b. Menaḥ.* 28b; *Pesiq. Rab.* 2.5: P. S. Alexander 1999a). Clearly messianism has moved up the rabbinic theological agenda.

Two passages in the Babylonian Talmud will serve to illustrate this religious revolution. The first is *b. Sanh.* 96b–99a, the most extended and systematic rabbinic treatise on the Messiah to survive from the Talmudic era. This gathers together the scattered earlier rabbinic dicta about the Messiah, arranges them topically and augments them. It is dominated by a number of themes: the birth-pangs of the Messiah; calculations about when the Messiah will come; the signs in nature, society and history that will herald his advent (the so-called 'footsteps of the Messiah': *m. Soṭah* 9.9–15); the length and nature of his reign. However, what this rich messianic collection does not give is a clear scenario of the end-

---

14 Note also the late emergence of a festal scroll for Hanukkah, the *Megillat Antiochus*.

time. That is provided in the second passage in *b. Meg.* 17b. To construct this scenario the Rabbis simply accepted the framework provided by the messianic benedictions of the Amidah. *b. Meg.* 17b offers a brief commentary on these, which consists of providing proof-texts for each of them from Scripture. This is a neat way of systematizing the biblical messianic data in terms of the Amidah's schema, but at the same time of biblicizing the Amidah, and rendering it rabbinically *kosher*. The Amidah, as I suggested earlier, was the main vehicle of popular messianism throughout the Talmudic period, so its adoption here marks a significant moment in the Rabbis' acceptance of the popular view. But it is noticeable that when the rabbinic doctrine finally emerges it tends to be ultra-realist, anti-utopian and anti-supernaturalist. The Babli's messianic doctrine is stated in a rather cool and objective way. The same themes are worked over in more vivid detail, and invested with a more powerful emotional charge, in the later midrashim such as *Lamentations Rabbah* and *Song of Songs Rabbah*, both of which dramatically demonstrate the new rabbinic interest in exploiting the messianic resonances of the Ninth of Ab and of Passover.

The Rabbis basically took over the popular view, but they stamped upon it their own moral and religious values. This is seen in the consistent anti-militarism of the rabbinic doctrine. Anti-militarism is implicit in many of the earliest rabbinic messianic dicta, but in the later sources it becomes much more insistent. The acceptance of messianism necessitated stronger and more explicit injunctions against hot-headed zealotry. Jews may emigrate to the Land of Israel *individually* but not *en masse*, because that would suggest that they were trying to force the redemption. They may not rebel against the nations of the world (*b. Ketub.* 111a). It is Israel's patient and meek acceptance of oppressive Gentile rule that will finally move God to send the Messiah. If she rebels, and tries to force the redemption, he will take it that the Messiah is not wanted: Israel feels she can work out her own salvation (*Song Rab.* 2.7.1).

Interestingly the Mourners for Zion would probably have agreed with this pacifist approach, which is also, arguably, implicit in the Amidah. But there is a profound difference between the three viewpoints with regard to the instrumentalities involved. In the case of the Amidah, Israel gathers in her synagogues and humbly petitions God her heavenly king, urging the merits of the fathers, to bring the Messiah. In the case of the Mourners for Zion, the Mourners hope that by adopting extreme forms of penance and fervent expressions of repentance they will move God to pity. The relationship is more intense, intimate and emotional. It may well have been among the Mourners for Zion that the traditions originated, which depict God himself as weeping and mourning for Zion, and regretting the harm he has done his people, though these were later adopted by the Rabbis (*b. Ber.* 3a; *Lam. Rab.*, *Proem* 24: Kuhn 1978). For the Rabbis, however, the supreme instrument for bringing the Messiah is the study and observance of the Torah. If all Israel repents for one day or keeps the Sabbath for one day, the Messiah will immediately come (*y. Ta'an.* 1.1).[15] Time and again

---

15   These statements are cast in both a positive and a negative form: (1) 'If all Israel does X [= a commandment] the Messiah will come'; and (2) 'X [= a sin] retards the coming of the Messiah.'

it is stated that if Israel keeps this *mitzvah* or upholds that rabbinic value, the Messiah will come (*y. Ta'an.* 2.1; *b. Yoma* 19b; *b. Šabb.* 118b; *b. Nid.* 13b). I have already hinted how uneasily this doctrine, which seems to make the coming of the Messiah dependent on the moral and religious condition of Israel, sits with the doctrine of the birth-pangs of the Messiah, which implies that the Messiah will come at a time when apostasy and immorality are rife, even within Israel. The former takes a gradualist view of the introduction of the messianic age (it is like the dawning of the day: *y. Yoma* 3.2; *y. Ber.* 1.1; *Song. Rab.* 6.10.1); the latter sees it as a more abrupt, cataclysmic event.[16]

The issue is earnestly debated in the later rabbinic texts. The Rabbis had inherited the idea of the messianic birth-pangs from the Mishnah (*b. Pesaḥ* 118a; *b. Šabb.* 118a; *b. Ketub.* 111a, 112b), so they would have found it difficult to jettison or ignore. But how were they to reconcile it with their desire to link the coming of the Messiah with the moral condition of the people, which implies that the advent is in the people's own hands, and will be achieved gradually? One solution was to argue that through repentance, good deeds and the performance of the *mitzvot* Israel could negate the birth-pangs, but if she failed to do what is right they would surely come upon her. Thus the birth-pangs are cleverly turned to reinforce the rabbinic values. Saʿadya was later to work out a widely accepted compromise (*Book of Beliefs and Opinions*, Treatise 8). God has fixed an absolute term for the Messiah's advent, a point in time beyond which he will not be delayed. But Israel has it in her power to hasten his coming, by repentance, good works and the observance of the *mitzvot*, though it will still lie with God to decide just when Israel has done enough. By hastening the coming of the Messiah Israel may well negate the birth-pangs of the Messiah, but if she does not repent she will go through them, and the Messiah's advent will be attended by trauma and catastrophe.

The rabbinization of the popular doctrine of the Messiah comes out in other ways, most notably in casting David and the Messiah as fundamentally Torah

---

16 These two views as to how the messianic era will be brought in – gradually through human effort or catastrophically through cataclysmic events and miraculous divine interventions – run through the history of Jewish thought. The former, though well rooted in the tradition, has been largely ignored, so much so that Scholem could assert: 'Jewish messianism in its origins and by its nature – this cannot be sufficiently emphasized – is a theory of catastrophe. This theory stresses the revolutionary, cataclysmic element in the transition from every historical present to the Messianic future. ... The elements of the catastrophic and the vision of the doom are present in peculiar fashion in the Messianic vision' (Scholem 1971: 7–8). But gradualism, as we have seen, is found at least as early as the Mishnah (*m. Soṭah* 9.15). It was taken up later by Maimonides in his *Mishneh Torah*, (*Laws of Kings* 11–12), though his *Epistle to the Yemen* is more 'catastrophic' in tone, and in modern times was reaffirmed by movements as diverse as early Reform Judaism and Zionism, both secular and religious (Ravitzky 2003). The gradualist view has certain similarities to Christian post-millenarianism, and the catastrophic to Christian pre-millenarianism, and like these two forms of Christian eschatology, a correlation with two very different attitudes towards engagement with the world is probably entailed. Gradualists, like post-millenarians, are more ready to get politically involved, since the coming of the Messiah depends crucially on their efforts to improve themselves and society. Catastrophists, on the other hand, like pre-millenarians, are more inclined to withdraw from the world, to keep themselves free from its taint, so as to escape the intervention of God in judgement.

scholars (*y. Sanh.* 2.3; *y. Šeqal.* 2.4; *y. Ber.* 1.1; *y. Ḥag.* 2.1; *b. Ber.* 4a; *b. Mo 'ed Qaṭ.* 16b; *Pesiq Rab Kah.* 18.6). The rabbinic rewriting of the popular doctrine of the Messiah is illustrated by the Targum of Song of Songs. The rabbinic credentials of this late Targum, composed possibly in the seventh or early eighth century in Palestine, are beyond dispute. It is a paean of praise for the rabbinic academy at Tiberias. Messianism is one of its major motifs, and its final chapter is a mini-apocalypse which is very much at home among the texts of the apocalyptic revival. But its Messiah is a very rabbinic figure. He is a great Torah-scholar. When the exiles will be gathered in it is to take part in a grand Talmudic *shiʿur* – a study-session – with the Messiah in the Jerusalem Temple (8.1–2). The Messiah's military prowess and the wars he fights to redeem Israel are at most only muffled noises off-stage. There is much about the Temple in Targum Song of Songs, but the Temple seems to be envisaged more as a *Beit Midrash* than as a place where sacrifices are offered to God. Temple imagery is freely transferred to the *Beit Midrash* even in the present age: the *Beit Midrash* is the *omphalos* of the world, and its head performs a high priestly role of mediation between heaven and earth (7.3). The boundaries between the two institutions are constantly blurred. The pacifism of the text is explicit. The readers are reminded of the disaster that befell the Ephraimites who went up to the Land prematurely. The implication is clear: such will be the fate of all who try to force the redemption (2.7; cf. 3.5; 8.4). Even in this age it is the scholars, and above all the school-children conning their Torah, who raise a defensive rampart around Israel (4.4). This is why the references to warfare in the messianic age are so muted. Even then it is Torah that will be Israel's sovereign defence (8.9–10). It is warfare on the spiritual plane that is most important (4.6) (P. S. Alexander 2003).

It is hard to overestimate the theological implications of this resurgence of messianism – messianism fundamentally of a realist variety – within rabbinic Judaism. It is a seismic shift, a move away from the essentially timeless Rabbinism of the Tannaitic and early Amoraic periods, to a re-engagement with history. The forward-looking, eschatological Judaism of late Second Temple times, sidelined by the Rabbis during the second and third centuries, thrust its way back into their theology in late Amoraic times. Evidence for this renewed interest in the historical process is all over the later rabbinic sources. We find it in Targum Song of Songs, which sets out an historical schema running from the first exodus, from Egypt, to the last exodus, from Edom, which will usher in the days of the Messiah. We find it in the new rabbinic fascination with the succession of world empires, culminating in the empire of the Messiah, which is often linked to interpretations of Daniel's visions, particularly of the four beasts (*b. Meg.* 11a, 17b; *b. ʿAbod Zar.* 9a–9b; *b.Pesaḥ.* 119a; *Lam. Rab.* 1.14.42; *Esth. Rab.* 1.1.12; *S. ʿOlam Rab.*: Cohen 1967: 223–62).[17]

---

17 The problem of messianism in rabbinic Judaism has certain intriguing similarities to the problem of messianism within modern Hasidism. Following the messianic debacle of seventeenth-century Sabbateanism, what was the attitude of early Hasidism towards messianism? Ben Zion Dinur argued that early Hasidism remained a full-blooded messianic movement. Martin Buber argued that it effectively liquidated or eliminated its messianic heritage. Scholem took a mediating view and argued that it neutralized it ('I am far from suggesting that the Messianic

The Historical Context

The general lines along which the rabbinic doctrine of the Messiah developed are reasonably clear. Between the second and sixth century the Rabbis managed to effect a complete U-turn in their attitude towards popular messianism. From marginalizing it and ignoring it wherever they could, they embraced it and moved it towards the centre of their theology. Why? The answer is far from clear, because the nexus between messianism and history remains obscure. Despite the fact that history is littered with messianic movements, no one has yet advanced a cogent, universal sociology of messianism.[18] However a number of pertinent points can be made.

(1) Messianism was an important element of the Rabbis' intellectual heritage from Second Temple times, and, as we have seen, that messianism had been preserved and was being promoted in their milieu by non-rabbinic tradition. It was basically realist and called for the overthrow of the imperial power. The Rabbis probably reacted against it for political reasons. The Talmudic period opened with a series of Jewish wars of liberation which had strong messianic overtones (the First Revolt of 66–74, the 'wars of Quietus' in the Diaspora in the time of Trajan, 115–17, and, clearest of all, the Bar Kokhba Revolt of 132–5). Running through the rabbinic traditions about these wars is a constant theme of the futility of armed struggle. There is no point taking up arms to resist Rome. Rather what Israel should concentrate on is the study and observance of the Torah. It is the Torah scholars who are the true 'guardians of the city' (*y. Ḥag.* 1:6; *Lam. Rab.* Proem 2; *Midr. Ps.* 127:1). The good life can be lived here and now. According to rabbinic legend Yohanan ben Zakkai left the stricken city of Jerusalem, made his peace with Titus, and requested and was granted the vineyard at Yavneh in which to set up his school (*'Abot de Rabbi Nathan* A 4). When his students asked him after the destruction of the Temple how the sins

---

hope and belief in Messianic redemption disappeared from the hearts of the Hasidim. That would be utterly untrue. ... But it is one thing to allot a niche to the idea of redemption, and quite another to have placed this concept with all it implies in the centre of religious life and thought.' Scholem 1971: 176–202). In this typology, my view of the situation in early rabbinic Judaism comes closest to Buber's 'liquidation of messianism'. What Buber says about early Hasidim comes fairly close to how I understand early rabbinic Judaism: 'Only the hallowing of all actions without distinction ... possesses redemptive power. Only out of the everyday does the All-Day of redemption grow. ... The Hasidic message of redemption stands in opposition to the Messianic self-differentiation of one man from other men, of one time from other times, of one act from other actions. ... Turning the whole of his life in the world to God and then allowing it to open and unfold in all its moments until the last – that is man's work towards redemption' (quoted in Scholem 1971: 178–9). This could be read as a perceptive comment on the dictum of Pinhas ben Ya'ir (*m. Soṭah* 9.15). If messianism was 'liquidated' or 'neutralized' within early Hasidism, it certainly re-emerged later (as it did in rabbinic Judaism), culminating in the last decades of the twentieth century when followers of the late Lubavitcher Rebbe, Menahem Mendel Schneerson, proclaimed him Messiah (Ravitzky 1996, 2003; Berger 2001; Lenowitz 1998: 199–224).

18 The problem is, as Ravitzky 2003 notes, that messianism can be a product as much of success as of failure. The twentieth century has witnessed one of the greatest revivals of Jewish messianism in history, yet the scholarly world has shown little interest in recording and analysing what has been happening before its eyes!

of Israel could now be atoned for, he famously replied, 'By acts of loving-kindness' (*'Abot de Rabbi Nathan* A 4). The Temple, in other words, was not so important. His ambivalence towards messianism was neatly encapsulated in the saying: 'If you have a sapling in your hand, and someone says to you, "Look, the Messiah has come!", first plant the sapling and then go out to greet him' ('Abot de Rabbi Nathan B 31). When Akiba proclaimed Bar Kokhba as Messiah, he was rebuked by Rabbi Yohanan ben Torta: 'Akiba, grass will grow on your cheeks, before the Messiah will come' (*y. Ta'an.* 4:5). Later rabbinic tradition sided with Yohanan: Bar Kokhba was a false Messiah, who disrespected the Torah sages (*y. Ta'an.* 4.5; *b. Sanh.* 93b; *Lam. Rab.* 2.2.4). The politics of the Rabbis post-Bar Kokhba became deeply pacifist. This led to a massive de-emphasizing of messianism, which was inherently politically explosive and had the potential to stir up disastrous armed rebellion.

(2) A second reason why the Rabbis may have initially marginalized messianism is that in their day it was seen largely as priestly doctrine. It is intriguing to note how much post-70 non-rabbinic messianism can be linked specifically with priestly traditions. There is a case to be made that the priesthood preserved its social cohesion after the destruction of the Temple to a greater degree than has usually been supposed, and may have gone on transmitting and studying its teachings, and offering spiritual leadership to the people, who continued to treat priests with marks of respect.[19] The priesthood constituted an alternative locus of spiritual authority to the Rabbinate. The Mourners for Zion were almost certainly dominated by priests. Heikhalot mysticism contains large elements of priestly lore. The synagogue may have been the powerbase for the priesthood in the Talmudic period and it has been argued that the Targums and the *Piyyutim* display a penchant for priestly themes. The Amidah is full of priestly motifs and may go back to a Temple prayer used in Second Temple times. The picture is complex and it would be wrong to oversimplify it. There is plenty of priestly interest in classic rabbinic literature: note, for example, the order *Qodashim* in the Mishnah. However, it would make sense to see messianism as a predominantly priestly as opposed to a strictly rabbinic concern post-70. After all it was the priests who had lost most by the destruction of the Temple, and who had most to gain when the Messiah came and rebuilt it.

(3) A third reason why the Rabbis may initially have de-emphasized messianism was the emergence of Christianity. Christianity was a radical form of messianic Judaism. Christ became for Christians the hermeneutical key to their understanding of the Old Testament, and was systematically read into it. The Rabbis may have responded by reading the Messiah out of it in order to cut off Christianity from its scriptural roots. This could be a factor in the conspicuous lack of messianic interest in the Tannaitic Midrashim. It may, for example, lie behind the exegesis which oddly refuses to see a messianic reference in the 'star' of Num. 24.17 (*y. Ned.* 3:8). It might also explain *Targum Jonathan*'s strange rendering of Isaiah 53, which, while conceding that the chapter speaks of the Messiah, systematically refuses to apply to him those elements in it which

---

19 Steven Fine 2005 is sceptical about this, but offers a good introduction, with abundant bibliography, to the debate.

Christians saw as conspicuously prefiguring Jesus. Involved here surely is an anti-Christian reworking of the text. This can be seen as part of a much wider attempt by the Rabbis to put clear water between themselves and Christianity. It is now widely recognized that emergent Christianity played a vital role in the self-definition of Rabbinic Judaism, just as Judaism played a decisive role in the self-definition of Christianity (P. S. Alexander 1992; Becker and Reed 2003).

Plausible reasons are to hand, then, for explaining, at least in part, why the Rabbis may have de-emphasized messianism, but this only serves to turn the spotlight back on to the question of why they changed their minds. It is surely significant that the renewed rabbinic engagement with messianism seems to have coincided with an upsurge of popular interest. Beginning probably sometime around the late fifth century Jews seemed to have developed once again a fascination with the end of time and the coming of the Messiah. This fascination continued for several centuries and amounted to nothing less than an apocalyptic revival in Judaism – a revival which somehow led to the rediscovery of 'lost' Second Temple apocalyptic traditions. It is to this period that the *Midreshei Ge'ullah* belong, as well as the late Targums with their substantial messianic references, many of the *piyyutim* of redemption, and a substantial part of the Heikhalot traditions. This eschatological interest was not confined to Jews, but affected other religious communities across the Middle East as well. We find it among Christians and Zoroastrians, and, after the rise of Islam, among Muslims as well (K. Berger 1976; P. J. Alexander 1985; Arjomand 2003; Olster 2003; Reeves 2005: 12–24).

The historical conditions which gave rise to the apocalyptic revival in Judaism are hard to pinpoint. From the early fourth century onwards we can easily identify events which could have stirred the messianic imagination of the Jewish people. The political triumph of Christianity under Constantine in the early fourth century, a triumph pushed in the faces of Palestinian Jews by the massive appropriation of the Holy Land as *Christian* sacred space inaugurated by Queen Helena, is referred to in a late interpolation in *m. Soṭah* 9:15 as 'the empire falling into heresy (*minut*)', and identified there as one of the signs of the imminent coming of the Messiah (Avi-Yonah 1976: 166–74). The Jews rose in revolt against Gallus in 351, but the revolt was short-lived and seemed to have been confined to a small band of zealots (Avi-Yonah 1976: 176–81). The emperor Julian's dramatic proclamation in 362 that he would allow the Jews to rebuild their temple in Jerusalem was met, by all accounts, with widespread enthusiasm and expectation throughout Jewry (Avi-Yonah 1976: 191–8). There were Samaritan revolts against Rome in 451, 484 and above all 529, but the extent to which Jews were drawn into these remains unclear (Avi-Yonah 1976: 241–3). The Persian-Roman wars of the early seventh century, leading to the Persian capture of Jerusalem in 614, certainly aroused intense messianic fervour, which spawned such late Hebrew apocalypses as the *Book of Elijah* and the *Book of Zerubbabel*, and the ferment was kept going by the Arab invasion of Palestine in 634 which ended with the surrender of Jerusalem four years later (Avi-Yonah 1976: 257–75). But the rabbinic reaction to these events was not predictable. As we have seen, after the disasters of earlier messianic wars, particularly the revolt of Bar Kokhba the Rabbis seem to have emphatically turned away from messianism. Now they turned towards it, and it is why this happened that remains obscure. They seem to have succumbed to the *Zeitgeist*, the *fin-de-siècle* mood that pervaded not only the Jewish communities but the whole of the Levant in the late fifth and sixth centuries,[20] and decided that the best defence against *dangerous* messianism was not to attempt to suppress or maginalize messianism but to define and promote a *rabbinically acceptable* doctrine of the Messiah. Messianism was finally decisively domesticated within rabbinic theology by the authority of Saᶜadya (*Book of Beliefs and Opinions*, Treatise 8), and its acceptability reaffirmed a little later by a responsum of Hai Gaon (Reeves 2005: 133–43). Saᶜadya may well have been stung by the criticisms of the Qaraite Mourners for Zion who claimed that the Rabbis were too smugly content with the status quo (the condition of exile and oppression), too interested in making money and living comfortable lives, too complacent about the ruined state of the Temple. Just as Saᶜadya stole the Qaraites' thunder by appropriating Islamic theology (the *Qalam*) to the defence of Rabbinism, so he tried to steal their thunder by integrating messianism into the rabbinic worldview. But the appropriation remained firmly on rabbinic terms.

20 On Messianic speculation in this period, see de Lange, this volume: 274–84.

Chapter 18

MESSIANISM IN ANCIENT BIBLE TRANSLATIONS IN GREEK AND LATIN

Alison Salvesen

Messianism in the Septuagint?

There is some controversy over the extent of messianic references in the books of the LXX translated from Hebrew and Aramaic. One reason for this is the sheer range of messianic ideas represented in literature dating to the same period as the LXX translations (roughly the third to late first centuries B.C.E.), and the difficulty of dating the stages of their development.[1] Therefore for the purpose of this study we will define a 'messiah' as a Davidic or priestly figure who will perform acts of deliverance for the Jewish people and establish God's kingdom on earth in the last days.[2] Another difficulty lies in the frequent ambiguity of the Greek texts, which can be understood in more than one way. It is important, therefore, to distinguish as far as possible between the following situations: messianic ideas in the original Hebrew text[3] that were faithfully represented in the Greek translation; concepts not present in the Hebrew but introduced by the translator; support for messianic beliefs read into the Greek text by later generations but not originating with the translator.[4] Distinguishing these possibilities involves an awareness of the surrounding context of each text, and of the translation techniques of each specific book.[5]

There are other, related issues. In places the Hebrew is rendered in a way that actually goes against an individual messianic interpretation, for instance in LXX Isa. 42.1, where the translator supplies the names Jacob and Israel to identify the servant of the Lord with the community as a whole.[6] A small number of passages

---

1   The beliefs of Greek-speaking Jews in Alexandria and elsewhere in the Diaspora may have differed somewhat from those of Palestinian Jews, which also varied considerably: for the situation at Qumran, see Evans 2000.
2   See Oegema 1998a: 290 and Lust 1985: 175.
3   See Gillingham 1998.
4   Dorival *et al.* 1988: 221–2 list passages that may reveal messianic readings or that facilitate a messianic reading of the text. Lust 2004b: 41 prefers to term these 'christological applications' and observes, 'It is difficult to detect in any of the texts listed by Harl a process of messianisation directly intended by the translator'. Elsewhere he remarks, 'often the LXX makes it more difficult to recognise in those texts a reference to an eschatological Messiah' (Lust 1997a).
5   See the comments on Schaper 1995 by Cox 2001, and the review by Pietersma 1997.
6   Mt. 12.18-21 cites Isa. 42.1-4, but the Greek does not coincide with that of LXX Isaiah. Dorival *et al.* 1988: 220–1 cite Hos. 11.1; Isa. 9.5; 42.1; Dan. 2.22 as examples of passages where the messianic idea is absent in the LXX.

that could be read messianically did not appear in the original LXX, such as Jer. 33.14-26, because they were absent in the Hebrew Vorlage of the translation, and had to be added by later revisers of the LXX. There is also the question of whether our modern critical editions of the LXX books invariably reflect what the original translators produced, as well as the attested introduction of christological readings by Christian scribes.[7] Comparison with messianic ideas in non-biblical literature is complicated by uncertainty about the date of some works or the layers within them. In particular, though the Aramaic Targumim contain many undoubtedly earlier traditions, their written form dates to the Talmudic period and beyond, and therefore may reflect different historical circumstances and theological preoccupations.

Such observations should not make us despair of the possibility of investigating messianism in the LXX, but great care is necessary if we are to reach sound conclusions.[8]

Considerations of space prevent a thorough survey of all passages thought to be significant, but the following section will examine texts forming the focus of recent discussion, with a view to ascertaining whether their apparent messianism was intended by the translators or read into the text at a later date. The principal texts occur mainly in the Pentateuch, Psalms and Prophets, and there are also certain terms that have been associated with messianic concepts, such as ἄνθρωπος,[9] υἱός τοῦ ἀνθρώπου,[10] μονόκερως,[11] ἄστρον, ῥάβδος, ἀνατολή, παιδεία. Some of these words can occur without theological significance in the LXX, and therefore the most persuasive cases occur where they are used to render quite different Hebrew words.

a) NRSV renders the MT of Gen. 49.10:

'The sceptre shall not depart from Judah, nor the ruler's staff from between his feet, until tribute comes to him; and the obedience of the peoples is his'.

In contrast, LXX has:

'a ruler (ἄρχων) shall not fail from Judah nor a leader (ἡγούμενος) from his thighs, until there comes what is set aside for him, and he is the expectation of peoples.'

It is not surprising to find that the LXX treats the sceptre and staff as metaphors for a person in authority. The question is whether this indicates that the translator intended the text to refer to a specifically messianic and royal figure, as in the explicit interpretation 'King Messiah' in the Targumim. In the second half of the verse the translator analyses the unusual word שִׁילֹה as לוֹ + שֶׁ,[12] and may have connected the construct form יְקְּהַת with the root קוה, 'hope'. The change in the next phrase from לוֹ to αὐτός is unexpected. The nominative pronoun in

---

7 See Ulrich 2000: 387 and Seeligmann's chapter on the transmission of the text of LXX Isaiah, where he discusses the likely existence of glosses and Christian interpolations. He comments on 'our utter inability to provide an adequate answer to the question: which elements in our text are we to attribute to the translator, and which not?' (Seeligmann 2004: 178).
8 Note the remarks of Gzella 2002: 78–9.
9 See Horbury 1998c: 50.
10 Cf. Horbury 1985.
11 See Schaper 1995 and Gzella 2001.
12 Cf. the Qere שֶׁלּוֹ.

all probability links the subject of the phrase with the dative (αὐτῷ) of the previous one, and with the ruler and leader of the first half of the verse. However, Johan Lust takes the pronoun to refer to Judah.[13] He also argues that the focus of v. 10c is on what has been set aside (τὰ ἀποκείμενα), rather than the identity of the person for whom it has been kept. Interestingly, the latter interpretation is brought out in an important variant 'until there comes the one for whom it is set aside' (ἕως ἂν ἔλθῃ ᾧ ἀπόκειται) which was known to early Christian writers and became an issue in debates with Jews.[14] Such a reading obviously enhances the importance of the figure and of his coming. As for προσδοκία ἐθνῶν, Monsengwo-Pasinya argues that elsewhere in LXX Genesis, ἔθνη refers to the Israelite tribes, and so here it is the Jews alone who expect the Messiah, and not foreign nations.[15] That it was understood in precisely this way in the late first century C.E. is supported by the reference in Acts 12.11 to προσδοκία τοῦ λαοῦ.

b) Num. 24.7 and 17 are often connected to Gen. 49.10, being also widely regarded as messianic.[16] They occur in the oracles of Balaam. The Hebrew of v. 7 is hard to interpret: NRSV translates:

'Water shall flow from his buckets, and his seed shall have abundant water, his king shall be higher than Agag, and his kingdom shall be exalted.'

The LXX, however, renders:

'A man (ἄνθρωπος) shall come forth from his seed, and he shall be lord over many peoples, and his kingdom shall be exalted over Gog, and his kingdom shall be increased.'

The question is whether the unexpected rendering 'man' is an intentional reference to the messiah. The term ἄνθρωπος also appears in LXX Num. 24.17, which reads, 'I shall show to him, and not now; I bless him, and he is not near. A star shall rise from Jacob and a man shall arise from Israel'.

Unlike Gen. 49.10, the sceptre of the Hebrew is not identified as a ruler, but only as a man (ἄνθρωπος), and thus as in v. 7 the question is whether 'man' is a messianic title.[17]

Johan Lust argues from citations in Philo and early Christian writers that ἄνθρωπος was not present in the original Greek form of v. 17 at all, and possibly not in v. 7 either.[18] He remarks that Heb. 8.2, which may allude to Num. 24.6c 'like the tents the Lord has planted' in the phrase 'the true tent that the Lord has set up', ignores v. 7. Therefore, Lust says, the verse could not have been one of the messianic proof-texts for Christians in the late first century.[19] However,

---

13   Lust 1997c: 40 and Harl 1986: 47, 309.
14   Harl 1986: 308–9 and Lust 1997c: 41, on Justin Martyr, who uses this variant version in *Dial.* 120.3–4, and accuses Jews of using another text here, no doubt because it does not favour his messianic interpretation. See the first apparatus in Wevers' edition of LXX Genesis (Wevers 1974: 460).
15   Monsengwo-Pasinya 1980: 366.
16   See Dorival *et al.* 1988: 288; Vermes 1973: 59–60; 159–66.
17   As argued by Horbury 1985: 49 and Horbury 1998c: 45–51, 137, citing also Isa. 32.2 and Ps. 86 (87).5. He also notes the use of ἐξελεύσεται in another passage said to be messianic in the LXX, Isa. 11.1 (Horbury 1998c: 101).
18   Lust 1995: 241–2.
19   Lust 1995: 241–2.

even if we accept the very vague allusion to Num. 24.6c, v. 7 would not have served the writer's purpose since Num. 24.7 speaks of 'a man': the writer has just stated that the heavenly tent was *not* pitched by man (ἄνθρωπος), and is stressing the priesthood and sonship of Jesus, not his humanity. More persuasive is Lust's observation that Justin Martyr has for v. 17 ἀνατελεῖ ἄστρον ἐξ Ἰακωβ καὶ ἡγούμενος ἐξ Ἰσραήλ,[20] and that Christian proof-texts in the early period centre on the titles ἄστρον (Num. 24.17), ἄνθος (Isa. 11.1) and ἀνατολή (Zech. 6.12), not ἄνθρωπος.[21] Although Philo cites 24.7 using the word ἄνθρωπος, his interpretation does not concern a royal or Davidic messiah, but a kind of restoration of Primeval Man by the Eschatological Man, and is thus more universalist.[22] Lust speculates that it was Philo's use of ἄνθρωπος that may have caused the word's introduction into the Greek of Num. 24.7,17: it is then found in Origen and Eusebius, where it is used to stress the humanity of Christ, rather than his messiahship.

The star of Bethlehem (Mt. 2.2, 8, 9, 10) is a likely allusion to this passage, though normally the Gospel writer cites a passage explicitly, then states that it has been fulfilled.

One other difference between the MT and the LXX in Num. 24.7 is that the Greek compares the kingdom to come with that of Gog, a prince in Ezekiel 38–39, instead of MT's Agag, king of Amalek in 1 Samuel 15. Lust notes that this change projects the event into the eschatological future. However, since the Samaritan Pentateuch also has the reading 'Gog', the name may have originated with the Hebrew Vorlage of the LXX rather than being an innovation of the Greek.

There are three further texts in the Pentateuch where messianic ideas have been perceived, but are less likely to have been due to the conscious decision of the translator.

c) Gen. 3.15 has been seen as a reference to the Christian idea that at the very moment of the Fall, God not only spoke of the enmity between humanity and Satan, but also hinted at the coming of the Saviour.[23] The Greek is close to the Hebrew:

'I will place hostility between you and the woman, and between your seed and her seed. He shall watch [Heb. 'bruise', 'strike'] your head and you will watch his heel.'

Since the gender of the pronoun αὐτός does not match the neuter σπέρμα, 'seed', the issue is whether αὐτός was chosen merely as a literal rendering of הוא,[24] or as an allusion to a coming messianic saviour. However, the choice of τηρεῖν, 'watch', to render שוף 'strike, bruise', has the consequence that the Greek has no suggestion of the overcoming of the serpent. The masculine pronoun may have been chosen to personalize the 'seed' in the sense of 'descendants',[25] or even to

---

20 *Dial.* 106.4. Similarly, Irenaeus reads *dux*.
21 Lust 1995: 241–2.
22 Philo, *Praem.* 95; *Mos.* 1.290. Lust 1995: 245–7, 250–1.
23 Martin 1965: 425–7 argues that the LXX represents the earliest form of this belief.
24 See Rösel 1994: 94–5.
25 Wevers 1993: 44.

point to an individual descendant, as Lust suggests.[26] However, it seems that the verse was only interpreted messianically in an indirect way, and never had the prominence of Gen. 49.10 among Christians.[27]

d) Another passage that became popular among Christians because it was seen as a foreshadowing of the crucifixion is Genesis 22. Schaper assumes from the use of ἀγαπητός in vv. 2, 12, 16 for יחיד and the appearance of the same word in Ps. 45(44).1 for ידידת, that there was a shift from the meaning 'loved one' to 'only son', and thus that ἀγαπητός has the associations of μονογενής.[28] Ausloos and Lemmelijn point out that the LXX translator of Genesis probably chose ἀγαπητός instead of the expected μονογενής in Genesis 22 to overcome the problem that Isaac was not in fact Abraham's only-begotten son, but the one he loved.[29]

e) The LXX renderings of Deut. 33.5, 26 raise similar questions concerning the exact significance of the term 'beloved'. Horbury renders v. 5:

'there shall be a ruler in the Beloved (ἠγαπημένος), when the rulers of the nations are gathered together at one time with the tribes of Israel'.

He notes the use of the future tense, against the sense of the MT.[30] Horbury believes 'ruler' could apply to an emperor-like ruler in Israel. On the other hand, the translator does not differentiate the nature of Israel's ruler from that of the rulers of the nations, since he uses ἄρχων for two different Hebrew expressions.[31] In vv. 5 and 26, ἠγαπημένος renders Jeshurun, which is a common term for Israel in the Hebrew Bible, and seems unlikely in either context to refer to a messianic figure rather than to Israel, the Beloved of God.[32] Moreover, ἠγαπημένος is used for Jeshurun again, in Deut. 33.15, where it clearly denotes Israel in an unflattering context.

There are a number of recent studies of the theology of the LXX Psalter, owing to its importance in liturgical and devotional use and its apparent influence on other Hellenistic Jewish literature. The present consensus seems to be that it dates from the mid-second century B.C.E. in Palestine.[33]

---

26   Lust 1997c: 37–8.
27   Alexandre 1988: 314–16 and Harl 1986: 47, 109. There is a possible allusion in Rev. 12.17. The Targumic interpretation takes the reference as a collective one, to the people of Israel who will observe Torah and thus strike the serpent's head. An eschatological significance was aided by the words ראש 'head; beginning' and עקב 'heel; end', but this was not noticed or taken up by the LXX. Rom. 16.20 is said to refer to Gen. 3.15, but if so, the wording and interpretation is very different from that of the LXX ('the God of peace will tread [συντρίψει] Satan under your feet'): God, not the Messiah, is the one who overcomes the serpent. For συντρίψει, compare Aquila's προστρίψει.
28   Schaper 1995: 78, 91–3.
29   Ausloos and Lemmelijn 2005.
30   Horbury 1998c 48, 50–1.
31   ἄρχων stands for מלך here, and ἀρχόντων λαῶν for ראשי עם.
32   The collective interpretation is also accepted by Dogniez and Harl 1992: 329, 345.
33   See most recently Gzella 2002: 48–55, who cites the arguments of Munnich, van der Kooij and Schaper. Though he doubts that there are concrete historical references in the LXX Psalms, he too favours a mid-second-century date, and situates the LXX Psalms in Palestine; Williams 2001 places the LXX Psalms prior to Isaiah and Proverbs, perhaps not long after 161 B.C.E.

f) Psalm 2 in its original setting offered a high view of the Israelite king, who was anointed and established by God and supported against his enemies. Psalm 2 even speaks of the king's divine sonship: 'you are my son: this day I have begotten you'. Re-application between the Seleucid and Hasmonean periods to a glorious future ruler is highly probable, and the two psalms must count as the cornerstones of subsequent royal messianism. The rendering of the LXX does not greatly add to what is already present in the Hebrew, in terms of a developing messianism.[34] מָשִׁיחַ 'anointed one' is accurately rendered by the standard LXX equivalent χριστός (2.2). Verses 6-7a in the LXX differ a little, in that the Anointed himself speaks:

'Yet I have been appointed as king by him, on Sion his holy mountain, announcing the command of the Lord.'

Gzella notes that the passive verb in the LXX emphasizes his divine legitimation.[35] The consonantal form of the verb תרעם in v. 9 could be interpreted in a number of ways, but the LXX takes it as ποιμανεῖς, 'you will shepherd them', rather than MT's more violent 'shatter'.[36] The rendering δράξασθε παιδείας 'take hold of discipline' does not bear much relation to the MT's difficult phrase בר נשקו: we do not know whether the translator had a different Hebrew Vorlage or chose to circumvent the problem by adopting this rendering. Both Schaper and Gzella, with some differences of emphasis, relate the phrase in the LXX to the Messiah's teaching of Torah.[37] Schaper concludes that the imagery of the LXX Psalm 2 was conceived of as messianic, citing its undoubted influence on *Psalms of Solomon* 17 and 18, especially ῥάβδον παιδείας χριστοῦ κυρίου in *Pss. Sol.* 18.6-7.[38] Nonetheless, δράξασθε παιδείας is hardly messianic in itself: the messianic colouring it later acquired may be due to the context and external theological developments, rather than originating with the translator.

g) Psalm 110(109) is the other key psalm in the development of messianism, and is particularly important for New Testament writers.[39] The Hebrew of v. 3 is obscure: NRSV renders:

'Your people will offer themselves willingly on the day you lead your forces on the holy mountains. From the womb of the morning, like dew, your youth will come to you.'

So the Greek here is striking:

'With you is rule on the day of your might, in the radiances of the holy ones. From the womb, before the Daystar, I begot you.'

The translator took ילדתיך as a verb plus object suffix, a more common form than the noun of the MT. It also harmonizes with Ps. 2.7 in both Greek and Hebrew. Some scholars argue that 'before the Daystar' (the preposition is as

---

34   Although Schaper 1995: 76 suggests that the imagery was employed already in the second century B.C.E. to illustrate ideas about the world to come, Psalm 2 in either Greek or Hebrew cannot be understood as speaking of the next world, only of the messianic age.
35   Gzella 2002: 337.
36   Note the use of the Greek of this verse in Rev. 12.5.
37   Schaper 1995: 73–6, and Gzella 2002: 333–50.
38   The *Psalms of Solomon* probably belong to the mid-first century B.C.E., and so are around a century later than the LXX Psalms: see Nickelsburg 2005: 238–47.
39   E.g. Mk 16.19; Mt. 22.44; Lk. 20.42-43; Heb. 7.21, cf. 24, 28; 8.1 .

ambiguous in Greek as it is in English) refers to the pre-existence of the Messiah, or at least his priority in creation.[40] Certainly the Hebrew of the MT has nothing to correspond to the preposition πρό at this point.

h) The use of ἀγαπητός in the title of Psalm 45(44) has been seen as a deliberate reference to a messianic figure by the translator.

Schaper believes that the rendering ὑπὲρ τοῦ ἀγαπητοῦ for שיר ידית is unexpected, and associates it with μονογενής and ἠγαπήμενος as synonymous messianic titles, with ὑπέρ representing a dedicatory formula 'in the wider context of Ptolemaic ruler-worship'.[41] However, ἀγαπητός is better explained as due to the etymologizing style of translation, reflected also in the rendering על־ששנים (as ὑπὲρ τῶν ἀλλοιωθησομένων, 'concerning those to be changed', as if from שנה + ש.[42] Certainly messianic and eschatological significance can be read into both words, but proving that this was what the translator had in mind is difficult. Schaper sees further messianism in the use of βασίλευε 'reign!' for רכב, 'ride!' (v. 5). However, the word occurs just after a short passage where the MT may be corrupt (והדרך והדרך: צלח) and the Greek does not correspond well to it. Βασίλευε may be an attempt at an *ad sensum* reading, associating riding forth with kingship.

Schaper also argues for 'a concept of divinized messianic king' in the LXX rendering of the same psalm.[43] For instance, in vv. 12-13, we find:
'And daughters of Tyre shall do reverence to him with gifts,
the rich of the earth shall supplicate your face.'

According to Schaper, the verb λιτανεύω is only used of prayer to divine beings. There appear to be some exceptions to this, however, involving entreaty to humans. It is difficult to establish who is addressed here, given the abrupt changes of person in v. 13. Yet the second person was used of the daughter/queen in previous verses:
'hear ... incline ... forget ...
the king desired your beauty, because he is your lord,'
and it is logical to suppose that this continues in v. 13b:
'and the daughters of Tyre will prostrate themselves to him with gifts,
the rich of the people will supplicate *your* face',
i.e. the face of the queen addressed previously. Therefore the parallelism created (against MT) by the LXX in 44.13 must describe the homage to be paid to the royal couple, first to the king and then to his consort.[44]

Another element in Schaper's argument for a divinized messiah king is that in Ps. 44(45).7a 'your throne, O God, is for ever and ever', the context indicates an address to the king as God. Schaper believes that it reflects Hellenistic concepts of the role of the ruler, and was not alien to contemporary Jewry.[45] Even

---

40 Schaper 1995: 101–7, following on from the views of Bousset and Volz.
41 Schaper 1995: 78, 82.
42 Similarly in the Psalm titles 60(59).1; 69(68).1; 80(79).1, but also Ps. 73(72).21, involving some very uneschatological kidneys, for MT אשתונן.
43 Schaper 1995: 79.
44 Similarly, MT understands פניך as a 2nd fem.
45 Schaper 1995: 80–2.

if this were true, the attitudes of Alexandrian Hellenism would not necessarily be replicated in the LXX Psalter if, as Schaper and others believe, it was created in Palestine.[46] It is more likely that both the Hebrew author and the Greek translator understood the line as an interjection or exclamation addressed to God, not the king.

i) The difficult Hebrew of Psalm 68 inevitably generated a good deal of exegesis in the versions, and LXX Ps. 67 is no exception. The title ἀγαπητός appears once more, in v. 13:

'the king of the armies of the beloved, of the beloved,
and for the beauty of the house to divide the spoils.'

But here it seems to correspond to the repeated verb יִדֹּדוּן יִדֹּדוּן, 'they flee, they flee'. Schaper points out that in Pss. 31(30).12 and 55(54).8 the translator recognized the root נדד, and so must have chosen to ignore it here to produce a deliberate exegetical rendering.[47] However, in those cases the root was clear, whereas in Ps. 68(67).13 the initial *nun* has assimilated. The triliteral root system was not fully appreciated in antiquity, and ancient translators and exegetes often worked on the basis of a biliteral root system, especially with 'weak' roots, so the translator may have connected the verb with דוד or ידד instead.

In the same verse, the LXX has a singular 'king' for Hebrew 'kings', but this may reflect a misreading or a difference in the Vorlage rather than indicating deliberate messianizing: for instance, in the uncontroversial passage, 1 Sam. 14.47, the MT has 'kings (of Sobah)' whereas the LXX has a singular, 'king'.[48]

j) In the case of Ps. 72(71).17, where the LXX has 'may his name be blessed forever, his name shall endure before the sun' (MT is a little obscure), Schaper suggests that LXX may refer to the pre-existence of the king's name, and relates it to the similar notion of his begetting before the Daystar in Ps. 110(109).3.[49] The difficulty is the ambiguity of the preposition πρό, and the future tense of διαμενεῖ, which looks forwards, not back, to the everlasting state of the name. Both the name of the king as well as that of God are said to be blessed in the LXX (vv. 17 and 19). However, the idea of the blessed name of the king may also have arisen from the idea of the nations being blessed in him (or it) in v. 17b, and it is no more messianic than LXX Gen. 12.2-3, where God promises to bless Abraham and to make his name great, that he will be a blessing and all the families of the earth will be blessed in him.[50]

---

46   Schaper 1995: 39.
47   Schaper 1995: 90–1.
48   Schaper cites the 'clearly messianic' use of ἀγαπητός in *T. Benj.* 11.2 as coming from 'another Jewish religious document of the second century BC', but Nickelsburg 2005: 314–15 believes that the present form of the *Testaments of the Twelve Patriarchs* is Christian, produced before 200 C.E., and has some cautionary remarks about using material from the *Testaments* to illustrate the forms of Judaism from which Christianity developed.
49   Schaper 1995: 93–4, with Volz, and more cautiously with Bousset.
50   Schaper's comparison with *1 Enoch* 48 (1995: 96) is not ideal, since the latter may date to the turn of the era and thus show a more developed messianism (see Nickelsburg 2005: 255). The use of the Targum to Psalms (1995: 95) is even more problematic: despite preserving 'a wealth of ancient material', the Targumim to the Writings require careful analysis themselves in order to ascertain to which periods various ideas belong. Moreover, in this case, the Targum is indeed looking back to the foreordaining of the Messiah's name, and thus is saying something quite different from the LXX.

The 'network of messianic texts' that Schaper suggests exists in the Greek Psalter[51] should be qualified as 'a network of texts that could be read messianically', since their form allowed such a reading, regardless of the translator's intention. Even if certain passages cannot fully support the interpretation he claims for them, Schaper's study still highlights some interesting renderings and has opened the eyes of many to the notion of exegesis by translation.

There is a measure of agreement on the date and provenance of LXX Isaiah, which scholars also place in the mid-second century B.C.E., but in Alexandria.[52]

k) The most famous passage is Isa. 7.14, in which παρθένος 'virgin' renders עלמה 'young woman'.[53] Did the translator consciously introduce a more miraculous element than suggested by the Hebrew, in view of the birth being a sign from God? Seeligmann sees it as an echo of the cry at Hellenistic Egyptian mysteries, ἡ παρθένος τέτοκεν.[54] Lust downplays the significance of the choice of word, noting that if παρθένος meant merely *virgo intacta*, it would give little sense when used at 62.5 (ὡς συνοικῶν νεανίσκος παρθένῳ). In LXX Gen. 24.14, 16, 55, παρθένος renders נערה while at 24.43 it is used for עלמה, while in 24.57 הנערה is represented by ἡ παῖς. This may suggest that the Genesis translator regarded παρθένος and παῖς as overlapping in sense if not actually synonymous.[55]

l) In Isa. 9.5-6, the LXX describes a child who is called only a 'messenger of great counsel', μεγάλης βουλῆς ἄγγελος, rather than the MT's 'Wonderful Counsellor, Mighty God'. 'Everlasting Father, Prince of Peace' in Hebrew has been rendered as '*I myself* [God] *shall bring* peace upon the rulers, peace and health to him', reading אבי as אביא. Lust notes that the LXX thus plays down the importance of the child to be born, since God is the main agent of blessing to both the rulers and the messiah himself.[56]

m) Isa. 11.1-6 is regarded as a messianic text in both Hebrew and Greek, though it is not quoted directly in the New Testament. The key terms in Greek in v. 1 are ῥάβδος 'staff' and ἄνθος 'flower' for חטר and נצר respectively. Horbury also sees a link between Gen. 49.9 ἀνέβης, referring to Judah, and the verb ἀναβήσεται here.[57] The minor differences between the Greek and the Hebrew do not make the LXX more messianic than the MT, however.

---

51 Schaper 1995: 107; cf. Horbury 1998c: 51, who speaks of 'a chain of exegetical interconnections' in the Pentateuch and the Prophets. Such connections were undoubtedly made by Jews and then Christians after the turn of the era, but it is hard to prove that the renderings under discussion were originally intended in such a sense, especially given that some others are passed over or downplayed.
52 Seeligmann 2004: 222–51 and van der Kooij 1981: 71–3 agree on a date around 140 B.C.E.
53 The term in Classical Greek seems to denote youth and the unmarried state rather than virginity per se: note the term παρθένιος in the *Iliad* for the offspring of an unmarried girl, παρθενιάς for a concubine's in Aristotle and Strabo and νόθον παρθένευμα with the same meaning in Euripides' *Ion* 1472 (LSJ 1339).
54 Seeligmann 2004: 292–3, following Kittel.
55 Though the Hebrew has בתולה, it speaks of a young man marrying (rather than cohabiting with) a virgin: Lust 2004b: 218–25.
56 Lust 1998: 159–62.
57 Lust 1998: 50.

n) Isa. 61.1-2 is quoted by Jesus and applied to himself in Lk. 4.18-19. The first part is the same as the LXX, but then the passage is abridged and combined with Isa. 58.6 plus Lev. 25.10. The writer of Luke evidently regarded Isa. 61.1-2 as messianic, whether the translator did or not.

o) The LXX rendering of Jer. 23.5-6, promising a righteous king in the days to come, is very similar to the Hebrew. The term 'righteous branch' appears, ἀνατολήν δικαίαν for צמח צדיק. In Zech 3.8 and 6.12, ἀνατολή/צמח is explicitly a title bestowed by God.[58] Thus ἀνατολή was frequently related to Jesus by early Christian writers, though as Lust points out, since the word could also be understood as the rising of the sun, this tended to be the sense taken up by commentators.[59] They were also able to relate it to the verb ἀνατέλλω used of the star of Num. 24.17, and of the rising of the star at Bethlehem in Mt. 2.2, 9.[60]

However, one notable feature of the Greek shows that the translator probably did not have an eschatological messianic figure in mind, because where the MT reads, '(this will be his name that he will call him): "The Lord our righteousness (צדקי׳נו)"', the LXX reads '... Josedek'. Lust argues that the LXX reflects an earlier form of the Hebrew, where Zedekiah was recognized as the legitimate heir, whereas the MT represents a reworked version referring to Jerusalem. The other reference to the 'righteous branch' which occurs in a very similar passage in Jeremiah, 33.14-16, is absent in the LXX.[61]

p) Ezek. 17.22-24, on the Lord's planting of the cedar tree, cannot be read messianically in the MT. However, according to Ziegler's critical edition of the LXX the Lord promises to take:

'from the choice ones of the cedar, from the crown of their heart I will pluck, and I myself will plant (it) on a high mountain, and *I will hang him on a lofty mountain of Israel*. And I will plant (him?) and he will put forth a shoot and make fruit and shall be a great cedar, and every animal shall rest beneath him, and every bird shall rest under his shade.'

Lust comments that although this passage would surely encourage Christian writers to think of the crucifixion, in fact during the early period they do not mention this text. He solves this conundrum through a comparison with the early papyrus 967, which has a different reading in v. 22:

'upon a high and hanging (κρεμαστόν) mountain; on the mountain height of Israel I will plant (them), and they shall take blossom and bear fruit.'

He believes that Christian scribes altered this earlier text to κρεμάσω as a deliberate reference to the crucifixion, and it is only after this alteration that the text is cited by writers such as Theodoret in relation to the Passion rather than to the parable of the mustard seed.[62]

---

58 ἰδοὺ ἐγὼ ἄγω τὸν δοῦλόν μου Ἀνατολήν and ἰδοὺ ἀνήρ, Ἀνατολὴ ὄνομα αὐτῷ.
59 Lust 2004a.
60 Dorival 1994: 452.
61 Lust 2004a.
62 Lust 1997a: 236–50.

q) Ezek. 21.30-32 speaks of taking away the high priest's turban and crown and giving it to one who was worthy of it: the LXX has the phrase ἕως οὗ ἔλθῃ ᾧ καθήκει (καὶ παραδώσω αὐτῷ) 'until he comes for whom it belongs (and I shall deliver it to him)', which as Monsengwo-Pasinya notes, is close to the wording of LXX Gen. 49.10 discussed above.[63] Lust suspects that the LXX reflects an anti-Hasmonean reaction, and is thus more inclined to see priestly than royal messianism in the Greek.[64]

r) One place where possible messianism in Ezekiel is removed rather than represented is in 21.15(10) and 20(15). The rather obscure Hebrew uses the term שֵׁבֶט, normally rendered here as 'sceptre' as a symbol of royal power, and seen by some as an allusion to the Messiah.[65] However, the LXX does not render the first occurrence at all, and translates the second as φυλή, 'tribe'.[66]

s) The Hebrew of Mic. 5.1-3 is commonly thought to reveal messianic expectation. 5.1, 3 are quoted in Mt. 2.6, but not in a form that corresponds to that of either the LXX or the Minor Prophets Scroll from Nahal Hever, and the Gospel writer may have drawn on both the Hebrew and Greek while paraphrasing rather freely (note especially Matthew's ἡγούμενος for the LXX's εἰς ἄρχοντα, representing מוֹשֵׁל). As for the LXX text of Mic. 5.1-3, most LXX witnesses present the Lord as the subject of v. 3, and not the implied messiah: 'the Lord shall stand and appear and shepherd his flock with strength', rather than MT's 'he shall stand and shepherd in the strength of the Lord'. The Hebrew at the end of v. 3, 'for now he shall be great (יִגְדַּל) to the ends of the earth' becomes in the LXX and the Nahal Hever Scroll 'because *they* shall be magnified (μεγαλυνθήσονται) to the ends of the earth'. For these reasons Lust argues that the LXX's deviations from the Hebrew reduce the messianic message overall.[67]

Messianism in the Versions of Aquila, Symmachus and Jerome?

The situation with the Greek versions of Aquila and Symmachus[68] is easier to assess, because we know they lived in the second century C.E. and were accused by Christians of altering the LXX text so as not to support christological interpretations.[69] The reality behind this charge may be more complex. Their

---

63 Monsengwo-Pasinya 1980: 367–76, and see also Moran 1958. The Hebrew of Ezek. 21.32 is also fairly close to MT Gen. 49.10: לֹא־בָא עַד אֲשֶׁר הַמִּשְׁפָּט.
64 Lust 1985: 180–91.
65 However, NRSV understands it differently: 'You have despised the rod and all discipline ... If you despise the rod, will it not happen?'
66 Lust 2003.
67 Lust 1997b: 75–88. He notes that the plural verb μεγαλυνθήσονται is the majority reading, against Ziegler and Rahlfs' editions (Lust 1997b: 80–1).
68 Aquila is known from both Christian and Jewish tradition to have been a Jewish convert. The testimony of the Church Fathers concerning Symmachus is less straightforward, and some sources make him an Ebionite, or Jewish Christian. The confusion may be due to a misunderstanding of a remark in Irenaeus: see Barthélemy 1974: 460. Symmachus's exegesis of the Pentateuch also has many more similarities with rabbinic Jewish tradition than with Christian interpretations: see Salvesen 1991.
69 Epiphanius, *de Mens. et Pond.*, 16–17.

renderings in fact reflect the need of the early rabbinic movement in Palestine for a faithful Greek translation of the emerging standard Hebrew text. Symmachus' version additionally reflects contemporary rabbinic exegesis. Their Greek versions thus inevitably diverge from that of the LXX, and not merely for reasons of anti-Christian polemic. We have a clearer picture of the messianic ideas current in the second century C.E. than at the time of the LXX translations, and so it may be easier to identify conscious messianic or anti-messianic renderings in the work of Aquila and Symmachus. The experience of the revolt under Simon bar Kosiba, whose identification with the star of Num. 24.17 gave him the name Bar Kokhba, may have affected these translators' messianic outlook.

Aquila's (*ca.* 130 C.E.) style is very literal and more etymological than exegetical. The case of Symmachus (fl. *ca.* 180–200 C.E.) is rather different: it was recognized even in antiquity by writers such as Jerome that he conveyed the sense of the Hebrew while also providing a faithful rendering. Though the versions of Aquila and Symmachus did not survive as continuous texts, many individual words and phrases were recorded by Christians in their exegetical works and in the margins of manuscripts of the LXX and the Syrohexapla, a literal Syriac rendering of Origen's 'restored' LXX text. Though Christian writers and scribes were interested in the renderings of Aquila and Symmachus for passages which were thought to have christological significance, what is preserved is very fragmentary, and therefore often hard to interpret.

Jerome translated the Hebrew Bible into Latin, and although his version is often known as the Vulgate the more correct title is the *Iuxta Hebraeos* (IH), the version 'according to the Hebrews'. For it he drew on his own patiently acquired knowledge of Hebrew, and on the LXX text as revised by Origen along with the later Greek revisions, especially those of Aquila, Symmachus and Theodotion. From the evidence of the IH itself, his aim seems to have been a text that was objectively rendered, in terms of not including readings that the Church considered proofs of the messiahship of Jesus but which were rejected by Jews because there was no base for such an understanding in the Hebrew text. On the other hand, he claimed that there were trinitarian texts in the Hebrew that the Seventy rendered differently or omitted in the LXX, in order not to reveal the *arcanum fidei* to the monotheist King Ptolemy. Now, however, as a Christian living after the fulfilment of these things by Christ, Jerome could render Scripture unambiguously, as history rather than prophecy.[70] In this way Jerome bolstered his argument for a Latin version taken directly from the Hebrew rather than from the hallowed text of the LXX.

a) Jerome's IH version has an implicit but clearly Christian understanding of Gen. 3.15. Instead of the pronoun 'he' (LXX αὐτός, whose significance was debated earlier), we find *ipsa* 'she', referring to Mary as the mother of the messiah, the 'seed'. Obviously this does not correspond to the masculine pronouns used in the MT or LXX, but appears to be a reading taken over from the Vetus Latina version.[71] It also violates the masculine gender of the verb ישׁופך, which

---

70 E.g. *Praef. in Pent.*, = *Apol.* II.25.
71 See Fischer 1949 67–9. The variant readings *ipse* and *illa* are present in the manuscript and citation traditions. Jerome notes in *Quaest. Hebr. Gen.* that the Hebrew has *ipse*, i.e. הוא, which is a variant in the Vulgate text.

Jerome interprets as Aquila προστρίψει and Symmachus θλίψει, with *conteret*, before returning to the LXX's rendering with the second verb *insidiaberis*: 'she will bruise your head, and you will watch her/his heel'.

b) For Gen. 49.10, Aquila's reading is preserved by Eusebius as 'a sceptre shall not arise in Judah and one proved accurate from between his feet, until he comes, and to him is the gathering (as if from קוה 'gather') of the nations'. The literal, non-personal renderings σκῆπτρον and ἀκριβαζόμενος for שבט and מחקק are to be expected from Aquila, and do not tell us whether he understood the verse messianically or not. However, ἀναστήσεται is not a literal rendering of יסור,[72] ἕως ἂν ἔλθῃ looks very like the LXX, and there is no rendering of שילה included in the citation, so the reliability of Eusebius' witness is doubtful. Symmachus treats שבט as a metaphor for authority (ἐξουσία), but does not personalize it. The Syrohexapla supplies the equivalents for שילה: Aq. 'as what is to him' and Symmachus 'of him whose it is'. Jerome has a rendering which is surely to be understood messianically and is in part a combination of other versions: 'the sceptre shall not be removed from Judah and a leader from his thigh, until he comes who is to be sent (*qui mittendus est*, as if from שלוח or של יח), and he shall be the expectation of the nations'.

c) In Genesis 22, the readings for Aquila and Symmachus in vv. 2, 12 are confused, but it is clear that they replaced the ἀγαπητός of the LXX for יחיד with μονογενής, or by μοναχόν or μόνον, 'only'. This is in spite of the fact that μονογενής would open up the passage to Christian typological exegesis. On the other hand, Symmachus's rendering in v. 13, 'a ram appeared after this, held fast by its horns in a *net*' avoids the type of the Lamb hanging from the Tree that some Christians extracted from the verse by associating any form of wood with the Cross. While employing *unigenitus* for Isaac, Jerome keeps close to the MT with 'a ram held by the horns among briars', *post tergum arietem inter vepres hærentem cornibus*.

d) For Num. 24.7, Aquila, Symmachus and Jerome all keep close to the Hebrew of v. 7a in contrast to the LXX. Aquila and IH have 'water will flow from his bucket and his seed shall be on many waters'.[73] Jerome, and Aquila and Symmachus according to the witness of the Syrohexapla and MS 58, follow the 'Agag' of the MT rather than the more eschatological reading 'Gog'.[74] Jerome, however, renders the rest as 'His king shall be raised up through (*propter*) Agag, and his (Agag's?) kingdom shall be taken away'. This may relate better to David, whose predecessor Saul lost the kingship through his disobedience over Agag, than to Christ.

e) In Num. 24.17a Jerome is again closer to the MT, but for the rest of the verse he follows the LXX. However, both Symmachus and Jerome replace the LXX's ἄνθρωπος with a literal and impersonal rendering of שבט (*virga*/σκῆπτρος). *Virga*

---

72 There may be some contamination from Num. 24.17, where Symmachus has ἀναστήσεται σκῆπτρον.

73 Symmachus has the barely intelligible rendering 'dripping on the shoots of each, but for the seed of each within many waters', but then continues as Aquila.

74 There is some confusion in the witnesses: for instance, Theodoret has Og (king of Bashan) for Symmachus, which if genuine would historicize the whole reading. Though influence from the Peshitta's own reading Agag is conceivable, 58 also records Ἀγάγ for the 'Three'. See Wevers 1982, apparatus.

would not seem to support a royal messianic interpretation, but note the use of the word in a passage that was important for Christians, Isa. 11.1, *et egredietur virga de radice Jesse, et flos de radice ejus ascendet*.

f) For Deut. 33.5, where the LXX had 'beloved' for יְשֻׁרוּן, Jerome translates etymologically, while restoring the translation 'king' for מֶלֶךְ: 'he will be/there will be a king with the most upright one', *erit apud rectissimum rex*. In this he may be following Symmachus and Theodotion, who have ἐν τῷ εὐθεῖ βασιλεύς. It is hard to say whether this was considered messianically, or refers to Moses in the previous verse, or even to God.

The situation in Psalms is especially interesting because we have two Latin versions from Jerome. The first was based on the LXX Psalter (*Iuxta Septuagintam*, ILXX, or Gallican Psalter) and was the one eventually adopted by the Latin Church. The other was directly translated from the Hebrew text, and influenced by the readings of the later Greek versions.[75]

g) In Psalm 2, Jerome maintains the ILXX rendering *adversus Dominum, et adversus christum ejus* in v. 2 as it agrees with the Hebrew. However, in v. 6 he follows Aquila and Quinta: 'but I have woven (*orditus sum*) my king', a possible meaning of נָסַכְתִּי, but unexpected here. Oddly, ILXX has *reges*, 'you will rule', while IH changes this to *pasces*, as in LXX ποιμανεῖς. In v. 11 for נַשְּׁקוּ בַר Jerome adopts the understanding of Symmachus, 'worship in a pure manner', *adorate pure*.

h) Psalm 45(44): In the title, Jerome alters the ILXX rendering that could be taken in an eschatological sense, *in finem pro his qui commutabuntur*, into *victori pro liliis*, in line with the sense of the readings of Aquila and Symmachus. Instead of ILXX's *canticum pro dilecto*, IH has 'a song of the most beloved', *canticum amantissimi*, which provides a link with Jerome's version of Deut. 33.12, *Amantissimus Domini* (יְדִיד יְ״) (though this latter passage is not messianic). Jerome's IH v. 5 eliminates 'reign!' for רְכַב: in v. 5 and follows Aquila with *ascende*. Verse 8 'therefore God, your God, has anointed you', מְשָׁחֲךָ, is rendered by ἔχρισέν σε/*unxit te* by all the versions, except Aquila. The latter has an aversion to using χρίω 'anoint' and χριστός 'anointed; > Christ' (hence his reputation in the Church for being anti-Christian in his renderings), and here as elsewhere he uses forms of ἀλείφω, a synonym without christological associations.

i) Ps. 60(59).9 in the LXX ('Judah [is] my king') is effectively de-messianized by the Three and Jerome: IH has *dux meus* for מְחֹקְקִי, while the Three adopt etymological renderings (Aquila ἀκριβαστής, Symmachus προτάσσων, and Theodotion ἀκριβαζόμενοι).

j) Ps. 68(67).12-13 was a passage where the name 'beloved' occurred in the LXX, but for the unrecognized verb יִדֹּדוּן (see above). Jerome renders non-messianically: *reges exercituum foederabuntur foederabuntur*, 'kings of armies will form alliances, form alliances'. The only other reading that survives is for Symmachus, and is a little uncertain, but maintains the incorrect derivation from ידד: '(kings of the armies) were beloved, they were loved'.[76]

---

75 See Estin 1984.
76 ἠγαπήθησαν ἀγαπητοί ἐγένοντο. See Field 1875, vol. 2, *ad loc*. Unlike other volumes, the current Göttingen edition of the LXX Psalms (ed. Rahlfs, 1967) lacks a hexaplaric apparatus, and so there is no convenient reference work for the Three in Psalms, although there is much new material that has come to light since Field's work.

k) For Psalm 110, since the first few verses in the LXX and therefore the ILXX are close to the Hebrew, Jerome has no need to alter the text of IH. Symmachus, however, changes v. 1 'sit (שׁב)' at my right hand' to *wait* at my right hand', which may imply that the work of suppressing the enemies of the messiah is not yet accomplished. Aquila, Symmachus and Jerome all move closer to the MT in v. 3, and shift the focus onto the nation in comparison with the LXX: Aquila 'with you (are) willing ones in the day of your abundance', Symmachus 'your people (are) leaders in the day of your strength', combined in IH *populi tui spontanei erunt in die fortitudinis tuae*. Jerome continues, 'in the holy mountains, as if from the womb, the dew of your youth will rise for you'. Again this combines Aquila and Symmachus,[77] and removes the reading of ילדתיך as 'I have begotten you' (= LXX here, and MT Ps. 2.7). Thus it diminishes the possible christological associations.

l) However, as John Cameron observes, while Jerome is scrupulous in the IH Psalter about not introducing christological readings which cannot be justified from the Hebrew, he brazenly introduces the name of Jesus for ישׁע instead. For instance at Pss. 79(78).9 and 85(84).5 we find '*auxiliare nobis Deus Iesus noster* and *converte nos Deus Iesus noster* as 'renderings' of ישׁענו אלהי עזרנו and ישׁענו אלהי שׁובנו.[78]

m) Jerome's practice in Isaiah differs from that in Psalms. In Isa. 7.14 he retained the LXX reading beloved of Christians for the IH: *ecce virgo concipiet*. This was in the full knowledge that Aquila, Symmachus and Theodotion all rendered העלמה as ἡ νεᾶνις, 'the young woman', and he therefore tried to justify his rendering on etymological grounds in his commentary.[79] Jerome also uses the passive, 'his name shall be called' instead of the active second person 'you shall call' of the LXX and MT. It is possible that this was done deliberately to connect it to Isa. 9.6,

et vocabitur[80] *nomen ejus, Admirabilis, Consiliarius, Deus, Fortis, Pater futuri sæculi, Princeps pacis.*

By following the Hebrew here (as supported by the renderings of Aquila, Symmachus and Theodotion), Jerome produces a rendering that is more messianic than the LXX, and he insists, on the basis of his Hebrew knowledge, that there are fully six titles listed. He defends the very different rendering of the Seventy by saying that they did not dare say that the boy was to be called 'God', and so substituted a different reading. This then may be one of the passages where Jerome can justify a return to the Hebrew Truth because it reveals mysteries of Christ that had been hidden by the Seventy translators.[81]

---

77 Aquila ἀπὸ μήτρας ἐξωρθρισμένης σοι δρόσος παιδιότητος σου; Symmachus ἐν ὄρεσιν ἁγίοις ὡς κατὰ ὄρθρον σοι δρόσος ἡ νεότης.
78 'The Vir Tricultus: an investigation of the Jewish, Classical and Christian Influences on the Iuxta Hebraeos Psalter', Oxford D.Phil. thesis, submitted 2007.
79 Gryson and Deproost 1993: 346–9.
80 Also active 3rd masc. sing. in the MT, though this would not be apparent in the consonantal text.
81 Gryson and Deproost 1993: 394: *qua nominum maiestate perterritos LXX reor non esse ausos de puero dicere quod aperte deus appellandus sit et cetera.*

n) As noted above, Jerome's version of Isa. 11.1 is 'a staff shall come forth from the root of Jesse, and a flower shall go up from his root'. This is almost an exact translation of the LXX, and not of the MT: the LXX renders two different Hebrew words as 'root' (גזע and שרש), and the verb פרה 'be fruitful' as 'go up', while 'flower' is hardly the correct translation of נצר: elsewhere, and especially in Isaiah, *flos* is a metaphor for what is passing away. He clarifies the rendering in his commentary, where he states that the *virga* is Mary (with a play on *virgo*), and the *flos* is the Saviour, but that the Jews consider the two items to indicate the same lord under two aspects. He is aware that the readings of the 'Three' (*truncum* and *germen*) could be used to sustain a messianic interpretation, but he prefers to stay with that of the LXX.[82]

o) It was noted above that Isa. 42.1 was given a collective interpretation by the LXX by the insertion of the names Jacob and Israel. Jerome notes that neither the Hebrew nor Mt. (12.18-20) has these.[83] ὁ παῖς μου was also used for עבדי, as elsewhere in LXX Isaiah, but the word can mean 'child' as well as 'servant'. Aquila and Symmachus revise to ὁ δοῦλος, though this is probably part of a wider standardization of renderings rather than an avoidance of a term that could be exploited by Christians. Jerome also has *servus meus* in IH, but retains *puer meus* alongside it in his Isaiah Commentary on 52.13.[84] In the latter passage on the Suffering Servant, Jerome stays close to the LXX except for his interpretation of 52.15: *iste asperget gentes multas*, 'he shall sprinkle many peoples' for כן יזה גוים רבים, against the LXX 'thus many peoples shall be amazed'. There is warrant in the Hebrew for this, and it matches the reading of Aquila and Theodotion (though Symmachus has 'he will reject'), but it also accords with the priestly salvific function of Jesus, as borne out in Jerome's commentary.[85]

p) However, in Isa. 53.2 Jerome discards the LXX's interpretation of כיונק as ὡς παιδίον, '(he sprang up before him) like a small child' for 'he will go up like a sapling (*virgultum*) before him', perhaps influenced by Symmachus's κλάδος. Other differences from the LXX are mainly attributable to Jerome's understanding of the Hebrew, but at the end of v. 8 he has *propter scelus populi mei percussi eum*, 'because of the wickedness of my people I struck him' for למו נגע מפשע עמי, a theological rendering that does not agree with any other version.[86]

q) In Lam. 4.20 the construct phrase 'the anointed of the Lord' משיח י״ occurs: with LXX (χριστὸς κύριος), Jerome ignores the construct and renders 'the spirit of our mouth, Christ the Lord, was captured in our sins, to whom we said "let us live among the nations in your shadow"'.[87] However, in Amos 4.13 where the MT has ומגיד לאדם מה־שחו and the LXX has the rendering καὶ ἀπαγγέλων

---

82   In Greek the equivalents for נצר are preserved as Aquila ἀκρεμών; Symmachus βλαστός.
83   (Eds) Gryson and Gabriel 1998: 1311–12.
84   (Eds) Gryson and Gabriel 1998: 1512, on 52.13.
85   (Eds) Gryson and Gabriel 1998: 1513, *mundans eas sanguine suo in baptismate dei consecrans seruituti*.
86   However, the variant *percussit* is also attested: see the apparatus in (eds) Gryson and Gabriel 1998: 1525. Jerome also renders מן in Num. 24.17 by *propter* (מאנג).
87   Lust 1985: 179 notes that Ziegler's edition relegates this majority reading (which he considers Christian in origin) to the footnotes, in favour of the unsupported χριστὸς κυρίου.

εἰς ἀνθρώπους τὸν χριστὸν αὐτοῦ, Jerome is aware of the error and translates, (*et adnuntians homini*) *eloquium suum*, in line with the sense of the Three and Quinta.[88]

Overall, then, we have a mixed picture of the attitudes and procedures of later versions, both Jewish and Christian. Aquila and Symmachus, like the LXX, are translators, not authors,[89] and from the isolated words and phrases that remain from their versions it is difficult to build up a clear picture of their messianic beliefs, though they do not seem to avoid every rendering that might play into Christian hands. In the case of Jerome we have not only his complete *Iuxta Hebraeos* version but also extensive writings and commentaries where he often clarifies renderings. His own choices can be surprising: sometimes non-messianic readings replace traditional Christian interpretations, while christological renderings can appear in unexpected places.

---

88 Lust 1985: 177–8 thinks it possible that the problem lay in the Hebrew Vorlage of the LXX.
89 Cf. Pietersma 1997: 190.

Chapter 19

MESSIANISM IN ANCIENT BIBLE TRANSLATIONS IN ARAMAIC AND SYRIAC

Robert P. Gordon

The Targums

The Aramaic Targums are paraphrases of the books of the Hebrew Bible – though none is extant for Daniel, Ezra and Nehemiah – some of which are relatively literal, while others are free, expansive and given to midrashic elaboration. The earliest of the extant Targums – saving a few Qumran fragments and the Qumran Aramaic version of Job (11Q10) whose status as 'Targum' has been questioned – probably began to assume written form in the century after the second Roman-Jewish war. Evidence of various kinds supports the claim that some writing down of Targum took place at an earlier stage, with perhaps already a tradition of oral Targum as background. One way or another, this early 'targumizing' appears to have left its mark upon a few New Testament texts (cf. Mk 4.12; Eph. 4.8).

Since it was part of the conceptuality of 'Targum' that the text of Scripture should be explained and contemporized, ideas that were post-biblical in origin or that had developed significantly beyond their biblical expression were freely introduced. Messianism is one such topic, beloved of the Targums generally. Rather than provide a summary of the main aspects of Targumic messianism, the discussion that follows highlights a number of features that are of particular interest when the subject is reviewed in the context of Jewish and Christian interpretation.

The Origins of the Messiah

The messiah of the extant Targums is typically presented in purely human terms, and this is very evident in some texts that became important in Christian apologetic. It is still sometimes surmised that the original Targumic interpretation of certain key passages was altered for polemical reasons, but this is very difficult to demonstrate. A human messiah is certainly preferred by *Tg. Isa.* 9.5(6), where the Targumist has not withheld his hand in order to obtain a satisfactory rendering of the Hebrew. First, however, there is a translation issue affecting the Aramaic to be resolved. Stenning 1949: 32 translates in this verse: 'and his name has been called from of old, Wonderful Counsellor ...', taking the Targumic *q°dām* to mean 'previous time, antiquity', and he was not the first to handle the Aramaic in this way. However, when *qdm* is used in *Targum Isaiah* with this sense it comes in the expression 'the days of old' and is vocalized as a noun (*q°dam*; cf. 23.7; 37.26; 51.9), in translations of identical phrases in the MT using the

Hebrew *qedem*. Moreover, in *Tg. Isa.* 9.5(6) not only does the pointing in the vocalized MS used in the editions by Stenning and Sperber indicate the preposition *q°dām* ('before'), but the whole phrase is a typical Targumic circumlocution: 'has been called from before the Wonderful in counsel ...' (cf. Levey 1974: 153 n. 31; Chilton 1987: 21). The Targum so rendered could still be taken to imply that the name of the messiah was appointed in advance of his appearing, just as is expressly indicated in those texts that say that it was 'called from of old' or similar (Ps. 72.17; cf. Mic. 5.1; Zech. 4.7). There is therefore good reason to translate the Targumic *'tqry* in Isa. 9.5(6) as the past tense that it is, rather than treat it as a future (*pace* Chilton 1987: 21). What the Targumist has done, therefore, is to engage in an exegetical manoeuvre of the 'alternative attribution' variety (cf. Gordon 1978: 114), referring the biblical 'cartouche' away from the messianic child to God himself as the appropriate bearer of titles such as 'Wonderful Counsellor' and 'Mighty God'. It would be easy to conclude that this was done in reaction to christological use of this Isaiah passage by the church of the early Christian centuries, but since the messiah is not presented as divine in the Targums generally, it is likely that any Targumic version of Isa. 9.5(6), even in 'pre-Christian' times, would have avoided any seeming ascription of divinity to the messiah. It is the singular manuscript Sperber MS c that, by omitting the words *mn qdm* ('from before'), produces a text that associates the messiah directly with the sublime titles that the bulk of the Targumic tradition denies him. Whether this implies anything about the stance of a copyist or editor, other than a rapprochement – albeit at a highly sensitive point – of the Targum with the parent Hebrew text, is hard to judge: the interest value of the unique readings of MS c has already been commented upon (Cathcart and Gordon 1989: 19).

The Targumic version of Mic. 5.1(2) is expressly 'messianic' despite its importance in the Matthaean nativity narrative and subsequently as a proof-text for the Davidic pedigree and antemundane origins of Christ: 'And you, Bethlehem Ephrath, were as one too small to be counted among the thousands of the house of Judah; from you the messiah will come forth before me in order to exercise rule over Israel, whose name is mentioned from of old, from ancient times.' The major difference from the Hebrew text is in the substitution of the motif of the messianic name for the reference to the 'goings forth' of the Bethlehemite ruler. So the biblical text is treated messianically in the Targum, while at the same time any suggestion of pre-existence is avoided. As to whether this is a deliberate interpretative move in response to Christian use of the verse, a couple of points are relevant. First, it should be noted that, as implied already in the use of the word 'motif', the idea of the antemundane origin of the name of the messiah is a Targumic commonplace (cf. above on Isa. 9.5[6]; see also *b. Pes.* 54a). Second, the antemundane origin of the name of the Son of Man is asserted in *1 En.* 48.3 ('Indeed, before the sun and signs were created, before the stars of the heavens were made, his name was named before the Lord of Spirits'), yet the same section goes on to affirm the antemundane origin of the messianic Son of Man himself (48.6). The Enochic passage is, therefore, a warning against reading too much into the attributing of antemundane origin to the *name* of the messiah, as if this excluded the idea of the antemundane origin of the messiah himself. At the same time, it must be conceded that the Targums generally maintain a consistent position in their depiction of a non-divine messiah. In other words, their messianism is closer to that of the *Psalms of Solomon* than to that of *1 Enoch* (cf. Charles 1913: 185, with the possible qualification mentioned by Horbury 1998d: 97–8).

Consistency of this sort rather than anti-Christian polemic may account for the Targumic handling of the Davidic dynastic oracle at 2 Sam. 7.14, where the metaphorical-sounding 'I shall be a father to him and he will be a son to me' shades off into simile in a good part of the manuscript tradition: 'I shall be like (MSS "for") a father to him, and he will be like (MSS "for") a son before me.' The text thus rendered is spoiled for use in the christological manner of Heb. 1.5, but then it is a strongly decontextualized use of 2 Sam. 7.14 that we have in Hebrews, as the remainder of the Old Testament text indicates, and the Targum behaves in consistency with its own views of messianism. Even so, Levey 1974: 37 thinks that the Targumist may have been familiar with Christian exegesis and was seeking to counteract it. However, while it is indeed probable that the Targum to this and most other texts took shape in the early Christian period, it remains possible that this Targumist was translating consistently with a Jewish tradition of interpretation that would have developed much as it did regardless of Christian involvement.

In *Tg. Ps.* 2.7 there is also a shading off into simile in a way that distinguishes the Targumic interpretation from the christological use of the verse in the New Testament: 'I shall recount the decree of the Lord. He said, "You are dear to me as a son is to a father, worthy as though I had created you today."' Again, it is not self-evident that the Targum is reacting to Christianizing of the text (cf. Heb. 1.5). Consistently with this general approach, *Tg. Ps.* 45.7 interrupts the psalm's address to the messiah with a statement directed to YHWH concerning 'your glorious throne', so preventing any possibility of divinity being ascribed to the messiah as a result of too close adherence to the wording of the MT. This is perfectly compatible with the atomistic approach of the Targums generally, and especially where an apparent misstatement on a point of theological importance had to be avoided.

The Messianic Community

Not surprisingly, the Targums to Gen. 3.15 see more than an anthropological axiom about mutual antipathy between snakes and humans, in what elsewhere became known as the *protevangelium*. Whereas *Onqelos* proceeds unmessianically with a statement about unremitting hostility between the serpent and humans, who will not forget what the serpent did to them at the beginning, the Palestinian Targums envisage healing for humanity in messianic times, for they 'will appease (using *šwpyyt*, punning on MT's use of *šwp*, "crush") one another at the very end of days, in the days of the King Messiah' (*Fragmentary-Targum* [Klein 1980: 46, 127]; cf. *Neofiti, Pseudo-Jonathan*). Success, meanwhile, in this struggle with the serpent will be contingent on the adherence of the human element to Torah. Now, while the Palestinian Targums introduce the messianic dimension, the 'seed' of the woman (MT) is plainly given a collective, i.e. non-messianic, interpretation, just as McNamara notes of Rev. 12.17, where there is a clear reference to Gen. 3.15 in 'the rest of [the woman's] seed' (McNamara 1966: 221–2) – though a more individualized sense of the 'seed' of Gen. 3.15 may be reflected in the earlier verses of Revelation 12 where the attentions of the great dragon are directed against the male child born to the portentous Woman (vv. 4-5). Thematically this has much in common with some sentences in Rom. 16.18-20 where Paul has Genesis 3 in mind, not just in his reference to the crushing of Satan under the feet of Christian believers (v. 20), but also in the immediately preceding verses. He talks of deception of the simple-minded (v. 18) and of his concern that his addressees should be wise as to what is good and innocent in relation to evil (v. 19; cf. Gen. 3.5). However, in Romans 16 there appears to be outright identification of the 'seed' of Gen. 3.15 with the church as the community of the messiah. Since this community is now, with the coming of the messiah, already 'in place', the note of eschatological imminence ('will *soon* crush'; contrast the Targumic 'at the very end of days') is judged all the more appropriate (cf. Rom. 13.11-12). Moreover, the correspondence between the Pauline text and the Targums – though no direct dependence need be envisaged – extends to the theme of human harmony, for Paul's starting point in Rom. 16.17-20 is the problem of dissension that threatened the Christian community addressed.

Messiah and the Nations

In the Targums the function of the messiah in relation to the nations is primarily to end their subjugation of the people of Israel. In the Palestinian Targums to the Pentateuch and the various Targums to the Hagiographa this is almost universally the work of the 'King Messiah' (or 'Messiah son of David').[1] While the 'standard' Targums (*Onqelos* and *Jonathan* to the *Prophets*) do not use the term 'King Messiah', their messianism differs hardly at all in this respect. The *Onqelos* version of Gen. 49.10 is expressly messianic and envisages the subjection of the Gentile peoples to the rule of the messiah:

> The ruler will never cease from the house of Judah, nor the scribe from his children's children, until the messiah comes, to whom the kingdom belongs, and him shall the nations obey (*y štmʿwn*).

The obedience motif is also represented in the *Fragmentary Targum* (Klein 1980: 158) and *Neofiti* renderings of the verse, albeit according to these texts the nations will be 'subjected' to the King Messiah. In this respect *Onqelos* may represent more closely the significance of MT *yqht* – which is given the sense of 'expectation' in the other major versions (LXX, Vg, Pesh) – though the influence of Deut. 18.15 ('him you shall obey', referring to the prophetic successor[s] of Moses) could be suspected in *Onqelos* (cf. Syrén 1986: 115). This idea of obedience to the messiah, whether it is by Israel or by Gentiles, almost acquires the status of a *topos* in the Targums. So the reference to the king in Jeshurun in Deut. 33.5 becomes the basis of a prediction, in the *Fragmentary Targum* (Klein 1980: 231) and in *Neofiti*, of a king who would arise from the house of Jacob, whom the tribes of Israel would obey. Again, in Isa. 11.10 the nations that will 'seek' the root of Jesse (MT) will, according to *Targum Jonathan*, 'obey' the

---

1   On the King Messiah in the Targumim and elsewhere, see Brock, this volume: 171–82.

descendant of Jesse, already dignified in v. 1 as 'messiah'. In Jer. 30.9 MT 'They will serve the Lord their God and David their king' takes on a messianic significance: 'They will serve before the Lord their God *and will obey the messiah son of David their king* whom I shall raise up for them.' I have noted elsewhere (Gordon 1986: 52–3), with particular reference to *Onqelos* at Gen. 49.10, the correspondence between this Targumic idea of obedience to the messiah and the Pauline term 'the obedience of faith', which has some importance in the development of Paul's argument in his letter to the Romans (1.5; 15.18; 16.19, 26, this latter forming an inclusio with 1.5). In Romans Paul is conscious of the fact that he is writing to the imperial capital, yet is not willing to play down the claim of Christ to universal obedience, and so writes of 'the obedience of faith among all the nations' to Jesus Christ 'of the seed of [the king-emperor] David' (1.3, 5). If 'the obedience of faith' involves a 'qualifying genitive' – corresponding to the seventh in Cranfield's list of possible candidates (Cranfield 1975–9: 1. 66) – it becomes the clearer that Paul is stressing that the kingdom of Christ does not involve political or territorial domination, but rather a subjection expressed in terms of faith. In its *Onqelos* version, Gen. 49.10, which is not quoted in the New Testament, provides as good a companion text as any from the Old Testament for the complex of ideas expressed in Rom. 1.1-5.

Servant and Messiah

The principal text is Isa. 52.13–53.12, where the term 'messiah' is introduced early into the Targumic version in the phrase 'my servant *the messiah*', in 52.13; thereafter a version of messianism is followed through in terms of the 'prospering' of which the verse speaks, 'prosper' becoming for the Targumist the clef sign of the whole section. Moreover, whereas the MT makes substantial use of the 'perfect' tense throughout the poem, and so naturally is translated as if referring to past action, in ch. 53, from v. 2 onwards, the Targum – saving a couple of clauses in v. 12 (see below) – adopts a basically future orientation in keeping with its messianic interpretation of the chapter. The sufferings of the servant are associated either with Israel in the past and present or, where the note is more punitive, with the nations in the future. Thus in 53.3 the preferred translation is 'Then the glory of all the kingdoms will be for contempt and will cease', where *(w)ypswq* (MSS) is intransitive. Levey's 'Then he shall be contemptuous of, and bring to an end, the glory of all the kingdoms' (Levey 1974: 64) can be justified insofar as it represents the alternative (transitive) reading *(w)ypsyq* ('will bring to an end'), but it misrenders *yhy lbwsrn*, which should mean 'will be for (= held in) contempt' and refers, consistently with the remainder of the chapter, to the nations whose glory will come to an end when the messiah intervenes (cf. Ådna 2004: 191 n. 6).

Most debate has, however, centred on the Targumic clause 'because he handed himself over to death' in 53.12. In this verse the Targum follows the tense sequence of the MT in a way that does not apply for most of the chapter: two future imperfects are followed by two retrospective explanatory clauses beginning 'because', whereas in the remainder of the verse the perfect-imperfect tense sequence of the MT ('bore'/'makes intercession') is thrown into the future in keeping with the Targum's envisaging of a future intercessory role for the messiah (vv. 4, 7, 11). But it is difficult to judge the full significance of this handling of the tenses. The actual expression 'hand oneself over to death' seems not necessarily to indicate literal death or martyrdom. One of the closest parallel occurrences comes in Judg. 5.18, where it is said that the people of Zebulun 'despised their life to the point of dying', which is generally taken to mean that they hazarded their lives in the battle against Sisera, and for this the Targum has 'handed over their life to killing' (cf. Judg. 9.17). Other comparable occurrences also suggest something distinct from actual acceptance of, or submission to, death. It is also questionable whether the Targumic expression is as strong as the underlying 'poured out (h^crh) his soul' of the MT, which normally is taken to imply literal death.

In the Targum, as in the MT, this selfless act or intention, however defined, forms the basis for the sharing of goods and spoil with the servant/messiah, and explanations of 'handed himself over to death' that relate the expression to its Targumic context have been sought. Since the Targum also associates the spoil of the MT with 'many peoples' and 'strong cities', it is possible that the messiah's 'handing himself over to death' takes place in the context of battle. Ådna (2004: 219–22), however, thinks of an intercessory role for the messiah comparable with that of Moses in Exod. 32.30-34, and the Targumic reference in Isa. 53.12 to subjecting Israel's rebellious – Israel's, since they are forgiven for the sake of the messiah – to the Torah lends plausibility to the interpretation. Moreover, Ådna (221) quotes a similar-sounding phrase from the Mekilta (on Exod. 12.1) to the effect that Moses and others of the patriarchs and prophets 'offered their life for Israel' when they engaged in intercession with God for their fellows (Horovitz and Rabin 1931: 4). This explanation is at least as contextually appropriate as that which seeks to explain the messiah's risk-taking in relation to his military undertakings.

The main functions of the messiah in *Tg. Isa.* 52.13–53.12 are the removal of Gentile domination, the assembling of the exiles, intercession on behalf of Israel, the building of the temple, instruction in Torah, and the judgement of the wicked. Alongside this there is significant emphasis in ch. 53 on the forgiveness of sins ('Then he will beseech concerning our sins, and for his sake our iniquities will be forgiven', v. 4; 'and when we give attention to his words our sins will be forgiven us', v. 5; 'and from before the Lord it was a pleasure to forgive the sins of us all on his account', v. 6; 'and he will beseech concerning their sins', v. 11; 'and he will beseech concerning many sins, and the rebels will be forgiven on his account', v. 12). A very definite relationship between the activity of the messiah and the forgiving of sins is therefore established in the Targum – to the extent that at one point he is even said to transfer the sins 'which my people committed' to the Gentile oppressors of Israel (v. 8). This emphasis on sin and forgiveness is especially strong in vv. 4-6, where also the Targum talks of the messiah building the sanctuary 'which was profaned because of our sins' (v. 5), and the situating of this last element encouraged Koch to characterize the messiah of this passage in priestly terms, since forgiveness of sins was particularly linked with the ritual of the Temple (Koch 1972: 135–6, 140, 144).

The responsibility for the rebuilding of the Temple is also given to the messiah at *Tg. Zech.* 6.12-13: 'and he will be raised up (or "anointed") and will build the temple of the Lord' (v. 12); 'He will build the temple of the Lord' (v. 13). In both instances the Targum keeps close to the biblical text, which is speaking of the post-exilic high priest, Joshua ben Jehozadak. Given that Zech. 6.12-13 is the probable matrix for the linking of the eschatological temple with the messiah, it is likely that *Tg. Isa.* 53.5 is beholden to the Zechariah passage on this point. The connection of the messiah with temple building is also represented in *Tg. Cant.* 1.17, where the rebuilding takes place 'in the days of the King Messiah'. A similar association of messiah and rebuilt temple is made in *b. Pesaḥ* 5a, where Israel is said to merit three rewards: the destruction of Esau, the building of the Temple and the name of the messiah. As in *Targum Canticles*, the reference falls short of attributing responsibility for the construction of the temple to the messiah himself.

However, while *Tg. Isa.* 53.5 envisages the messiah building the Temple, there is little to encourage the view that the messiah's intercessions have to be seen in a priestly context. Indeed, the companion text in *Tg. Zech.* 6.13 makes a distinction between the messiah and an end-time priestly figure: 'and there will be a high priest (MS "priest serving") beside his throne'. This is the likely rendering of the Aramaic, which follows the MT quite closely and probably should be translated in line with it, in preference to 'and he will be a high priest upon his throne'.[2] This civil-priestly diarchy is clearly in evidence in the Targumic version of 1 Sam. 2.35, where the faithful priest predicted in the speech of the man of God will '*serve* before my anointed forever'. If there is some merging of the civil and the priestly in the substantially reworked *Tg. Isa.* 22.15-25, it is not expressed with sufficient clarity to amount to an alternative position. Moreover, as Smolar and Aberbach 1983: 64–6 suggest (cf. Chilton 1987: 45), the Targum may be alluding to the Hasmonean rulers, with their combining of royal and priestly authority, in which case the 'annulment' of the prophecy in v. 25 takes account of the disfavour into which the Hasmonean house descended. In other words, the passage is not expressive of properly messianic sentiment.

Finally, if the messiah of *Tg. Isa.* 52.13–53.12 were a priestly character, we might have expected this to become apparent when the Targumist was rendering the verb *yzh* (presumed root *nzh*) in 52.15. The word is commonly listed separately from the familiar root *nzh* ('sprinkle'), but this was not always so, and the AV rendering by 'sprinkle' has precedent in the minor Greek versions of Aquila and Theodotion (*rantisei*) and the Vulgate (*asperget*). *nzh* ('sprinkle') is used a number of times in priestly texts for ritual manipulation of blood, and the occurrence of *yzh* in 52.15 certainly offered the Targumist the opportunity to associate a priestly function with the messiah, if he had so desired. Since the verb has 'many nations' as its direct object, there would have been need for some translational dexterity, but no more than at many other points throughout the chapter.

The Ephraimite Messiah

While the Targums overwhelmingly associate the messiah with victory over Israel's enemies and the inauguration of a new era of peace, prosperity and Torah-observance, at some point there began to develop ideas of a different type of messiah who would precede the Davidic messiah or would work in concert with him, and who, according to some texts, would actually suffer defeat and death at the hand of the end-time assailant Gog (cf. Ezek. 38–39). In keeping with the

---

2 LXX 'and the priest will be on his right hand' makes the distinction still more explicit.

biblical account of Gog's defeat on the mountains of Israel (cf. Ezek. 38.21; 39.4), a number of Targumic references to Gog mention his destruction, whether directly by God himself (1 Sam. 2.10; 2 Sam. 22.49; *Tg. Ps.-J.* Num. 11.26) or through the agency of the King Messiah, as in *Frg.Tg.* Num. 11.26 (Klein 1980: 194), or of the messiah son of Ephraim, as in *Ps.-J.* Exod. 40.11. Twice in *Targum Canticles* (4.5; 7.4) the messiah son of David and the messiah son of Ephraim are mentioned conjointly as the deliverers of Israel, but without specific reference to Gog.

Without doubt, the most interesting Targumic statement about this lesser-known messiah comes in a marginal reading introduced by the siglum *trg yrwš* ('Jerusalem Targum') in the margin of Codex Reuchlinianus (Sperber's MS f) (Sperber 1962: 495):

> And I shall cause to rest upon the house of David and upon the inhabitants of Jerusalem the spirit of prophecy and true prayer. And afterwards the messiah son of Ephraim will go out to do battle with Gog, and Gog will kill him in front of the gate of Jerusalem. And they will look to me and will inquire from me why the nations pierced the messiah son of Ephraim. And they will mourn for him just as a father and mother mourn for an only son, and they will lament for him just as they lament for a firstborn.

This interest in the fate of the Ephraimite messiah is thrown into relief by the fact that the standard Targum text of Zech. 12.10 is non-messianic, focusing instead on the exile: 'And they will entreat from before me because they were exiled.' Other proposed translations of the standard version at this point are less likely, and still less probable is the suggestion that there is an indirect reference to the Ephraimite messiah here, if the text is translated, 'And they will entreat from before me concerning him on whose account they were exiled' (cf. Gordon 2003: 187). So it is the marginal reading of Reuchlinianus, paralleled by a tradition reported in *b. Sukkah* 52a, that is our basic text for the identification of the pierced one in Zech. 12.10 with the messiah son of Ephraim.

It is difficult to date this marginal reading with any confidence, even in relation to the standard text. The siglum 'Jerusalem Targum' in the Reuchlinianus margins introduces material of varied date and, probably, provenance, and may or may not relate to a now largely lost Palestinian Targum ancestral to the extant, Babylonianized, *Targum to the Prophets*. The case for the existence of such a 'Palestinian Targum to the Prophets' rests mainly on scattered quotes and references and haftaric passages, in which ascription to a Jerusalemite/Palestinian source, deviations from the standard Targum and identifiable dialectal differences all play a part. This particular variant is of mixed dialect and is not connected with any haftaric text or tradition (Kasher 1996: 223); and even if its origin in a Palestinian Targum could be demonstrated, the problem of dating would persist, since the text of the 'non-standardized' Palestinian Targum tradition – witness the Palestinian Pentateuchal Targums – remained fluid for rather longer than the Babylonianized texts.

The circumstances in which the minor messianic figure of the Ephraimite messiah came in as a complement or foil to the dominant Davidic model have been frequently discussed. Duality in the conception of the messianic role is well attested in a range of ancient literature, including the Dead Sea writings, and its roots are usually traced to biblical texts like Zech. 4.14; 6.13 and the civil-priestly diarchy mentioned above. The term 'messiah son of Ephraim (or "Joseph")' itself does not point to a priestly figure, while a lay character is suggested by *Ps.-J.* Exod. 40.11, which traces the lineage of the Ephraimite messiah back to Joshua, of the tribe of Ephraim, who is said to be symbolized in the laver of the Tent of Meeting ('the laver and base represent the more menial, the servant Joshua the Ephraimite, and his descendant, the messiah son of Ephraim' [Levey 1974: 15]). Potentially more significant are *Tg. Ps.-J.* Deut. 30.4 and *Tg. Lam.* 4.22, both of which attribute the end-time deliverance of Israel to 'Elijah the high priest' and the King Messiah. This involvement of Elijah, somewhat improbably as *high priest*, relates to a line of tradition especially favoured in *Pseudo-Jonathan*, according to which Phinehas ('he is Elijah the great priest') would be sent to gather in the exiles at the end of days (*Tg. Ps.-J.* Exod. 6.18; cf. 4.13; 40.10). However, an equation of Phinehas/Elijah with the Ephraimite messiah is not in question, and there is no evidence that this quasi-messianic role for Phinehas/Elijah contributed to the theme of the dying Ephraimite messiah. Nor is there anything in the Phinehas/Elijah tradition, or in that of the civil-priestly diarchy, that should predispose either to develop in the direction of suffering and dying messiahship.

The cutting off of 'an anointed one' is mentioned in Dan. 9.26, and the death of 'my son the messiah' is envisaged in *4 Ezra* 7.28-29, but the relationship of these texts to the tradition of the Ephraimite messiah, or their potential for influencing that tradition, is far from clear, for reasons that need not be rehearsed here. Mostly, the introduction of the Ephraimite messiah, especially in his dying mode, is explained as a response to historical circumstances, whether the preaching of Christian messianism or the disappointed hopes associated with the messianic pretender Bar Kokhba in 132–5 C.E. If it was the former, then the sheer weight of Christian evangelizing and apologetic has produced in a tiny and unrepresentative sector of Jewish thinking – and I am not overlooking the later references to the dying Ephraimite messiah in the like of *Leqach Tov* on Num. 24.17 – a mirror-imaged concept based on Zech. 12.10, already favoured as a proof-text in the earliest Christian tradition (cf. Jn 19.37; Rev. 1.7). There are, to be sure, fundamental differences between this underdeveloped figure of the Ephraimite messiah and the messiah of Christian faith (cf. Dalman 1888: 22–3), but conceptual overlap beyond a limited extent is hardly to be expected. Even so, it remains more likely that the fates of Bar Kokhba and others like him convinced a few in rabbinical circles that victory in the days of the messiah would be achieved in two stages, involving first a dying Ephraimite messiah (cf. Dan. 9.26; Zech. 13.7?) and then, decisively, the King Messiah.

The Peshitta

Little or nothing is known of the early history of the Peshitta; the earliest extant manuscripts come from the fifth century and, as it happens, are among the oldest dated manuscripts of any version of the Bible (Gordon 1998: 355–6). Even discussion of the merits of Jewish or Christian provenance for the version, or for individual books or groups of books (notably the Pentateuch), has produced contrasting conclusions. And whether it is easier to identify readings supposedly pointing in one direction or the other, or to come behind and knock such proposals down, is, as in many another undertaking, a moot point. In point of fact, a survey of the main texts patient of messianic interpretation in the Old Testament discloses minimal difference between the MT and the Syriac. This would suggest that, whatever the interpretative leanings of the translators, these have affected their rendering of the biblical text to only a limited extent.

At a few points the differences between the MT and the Syriac at the least confirm that the version is interpreting messianically even if, by contrast with the Targums, the term 'messiah' is not normally imported into the translation. For example, at Gen. 49.10 the interpretation of 'Shiloh' by 'he to whom it (MSS "the kingdom") belongs' is compatible with a messianic interpretation of the verse; the MSS addition of 'the kingdom', in elucidation of an otherwise unexplained feminine pronoun in the Syriac, produces a reading very similar to that of *Onqelos*, which is expressly messianic (cf. *Fragmentary Targum* [Klein 1980: 158], *Neofiti*).[3] The orientation of the verse in the MT is, in any case, already towards a future ruler who would be the focus of international expectation (cf. Pesh 'and the nations will look for him', at the end of the verse). Again, at Num. 24.17 the 'sceptre' of the MT is personalized as a 'prince' in a text that, even if not messianic according to strict definition, plainly refers to a future Israelite ruler of quasi-messianic importance.

I have commented elsewhere on the challenging case of the Peshitta version of 1 Sam. 2.35 (Gordon 1996: 170–4).

> And I shall raise up for myself a faithful priest, who will act according to what is in my heart and in my mind. And I shall build him a sure house, and he will go in and out before my anointed forever. (MT)

> And I shall raise up for myself a priest who is faithful according to my heart, and he will act according to what is in my heart and mind. And I shall build him a sure house. And my anointed will walk before me forever. (Pesh)

There is a high degree of correspondence between the two texts, but the translation of *lpny* – no doubt, in an unpointed text – by 'before *me*' opens up the possibility that there is a merging of the kingly and priestly personae in the Peshitta of this verse, and in a way that would be specially attractive to a Christian translator or reader. However, it would be very difficult, first to be certain as to the real implications of the Peshitta rendering, and second to establish that the translation originated in Christian circles. In the study already cited (Gordon 1996: 170–4), I have discussed a couple of other features of 1 Sam. 2.35-36 that have a bearing on this issue.[4]

In recent publications Peshitta specialists have been proceeding very circumspectly on this issue of Christian elements within the Peshitta. Weitzman 1999: 240–6 examines a range of texts of special importance to Christian messianic interpretation of the Old Testament and concludes that there is very little to suggest Christian

---

3   Cf. 4Q252: 'until the messiah of justice (= rightful messiah?), the branch of David, comes, for to him and his descendants has been given the covenant of kingship ...' (cf. Syrén 1986: 56–7).

4   My discussion of the phrase 'according to my heart' in 2.35 is more nuanced than Morrison (2001: 158) allows.

influence upon their translation into Syriac. He thinks that the Peshitta Old Testament was translated within a closed, non-rabbinic Jewish community 'estranged from the Jewish people as a whole' (246). The texts considered include Ps. 110.3, Isa. 7.14, Dan. 9.26 and Zech. 12.10. In all such cases apparent christological elements are without much difficulty explained as being applied equally to God in other passages, as attributable to translation technique or as resulting less exaltedly from the translator's attempt to represent a difficult Hebrew *Vorlage*. Others have reached similar conclusions in studies dedicated to particular Old Testament books (Gelston 1997 [Isaiah]; Morrison 2001 [1 Samuel]). For example, Gelston 1997: 563–82 is sceptical of attempts to find Christian elements in the Peshitta of Isaiah, though he is open to the possibility that 'specifically Christian changes were made in particular manuscripts during the course of the transmission' (p. 566, with reference to Isa. 9.5[6], p. 573, referring to Isa. 60.16). A rendering that may actually point away from Christian influence on the Peshitta comes at Isa. 53.9 ('A wicked man provided his grave, even a rich man at his death'), which agrees ill with the Gospel tradition about Joseph of Arimathaea (Gelston 1997: 577; Weitzman 1999: 244).

A possible instance of Christianizing of the text during transmission, in the way envisaged by Gelston, comes in 1 Chr. 5.2 (Gordon 1998: 360–1). The significance of the reference lies partly in the fact that it is clearly translational and interpretative vis-à-vis the MT. In this case it is not a matter of determining how much new translational content there is in a rendering that reproduces most or all features of the parent text, as is often the situation in the kinds of passages discussed in the preceding paragraph. 1 Chr. 5.1-2 is prefatorial, and partly parenthetical, in relation to the genealogy of Reuben in the verses that follow. The business of v. 2 is to explain that, although Judah was strong among his brothers and produced 'a ruler', yet the birthright belonged to Joseph. For this, and rather freely in the first clause, the Peshitta offers: 'The King Messiah will come forth (*npwq*) from Judah, and the birthright will be given to Joseph.' First, we should note the expression 'King Messiah', which is quite common in the Palestinian Targums to the Pentateuch and in the Targums to the Hagiographa, but absent from *Onqelos* and *Targum Jonathan* to the *Prophets*. In other words, and in purely versional terms, the Peshitta has a strikingly Targumic expression here. Weitzman 1999: 114, consistent with his general view of Peshitta Chronicles, attributes the looseness of the Syriac in relation to the Hebrew to a damaged *Vorlage*. However, even proof of a damaged *Vorlage* would not reduce the significance of the reading, since it is precisely in such circumstances, when a translator is forced to guess or innovate, that beliefs important to him and not necessarily fathered on the underlying text are likely to come through.

The Peshitta rendering of 1 Chr. 5.2 not only has the rabbinic, and Targumic, expression 'King Messiah', but also by its use of the future tense ('will come forth') – where the Hebrew has the perfect tense – represents a Jewish perspective on messianism. Moreover, this future reference is followed by another future in the next clause ('will be given'), so that there is a consistency of perspective in the standard version. On the other hand, MS 9a of the Biblioteca Medicea Laurenziana, Florence, has the reading '*has* come forth': 'The King Messiah has come forth (*npq*) from Judah.' Apparently, a personal, scribal, perspective on the coming of the messiah is being expressed here. This would seem to be confirmed by the fact that

MS 9a1, like the rest of the MS tradition, uses the future tense in the second clause. The conclusion is hard to avoid that the originally Jewish perspective on messianism represented by the majority text has been altered in 9a1 to express a Christian viewpoint. For it is unlikely that a text expressing the (almost certainly Christian) view that the messiah (*sub specie* the Jewish 'King Messiah') had already come would be altered to imply that he had not yet come, since this alteration would very probably have to be located in that phase of the transmission of the Old Testament Peshitta when it had passed from Jewish to Christian custody. Equally, the use of 'come forth', recalling the prophecy in Mic. 5.1(2) much cited in Christian circles, makes it less likely that some Jewish messianic view, such as that the messiah was already existent but had yet to be revealed, is reflected in the minority reading.

In Conclusion

Insofar as 'resistance' features in this exposition of messianism in the Targum and Peshitta, discussion has operated at two levels. At the purely textual level, differences between the Targumic and Christian (essentially New Testament) interpretations of key Old Testament texts have been noted, but rushed judgements about anti-Christian polemic in the Targums have been resisted, if only because of the extent of the Targumic self-consistency on the disputed points. The Peshitta, for its part, gives little indication of *Tendenz* in these or other matters messianic, and since it substantially follows its Hebrew parent text, further summarizing comment will focus on the Targums.

The resistance that issues in the final redemption of Israel is repeatedly associated in the Targums with the figures of the Ephraimite Messiah and, mostly, the 'King Messiah', but this normally from a very 'end of days' perspective. There is little that could be construed as encouragement to 'hasten the coming' of the messiah by means of opposition and militancy in the face of Gentile oppression. Historical experience rather than more directly theological motivation, as in Christian circles (see above on Rom. 1.5), will have contributed strongly to this attitude. It is in the relatively late *Targum Canticles*, originating in the seventh or (more probably) eighth century C.E. (Alexander 2003: 55), that the dangers of messianically inspired activism most noticeably exercise the mind of a Targumist. This Targumist, in common with a great deal of rabbinic opinion, saw righteousness, prayer and the study of, and adherence to, Torah as the appropriate preparation for the revelation of the messiah (see 1.8; 7.13-14; 8.4):

> The King Messiah will say: 'I adjure you, O my people of the House of Israel, not to be stirred up against the nations of the world, in order to escape from exile, nor to rebel against the hosts of Gog and Magog. Wait yet a little till the nations that have come up to wage war against Jerusalem are destroyed, and after that the Lord of the World will remember for your sake the love of the righteous, and it shall be the Lord's good pleasure to redeem you.' (Alexander 2003: 193)

It is a pleasure to contribute to a volume that honours William Horbury and the vast erudition that he brings to the study of Jewish and Christian origins.

Chapter 20

JEWISH AND CHRISTIAN MESSIANIC HOPES IN PRE-ISLAMIC BYZANTIUM[1]

Nicholas de Lange

Both Judaism and Christianity grew up with a deep-seated messianic tension embedded in their very muscles and sinews. Every now and then this tension flares up until it becomes intense and in extreme cases unbearable. It is tempting to attribute these flare-ups to external causes, such as political oppression, or a generalized malaise in society due to rapid change or uncertain prospects. Such links may well seem fanciful, and it is never easy to establish them with confidence; often they have a strong whiff of the *post eventum* explanation about them. Messianic fervour may spread spontaneously, or it may be deliberately stirred up. It is always characterized by a dissatisfaction with the established order, ranging from impatience to deep despair.

Looking at the first Byzantine centuries from this viewpoint we might expect to be able to predict that as Christianity dramatically gained official acceptance after the great persecution and then gradually achieved political power in the Roman empire the stimulus to acute messianism would die away, while in Judaism the same political development would produce a contrary effect, official intolerance, isolation and marginalization giving rise to resentment and a powerful desire for change. But such expectations would be based on a simplistic view of the triumph of Christianity and the subjugation of the Jews. Christian history in the period from Constantine to Heraclius is marked by successive strains and crises: internal political and religious conflicts expressed in anathemas, schisms and occasional violence, not to mention foreign invasions and military defeats. The so-called barbarian invasions and the seemingly endless fighting with Persia must have stirred anyone with apocalyptic leanings. As for the Jews, despite an observable deterioration in their legal and social position, they enjoyed a good deal of stability at certain times and places. The background, then, is much more complicated than it may appear, and the story of Jewish and Christian messianism during this period is also a complicated one. In untangling the

---

1 It gives me special pleasure to dedicate this essay to a dearly loved colleague and friend, whose acuity, sagacity, encyclopaedic knowledge and unfailing good humour have accompanied me through thirty-five collegiate years. William Horbury's study of the theme of messianism in the liturgical poems of Yose ben Yose (which in his multifarious published *oeuvres* represents an isolated foray into this terrain) represents a pioneering contribution to the subject of these lines, and remains the best (and virtually the only) study of the theme in any of the early synagogue poets.

complexities there may be some benefit in considering the Jewish and Christian material together.[2]

It is indeed not easy to find firm evidence of a direct link between messianism and political events between the reign of Constantine I and that of Justinian I. To take first the case of the Jews, the apparently widespread Jewish yearning for the restoration of the Jerusalem temple and the Davidic kingdom may be naturally seen as a response to the loss of political autonomy and the destruction of the temple by the Romans, followed by centuries of subjugation, fiscal exactions and dispersion. Does that mean that the peaks of acute, urgent messianic expectation correspond necessarily with political events, such as rebellions, or with the anticipation of wars and possible regime change? This has often been asserted, both in general and in relation to specific episodes; the evidence, however, is generally too flimsy to support such claims in our period, at any rate before the sixth century.

A case in point is the assertion found in a number of histories that a Jewish revolt in Palestine during the period 351–3 had a messianic character, on the evidence of the statement of Aurelius Victor that the Jews 'nefariously raised Patricius to a kind of royalty'.[3] A series of recent studies has demonstrated that there is no basis for this assertion,[4] and it has even been denied that a Jewish rebellion against Roman rule took place at this time.[5]

The emperor Julian's planned rebuilding of the Jerusalem temple, frustrated by an earthquake datable probably in May 363, has often been interpreted in a messianic light. Careful recent studies of the evidence have, however, discounted this interpretation.[6]

Interestingly for the thesis of a link between political events and messianism, there is no hint in our sources of any Jewish messianic interpretation of the sack of Rome by Alaric in 410, and again by Gaiseric in 455.

Referring to a series of ominous floods, famines, comets and earthquakes during the reign of Justinian I in the sixth century, the historian S. W. Baron writes: 'If the Christian masses viewed these awesome events as messianic portents, how much more prepared were the minds of harassed Jewry to see in them signs of approaching redemption ... That is why large segments of the populace were

---

2 In what follows I adopt a deliberately broad definition of messianism. The focus is mainly on the eastern part of the Roman Empire. I have opted to treat Jewish and Christian messianism as two distinct topics bound together mainly by time and place; it seems to me that any study of mutual influences in this period would have to be built on dangerously slim foundations. For reasons of space I have omitted all discussion of the role of Jewish messianism in the Christian literature of the period, a large subject that deserves a study of its own. For an important illustration of some of the complexities of the topic see Kinzig 2003.
3 Aurelius Victor, *Caes.* 42.11.
4 Geiger 1979; Stemberger 1987: 132–50 (ET Stemberger 2000: 161–84); Arce 1987; Mor 1989.
5 Schäfer 1983, 1986: 197 (ET Schäfer 1995: 182).
6 'The Christian reports of the attempt to rebuild the Temple contain no reliable information about Julian's motivation for undertaking the project or Jewish reactions to it', Levenson 2004: 453. See also Stemberger 1987: 151–74 (ET Stemberger 2000: 185–216); Penella 1999; Borelli 2000. The attempt by Laceranza 2002 to discern a messianic interpretation in certain rabbinic sources relating to Rabbi Ahai of Lydda, while suggestive, remains speculative.

ready to follow any messianic pretender. It is almost unbelievable how many of these false messiahs, whether genuine ecstatics or ruthless careerists ... found immediate acceptance among the masses and little overt opposition on the part of the more sophisticated leaders.'[7] That the sixth century was a time of intense eschatological excitement among Christians is not in doubt,[8] but so far as the Jews are concerned Baron's sweeping claim is unsupported by any evidence, and the only example cited from the period before the Arab conquest is a false messiah in Crete who appeared a century earlier than the period under discussion, around 440, and who according to a contemporary Christian chronicler proclaimed himself a new Moses and promised to lead the Jews dryshod to Palestine; they threw themselves into the sea, and many were drowned, the remainder accepting baptism, according to our single source.[9] While there is no particular reason to doubt the historicity of the account, and while it certainly seems to indicate an interest in messianism at the time, it is hardly sufficient to sustain the edifice of Baron's speculation. A letter purportedly written about this time by the Jewish priests and leaders in Galilee announcing the end of the dispersion of the Jews and inviting them to hasten to Jerusalem for the feast of Tabernacles, 'since our kingdom will be restored in Jerusalem', is of very doubtful historical value.[10]

Moving on to the sixth century, a suggestion that from messianic motives a supposed descendant of King David, a son of the exilarch in Babylon, was appointed head of the rabbinic school or 'sanhedrin' in Tiberias in 520 must be judged highly speculative.[11] The event itself is only reported in a single medieval source.

We are on firmer ground as we progress towards the cataclysmic events of the early seventh century. Wars between Byzantium and Persia flared up under Anastasius I (reigned 491–518) and again under Justin II (reigned 565–78), and under Phocas (reigned 602–10) in 603. This extended period of alternating warfare and uneasy phases of peace and diplomacy evidently raised for some Jews a real prospect of an end to Christian rule; it culminated in a series of dramatic events under Heraclius (reigned 610–41) that had a marked impact on Jews and Christians alike. Jerusalem was captured by the Persians in 614. The supposed relic of the Cross of Christ, preserved in a silver casing in the Church of the Holy Sepulchre, was carried off to Persia, and the city was apparently handed over (for a period of some three years) to the Jews, who, according to Christian sources, exacted a bloody revenge on the remaining Christians of the city for long years of oppression.[12] It is not hard to guess at the feelings inspired by these events in those sensitive to the messianic beliefs of both religions. Within a few years the

7   Baron 1957: 3.16.
8   See below, and Mango 1980: 203–7.
9   Socrates, *HE* 7.38.
10   The letter is only mentioned in the Syriac life of the monk Barsauma: see Stemberger 1987: 247–50 (ET Stemberger 2000: 310–12). On Jewish life and letters generally at this time see de Lange 2005.
11   Irshai 2002: 207. See also Rabello 1987: 1.479–82.
12   On the interpretation of these sources in modern historiography see Horowitz 1998, 2006: 228–46.

Persians had taken Alexandria and were marching on Constantinople. Heraclius, playing on apocalyptic feelings fuelled by the capture of Jerusalem and the Cross, rallied Christians for a holy war on the infidel. His impressive victory over Persia (which some calculated had taken a symbolic six years to achieve, corresponding to the days of creation) was crowned by the calculatedly apocalyptic return of the True Cross to its place on Golgotha in 630. This was said to have been accompanied by a massacre of Jews in the Holy Land, and closely followed by a decree that all Jews in the empire should be baptized.[13] A great deal has been written about this period, and some of the echoes of political expectations in contemporary Jewish writings will be mentioned below. It must be stressed that the writings in question are not easily datable, and indeed attempts to date them have largely hinged on the assumption that acute messianism must be associated with political upheavals. Some of them are composite works that seem to have evolved in stages over some time, and sometimes there is no single definitive form of the text. Generally speaking, there is no reason to doubt that many of these works originated, in part at least, during the long period from 502 to 630, and the closer we approach the finale under Heraclius the closer the visible links between at least certain apocalyptic texts and the anticipated outcome of the fighting.[14]

In Christianity, too, it is difficult to identify explicit instances of acute messianism before at least the beginning of the sixth century. There is one fairly obvious explanation for this. There was an old belief that the world would last for six thousand years, corresponding to the six days of the creation (since from the divine perspective a thousand years are like a single day, Ps. 90.4). It was generally agreed that the advent of Christ came in the middle of the sixth and last of these millennia, indeed elaborate chronological systems were constructed to accommodate this date. Thus the end of the present order was not due until *ca.* 500 A.D. Hippolytus had spelt this out in his commentary on Daniel (4.23f.): the end of the sixth millennium would be followed by the 'sabbath', when Christ would come down from heaven and reign together with the saints (Rev. 20.4-5). But when Hippolytus was writing, at the beginning of the third century, the present order still had three centuries to run and the expected end was relatively remote. Similar views were expressed a little later by the chronographer Sextus Julius Africanus and others.

It is true that some others, like Hippolytus's contemporary Tertullian, saw the end as very near: the present world is worn out with age, and will soon be consumed with a great flame; the Antichrist is close at hand, gasping for Christian blood. Tertullian also mentions eyewitnesses who have seen something looking like a city suspended above Judaea, an allusion to a persistent Christian belief in the future restoration of the earthly Jerusalem (cf. Rev. 21.2).[15] Various beliefs of this kind were maintained in the early Church, and what they tended to have

---

13   See Dagron and Déroche 1991, esp. 28–32.
14   See van Bekkum 2002.
15   For a summary of the eschatological beliefs of Tertullian, Hippolytus and other early Fathers see Daley 1991: 25–43. On the restoration of Jerusalem in Christian thought see Wilken 1992, esp. 65–100.

in common was a belief in a two-stage Second Coming, in which the last judgement would be preceded by a thousand-year reign of the Messiah in this world. They were attacked by Origen, as resulting from a 'Jewish' reading of Scripture, in the name of an allegorizing Christian Platonism which categorically exalted the spiritual over the 'carnal' or material.[16]

While the allegorizing tendency did not completely crush millennial beliefs, it did tend to predominate in the Church. Eusebius (*Hist. eccl.* 7.24–5) mentions a bishop in the Fayyum named Nepos who wrote a *Refutation of the allegorists*, based on the visions of the Apocalypse, and looking forward to an earthly rule of Christ. Eusebius, following in the footsteps of Origen, describes his interpretation as 'rather Jewish', and explains that it was combated by Dionysius of Alexandria, a pupil of Origen, in a work entitled *On the promises*. Dionysius discovered that the millennarian doctrine propounded by Nepos had taken such hold in the region that entire churches had turned to 'schism and apostasy', a rather extreme point of view on the part of the allegorists, indicating, like the title of Nepos's work, an acute conflict within the Church. In his counterblast Dionysius undermined the authority of the Apocalypse, arguing that it was not a genuine work of the apostle John, and interpreting its visions allegorically. The story of Bishop Nepos, related by Eusebius, opens an all-too-rare window for us on this conflict in the church of the third century. From sparse references it is clear that the victory of the allegorists was not complete,[17] but it was very considerable, and indeed the scarcity of surviving millenarian literature from the church of the fourth and fifth centuries is a tribute to their success.

With the approach of the year 500, the end of the sixth millennium, however, urgent eschatological interest intensified. The Apocalypse, previously viewed with some suspicion in the eastern churches and often excluded from the canon of Scripture, was more widely read and commented on. The earliest extant Greek commentary (one of only three surviving) is by the sixth-century author Oecumenius: it accepts the book as part of the divinely inspired Scripture and expounds its relevance to the current situation, although Oecumenius does not specifically accept the view, propounded by others in his time, that the end of history is imminent.[18]

The year 500 fell during the reign of Anastasius. A very few years after this fateful date an unknown Greek writer took up an older Latin work, now lost, known as the *Tiburtine Sibyl*, and recast it as a prophecy of the last times. The 'birth pangs of the world', according to this 'Oracle of Baalbek', have already begun; the last times will begin in earnest after the death of Anastasius (predicted for the year 522). Savage fighting will break out; a series of kings, bearing the marks traditionally attached to the Antichrist, will rule during this period of violent destruction, culminating in a nameless 'king with the changing shape'. This

---

16   The relevant texts from the *First Principles* are clearly set out by Simonetti 1975. See also Wilken 1992: 76.
17   See, for example, the passage of Methodius of Olympus (d. *ca.* 311) discussed by Simonetti 1975: 54–8. For some examples of millenarianism outside the Greek-speaking churches in the fifth century see Daley 1991: 169 (Agathangelos) and 172 (Narsai). For further discussion of this incident, see Carleton Paget, this volume: 193–4.
18   See Daley 1991: 179–83.

terrible ruler will slay Enoch and Elijah, who have risen to fight against him, but he will be killed in turn by Christ, who will come from heaven 'like a great flashing star'. After the last judgement, Christ will rule with his holy angels.[19]

Elements of this apocalyptic vision, including the return of Enoch and Elijah, can be traced in earlier prophecies. The Antichrist, in particular, is a familiar figure in Christian speculation about the last times, rooted in the prophetic visions of Daniel and the Apocalypse, and assuming many different forms in different contexts.[20] Whereas for Origen and his followers the name encompasses a multitude of abstract, impersonal ills that can be summed up as false ways of reading the sacred Scriptures, for other Christian writers it refers to a real person, a future tyrannical figure, probably of Jewish origin (although some identified him with the emperor Nero), who will secure absolute power over the world until the coming of his cosmic enemy, the true Christ. It has often been suggested that this interpretation is particularly associated with times of persecution of Christians, or, in the Christian empire, political crisis.

In the troubled century following the death of Anastasius eschatological predictions intensified, and there were some Christians who even identified emperor Justinian I (reigned 527–65) with the expected Antichrist.[21] When in 557 the city of Constantinople was shaken by a terrible earthquake prophecies of the end of the world proliferated and the population panicked. It was around this time that Romanos the Melodist composed his *kontakion* on the Second Coming, which dwells at length on the figure of the Antichrist:

> Then he will make for himself a special temple, deceiving the Hebrew nation and others – the lawless one,
> when he performs fabricated illusions and signs, the tyrant.
> He changes himself from one form to another, he flies into the air,
> and cunningly gives the demons the appearance of angels
> to carry out his orders with zeal.
> Tribulation and constraint there will be for humankind, great and without measure,
> through which all your servants are tested,
>   *Judge most just.*[22]

With the resumption of the Persian wars in the second half of the sixth century an intensified mood of anxiety and apocalyptic speculation can be discerned in Christian literature, centring, as we have already observed, on the holy city of Jerusalem.

The foregoing remarks may serve to place the Jewish messianism of the age of Justinian and Heraclius into some kind of perspective. This messianism may be discerned in various writings: I shall concentrate here on three genres: liturgy, hymnography and apocalypse.

The Hebrew liturgy of the synagogue, so far as we can reconstruct it, expresses a strong sense of longing for redemption (*ge'ullah*).[23] This is particularly felt in some

19   Alexander 1967.
20   See McGinn 1994; Badilita 2005.
21   Procopius, *Secret History* 8.13; 12.19–32. See Rubin 1961.
22   Lash 1995: 224.
23   On what follows see particularly Heinemann 1977. See also Reif 1998.

of the petitionary prayers of the *amidah* (the main statutory prayer), in such formulations as these:[24]

> Sound the great ram's horn for our liberation, and raise a banner to gather in our exiles, [and gather us together from the four corners of the world to your holy abode]. Blessed are you, Lord who gathers the dispersed ones of his people Israel.
> Restore our judges as in olden times and our counsellors as at the beginning, [and remove from us sorrow and sighing; and reign over us as king, O Lord, you alone with compassion, righteousness and justice]. Blessed are you, Lord, the king who loves [righteousness and] justice.
> But for the apostates let there be no hope [if they do not return to your Torah;] [and may you speedily uproot, smash and humble the arrogant empire in our days]. [And may the Christians and the *minim* [heretics] perish in an instant and may all the foes of your people and their persecutors be speedily cut off, and break the yoke of the gentiles from off our necks.] Blessed are you, Lord who smashes the wicked and humbles the arrogant ...
> Return in mercy to Jerusalem your city, and rebuild it soon in our time to last for ever. Blessed are you, Lord who rebuilds Jerusalem. [*Some texts read:* Have mercy O Lord upon us and on Israel your people and on Jerusalem your city and on your shrine and your temple and your abode, and on Zion the dwelling place of your glory, and rebuild it *etc.*]
> Cause the scion of David your servant to spring up [speedily], and exalt his horn with your salvation, [for we await your salvation all day long]. Blessed are you, Lord who makes the horn of salvation to spring up.

The following words are preserved among the prayers following the prophetic reading (*haftarah*):

> Show compassion to Zion, for she is the home of our lives, and save her who is grieved in spirit speedily in our days. Blessed are you, Lord who makes Zion rejoice in her children.
> Make us rejoice, O Lord our God, through Elijah the prophet your servant and through the kingdom of the house of David your messiah, speedily may he come and gladden our hearts; on his throne let no stranger sit and let others no longer inherit his glory, for you have sworn to him by your holy Name that his lamp shall never be extinguished. Blessed are you, Lord, the Shield of David.

Other similarly worded prayers may be found, for instance in the worship for the New Year and Atonement Day festivals.

While the wording of these prayers is definitely messianic (we may note particularly the mention of Elijah and David) and contains a repeated note of urgency, it is far removed from the elaborate apocalypticism to be found in some other writings, and even biblical allusions are handled with severe restraint. The prayers may be seen as striking a compromise between the quietism that can be discerned in some rabbinic writings[25] and the full-blooded visions of the apocalypses.

Hebrew hymnography (*piyyut*) of this period, as one might expect, reflects the expectations of the liturgy, with each author contributing his own perspective.[26]

---

24   The translations are based on the edition by Luger 2001 (5761). Wording enclosed in square brackets is found in some but not all texts.
25   On which see de Lange 1978.
26   On the place of the *piyyut* in the late antique synagogue see Levine 2000a, esp. 552–6; Yahalom 1999. On Hebrew hymnography in general see Weinberger 1998. See also Alexander, this volume: 231–2.

William Horbury, in a masterly study, has analysed messianic elements in the *piyyutim* of Yose ben Yose (5th century?), which he summarizes in the following words:

> Yose's messianism hopes above all for the establishment of God's kingdom and the return of the divine Bridegroom to his sanctuary and people. This hope embraces a series of expectations, from the downfall of Edom [the Roman empire] and the return of the Shekhinah [the divine presence] to the resurrection of the dead, the defeat of antichrist and God's sole rule. His presentation of them is urgent, nationalistic but theocentric; concerned with God's Law, and concerned still more obviously with sanctuary, sacrifice, sin and atonement.[27]

Most of these elements echo themes already noted in the synagogue liturgy, but a few demand further comment. The 'divine Bridegroom' points to the rich use of biblical imagery in the *piyyutim*, which indeed often integrate entire biblical verses cited ostensibly in confirmation of the ideas set forth. Each biblical citation or allusion carries its baggage of pre-existing interpretation, often heavily messianic, but the poet has the freedom to rework both citations and interpretations. Thus, in Yose, the Bridegroom of the Song of Songs is more liable to represent God himself than the messiah, as in some other interpretations. Edom or Esau is a common designation, in rabbinic midrash as well as in *piyyut*, of Rome, denoting at first the pagan empire and later, naturally enough, its Christian successor.[28] 'Antichrist' (never so named in the Jewish sources) is shorthand for a powerful enemy who will achieve dominion in the last days, to be eventually overcome and slain by the messiah; he can sometimes be identified with the Roman emperor.

The *urgency* of Yose's messianic tone deserves closer attention, as it may at first sight appear to represent a departure from the standard messianic expectations of the midrash and the liturgy. It is discerned by Horbury in such lines as:

> Stir and awake the *joy of the whole earth* [Jerusalem, Ps. 48.3],
> and establish thy throne in the city of the KINGDOM

or:

> Contend, O *saviours* [Obad 21], take the glory from Edom:
> and set upon the Lord the majesty of the KINGDOM[29]

Yet these are relatively conventional petitions, and they lack even the adverb 'speedily' that is so often repeated in the liturgy. A more explicit urgency is found in the *piyyutim* of Yehudah, an otherwise unknown poet whose works have been recovered from the Cairo Genizah. His *qedushta'ot* (hymns to embellish the *'amidah*) follow a very strict and regular form, in which the fourth element always begins with the words *'ad matai* ('how long?'), and expresses genuine impatience for redemption. Here are some examples:

27 Horbury 1981: 178 (repr. in Horbury 2003b: 323).
28 See de Lange 1978; Hadas-Lebel 1984.
29 Horbury 1981: 160–1, 175 (=Horbury 2003b: 306–7, 320) [the translation is Horbury's].

> How long will the perpetual offering fail from your throngs,
> and your lodging place be given over to eaters of pigs' flesh?
> Be zealous on account of our zeal to restore it to your abode,
> let my prayer be set forth before you as incense [Ps. 141.2].
>
> From the four corners of the world to my holy house
> gather to Zion all the seed of my holy ones
> and on the three pilgrim festivals may my assembled ones be seen;
> kings shall bring presents to you [Ps. 68.30] ...
>
> How long will our Land be desolate,
> and she who is fair as the moon and pure as the sun cry out?
> Her firstfruits count for naught until you quicken those who lie fast asleep,
> you send forth your spirit and they are created, and renew the face of the earth [Ps. 104.30]
> ...
>
> How long shall we dwell outside the Land,
> while the ruler [or guardian angel?] of Edom is exalted unto heaven?
> Humble him and cause him to descend to the depths of the earth,
> and let heaven be glad and the earth rejoice [Ps. 96.10].[30]

Despite these expressions of impatience, Yehudah, who probably lived and wrote in the sixth century, shares with his predecessor Yose ben Yose a tendency to focus on God's return to Zion, rather than the person of the messiah, to whom he rarely alludes. A contemporary of Yehudah's, Simeon bar Megas, is more explicit, as in this poetic elaboration on the theme of Esau, the elder brother, and Jacob (Israel), the lesser:

> His mother and father called him elder,
> but you said, I will make you [Esau] least [Obad. 2] ...
> Hasten the great day,
> Hurry, that the smallest [Israel] become a mighty nation ...
> The prince [Joseph] who began [his search] with the eldest [Gen. 44.12]
> [bring nigh] the time when the lesser Messiah will issue from him ...
> send the mighty prince [Michael, Dan. 12.1],
> that he may save both great and small.[31]

The messiah of the tribe of Joseph (or Ephraim), who will die in battle with Israel's enemies, before the latter are defeated by the messiah of the house of David, is found in various sources, rabbinic, targumic and apocalyptic. It is the Davidic messiah who is referred to under the name Menahem, 'the comforter', in this poem by Simeon bar Megas:

> Send us the man called Menahem;
> vengeance will sprout from him.
> Let him come in our day
> and may authority rest on his shoulders [Isa. 9.5].[32]

30 Cf. van Bekkum 1998: 45 (cf. xv), 87, 104 (cf. xvi).
31 Translation by Weinberger 1998: 37.
32 Translation by Weinberger 1998: 38.

There may be an allusion to the antichrist-figure in a poem on the tenth plague (the slaying of the firstborn): just as the tenth plague led to the Exodus, so may the tenth king come soon, heralding Israel's latter-day redemption.[33] Yet although he is freer in mentioning the messiah than some other poets, Simeon too places the emphasis firmly on God, his return to Zion, and the restoration of sacrificial worship.

Quite different in character are the apocalyptic texts that have been dated to the period of Heraclius on the basis of references to contemporary events. The best-known of these is the *Prophecy and dream of Zerubbabel son of Shealtiel*.[34] Zerubbabel is carried miraculously to Rome, where he meets the Davidic messiah, named as Menahem son of Ammiel, together with the archangel Michael, who tells him of the future salvation of Israel. The scenario is confused in the extreme in the text as it has come down to us. Hephzibah, the mother of the messiah, will attack and kill two kings. Five years later the messiah of the house of Joseph and Ephraim, by name Nehemiah son of Hushiel, will appear and gather all Israel; they will stay in Jerusalem and offer sacrifices. Five years later, however, the king of Persia will attack them, but thanks to Hephzibah and her magical staff, the 'wicked one', who is the ninth king, will die. But there is worse to come. The tenth king, Armilos,[35] the offspring of Satan and the image of a virgin, will dominate the world with violence and will kill Nehemiah son of Hushiel and his righteous companions, and the people of Israel will flee to the wilderness. But Menahem, the Davidic messiah, will make his appearance with Elijah the prophet; he will bring Nehemiah son of Hushiel back to life and Israel will be saved. The Lord will descend upon the Mount of Olives and blow a great ram's horn; he will do battle against Gog and Magog and the forces of Armilos (who will have been slain by Menahem). After this final war the dead will be brought back to life and the two messiahs, with Elijah, will go up to Jerusalem. Israel will offer sacrifices to God once more, and he will rejoice at their smell and bring down to earth the temple that was built above.

This apocalypse, and others like it,[36] are far removed from the restrained and learned language of liturgy and piyyut (with which, however, they share many elements), and are closer to that of Christian apocalypses from this period that are preserved in Greek and Syriac, such as the *Oracle of Baalbek* mentioned above. This is a popular genre, spread by seers and holy men, rather than an expression of official religion; it is clearly born of the excitement and uncertainties of very troubled times.

To summarize: messianism takes varied forms, and these may readily co-exist. As comparative study underlines, for both Jews and Christians the sixth and early seventh centuries mark a high point in acute, urgent messianic fervour resulting

---

33   Yahalom 1984: 182.
34   The text has been edited by Israël Lévi from the so-called *Chronicles of Yerahmeel* (conveniently reprinted in Patlagean 1994). It is translated by M. Himmelfarb in Stern and Mirsky 1990. A more recent edition by Even-Shmuel (Kaufman) 1954 is largely the product of the editor's imagination and cannot be relied on.
35   See Dan 1998.
36   See now Spurling 2004.

at times in elaborate apocalyptic visions. This development coincides with political events and is clearly related to them; indeed it is sometimes exploited by political leaders.

Heraclius's reconquest of Jerusalem was short-lived. Already a new enemy had made its appearance in the form of the Arabs or 'Saracens', and it was said that a prophet had appeared among them proclaiming the advent of the coming anointed one or messiah. Under Arab rule both Jews and Christians – but particularly the Christians, compelled to accustom themselves to the condition of a subject people long familiar to the Jews – experienced new manifestations of messianic speculation. But that is another story.

Chapter 21

False Prophet, False Messiah and the Religious Scene in Seventh-Century Jerusalem

Guy G. Stroumsa

The early Christian figure of Antichrist, like that of Christ, owes much to concepts current among Jews from before the time of Pompey. William Horbury has followed the early traces of the myth of a messianic opponent, which would remain active throughout the Roman period.[1] While the birth of Christianity might well have been the most potent historical consequence of Jewish Messianism, it was certainly not the last. Sometimes dormant, Jewish and Christian eschatological expectations never died out: Jewish messianic movements and Christian intense expectations of the *parousia*, or Second Coming of Christ, have punctuated the history of the two religions. In some cases, a combination of these two phenomena has had an explosive effect and some dramatic consequences. Such a combination occurred in seventh-century Palestine, and bears directly upon the earliest stages of Islam.

The purpose of the following pages is to highlight some aspects of Jewish and Christian late antique eschatological conceptions, in particular the figures of the false prophet and of the false Messiah. More precisely, I shall try to focus on conflicting beliefs and expectations regarding the Temple Mount in Jerusalem.

As in our own days, there existed in the seventh century a direct link between Messianism and geo-politics. From the two empires which clashed in the early years of the seventh century, one would disappear before its end, to be replaced by a new one. The Byzantines were able to understand the Islamic invaders only as the bearers of a yet unknown kind of Christian heresy – as is clear from John of Damascus, writing in the first half of the eighth century.[2] The fundamental difficulty for Christian intellectuals to understand Islam on its own terms points to the fact that what we call today the 'clash of civilizations' was also a conflict of interpretations within the monotheistic traditions. This conflict, however, was not simply one between Christians and Muslims; it also involved the Jews, who sat on both sides of the political, cultural and linguistic divide. While we still ignore much of the state of affairs in Arabia, the importance of the presence

---

1   See Horbury 1998d. For an excellent collection of the early Christian texts on Antichrist, with translation and notes, see Potestà and Rizzi 2005. I should like to thank James Carleton Paget for his useful remarks on the draft of this text.
2   See Sahas 1972; see also G. Stroumsa forthcoming (a).

of both Jews and Jewish religious ideas in pre-Islamic Arabia is now being recognized.[3] While it remains difficult to identify precisely the kind of Judaism involved, it probably did not include only 'orthodox' Rabbinic Judaism (whether one can speak about such a thing in Arabia at all), but also Jewish Christianity, perhaps of different kinds.

Prophecy was one of the central concepts around which polemics raged between the different groups claiming to possess wisdom and truth from divine revelation. For each group, the others' claim to knowledge was a false one, as it was based upon false prophecy. While the concept of prophecy has been much studied, the same cannot be said about its reverse, the idea of false prophecy.[4]

I

From the New Testament on, early Christian texts reflect a constant preoccupation with false prophets.[5] It is however for the Jewish Christians, and in particular for the Ebionites, that the problem of false prophecy was of crucial importance in the economy of salvation. 'They seek to comment on the prophecies with an excessive attention', notes Irenaeus.[6] The idea of prophecy is absolutely essential to Ebionite theology, in particular as it appears in the Pseudo-Clementine *Homilies*. For the Ebionites, the identity of Jesus is defined by his prophecy. Jesus is for them the last incarnation of the 'True Prophet', who, since Adam, from generation to generation, presents the divine message to mankind. In each generation, however, the True Prophet is preceded by a false prophet, an impostor sent by Satan, who claims to be the True Prophet. Truth and Lie are thus for ever coupled, throughout the ages, in 'syzygies' of opposites. The false prophets are 'the prophets of this world', who remain for ever ignorant of eternal truths.[7] Thus Cain precedes Abel, Ishmael precedes Isaac, Esau precedes Jacob, Aaron precedes Moses, and Paul precedes Peter. False prophets are feminine, and are born from women. False prophecy, indeed, stems from Eve, just as true prophecy stems from Adam. False prophets are impostors, who bring a false doctrine. Hence, a false gospel precedes the revelation of the True Gospel.[8]

---

3   See for instance Robin 2003. Contemporary research on the Jewish and Christian background of the earliest strata of Islam owes probably more to the iconoclastic approach of Crone and Cook 1977 than to any other single work.
4   On false prophets in the Hebrew Bible, see for instance Buber 1964; von Rad 1933; Quell 1952; Osswald 1962. Cf. Mendelsohn 1973, and Paul 1973, who both point out the weakness of the differentiation criteria between true and false prophets as presented by the Deuteronomist.
5   In the New Testament, see in particular Mt. 7.15, 1 Cor. 12.27-28, 1 Jn 2.18, 2 Pet. 2.1. Further references include *Did.* 11: 3-10 (cf. 12: 1-2; 16: 3); Hermas, *Mand.* 11.7–8, 11; Justin Martyr, *Dial.* 69.1; Origen, *Cels.* 7.9. William Horbury has called attention to the symmetry between the behaviour of false prophets and that of itinerant philosophers such as the Cynics; see Horbury 1998d, 111–26.
6   Irenaeus, *Haer.* 1.26.2; (2, 346–7 Rousseau-Doutreleau).
7   Ps.-Clement, *Hom.* 2.15.4.
8   Ps.-Clement, *Hom.* 2.17.4. Cf. *Hom.* 1.18.1–19.8; 3.17.25.

Although this doctrine of the syzygies is well known, it has been granted too little attention in the context of polemics against false prophets in ancient Christian literature. If the many false prophets are so dangerous for humankind, it is because they mislead men, as they succeed in presenting error as truth, in order to ensure the acceptance of their doctrines (cf. Mt. 7.15). Truth and error thus appear as mixed (*Hom.* 1.19), and a test is necessary in order to distinguish true prophets from impostors (*Hom.* 2.5.10).[9]

A remarkably similar conception is found in a text from Nag Hammadi, the *Second Treatise of the Great Seth*.[10] In this text, Adam, then Abraham, Isaac, Jacob, David, Solomon, the twelve prophets, Moses and John the Baptist, are called 'laughing stocks' (*côbe*), as they have been created by the Hebdomad as so many imitations of the true prophets. This text probably reflects the Gnostic reinterpretation of a Jewish-Christian *theologoumenon*.

It is in this context that we must see the Christian perception of Mani, false prophet, magician and impostor (*goès*), who had learned his craft from his master Scythianus, trying in vain to accomplish true miracles. For the heresiologists, his very name reveals his folly, his *mania*.[11] The chain of the true prophets is indeed a Jewish-Christian *theologoumenon*, which is found also in the Manichaean conception of the succession of prophets from Adam to Mani. But the Manichaean conception is more complex, as it involves a *double* chain of prophecy.

A double list of prophets, sent throughout history and to the different regions of the world, is typical of the Manichaean structure of prophecy. On the one hand, there is a diachronic list of prophets, from Adam to Christ to Mani, which includes prophets of the antediluvian times such as Enoch – but not the biblical prophets properly so called. The synchronic list, on the other hand, mentions Buddha in the East, Zarathustra in the central lands, and Jesus in the West, all preceding Mani. Each was sent only to one area of the world, while Mani, the only prophet to offer a total revelation, valid for all peoples, in the entire *oikoumenè*, seals prophecy. The double chain of prophecy, which was known for a long time from various Manichaean texts, is epitomized in a recently published Coptic *Kephalaion*.[12]

The Manichaean double chain of prophecy, both through the ages and through the universe, has always been considered by scholars to be an original theme, devised by Mani himself, the first thinker to have established a consciously

---

9   On the importance of syzygies in Ebionite theology, see in particular the work of H. J. Schoeps, well synthesized in Schoeps 1969: 88–91.
10   CG VII.2, 62–3.
11   Epiphanius, *Panarion* 66. A similar etymology is found in the *Acta Archelai*.
12   See Tardieu 1988: 153–82. As Tardieu points out, this very important text represents the oldest literary document on the expansion of Buddhism in the Kushan empire. The Kushan empire was from the late first to the third centuries C.E. an important Buddhist power, where Graeco-Roman, Indian and Iranian cultures mixed to a remarkable extent, and known for its widespread cultural, artistic and religious syncretism. Moreover, the *Kephalaion* emphasizes the formative importance of Buddhist influence in the early stages of Manichaeism.

universal religion. If my analysis above is correct, this *communis opinio* should be qualified. The Manichaean double chain of prophecy is highly reminiscent of Tatian's and Clement's conception of two kinds of *barbaros philosophia*, that of the Hebrews and those of the Eastern barbarian peoples. The similarities between these two mythological frames seem too close to be the fruit of chance.[13] The basic structure of Manichaean revelation throughout the generations and among the different cultures appears to have been, rather than a total novelty, a new development, stemming from an already existing Christian scheme. This scheme had been accepted, in particular, by those Christian thinkers who kept a particular interest in traditions of the East.

For the Christian eschatological tradition, the false prophet, who according to Jewish-Christian theology appears at different stages in history, each time preceding the coming of a true prophet, makes a final appearance at the end of times. According to the book of Revelation, (Rev. 13.11-18), the false prophet is the lieutenant of the Antichrist, an enormous beast coming from the earth, but masquerading as a sheep, i.e., taking the appearance of justice. Simulacra, lying prodigies, counterfeit prophecies, reflect the character of this false Messiah, who seeks to imitate, one last time, the deeds of Christ. As shown in the writings of Victorinus of Poetovio, the false prophet, then, is also a central figure of Christian eschatological thought.[14] It is in this eschatological context that one must understand the 'false prophecy' of such figures as Montanus, Mani and Muhammad.

II

After the Montanist crisis, the possibility of Christian prophecy must have been much weakened, and relegated to heretical trends. Yet, the impressive resilience and continued impact of the topic of false prophecy shows that such movements were not quite marginalized. Since, for the Rabbis, too, the age of prophecy was officially closed, one finds in Rabbinic as well as in Patristic literature relatively few discussions on 'the signs of prophecy', the criteria which permit one to distinguish between true and false prophets. Such discussions will become absolutely capital in Islamic theological literature, as Muhammad is defined as a prophet.[15] The main accusation against Muhammad, throughout centuries of Christian anti-Muslim polemics, in the Middle Ages and until the early Modern times, has always been the accusation of false prophecy: for both Christians (and also, to some extent, for Jews), Muhammad was an impostor, who succeeded in appearing as a prophet. In the Qur'an, and then in the Kalam, Muhammad is identified not simply as a prophet, but as the seal of the prophets, the *ḫātam al-nabiyîn*, even if this expression seems to have meant, originally, 'confirmation' rather than 'end' of prophecy.[16] Actually, Muhammad is not the first to have used

---

13   For a detailed argumentation, see G. Stroumsa 1996.
14   See Dulaey 1993, vol. I: 204–6, vol. II: 101.
15   See S. Stroumsa 1999: 22–4 and nn. 16, 23.
16   See Friedmann 1986.

this expression, which appears already in Manichaean texts, where it is Mani's disciples who are the 'seal' of his prophecy, i.e., its testimony and authentification.[17]

We have seen how the idea of true and false prophecy was absolutely central for the Jewish Christians. Indeed, for them (and for them only) there was an adequacy between the concept of prophet and that of messiah. We have known for some time that some Jewish Christian groups remained in existence quite late, certainly in Palestine, until at least the eighth century, when John of Damascus, sitting in the monastery of Mar Saba in the Judaean wilderness, testifies to their presence on the shores of the Dead Sea.[18] Shlomo Pines, on his side, has argued for the presence of a Jewish Christian community in Jerusalem during the reign of Mu'awwiyah.[19]

The fact that these late Jewish Christians might have been only a small sect does in no way mean that they remained marginalized, having no impact on society at large. Warnings against Judaizing practices were common in seventh-century Christian literature, and might point to the continued presence and influence of Jewish-Christian groups. Thus, the *Doctrina Jacobi* reflects a preoccupation with Judaizers who observed the sabbath as they were expecting the second coming of the Anointed One, i.e., the Messiah. (1.19).[20] It stands to reason, then, to postulate that they may have played some role in the polemic on true and false prophecy and Messianism between Jews and Christians in the seventh century.

As Shlomo Pines has pointed out, for instance, Abu Isa al-Isfahani (d. *ca.* 750), a leader of a Jewish sect who led a rebellion against the Caliph 'Abd al-Malik b. Marwan, was probably influenced in his self-conception by Jewish-Christian beliefs when he presented Jesus and Muhammad as true prophets.[21] Pines then asks himself whether 'the views held on the evidence of the *Doctrina Jacobi* at the time of the advent of Islam may be regarded as a form of reaction to this event or may have preceded it', and perhaps at some stage helped to shape the beliefs of the followers of the new religion. He answers that 'in our present state of knowledge, no conclusive answer to this complex of questions is possible.'[22] I propose here to review the evidence, in the hope that it might shed some new light on the question at hand.

Since at least the Iranian conquest of Jerusalem in 614, and the taking of the Holy Cross in captivity, both Jews and Christians in Palestine felt they were living in apocalyptic times. The Apocalyptic trends of early Christianity, which had gone dormant in the aftermath of the Constantinian revolution, were reactivated. The Christian world was rife with expectations of the *Endzeit*, with its traditional imagery of cosmic war between the forces of light and those of darkness. In Averil

---

17 See G. Stroumsa 1986. See also Colpe 1990. Colpe and I reached the same conclusions simultaneously, and independently of one another. See further R. Simon 1997.
18 See G. Stroumsa 1985.
19 See Pines 1984.
20 The best edition of this capital text is that of Déroche 1991.
21 Pines 1968, esp. 254. Cf. Starr 1937.
22 See Pines 1984: 152.

Cameron's words, 'Islam took shape within a context of extreme religious and cultural tension.'[23]

The new clash between the Christian and the Islamic imperial states was indeed nurtured in the cocoon of the Jewish-Christian conflict of interpretations, which only superficially appear to repeat in essence, and ad nauseam, old arguments over an issue decided long previously. The argumentation of these early polemics, centred upon the interpretation of biblical prophecies, revolved mainly around the figure of Christ as the Messiah announced by the prophets of Israel. For the Jews, the Messiah was yet to come, while for the Christians, he was to return in full glory, and establish his kingdom, at long last, over the earth. For the Chiliasts of the first centuries, most clearly exemplified, perhaps, by Irenaeus, Jerusalem, and in particular the Temple Mount, would become at the end of times the epicentre of dramatic events at the cosmic level (see *Haer.* 5.25–30). The Chiliastic debate which had raged in the first Christian centuries focused on issues of inheritance of the Holy Land and restoration of the Jews to their own land.[24] Early Christian Chiliastic expectations had very strong Jewish roots.[25]

A comparative study of late antique Jewish and Christian eschatology remains a desideratum, which should emphasize the differences as well as the similarities between the two movements: indeed, the political situation of the Jews was vastly different from that of the Byzantine Christians. The former did not have anything to lose from the change of political and religious power. On the contrary, they had much to gain, and it was easier for them to bet on the new, previously unknown force. They could thus easily have placed their hopes of religious and political renewal with the Muslim conquerors.

For Byzantine Christians, the Messiah expected by the Jews would be the last impostor, the Antichrist. From the fourth century on, the Jews, on the other hand, believed that they were ruled by believers in a false Messiah. Victory for one side meant defeat for the other: a zero-sum game, in modern strategic terminology. The clearest expression of a Jewish vindication would be the re-establishment of the Temple. For the Christians, such a threat was tantamount to the coming of the Antichrist, who had been described, in Irenaeus' classical version of the myth, as well as in the slightly later version of Hippolytus, as establishing his throne, for three and a half years, until he would be finally defeated by Jesus Christ, in the Temple itself. For the Christian *psyche*, such a threat did not belong only to the ancient past. The memories of the great anxiety generated by Julian's authorization to rebuild the Temple, and the fact that work had actually started, before a providential earthquake had brought these efforts to naught, do not seem to have quite disappeared for a long time.[26] In the seventh century, with the Iranian violent conquest and its deeply humiliating result, the Holy Cross in

---

23 Cameron 1991. On this, see de Lange, this volume: 274–84.
24 See Heid 1993.
25 For a recent study of a particularly interesting aspect of early Christian eschatology, see Vianès-Abou Samra 2004. See further Hill 1992.
26 See Wilken 1992.

enemy custody, and the new wave of successful invasion by the barbarian Arabs, the old questions were raised again, with a new urgency.[27] Who could these Arabs really be, the Christians asked themselves, who stemmed from their Southern desert, claiming to follow the lead of their prophet? Might they not really represent, in disguise, the powerful arm of the Jews, sent to reclaim their pretensions on the Holy Land and in the Holy City? Paradoxically, the great fear of the Christians had more to do with the shadow of the Jews than with the Arab invaders.

For the Jews, the end of Christian domination offered a chance, or so they thought, to rebuild the Temple.[28] This possibility could not have been envisaged with equanimity by the Christians, for whom such an event would be tantamount to the belated victory of the despised old religion. Such a victory would announce the coming of the Antichrist before Christ's *parousia* at the end of times – an eschatological imagery inherited from the earliest stages of Christian literature. It is often assumed that the coming of the Arabs meant the end of the Jewish hopes in the city.[29] Such a view, however, reflects the eventual outcome of Islamic rule, compressing and flattening the dramatic events of the seventh century. For some time, at least, it seems that the Arab invasion presented the Jews with a new chance of finally getting rid of the hated Byzantines, and an opportunity to rebuild their Temple.

A generation ago, Michael Cook and Patricia Crone showed, in their groundbreaking *Hagarism*, the extent to which earliest Islam must be understood as the product of the preaching of Judaic Messianism in a Gentile environment.[30] In recent years, important epigraphic studies have done much to sharpen our perception of the Jewish element in the Arabian background of Muhammad's preaching. Christian Robin notes the importance, as revealed by these findings, of both Jewish presence and Jewish ideas in the Arabic peninsula as early as the fourth century. For him, this weakens the need for appeal to Jewish ideas imported from Palestine, as proposed by Cook and Crone.[31] Here, adopting another perspective, I wish to emphasize the cross-fertilization of Jewish and Christian beliefs in the Holy Land, with particular reference to the eschatological expectations of both Jews and Christians around the Temple Mount.[32]

The Byzantines were slow in understanding the true faith of their new conquerors. The Arabs remained for them, for too long, barbarians coming from the desert, and Muhammad was perceived as a false prophet, whose faith could be understood only in the categories of Christian theology, namely, as a heresy.[33] Although it would

---

27 See Kaegi 2003: 79–80 and 204–7.
28 On the state of Byzantine Jewry in the seventh century, Starr 2003 is still valid.
29 See for instance Cameron 1998, esp. 204.
30 Crone and Cook 1977.
31 See Robin 2003.
32 On the Temple Mount and its complex and highly charged religious significance, see G. Stroumsa forthcoming (b).
33 See Hoyland 1997. On Muhammad, see esp. John of Damascus, *Adv. Haer.*, Heresy 101 (the last and worst heresy, according to the author, invented by the false prophet Muhammad, who, having learned some elements of biblical religion, convinced the pagan Arabs by simulating piety).

eventually settle down, for centuries, there was a deep-seated political and religious conflict, sometimes more overt, sometimes relatively dormant, which started as a 'big bang', epitomized, more than anything else, by Omar's conquest of Jerusalem and the ensuing dramatic changes in the religious topography of the city.

In recent years, much scholarly effort has been spent on analysing the complex relationship between Jews and Christians in seventh-century Byzantium.[34] In a series of important publications, distinguished Byzantinists such as Gilbert Dagron, Averil Cameron, Cyril Mango or Vincent Déroche have done much to provide us with a clearer understanding of the complex interface between Jews and Christians in the seventh century, in particular from the perspective of the Greek texts.[35] These and other scholars have underlined the renewed importance of disputes between Jews and Christians in the Eastern Roman Empire of the seventh century. In particular, they have highlighted the centrality of the Holy Land, of the Holy City, and of its core, the Temple Mount, in these disputes, as well as their direct impact on the earliest stages of Islam. The spiritual demotion of *vetus Israel* by *Verus Israel* had been symbolized by the relocation of the sanctified *locus*, from the Temple Mount, whose emptiness should remain striking, visible to all, by the new basilica of the *Anastasis*. Oleg Grabar has called this process of relocation an *eislithosis*,[36] while Annabel Warthon has referred to the Byzantine *erasure* of the Jewish dimension of Jerusalem.[37]

More work, however, is needed for a careful synoptic analysis of both the Christian and the Jewish sources, in Hebrew and Aramaic as well as in Greek and Syriac. The Jewish sources, in particular, are much less understood than the Christian ones. For some of the most important ones (such as the *Book of Zerubbabel*), we even lack a critical edition, and the texts are difficult to date with precision.[38] A comparative view of all the available sources relevant to the renewed tensions between Jews and Christians in seventh-century Jerusalem could shed new light on the cultural and religious tensions which were in the background of the emergence and early development of Islam.[39]

The Islamic conquest of Jerusalem in 638 at once rekindled the fears of the Christians and the hopes of the Jews, bringing them to new levels of intensity. The conquerors, seeking to do what we could call, in the Hegelian sense, an *Aufhebung* of both Judaism and Christianity, moved back its sacred core from the Basilica of the *Anastasis* to the Temple Mount. For the Byzantine historiographer Theophanes, it was Omar's devilish pretence which made him seek to emulate Solomon.[40]

---

34 See for instance Stemberger 1999.
35 See for instance Dagron and Déroche 1991; Mango 1999; Déroche 1999.
36 Grabar 1999.
37 Warthon 2000.
38 See Lévi 1915–35. See further Dan 1998 and Himmelfarb 1990.
39 Cameron 2002.
40 See De Boor 1883, and Mango and Scott 1997.

Indeed, other sources indicate that the Muslim building activity on the Mount was at first perceived by some Jews and some Christians, as an attempt at rebuilding the Jewish Temple.[41] Anastasius of Sinai refers to 'those who think and say that it is the Temple of God (*naos theou*) being built now in Jerusalem'.[42] This perception is reflected very early in both the Coptic *Apocalypse of Shenute*, and the *Secrets of Rabbi Simeon bar Yohai*.[43] Of course, what was perceived as a tragedy by the Christians was considered a divine miracle by the Jews.

It should come as no surprise that for both Jews and Christians, architectural structures on the Temple Mount erected in the name of the God of Abraham would be understood to be the direct successors of Solomon's Temple. What is more striking is that these structures were understood in the same way by the Muslims. A number of early Islamic sources indicate quite clearly that the Muslims attempted to rebuild the Temple as a mosque, and that in the Umeyyad period, up to the early ninth century, the Temple Mount was considered to be both the Temple rebuilt and the Mosque of Jerusalem. As shown by Andreas Kaplony, it is only with the Abbasids that the conception of the Temple fell into oblivion, the Haram thus losing some of its charisma.[44] Until then, the very architecture stressed the direct relation of the Haram to the Temple, for instance by integrating pieces of bedrock and ruins, and in particular inside the Dome of the Rock, which was 'specially loaded with Temple traditions'. Kaplony stresses that the assertion that the Haram is the rebuilt Temple continues the Byzantine idea that the emperor builds a new Temple, thereby declaring himself the legitimate heir of King David. This is certainly true. Kaplony adds, however, and this is more directly relevant to my argument, that the rebuilding was directly aimed at a Jewish public, who was expecting the eschatological Temple at the end of time. The Caliph, in such a mindset, could also be perceived by the Jews as their expected Messiah. Attitudes changed when it became clear, however, that the Muslims did not intend to rebuild the Jewish Temple, but rather to build a structure of their own. For the Jews, the construction of a new kind of Temple, rather than the reconstruction of Solomon's Temple, would not have been perceived as less shocking than the Christian total lack of interest in the Temple Mount and the transfer of the sacred place to the Basilica of the *Anastasis*. Moreover, as the *Anastasis* remained standing, it would retain its sacredness (although a lesser one, of course, under the Islamic regime). Building activity, however, did not remain the privilege of the conquerors. The seventh-century Armenian historian Sebeos, one of our best sources, indicates that the Jews started to build a synagogue on the Temple Mount in the first years after the conquest. It is only later that the first Al-Aqsa mosque seems to have been built.[45]

---

41 Déroche 1999: 158; cf. Flusin 1991: 408.
42 Anastasius of Sinai, *Narrationes*, C3, quoted by Hoyland 2000: 289 and n. 54. The testimony of Anastasius is significant, as he was then living on the Mount of Olives.
43 See Hoyland 1997: 279–82 (*Ps. Shenute*) and 308–12 (*Secrets of Sh. Bar Yohai*).
44 Kaplony 2002.
45 Badrosian 1985, ch. 31.

The Jews could have perceived Muhammad either as a prophet or as the Messiah. Both these titles, indeed, had been attached in the Hebrew Bible to non-Israelite figures, such as the prophet Balaam or King Cyrus, who had been called 'God's anointed'. The Jewish sources from Arabia are scarce and difficult to interpret, but it seems that some Jews, at least, did see in Muhammad, at first, a messianic (or a pre-messianic) figure. Now, according to the *Doctrina Jacobi*, a crucial Greek document from the very first days of the Islamic conquests, the Jews considered Muhammad to be a false prophet (*pseudoprophètès*). In this text, we read that 'the Jews speak of a prophet from the Saracens, and consider him a false prophet, because of his massacres.' In the same passage, Abraham, a Palestinian Jew, says that 'a false prophet has appeared among the Saracens. He is proclaiming the advent of the anointed one who is to come.'[46]

It is of course possible to understand this literally, although it seems that in the seventh century, the Jews thought more in messianic than in prophetic terms. Indeed, the concept of a false prophet seems to be absent from rabbinic literature. And in the mid-seventh century, the *Sefer Zerubbabel* uses a very rare term, *mashiaḥ sheker*, false Messiah.[47] The Syriac *Apocalypse* of Pseudo-Methodius, a contemporary text destined to exert a powerful influence, East and West, also mentions how the 'son of perdition, false Messiah (*meshiḥa degala*) will enter Jerusalem and sit on God's throne'.[48] *Degala*, here, seems to be at the origin of the figure parallel to the Antichrist in Islamic eschatological texts, the *Dajjāl*.[49] Similarly, the *Edessene Apocalyptical Fragment* (dating from 683) refers to the appearance, at the end of time, of the son of perdition, who is named 'false Messiah'.[50] The Antichrist of early Christian literature had become the false Messiah of the late antique Jewish sources.

One may then suggest also another possible interpretation of this testimony. Some Jews might have considered Muhammad, at first, to be the Messiah, later to call him a false Messiah, when they realized that he did not bring about a fulfilment of the promises. The Christians could not possibly understand what the term 'Messiah' meant, since Christos was the name of the Saviour, and might have understood this term as identical to 'false prophet'. For the Christians, Muhammad could only be a *pseudoprophētēs*. Thus Theophanes relates how some Jews took Muhammad, the leader and false prophet (*archegos kai pseudo-*

---

46 Déroche 1991: 203–9.
47 See Lévi 1914–35. We possess only remnants of what must have been a whole Jewish literature dealing with the Messiah from that period. See for instance Marmorstein 1906.
48 I quote according to Reinink 1993. On Pseudo-Methodius' *Apocalypse*, see Reinink 2005. See also Palmer 1993. On the powerful and long-lasting influence of this text on Western Medieval eschatology, see Möhring 2000.
49 See Rabin 1957, esp. 120.
50 See Palmer 1993: 243–53, esp. 247.

prophētēs) of the Saracens, to be 'the Messiah who is expected by them'.[51] The language of this passage shows quite clearly that the Christians could think of Muhammad only within the category of prophecy, while for the Jews, it was the Messianic expectation which was most pregnant.[52]

The main thrust of the debates between Jews and Christians, then, had evolved, since the second century, when Justin's *Dialogue with Trypho* emphasized the idea of prophecy. In the seventh century, the focus was not so much on true prophecy as on messianism: the *Endzeit* was now of more immediate importance than that of the past. While in its earlier stages, Jewish-Christian polemics had dealt with false prophecy, it aimed now at identifying the false Messiah, the impostor of the end-times. The mythological images inherited from the earliest Christian texts emerged with renewed power. The son of perdition sitting in the Temple of the Lord (2 Thess. 2.4) became a direct inspiration of the Pseudo-Methodius *Apocalypse*.

The intense discussion between Jews and Christians reflected in the *Doctrina Jacobi* is not on prophecy, but on the coming of the Messiah and on the Messiahship of Jesus. For Ioustos, who comes 'from the East', the first coming of Christ meant the end of prophecy (3.8). For the author of this work, as for the *Trophies of Damascus*, a text from the late seventh century, the Jews still expect 'their Christ'.[53] A similar view is expressed by Jacob of Edessa, in his *Letter to John the Stylite* (written around 708). The figure of the Messiah (*mashiḥā*) is fundamental for Jews, Christians and also Muslims. The Jews, however, contend that he has not yet come, while the Muslims do not consider Jesus to have been the Son of God, but rather a prophet, announced by the prophets.[54]

In his *Letter 14*, dated from 634, Maximus Confessor expects the imminent coming of the Antichrist, who will announce the *parousia* of Christ. Another of his letters, from 632, is replete with eschatological context.[55] The so-called Coptic *Apocalypse of Shenute* (from about 644) mentions that a figure arising from the sons of Ishmael will hound the Christians and will seek to rebuild the Temple in Jerusalem, announcing the end of times, while the Jews will expect the deceiver.[56] Toward the end of the century, the Syriac *Apocalypse* of Pseudo-Ephrem (probably written after 692) mentions the messenger (*izgadā*) of the son of perdition among the offspring of Hagar, while John of Damascus refers to the people-deceiving cult (*thrēskeia*) of the Ismaelites, a forerunner of the Antichrist.[57]

---

51   *ton par auton prosdokomenon Christon*, 333 de Boor. See also Mango and Scott 1997: 464–5.
52   Cf. Lewis 1976.
53   *ho Christos auton erchomenos*, IV.2; *ho erchomenos elimmenos humon*, IV.3. I quote according to Bardy 1927: 242–3.
54   See Hoyland 1997: 160–7.
55   On both these letters, see Dagron in Dargon and Déroche 1991: 38–41.
56   Hoyland 1997: 308–12.
57   *De Haeresibus* 60–1.

Some Jewish sources concur in perceiving Muhammad as a prophet announcing the redemption of Israel. In the *Secrets of Rabbi Simeon bar Yohai* (probably written after 680), the archangel Metatron is quoted as saying: 'In order to save you from Edom, God raises over the Ismaelites a prophet according to his will ... The second king who arises from Ishmael will be a lover of Israel ... he restores their breaches and the breaches of the Temple. He hews Mount Moriah, makes it level and builds a mosque *hishtaḥawaya* (ritual prostration) there on the Temple rock.'[58] Indeed, Sunni and Shi'i sources relate that a Yemenite Jew named 'Abdallah b. Saba' was the first to publicly proclaim that Muhammad himself was the Messiah who would return at the end of times.[59]

Our sources, then, do not offer a single and clear-cut image of Muhammad, who can be perceived either through the category of prophet or through that of Messiah. As we have seen, however, there was one – and only one – group whose theology retained a place for the coming of a false prophet, announcing the last and true prophet, the Messiah, at the end-times: the Jewish Christians, in particular the Ebionites and the various groups which succeeded them. In this respect, the 'Jewish-Christian' formulations and Docetic conceptions in the Qur'an deserve fresh consideration. The perception of Muhammad as a false prophet in an eschatological context suggests, then, that this theologoumenon was developed in a Jewish-Christian milieu.

In the intense revival of competition for the holy places (and in particular for the Temple Mount) between Jews and Christians, what was a Messianic hope for some represented the threat of eschatological nightmare for others. What is of special interest in our present context is the interplay between the eschatological visions of both Jews and Christians.[60] The preceding pages have sought to show, through a particularly pregnant example, the historical recurrence of mythical thought patterns inherited from early Jewish eschatology and Messianism.

---

58   See Hoyland 1997: 308–12.
59   See Wasserstrom 1995: 55, who refers to studies by J. Van Ess and I. Friedländer.
60   See Irsai 2000.

APPENDIX:
WILLIAM HORBURY'S PUBLICATIONS

Horbury, William (1970), 'A Critical Examination of the Toledoth Yeshu.' Ph.D. dissertation, University of Cambridge.

——— (1970), 'The Trial of Jesus in Jewish Tradition.' In *The Trial of Jesus: Cambridge Studies in Honour of C. F. D. Moule*, 103–21. Ed. E. Bammel. London: SCM.

Horbury, William and Jörg-Ulrich Fechner (1971), 'A Hebrew MS Binding on a Sixteenth-Century Volume in Clare College Library.' *Transactions of the Cambridge Bibliographical Society* 5: 217–29.

Horbury, William (1972), 'The Passion Narratives and Historical Criticism.' *Theology* 75: 58–71.

——— (1972), 'Tertullian on the Jews in the Light of *De Spectaculis* xxx. 5–6.' *JTS* 23: 455–59.

——— (1974), 'Jesus the Jew.' *Theology* 77: 227–32.

——— (1974), 'The Temple.' *ExpTim* 86: 36–42.

——— (1979), 'Paul and Judaism.' *ExpTim* 90: 116–18.

——— (1980), 'Keeping Up With Recent Studies: Rabbinics.' *ExpTim* 91: 233–40.

——— (1981), 'Suffering and Messianism in Yose ben Yose.' In *Suffering and Martyrdom in the New Testament: Studies Presented to G. M. Styler by the Cambridge New Testament Seminar*, 143–82. Ed. W. Horbury and B. McNeil. Cambridge: Cambridge University Press.

Horbury, William and Brian McNeil, eds, (1981), *Suffering and Martyrdom in the New Testament: Studies Presented to G.M. Styler by the Cambridge New Testament Seminar*. Cambridge: Cambridge University Press.

Horbury, William (1982), '1 Thessalonians ii.3 as Rebutting the Charge of False Prophecy.' *JTS* 33: 492–508.

——— (1982), 'The Benediction of the *Minim* and Early Jewish-Christian Controversy.' *JTS* 33: 19–61.

Horbury, William and Christopher Rowland, eds, (1983), *Essays in Honour of Ernst Bammel*. *JSNT* 19. Sheffield: Sheffield Academic Press.

Horbury, William (1983), 'The Aaronic Priesthood in the Epistle to the Hebrews.' *JSNT* 19: 43–71.

——— (1983), 'The Basle Nizzahon.' *JTS* 34: 497–514.

——— (1984), 'Christ as Brigand in Ancient Anti-Christian-Polemic.' In *Jesus and the Politics of His Day*, 183–95. Ed. E. Bammel and C. F. D. Moule. Cambridge: Cambridge University Press.

——— (1984), 'The Temple Tax.' In *Jesus and the Politics of His Day*, 265–86. Ed. E. Bammel and C. F. D. Moule. Cambridge: Cambridge University Press.

—— (1985), 'Extirpation and Excommunication.' *VT* 35: 13–38.
—— (1985), 'The Messianic Associations of "The Son of Man".' *JST* 36: 34–55.
—— (1986), 'Ezekiel Tragicus 106: ‰´Ú?Ì·Ù·.' *VT* 36: 37–51.
—— (1986), 'The Revision of Shem Tob ibn Shaprut's *Eben Bohan*.' *Sefarad* 43 (1983; issued 1986): 221–37.
—— (1986), 'The Twelve and the Phylarchs.' *NTS* 32: 503–27.
—— (1988), 'Messianism among Jews and Christians in the Second Century.' *Augustinianum* 28: 71–88.
—— (1988), 'Old Testament Interpretation in the Writings of the Church Fathers.' In *Mikra: Text, Translation, Reading, and Interpretation of the Hebrew Bible in Ancient Judaism and Early Christianity*, 727–87. Ed. M. J. Mulder and H. Sysling. CRINT 2:1. Assen and Philadelphia: Van Gorcum and Fortress Press.
—— (1989), 'The Purpose of Pseudo-Cyprian, *Adversus Iudaeos*.' *Studia Patristica* 18.3: 291–317.
—— (1991), 'Herod's Temple and Herod's Days.' In *Templum Amicitiae: Essays on the Second Temple presented to Ernst Bammel*, 103–49. Ed. W. Horbury. JSNTSup 48. Sheffield: JSOT Press.
—— (1991), 'The Jewish Dimension.' In *Early Christianity: Origins and Evolution to AD 600: In Honour of W.H.C. Frend*, 40–51. Ed. I. Hazlett. London: SPCK.
—— (1991), 'The Name Mardochaeus in a Ptolemaic Inscription.' *VT* 41: 220–26.
Horbury, William, ed., (1991), *Templum Amicitiae: Essays on the Second Temple Presented to Ernst Bammel*. JSNTSup 48. Sheffield: JSOT Press.
Horbury, William (1992), 'Jewish-Christian Relations in Barnabas and Justin Martyr.' In *Jews and Christians : the parting of the ways, A.D. 70 to 135 : the Second Durham-Tübingen Research Symposium on Earliest Christianity and Judaism, Durham, September, 1989*, 315–45. Ed. J. D. G. Dunn. WUNT 66. Tübingen: Mohr Siebeck.
—— (1992), 'Jews and Christians on the Bible: Demarcation and Convergence.' In *Christliche Exegese zwischen Nicaea und Chalcedon*, 72–103. Ed. J. v. Oort and U. Wickert. Kampen: Kok Pharos.
—— (1993), 'Constitutional Aspects of the Kingdom of God.' In *The Kingdom of God and Human Society*, 60–79. Ed. R. S. Barbour. Edinburgh: T&T Clark.
Horbury, William and David Noy (1992), *Jewish Inscriptions of Graeco-Roman Egypt: With an Index of the Jewish Inscriptions of Egypt and Cyrenaica*. Cambridge etc.: Cambridge University Press.
Horbury, William (1994), 'The "Caiaphas" Ossuaries and Joseph Caiaphas.' *PEQ* 126: 32–48.
—— (1994), 'Jewish Inscriptions and Jewish Literature in Egypt, with Special Reference to Ecclesiasticus.' In *Studies in Early Jewish Epigraphy*, 9–43. Ed. J. W. van Henten and P. W. van der Horst. AGJU 21. Leiden: Brill.
—— (1994), 'Judah Briel and Seventeenth-Century Jewish Anti-Christian Polemic in Italy.' *JSQ* 1: 171–92.

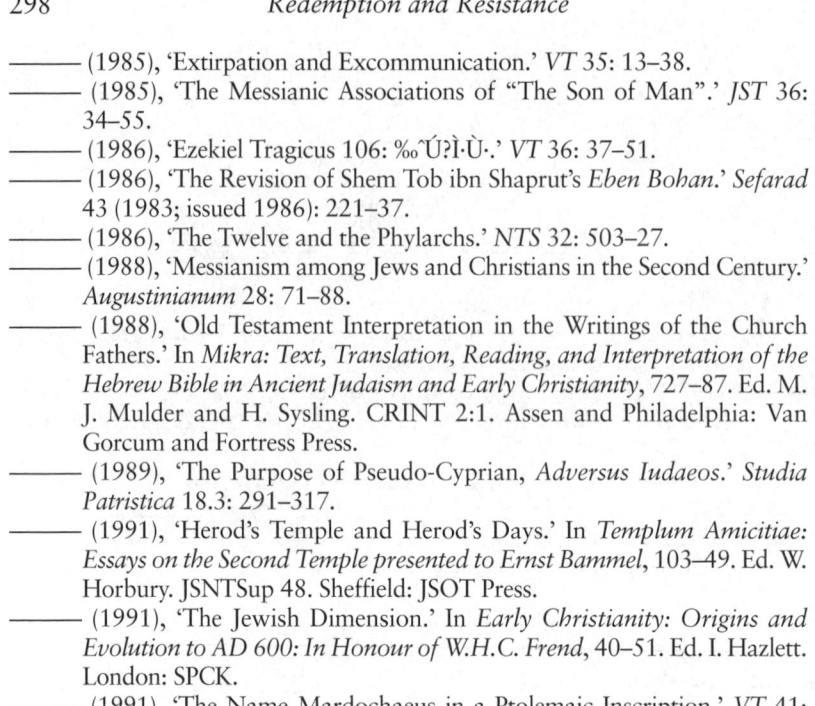

―――― (1994), 'A Personal Name in a Jar-inscription in Hebrew Characters from Alexandria?' *VT* 44: 103–07.

―――― (1994), 'The Wisdom of Solomon in the Muratorian Fragment.' *JTS* 45: 149–59.

―――― (1995), 'The Christian Use and the Jewish Origins of the Wisdom of Solomon.' In *Wisdom in Ancient Israel: Essays in Honour of J. A. Emerton*, 182–96. Ed. J. Day *et al.* Cambridge: Cambridge University Press.

―――― (1996), 'The Beginnings of the Jewish Revolt under Trajan.' In *Geschichte – Tradition – Reflexion: Festschrift für Martin Hengel zum 70. Geburtstag* 1:283–304. Ed. H. Cancik et al. Tübingen: Mohr Siebeck.

―――― (1996), 'Land, Sanctuary and Worship.' In *Early Christian Thought in its Jewish Context*, 207-24. Ed. J. Barclay and J. Sweet. Cambridge, etc.: Cambridge University Press.

Horbury, William and Samuel Krauss (1996), *The Jewish-Christian Controversy from the Earliest Times to 1789*. TSAJ 56. Tübingen: Mohr Siebeck.

Horbury, William (1997), 'Appendix: The Hebrew Text of Matthew in Shem Tob Ibn Shaprut's *Eben Bohan*.' In *A Critical and Exegetical Commentary on the Gospel According to Saint Matthew*, 3:729–38, by W. D. Davies and D. C. Allison. ICC. Edinburgh: T & T Clark.

―――― (1997), 'A Proselyte's *Heis Theos* Inscription near Caesarea.' *PEQ* 130: 133–37.

―――― (1997), 'Septuagintal and New Testament Conceptions of the Church.' In *A Vision for the Church: Studies in Early Christian Ecclesiology in Honour of J. P. M. Sweet*, 1–17. Ed. M. Bockmuehl and M. B. Thompson. Edinburgh: T&T Clark.

―――― (1998), 'Antichrist Among Jews and Gentiles.' In *Jews in a Graeco-Roman World*, 113–33. Ed. M. Goodman. Oxford/New York: Oxford University Press.

―――― (1998), 'The Benediction of the Minim.' In *Jews and Christians in Contact and Controversy*, 67–110. Edinburgh: T&T Clark.

―――― (1998), 'Christ as Brigand in Ancient Anti-Christian Polemic.' In *Jews and Christians in Contact and Controversy*, 162–73. Edinburgh: T&T Clark.

―――― (1998), 'The Cult of Christ and the Cult of the Saints.' *NTS* 44: 444–69.

―――― (1998), 'Early Christians on Synagogue Prayer and Imprecation.' In *Tolerance and Intolerance in Early Judaism and Christianity*, 296–317. Ed. G. N. Stanton and G. G. Stroumsa. Cambridge: Cambridge University Press.

―――― (1998), *Jewish Messianism and the Cult of Christ*. London: SCM.

―――― (1998), *Jews and Christians in Contact and Controversy*. Edinburgh: T&T Clark.

―――― (1998), 'Messianism in the Old Testament Apocrypha and Pseudepigrapha.' In *King and Messiah in Israel and the Ancient Near East: Proceedings of the Oxford Old Testament Seminar*, 402–33. Ed. J. Day. JSOTSup 270. Sheffield: Sheffield Academic Press.

Horbury, William, John Sturdy and W. D. Davies, eds, (1999), *The Cambridge History of Judaism*. Vol. 3: *The Early Roman Period*. Cambridge: Cambridge University Press.

Horbury, William (1999), *Christianity in Ancient Jewish Tradition: An Inaugural Lecture Delivered Before the University of Cambridge in the Divinity School, St John's Street on Thursday 4th February 1999.* Cambridge etc.: Cambridge University Press.

—— (1999), 'Der Tempel bei Vergil und im herodianischen Judentum.' In *Gemeinde ohne Tempel = Community Without Temple: Zur Substituierung und Transformation des Jerusalemer Tempels und seines Kults im Alten Testament, antiken Judentum und frühen Christentum*, 149–68. Ed. B. Ego *et al.* WUNT 118. Tübingen: Mohr Siebeck.

—— (1999), 'The Hebrew Matthew and Hebrew Study.' In *Hebrew Study from Ezra to Ben-Yehuda*, 122–31. Ed. W. Horbury. Edinburgh: T&T Clark.

Horbury, William, ed., (1999), *Hebrew Study from Ezra to Ben-Yehuda*. Edinburgh: T&T Clark.

Horbury, William (1999), 'Introduction.' In *Hebrew Study from Ezra to Ben-Yehuda*, 1–12. Ed. W. Horbury. Edinburgh: T&T Clark.

—— (1999), 'John Spencer (1630–1693) and Hebrew Study.' *Letter of the Corpus Association* 78: 12–23.

—— (1999), 'Pappus and Lulianus in Jewish Resistance to Rome.' In *Jewish Studies at the Turn of the Twentieth Century: Proceedings of the 6th EAJS Congress, Toledo, July 1998*, 1:289–95. Ed. J. Targarona Borrás and A. Sáenz-Badillos. Leiden/Boston: Brill.

—— (1999), 'Preface.' In *The Cambridge History of Judaism*. Vol. 3: *The Early Roman Period*:xi–xvii. Ed. W. Horbury *et al.* Cambridge: Cambridge University Press.

—— (1999), 'The Proper Name in 4Q468g: Peitholaus?' *JJS* 50: 310–11.

—— (1999), 'Women in the Synagogue.' In *The Cambridge History of Judaism*. Vol. 3: *The Early Roman Period*: 358–401. Ed. W. Horbury *et al.* Cambridge: Cambridge University Press.

—— (2001), 'Hebrew Apologetic and Polemical Literature.' In *Hebrew Scholarship in the Medieval World*, 189–209. Ed. N. R. M. De Lange. Cambridge: Cambridge University Press.

—— (2001), 'Jesus Christus in der Sicht des Judentums.' *Die Religion in Geschichte und Gegenwart*[4] 4: 483–84.

—— (2001), 'Macbride Sermon on Messianic Prophecy 1998.' *Hertford College Magazine* 83 (1997–98, issued 2001): 57–64.

—— (2001), 'The Wisdom of Solomon.' In *The Oxford Bible Commentary*, 650–67. Ed. J. Barton et al. Oxford/New York: Oxford University Press.

—— (2003), 'The Books of Solomon in Ancient Mysticism.' In *Reading Texts, Seeking Wisdom: Scripture and Theology*, 185–201. Ed. G. Stanton and D. F. Ford. London: SCM.

—— (2003), 'The Depiction of Judaeo-Christians in the Toledot Yeshu.' In *The Image of the Judaeo-Christians in Ancient Jewish and Christian Literature: Papers Delivered at the Colloquium of the Institutum Iudaicum, Brussels 18–19 November, 2001*, 280–86. Ed. P. J. Tomson and D. Lambers-Petry. Tübingen: Mohr Siebeck.

—— (2003), *Messianism among Jews and Christians: Twelve Biblical and Historical Studies*. London/New York: T&T Clark.

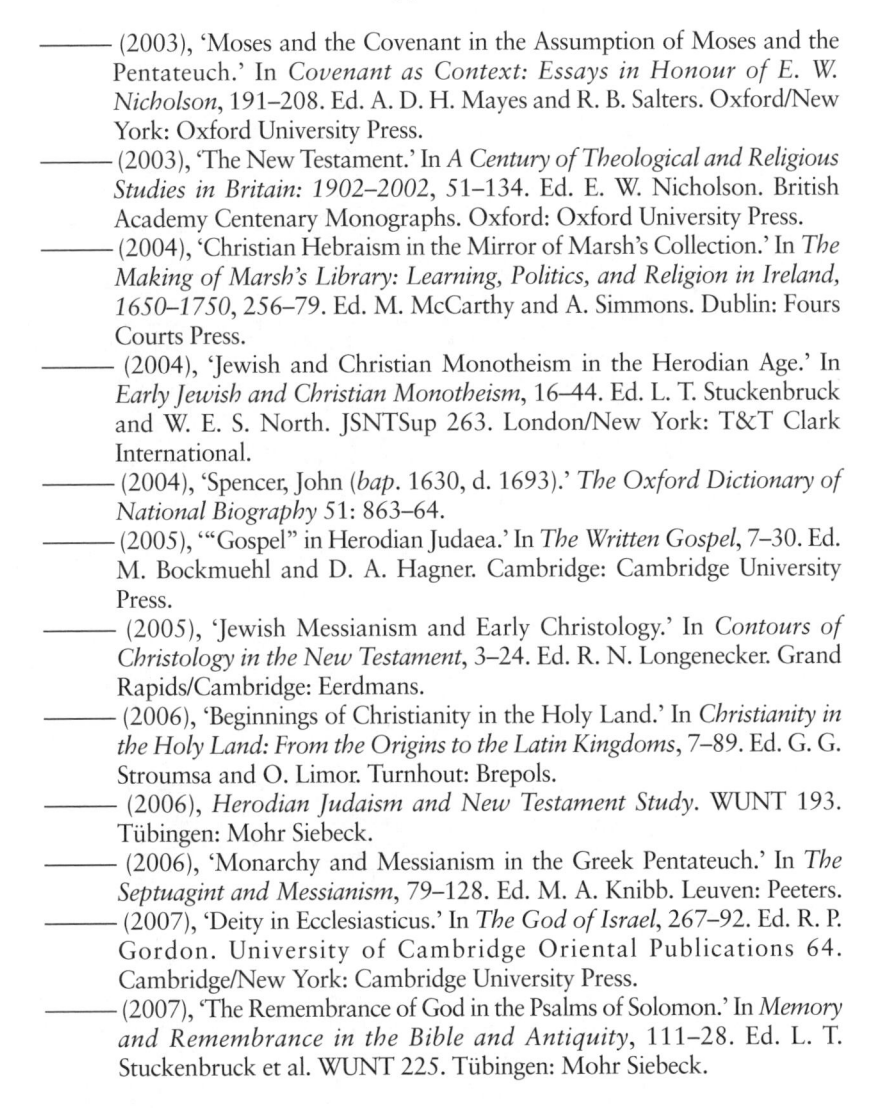

―――― (2003), 'Moses and the Covenant in the Assumption of Moses and the Pentateuch.' In *Covenant as Context: Essays in Honour of E. W. Nicholson*, 191–208. Ed. A. D. H. Mayes and R. B. Salters. Oxford/New York: Oxford University Press.

―――― (2003), 'The New Testament.' In *A Century of Theological and Religious Studies in Britain: 1902–2002*, 51–134. Ed. E. W. Nicholson. British Academy Centenary Monographs. Oxford: Oxford University Press.

―――― (2004), 'Christian Hebraism in the Mirror of Marsh's Collection.' In *The Making of Marsh's Library: Learning, Politics, and Religion in Ireland, 1650–1750*, 256–79. Ed. M. McCarthy and A. Simmons. Dublin: Fours Courts Press.

―――― (2004), 'Jewish and Christian Monotheism in the Herodian Age.' In *Early Jewish and Christian Monotheism*, 16–44. Ed. L. T. Stuckenbruck and W. E. S. North. JSNTSup 263. London/New York: T&T Clark International.

―――― (2004), 'Spencer, John (*bap.* 1630, d. 1693).' *The Oxford Dictionary of National Biography* 51: 863–64.

―――― (2005), '"Gospel" in Herodian Judaea.' In *The Written Gospel*, 7–30. Ed. M. Bockmuehl and D. A. Hagner. Cambridge: Cambridge University Press.

―――― (2005), 'Jewish Messianism and Early Christology.' In *Contours of Christology in the New Testament*, 3–24. Ed. R. N. Longenecker. Grand Rapids/Cambridge: Eerdmans.

―――― (2006), 'Beginnings of Christianity in the Holy Land.' In *Christianity in the Holy Land: From the Origins to the Latin Kingdoms*, 7–89. Ed. G. G. Stroumsa and O. Limor. Turnhout: Brepols.

―――― (2006), *Herodian Judaism and New Testament Study*. WUNT 193. Tübingen: Mohr Siebeck.

―――― (2006), 'Monarchy and Messianism in the Greek Pentateuch.' In *The Septuagint and Messianism*, 79–128. Ed. M. A. Knibb. Leuven: Peeters.

―――― (2007), 'Deity in Ecclesiasticus.' In *The God of Israel*, 267–92. Ed. R. P. Gordon. University of Cambridge Oriental Publications 64. Cambridge/New York: Cambridge University Press.

―――― (2007), 'The Remembrance of God in the Psalms of Solomon.' In *Memory and Remembrance in the Bible and Antiquity*, 111–28. Ed. L. T. Stuckenbruck et al. WUNT 225. Tübingen: Mohr Siebeck.

WORKS CITED

Abegg, Martin G., Jr. (1995), 'The Messiah at Qumran: Are We Still Seeing Double?' In *DSD* 2: 125–44.
Abegg, Martin G., Jr. and Craig A. Evans (1998), 'Messianic Passages in the Dead Sea Scrolls.' In *Qumran-Messianism: Studies on the Messianic Expectations in the Dead Sea Scrolls*, 204–14. Ed. J. H. Charlesworth *et al*. Tübingen: Mohr Siebeck.
Achtemeier, Paul J. (1996), *1 Peter: A Commentary on First Peter*. Hermeneia. Minneapolis: Fortress Press.
——— (1999), 'The Christology of 1 Peter: Some Reflections.' In *Who Do You Say that I Am? Essays on Christology*, 140–54. Ed. M. A. Powell and D. R. Bauer. Louisville: Westminster John Knox Press.
Adamson, James B. (1976), *The Epistle of James*. NICNT. Grand Rapids: Eerdmans.
Ådna, Jostein (2004), 'The Servant of Isaiah 53 as Triumphant and Interceding Messiah: The Reception of Isaiah 52:13–53:12 in the Targum of Isaiah with Special Attention to the Concept of the Messiah.' In *The Suffering Servant: Isaiah 53 in Jewish and Christian Sources*, 189–224. Ed. B. Janowski and P. Stuhlmacher. Trans. D. P. Bailey. Grand Rapids: Eerdmans.
Aescoly, Aaron Zeev (1987), *Jewish Messianic Movements*. (Hebr.) 2nd edn. Jerusalem: Mosad Bialik.
Alexander, Paul J. (1967), *The Oracle of Baalbek: The Tiburtine Sibyl in Greek Dress*. Dumbarton Oaks Studies 10. Washington: Dumbarton Oaks Center for Byzantine Studies.
——— (1985), *The Byzantine Apocalyptic Tradition*. Berkeley: University of California Press.
Alexander, Philip S. (1983), '3 Enoch.' In *OTP*, 1: 223–315. Ed. J. H. Charlesworth. New York: Doubleday.
——— (1990), 'Late Hebrew Apocalyptic: A Preliminary Survey.' In *La fable apocryphe*, 1: 197–217. Ed. P. Geoltrain *et al*. Apocrypha 1–2. Turnhout: Brepols.
——— (1991), 'The Family of Caesar and the Family of God: The Image of the Emperor in early Jewish Mystical Literature.' In *Images of Empire: The Roman Empire in Jewish, Christian and Greco-Roman Sources*, 276–97. Ed. L. Alexander. JSOTSup 122. Sheffield: Sheffield Academic Press.
——— (1992), '"The Parting of the Ways" from the Perspective of Rabbinic Judaism.' In *Jews and Christians: The Parting of the Ways, A.D. 70 to 135*, 1–25. Ed. J. D. G. Dunn. WUNT 66. Tübingen: Mohr Siebeck.
——— (1998), 'The King Messiah in Rabbinic Judaism.' In *King and Messiah in Israel and the Ancient Near East: Proceedings of the Oxford Old Testament Seminar*, 456–73. Ed. J. Day. JSOTSup 270. Sheffield: Sheffield Academic Press.

―― (1999a), 'From Poetry to Historiography: The Image of the Hasmoneans in Targum Canticles and the Question of the Targum's Provenance and Date.' *JSP* 19: 103–28.
―― (1999b), 'How Did the Rabbis Learn Hebrew?' In *Hebrew Study from Ezra to Ben-Yehuda*, 71–89. Ed. W. Horbury. Edinburgh: T&T Clark.
―― (2001), 'Tora and Salvation in Tannaitic Literature.' In *Justification and Variegated Nomism: A Fresh Appraisal of Paul and Second Temple Judaism*, 1: 261–301. Ed. D. A. Carson *et al.* WUNT 2: 140, 181. Tübingen/Grand Rapids: Mohr Siebeck/Baker Academic.
―― (2003), *The Targum of Canticles: Translated, with a Critical Introduction, Apparatus, and Notes*. ArBib 17A. London: T&T Clark.
―― (2006), *Mystical Texts*. Companion to the Qumran Scrolls 7. London: T&T Clark International.
―― (2007), 'Jewish Christians in Early Rabbinic Literature.' In *Jewish Believers in Jesus—The Early Centuries*, 659–709. Ed. O. Skarsaune and R. Hvalvik. Peabody: Hendrickson.
Alexandre, Monique (1988), *Le commencement du livre Genèse I-V: La version grecque de la Septante et sa réception*. Christianisme Antique 3. Paris: Beauchesne.
Alföldi, Andreas (1980), *Die monarchische Repräsentation im römischen Kaiserreiche*. 3rd edn, Darmstadt: Wissenschaftliche Buchgesellschaft.
Allison, Dale C. (2000), 'The Secularizing of the Historical Jesus.' *Perspectives in Religious Studies* 27: 135–52.
Altheim, Franz (1930), *Griechische Götter im alten Rom*. Giessen: Töpelmann.
Altmann, Alexander (1968), '*Homo Imago Dei* in Jewish and Christian Theology.' *JR* 48: 235–59.
Altmann, Alexander, ed. (1966), *Biblical Motifs: Origins and Transformations*. Cambridge: Harvard University Press.
Ameling, Walter (2003), 'Jerusalem als hellenistische Polis: 2 Makk 4,9-12 und eine neue Inschrift.' *BZ* 47: 105–11.
Anderson, Paul N. (1996), *The Christology of the Fourth Gospel: Its Unity and Disunity in the Light of John 6*. WUNT 2:78. Tübingen: Mohr Siebeck.
Applebaum, Shimon (1979), *Jews and Greeks in Ancient Cyrene*. SJLA 28. Leiden: E. J. Brill.
Arce, Javier (1987), 'La rebelión de los Judíos durante el gobierno de Constancio Galo César, 353 d.C.' *Athenaeum* n.s. 65: 109–25.
Arjomand, Said Amir (2003), 'Islamic Apocalypticism in the Classical Period.' In *The Continuum History of Apocalypticism*, 380-416. Ed. B. McGinn *et al.* New York: Continuum.
Arnal, William. E. (2005a), 'The Cipher "Judaism" in Contemporary Historical Jesus Scholarship.' In *Apocalypticism, Anti-Semitism and the Historical Jesus: Subtexts in Criticism*, 24–54. Ed. J. S. Kloppenborg and J. W. Marshall. *JSHJSup* 1. London/New York: T&T Clark.
―― (2005b), *The Symbolic Jesus: Historical Scholarship, Judaism, and the Construction of Contemporary Identity*. Religion in Culture. London/Oakville: Equinox.
Ashton, J. (1991), *Understanding the Fourth Gospel*. Oxford: Clarendon.

Atkinson, Kenneth R. (1996), 'Herod the Great, Sosius, and the Siege of Jerusalem (37 B.C.E.) in Psalm of Solomon 17.' *NovT* 38: 313–22.

—— (1999), 'On the Herodian Origin of Militant Davidic Messianism at Qumran: New Light from *Psalm of Solomon 17*.' *JBL* 118: 435–60.

Attridge, Harold W. (1989), *The Epistle to the Hebrews: A Commentary on the Epistle to the Hebrews*. Hermeneia. Philadelphia: Fortress Press.

Auffarth, Christoph et al. (2002), 'Messias/Messianismus.' *RGG*[4] 5: 1143–62.

Aune, David E. (1983), *Prophecy in Early Christianity and the Ancient Mediterranean World*. Grand Rapids: Eerdmans.

—— (1992), 'Christian Prophecy and the Messianic Status of Jesus'. In *The Messiah: Developments in Earliest Judaism and Christianity*, 404–22. Ed. J. H. Charlesworth. Minneapolis: Fortress Press.

—— (1997–8), *Revelation*. WBC 52. 3 vols. Dallas: Word Books.

Ausloos, Hans and Bénédicte Lemmelijn (2005), '"Your Only Son, Your Beloved One" (Genesis 22): When Septuagint and Messianism Meet.' In *Interpreting Translation: Studies on the LXX and Ezekiel in Honour of Johan Lust*, 19–31. Ed. F. García Martínez and M. Vervenne. BETL 192. Leuven: Peeters.

Avi-Yonah, Michael (1976), *The Jews of Palestine: A Political History from the Bar Kokhba War to the Arab Conquest*. Oxford: Blackwell.

Bacher, W. (1890), 'The Church Fathers, Origen, and Rabbi Hoshaya.' *JQR* 3: 357–60.

Badilita, Cristian (2005), *Métamorphoses de l'antichrist chez les pères de l'église*. Théologie historique 116. Paris: Beauchesne.

Badrosian, R., tr., (1985), *Sebeos' History*. Sources of the Armenian Tradition; New York.

Baer, Y. F. (1961), 'Israel, the Christian Church, and the Roman Empire.' *ScrHier* 7: 79–145.

Bakhos, Carol (2006), Review of Review of William Horbury, *Jews and Christians: In Contact and Controversy* (Edinburgh: T&T Clark, 1998). *SJT* 59: 100–2.

Balch, David L. (1981), *Let Wives be Submissive: The Domestic Code in 1 Peter*. SBLMS 26. Chico: Scholars Press.

—— (1986), 'Hellenization/Acculturation in 1 Peter.' In *Perspectives on First Peter*, 79–101. Ed. C. H. Talbert. Macon: Mercer University Press.

Bammel, Ernst (1984a), 'The Revolution Theory from Reimarus to Brandon.' In *Jesus and the Politics of his Day*, 11–68. Ed. E. Bammel and C. F. D. Moule. Cambridge etc.: Cambridge University Press.

—— (1984b), 'The Titulus.' In *Jesus and the Politics of his Day*, 353–64. Ed. E. Bammel and C. F. D. Moule. Cambridge etc.: Cambridge University Press.

Barclay, John M. G. (1996), *Jews in the Mediterranean Diaspora: From Alexander to Trajan (323 BCE – 117 CE)*. Edinburgh: T&T Clark.

Bardy, G. (1925), 'Les traditions juives dans l'œuvre d'Origène.' *RB* 34: 217–52.

—— (1927), *Les Trophées de Damas: Controverse judéo-chrétienne du VIIe siècle*. Patrologia orientalis 15:2. Paris: Firmin-Didot.

Barker, Margaret (2000), *The Revelation of Jesus Christ: which God gave to him to show to his servants what must soon take place (Revelation I.I)*. Edinburgh: T&T Clark.

Barnard, L.W. (1968), 'The Origins and the Emergence of the Church in Edessa.' VC 22: 161–75.
Barnes, T. D. (1989), 'Trajan and the Jews.' JJS 40: 145–62.
Baron, Salo Wittmayer (1957) vol. III, *A Social and Religious History of the Jews.* 2nd edn, New York: Columbia University Press.
Barrett, C. K. (1975), *The Gospel of John and Judaism.* London: SPCK.
—— (1994–8), *The Acts of the Apostles.* ICC. 2 vols; Edinburgh: T&T Clark.
—— (1999), 'The Christology of Hebrews.' In *Who Do You Say that I Am? Essays on Christology*, 110–27. Ed. M. A. Powell and D. R. Bauer. Louisville: Westminster John Knox Press.
Barthélemy, Dominique (1974), 'Qui est Symmaque?' CBQ 36: 451–65.
Bartlett, John R. (1973), *The First and Second Books of the Maccabees.* CBC. Cambridge: Cambridge University Press.
Barton, John (1998), 'The Messiah in Old Testament Theology.' In *King and Messiah in Israel and the Ancient Near East: Proceedings of the Oxford Old Testament Seminar*, 365–79. Ed. J. Day. JSOTSup. 270 Sheffield: Sheffield Academic Press.
Bauckham, Richard J. (1980), 'The Delay of the Parousia.' TynBul 31: 3–36.
—— (1988), 'James, 1 and 2 Peter, Jude.' In *It is Written–Scripture Citing Scripture: Essays in Honour of Barnabas Lindars, SSF*, 303–17. Ed. D. A. Carson and H. G. M. Williamson. Cambridge etc.: Cambridge University Press.
—— (1990), *Jude and the Relatives of Jesus in the Early Church.* Edinburgh: T&T Clark.
—— (1993a), *The Climax of Prophecy: Studies on the Book of Revelation.* Edinburgh: T&T Clark.
—— (1993b), *The Theology of the Book of Revelation.* New Testament Theology. Cambridge: Cambridge University Press.
—— (1998a), 'The Apocalypse of Peter: A Jewish Christian Apocalypse from the Time of Bar Kokhba.' In *The Fate of the Dead: Studies on the Jewish and Christian Apocalypses*, 160–258. NovTSup 93. Leiden/Boston: Brill.
—— (1998b) 'Jews and Jewish Christians in the Land of Israel at the Time of the Bar Kochba War, with Special Reference to the *Apocalypse of Peter.*' In *Tolerance and Intolerance in Early Judaism and Christianity*, 228–38. Ed. G. N. Stanton and G. G. Stroumsa. Cambridge etc.: Cambridge University Press.
—— (1999), *James: Wisdom of James, Disciple of Jesus the Sage.* New Testament Readings. London/New York: Routledge.
—— (2004), 'The Wisdom of James and the Wisdom of Jesus.' In *The Catholic Epistles and Tradition*, 75–92. Ed. J. Schlosser. BETL 176. Leuven: Peeters.
Bauckham, Richard and Trevor Hart (1999), *Hope Against Hope: Christian Eschatology in Contemporary Context.* London/Grand Rapids: Darton, Longman & Todd/Eerdmans.
Beall, Todd S. (1988), *Josephus' Description of the Essenes Illustrated by the Dead Sea Scrolls.* Cambridge etc.: Cambridge University Press.
Beaton, Richard (2002), *Isaiah's Christ in Matthew's Gospel.* SNTSMS 123. Cambridge/New York: Cambridge University Press.

Beavis, Mary Ann (2006), *Jesus and Utopia: Looking for the Kingdom of God in the Roman World.* Minneapolis: Fortress Press.
Becker, Adam H. and Annette Yoshiko Reed, eds, (2003), *The Ways That Never Parted: Jews and Christians in Late Antiquity and the Early Middle Ages.* Tübingen: Mohr Siebeck.
Bedjan, Paul (1902), *S. Martyrii qui et Sahdona quae supersunt omnia.* Paris/Leipzig: Harrassowitz.
Beker, Johan Christiaan (1980), *Paul the Apostle: The Triumph of God in Life and Thought.* Philadelphia: Fortress Press.
Bedrosian, Robert (1985), *Sebeos' History.* New York: Sources of the Armenian Tradition.
Belayche, Nicole (2001), *Iudaea-Palaestina: The Pagan Cults in Roman Palestine (Second to Fourth Century).* Tübingen: Mohr Siebeck.
Bellinger, William H. and William R. Farmer, eds, (1998), *Jesus and the Suffering Servant: Isaiah 53 and Christian Origins.* Harrisburg: Trinity Press.
Berger, David (2001), *The Rebbe, the Messiah, and the Scandal of Orthodox Indifference.* London: Littman Library of Jewish Civilization.
Berger, Klaus (1976), *Die griechische Daniel-Diegese: Eine altkirchliche Apokalypse. Text, Übersetzung und Kommentar.* StPB 27. Leiden: Brill.
Bertram, G. (1966), 'Erhöhung.' *RAC* 6: 22–43.
Best, Ernest (1969), '1 Peter II,4-10 - A Reconsideration.' *NovT* 11: 270–93.
Betz, Hans Dieter (1995), *The Sermon on the Mount: A Commentary on the Sermon on the Mount, Including the Sermon on the Plain (Matthew 5:3-7:27 and Luke 6:20-49).* Ed. A. Y. Collins. Hermeneia. Minneapolis: Fortress Press.
Bichler, Reinhold (1983), *'Hellenismus': Geschichte und Problematik eines Epochenbegriffs.* Impulse der Forschung 41. Darmstadt: Wissenschaftliche Buchgesellschaft.
Bickerman, Elias (1929), 'Die römische Kaiserapotheose.' *ARW* 27: 1–31.
Bietenhard, Hans (1974), *Caesarea, Origenes und die Juden.* Franz Delitzsch-Vorlesungen 1972. Stuttgart: Kohlhammer.
Bilde, Per, ed., (1996), *Aspects of Hellenistic Kingship.* Studies in Hellenistic Civilization 7. Aarhus: Aarhus University Press.
Biller, Gerhard and Ulrich Dierse (1980), 'Messianismus, messianisch.' *Handwörterbuch der Philosophie* 5: 1163–6.
Blanc, Cécile (1975), *Commentaire sur saint Jean.* SC 222. Vol. 3, Paris: Editions du Cerf.
Blowers, Paul M. (1988), 'Origen, the Rabbis, and the Bible: Toward a Picture of Judaism and Christianity in Third-Century Caesarea.' In *Origen of Alexandria: His World and His Legacy,* 96–116. Ed. C. Kannengiesser and W. L. Petersen. Christianity and Judaism in Antiquity 1. Notre Dame: University of Notre Dame Press.
Böcher, Otto, *et al.* (1981), 'Chiliasmus.' *TRE* 7: 723–45.
Bockmuehl, Markus (1992), 'A "Slain Messiah" in 4Q Serekh Milhamah (4Q285)?' *TynBul* 43: 155–69.
——— (2001), '1 Thessalonians 2:14-16 and the Church in Jerusalem.' *TynBul* 52: 1–31.
——— (2004), 'Simon Peter's Names in Jewish Sources.' *JJS* 55: 58–80.

―― (2006), *Seeing the Word: Refocusing New Testament Study*. Grand Rapids: Baker Academic.
Bogaert, Pierre (1969), *Apocalypse de Baruch: Introduction, Traduction du Syriaque et Commentaire*. SC 144–5. 2 vols; Paris: Cerf.
Bonhoeffer, Dietrich (1949), *Ethik*. Ed. E. Bethge. Munich: Kaiser.
―― (1965), *Ethics*. Trans. N. H. Smith. Ed. E. Bethge. New York: Macmillan.
Boor, Carl (1883), *Theophanis Chronographia*. Leipzig: Teubner.
Borelli, D. (2000), 'In margine alla questione ebraica in Giuliano imperatore.' *Koinonia* 24: 94–116.
Borg, Marcus J. (1994), *Meeting Jesus Again for the First Time: The Historical Jesus & the Heart of Contemporary Faith*. 1st edn. San Francisco: HarperSanFrancisco.
―― (1998), *Conflict, Holiness, and Politics in the Teachings of Jesus*. 2nd edn, Harrisburg: Trinity Press International.
Bornkamm, Günther (1952), *Das Ende des Gesetzes: Paulusstudien*. BEvT 16. Munich: Kaiser.
Boyarin, D. (2001), 'The Gospel of the *Memra*: Jewish Binitarianism and the Prologue to John.' *HTR* 94: 243–84.
Brandon, S. G. F. (1957), *The Fall of Jerusalem and the Christian Church: A Study of the Effects of the Jewish Overthrow of A.D. 70 on Christianity*. 2nd edn, London: SPCK.
―― (1967), *Jesus and the Zealots: A Study of the Political Factor in Primitive Christianity*. Manchester: Manchester University Press.
―― (1968), *The Trial of Jesus of Nazareth*. Historic trials series. London: Batsford.
Brandt, O. (2004), 'Jews and Christians in Late Antique Rome and Ostia: Some Aspects of Archaeological and Documentary Evidence.' *Opuscula Romana* 29: 7–27.
Bredin, Mark (2003), *Jesus, Revolutionary of Peace: A Nonviolent Christology in the Book of Revelation*. Paternoster Biblical and Theological Monographs. Carlisle: Paternoster.
Brock, Sebastian P. (1979), 'Jewish Traditions in Syriac Sources.' *JJS* 30: 212–32.
―― (1982), 'An Early Interpretation of *pasah: aggen* in the Palestinian Targum.' In *Interpreting the Hebrew Bible: Essays in Honour of E. I. J. Rosenthal*, 27–34. Ed. J. A. Emerton and S. Reif. Cambridge: Cambridge University Press.
―― (1995), 'A Palestinian Targum Feature in Syriac.' *JJS* 46: 271–82.
―― (1998), 'The Peshitta Old Testament: Between Judaism and Christianity.' *CNS* 19: 483–502.
―― (2002), 'Jacob of Serugh's Verse Homily on Tamar (Gen 38).' *Mus* 115: 279–313.
―― (2005), 'The Bridal Chamber of Light: A Distinctive Feature of Syriac Liturgical Tradition.' *The Harp: A Review of Syriac and Oriental Studies* 18: 179–91.
Brockington, L. H. (1955), 'The Septuagintal Background to the New Testament use of *doxa*.' In *Studies in the Gospels: Essays in Memory of R. H. Lightfoot*, 1–8. Ed. D. Nineham. Oxford: Blackwell.

Brooke, George J. (1985), *Exegesis at Qumran: 4QFlorilegium in its Jewish Context*. JSOTSup 29. Sheffield: JSOT Press.

────── (1991), 'The Kittim in the Qumran Pesharim.' In *Images of Empire*, 135–59. Ed. L. Alexander. JSOTSup 122. Sheffield: JSOT Press.

────── (1998), 'Kingship and Messianism in the Dead Sea Scrolls.' In *King and Messiah in Israel and the Ancient Near East*, 434–55. Ed. J. Day. Sheffield: Sheffield Academic Press.

Brooks, Roger (1988), 'Straw Dogs and Scholarly Ecumenism: The Appropriate Jewish Background for the Study of Origen.' In *Origen of Alexandria: His World and His Legacy*, 63–95. Ed. C. Kannengiesser and W. L. Petersen. Christianity and Judaism in Antiquity 1. Notre Dame: University of Notre Dame Press.

Brown, Raymond E. (1982), *The Epistles of John: A New Translation with Introduction and Commentary*. AB 30. Garden City: Doubleday.

────── (1993), *The Birth of the Messiah: A Commentary on the Infancy Narratives in the Gospels of Matthew and Luke*. 2nd edn, New York: Doubleday.

Brox, Norbert (1979), *Der erste Petrusbrief*. EKKNT 21. Zurich etc./Neukirchen-Vluyn: Benziger/Neukirchener.

Buber, Martin (1964), 'Falsche Propheten.' In *Werke*, 2: *Schriften zur Bibel*:1234–**. München: Kösel.

Buchanan, George Wesley (1978), *Revelation and Redemption: Jewish Documents of Deliverance from the Fall of Jerusalem to the Death of Nahmanides*. 1st edn. Dillsboro: Western North Carolina Press.

Buchheit, V. (1993), 'Numa-Pythagoras in der Deutung Ovids.' *Hermes* 121: 77–99.

Büchler, Adolf (1912), 'Über die Minim von Sepphoris und Tiberias im zweiten und dritten Jahrhundert.' In *Judaica : Festschrift zu Hermann Cohens Siebzigstem Geburtstage*, 271–95. Ed. n. d. Berlin: Cassirer.

Buitenwerf, Rieuwerd (2003), *Book III of the Sibylline Oracles and its Social Setting*. SVTP 17. Leiden/Boston: Brill.

Bultmann, Rudolf (1967), 'Bekenntnis- und Liedfragmente im ersten Petrusbrief.' In *Exegetica: Aufsätze zur Erforschung des Neuen Testaments*, 285–97. Tübingen: Mohr Siebeck.

Burger, Christoph (1972), *Jesus als Davidssohn*. Göttingen: Vandenhoeck & Ruprecht.

Burkert, Walter (1961), 'Hellenistische Pseudopythagorica.' *Philologus* 105: 16-43, 226–46.

Butcher, Kevin (2003), *Roman Syria and the Near East*. London: British Museum.

Caird, G. B. (1966), *A Commentary on the Revelation of St. John the Divine*. New York: Harper and Row.

Cameron, Averil (1991), 'The Eastern Provinces in the Seventh Century: Hellenism and the Emergence of Islam.' In *Hellenismos: Quelques jalons pour une histoire de l'identité grecque. Actes du Colloque de Strasbourg, 25–27 octobre 1989*, 287–313. Ed. S. Saïd. Travaux du Centre de recherche sur le Proche-Orient et la Grèce antiques 11. Leiden/New York: E.J. Brill.

―― (1995), 'The Trophies of Damascus: The Church, the Temple and Sacred Space.' In *Le Temple Lieu de conflit: Actes du colloque de Cartigny 1991*, 203–12. Les cahiers du CEPOA 7. Leuven: Editions Peeters.

―― (2002), 'Blaming the Jews: The Seventh-Century Invasions of Palestine in Context.' In *Mélanges Gilbert Dagron: Travaux et Mémoires*, 14:57–78. Ed. V. Déroche. Paris: Association des amis du Centre d'histore et civilisation de Byzance.

Camery-Hoggatt, Jerry (1992), *Irony in Mark's Gospel: Text and Subtext*. SNTSMS 72. Cambridge: Cambridge University Press.

Cancik, Hubert and Konrad Hitzl, eds, (2003), *Die Praxis der Herrscherverehrung in Rom und seinen Provinzen*. Tübingen: Mohr Siebeck.

Carleton Paget, James (1994), *The Epistle of Barnabas: Outlook and Background*. WUNT 2:64. Tübingen: Mohr Siebeck.

Carmi, T. (1981), *The Penguin Book of Hebrew Verse*. Harmondsworth: Penguin Books.

Carmichael, Joel (1963), *The Death of Jesus*. London: V. Gollancz.

Carnegie, D. R. (1982), 'Worthy is the Lamb: The Hymns in Revelation.' In *Christ the Lord: Studies in Christology presented to Donald Guthrie*, 243–56. Ed. H. H. Rowdon. Leicester: Inter-Varsity Press.

Carrell, Peter R. (1997), *Jesus and the Angels: Angelology and the Christology of the Apocalypse of John*. SNTSMS 95. Cambridge etc.: Cambridge University Press.

Carson, D. A. (2005), 'Syntactical and Text-Critical Observations on John 20.30-31: One More Round on the Purpose of the Fourth Gospel.' *JBL* 124: 693–714.

Carson, D. A. and H. G. M. Williamson, eds, (1988), *It is Written—Scripture Citing Scripture: Essays in Honour of Barnabas Lindars, SSF*. Cambridge etc.: Cambridge University Press.

Carter, Warren (2004), 'Going All the Way? Honouring the Emperor and Sacrificing Wives and Slaves in 1 Peter 2.13–3.6.' In *A Feminist Companion to the Catholic Epistles*, 14–33. Ed. A.-J. Levine and M. M. Robbins. London/New York: T&T Clark.

Cathcart, Kevin J. and Robert P. Gordon, eds, (1989), *The Targum of the Minor Prophets: Translated, with a Critical Introduction, Apparatus, and Notes*. ArBib 14. Wilmington: Michael Glazier.

Chancey, Mark A. (2002), *The Myth of a Gentile Galilee: The Population of Galilee and New Testament Studies*. STNSMS 118. Cambridge etc.: Cambridge University Press.

―― (2005), *Greco-Roman Culture and the Galilee of Jesus*. SNTSMS 134. Cambridge etc.: Cambridge University Press.

Chadwick, Henry, ed., (1953), *Origen: Contra Celsum*. Cambridge: Cambridge University Press.

Charles, R. H., ed., (1913), *The Apocrypha and Pseudepigrapha of the Old Testament*. Vol. 2: *Pseudepigrapha*. Oxford: Clarendon.

Charlesworth, James H. (2001), 'Messianology in the Biblical Pseudepigrapha.' In *Qumran-Messianism: Studies on the Messianic Expectations in the Dead Sea Scrolls*, 21–52. Ed. J. H. Charlesworth *et al*. Tübingen: Mohr Siebeck.

Charlesworth, James H., ed., (1992), *The Messiah: Developments in Earliest Judaism and Christianity*. Minneapolis: Fortress.

Chester, Andrew (1991), 'Jewish Messianic Expectations and Mediatorial Figures and Pauline Christianity.' In *Paulus und das antike Judentum: Tübingen-Durham-Symposium im Gedenken an den 50. Todestag Adolf Schlatters*, 17–89. Ed. M. Hengel and U. Heckel. WUNT 58. Tübingen: Mohr Siebeck.

—— (1992), 'The Parting of the Ways: Eschatology and Messianic Hope.' In *Jews and Christians: The Parting of the Ways A.D. 70-135*, 239–313. Ed. J. D. G. Dunn. WUNT 66. Tübingen: Mohr Siebeck.

Chester, Andrew and Ralph P. Martin (1994), *The Theology of the Letters of James, Peter and Jude*. New Testament Theology. Cambridge, etc.: Cambridge University Press.

Chilton, Bruce (1983), *The Glory of Israel: The Theology and Provenance of the Isaiah Targum*, JSOTSup 23. Sheffield: JSOT Press.

—— (1987), *The Isaiah Targum: Introduction, Translation, Apparatus and Notes*. ArBib 11. Edinburgh: T&T Clark.

Christ, Karl (1994), *Caesar: Annäherungen an einen Diktator*. München: Beck.

Cohen, Gerson D., ed., (1967), *A Critical Edition with a Translation and Notes of the Book of Tradition (Sefer Ha-Qabbalah) by Abraham Ibn Daud*. Judaica 1:3. Philadelphia: Jewish Publication Society of America.

Cohen, Shaye J. D. (1992), 'Judaism to the Mishnah, 135-220 C.E.' In *Christianity and Rabbinic Judaism: A Parallel History of Their Origins and Early Development*, 195–223. Ed. H. Shanks. Washington: Biblical Archaeological Society.

—— (1999), 'The Rabbi in Second-Century Jewish Society.' In *The Cambridge History of Judaism*, 3: *The Early Roman Period*: 922–90. Ed. W. Horbury et al. Cambridge: Cambridge University Press.

Cohn, Norman R. C. (1957), *The Pursuit of the Millennium*. London: Secker & Warburg.

—— (1961), *The Pursuit of the Millennium: Revolutionary Messianism in Medieval and Reformation Europe and its Bearing on Modern Totalitarian Movements*. Harper Torchbooks. 2nd edn, New York: Harper & Row.

Collins, John J. (1974), *The Sibylline Oracles of Egyptian Judaism*. Missoula: Society of Biblical Literature.

—— (1983), 'The Sibylline Oracles.' In *The Old Testament Pseudepigrapha*, 1: 354–405. Ed. J. H. Charlesworth. Garden City: Doubleday.

—— (1987), 'Messianism in the Maccabean Period.' In *Judaisms and Their Messiahs at the Turn of the Christian Era*, 97–110. Ed. J. Neusner et al. Cambridge etc.: Cambridge University Press.

—— (1993a), *A Commentary on the Book of Daniel*. Hermeneia. Minneapolis: Fortress.

—— (1993b), 'The *Son of God* Text from Qumran.' In *From Jesus to John: Essays on Jesus and New Testament Christology in Honour of Marinus de Jonge*, 65–82. Ed. M. C. de Boer. JSNTSup 84. Sheffield: Sheffield Academic Press.

—— (1995), *The Scepter and the Star: The Messiahs of the Dead Sea Scrolls and Other Ancient Literature*. New York: Doubleday.

—— (1996), 'Jesus and the Messiahs of Israel.' In *Geschichte - Tradition - Reflexion: Festschrift für Martin Hengel zum 70. Geburtstag*, 3: 287–302. Ed. H. Cancik *et al.* Tübingen: Mohr Siebeck.

——— (1998), 'Jesus, Messianism and the Dead Sea Scrolls.' In *Qumran–Messianism: Studies on the Messianic Expectations in the Dead Sea Scrolls*, 100–19. Ed. J. H. Charlesworth *et al.* Tübingen: Mohr Siebeck.

—— (2000), *Between Athens and Jerusalem: Jewish Identity in the Hellenistic Diaspora*. The Biblical Resource Series. 2nd edn, Grand Rapids: Eerdmans.

—— (2001), 'Cult and Culture: The Limits of Hellenization in Judea.' In *Hellenism in the Land of Israel*, 38–61. Ed. J. J. Collins and G. E. Sterling. Notre Dame: University of Notre Dame Press.

—— (2002), 'Temporality and Politics in Jewish Apocalyptic Literature.' In *Apocalyptic in History and Tradition*, 26–43. Ed. C. Rowland and J. Barton. JSPSup 43. Sheffield: Sheffield Academic Press.

Colpe, Carsten (1990), *Das Siegel der Propheten: Historische Beziehungen zwischen Judentum, Judenchristentum, Heidentum und frühem Islam*. Arbeiten zur neutestamentlichen Theologie und Zeitgeschichte 3. Berlin: Institut Kirche und Judentum.

—— (1991), 'Himmelfahrt.' *RAC* 15: 212–19.

—— (1996), 'Jenseitsfahrt II (Unterwelts- oder Höllenfahrt).' *RAC* 17: 466–89.

Colpe, Carsten *et al.* (1996a), 'Jenseitsfahrt I (Himmelfahrt).' *RAC* 17: 407–66.

—— (1996b), 'Jenseits.' *RAC* 17: 246–407.

Colpe, Carsten and Peter Habermehl (1996), 'Jenseitsreise.' *RAC* 17: 490–543.

Conzelmann, Hans (1955), 'Was glaubte die frühe Christenheit?' *SThU* 25: 61–74.

Corley, Kathleen E. (1995), '1 Peter.' In *Searching the Scriptures*, 2: *A Feminist Commentary*, 349–60. Ed. E. Schüssler Fiorenza. London: SCM.

Cotton, H. M. (1998), 'The Rabbis and the Documents.' In *Jews in the Graeco-Roman World*, 167–79. Ed. M. Goodman. Oxford: Clarendon.

Court, John (1979), *Myth and History in the Book of Revelation*. Atlanta: John Knox.

Cox, Claude E. (2001), 'Schaper's *Eschatology* meets Kraus's *Theology of the Psalms*.' In *The Old Greek Psalter: studies in honour of Albert Pietersma*, 289–311. Ed. R. J. V. Hiebert *et al.* JSOTSup 332. Sheffield: Sheffield Academic Press.

Cranfield, C. E. B. (1975–9), *A Critical and Exegetical Commentary on the Epistle to the Romans*. 2 vols; Edinburgh: T&T Clark.

Crone, Patricia and M. A. Cook (1977), *Hagarism: The making of the Islamic world*. Cambridge/New York: Cambridge University Press.

Crossan, John Dominic and Jonathan L. Reed (2004), *In Search of Paul: How Jesus's Apostle Opposed Rome's Empire with God's Kingdom. A New Vision of Paul's Words & World*. New York: HarperSanFrancisco.

Crossley, James G. (2004), *The Date of Mark's Gospel: Insights From the Law in Earliest Christianity*. JSNTSup 266. London/New York: T&T Clark.

—— (2006), *Why Christianity Happened: A Sociohistorical Account of Christian Origins 26-50 CE*. Louisville: Westminster John Knox.

Cullmann, Oscar (1963), *The Christology of the New Testament*. Trans. S. C. Guthrie and C. A. M. Hall. Rev. edn, Philadelphia: Westminster Press.

Cullmann, Oscar (1970), *Jesus and the Revolutionaries*. Trans. G. Putnam. New York: Harper & Row.

Cureton, William (1864), *Ancient Syriac Documents Relative to the Earliest Establishment of Christianity in Edessa and the Neighbouring Countries*. Ed. W. Wright. London/Edinburgh: Williams & Norgate.

Dagron, Gilbert and Vincent Déroche (1991), 'Juifs et chrétiens dans l'Orient du VIIe siècle.' *Travaux et Mémoires* 11: 17–274.

Dahl, Nils Alstrup (1974), *The Crucified Messiah, and Other Essays*. Minneapolis: Augsburg.

—— (1991), *Jesus the Christ: The Origins and Development of New Testament Christology*. Minneapolis: Fortress.

Daley, Brian (1991), *The Hope of the Early Church: A Handbook of Patristic Eschatology*. Cambridge etc.: Cambridge University Press.

Dalman, G. (1888), *Der leidende und der sterbende Messias der Synagoge im ersten nachchristlichen Jahrtausend*. Berlin: H. Reuther.

Dalton, William J. (1989), *Christ's Proclamation to the Spirits: A Study of 1 Peter 3:18–4:6*. AnBib 23. 2nd edn, Rome: Pontifical Biblical Institute.

Dan, Joseph (1998), 'Armilus: the Jewish Antichrist and the Origins and Dating of the Sefer Zerubbavel.' In *Toward the Millennium: Messianic Expectations from the Bible to Waco*, 73–104. Ed. P. Schäfer and M. R. Cohen. Leiden: Brill.

Davids, Peter H. (1982), *The Epistle of James: A Commentary on the Greek Text*. Grand Rapids: Eerdmans.

Day, John (2004), 'How Many Pre-exilic Psalms Are There?' In *In Search of Pre-exilic Israel: Proceedings of the Oxford Old Testament Seminar*, 225–50. Ed. J. Day. JSOTSup 406. London/New York: T&T Clark International.

De Boor, C. (1883), *Theophanis Chronographia*. Leipzig.

de Jonge, M. (1986), 'The Earliest Christian Use of *Christos*: Some Suggestions.' *NTS* 32: 321–43.

de Jonge, Marinus (1966), 'The Use of the Word "Anointed" in the Time of Jesus.' *NovT* 8: 132–48.

—— (1977), *Jesus: Stranger from Heaven and Son of God. Jesus Christ and the Christians in Johannine Perspective*. Sources for Biblical Study 11. Missoula: Scholars Press.

—— (1980), 'The Use of the Expression ὁ χριστός in the Apocalypse of John.' In *L'Apocalypse johannique et l'Apocalyptique dans le Nouveau Testament*, 267–81. Ed. J. Lambrecht. BETL 53. Leuven: Leuven University Press.

—— (1988), *Christology in Context: The Earliest Christian Response to Jesus*. Philadelphia: Westminster Press.

—— (1991), *Jewish Eschatology, Early Christian Christology, and the Testaments of the Twelve Patriarchs: Collected Essays of Marinus de Jonge*. NovTSup 63. Leiden/New York: E. J. Brill.

de Lange, Nicholas R. M. (1976), *Origen and the Jews: Studies in Jewish-Christian Relations in Third-Century Palestine*. Cambridge/New York: Cambridge University Press.

—— (1978), 'Jewish Attitudes to the Roman Empire.' In *Imperialism in the Ancient World*, 255–81. Ed. P. D. A. Garnsey and C. R. Whittaker. Cambridge: Cambridge University Press.

—— (2005), 'Jews in the Age of Justinian.' In *The Cambridge Companion to the Age of Justinian*, 401–29. Ed. M. Maas. Cambridge: Cambridge University Press.

de Savignac, J. (1959), 'Le Messianisme de Philon d'Alexandrie.' *NovT* 4: 319–24.

de Ste. Croix, G. E. M. (1963), 'Why Were the Early Christians Persecuted?' *Past & Present* 26, 6–38.

Dehandschutter, B. (1980), 'The Meaning of Witness in the Apocalypse.' In *L'Apocalypse johannique et l'Apocalyptique dans le Nouveau Testament*. Ed. J. Lambrecht. BETL 53. Leuven: Leuven University Press.

Déroche, Vincent (1991), 'Doctrina Jacobi.' *Travaux et Mémoires* 11: 69–219.

—— (1999), 'Polémique anti-judaïque et emergence de l'Islam (7e-8e s.)', *Revue des Etudes Byzantines* 57, 141–61.

—— ed. and tr. (1991), *Doctrina Jacobi*, *Travaux et Mémoires* 11, 69–219.

Desroche, Henri (1969), *Dieux d'hommes: Dictionnaire des messianismes et millénarismes de l'ère chrétienne*. Paris: Mouton.

Dibelius, Martin and Heinrich Greeven (1976), *James: A Commentary on the Epistle of James*. Hermeneia. Philadelphia: Fortress Press.

DiTommaso, Lorenzo (2005), *The Book of Daniel and the Apocryphal Daniel Literature*. SVTP 20. Leiden/Boston: Brill.

Doble, Peter (1996) *The Paradox of Salvation: Luke's Theology of the Cross*. SNTSMS 87. Cambridge: Cambridge University Press.

—— (2006), 'Luke 24.26, 44 – Songs of God's Servant: David and his Psalms in Luke-Acts.' *JSNT* 28: 267–83.

Dodd, C. H. (1953), *The Interpretation of the Fourth Gospel*. Cambridge: Cambridge University Press.

—— (1963), *Historical Tradition in the Fourth Gospel*. Cambridge: Cambridge University Press.

Dogniez, Cécile and Marguerite Harl (1992), *La Bible d'Alexandrie*. Vol. 5: *Le Deutéronome*. Paris: Editions du Cerf.

Dorival, Gilles (1994), *La Bible d'Alexandrie*. Vol. 4: *Les Nombres*. Paris: Editions du Cerf.

Dorival, Gilles, Marguerite Harl, and Olivier Munnich (1988), *La Bible grecque des Septante: Du Judaïsme Hellénistique au Christianisme ancien*. Initiations au Christianisme ancien. Paris: Cerf/C.N.R.S.

Drijvers, H. J. W. (1992), 'Syrian Christianity and Judaism.' In *The Jews among Pagans and Christians*, 124–46. Ed. J. Lieu *et al.* London: Routledge.

—— (1996), 'Early Syriac Christianity: Some Recent Publications.' *VC* 50: 159–77.

Droysen, Johann Gustav (1877–8), *Geschichte des Hellenismus*. 3 vols; 2nd edn, Gotha: Perthes.

Duff, Tim (1999), *Plutarch's Lives: Exploring Virtue and Vice*. Oxford: Clarendon Press.

Dulaey, Martine (1993), *Victorin de Poetovio, premier exégète latin*. Collection des études augustiniennes. Série Antiquité 139–140. 2 vols. Paris: Institut d'études augustiniennes.

Duling, Dennis C. (1978), 'The Therapeutic Son of David: An Element in Matthew's Christological Apologetic.' *NTS* 24: 392–409.
Dunn, James D. G. (1988), *Romans*. WBC 38. 2 vols; Dallas: Word Books.
—— (1994), 'Jesus Tradition in Paul.' In *Studying the Historical Jesus: Evaluations of the State of Current Research*, 155–78. Ed. B. Chilton and C. A. Evans. Leiden etc.: Brill.
—— (1998), *The Theology of Paul the Apostle*. Grand Rapids: Eerdmans.
Dürr, Lorenz (1925), *Ursprung und Ausbau der israelitisch-jüdischen Heilandserwartung: Ein Beitrag zur Theologie des Alten Testaments*. Berlin: Schwetschke.
Durst, Michael (1987), *Die Eschatologie des Hilarius von Poitiers: Ein Beitrag zur Dogmengeschichte des vierten Jahrhunderts*. Bonn: Borengässer.
Eger, Hans (1933), *Die Eschatologie Augustins*. Greifswalder theologische Forschungen 1. Greifswald: Bamberg.
Eisenman, Robert H. (1996), *The Dead Sea Scrolls and the First Christians: Essays and Translations*. Shaftesbury: Element.
—— (1997), *James, the Brother of Jesus*. London: Faber and Faber.
Eisler, Robert (1929), *Iesous basileus ou basileusas: Die messianische Unabhängigkeitsbewegung vom Auftreten Johannes des Täufers bis zum Untergang Jakobs des Gerechten*. Religionswissenschaftliche Bibliothek 9.1–2. Heidelberg: C. Winter.
—— (1931), *The Messiah Jesus and John the Baptist According to Flavius Josephus' Recently Rediscovered 'Capture of Jerusalem' and the Other Jewish and Christian Sources*. Trans. A. H. Krappe. London: Methuen.
Eliav, Y. Z. (2003), 'The Urban Layout of Aelia Capitolina: A New View from the Perspective of the Temple Mount.' In *The Bar Kokhba War Reconsidered: New Perspectives on the Second Jewish Revolt against Rome*, 241–77. Ed. P. Schäfer. Tübingen: Mohr Siebeck.
Elliott, John H. (1966), *The Elect and the Holy: An Exegetical Examination of I Peter 2:4-10 and the Phrase Basileion Hierateuma*. NovTSup 12. Leiden: Brill.
—— (1981), *A Home for the Homeless: A Sociological Exegesis of 1 Peter, Its Situation and Strategy*. Philadelphia/London: Fortress/SCM.
—— (1986), '1 Peter, its Situation and Strategy: a Discussion with David Balch.' In *Perspectives on First Peter*, 61–78. Ed. C. H. Talbert. Macon: Mercer University Press.
—— (2000), *1 Peter: A New Translation with Introduction and Commentary*. AB 37B. 1st. New York: Doubleday.
Elsdon, Ron (2001), 'Was Paul "Converted" or "Called"? Questions of Methodology.' *PIBA* 24: 17-47.
Elsner, Jas (2001), 'Cultural Resistance and the Visual Image: The Case of Dura Europos.' *CP* 96: 269–304.
Epstein, Isidore (1935), *The Babylonian Talmud: Seder Nezikin*. Vol. 3: *Sanhedrin*. London: Soncino Press.
Erder, Yoram (2003), 'The Mourners of Zion: The Karaites in Jerusalem in the Tenth and Eleventh Centuries.' In *Karaite Judaism: A Guide to its History and Literary Sources*, 213–35. Ed. M. Polliack. Handbuch der Orientalistik 1:73. Leiden: Brill.

—— (2004), *Karaite Mourners of Zion and the Qumran Scrolls*. (Hebr.). Tel-Aviv: Kibbutz Ha-Meuchad.
Eskola, Timo (2001), *Messiah and the Throne: Jewish Merkabah Mysticism and Early Christian Exaltation Discourse*. WUNT 2:142. Tübingen: Mohr Siebeck.
Estin, Colette (1984), *Les psautiers de Jérôme à la lumière des traductions juives antérieures*. Collectanea Biblica Latina 15. Rome: San Girolamo.
Evans, Craig A. (1999), 'Jesus and the Dead Sea Scrolls.' In *The Dead Sea Scrolls after Fifty Years*, 573–98. Ed. P. W. Flint and J. C. VanderKam. Leiden: Brill.
—— (2000), 'Messiahs.' *Encyclopedia of the Dead Sea Scrolls* 1: 537–42.
Evans, Richard J. (1997), *In Defence of History*. London: Granta Books.
Even-Shmuel (Kaufman), Yehuda (1954), *Midreshei Ge'ullah*. 2nd edn, Jerusalem/Tel Aviv: Mosad Bialik.
Feldman, Louis H. (1977), 'Hengel's Judaism and Hellenism in retrospect.' *JBL* 96: 371–82.
—— (1986), 'How much Hellenism in Jewish Palestine?' *HUCA* 57: 83–111.
Feldmeier, Reinhard (1992), *Die Christen als Fremde: Die Metapher der Fremde in der antiken Welt, im Urchristentum und im 1. Petrusbrief*. WUNT 64. Tübingen: Mohr Siebeck.
Ferrua, Antonio (1991), *The Unknown Catacomb: A Unique Discovery of Early Christian Art*. New Lanark: Geddes & Grosset.
Fiedrowicz, Michael (2000), *Apologie im frühen Christentum: Die Kontroverse um den christlichen Wahrheitsanspruch in den ersten Jahrhunderten*. Paderborn: Ferdinand Schöningh.
Field, Frederick (1875), *Origenis Hexaplorum quae supersunt: Veterum interpretum graecorum in totum Vetus Testamentum fragmenta*. 2 vols; Oxford: Clarendon.
Filoramo, G. (1998), 'Riflessioni in margine al profetismo cristiano primitivo', *Rivista di Storia e Letteratura Religiosa* 34: 95–107.
—— (2005), *Veggenti, profeti, gnostici: Identità e conflitti nel cristianesimo antico*. Scienze e storia delle religioni N.S. 1. 1. Brescia: Morcelliana.
Fine, Steven (1997), *This Holy Place: On the Sanctity of the Synagogue During the Greco-Roman Period*. Notre Dame: University of Notre Dame Press.
—— (2005), 'Between Liturgy and Social History: Priestly Power in Late Antique Palestinian Synagogues?' *JJS* 56: 1–9.
Fiocchi Nicolai, Vincenzo (2001), *Strutture funerarie ed edifici di culto paleocristiani di Roma dal IV al VI secolo*. Vatican City: Pontificia Commissione di Archeologia Sacra.
Fischer, Bonifatius (1949), *Vetus Latina: Die Reste der altlateinischen Bibel*. Vol. 1: *Genesis*. Freiburg: Herder.
Fishbane, Michael A. (1985), *Biblical Interpretation in Ancient Israel*. Oxford: Clarendon.
Fishwick, Duncan (1987), *The Imperial Cult in the Latin West: Studies in the Ruler Cult of the Western Provinces of the Roman Empire*. Etudes Préliminaires aux Religions Orientales dans l'Empire Romain 108. Vol. 1.1. Leiden/New York: Brill.

Fitzmyer, Joseph A. (1981–5), *The Gospel According to Luke: A New Translation with Introduction and Commentary*. AB 28. 2 vols; New York: Doubleday.
——— (1993a), '4Q246: The "Son of God" Document from Qumran.' *Bib* 74: 153–74.
——— (1993b), *Romans: a New Translation with Introduction and Commentary*. AB 33. New York: Doubleday.
——— (1997), *The Semitic Background of the New Testament*. The Biblical Resource Series. Combined. Grand Rapids/Livonia: Eerdmans/Dove.
——— (2007), *The One Who Is to Come*. Grand Rapids: Eerdmans
Fleischer, Ezra (1984–5), 'אלעזר י׳ של פעילותו ומקום זמנו שאלת לפתרון קיליר ברבי' *Tarbiz* 54: 383–427.
Flusin, B. (1991), 'Démons et Sarrasins: l'auteur et le propos des Diègèmata stèriktika d'Anastase le Sinaïte', *Travaux et Mémoires* 11, 381–410.
Foerster, Gideon (1976), 'Art and Architecture in Palestine.' In *The Jewish People in the First Century*, 2: 971–1006. Ed. S. Safrai and M. Stern. Philadelphia: Fortress Press.
——— (1992), 'The Ancient Synagogues of the Galilee.' In *The Galilee in Late Antiquity*, 289–319. Ed. L. I. Levine. New York: Jewish Theological Seminary of America.
Fonrobert, Charlotte Elisheva (2001), 'The *Didascalia Apostolorum*: A Mishnah for the Disciples of Jesus.' *JECS* 9: 483–509.
Fortna, Robert T. (1989), *The Fourth Gospel and its Predecessor*. Edinburgh: T&T Clark.
Fossum, Jarl E. (1999), 'Glory.' In *Dictionary of Deities and Demons in the Bible*, 348–52. 2nd edn, Leiden/Grand Rapids: Brill/Eerdmans.
Fowler, Robert (1981), *Loaves and Fishes: The Function of the Feeding Stories in the Gospel of Mark*. Chico: Scholars Press.
Frank, Daniel (2004), *Search Scripture Well: Karaite Exegetes and the Origins of the Jewish Bible Commentary in the Islamic East*. Etudes sur le Judaïsme Médiéval 29. Leiden/Boston: Brill.
Frankfurter, David (1992), 'Lest Egypt's City Be Deserted: Religion and Ideology in the Egyptian Response to the Jewish Revolt (116–117 C.E.).' *JJS* 43: 203–20.
——— (1993), *Elijah in Upper Egypt: The Apocalypse of Elijah and Early Egyptian Christianity*. SACStudies. Minneapolis: Fortress Press.
——— (1996), 'The Legacy of Jewish Apocalypses in Early Christianity: Regional Trajectories.' In *The Jewish Apocalyptic Heritage in Early Christianity*, 129–200. Ed. J. C. VanderKam and W. Adler. CRINT 3:4. Assen/Minneapolis: Van Gorcum/Fortress Press.
——— (1998), 'Early Christian Apocalypticism: Literature and Social World.' In *The Encyclopedia of Apocalypticism*, 1: The Origins of Apocalypticism in Judaism and Christianity: 415–56. Ed. J. J. Collins. New York: Continuum.
Fredriksen, Paula (1988), *From Jesus to Christ: The Origins of the New Testament Images of Jesus*. New Haven/London: Yale University Press.
Frend, W. H. C. (2000), 'Martyrdom and Political Oppression.' In *The Early Christian World*, 815–39. Ed. P. F. Esler. London/New York: Routledge.
Freyne, Sean (1998), *Galilee from Alexander the Great to Hadrian, 323 B.C.E. to 135 C.E.: A Study of Second Temple Judaism*. 2nd edn, Edinburgh: T&T Clark.

——— (2000), *Galilee and Gospel: Collected Essays*. WUNT 125. Tübingen: Mohr Siebeck.
——— (2001), 'A Galilean Messiah?' *ST* 55: 198–218.
——— (2004), *Jesus, a Jewish Galilean: A New Reading of the Jesus-Story*. London/New York: T&T Clark International.
Friedmann, Y. (1986), 'Finality of Prophethood in Sunni Islam', *JSAI* 7: 177–215.
Friesen, Steven J. (2001), *Imperial Cults and the Apocalypse of John: Reading Revelation in the Ruins*. Oxford: Oxford University Press.
Frost, S. B. (1952), *Old Testament Apocalyptic, its Origins and Growth*. The Fernley-Hartley Lecture 1952. London: Epworth Press.
Fuks, Alexander (1961), 'Aspects of the Jewish Revolt in A. D. 115 – 117.' *JRS* 51: 98–104.
Gaddis, Michael (2005), *There is no Crime for Those Who Have Christ: Religious Violence in the Christian Roman Empire*. The Transformation of the Classical Heritage 39. Berkeley: University of California Press.
Gafni, Isaiah M. (1992), 'The World of the Talmud: From the Mishnah to the Arab Conquest.' In *Christianity and Rabbinic Judaism: A Parallel History of Their Origins and Early Development*, 225–65. Ed. H. Shanks. Washington: Biblical Archaeological Society.
Gager, John G. (1998), 'Messiahs and Their Followers.' In *Toward the Millennium: Messianic Expectations from the Bible to Waco*, 37–46. Ed. P. Schäfer and M. R. Cohen. Leiden/Boston: Brill.
——— (2000), *Reinventing Paul*. Oxford/New York: Oxford University Press.
García Martínez, Florentino (1988), 'Qumran Origins and Early History: A Groningen Hypothesis.' *FO* 25: 111–36.
García Martínez, Florentino and E. J. C. Tigchelaar (1996), *The Dead Sea Scrolls Translated: The Qumran Texts in English*. Trans. W. G. E. Watson. 2nd edn, Leiden etc./Grand Rapids: Brill/Eerdmans.
García Martínez, Florentino and Eibert J. C. Tigchelaar, eds, (1997–8), *The Dead Sea Scrolls Study Edition*. 2 vols; Leiden/Grand Rapids: Brill/Eerdmans.
Gaston, Lloyd (1987), *Paul and the Torah*. Vancouver: University of British Columbia Press.
Gathercole, Simon (2005), 'The Heavenly ἀνατολή (Luke 1:78-9).' *JTS* 56: 471–88.
Gatz, Bodo (1967), *Weltalter, goldene Zeit und sinnverwandte Vorstellungen*. Spudasmata 16. Hildesheim: Olms.
Geiger, Joseph (1979), 'The last Jewish revolt again Rome: A Reconsideration.' *Scripta Classica Israelica* 5: 250–7.
Gelston, A. (1997), 'Was the Peshitta of Isaiah of Christian Origin?' In *Writing and Reading the Scroll of Isaiah: Studies of an Interpretive Tradition*, 563–82. Ed. C. C. Broyles and C. A. Evans. VTSup 70.2. Leiden: Brill.
Gera, Dov (1998), *Judaea and Mediterranean Politics, 219 to 161 B.C.E.* Brill's Series in Jewish Studies 8. Leiden/New York: Brill.
Gesche, Helga (1968), *Die Vergottung Caesars*. Frankfurter althistorische Studien 1. Kallmünz: Lassleben.
——— (1976), *Caesar*. Darmstadt: Wissenschaftliche Buchgesellschaft.

Gese, Hartmut (1983), 'Der Messias.' In *Zur biblischen Theologie: Alttestamentliche Vorträge*, 128–51. 2nd edn, Tübingen: Mohr Siebeck.

——— (1984a), 'Anfang und Ende der Apokalyptik, dargestellt am Sacharjabuch.' In *Vom Sinai zum Zion: Alttestamentliche Beiträge zur biblischen Theologie*, 202–30. Munich: Kaiser.

——— (1984b), 'Der Davidsbund und die Zionserwählung.' In *Vom Sinai zum Zion: Alttestamentliche Beiträge zur biblischen Theologie*, 113–29. Munich: Kaiser.

——— (1984c), 'Natus ex Virgine.' In *Vom Sinai zum Zion: Alttestamentliche Beiträge zur biblischen Theologie*, 130–46. Munich: Kaiser.

Gibbs, J. M. (1964), 'Purpose and Pattern in Matthew's Use of the Title "Son of God".' *NTS* 10: 446–64.

Gillingham, S. E. (1998), 'The Messiah in the Psalms: A Question of Reception History and the Psalter.' In *King and Messiah in Israel and the Ancient Near East: Proceedings of the Oxford Old Testament Seminar*, 209–37. Ed. J. Day. JSOTSup 270. Sheffield: Sheffield Academic Press.

Giovannini, A. (1996), 'L'interdit contre les chrétiens: raison d'état ou mesure de police?' *Cahiers du Centre Glotz* 7: 103–34.

Glaser, K. (1936), 'Numa Pompilius.' *PW* 17.1: 1242–52.

Goldberg, Arnold (1978), *Erlösung durch Leiden: Drei rabbinische Homilien über die Trauernden Zions und den leidenden Messias Efraim (PesR 34. 36. 37)*. Frankfurter judaistische Studien 4. Frankfurt: Gesellschaft zur Förderung Judaistischer Studien.

——— (1979), 'Die Namen des Messias in der rabbinischen Traditionsliteratur: Ein Beitrag zur Messianologie des rabbinischen Judentums.' *Frankfurter Judaistische Beiträge* 7: 1–93.

Goldman, J. (1973), 'The Dura Synagogue Costumes and Parthian Art.' In *The Dura-Europos Synagogue: A Re-evaluation (1932–1972)*, 53–77. Ed. J. Gutmann. Religion and the Arts 1. Chambersburg: American Academy of Religion.

Goldstein, Jonathan A. (1987), 'How the Authors of 1 and 2 Maccabees Treated the "Messianic" Promises.' In *Judaisms and Their Messiahs at the Turn of the Christian Era*, 69–96. Ed. J. Neusner *et al*. Cambridge etc.: Cambridge University Press.

Goodacre, M. (2002), *The Case Against Q*. Harrisburg: Trinity Press International.

Goodblatt, David M. (1994), *The Monarchic Principle: Studies in Jewish Self-Government in Antiquity*. TSAJ 38. Tübingen: Mohr Siebeck.

Goodenough, E. R. (1938), *The Politics of Philo Judaeus: Practice and Theory*. New Haven/London: Yale University Press/Oxford University Press.

——— (1988), *Jewish Symbols in the Greco-Roman Period*. Ed. J. Neusner. Bollingen Series. Abridged edn, Princeton: Princeton University Press.

Goodman, Martin (1983), *State and Society in Roman Galilee, A.D. 132–212*. Totowa, NJ: Rowman and Allenheld.

——— (1987), *The Ruling Class of Judaea: The Origins of the Jewish Revolt Against Rome, A.D. 66–70*. Cambridge: Cambridge University Press.

——— (1994), 'Sadducees and Essenes after 70.' In *Crossing the Boundaries: Essays in Biblical Interpretation in Honour of Michael D. Goulder*, 347–56. Ed. S. E. Porter *et al*. Leiden: Brill.

—— (2004), 'Trajan and the Origins of Roman Hostility to the Jews.' *Past & Present* 182: 3–29.
Goodspeed, Edgar Johnson (1966), *A History of Early Christian Literature*. Ed. R. M. Grant. Rev. edn, Chicago: University of Chicago Press.
Goranson, Stephen (1999), 'Joseph of Tiberias Revisited: Orthodoxies and Heresies in Fourth-Century Galilee.' In *Galilee through the Centuries: Confluence of Cultures*, 335–43. Ed. E. M. Meyers. Duke Judaic Studies Series 1. Winona Lake: Eisenbrauns.
Gordon, Robert P. (1978), 'The Targumists as Eschatologists.' In *Congress Volume: Göttingen 1977*, 113–30. Ed. J. A. Emerton. VTSup 29. Leiden: Brill.
—— (1986), *1 & 2 Samuel: A Commentary*. Exeter: Paternoster.
—— (1996), 'Translational Features of the Peshitta in 1 Samuel.' In *Targumic and Cognate Studies: Essays in Honour of Martin McNamara*, 163–76. Ed. K. J. Cathcart and M. Maher. JSOTSup 230. Sheffield: Sheffield Academic Press.
—— (1998), 'The Syriac Old Testament: Provenance, Perspective and Translation Technique.' In *The Interpretation of the Bible: The International Symposium in Slovenia*, 355–69. Ed. J. Krašovec. JSOTSup 289. Sheffield: Sheffield Academic Press.
—— (2003), 'The Ephraimate Messiah and the Targum(s) to Zechariah 12.10.' In *Reading Right to Left: Essays on the Hebrew Bible in Honour of David J. A. Clines*, 184–95. Ed. J. Cheryl Exum and H. G. M. Williamson. JSOTSup. 373. London: Sheffield Academic Press.
Grabar, O. (1999), 'Space and Holiness in Medieval Jerusalem.' In *Jerusalem: Its sanctity and centrality to Judaism, Christianity, and Islam*, 275–86 [also published in *Islamic Studies* 40 (2001), 681–692]. Ed. L. I. Levine. New York/London: Continuum.
Graf, F. (1997), 'Egeria.' *DNP* 3: 888.
Green, William Scott (1987), 'Introduction: Messiah in Judaism. Rethinking the Question.' In *Judaisms and Their Messiahs at the Turn of the Christian Era*, 1–14. Ed. J. Neusner *et al*. Cambridge etc.: Cambridge University Press.
Gressmann, Hugo (1929), *Der Messias*. Göttingen: Vandenhoeck & Ruprecht.
Griffith, Terry (2002), *Keep Yourselves from Idols: A New Look at 1 John*. JSNTSup 233. London/New York: Sheffield Academic Press.
Grillmeier, Alois (1978), 'Der Gottessohn im Totenreich.' In *Mit ihm und in ihm: Christologische Forschungen und Perspektiven*, 76–174. 2nd edn, Freiburg im Breisgau: Herder.
—— (1990), *Jesus der Christus im Glauben der Kirche*. 3rd edn, Vol. 1: *Von der apostolischen Zeit bis zum Konzil von Chalcedon (451)*. Freiburg etc.: Herder.
Gruen, Erich S. (1996), 'Hellenistic Kingship: Puzzles, Problems and Possibilities.' In *Aspects of Hellenistic Kingship*, 116–25. Ed. P. Bilde. Studies in Hellenistic Civilisation 7. Aarhus: Aarhus University Press.
—— (1998), *Heritage and Hellenism: The Reinvention of Jewish Tradition*. Berkeley: University of California Press.
Grundmann, Walter (1974), 'Χρίω κτλ., D: The Christ-Statements of the New Testament.' *TDNT* 9: 527–73.

Gryson, Roger and Paul-Augustin Deproost, eds, (1993), *Commentaires de Jérôme sur le prophète Isaïe: Livres I-IV*. AGLB 23. Freiburg: Herder.
Gryson, Roger and C. Gabriel (1998), *Commentaires de Jérôme sur le prophète Isaïe: Livres XII-XV*. AGLB 35. Freiburg: Herder.
Guthrie, Donald (1994), 'The Christology of Revelation.' In *Jesus of Nazareth: Lord and Christ. Essays on the Historical Jesus and New Testament Christology*, pp. 397–409. Ed. J. B. Green and M. Turner. Grand Rapids/Carlisle: Eerdmans/Paternoster.
Gutmann, Joseph (1973), 'Programmatic Painting in the Dura Synagogue.' In *The Dura-Europos Synagogue: A Re-evaluation (1932–1972)*, 137–53. Ed. J. Gutmann. Religion and the Arts 1. Chambersburg: American Academy of Religion.
Gzella, Holger (2001), 'Das Kalb und das Einhorn: Endzeittheophanie und Messianismus in der Septuaginta-Fassung von Ps. 29(28).' In *Der Septuaginta-Psalter: Sprachliche und theologische Aspekte*, 257–90. Ed. E. Zenger. Herders biblische Studien 32. Freiburg etc.: Herder.
—— (2002), *Lebenszeit und Ewigkeit: Studien zur Eschatologie und Anthropologie des Septuaginta-Psalters*. BBB 134. Berlin: Philo.
Haas, Christopher (1997), *Alexandria in Late Antiquity: Topography and Social Conflict*. Ancient Society and History. Baltimore: Johns Hopkins University Press.
Habas-Rubin, Ephrat (1994), 'The Jewish Origin of Julius Africanus.' *JJS* 45: 86–91.
Haber, Susan (2005), 'From Priestly Torah to Christ Cultus: The Re-Vision of Covenant and Cult in Hebrews.' *JSNT* 28: 105–24.
Hachlili, Rachel (1998), *Ancient Jewish Art and Archaeology in the Diaspora*. Handbuch der Orientalistik 7.1.2, B9. Leiden/Boston: Brill.
Hadas-Lebel, Mireille (1984), 'Jacob et Esaü, ou Israël et Rome dans le Talmud et le Midrash.' *RHR* 201: 369–92.
Hagner, Donald Alfred (1984), *The Jewish Reclamation of Jesus: An Analysis and Critique of Modern Jewish study of Jesus*. Grand Rapids: Academie Books.
Hahn, August and G. Ludwig Hahn (1897), *Bibliothek der Symbole und Glaubensregeln der Alten Kirche*. 3rd edn, Breslau: Morgenstern.
Hamacher, Elisabeth (1999), *Gershom Scholem und die allgemeine Religionsgeschichte*. Religionsgeschichtliche Versuche und Vorarbeiten 45. Berlin/New York: de Gruyter.
Hanson, K. C. and Douglas E. Oakman (1998), *Palestine in the Time of Jesus: Social Structures and Social Conflicts*. Minneapolis: Fortress Press.
Hardin, Justin K. (2006), 'Decrees and Drachmas at Thessalonica: An Illegal Assembly in Jason's House (Acts 17.1-10a).' *NTS* 52: 29–49.
Harl, Marguerite (1986), *La Bible d'Alexandrie*. Vol. 1: *La Genèse*. Paris: Cerf.
Harnack, Adolf von (1924), *Marcion: Das Evangelium vom fremden Gott*. TU 45. 2nd edn, Leipzig: J. C. Hinrichs.
Hays, Richard B. (1996), *The Moral Vision of the New Testament: Community, Cross, New Creation*. New York: HarperSanFrancisco.
—— (2005), *The Conversion of the Imagination: Essays on Paul as Interpreter of Israel's Scripture*. Grand Rapids: Eerdmans.

Hecht, Richard D. (1987), 'Philo and Messiah.' In *Judaisms and Their Messiahs at the Turn of the Christian Era*, 139–68. Ed. J. Neusner *et al*. Cambridge etc.: Cambridge University Press.

Heid, Stefan (1993), *Chiliasmus und Antichrist-Mythos: Eine frühchristliche Kontroverse um das Heilige Land*. Hereditas 6. Bonn: Borengässer.

Heinemann, Joseph (1975), 'The Messiah of Ephraim and the Premature Exodus of the Tribe of Ephraim.' *HTR* 68: 1–15.

—— (1977), *Prayer in the Talmud: Forms and Patterns*. Trans. R. Sarason. SJ 10. Berlin/New York: de Gruyter.

Hemer, Colin J. (1986), *The Letters to the Seven Churches of Asia in their Local Setting*. Sheffield: JSOT Press.

Hengel, Martin (1961), *Die Zeloten: Untersuchungen zur jüdischen Freiheitsbewegung in der Zeit von Herodes I bis 70 n. Chr*. AGSU 1. Leiden: Brill.

—— (1971), *Was Jesus a revolutionist?* Trans. W. Klassen. Philadelphia: Fortress Press.

—— (1973), *Victory over Violence: Jesus and the Revolutionists*. Trans. D. E. Green. Philadelphia: Fortress Press.

—— (1983), *Between Jesus and Paul: Studies in the Earliest History of Christianity*. Trans. J. Bowden. London: SCM.

—— (1988), *Judentum und Hellenismus: Studien zu ihrer Begegnung unter besonderer Berücksichtigung Palästinas bis zur Mitte des 2. Jh.s v. Chr*. WUNT 10. 3rd edn, Tübingen: Mohr Siebeck.

—— (1989a), *The 'Hellenization' of Judaea in the First Century after Christ*. Trans. J. Bowden. London/Philadelphia: SCM Press/Trinity Press International.

—— (1989b), *The Zealots: Investigations into the Jewish Freedom Movement in the Period from Herod I until 70 A.D*. Trans. D. Smith. Edinburgh: T&T Clark.

—— (1995), *Studies in Early Christology*. Trans. R. Kearns. Edinburgh: T&T Clark.

—— (1996), 'Messianische Hoffnung und politischer "Radikalismus" in der "jüdisch-hellenistischen Diaspora". Zur Frage der Voraussetzungen des jüdischen Aufstandes unter Trajan 115 – 117 n. Chr.' In *Judaica et Hellenistica: Kleine Schriften*, 1: 314–43.

—— (2000), *The Four Gospels and the One Gospel of Jesus Christ: An Investigation of the Collection and Origin of the Canonical Gospels*. Trans. J. Bowden. London: SCM Press.

—— (2001), 'Judaism and Hellenism Revisited.' In *Hellenism in the Land of Israel*, 6-37. Ed. J. J. Collins and G. E. Sterling. Notre Dame: University of Notre Dame Press.

Hengel, Martin and Roland Deines (1991), *The Pre-Christian Paul*. Trans. J. Bowden. London: SCM Press.

Hennecke, Edgar (1973), *New Testament Apocrypha*. Trans. R. M. Wilson. Ed. W. Schneemelcher. 2 vols; 2nd edn, London: SCM Press.

Henze, Matthias (2001), *The Syriac Apocalypse of Daniel*. Studien und Texte zu Antike und Christentum 11. Tübingen: Mohr Siebeck.

Hertling, Ludwig and Engelbert Kirschbaum (1960), *The Roman Catacombs and Their Martyrs*. Trans. J. Costelloe. Rev. edn, London: Darton, Longman & Todd.

Hill, Charles E. (1992), *Regnum Caelorum: Patterns of Future Hope in Early Christianity*. Oxford.

——— (2000), 'Cerinthus, Gnostic or Chiliast? A New Solution to an Old Problem.' *JECS* 8: 135–72.

——— (2001), *Regnum Caelorum: Patterns of Millennial Thought in Early Christianity*. 2nd edn, Grand Rapids: Eerdmans.

Himmelfarb, Martha (1990), 'Sefer Zerubbabel.' In *Rabbinic Fantasies: Imaginative Narratives from Classical Hebrew Literature*, 69–90. Ed. D. Stern and M. Mirsky. Philadelphia: Jewish Publication Society.

——— (1993), *Ascent to Heaven in Jewish and Christian Apocalypses*. New York/Oxford: Oxford University Press.

——— (2002), 'The Mother of the Messiah in the Talmud Yerushalmi and Sefer Zerubbabel.' In *The Talmud Yerushalmi and Graeco-Roman culture*, 3: 369–89. Ed. P. Schäfer and C. Hezser. TSAJ 71, 79, 93. Tübingen: Mohr Siebeck.

Hooker, Morna Dorothy (1990), *From Adam to Christ : Essays on Paul*. Cambridge etc.: Cambridge University Press.

——— (1991), *A Commentary on the Gospel According to St. Mark*. Black's New Testament commentaries. London: A & C Black.

Horbury, William (1970), 'A Critical Examination of the Toledoth Yeshu.' Ph.D. dissertation, University of Cambridge.

——— (1981), 'Suffering and Messianism in Yose ben Yose.' In *Suffering and Martyrdom in the New Testament: Studies Presented to G. M. Styler by the Cambridge New Testament Seminar*, 143–82. Ed. W. Horbury and B. McNeil. Cambridge: Cambridge University Press.

——— (1982), 'The Benediction of the *Minim* and Early Jewish-Christian Controversy.' *JTS* 33: 19–61.

——— (1984), 'The Temple Tax.' In *Jesus and the Politics of His Day*, 265–86. Ed. E. Bammel and C. F. D. Moule. Cambridge: Cambridge University Press.

——— (1985), 'The Messianic Associations of "The Son of Man".' *JTS* 36: 34–55.

——— (1991), 'Herod's Temple and Herod's Days.' In *Templum Amicitiae: Essays on the Second Temple presented to Ernst Bammel*, 103–49. Ed. W. Horbury. JSNTSup 48. Sheffield: JSOT Press.

——— (1996), 'The Beginnings of the Jewish Revolt under Trajan.' In *Geschichte - Tradition - Reflexion: Festschrift für Martin Hengel zum 70. Geburtstag* 1: 283–304. Ed. H. Cancik *et al.* Tübingen: Mohr Siebeck.

——— (1998), 'Antichrist among Jews and Gentiles', in M. Goodman, ed., *Jews in a Graeco-Roman World*. Oxford, 113–33.

——— (1998a), 'The Benediction of the Minim.' In *Jews and Christians in Contact and Controversy*, 67–110. Edinburgh: T&T Clark.

——— (1998b) 'Christ as Brigand in Ancient Anti-Christian Polemic.' In *Jews and Christians in Contact and Controversy*, 162–73. Edinburgh: T&T Clark.

——— (1998c), *Jewish Messianism and the Cult of Christ*. London: SCM.

——— (1998d), *Jews and Christians in Contact and Controversy*. Edinburgh: T&T Clark.

——— (1999), *Christianity in Ancient Jewish Tradition: An Inaugural Lecture Delivered Before the University of Cambridge in the Divinity School, St John's Street on Thursday 4th February 1999*. Cambridge: Cambridge University Press.

——— (2003a), 'The Aaronic Priesthood in the Epistle to the Hebrews.' In *Messianism Among Jews and Christians: Biblical and Historical Essays*, 27–54. London/New York: T&T Clark.

——— (2003b), *Messianism among Jews and Christians: Twelve Biblical and Historical Studies*. London/New York: T&T Clark.

——— (2003c), 'Antichrist among Jews and Gentiles.' In *Messianism Among Jews and Christians: Biblical and Historical Studies* 329–50. London/New York: T&T Clark International.

——— (2005), 'Jewish Messianism and Early Christology.' In *Contours of Christology in the New Testament*, 3–24. Ed. R. N. Longenecker. Grand Rapids/Cambridge: Eerdmans.

——— (2006a), 'Beginnings of Christianity in the Holy Land.' In *Christianity in the Holy Land: From the Origins to the Latin Kingdoms*, 7–89. Ed. G. G. Stroumsa and O. Limor. Turnhout: Brepols.

——— (2006b), 'Monarchy and Messianism in the Greek Pentateuch.' In *The Septuagint and Messianism*, 79–128. Ed. M. A. Knibb. Leuven: Peeters.

Horovitz, S. and I. A. Rabin, eds, (1931), *Mechilta d'Rabbi Ismael*. Corpus Tannaiticum 3.3. Frankfurt: Kauffmann.

Horowitz, Elliott S. (1998), '"The Vengeance of the Jews Was Stronger Than Their Avarice": Modern Historians and the Persian Conquest of Jerusalem in 614.' *Jewish Social Studies*, n.s., 4: 1–39.

——— (2006), *Reckless Rites: Purim and the Legacy of Jewish Violence*. Jews, Christians, and Muslims from the Ancient to the Modern World. Princeton: Princeton University Press.

Horrell, David G. (1997), 'Leadership Patterns and the Development of Ideology in Early Christianity.' *Sociology of Religion* 58: 323–41.

——— (1998), *The Epistles of Peter and Jude*. Epworth Commentaries. London: Epworth.

——— (2002), 'The Product of a Petrine Circle? A Reassessment of the Origin and Character of 1 Peter.' *JSNT*, 86: 29–60.

——— (forthcoming), 'The Label Χριστιανός: 1 Pet. 4.16 and the Formation of Christian Identity', *JBL*.

Horsley, Richard A. (1984), 'Popular Messianic Movements Around the Time of Jesus.' *CBQ* 46: 471–95.

——— (1985a), '"Like One of the Prophets of Old" : Two Types of Popular Prophets at the Time of Jesus.' *CBQ* 47: 435–63.

——— (1985b), 'Menachem in Jerusalem: A Brief Messianic Episode Among the Sicarii - not "Zealot Messianism".' *NovT* 27: 334–48.

——— (1993), *Jesus and the Spiral of Violence: Popular Jewish Resistance in Roman Palestine*. Minneapolis: Fortress Press.

——— (1995), *Galilee: History, Politics, People*. Valley Forge: Trinity Press International.

—— (2003), *Jesus and Empire: The Kingdom of God and the New World Disorder*. Minneapolis, MN: Fortress Press.

—— (2004), *Hidden Transcripts and the Arts of Resistance: Applying the Work of James C. Scott to Jesus and Paul*. SemeiaSt 48. Leiden/Boston: Brill.

Horsley, Richard A., ed., (1997), *Paul and Empire: Religion and Power in Roman Imperial Society*. Harrisburg: Trinity Press International.

—— (2000), *Paul and Politics: Ekklesia, Israel, Imperium, Interpretation. Essays in Honor of Krister Stendahl*. Harrisburg: Trinity Press International.

Horsley, Richard A. and John S. Hanson (1985), *Bandits, Prophets & Messiahs: Popular Movements in the Time of Jesus*. Minneapolis: Winston Press.

—— (1999), *Bandits, Prophets & Messiahs: Popular Movements in the Time of Jesus*. 2nd edn, Harrisburg: Trinity Press International.

Hossfeld, Frank-Lothar and Erich Zenger (1993), *Die Psalmen I : Psalm 1-50*. Die Neue Echter Bibel. Würzburg: Echter Verlag.

—— (2000), *Psalmen 51-100*. HTKNT. Freiburg: Herder.

Hoyland, Robert G. (1997), *Seeing Islam as Others Saw It: A Survey and Evaluation of Christian, Jewish, and Zoroastrian Writings on Early Islam*. Studies in late antiquity and early Islam 13. Princeton: Darwin Press.

—— (2000), 'The Earliest Christian Writings on Muhammad: An Appraisal.' In *The Biography of Muhammad : the issue of the sources*, 277–97. Ed. H. Motzki. Islamic History and Civilization, Studies and Texts 32. Leiden/Boston: Brill.

Hughes, Kevin L. (2005), *Constructing Antichrist: Paul, Biblical commentary, and the Development of Doctrine in the Early Middle Ages*. Washington: Catholic University of America Press.

Hurst, David (1990), *The Epistle to the Hebrews: Its Background of Thought*. SNTSMS 65. Cambridge etc.: Cambridge University Press.

Hurtado, Larry W. (2003), *Lord Jesus Christ: Devotion to Jesus in Earliest Christianity*. Grand Rapids: Eerdmans.

Hvalvik, Reidar (1996), *The Struggle for Scripture and Covenant: The Purpose of the Epistle of Barnabas and Jewish-Christian Competition in the Second Century*. WUNT 2:82. Tübingen: Mohr Siebeck.

Idel, Moshe (1998), *Messianic Mystics*. New Haven: Yale University Press.

—— (2003), 'Jewish Apocalypticism 670–1670.' In *The Continuum History of Apocalypticism*, 354–79. Ed. B. McGinn et al. New York: Continuum.

Irsai, Oded (1993), 'Narcissus of Jerusalem and His Role in the Enhancement of the Apostolic Image of the Church of Jerusalem: The Church of Aelia between Marcus and Narcissus (ca 135-190 C.E.).' In *Aux origines juives du Christianisme*, 111–31. Ed. F. Blanchetière and M. D. Herr. Jerusalem: Centre de recherche Français de Jérusalem.

—— (2000), 'Dating the Eschaton: Jewish and Christian Apocalyptic Calculations in Late Antiquity.' In *Apocalyptic Time* 113–53. Ed. A. I. Baumgarten. Leiden/Boston: Brill.

—— (2002), 'Confronting a Christian Empire.' In *Cultures of the Jews: A New History*, 181–219. Ed. D. Biale. New York: Schocken Books.

Jacobs, Martin (1995), *Die Institution des jüdischen Patriarchen: Eine quellen- und traditionskritische Studie zur Geschichte der Juden in der Spätantike*. TSAJ 52. Tübingen: Mohr Siebeck.
Janowski, Bernd (2002), 'Die Frucht der Gerechtigkeit: Psalm 72 und die judäische Königsideologie.' In *'Mein Sohn bist du' (Ps 2,7): Studien zu den Königspsalmen*, 94–134. Ed. E. Otto and E. Zenger. SBS 192. Stuttgart: Katholisches Bibelwerk.
Jansma, T. (1973), 'Ephraem on Genesis XLIX, 10: An Enquiry into the Syriac Text Forms as Presented in his Commentary on Genesis.' *ParOr* 4: 247–56.
Japhet, Sara (1993), *I & II Chronicles: A Commentary*. OTL. London: SCM Press.
Jenkins, R. G. (1995), 'The Prayer of the Emanations in Greek from Kellis (T.Kellis 22).' *Mus* 108: 243–63.
Jeremias, Joachim (1966), 'Artikelloses Christos.' *ZNW* 57: 211–15.
—— (1969), 'Nochmals: Artikelloses Christos in 1 K 15,3.' *ZNW* 60: 215–17.
—— (1976), *The Prayers of Jesus*. London: SCM.
Johnson, Aubrey Rodway (1967), *Sacral kingship in ancient Israel*. 2nd edn, Cardiff: University of Wales Press.
Johnson, Luke Timothy (1995), *The Letter of James: A New Translation With Introduction and Commentary*. AB 37A. New York: Doubleday.
Jones, C. P. (1986), *Culture and Society in Lucian*. Cambridge: Harvard University Press.
Jörns, Klaus-Peter (1971), *Das hymnische Evangelium: Untersuchungen zu Aufbau, Funktion und Herkunft der hymnischen Stücke in der Johannesoffenbarung*. SNT 5. Gütersloh: Mohn.
Joyce, Paul M. (1998) 'King and Messiah in Ezekiel.' In *King and Messiah in Israel and the Ancient Near East: Proceedings of the Oxford Old Testament Seminar*, 323–37. Ed. J. Day. JSOTSup 270. Sheffield: Sheffield Academic Press.
Juel, Donald H. (1992), 'The Origin of Mark's Christology.' In *The Messiah: Developments in Earliest Judaism and Christianity*, 449–60. Ed. J. H. Charlesworth. Minneapolis: Fortress.
Kaegi, Walter Emil (2003), *Heraclius, Emperor of Byzantium*. Cambridge/New York: Cambridge University Press.
Kaplony, Andreas (2002), *The Haram of Jerusalem, 324–1099: Temple, Friday Mosque, Area of Spiritual Power*. Freiburger Islamstudien 22. Stuttgart: Franz Steiner Verlag.
—— (forthcoming), 'The Temple Mount/al-Haram al-Sharif in Jerusalem 635–1099.' In *Where Heaven and Earth Meet: Jerusalem's Sacred Esplanade*. Ed. O. Grabar and B. Z. Kedar. Jerusalem.
Karrer, Martin (1991), *Der Gesalbte: Die Grundlagen des Christustitels*. FRLANT 151. Göttingen: Vandenhoeck & Ruprecht.
Käsemann, Ernst (1984), *The Wandering People of God: An Investigation of the Letter to the Hebrews*. Trans. R. A. Harrisville and I. L. Sandberg. Minneapolis: Augsburg.
Kasher, Rimon (1996), *Targumic Toseftot to the Prophets*. Sources for the Study of Jewish Culture 2. Jerusalem: World Union of Jewish Studies.
Kellermann, Ulrich (1967), *Nehemia: Quellen, Überlieferung und Geschichte*. BZAW 102. Berlin: Töpelmann.

Kerkeslager, Allen (2006), 'The Jews in Egypt and Cyrenaica.' In *The Cambridge History of Judaism*, 4: 53–68. Ed. S. T. Katz. Cambridge etc.: Cambridge University Press.

Kerner, Jürgen (1998), *Die Ethik der Johannes-Apokalypse im Vergleich mit der des 4. Esra: Ein Beitrag zum Verhältnis von Apokalyptik und Ethik*. BZAW 94. Berlin/New York: de Gruyter.

Kessler, Edward (2004), *Bound by the Bible: Jews, Christians and the Sacrifice of Isaac*. Cambridge etc.: Cambridge University Press.

Kessler, Herbert L. (1987), 'Prophetic Portraits in the Dura Synagogue.' *JAC* 30: 149–55.

Kessler, John (2006), 'Haggai, Zerubbabel and the Political Status of Yehud: The Signet Ring in Haggai 2:23.' In *Prophets, Prophecy, and Prophetic Texts in Second Temple Judaism*, 102–19 Ed. M. H. Floyd and R. L. Haak. Library of Hebrew Bible/Old Testament Studies 427. London/New York: T&T Clark.

Kim, Seyoon (2002), *Paul and the New Perspective: Second Thoughts on the Origin of Paul's Gospel*. WUNT 140. Tübingen: Mohr Siebeck.

Kimelman, Reuven R. (1980), 'Rabbi Yohanan and Origen on the Song of Songs: A Third-Century Jewish-Christian Disputation.' *HTR* 73: 567–95.

——— (1997), 'The Messiah of the Amidah: A Study in Comparative Messianism.' *JBL* 116: 313–24.

Kingsbury, Jack D. (1976), 'The Title "Son of David" in Matthew's Gospel.' *JBL* 95: 591–602.

——— (1987), 'The Developing Conflict between Jesus and the Jewish Leaders in Matthew's Gospel.' *CBQ* 49: 57–73.

Kinzig, Wolfram (1998), 'Philosemitismus angesichts des Endes? Bemerkungen zu einem vergessenen Kapitel jüdisch-christlicher Beziehungen in der Alten Kirche.' In *Kaum zu glauben: Von der Häresie und dem Umgang mit ihr*, 59–95. Ed. A. Lexutt and V. Bülow. Arbeiten zur Theologiegeschichte 5. Rheinbach-Merzbach: CMZ-Verlag.

——— (2003), 'Jewish and "Judaizing" Eschatologies in Jerome.' In *Jewish Culture and Society under the Christian Roman Empire*, 409–29. Ed. R. L. Kalmin and S. Schwartz. Interdisciplinary Studies in Ancient Culture and Religion 3. Leuven: Peeters.

——— (2007), 'The Nazoreans.' In *Jewish Believers in Jesus—The Early Centuries*, 463–87 Ed. O. Skarsaune and R. Hvalvik. Peabody: Hendrickson.

Kippenberg, Hans G. (1990), 'Apokalyptik/Messianismus/Chiliasmus.' *Handbuch religionswissenschaftlicher Grundbegriffe* 2: 9–26.

Klausner, Joseph (1925), *Jesus of Nazareth: His Life, Times, and Teaching*. Trans. H. Danby. London: Allen & Unwin.

——— (1955), *The Messianic Idea in Israel, from its Beginning to the Completion of the Mishnah*. New York: Macmillan.

Klein, Michael L. (1980), *The Fragment-Targums of the Pentateuch According to Their Extant Sources*. Text, Indices and Introductory Essay. AnBib 76. Rome: Biblical Institute Press.

Klijn, A. F. J. (1972), 'Jerome's Quotations from a Nazorean Interpretation of Isaiah.' *RSR* 60: 241–55.

Klijn, A. F. J. and G. J. Reinink (1973), *Patristic evidence for Jewish-Christian Sects.* NovTSup 36. Leiden: Brill.

Kobelski, Paul J. (1981), *Melchizedek and Melchireša.* CBQMS 10. Washington: Catholic Biblical Association of America.

Koch, Ernst (1986), 'Höllenfahrt Christi.' *TRE* 15: 455–61.

Koch, Glenn Alan (1976), 'A Critical Investigation of Epiphanius' Knowledge of the Ebionites: A Translation and Critical Discussion of Panarion 30.' Ph.D. dissertation, University of Pennsylvania.

Koch, Klaus (1972), 'Messias und Sündenvergebung in Jesaja 53 - Targum: Ein Beitrag zu der Praxis der aramäischen Bibelübersetzung.' *JSJ* 3: 117–48.

—— (2002), 'Der König als Sohn Gottes in Ägypten und Israel.' In *'Mein Sohn bist du' (Ps 2,7): Studien zu den Königspsalmen,* 1–32. Ed. E. Otto and E. Zenger. SBS 192. Stuttgart: Katholisches Bibelwerk.

Koep, Leo (1952), *Das himmlische Buch in Antike und Christentum: Eine religionsgeschichtliche Untersuchung zur altchristlichen Bildersprache.* Bonn: Hanstein.

Kokkinos, Nikos (1998), *The Herodian Dynasty: Origins, Role in Society, and Eclipse.* JSPSup 30. Sheffield: Sheffield Academic Press.

Koschaker, P. (1942), 'Persönlichkeitszeichen.' *FF* 18: 246–8.

Kötting, Bernhard (1958), 'Endzeitprognosen zwischen Lactantius und Augustinus.' *Historisches Jahrbuch* 77, 125–39.

Kraeling, Carl H. et al. (1956), *The Excavations at Dura-Europos: Final Report.* Vol. 8.1: *The Synagogue.* New Haven: Yale University Press.

—— (1967), *The Excavations at Dura-Europos: Final Report.* Vol. 8.2: *The Christian Building.* New Haven: Yale University Press.

Kramer, Werner R. (1966), *Christ, Lord, Son of God.* Trans. B. Hardy. SBT 50. London: SCM.

Kroll, John H. (2001), 'The Greek Inscriptions of the Sardis Synagogue.' *HTR* 94: 5–55.

Kuhn, Peter (1978), *Gottes Trauer und Klage in der rabbinischen Überlieferung (Talmud und Midrasch).* AGAJU 13. Leiden: Brill.

Kutsch, Ernst (1963), *Salbung als Rechtsakt im Alten Testament und im alten Orient.* BZAW 87. Berlin: de Gruyter.

—— (1979), 'Wie David König wurde: Beobachtungen zu 2. Sam 2,4a und 5,3.' In *Textgemäss: Aufsätze und Beiträge zur Hermeneutik des Alten Testaments. Festschrift für Ernst Würthwein zum 70. Geburtstag,* 75–93. Ed. A. H. J. Gunneweg and O. Kaiser. Göttingen: Vandenhoeck & Ruprecht.

Laceranza, G. (2002), 'Giuliano Messia dei Giudei.' *Materia Giudaica* 7: 74–8.

Lahey, Lawrence L. (2001), 'The Dialogue of Timothy and Aquila: Critical Greek Text and English Translation of the Short Recension, with an Introduction Including a Source-Critical Study.' Ph.D. dissertation, University of Cambridge.

Lane, William L. (1991), *Hebrews.* WBC 47. 2 vols. Waco: Word.

Lane Fox, R. (1986), *Pagans and Christians.* London: Viking.

Lash, Ephrem, ed., (1995), *Kontakia: On the Life of Christ. Chanted Sermons by the Great Sixth Century Poet and Singer St. Romanos.* The Sacred Literature Series. San Francisco/London: HarperCollins.

Latte, Kurt (1960), *Römische Religionsgeschichte*. Handbuch der Altertumswissenschaft 5.4. München: Beck.

Lawlor, Hugh Jackson (1912), 'The *Hypomnemata* of Hegesippus.' In *Eusebiana: Essays on the Ecclesiastical History of Eusebius Pamphili, ca 264–349 A.D. Bishop of Caesarea*, 1–107. Oxford: Oxford University Press.

Lawlor, Hugh Jackson and John Ernest Leonard Oulton (1927), *Eusebius, Bishop of Caesarea: The Ecclesiastical History and the Martyrs of Palestine*. 2 vols; London/New York: SPCK/Macmillan.

Laws, Sophie (1980), *A Commentary on the Epistle of James*. BNTC. London: A&C Black.

Lehnart, Andreas (1999), 'Esra/Esrabücher: IV. Viertes Esrabuch.' *RGG*⁴ 2: 1586–88.

Lenowitz, Harris (1998), *The Jewish Messiahs: From the Galilee to Crown Heights*. Oxford/New York: Oxford University Press.

Levenson, David (2004), 'The Ancient and Medieval Sources for the Emperor Julian's Attempt to Rebuild the Jerusalem Temple.' *JSJ* 35: 409–60.

Levey, Samson H. (1974), *The Messiah: An Aramaic Interpretation. The Messianic Exegesis of the Targum*. Cincinnati: Hebrew Union College-Jewish Institute of Religion.

Lévi, I. (1914, 1919, 1920), 'L'Apocalypse de Zorobabel et le roi de Perse Siroès.' *Revue des Études Juives* 68, 69, 71: 129–60, 08–21, 57–65.

Levine, Lee I. (1975), 'R. Abbahu of Caesarea.' In *Christianity, Judaism and Other Greco-Roman Cults*, 4: 56–76. Ed. J. Neusner. SJLA 12. Leiden: Brill.

——— (1981), 'Towards an Appraisal of Herod the Builder.' In *The Jerusalem Cathedra: Studies in the History, Archaeology, Geography and Ethnography of the Land of Israel*, 1: 62–7. Ed. L. I. Levine. Jerusalem: Yad Izhak Ben-Zvi Institute.

——— (1998), *Judaism and Hellenism in Antiquity: Conflict or Confluence?* Peabody: Hendrickson.

——— (2000a), *The Ancient Synagogue: The First Thousand Years*. New Haven/London: Yale University Press.

——— (2000b), 'The History and Significance of the Menorah in Antiquity.' In *From Dura to Sepphoris: Studies in Jewish Art and Society in Late Antiquity*, 131–53. Ed. L. I. Levine and Z. Weiss. Journal of Roman Archaeology Supplementary Series 40. Portsmouth: Journal of Roman Archaeology.

Levine, Lee I. and Zeev Weiss, eds, (2000), *From Dura to Sepphoris: Studies in Jewish Art and Society in Late Antiquity*. Journal of Roman Archaeology Supplementary Series 40. Portsmouth: Journal of Roman Archaeology.

Levit-Tawil, Dalia (1979), 'The Purim Panel in Dura in the Light of Parthian and Sasanian Art.' *JNES* 38: 93–109.

Lewis, Bernard (1974), 'On that Day: A Jewish Apocalyptic Poem on the Arab Conquests.' In *Mélanges d'islamologie: Volume dédié à la mémoire de Armand Abel par ses collègues, ses élèves et ses amis*, 197–200. Ed. P. Salmon. Leiden: Brill.

────── (1976), 'An Apocalyptic Vision of Islamic History.' In *Studies in Classical and Ottoman Islam, 7th–16th centuries*, 308–38. London: Variorum.
Lieberman, Saul (1939-44), 'The Martyrs of Caesarea.' *Annuaire de l'institut de philologie et d'histoire orientales et slaves* 7: 395–446.
Lieu, Judith (2004), *Christian Identity in the Jewish and Graeco-Roman World*. Oxford: Oxford University Press.
────── (2005), 'How John Writes.' In *The Written Gospel*, 171–83. Ed. M. Bockmuehl and D. A. Hagner. Cambridge: Cambridge University Press.
Lilius, Henrik (1981), *Villa Lante al Gianicolo: L'architettura e la decorazione pittorica*. Acta Instituti Romani Finlandiae 10: 1–2. 2 vols in 1. Rome: Institutum Romanum Finlandiae.
Lindars, Barnabas (1991), *The Theology of the Letter to the Hebrews*. New Testament Theology. Cambridge etc.: Cambridge University Press.
Loader, William R. G. (1992), *The Christology of the Fourth Gospel: Structure and Issues*. BBET 23. 2nd rev. edn. Frankfurt/New York: P. Lang.
Loffreda, Stanislao (1985), *Recovering Capharnaum*. Studium Biblicum Franciscanum guides 1. Jerusalem: Franciscan Printing Press.
Lohfink, Gerhard (1971), *Die Himmelfahrt Jesu: Untersuchungen zu den Himmelfahrts- und Erhöhungstexten bei Lukas*. SANT 26. Munich: Kösel-Verlag.
Lona, Horacio E. (2005), *Die 'Wahre Lehre' des Kelsos: Übersetzt und erklärt*. Kommentar zu frühchristlichen Apologeten: Ergänzungsband 1. Freiburg etc.: Herder.
Lorein, Geert Wouter (2003), *The Antichrist Theme in the Intertestamental Period*. JSPSup 44. London/New York: T&T Clark International.
Lucian (1961), *Lucian: in eight volumes*. Ed. A. M. Harmon and K. Kilburn. LCL. Repr. London: Heinemann.
Luger, Yechezkel (2001), (5761), *The Weekday Amidah in the Cairo Genizah*. (Hebr.). Jerusalem: Orhot.
Luneau, Auguste (1964), *L'histoire du salut chez les Pères de l'Église: La doctrine des âges du monde*. ThH 2. Paris: Beauchesne.
Lust, Johan (1985), 'Messianism and Septuagint.' In *Congress Volume (Salamanca) 1983*, 174–91. Ed. J. A. Emerton. VTSup 36. Leiden: Brill.
────── (1995), 'The Greek Version of Balaam's Third and Fourth Oracles: The ἄνθρωπος in Num 24:7 and 17. Messianism and Lexicography.' In *VIII Congress of the International Organization for Septuagint and Cognate Studies, Paris 1992*, 233–52. Ed. L. Greenspoon and O. Munnich. SBLSCS 41 Atlanta: Scholars.
────── (1997a), '"And I shall hang him on a lofty mountain": Ezek 17:22–24 and Messianism in the Septuagint.' In *IX Congress of the IOSCS Cambridge 1995*, 231–50. Ed. B. A. Taylor. SBLSCS 45. Atlanta: Scholars.
────── (1997b), 'Mic 5,1–3 in Qumran and in the New Testament and Messianism in the Septuagint.' In *The Scriptures in the Gospels*, 65–88. Ed. C. M. Tuckett. BETL 131. Leuven: Peeters.
────── (1997c), 'Septuagint and Messianism, With a Special Emphasis on the Pentateuch.' In *Theologische Probleme der Septuaginta und der hellenistischen Hermeneutik*, 26–45. Ed. H. G. Reventlow.

Veröffentlichungen der Wissenschaftlichen Gesellschaft für Theologie 11. Gütersloh: Kaiser/Gütersloher Verlagshaus.

—— (1998), 'Messianism in the Septuagint: Isaiah 8:23b–9:6 (9:1–7).' In *The Interpretation of the Bible: The International Symposium in Slovenia*, 147–63. Ed. J. Krašovec. JSOTSup 289. Sheffield: Sheffield Academic Press.

—— (2003), 'Messianism in Ezekiel in Hebrew and Greek, Ezek 21:15(10) and 20 (15).' In *Emanuel: Studies in Hebrew Bible, Septuagint and Dead Sea Scrolls in Honor of Emanuel Tov*, 619–31. Ed. S. M. Paul et al. VTSup 94. Leiden/Boston: Brill.

—— (2004a), 'Messianism and the Greek version of Jeremiah: Jer 23,5–6 and 33,14–26.' In *Messianism in the Septuagint: Collected Essays by J. Lust*, 41–67. Ed. K. Hauspie. Leuven: Peeters.

—— (2004b), 'A Septuagint Christ preceding Christ? Messianism in the Septuagint exemplified in Isa 7,10–17.' In *Messianism in the Septuagint: Collected Essays by J. Lust*, 211–26. Ed. K. Hauspie. Leuven: Peeters.

Luz, Ulrich (1991), 'Eine thetische Skizze der matthäischen Christologie.' In *Anfänge der Christologie*, 223–26. Ed. C. Breytenbach and H. Paulsen. Göttingen: Vandenhoeck & Ruprecht.

—— (2002), *Das Evangelium nach Matthäus (Mt. 1-7)*. Rev. edn, Vol. I/1. Düsseldorf/Zürich: Benziger.

Maccoby, Hyam (1973), *Revolution in Judaea: Jesus and the Jewish Resistance*. London: Orbach & Chambers.

—— (2003), *Jesus the Pharisee*. London: SCM Press.

MacRae, George W. (1987), 'Messiah and Gospel.' In *Judaisms and Their Messiahs at the Turn of the Christian Era*, 169–85. Ed. J. Neusner et al. Cambridge etc.: Cambridge University Press.

Madec, Goulven (1986–94), 'Christus.' *Augustinus-Lexikon* 1: 846–908.

Magness, Jodi (2002), *The Archaeology of Qumran and the Dead Sea Scrolls*. Studies in the Dead Sea Scrolls and Related Literature. Grand Rapids: Eerdmans.

Mango, Cyril A. (1980), *Byzantium: The Empire of New Rome*. History of Civilization. London: Weidenfeld and Nicolson.

—— (1992), 'The Temple Mount, AD 614–638.' In *Bayt al-Maqdis*, 1–16. Ed. J. Raby and J. Johns. Oxford Studies in Islamic Art 9. Oxford/New York: Oxford University Press.

Mango, C. and R. Scott, tr., com., (1997), *The Chronicle of Theophanes Confessor: Byzantine and Near Eastern History, AD 284–813*. Oxford/New York: Clarendon/Oxford University Press.

Manson, Thomas Walter (1962), *Studies in the Gospels and Epistles*. Manchester: Manchester University Press.

Markschies, Christoph (1998), 'Kerinth: Wer war er und was lehrte er?' *JAC* 41: 48–76.

—— (2000), *Alta Trinità Beata: Gesammelte Studien zur altkirchlichen Trinitätstheologie*. Tübingen: Mohr Siebeck.

—— (2004), 'Kerinthos.' *RAC* 20: 755–66.

Marmorstein, A. (1906), 'Les signes du Messie', *Revue des Études Juives* 52: 176–86.

—— (1920), 'Deux renseignements d'Origène concernant les Juifs.' *REJ* 71: 190–99.
Marshall, I. Howard and Philip Towner (1999), *A Critical and Exegetical Commentary on the Pastoral Epistles*. ICC. Edinburgh: T&T Clark.
Martin, R. A. (1965), 'The Earliest Messianic Interpretation of Genesis 3:15.' *JBL* 84: 425–27.
Mason, Rex (1982), 'The Prophets of the Restoration.' In *Israel's Prophetic Tradition: Essays in Honour of Peter R. Ackroyd*, 140–45. Ed. R. Coggins *et al.* Cambridge: Cambridge University Press.
—— (1998), 'The Messiah in the Postexilic Old Testament Literature.' In *King and Messiah in Israel and the Ancient Near East: Proceedings of the Oxford Old Testament Seminar*, 338–64. Ed. J. Day. JSOTS 270. Sheffield: Sheffield Academic Press.
Mason, Steve (1994), 'Josephus, Daniel, and the Flavian House.' In *Josephus and the History of the Greco-Roman Period: Essays in Memory of Morton Smith*, 161–91. Ed. F. P. a. J. Sievers. SPB 41. Leiden: Brill.
—— (2003), 'Contradiction or Counterpoint? Josephus and Historical Method.' *Review of Rabbinic Judaism* 6: 145–88.
Massyngberde Ford, J. (1975), *Revelation: Introduction, Translation and Commentary*. AB 38. Garden City, NY: Doubleday and Co.
Maynard-Reid, Pedrito U. (1987), *Poverty and Wealth in James*. Maryknoll: Orbis.
Mazzaferri, Frederick David (1989), *The Genre of the Book of Revelation from a Source-Critical Perspective*. BZNW 54. Berlin/New York: de Gruyter.
McCasland, S. V. (1946), 'Christ Jesus.' *JBL* 65: 373–83.
McGing, Brian C. (1995), 'Hellenism, Judaism and the Hasmoneans.' In *Simblos: Scritti di Storia Antica*, 57–74. Bologna: Università degli Studi di Bologna.
McGinn, Bernard (1994), *Antichrist: Two Thousand Years of the Human Fascination with Evil*. San Francisco: HarperSanFrancisco.
McGrath, James F. (2001), *John's Apologetic Christology: Legitimation and Development in Johannine Christology*. SNTSMS 111. Cambridge etc.: Cambridge University Press.
McHugh, Michael P., ed., (1972), *Ambrose: Seven Exegetical Works*. Washington: Catholic University of America Press.
McKnight, Scot (1999), *A New Vision for Israel: The Teachings of Jesus in National Context*. Grand Rapids: Eerdmans.
McNamara, Martin (1966), *The New Testament and the Palestinian Targum to the Pentateuch*. AnBib 27. Rome: Pontifical Biblical Institute.
Meadors, E. P. (1999), 'The 'Messianic' Implications of the Q Material.' *JBL* 118, no. 2: 253–77.
Meeks, Wayne A. (1967), *The Prophet-King: Moses Traditions and the Johannine Christology*. NovTSup 14. Leiden: Brill.
—— (1972), 'The Man from Heaven in Johannine Sectarianism.' *JBL* 91: 44–72.
Meiggs, Russell (1973), *Roman Ostia*. 2nd edn, Oxford: Clarendon Press.

Mélèze-Modrzejewski, Joseph (1997), *The Jews of Egypt : From Rameses II to Emperor Hadrian*. Trans. R. Cornman. Princeton: Princeton University Press.

Mendels, Doron (1992a), 'Pseudo-Philo's *Biblical Antiquities*, the "Fourth Philosophy", and the Political Messianism of the First Century C.E.' In *The Messiah: Developments in Earliest Judaism and Christianity*, 261–75. Ed. J. H. Charlesworth. Minneapolis: Fortress Press.

—— (1992b), *The Rise and Fall of Jewish Nationalism*. ABRL. 1st edn. New York: Doubleday.

Mendelssohn, S. (1973), 'Prophet (false)' *EJ* 10: 212–13.

Meshorer, Ya'akov (2001), *A Treasury of Jewish Coins from the Persian Period to Bar Kokhba*. Jerusalem/Nyack: Yad ben-Zvi/Amphora.

Mettinger, Tryggve N. D. (1976), *King and Messiah: The Civil and Sacral Legitimation of the Israelite Kings*. ConBOT 8. Lund: Gleerup.

Mildenberg, Leo and Patricia Erhart Mottahedeh (1984), *The Coinage of the Bar Kokhba War*. Aarau: Sauerländer.

Millar, Fergus (1993), *The Roman Near East, 31 BC – AD 337*. Cambridge: Harvard University Press.

—— (2006), 'Transformations of Judaism under Graeco-Roman Rule: Responses to Seth Schwartz's *Imperialism and Jewish Society*.' *JJS* 57: 139–58.

Möhring, H. (2000), *Der Weltkaiser der Endzeit: Entstehung, Wandel und Wirkung einer tausendjährigen Weissagung*. Mittelalter-Forschungen 3. Stuttgart: Thorbecke.

Moloney, F. (1998), *The Gospel of John*. SP 4. Collegeville: Liturgical Press.

Momigliano, Arnaldo (1975), *Alien Wisdom: The Limits of Hellenization*. Cambridge: Cambridge University Press.

—— (1993), *The Development of Greek Biography*. 2nd edn, Cambridge/London: Harvard University Press.

Mommsen, Theodor (1887), *Römisches Staatsrecht*. 3 vols in 5. 3rd edn, Leipzig: Hirzel.

Monsengwo-Pasinya, Laurent (1980), 'Deux textes messianiques de la Septante: Gn 49,10 et Ez 21,32.' *Bib* 61: 357–76.

Moore, George Foot (1927–30), *Judaism in the First Centuries of the Christian Era: The Age of the Tannaim*. 3 vols; Cambridge: Harvard University Press.

Mor, Menachem (1989), 'The Events of 351–352 in Palestine: The Last Revolt Against Rome?' In *The Eastern Frontier of the Roman Empire: Proceedings of a Colloquium Held at Ankara in September 1988*, 335–53. Ed. D. H. French and C. S. Lightfoot. B.A.R. International Series 553. Oxford: B.A.R.

Moran, W. L. (1958), 'Gn 49,10 and its use in Ez 21,32'.' *Bib* 39: 406–11.

Morrison, Craig E. (2001), *The Character of the Syriac Version of the First Book of Samuel*. Monographs of the Peshitta Institute Leiden 11. Leiden/Boston: Brill.

Moule, C. F. D. (1977), *The Origin of Christology*. Cambridge: Cambridge University Press.

Mowinckel, Sigmund (1922), *Psalmenstudien*. Videnskapsselskapets skrifter. II, Hist.-filos. klasse 6. Vol. 2: *Das Thronbesteigungsfest Jahwäs und der Ursprung der Eschatologie*. Kristiania: Dybwad.

—— (1956), *He That Cometh: The Messiah Concept in the Old Testament and Later Judaism*. Oxford: Blackwell.
Moxnes, Halvor (1988), *The Economy of the Kingdom: Social Conflict and Economic Relations in Luke's Gospel*. OBT 23. Philadelphia: Fortress Press.
—— (2003), *Putting Jesus in his Place: A Radical Vision of Household and Kingdom*. Louisville/London: Westminster John Knox.
Musurillo, Herbert A. (1954), *The Acts of the Pagan Martyrs: Acta Alexandrinorum*. Oxford: Clarendon Press.
Myers, Ched (1988), *Binding the Strong Man: A Political Reading of Mark's Story of Jesus*. Maryknoll: Orbis Books.
Nash, Ernest (1961), *Bildlexikon zur Topographie des antiken Rom*. Tübingen: Wasmuth.
Nestori, Aldo (1975), *Repertorio topografico delle pitture delle catacombe romane*. Roma Sotterranea Cristiana 5. Vatican City: Pontificio Istituto di archeologia cristiana.
Neugebauer, Friedrich (1958), 'Das Paulinische "in Christo".' *NTS* 4: 124–38.
Neusner, Jacob (1981), *Judaism: The Evidence of the Mishnah*. Chicago: University of Chicago Press.
—— (1984), *Messiah in Context: Israel's History and Destiny in Formative Judaism*. Philadelphia: Fortress Press.
—— (1987), 'Mishnah and Messiah.' In *Judaisms and Their Messiahs at the Turn of the Christian Era*, 265–82. Ed. J. Neusner et al. Cambridge etc.: Cambridge University Press.
Neusner, Jacob, William Scott Green, and Ernest S. Frerichs, eds, (1987), *Judaisms and their Messiahs at the Turn of the Christian Era*. Cambridge etc.: Cambridge University Press.
Newman, Carey C. (1992), *Paul's Glory-Christology: Tradition and Rhetoric*. NovTSup 69. Leiden/New York: Brill.
Newman, Hillel I. (2001), 'Jerome's Judaizers.' *JECS* 9: 421–52.
Neyrey, Jerome H. (1988), *An Ideology of Revolt: John's Christology in Social-Science Perspective*. Philadelphia: Fortress Press.
Nickelsburg, George W. E. (1981), *Jewish Literature Between the Bible and the Mishnah: A Historical and Literary Introduction*. London: SCM.
—— (1987), 'Salvation Without and With a Messiah.' In *Judaisms and Their Messiahs at the Turn of the Christian Era*, 49–68. Ed. J. Neusner et al. Cambridge etc.: Cambridge University Press.
—— (2005), *Jewish Literature Between the Bible and the Mishnah: A Literary and Historical Introduction*. 2nd. Minneapolis: Fortress Press.
Niebuhr, Karl Wilhelm (1993), 'Jesus Christus und die vielfältigen messianischen Erwartungen Israels: Ein Forschungsbericht.' *Jahrbuch für Biblische Theologie* 8: 337–45.
Nock, Arthur Darby (1972), 'Cremation and Burial in the Roman Empire.' In *Essays in Religion and the Ancient World*, 1:277–307. Ed. Z. Stewart. Cambridge: Harvard University Press.
Nogalski, James (1993a), *Literary Precursors to the Book of the Twelve*. Berlin/New York: de Gruyter.

―――― (1993b), *Redactional Processes in the Book of the Twelve*. Berlin/New York: de Gruyter.
Noy, David and Hanswulf Bloedhorn (2004), *Inscriptiones Judaicae Orientis*. TSAJ 102. Vol. 3. Tübingen: Mohr Siebeck.
Noy, David and Susan Sorek (2003), '"Peace and Mercy Upon All Your Blessed People": Jews and Christians at Apamea in Late Antiquity.' *Jewish Culture and History* 6, no. 2: 11–24.
O'Connell, John P. (1948), *The Eschatology of St Jerome*. Dissertationes ad Lauream 16. Mundelein: Pontificia Facultas Theologica Seminarii Sanctae Mariae ad Lacum.
O'Donovan, Oliver (1996), *The Desire of the Nations: Rediscovering the Roots of Political Theology*. Cambridge etc.: Cambridge University Press.
Oakes, Peter. 2001. *Philippians: From People to Letter*. SNTSMS 110. Cambridge: Cambridge University Press.
Oegema, Gerbern S. (1994), *Der Gesalbte und sein Volk: Untersuchungen zum Konzeptualisierungsprozess der messianischen Erwartungen von den Makkabäern bis Bar Koziba*. Schriften des Institutum Judaicum Delitzschianum 2. Göttingen: Vandenhoeck & Ruprecht.
―――― (1998a), *The Anointed and His People: Messianic Expectations from Maccabees to Bar Kochba*. JSPSup 27. Sheffield: Sheffield Academic Press.
―――― (1998b), 'Messianic Expectations in the Qumran Writings: Theses on their Development.' In *Qumran-Messianism: Studies on the Messianic Expectations in the Dead Sea Scrolls*, 53–82. Ed. J. H. Charlesworth et al. Tübingen: Mohr Siebeck.
Olster, David (2003), 'Byzantine Apocalypses.' In *The Continuum History of Apocalypticism*, 254–72. Ed. B. McGinn et al. New York: Continuum.
Origen, (1953), *Contra Celsum* H. Chadwick, tr. Cambridge.
Osswald, E. (1962), *Falsche Prophetie im Alten Testament*. Sammlung gemeinverständlicher Vortrage und Schriften aus dem Gebiet der Theologie und Religionsgeschichte 237. Tübingen: J.C.B. Mohr (Paul Siebeck).
Oz, Amos (2005), *A Tale of Love and Darkness*. Trans. N. de Lange. First Harvest. Orlando: Harcourt.
Painter, John (1991), *The Quest for the Messiah: The History, Literature and Theology of the Johannine Community*. Edinburgh: T&T Clark.
Palmer, Andrew, Sebastian P. Brock, and Robert G. Hoyland, eds., (1993), *The Seventh Century in the West-Syrian Chronicles*. Translated Texts for Historians 15. Liverpool: Liverpool University Press.
Paltiel, Eliezer (1991), *Vassals and Rebels in the Roman Empire: Julio-Claudian Policies in Judaea and the Kingdoms of the East*. Collection Latomus 212. Brussels: Latomus.
Patai, Raphael (1988), *The Messiah Texts*. Detroit: Wayne State University Press.
Patlagean, Evelyne, ed., (1994), *Le ravissement du Messie à sa naissance et autres essais*. Collection de la Revue des Études Juives 13. Leuven: Peeters.
Paul, Sh. (1973), 'Prophets and Prophecy', *EJ* 13: 1168–9.
Pavia, Carlo (2000), *Guida delle Catacombe Romane*. Rome: Gangemi.
Pearson, Birger A. (2003), 'Cracking a Conundrum: Christian Origins in Egypt.' *ST* 57: 61–75.

―――― (2006), 'Egypt.' In *The Cambridge History of Christianity: Origins to Constantine.* Ed. M. M. Mitchell and F. M. Young. Cambridge etc.: Cambridge University Press.
Pearson, Birger Albert and James E. Goehring, eds, (1986), *The Roots of Egyptian Christianity.* Studies in Antiquity and Christianity. Philadelphia: Fortress Press.
Penella, Robert J. (1999), 'Emperor Julian, the Temple of Jerusalem and the God of the Jews.' *Koinonia* 23: 15–31.
Pérez Fernández, Miguel (1981), *Tradiciones mesiánicas en el Targum Palestinense: Éstudios exegéticos.* Valencia/Jerusalem: Institución San Jerónimo.
Pergola, Philippe (1998), *Le Catacombe Romane: Storia e Topografia.* Rome: Carocci.
Perrin, Bernadotte (1914), *Plutarch's Lives.* 11 vols. Frequent reprints. London/Cambridge: Heinemann/Harvard University Press.
Peter, Hermann Wilhelm Gottlob (1865), *Die Quellen Plutarchs in den Biographieen der Römer.* Halle: Buchhandlung des Waisenhauses.
Pietersma, Albert (1997), Review of Joachim Schaper, *Eschatology in the Greek Psalter,* WUNT 2:76 (Tübingen: Mohr Siebeck, 1995). *BO* 54: 185–90.
Pines, Shlomo (1968), 'The Jewish Christians of the Early Centuries of Christianity According to a New Source.' *Proceedings of the Israel Academy of Sciences and Humanities* 2: 237–310.
―――― (1984), 'Notes on Islam and on Arabic Christianity and Judaeo-Christianity.' *JSAI* 4: 135–52.
―――― (1996a), 'The Jewish Christians of the Early Centuries of Christianity According to a New Source.' In *Studies in the History of Religion,* 211–84. Ed. G. G. Stroumsa. Jerusalem: Hebrew University Magnes Press.
―――― (1996b), 'Notes on Islam and on Arabic Christianity and Judaeo-Christianity.' In *Studies in the History of Religion,* 316–33. Ed. G. G. Stroumsa. Jerusalem: Hebrew University Magnes Press.
Polliack, Meira (1997), *The Karaite Tradition of Arabic Bible Translation: A Linguistic and Exegetical Study of Karaite Translations of the Pentateuch from the Tenth and Eleventh Centuries C.E.* Etudes sur le Judaïsme Médiéval 17. Leiden/New York: Brill.
Posnanski, Adolf (1904), *Schiloh: Ein Beitrag zur Geschichte der Messiaslehre.* Vol. 1: *Die Auslegung von Genesis 49,10 im Altertume bis zu Ende des Mittelalters* Leipzig: Hinrichs.
Potestà, Gian Luca and Marco Rizzi (2005), *L'Anticristo.* 3 vols. Vol. 1: *Il nemico dei tempi finali, testi dal II al IV secolo.* Milano: Fondazione Lorenzo Valla/Mondadori.
Préaux, Claire (1978), *Le monde hellénistique: la Grèce et l'Orient de la mort d'Alexandre à la conquête romaine de la Grèce <323-145 av. J.-C.* 2 vols; Paris: Presses Universitaires de France.
Price, Jonathan T. (1992), *Jerusalem under siege : the collapse of the Jewish state, 66–70 C.E.* Leiden/New York: Brill.
Price, S. R. F. (1984), *Rituals and Power: The Roman Imperial Cult in Asia Minor.* Cambridge: Cambridge University Press.
Pritz, Ray A. (1985), 'Joseph of Tiberias: The Legend of a 4th Century Jewish Christian.' *Mishkan* 2: 47–54.

――― (1988), *Nazarene Jewish Christianity: From the End of the New Testament Period Until its Disappearance in the Fourth Century*. SPB 37. Jerusalem/Leiden: Magnes/Brill.
Prostmeier, Ferdinand R. (1999), *Der Barnabasbrief*. Kommentar zu den Apostolischen Vätern 8. Göttingen: Vandenhoeck & Ruprecht.
Pucci Ben Zeev, Miriam (2005), *Diaspora Judaism in Turmoil, 116/117 CE: Ancient Sources and Modern Insights*. Interdisciplinary Studies in Ancient Culture and Religion 6. Leuven: Peeters.
Quell, G. (1952), *Wahre und Falsche Propheten: Versuch einer Interpretation*. BFCT 46: 1. Gütersloh: Bertelsmann.
Raban, Avner and Kenneth G. Holum (1996), *Caesarea Maritima: A Retrospective after Two Millennia*. Documenta et Monumenta Orientis Antiqui 21. Leiden/New York: Brill.
Rabello, Alfredo Mordechai (1987–8), *Giustiniano, Ebrei e Samaritani alla luce delle fonti storico-letterarie, ecclesiastiche e giuridiche*. Monografie del Vocabolario di Giustiniano 1–2. 2 vols. Milano: A. Giuffrè.
Rabin, Chaim (1957), *Qumran Studies*. Scripta Judaica 2. Oxford: Oxford University Press.
Rad, G. von (1933), 'Die falsche Propheten', *ZAW* 51, 109–20.
Rajak, Tessa (1996), 'Hasmonean Kingship and the Invention of Tradition.' In *Aspects of Hellenistic Kingship*, 99–115. Ed. P. Bilde. Studies in Hellenistic Civilisation 7. Aarhus: Aarhus University Press.
――― (2002), 'Jewish Millenarian Expectations.' In *The First Jewish Revolt: Archaeology, History, and Ideology*, 164–88. Ed. A. M. Berlin and J. A. Overman. London/New York: Routledge.
Ravitzky, Aviezer (1996), *Messianism, Zionism, and Jewish Religious Radicalism*. Chicago Studies in the History of Judaism. Chicago: University of Chicago Press.
――― (2003), 'The Messianism of Success in Contemporary Judaism.' In *The Continuum History of Apocalypticism*, 563–81. Ed. B. McGinn et al. New York: Continuum.
Reeves, John C. (2005), *Trajectories in Near Eastern Apocalyptic: A Postrabbinic Jewish Apocalypse Reader*. RBS 45. Atlanta: Society of Biblical Literature.
Reif, Stephan C. (1998), 'Jerusalem in Jewish liturgy.' In *Jerusalem: Its Sanctity and Centrality in Judaism, Christianity, and Islam*, 424–37. Ed. L. I. Levine. New York: Continuum.
Reiling, J. (1971), 'The use of *pseudoprophètes* in the Septuagint, Philo and Josephus', *Novum Testamentum* 13: 147–56.
――― (1973), *Hermas and Christian Prophecy: A Study of the Eleventh Mandate*. NovTSup 37. Leiden: Brill.
Reimarus, Hermann Samuel (1772), *Von dem Zwecke Jesu und seiner Jünger, noch ein Fragment des Wolfenbüttelschen ungenannten*. Ed. G. E. Lessing. Braunschweig.
――― (1970), *The Goal of Jesus and His Disciples*. Trans. G. W. Buchanan. Leiden: E. J. Brill.
Reinink, G. J. (1993), *Die Syrische Apokalypse des Pseudo-Methodius*. CSCO 540–41. 2 vols. Louvain: E. Peeters.

―――― (2005), *Syriac Christianity under Late Sasanian and Early Islamic Rule.* Aldershot/Burlington: Ashgate/Variorum.

Renov, I. (1970), 'A View of Herod's Temple from Nicanor's Gate in a Mural Panel of the Dura Europos Synagogue.' *IEJ* 20: 67–74.

Rensberger, David K. (1989), *Overcoming the World: Politics and Community in the Gospel of John.* London: SPCK.

Reumann, John (1999), 'Christology of James.' In *Who Do You Say that I Am? Essays on Christology*, 128–39. Ed. M. A. Powell and D. R. Bauer. Louisville: Westminster John Knox Press.

Revel-Neher, E. (2000), 'From Dream to Reality: Evolution and Continuity in Jewish Art.' In *From Dura to Sepphoris: Studies in Jewish Art and Society in Late Antiquity*, 53–63. Ed. L. I. Levine and Z. Weiss. Journal of Roman Archaeology Supplementary Series 40. Portsmouth: Journal of Roman Archaeology.

Rhoads, David M. (1976), *Israel in Revolution, 6–74 C.E.: A Political History Based on the Writings of Josephus.* Philadelphia: Fortress Press.

Richardson, Peter (1999), *Herod: King of the Jews and Friend of the Romans.* Personalities of the New Testament. Minneapolis: Fortress Press.

Riedo-Emmenegger, Christoph (2005), *Prophetisch-messianische Provokateure der Pax Romana: Jesus von Nazaret und andere Störenfriede im Konflikt mit dem Römischen Reich.* NTOA/SUNT 56. Fribourg/Göttingen: Academic Press/Vandenhoeck & Ruprecht.

Riedweg, Christoph (2002), *Pythagoras: Leben, Lehre, Nachwirkung. Eine Einführung.* Munich: Beck.

Riley, William (1993), *King and Cultus in Chronicles: Worship and the Reinterpretation of History.* JSOTSup 160. Sheffield: JSOT Press.

Robin, C. J. (2003), 'Le judaïsme de Himyar', *Arabia* 1: 97–172.

Robinson, John A. T. (1962), 'The Destination and Purpose of St John's Gospel.' In *Twelve New Testament Studies*, 107–25 London: SCM.

Rocca, Samuele (2006), 'Josephus and the Psalms of Solomon on Herod's Messianic Aspirations: An Interpretation.' In *Making History: Josephus and Historical Method*, 313–33. Ed. Z. Rodgers. Leiden etc.: Brill.

Roller, Duane W. (1998), *The Building Program of Herod the Great.* Berkeley: University of California Press.

Ropes, James H. (1916), *A Critical and Exegetical Commentary on the Epistle of St. James.* ICC. Edinburgh: T&T Clark.

Rösel, Martin (1994), *Übersetzung als Vollendung der Auslegung: Studien zur Genesis-Septuaginta.* Berlin/New York: de Gruyter.

Rosen, K. (1985), 'Die falschen Numabücher: Politik, Religion und Literatur in Rom 181 v. Chr.' *Chiron* 15: 65–90.

Rowe, C. Kavin (2005), 'History, Hermeneutics and the Unity of Luke-Acts.' *JSNT* 28: 131–57.

Rowland, Christopher (1993), *Revelation.* Epworth Commentaries. London: Epworth Press.

―――― (1997), 'The Lamb and the Beast, the Sheep and the Goats: "The Mystery of Salvation" in Revelation.' In *A Vision for the Church: Studies in Early Christian Ecclesiology in Honour of J.P.M. Sweet*, 181–91. Ed. M. Bockmuehl and M. B. Thompson. Edinburgh: T&T Clark.

——— (1998), 'Christ in the New Testament.' In *King and Messiah in Israel and the Ancient Near East: Proceedings of the Oxford Old Testament Seminar*, 474–96. Ed. J. Day. JSOTSup 270. Sheffield: Sheffield Academic Press.
Rubin, B. (1961), 'Der Antichrist und die "Apocalypse" des Prokopios von Kaisareia.' *ZDMG* 110: 55–63.
Runesson, A. (2001), 'The Synagogue at Ancient Ostia: The Building and its History from the First to the Fifth Century.' In *The Synagogue of Ancient Ostia and the Jews of Rome: Interdisciplinary Studies*, 29–99. Ed. B. Olsson et al. Acta Instituti Romani Regni Sueciae 57. Jonsered: Paul Åströms Förlag.
Rutgers, Leonard Victor (1995), *The Jews in Late Ancient Rome: Evidence of Cultural Interaction in the Roman Diaspora*. Religions in the Graeco-Roman World 126. Leiden etc.: Brill.
Sabar, S. (2000), 'The Purim Panel at Dura: A Socio-Historical Interpretation.' In *From Dura to Sepphoris: Studies in Jewish Art and Society in Late Antiquity*, 155–63. Ed. L. I. Levine and Z. Weiss. Journal of Roman Archaeology Supplementary Series 40. Portsmouth: Journal of Roman Archaeology.
Sahas, D. J. (1972), *John of Damascus on Islam: The 'Heresy of the Ishmaelites'*. Leiden: Brill.
Salvesen, Alison (1991), *Symmachus in the Pentateuch*. JSS Monograph 15. Manchester: University of Manchester.
Sanders, E. P. (1977), *Paul and Palestinian Judaism*. London: SCM.
Sänger, Dieter (1994), *Die Verkündigung des Gekreuzigten und Israel: Studien zum Verhältnis von Kirche und Israel bei Paulus und im frühen Christentum*. WUNT 75. Tübingen: Mohr Siebeck.
Scardigli, Barbara, ed., (1995), *Essays on Plutarch's Lives*. Oxford: Clarendon.
Schäfer, Peter (1981), *Der Bar Kokhba-Aufstand: Studien zum zweiten jüdischen Krieg gegen Rom*. TSAJ 1. Tübingen: Mohr Siebeck.
——— (1983), *Geschichte der Juden in der Antike: Die Juden Palästinas von Alexander dem Grossen bis zur arabischen Eroberung*. Stuttgart/Neukirchen-Vluyn: Katholisches Bibelwerk/Neukirchener Verlag.
——— (1986), 'Der Aufstand gegen Gallus Caesar.' In *Tradition and Re-Interpretation in Jewish and Early Christian Literature: Essays in Honour of Jürgen C.H. Lebram*, 184–201. Ed. J. W. van Henten et al. SPB 36. Leiden: Brill.
——— (1995), *The History of the Jews in Antiquity: The Jews of Palestine from Alexander the Great to the Arab Conquest*. Luxembourg: Harwood Academic Publishers.
——— (2003), 'Bar Kokhba and the Rabbis.' In *The Bar Kokhba War Reconsidered: New Perspectives on the Second Jewish revolt against Rome*, 1–22. Ed. P. Schäfer. Tübingen: Mohr Siebeck.
Schäfer, Peter and Mark R. Cohen (1998), *Toward the Millennium: Messianic Expectations from the Bible to Waco*. Leiden/Boston: Brill.
Schalit, Abraham (1969), *König Herodes: Der Mann und sein Werk*. Berlin: De Gruyter.
Schaper, Joachim (1995), *Eschatology in the Greek Psalter*. WUNT 2:76. Tübingen: Mohr Siebeck.

—— (2000), *Priester und Leviten im achämenidischen Juda: Studien zur Kult- und Sozialgeschichte Israels in persischer Zeit*. FAT 31. Tübingen: Mohr Siebeck.

—— (2004), *'Wie der Hirsch lechzt nach frischem Wasser': Studien zu Ps 42/43 in Religionsgeschichte, Theologie und kirchlicher Praxis*. BibS(N) 63. Neukirchen-Vluyn: Neukirchener.

Schart, Aaron (1998), *Die Entstehung des Zwölfprophetenbuchs: Neubearbeitungen von Amos im Rahmen schriftenübergreifender Redaktionsprozesse*. BZAW 260. Berlin/New York: de Gruyter.

Schendel, Eckhard (1971), *Herrschaft und Unterwerfung Christi: 1. Korinther 15, 24-28 in Exegese und Theologie der Väter bis zum Ausgang des 4. Jahrhunderts*. Tübingen: Mohr Siebeck.

Schmidtke, Alfred (1911), *Neue Fragmente und Untersuchungen zu den judenchristlichen Evangelien: Ein Beitrag zur Literatur und Geschichte der Judenchristen*. TU 37:1. Leipzig: Hinrichs.

Schneemelcher, Wilhelm (1991), *New Testament Apocrypha*. Ed. R. M. Wilson. 2 vols. Rev. edn. Cambridge/Louisville: James Clark/Westminster John Knox Press.

—— (1992), *New Testament Apocrypha* II. Cambridge/Louisville: Westminster John Knox Press.

Schnelle, Udo (1992), *Antidocetic Christology in the Gospel of John: An Investigation of the Place of the Fourth Gospel in the Johannine School*. Trans. L. M. Maloney. Minneapolis: Fortress Press.

—— (2005), *Apostle Paul: His Life and Theology*. Grand Rapids: Baker Academic.

Schniedewind, William M. (1994), 'King and Priest in the Book of Chronicles and the Duality of Qumran Messianism.' *JJS* 45: 71–8.

Schoeps, Hans Joachim (1969), *Jewish Christianity: Factional Disputes in the Early Church*. Philadelphia: Fortress Press.

Scholem, Gershom (1971), *The Messianic Idea in Judaism: And Other Essays on Jewish Spirituality*. London/New York: Allen and Unwin/Schocken.

—— (1973), *Sabbatai Sevi: the mystical messiah, 1626-1676*. Bollingen Series 93. Princeton: Princeton University Press.

Schreiber, Stefan (2000), *Gesalbter und König: Titel und Konzeptionen der königlichen Gesalbtenerwartung in frühjüdischen und urchristlichen Schriften*. BZNW 105. Berlin: Walter de Gruyter.

Schreiner, Thomas R. (2001), *Paul, Apostle of God's Glory in Christ: A Pauline Theology*. Downers Grove/Leicester: InterVarsity Press/Apollos.

Schröder, Wilt Aden (1971), *M. Porcius Cato, das erste Buch der Origines: Ausgabe und Erklärung der Fragmente*. Beiträge zur Klassischen Philologie 41. Meisenheim am Glan: Hain.

Schürer, Emil (1973–87), *The History of the Jewish People in the Age of Jesus Christ*. Ed. G. Vermes *et al*. 3 vols; rev. edn, Edinburgh: T&T Clark.

Schüssler Fiorenza, Elisabeth (1972), *Priester für Gott: Studien zum Herrschafts- und Priestermotiv in der Apokalypse*. NTAbh, n.s. 7. Münster: Aschendorff.

Schutter, William L. (1989), *Hermeneutic and Composition in 1 Peter*. WUNT 2:30. Tübingen: Mohr Siebeck.

Works Cited

Schwarte, Karl-Heinz (1966), *Die Vorgeschichte der augustinischen Weltalterlehre.* Antiquitas 1:12. Bonn: Habelt.

——— (1978), 'Apokalyptik/Apokalypsen: V. Alte Kirche.' *TRE* 3: 257–75.

Schwartz, Daniel R. (1992), *Studies in the Jewish Background of Christianity.* WUNT 60. Tübingen: Mohr Siebeck.

Schwartz, Seth (2001), *Imperialism and Jewish Society, 200 B.C.E. to 640 C.E.* Princeton: Princeton University Press.

Schwegler, Albert. 1853. *Römische Geschichte.* 3 vols; Tübingen: Laupp.

Scott, James C. (1985), *Weapons of the Weak: Everyday Forms of Peasant Resistance.* New Haven/London: Yale University Press.

——— (1986), 'Everyday Forms of Peasant Resistance.' In *Everyday Forms of Peasant Resistance in Southeast Asia*, 5–35. Ed. J. C. Scott and B. J. Kerkvliet. London: Cass.

——— (1987), 'Resistance Without Protest and Without Organization: Peasant Opposition to the Islamic Zakat and the Christian Tithe.' *Contemporary Studies in History and Society* 29: 417–52.

——— (1990), *Domination and the Arts of Resistance: Hidden Transcripts.* New Haven: Yale University Press.

Seeligmann, Isaac Leo (2004), *The Septuagint Version of Isaiah and Cognate Studies.* Ed. R. Hanhart and H. Spieckermann. FAT 40. Tübingen: Mohr Siebeck.

Segal, Alan F. (1977), *Two Powers in Heaven: Early Rabbinic Reports about Christianity and Gnosticism.* SJLA 25. Leiden: Brill.

——— (1980), 'Heavenly Ascent in Hellenistic Judaism, Early Christianity and their Environment.' *ANRW* 2.23.2: 1333–94.

——— (1990), *Paul the Convert: The Apostolate and Apostasy of Saul the Pharisee.* New Haven: Yale University Press.

——— (1992a), 'Conversion and Messianism: Outline for a New Approach.' In *The Messiah: Developments in Earliest Judaism and Christianity*, 296–340. Ed. J. H. Charlesworth. Minneapolis: Fortress Press.

——— (1992b), 'The Risen Christ and the Angelic Figures in Light of Qumran.' In *Jesus and the Dead Sea Scrolls*, 302–28. Ed. J. H. Charlesworth. New York: Doubleday.

——— (1996), 'The Akedah: Some Reconsiderations.' In *Geschichte - Tradition - Reflexion: Festschrift für Martin Hengel zum 70. Geburtstag*, 1:99–116. Ed. H. Cancik *et al.* Tübingen: Mohr Siebeck.

Segundo, Juan Luis (1985), *The Historical Jesus of the Synoptics.* Maryknoll: Orbis Books.

——— (1988), *An Evolutionary Approach to Jesus of Nazareth.* Ed. J. Drury. Maryknoll: Orbis Books.

Sehlmeyer, M. (1999), 'Statua: Romulus Tropaiophorus.' In *Lexicon Topographicum Urbis Romae*, 4: 369. Ed. E. M. Steinby. Rome: Quasar.

Seland, Torrey (2005), *Strangers in the Light: Philonic Perspectives on Christian Identity in 1 Peter.* Biblical Interpretation Series 76. Leiden/Boston: Brill.

Selwyn, E. G. (1952), *The First Epistle of St. Peter.* London: Macmillan.

Siber, Heinrich (1952), *Römisches Verfassungsrecht in geschichtlicher Entwicklung.* Juristische Handbibliothek. Lahr: Schauenburg.

Simon, R. (1997) 'Mānī and Muhammad', *JSAI* 21: 118–41.
Simonetti, Manlio (1975), 'Il millenarismo in Oriente da Origene a Metodio.' In *Corona Gratiarum: Miscellanea patristica, historica et liturgica Eligio Dekkers O.S.B. XII lustra complenti oblata*, 1:37–58. Ed. A. J. de Smedt. Bruges, The Hague: Sint Pietersabdij/Nijhoff.
Skarsaune, Oskar (1987), *The Proof from Prophecy: A Study in Justin Martyr's Proof-Text Tradition: Text-Type, Provenance, Theological Profile*. NovTSup 56. Leiden: Brill.
Slingerland, H. Dixon (1997), *Claudian Policymaking and the Early Imperial Repression of Judaism at Rome*. South Florida Studies in the History of Judaism 160. Atlanta: Scholars Press.
Smith, Morton (1987), *Palestinian Parties and Politics that Shaped the Old Testament*. 2nd edn, London: SCM.
Smolar, Leivy and Moses Aberbach (1983), *Studies in Targum Jonathan to the Prophets*. The Library of Biblical Studies. New York: Ktav.
Sonne, I. (1947), 'The Paintings of the Dura Synagogue.' *HUCA* 20: 255–362.
Sperber, Alexander, ed., (1962), *The Bible in Aramaic: Based on Old Manuscripts and Printed Texts*. Vol. 3: *The Latter Prophets according to Targum Jonathan*. Leiden: Brill.
Speyer, Wolfgang (1970), *Bücherfunde in der Glaubenswerbung der Antike: Mit einem Ausblick auf Mittelalter und Neuzeit*. Hypomnemata 24. Göttingen: Vandenhoeck & Ruprecht.
────── (1981), *Büchervernichtung und Zensur des Geistes bei Heiden, Juden und Christen*. Bibliothek des Buchwesens 7. Stuttgart: Hiersemann.
Spilsbury, Paul (2003), 'Flavius Josephus on the Rise and Fall of the Roman Empire.' *JTS* 54: 1–24.
Spurling, Helen (2004), 'Pirqe Mashiah: A Translation, Commentary and Introduction.' Ph.D. dissertation, University of Cambridge.
Staerk, Willy (1938), *Die Erlöserwartung in den östlichen Religionen: Untersuchungen zu den Ausdrucksformen der biblischen Christologie (Soter II)*. Stuttgart/Berlin: Kohlhammer.
Stählin, Gustav (1962), *Die Apostelgeschichte übersetzt und erklärt*. NTD 5. Göttingen: Vandenhoeck & Ruprecht.
Stanton, Graham N. (1973), 'On the Christology of Q.' In *Christ and Spirit in the New Testament*, 27–42. Ed. B. Lindars and S. S. Smalley. Cambridge: Cambridge University Press.
────── (1992), *A Gospel for a New People: Studies in Matthew*. Edinburgh: T&T Clark.
────── (2004), *Jesus and Gospel*. Cambridge/New York: Cambridge University Press.
Stanton, V. H. (1886), *The Jewish and the Christian Messiah*. Edinburgh: T&T Clark.
Starr, J. (1935), 'Byzantine Jewry on the Eve of the Arab Conquest (565–638)', *Journal of the Palestine Oriental Society* 15: 280–93.
────── (1937), 'Le mouvement messianique au début du VIIIe siècle', *Revue des Études Juives* 102: 81–92.
Ste Croix, G. E. M. de (1963), 'Why were the Christians persecuted?', *Past and Present* 26: 6–38.

Stegemann, Ekkehard (1985), '"Kindlein, hütet euch vor den Götterbildern".' *TZ* 41: 284–94.

—— (1993), 'Welchen Sinn hat es, von Jesus als Messias zu reden?' In *Messias-Vorstellungen bei Juden und Christen*, 81–102. Ed. E. Stegemann. Stuttgart: Kohlhammer.

Stegemann, Hartmut (1993), *Die Essener, Qumran, Johannes der Täufer und Jesus: Ein Sachbuch*. Herder Spektrum. Freiburg: Herder.

Steinby, Eva Margareta, ed., (1993–2000), *Lexicon topographicum urbis Romae*. 6 vols; Roma: Quasar.

Stemberger, Günter (1987), *Juden und Christen im heiligen Land: Palästina unter Konstantin und Theodosius*. Munich: Beck.

—— (1999), 'Jerusalem in the Early Seventh Century: Hopes and Aspirations of Christians and Jews.' In *Jerusalem: Its Sanctity and Centrality to Judaism, Christianity, and Islam*, 260–70. Ed. L. I. Levine. New York/London: Continuum.

—— (2000), *Jews and Christians in the Holy Land: Palestine in the Fourth Century*. Trans. R. Tuschling. Edinburgh: T&T Clark.

Stenning, John Frederick (1949), *The Targum of Isaiah*. Oxford: Clarendon Press.

Stern, David and Mark Mirsky, eds, (1990), *Rabbinic Fantasies: Imaginative Narratives from Classical Hebrew Literature*. Philadelphia: Jewish Publication Society.

Stern, Ephraim (1984), 'The Persian Empire and the Political and Social History of Palestine in the Persian Period.' In *The Cambridge History of Judaism*, 1:70–87. Ed. W. D. Davies and L. Finkelstein. Cambridge: Cambridge University Press.

Stone, Michael E. (1987), 'The Question of the Messiah in 4 Ezra.' In *Judaisms and Their Messiahs at the Turn of the Christian Era*, 209–24. Ed. J. Neusner et al. Cambridge etc.: Cambridge University Press.

—— (1990), *Fourth Ezra: A Commentary on the Book of Fourth Ezra*. Hermeneia. Minneapolis: Fortress Press.

Strauß, Hans et al. (1992), 'Messias/Messianische Bewegungen.' *TRE* 22: 617–38.

Strauss, M. L. (1995), *The Davidic Messiah in Luke-Acts: The Promise and its Fulfilment in Lukan Christology*. JSNTSup. Vol. 110. Sheffield: Sheffield Academic Press.

Strecker, Georg (1962), 'Entrückung.' *RAC* 5: 461–76.

—— (1996), *The Johannine Letters: A Commentary on 1, 2, and 3 John*. Trans. L. M. Maloney. Ed. H. W. Attridge. Hermeneia. Minneapolis: Fortress Press.

Stroumsa, Guy. G. (1985), 'Gnostics and Manichaeans in Byzantine Palestine.' *Studia Patristica* 10: 273–78.

—— (1986),'Seal of the Prophets: the Nature of a Manichaean Metaphor.' *JSAI* 7: 61–74.

—— (1996), 'Philosophy of the Barbarians: On Early Christian Ethnological Representations.' In *Geschichte – Tradition – Reflexion: Festschrift für Martin Hengel zum 70. Geburtstag*, 2: 339–68. Ed. H. Cancik et al. Tübingen: Mohr Siebeck.

——— (1999), *Barbarian Philosophy: The Religious Revolution of Early Christianity*. WUNT 112. Tübingen: Mohr Siebeck.
——— (forthcoming a), 'Barbares ou hérétiques: juifs et arabes dans la conscience byzantine (IVe–VIIIe s.).' *Revue Internationale de Philosophie*.
——— (forthcoming b), 'The Temple Mount: A Case of Religious Over-Determination.' In *Where Heaven and Earth Meet: Jerusalem's Sacred Esplanade*. Ed. O. Grabar and B. Z. Kedar. Jerusalem.
Stroumsa, Sarah (1999), *Freethinkers of Medieval Islam: Ibn al-Rawandi, Abu Bakr al-Razi and Their Impact on Islamic Thought*. Islamic Philosophy, Theology, and Science 35. Leiden/Boston: Brill.
Stuckenbruck, Loren T. (1995), *Angel Veneration and Christology: A Study in Early Judaism and in the Christology of the Apocalypse of John*. WUNT 2:70. Tübingen: Mohr Siebeck.
Stuhlmacher, Peter (1983), 'Jesustradition im Römerbrief.' *TBei* 14: 240–50.
——— (1989), 'Die Stellung Jesu und des Paulus zu Jerusalem: Versuch einer Erinnerung.' *ZTK* 86: 140–156.
——— (1993), 'Der messianische Gottesknecht.' *Jahrbuch für Biblische Theologie* 8: 131–54.
Swartz, Michael D. and Joseph Yahalom (2004), *Avodah: Ancient Poems for Yom Kippur*. University Park: Pennsylvania State University Press.
Sweet, J. P. M. (1979), *Revelation*. Philadelphia: Westminster.
——— (1981), 'Maintaining the Testimony of Jesus: the Suffering of Christians in the Revelation of St John.' In *Suffering and Martyrdom in the New Testament: Studies Presented to G.M. Styler*, 101–17. Ed. W. Horbury and B. McNeil. Cambridge: Cambridge University Press.
——— (1984), 'The Zealots and Jesus.' In *Jesus and the Politics of his Day*, 1–9. Ed. E. Bammel and C. F. D. Moule. Cambridge etc.: Cambridge University Press.
Syrén, Roger (1986), *The Blessing in the Targums: A Study on the Targumic Interpretations of Genesis 49 and Deuteronomy 33*. Acta Academiae Aboensis A 64:1. Åbo: Åbo Akademi.
Tardieu, M. (1988), 'La diffusion du bouddhisme dans l'empire kouchan, l'Iran et la Chine d'après un kephalaion manichéen inédit', *Studia Iranica* 17: 153–82.
Taylor, Justin (1998), 'Why Did Paul Persecute the Church?' In *Tolerance and Intolerance in Early Judaism and Christianity*, 99–120. Ed. G. N. Stanton and G. G. Stroumsa. Cambridge: Cambridge University Press.
Telfer, W. (1960), 'Was Hegesippus a Jew?' *HTR* 53: 143–53.
ter Haar Romeny, B. (2005), 'Hypotheses on the Development of Judaism and Christianity in Syria.' In *Matthew and the Didache: Two Documents from the Same Jewish-Christian Milieu?*, 13–33. Ed. H. van de Sandt. Assen/Minneapolis: Royal Van Gorcum/Fortress.
Theissen, Gerd (1978), *Sociology of Early Palestinian Christianity*. 1st US edn. Philadelphia: Fortress Press.
——— (1991), *The Gospels in Context: Social and Political History in the Synoptic Tradition*. Trans. L. M. Maloney. Minneapolis: Fortress Press.
——— (1992a), 'Gruppenmessianismus: Überlegungen zum Ursprung der Kirche im Jüngerkreis Jesu.' *Jahrbuch für Biblische Theologie* 7: 101–23.

―――― (1992b), *Social Reality and the Early Christians: Theology, Ethics, and the World of the New Testament*. Minneapolis: Fortress Press.

―――― (2004), *Die Jesusbewegung : Sozialgeschichte einer Revolution der Werte*. Gütersloh: Gütersloher Verlagshaus.

Theissen, Gerd and Annette Merz (1998), *The Historical Jesus: A Comprehensive Guide*. Trans. J. Bowden. London: SCM Press.

Thomas, L. A. R. (1978), 'The Legends Concerning Peter and Antioch in Syriac Tradition, with an Edition and Translation of Jacob of Serug's Homily on the Conversion of Antioch.' M.Litt. thesis, University of Oxford.

Thompson, Leonard. L. (1990), *The Book of Revelation: Apocalypse and Empire*. New York/Oxford: Oxford University Press.

Thompson, Michael (1991), *Clothed with Christ: The Example and Teaching of Jesus in Romans 12.1-15:13*. JSNTSup 59. Sheffield: JSOT Press.

Thornton, Timothy C. G. (1990), 'The Stories of Joseph of Tiberias.' VC 44: 54–63.

Thyen, Hartwig (2005), *Das Johannesevangelium*. HNT 6. Tübingen: Mohr Siebeck.

Torrey, C. C. (1937), 'Χριστός' In *Quantulacumque: Studies Presented to Kirsopp Lake*, 317–24. Ed. R. P. Casey *et al*. London: Christophers.

Toynbee, J. M. C. (1996), *Death and Burial in the Roman World: Aspects of Greek and Roman Life*. 2nd edn, Ithaca: Cornell University Press.

Tuckett, Christopher M. (1996), *Q and the History of Early Christianity*. Edinburgh: T&T Clark.

―――― (2001a), *Christology and the New Testament: Jesus and His Earliest Followers*. Edinburgh: Edinburgh University Press.

―――― (2001b), 'The Christology of Luke-Acts.' In *The Unity of Luke-Acts*, 133–64. Ed. J. Verheyden. BETL 142. Leuven: Leuven University Press & Peeters.

Ulrich, Eugene (2000), 'Isaiah, Book of.' *Encyclopedia of the Dead Sea Scrolls* 1: 384–8.

Urbach, Ephraim E. (1971), 'The Homiletical Interpretations of the Sages and the Expositions of Origen on Canticles and the Jewish-Christian Disputation.' *ScrHier* 22: 247–75.

―――― (1975), *The Sages: Their Concepts and Beliefs*. Cambridge: Harvard University Press.

van Bekkum, Wout Jac. (1998), *Hebrew Poetry from Late Antiquity: Liturgical Poems of Yehudah. Critical Edition with Introduction and Commentary*. AGJU 43. Leiden/Boston: Brill.

―――― (2002), 'Jewish Messianic Expectations in the Age of Heraclius.' In *The Reign of Heraclius (610–641): Crisis and Confrontation*, 95–112. Ed. G. J. Reinink and B. H. Stolte. Groningen Studies in Cultural Change 2. Leuven: Peeters.

van der Horst, Pieter W. (2001), 'Judaism and Hellenism Revisited.' In *Hellenism in the Land of Israel*, 154–74. Ed. J. J. Collins and G. E. Sterling. Notre Dame: University of Notre Dame Press.

van der Kooij, Arie (1981), *Die alten Textzeugen des Jesajabuches: Ein Beitrag zur Textgeschichte des Alten Testaments*. OBO 35. Fribourg/Göttingen: Universitätsverlag/Vandenhoeck & Ruprecht.

van der Woude, A. S. (1957), *Die messianischen Vorstellungen der Gemeinde von Qumran*. Studia Semitica Neerlandica 3. Assen: Van Gorcum.
Van Egmond, Richard (2006), 'The Messianic 'Son of David' in Matthew.' *JGRChJ* 3: 41–71.
van Henten, Jan Willem (1997), *The Maccabean Martyrs as Saviours of the Jewish People: A Study of 2 and 4 Maccabees*. JSJSup 57. Leiden/New York: Brill.
—— (2001), 'The Honorary Decree for Simon the Maccabee (1 Macc 14:25-49) in its Hellenistic Context.' In *Hellenism in the Land of Israel*, 116–45. Ed. J. J. Collins and G. E. Sterling. Notre Dame: University of Notre Dame Press.
van Unnik, W. C. (1973), 'The Purpose of St. John's Gospel.' In *Sparsa Collecta*, 1:35–63. Leiden: Brill.
VanderKam, James C. (1992), 'Righteous One, Messiah, Chosen One, and Son of Man in *1 Enoch* 37–71.' In *The Messiah: Developments in Earliest Judaism and Christianity*, 169–91. Ed. J. H. Charlesworth. Minneapolis: Fortress Press.
—— (1994), *The Dead Sea Scrolls Today*. Grand Rapids: Eerdmans.
Vanni, Ugo (1999), 'Language, Symbol and Mystical Experience in the Book of Revelation.' In *1900th Aniversary [sic] of St. John's Apocalypse: Proceedings of the International and Interdisciplinary Symposium (Athens-Patmos, 17-26 September 1995)*, 605–27. Ed. n.d. Athens: Eptalophos.
Vermes, Geza (1973), *Scripture and Tradition in Judaism: Haggadic Studies*. StPB 4. 2nd edn, Leiden: Brill.
Verseput, Donald (1987), 'The Role and Meaning of the "Son of God" Title in Matthew's Gospel.' *NTS* 33: 533–7.
Vianès-Abou Samra, Laurence (2004), 'L'eschatologie d'Apollinaire de Laodicée à travers les Fragments sur les Psaumes.' *Annali di storia dell'esegesi* 21: 331–71.
Viellefond, Jean René (1970), *Les Cestes de Julius Africanus: Étude sur l'ensemble des fragments avec édition, traduction et commentaires*. Publications de l'Institut Français de Florence 1:20. Florence/Paris: Sansoni/Librairie M. Didier.
Vogels, Heinz-Jürgen (1976), *Christi Abstieg ins Totenreich und das Läuterungsgericht an den Toten: Eine bibeltheologisch-dogmatische Untersuchung zum Glaubensartikel "descendit ad inferos"*. Freiburger Theologische Studien 102. Freiburg: Herder.
Vogler, Werner (1988), *Jüdische Jesusinterpretationen in christlicher Sicht*. Weimar: H. Böhlaus.
von Rad, Gerhard (1933), 'Die falschen Propheten.' *Zeitschrift für die altttestamentliche Wissenschaft* 51: 109–20.
Wallace, Daniel B. (1996), *Greek Grammar Beyond the Basics: An Exegetical Syntax of the New Testament*. Grand Rapids: Zondervan.
Wanke, Gunther (1984), 'Prophecy and Psalms in the Persian Period.' In *The Cambridge History of Judaism*, 1: *Introduction*:162–88. Ed. W. D. Davies and L. Finkelstein. Cambridge: Cambridge University Press.
Warthon, A. (2000), 'Erasure: Eliminating the Space of Late Ancient Judaism', in L. I. Levine and Z. Weiss, eds, *From Dura to Sepphoris: Studies in Jewish Art and Society in Late Antiquity*. Portsmouth, RI, 195–213.

Waschke, Ernst-Joachim (2001), *Der Gesalbte: Studien zur alttestamentlichen Theologie.* BZAW 306. Berlin/New York: De Gruyter.
Wasserstrom, Steven M. (1995), *Between Muslim and Jew: the Problem of Symbiosis under Early Islam.* Princeton: Princeton University Press.
Wedderburn, A. J. M., ed., (1989), *Paul and Jesus: Collected Essays.* Sheffield: Sheffield Academic Press.
Weinberger, Leon J. (1998), *Jewish Hymnography: A Literary History.* London: Littman Library of Jewish Civilization.
Weinstock, Stefan (1971), *Divus Julius.* Oxford: Clarendon Press.
Weiser, Alfons and Hans-Georg Pöhlmann (1986), 'Höllenfahrt Christi.' *TRE* 15: 330–41.
Weitzman, Michael (1999), *The Syriac Version of the Old Testament: An Introduction.* UCOP 56. Cambridge etc.: Cambridge University Press.
Weitzmann, Kurt and Herbert L. Kessler (1990), *The Frescoes of the Dura Synagogue and Christian Art.* Dumbarton Oaks Studies 28. Washington: Dumbarton Oaks.
Wenham, David (1995), *Paul: Follower of Jesus or Founder of Christianity?* Grand Rapids: Eerdmans.
Wevers, John William (1982), *Numeri.* Septuaginta Vetus Testamentum Graecum auctoritate Academiae Scientiarum Gottingensis editum. Göttingen: Vandenhoeck & Ruprecht.
―― (1993), *Notes on the Greek Text of Genesis.* SBLSCS 35. Atlanta: Scholars Press.
Wevers, John William, ed., (1974), *Genesis.* Septuaginta Vetus Testamentum Graecum auctoritate Academiae Scientiarum Gottingensis editum 1. Göttingen: Vandenhoeck & Ruprecht.
Wharton, Annabel Jane (1995), *Refiguring the Post-Classical City: Dura Europos, Jerash, Jerusalem, and Ravenna.* Cambridge etc.: Cambridge University Press.
―― (2000), 'Erasure: Eliminating the Space of Late Ancient Judaism.' In *From Dura to Sepphoris: Studies in Jewish Art and Society in Late Antiquity,* 195–214. Ed. L. I. Levine and Z. Weiss. Journal of Roman Archaeology Supplementary Series 40. Portsmouth: Journal of Roman Archaeology.
Wilckens, Ulrich (2003), *Der Sohn Gottes und seine Gemeinde: Studien zur Theologie der Johanneischen Schriften.* FRLANT 200. Göttingen: Vandenhoeck & Ruprecht.
Wilken, Robert Louis (1992), *The Land Called Holy: Palestine in Christian History and Thought.* New Haven: Yale University Press.
Willi, A. (1998), 'Numa's Dangerous Books: The Exegetic History of a Roman Forgery.' *MH* 55: 139–72.
Williams, Rowan (2000), *On Christian Theology.* Oxford/Malden: Blackwell.
―― (2003), 'Historical Criticism and Sacred Text.' In *Reading Texts, Seeking Wisdom: Scripture and Theology,* 216–28. Ed. G. Stanton and D. F. Ford. London: SCM.
Williams, Tyler F. (2001), 'Towards a Date for the Old Greek Psalter.' In *The Old Greek Psalter: Studies in Honour of Albert Pietersma,* 248–76. Ed. R. J. V. Hiebert *et al.* JSOTSup 332. Sheffield: Sheffield Academic Press.

Williamson, H. G. M. (1977), 'Eschatology in Chronicles.' *TynBul* 28: 115–54.
—— (1983), 'The Dynastic Oracle in the Books of Chronicles.' In *Isac Leo Seeligmann Volume*, 3: 305–18. Ed. A. Rofé and Y. Zakovitch. Jerusalem: Rubinstein.
—— (1998), *Variations on a Theme: King, Messiah and Servant in the Book of Isaiah*. Didsbury Lectures 1997. Carlisle: Paternoster Press.
Windisch, Hans (1930), *Die katholischen Briefe*. HNT 15. 2nd edn, Tübingen: Mohr.
Wink, Walter (1992), *Engaging the Powers: Discernment and Resistance in a World of Domination*. Minneapolis: Fortress Press.
—— (2003), *Jesus and Nonviolence: A Third Way*. Minneapolis: Augsburg Fortress.
Wintermute, O. S. (1983), 'Apocalypse of Elijah.' In *The Old Testament Pseudepigrapha*, 1: 721–53. Ed. J. H. Charlesworth. Garden City: Doubleday.
Wlosok, Antonie, ed., (1978), *Römischer Kaiserkult*. Darmstadt: Wissenschaftliche Buchgesellschaft.
Wolff, Hans Walter (1991), *Dodekapropheton: 6, Haggai*. BKAT 14:6. 2nd edn, Neukirchen-Vluyn: Neukirchener Verlag.
Wolfson, Harry Austryn (1947), *Philo: Foundations of Religious Philosophy in Judaism, Christianity, and Islam*. 2 vols; Cambridge: Harvard University Press.
Wright, N. T. (1991), *The Climax of the Covenant: Christ and the Law in Pauline Theology*. Edinburgh: T&T Clark.
—— (1996), *Jesus and the Victory of God*. Christian Origins and the Question of God 2. Minneapolis: Fortress.
—— (2002), 'The Letter to the Romans: Introduction, Commentary, and Reflections.' *NIB* 10: 373–795.
—— (2003), *The Resurrection of the Son of God*. Christian Origins and the Question of God 3. London: SPCK.
Yahalom, Joseph (1999), *Poetry and Society in Jewish Galilee of Late Antiquity* (Hebr.). Ha-Kibbutz Ha-Meuchad: Tel Aviv.
Yahalom, Joseph, ed., (1984), *Liturgical poems of Sim'on Bar Megas*. (Hebr.). Jerusalem: Israel Academy.
Yahalom, Joseph and M. Sokoloff (1999), שירת בני מערבא: *Jewish Palestinian Aramaic Poetry from Late Antiquity*. Jerusalem: Israel Academy of Sciences and Humanities.
Yarbro Collins, Adela (1976a), *The Combat Myth in the Book of Revelation*. HDR 9. Missoula: Scholars Press.
—— (1976b), 'Composition and Redaction of the *Testament of Moses* 10.' *HTR* 69: 179–86.
—— (1984), *Crisis and Catharsis*. Philadelphia: Westminster.
—— (2001), 'Jesus' Action in Herod's Temple.' In *Antiquity and Humanity: Essays on Ancient Religion and Philosophy Presented to Hans Dieter Betz on his 70th Birthday*, 45–61. Ed. A. Yarbro Collins and M. M. Mitchell. Tübingen: Mohr Siebeck.
Yoder, John Howard (1972), *The Politics of Jesus: Vicit Agnus Noster*. Grand Rapids: Eerdmans.

Zakovitch, Yair (1992), *An Introduction to inner-Biblical interpretation*. [Hebrew]. Even Yehudah: Rekhes.

Zanker, Paul (1988), *The Power of Images in the Age of Augustus*. Ann Arbor: University of Michigan Press.

Zeller, Dieter (1993), 'Zur Transformation des Χριστός bei Paulus.' *Jahrbuch für Biblische Theologie* 8: 155–67.

Zenger, Erich (2002), '"Es sollen sich niederwerfen vor ihm alle Könige" (Ps 72,11): Redaktionsgeschichtliche Beobachtungen zu Psalm 72 und zum Programm des messianischen Psalters Ps 2-89.' In *'Mein Sohn bist du' (Ps 2,7): Studien zu den Königspsalmen*, 66–93. Ed. E. Zenger and E. Otto. SBS 192. Stuttgart: Katholisches Bibelwerk.

Zetterholm, Magnus (2001), 'A Struggle Among Brothers: An Interpretation of the Relations between Jews and Christians at Ostia.' In *The Synagogue of Ancient Ostia and the Jews of Rome: Interdisciplinary Studies*, 101–13. Ed. B. Olsson *et al*. Acta Instituti Romani Regni Sueciae 57. Jonsered: Paul Åströms Förlag.

—— (2004), *The Formation of Christianity in Antioch: A Social-Scientific Approach to the Separation Between Judaism and Christianity*. Routledge Early Church Monographs. London: Routledge.

Ziegler, Konrat (1964), *Plutarchos von Chaironeia*. 2nd edn, Stuttgart: Druckenmüller.

—— (1969–73), *Plutarchi Vitae Parallelae*. 4th edn, Vol. 3.1–2. Leipzig: Teubner.

Zimmermann, Johannes (1998), *Messianische Texte aus Qumran: Königliche, priesterliche und prophetische Messiasvorstellungen in den Schriftfunden von Qumran*. WUNT 2:104. Tübingen: Mohr Siebeck.

Index of Ancient Sources

HEBREW OLD TESTAMENT		33.18–34.8	124	33.26	249
Genesis		Leviticus		Judges	
1.1	164	16	129	2.18	21
1.26-27	214	19.18	123	3.9	21
1.26	165	25	23	5.18	267
3	265	25.10	254	6.12	37
3.5	265	26	187	6.36-37	21
3.15	248, 249, 256, 264			9.17	267
4.23	165	Numbers		15.18	21
6.1-4	133	11.26	230		
14.17-20	128	19.4	132	Ruth	
19.24	165	24	184	1.1	230
22	249, 257	24.6	247, 248	3.15	230
22.2	249, 257	24.7	13, 174, 184, 187, 230, 247, 248, 257	1 Samuel	
22.12	249, 257			2.35-36	271
22.13	257			2.35	268, 271
22.14	169			5	218
22.16	249	24.15-17	24, 26	12.3	143
28.18	209	24.16-19	151	14.47	252
44.12	282	24.17-19	25	15	248
49	*174*	24.17	22, 24, 25, 26, 88, 152, 156, 160, 163, 164, 174, 184, 189, 242, 248, 254, 256, 257, 260, 270	16	37
49.7	247				
49.9-11	182			2 Samuel	
49.9-10	184			2.4	54
49.9	174, 253			2.7	54
49.10-11	164			3.39	54
49.10	12, 22, 25, 164, 169, 176, 201, 246, 247, 249, 255, 257, 266			5.3	54
				7	27, 140
				7.11-14	111
		Deuteronomy		7.13-14	27
		13.1-5	99	7.14	27, 81, 87, 128, 264
		17.15	32		
Exodus		18.18-20	99	7.32-13	87
12	173	18.15	265	8.9-16	87
12.1	267	28	187	23.3	174
12.3	173	32.31	32	23.5	9
17.14	192	33.8-11	24, 26, 27		
19.6	142, 145	33.10	26	2 Kings	
24.3-8	132	33.4-5	184	2	199, 202
24.8	132	33.5	249, 258, 265		
32.30-34	267			1 Chronicles	
33.1	192	33.12	258	2.3-15	12
33.3	192	33.15	249	3.19-24	12

3.19	6	16.8-11	93	89.38	140	
3.24	230	16.14	141	89.39	143	
5.2	12	16.16	141	89.51-52	230	
9.10	19	17	31	89.52	10, 143	
14.2	12	18.28-32	230	90.4	277	
17.14	12	18.49	113	96.10	282	
24.7	19	18.51	143	104.30	28	
28.5	13	19	193	110	5, 128, 161, 169, 259	
28.7	12	19.15	141			
		20.7	143	110.1	93, 259	
2 Chronicles		21.1-8	230	110.3	5, 250, 252, 259	
1.9-10	12	24	161			
9.22	12	28.8	143	110.4	128	
10.19	174	31.12	252	110.17	252	
		37	125	110.19	252	
Ezra		42–89	10	118.22	133	
7.12	13	45	251, 258	118.25-26	106	
9.7	13	45.1-18	230	132	209	
		45.1	249	132.10	143	
Nehemiah		45.5	251, 258	132.11-18	230	
6.7	11	45.7	251	132.17	143	
9.32	13	45.8	258	136.2	219	
9.34	13	45.12-13	251	141.2	282	
		45.13	251	146.10	233	
Esther		46.7	9	147.2	175	
1.1	230	46.11	9	155	75	
		48.3	281			
Psalms		55.8	252	Proverbs		
1–2	27	60.1	251	8.22-31	127	
1.5	205	60.9	258	8.23	132	
2–89	10	61.7-9	230			
2	4, 10, 28, 40, 42, 91, 94, 114, 141, 250, 258	68	252	Ecclesiastes		
		68.12-13	258	1.11	230	
		68.13	252	7.24	230	
		68.30	282			
		68.31	175	Song of Songs		
2.2	10, 143, 250, 258	69.1	251	1.1–3.8	168	
		69.9	113	1.8	230	
2.6-7	250	72	10, 114, 161, 164, 180	1.17	230	
2.6	258			4.5	230	
2.7-9	5			7.4	230	
2.7	5, 22, 90, 91, 116, 127, 128, 250, 259	72.1-20	230	7.12–8.4	230	
		72.17	252, 263			
		73.21	251	Isaiah		
		79.9	259	3.14-15	126	
2.8-9	144	80.1	251	6.32	233	
2.9	40, 141, 250	80.15-18	230	7	9	
		82.1	128	7.10-17	5	
2.11	258	83.10	143	7.14	161, 253, 259	
2.18	141	85.5	259			
2.26-28	141	87.5	247	8.4	161	
3–41	10	89	10, 114, 140	8.14	133	
11.15	141			9.2	88, 163	
11.18	141	89.19	37	9.5-6	5	
12.10	141	89.20	140	9.5	161, 263, 282	
14.1	141	89.26-36	87			

Index of Ancient Sources

9.6-7	88	61.1-3	9	7.25-26	18
9.6	37, 161, 259	61.1-2	81, 254	8.26	38
		61.1	23, 81, 82	9.24-27	76, 192
11	42, 114	61.3	231	9.25-26	23
11.1-25	25	61.6	145	9.25	77
11.1-6	22, 253	62.10-12	208	9.26	270
11.1-2	87	65.8-9	178	11.28-39	18
11.1	164, 184, 248, 253, 258, 260, 266	65.16	140	11.30	18
		65.22-25	203	11.32	18
		66.15-16	208	12.1	82
		66.18-19	208	12.4	38
11.2-4	40				
11.4	25	Jeremiah		Joel	
11.10	111, 265	22.24	7	2.14-21	92
11.12	111	23.5-6	6, 7, 254	3.1-5	92
13.6	208	23.6	182		
16.13-14	76	25.11-12	76	Amos	
19.20	184	29.10	76	2.6-8	126
19.25	184	30.9	266	4.13	260
23.1	25	33.14-16	254		
23.12	25	33.15-16	6, 7	Obadiah	
24.1	208	46	184	2	282
26.9-10	208			21	281
26.19	208	Lamentations			
27.13	204	2.22	230	Micah	
28.16	133	4.20	260	3.11	9
29.18	81	4.22	230	4–5	8
31.5	173			4.8	8, 9
32.2	247	Ezekiel		5.1-3	9, 255
35.5-6	81	1–3	138	5.1	255, 263
40–55	9, 38, 42	1.10	32	5.3	255
41.2	185	1.26-28	124	5.4-5	9
41.25	185	17.7	32		
42	114	17.22-24	6, 254	Habbakuk	
42.1-4	85, 245	17.22	254	3.13	204
42.1	245, 260	21.15	255		
43.1	31	21.20	255	Zephaniah	
44.6	106	27.6	25	1.11-15	126
45.1-7	204	34.24	24	3.13	106
45.3	174	37.25	24	3.14-20	105
51.5	164	38–9	248	3.14	106
51.9	232	40–8	201	3.15	105, 106
52.7	23, 82, 236				
52.13–53.12	131, 132, 266	Daniel		Haggai	
		2	174	2.20-23	6-7, 9
52.13	260	2.34	177	2.23	7
52.15	260	4.23	277		
53	132, 242	7	23, 41, 42, 114, 136, 188, 189, 192, 202	Zechariah	
53.2	260			1.16-17	6
53.3-12	132			3.8	254
53.12	267			4.1-14	7, 9
56–66	201	7.8	36	4.7	263
58.6	254	7.9-11	36	4.14	270
60.1-3	188	7.13	52	6.12-13	267
60.19-20	188	7.1-17	203	6.12	248, 254
61	23, 82, 91	7.17	36	6.13	270

8.3	6	7.48-49	19	88	140
9.5	53	8.1–13.50	19	88.21	140
9.9	106	9.27	20	88.39	140
9.13	37	13.51-52	19	109.3	250, 252
10.7	37	14.25-49	19, 20	109.17	252
12.10	270	14.29	21	109.19	252
13.7	270	14.31-32	21	133	209
		14.32-40	20		
Malachi		14.33-34	21	Wisdom	
2.17–3.5	8	14.35-36	21	2.10–3.8	125
3.1	200	14.35	20	6.1-3	137
3.5	126	14.36-37	21		
3.13-21	8, 9	14.36	21	Sirach	
4.5	20	14.41-42	20	2.1-9	127
		14.41	20, 21	24.9	132
SEPTUAGINT		15.33	30	50.1-14	20
Genesis		15.38	20	50.5-21	20
12.2-3	252	16.2-3	21		
24.14	253			Hosea	
24.16	253	2 Maccabees		11.1	245
24.43	253	2.8	124		
24.55	253	2.21	18	Micah	
24.57	253	4.9	18	5.2	263
49.9-10	184	4.12	18		
49.10	255	4.13	18	Zechariah	
		4.19	18	6.12	33, 186
Numbers		5.15-16	18		
24.7	184	5.21	18	Isaiah	
24.17	184, 247	6.1-11	18	9.5-6	253
		8.1	18	9.5	245
Deuteronomy		14.38	18	9.6	263
33.4-5	184			11.11-16	190
		3 Maccabees	186	11.1	247
1 Chronicles		Psalms		49	114
3.19	6	15.8-11	93	Jeremiah	
		30.12	252	33.14-26	246
1 Maccabees		44.7-8	128		
1.11-15	18	44.13	251	Baruch	
1.20-28	19	44.1	249	1.16	13
1.29-40	19	44.5	258		
1.41-64	19	44.7	251	Ezekiel	
2.1	19	44.8	258	21.10	255
2.15-28	21	54.8	252	21.15	255
2.15-27	19, 21	59.1	251	21.30-32	255
2.47	21	59.9	258		
2.54	21	67	252	Daniel	
2.57	21	67.12-13	258	2.22	245
3.1–4.55	19	67.13	252		
3.3-4	21	68.1	251	PESHITTA	
3.4-8	21	71.17	252	Genesis	
4.25	21	72.21	251	49.10	271
4.30	21	78.9	259		
4.46	20	79.1	251	Numbers	
4.56-59	19	84.5	259	24.17	271
5.1–7.47	19	86.5	247		
5.62	21,30				

Index of Ancient Sources

1 Samuel			40.9	174, 182	Ezekiel	
2.35	271		40.10	270	38–39	268
			40.11	269, 270	38.21	269
1 Chronicles					39.4	269
5.1-2	272		Numbers			
5.2	272		11.26	269	Zechariah	
			23.21	174, 230	9.9	230
Psalms			24.17	174	12.10	269
110.3	272		24.20	174	6.12-13	267
			24.24	174	6.12	267
Isaiah					6.13	267, 268
7.14	272		Deuteronomy			
9.5	272		25.19	174, 230	Malachi	
53.9	272		30.4-9	230	4.5	230
60.16	272		30.4	174, 270		
					Targum Ruth	
Daniel			*Fragmentary Targum*		3.15	176
9.26	272		Genesis			
			3.15	230	*Targum Canticles*	
Micah			49.1	230	1.8	273
5.1	273		Exodus		1.17	268
			12.42	174, 230	2.7	240
Zechariah			Numbers		3.5	240
12.10	272		11.26	230, 269	4.4	240
			24.7	230	4.5	269
TARGUMS					4.6	240
Targum Neofiti			*Targum Jonathan*		7.3	240
Genesis			1 Samuel		7.4	269
3.15	174		2.10	269	7.13-14	273
49.10	174, 176				8.1-2	240
49.11	174		2 Samuel		8.4	240, 273
			22.49	269	8.9-10	240
Numbers						
11.26	174		Isaiah		*Targum Lamentations*	
24.7	174		9.5	262, 263	4.22	270
			22.15-25	268		
Targum Onqelos			22.25	268	*Targum Psalms*	
Genesis			23.7	262	2.7	264
49.10-12	230		37.26	262	45.7	264
49.10	265		51.9	262		
			52.13–53.12	267, 268	NEW TESTAMENT	
Numbers			52.13	266	Matthew	
24.17-20	230		52.15	268	1–2	47
24.23-24	230		53	267	1.1	79, 84, 85
			53.2	266	1.16	79
Targum Pseudo-Jonathan			53.3	266	1.17	79, 84
Genesis			53.4-6	267	1.18-25	84
3.15	230		53.4	266, 267	1.18	79
35.21	174, 230		53.5	267, 268	1.21	84
49.1	230		53.6	267	2.2-6	86
			53.8	267	2.2-3	51, 85
Exodus			53.11	266, 267	2.2	248, 254
4.13	270		53.12	266, 267	2.3	85, 86
6.18	270		54.7	266	2.4	79
17.16	230				2.6	255
40.9-11	230				2.8	248

2.9	248, 254	Mark		Luke	
2.10	248	1.1	82, 83, 84	1–2	47
3.16	54	1.9-11	54	1.26-38	87
4.1-11	49, 80	1.10	54	1.32-33	41, 87
4.8-10	50	1.12-13	49	1.32	54, 87
4.16	163	1.13	49	1.34-35	49
5–7	85	1.15	124	1.35	87, 173
5.41	74	1.37	54	1.36	173
5.44-45	74	3.15	76	1.47	89
7.15	286, 287	3.22	69	1.68-79	87
8–9	85	4.12	262	1.68	88, 89, 92
8.5-13	74	6.32-44	56	1.69	79, 88, 89
8.17	86, 132	8.1-10	56	1.70-71	88
9.27-28	86	8.27-33	50	1.71	88, 89
9.27	84, 85	8.29	83, 123	1.76-77	88
10.23	75, 76	9.1	75	1.78	88, 163
10.32	179	10.40	54	1.79	88, 163
11–3	85	10.45	132	2.1-20	89
11.2-6	81	10.47	85	2.11	51, 89, 90, 93
11.2	38, 85	10.48	85		
11.6	96	11.1-11	85	2.14	41
11.29	86	11.1-10	53	2.25-38	90
12.17-21	86	11.10	53,106	2.25	90
12.18-21	85, 245, 260	11.11	53	2.26	79
		12.10-11	133	2.30-32	90
12.23	84, 85, 86	12.13-7	74	2.34	90
12.28	80	12.17	74	2.35	41
12.41-42	80	12.31	123	2.38	90, 92
13.16-17	80	12.35	85	3.3-18	90
14.13-21	56	13	68, 73	3.15	79, 90
15.22	84, 85	13.26-27	76	3.21-32	90
15.32-39	56	13.30	75	3.22	54
17.25-26	74	13.32	76	3-24	90
19.28	54	14.3-9	54	4.1-13	49,80
20.30	85	14.9	76	4.5-8	50
20.31	85	14.32-42	56	4.16-30	91
21.1-11	85	14.65	50	4.18-19	254
21.5	86	14.61-62	123	4.18	54, 91
21.9	84, 85, 86	14.61	85	4.41	91
21.10	85	14.62	83	6.15	65
21.15	84, 85, 86	15.1-4	74	6.20-25	126
22.15-22	74	15.2	83	6.22	103
22.42	85	15.9	83	6.20	123
22.44	250	15.12	83	7.19	81
24-25	202	15.16-20	50	7.20	38
24	162	15.17	52	7.22-23	81
24.29-31	211	15.18	83, 96	7.23	96
25.31-46	75	15.26	52, 83, 175	9.31	95
25.31	54	15.27	83, 96	9.51	95
26.55	163	15.31-32	83, 84	10.18	75
27.29	52	15.32	51, 83, 96	10.23-24	80
27.37	52, 175	15.39	50, 83	11.20	80
28.5	52	16.1-8	60	11.31-32	80
28.10	52	16.8	52	13.3	74
		16.19	250	14.21	76
				16.19-31	75

Index of Ancient Sources

19.38	69	6.14	105	19.7	105
20.21-26	74	6.15	50	19.9-21	105
20.42-43	250	6.38-40	100	19.9	105
21.7-9	76	7	103	19.10-11	105
21.28	92	7.1	104	19.11	105
22.30	54	7.13	99	19.12	67, 105
22.67	85	7.14-9	99	19.14-22	52
22.70	85	7.26-27	97	19.14	105
22.37	132	7.26	99	19.15	52, 67, 105
23.2-4	69	7.27	101, 102	19.19-22	52
23.2	69, 89, 116, 174, 175	7.30	99, 104	19.19	175
		7.31	97, 98, 99, 101, 102	19.26-27	103
23.37-38	69			19.37	270
23.38	52, 175	7.32	104	20.19-23	52
23.47	125	7.41-42	97, 99, 101	20.26	52
24	92	7.42	102	20.28	100
24.21	50, 92	7.52	101, 102	20.30-31	97, 98, 103
24.26	92, 124	8.12	100	20.31-32	102
24.37-40	52	8.15-18	100	20.31	97, 99, 106
24.46	92	8.37	104	21.21-23	75
24.51	95	8.40	104		
		8.58	100	Acts of the Apostles	
John		9.22	97, 101, 103	1.6	92
1.1-18	127			1.6-8	50
1.1	97	9.33-34	103	1.13	65
1.14	97, 103, 173	9.35	102	2.14-36	92
		10.7-13	104	2.14-36	95
1.20	97	10.22	104	2.22	93
1.31	106	10.30	100	2.30	93
1.33	54	10.31-39	101	2.31	93
1.34	103	10.31	104	2.36	77, 89, 93, 136
1.41-51	102	11.47-53	104		
1.41	44, 54, 97, 98, 103, 105, 203, 204, 209	11.27	97, 102	2.43	93
		11.55	104	3.14	107, 125
		12.12-15	53	3.18	92
		12.12-16	102	4.11	133
		12.10	104	4.24-29	91
1.47	106	12.14	106	4.27	54
1.49	105	12.15	106	5.11	93
2.13	104	12.34	101, 102	5.31	51, 89
3.13	101	16.2	104, 105	*6.1*	*17*
3.35	100	17.5	124	7	129
4.10	103	17.16	104	7.52	107, 125
4.19-26	206	17.24	132	7.55	124
4.20	209	18-19	52	8.32-33	132
4.22	103	18.3	104	9.1-3	134
4.25	44, 54, 97, 103, 203, 204, 209	18.10	104	9.19-25	93
		18.20	67	9.19-22	91, 93
		18.23	67	9.20	93, 116
4.26	103	18.33-38	67, 105	9.22	*116*
4.29	103	18.33	52	10.36-43	91
4.42	51, 105	18.36-37	52, 105	10.38	54
5.17-18	101	18.39	52	11.26	110, 155
5.18	104	19.2	52	12.11	247
6	101	19.3	52	13.13-52	93
6.1-13	56	19.5	52	13.16-41	93, 95
6.4	104				

13.16	93	15.8	111	5.1	116
13.22-23	93, 116	15.9	113	5.11	55
13.23	51, 89	15.12	114, 117		
13.26	93	15.18	266	Ephesians	
13.32-33	94, 116	16.17-20	265	1.2	140
13.33-35	17	16.17	55	1.10	110, 133
13.33	91, 144	16.18-20	265	1.12	110
14.1	94	16.18	265	1.20	110
16.16-40	134	16.19	265, 266	1.22	203
17.1-10	68	16.20	249, 265	4.8	262
17.1-3	94	16.26	132, 266	5.2	142
17.3	92, 94, 116			5.5	114
17.5-9	134	1 Corinthians		5.14	110
17.7	116	1.3	140		
17.10	94	1.21-24	55	Philippians	
17.16-17	94	1.23	92, 110	1.2	140
18.2	199	2.8	124, 130	1.6	119
18.4-6	94	3.11	110	1.10	119
18.5	116	8.11-12	120	1.15	110
18.12-17	134	10.1-11	119	1.17	110
18.14-16	69	10.4	110, 131	1.28-30	68
18.28	116	12.3	115, 116	2	117
22.11	124	12.27-28	286	2.9-11	115, 117, 132, 133
22.14	125	13.13	130		
26.23	92, 94, 116	15	117	2.6-11	115, 117, 127
		15.3	92, 110, 112		
Romans				2.5-11	116
1.1-5	266	15.20-28	114, 117	2.11	116, 124
1.3-5	117	15.22	110	2.16	119
1.3-4	77, 111, 116	15.23	124	3.7	110
		15.23-28	111, 114	3.19-21	117
1.3	94, 266	15.24-28	202, 211	3.20	116
1.4	111, 132	15.25-28	133	3.21	124, 133
1.5	266, 273	15.27-28	203		
1.7	140	15.27	203	Colossians	
1.16-17	117	15.43	124	1.11	124
4.25	132	16.22	119, 123	1.15-20	125, 127
5.6	112			1.18	141
5.8	112	2 Corinthians		1.26	132
8.18-25	118	1.21	54, 112	2.15	133
8.29	130	4.4-5	116	2.18	127
9.5	111, 114, 116, 141	4.6	124	3.18–4.1	134
		5.10	110, 111, 119		
9.32-33	133			1 Thessalonians	
10.9	115, 116	8.1-2	68	1.6	68, 134
13	117	10.1	120	2.14	68, 134
13.1-8	74	11.2-3	110	2.19	124
13.1-7	134, 137	11.23-25	134	3.3	68
13.11-12	265	12	140	4	117
13.12	124	12.1	121	4.11-12	76
14.15	120	12.4	144	4.15–5.10	76
15.3-9	113			4.15-17	118, 119
15.3	113, 114	Galatians		4.15	117
15.7-12	111, 114, 116, 120	1.4	116	4.17	117, 211
		2.20	142	5	117
15.7	114	3.16	110, 111	5.3	117, 118

5.11-24	76	7.24	250	2.7	124		
5.23	119	7.28	250	2.8	123		
		8.2	247	2.14	125		
2 Thessalonians		8.6-13	129	2.19	123		
1.4	68	8.11	250	2.23	123		
2.1	76	9.1–10.18	129	3.13-18	125		
2.2	119	9.2-5	129	3.15	125		
2.4	295	9.11-5	129	3.17	125		
		9.11	127	4.4-5	126		
1 Timothy		9.12-4	131	4.10	125		
1.2	140	9.12	129	5.1-6	126		
3.16	125, 132	9.14	127	5.4	126		
6.14	117	9.24-6	129	5.6	124, 126		
		9.23	129	5.7-11	125, 126		
2 Timothy		9.24	127	5.7-8	124, 125		
1.10	117, 132	9.28	127, 129	5.13	125		
4.1	117	10.1-2	129	5.14-15	125		
4.8	117	10.1	129	5.15-20	125		
4.18	141	10.10	127, 129	5.16-18	125		
		10.19-20	129	5.16	125		
Titus		10.22-24	129				
1.4	140	10.22	129	1 Peter			
2.13	117, 123	10.24	130	1.1	130		
		10.26	129	1.2	132		
Philemon		10.32ff	130	*1.5-9*	*133*		
1.3	140	10.35	130	*1.5*	*131*		
		10.39	129	1.10-12	131		
Hebrews		11.1-40	130	1.11	124		
1.3	127	11.1ff	129	1.14	133		
1.5-14	127, 139	11.7	130	1.17	130		
1.5	127, 128,	11.13	130	1.18	133		
	144, 264	11.16	130	1.18-21	131, 132,		
1.8	128	11.26	127		133		
1.9	54	11.32-8	130	1.19	131		
2.5-9	139	12.1	130	1.20	131, 132,		
2.7	124	12.2	130		133		
2.8	130, 203	12.3-4	130	1.21	132		
2.10-18	130	12.3	130	2.4-10	133		
2.14	128	12.4	130, 134	2.4-8	131		
2.17	128, 129	13.8	127	2.4-5	133		
3.6	127, 130	13.12	129	2.6-10	133		
3.14	127, 130	13.21	127	2.6-8	133		
4.14-5.10	129			2.11–3.12	134		
4.15-5.4	128	James		2.11	130		
4.16	129, 130	1.1	123	2.12	134		
5–7	128	1.2-4	125	2.13-17	137		
5.5	127, 128,	1.3-4	125	2.13	134		
	144	1.5	125	2.18-21	132		
5.6	128	1.12	125	2.18	134		
6.4-6	129	1.18	125	2.21-24	131		
7.1-10	128	1.21	125	2.21-25	131, 132,		
7.3	128	1.27	125, 126		133		
7.5	128	2.1	123, 127	3.1	134		
7.10	128	2.5	126	3.15	134		
7.18-19	129	2.6-7	125	3.18-22	131, 132		
7.21	250	2.6	126	3.18-19	131		

3.18	125, 132	1.18	141				249, 264
3.19-21	132	2–3	139	13	117, 144
3.22	131, 133	2.2	136	13.2	144
4.2-4	133	2.10	136	13.4	137, 144
4.6	132	2.13	134, 136	13.5	144
4.7	124	2.13	136	13.7	137
4.14	124	2.14	142	13.8	143
4.16	134	2.19	136	13.10	136, 143
5.12	131	2.26	144	13.11	137
		2.28	144	13.11-18	288
2 Peter		3.3	136	13.12	137, 144
1.1	123	3.14	140, 141	13.14	137
1.2	140	3.19	136	14.4	142, 146
1.16	124	4.1	138, 139	14.10	143
2.1	286	4.2	137	14.12	136
3.4	75, 124	4.9	141	14.19-20	143
3.18	141-142	4.19	141	15.3	142
		5	138	15.7	141
1 John		5.6	143	16.2	142
2.1	107, 125	5.8-14	144	16.4	142
2.2	107	5.9-10	117	16.10-13	142
2.15-17	107	5.9	142, 143	16.13	137
2.18	106, 107, 286	5.11-14	139	16.14	141
		5.12	143	16.15-16	142
2.22	106	5.13	141	16.17-21	142
2.28	124	6	138	17	117
2.29	125	6.9	136, 143	17.1	139
3.7	125	6.11	136	17.3	137
4.2	106, 107	6.15	142	17.12	144
4.10	107	7.2-3	137	17.13	144
4.15	106	7.10	143	17.14	141, 143
5.1	106	7.14-17	136	18.24	136
5.6	*106*	7.14	142, 143	19	143
5.21	107	8.1	138	19.10	139, 140
		9.3-6	142	19.15	143, 144
2 John		10	138	19.16	141
3	140	10.2	138	19.19	141
7	106, 107	10.6	141	19.20	137
		10.8	138	20–22	202
Revelation		11.3	144	20.4-6	145
1.1-2	138	11.6	144	20.4-5	277
1.1	138	11.7	143	20.4	136, 138, 145
1.4-5	140	11.8	140, 142		
1.2	138	11.15	138, 143, 144	20.6	117, 138, 145
1.4	54, 136				
1.5-6	141, 144	12	264	20.10	137
1.5	138, 140, 151	12.5	141, 250	21–22	201
		12.7	139	21	194
1.6	142, 145	12.9	136, 139	*21.2*	*277*
1.7	140, 270	12.10-12	143	*21.9*	*139*
1.9	140	12.10	138, 143, 144	*21.10-21*	*193*
1.10	136, 137			21.10	137, 139
1.11	136	12.11	136, 143	21.22	139, 145
1.12-20	139	12.13-7	142	21.23	145, 146
1.13	142	12.14	142	22.1	139
1.15	141	12.17	136, 140,	22.3-4	144

22.3	139, 146	13	42	3.218-64	186
22.4	145	13.31-33	149	3.250-51	188
22.5	117	13.25-26	149	3.265-294	185
22.6	138, 139	13.26	132	3.276-80	188
22.8-9	139	13.29	149	3.282-294	186
22.8	139	13.35	149	3.283-85	188
22.16	139, 163	13.37	149	3.286-87	185
22.20	123, 140	14.52	115	3.318	184
				3.348-49	185

OLD TESTAMENT
PSEUDEPIGRAPHA
1 Enoch

		Apocalypse of Elijah		3.351-60	188
		3.2	194	3.361-85	188
		3.5	195	3.381-83	185
6-16	133	5.2-4	194	3.403-405	188
39	115	5.36-39	194	3.418-33	188
46	115			3.484-91	188
46.1-4	132	*Ezekiel the Tragedian*		3.492-511	188
46.5-8	42	36–41	186	3.545-72	185
48	115, 252	68–89	186	3.545-49	185
48.5-8	42	106–107	186	3.573-600	186
48.2-6	132			3.601-18	185
48.3	263	*Jubilees*	30	3.608	184
48.6-7	42			3.611-15	185
48.6	263	*Liber antiquitatum bibli-*		3.624-34	185
49.2-4	42	*carum*	42	3.652-56	185
49.4	199			3.669-731	186
53.6	33, 124	*Psalms of Solomon*		3.767-808	186
61.13	42	9.1	92	5	184
62.7	42, 132	17	30, 35, 40,	5.60-92	191
90.28-35	35		41, 69, 79,	5.108-109	189
94.6–99.16	126		250	5.158-61	189
		17.1-6	30	5.158-60	189
2 Enoch		17.7	30	5.179-86	191
45	232	17.23-51	33	5.249	188
48A	233	17.23-24	94, 141,	5.256-57	189
58A	232		144	5.258-60	188, 189
71.32-33	128	17.23	115	5.403-33	192
72.1-7	128	17.26	187	5.414-27	188
		17.32	89, 187	5.414-15	115
2 Baruch		17.37	187	5.414-15	189
1-12	232	17.47	115	5.414	188
29	43	18	40, 79, 250	5.420-21	188
30.1	132	18.5	132	5.429-31	188
40.1-3	42	18.6-7	250	5.432	188
77	232	21–22	40		

				Testament of Judah 30	
4 Ezra		*Sibylline Oracles*		24.1-6	88
2.40	76	3	184		
7.23	76	3.75-85	188	*Testament of Levi* 30	
7.28-29	132, 270	3.93-110	188		
7.28-29	42	3.137-54	188	*Testament of Moses*	
11-3	192	3.156-61	184	6-7	41
11.37–12.1	42	3.162-78	188	10.1	41
12	76	3.171-74	185	10.8	41
12.31-34	132	3.193	184		
12.32-34	42	3.211-17	186		
12.32	115	3.214-47	188		

DEAD SEA SCROLLS
1Q28 (1QS; 1QRule of the Community)
8.4-8   133
9   24, 28, 30
9.9-11   24
11   30

1Q28a (1QSa; 1QRule of the Congregation)
2   22, 115
2   28
2.11-22   144

1Q28b (1QSb; 1QRule of Benedictions)
5.21-29   25
5.27   25

1Q30 (1QLiturgical Texts)
1.2   23

1Q33 (1QM; 1QWar Scroll)
                 25
9.8   15
11.7-8   22

4Q58 (4QIsa^d; 4QIsaiah^d)
                 133

4Q161 (4QpIsa^a; 4QIsaiah Pesher^a)
8-10.iii.11-22   41
8-10.iii.15-22   26
8-10.iii.18-22   25

4Q169 (4QpNah; 4QNahum Pesher)
3+4.i.7-8   69

4Q174 (4QFlor; 4QFlorilegium)
                 11, 26, 27, 28, 81, 84
1-3.i.10-12   27
1-3.i.10-13   87
1-3.i.11-12   22, 88
1-3.i.17-18   28

4Q175 (4QTest; 4QTestimonia)
                 24, 28
9-13   25

4Q215a (4QTime of Righteousness)
1.ii.10   23

4Q246 (4QAramaic Apocalypse)
                 41, 79, 81, 100, 111
2.1   27
2.2-3   27
2.4-5   27
2.7-8   27

4Q252 (4QCommentary on GenesisA)
                 24, 271
5.1   25
5.3-4   23

4Q255-264   22

4Q256-273   23

4Q266 (4QD^a; 4QDamascus Document^a)
10.i.12   24

4Q267 (4QD^b; 4QDamascus Document^b)
3.ii.17   22

4Q270 (4QD^e;4QDamascus Document^e)
9.ii.14   22

4Q275 (4QCommunity Ceremony)
1.9   22

4Q285 (4QSM; 4QSefer ha-Milḥamah)
                 41
5.4-5   22
5.4   25, 26

4Q287 (4QBer^b; 4QBlessings^b)
10   13

4Q369 (4QPEnoch; 4QPrayer of Enoch)
                 84, 111

4Q375 (4QapocrMoses^a; 4QApocryphon of Moses^a)
1.9   15

4Q376 (4QapocrMoses^b; 4QApocryphon of Moses^b)
1.i.1-2   22
1.i.1   15

4Q377 (4QapocrPentB; 4Qapocryphon Pentateuch B)
2.ii.5   22

4Q381 (4QNon-Canonical Psalms)
15.7   22

4Q458 (4QNarrative A)
                 23

4Q491 (4QM^a; 4QWar Scroll^a)
11   23

4Q521 (4QMessianic Apocalypse)
                 40, 79
2.ii   23
2.ii.10-14   81
2.ii.12   81
8.9   22

4Q538 (4QTJud ar; 4QTTestament of Judah ar)
                 111

4Q541 (4QapocrLevi^b[?] ar; 4Qapocryphon of Levi^b[?] ar)
                 28
9   27
9.3-6   26
9.6-7   26

6Q15 (6QD; 6QDamascus Document)
3.4   22

11Q5 (11QPs^a)
24.10   75

11Q10 (11QtgJob; 11QTargum Job)
                 262

11Q13 (11QMelch; 11QMelchizedek)
                 91
2.9-10   128
2.15-16   23, 82

Index of Ancient Sources

2.15	23	2.56	36	*De virtutibus*	
2.18	23	2.261-63	187	75	186
2.2	23	2.433-34	153		
		2.442-44	153	Mishnah (*m.*)	
CD (Damascus Document)		2.443-44	39	*'Abot*	
2.12-3	22	2.444	39	3.2	74
5.21-vi 1	22	4.385	154		
6.7-11	26	5.367	137	*Berakot*	
7	28	6.283-85	154	4.3	229
7.18-20	22	6.285-87	38		
7.18-21	25, 26	6.300-10	38	*Bikkurim*	
12.23-13 1	23, 24	6.310	152	3.4	39
14.19	23, 24	6.311	152		
19.10-11	23, 24	6.312-15	150	*Ḥagigah*	
20.1	24	6.312-13	152	2.1	234
		6.312	40		
JOSEPHUS		6.399-407	152	*Megillah*	
Antiquities		7.29-33	154	4.6	230-231
4.115-16	187	7.262-70	36	4.9-10	230-231
12.265	19	7.410-11	188		
13.282-300	20			*Soṭah*	
13.288-300	30	*Against Apion*		7.8	39
13.301	20	2.193	154	9.9-15	237
13.318	30			9.15	161, 231,
13.372-74	30	*Life*			235, 239,
13.380-83	68	66	36		241, 243
14.9	32				
14.40-41	34	PHILO		*Ta'anit*	
14.41	38	*De confusione linguarum*		4.6-7	236
15.187-301	29	62–63	186	4.8	76
15.381-89	55			24a	76
15.382-88	33	*Legum allegoriae*			
15.388-90	32	3.79	128	*Yoma*	129
15.421-23	32				
15.421	34	*Legatio ad Gaium*		Tosefta (*t.*)	
16.183-87	33	149–51	34	*Soṭah*	
17.149-67	31			15.10-15	232, 236
17.271-2	36	*De vita Moisis*			
17.285	36, 42	1	188	BABYLONIAN TALMUD (B.)	
17.299-303	34	1.290	187, 248	*'Abodah Zarah*	
17.304	38	2.44	186	9a-9b	240
18.273-78	39	2.288	186	9b	237
18.116-19	38				
18.23	105	*De opificio mundi*		*Baba Batra*	
18.64	155	89–91	186	3b-4a	32
18.294-97	39				
19.278-91	39	*De praemiis et poenis*		*Berakot*	
19.328-34	39	79–172	186	3a	238
20.97-98	38	92	187	4a	240
20.168-72	38	95	186, 187,	29a	229
20.169-272	187		248	33a	229
		162–63	187	60b	75
War		162	187		
1.70	20	164	187	*Giṭṭin*	
1.97-98	69			55a–58b	237
1.282-85	55				

Hagigah		PALESTINIAN TALMUD (Y.)		2.2.4	242
11b–16a	234	*Berakot*			
		1.1	239, 240	*Esther Rabbah*	
Horayot		2.4	174, 229	1.1.12	240
11b	169	*Hagigah*			
		1.6	241	*Song of Songs Rabbah*	
Ketubbot		2.1	240	2.7.1	238
111a	238, 239			6.10.1	239
112b	239	*Ketubbot*			
		12.3	236	Other rabbinic writings	
Megillah				*'Aggadat ha-Mashiah*	
11a	240	*Kil'ayim*			232, 233
17b–18a	229	9.3	236		
17b	229, 238,			*'Aggadat Rabbi Yishma'el*	
	240	*Megillah*			232, 233
		4.1	230		
Menahot		4.1, 42d	231	*Amidah*	
28b	237			2	228
		Nedarim		7	228, 229
Mo'ed Qatan	240	3.8	242	10	228
				11	228
Niddah		*Sanhedrin*		12	228
13b	239	2.3	240	14	228
				16	228
Pesahim		*Šeqalim*			
5a	268	2.4	240	*'Abot deRabbi Natan*	
54a	263	3.3	236	A 4	241, 242
68a	236			B 31	227, 242
118a	239	*Ta'anit*			
119a	240	1.1	238	*Book of Beliefs and*	
		2.1	239	*Opinions,*	
Sanhedrin		2.4	169	Treatise 8	234, 239,
5a	169	4.5	242		244
38a	236	4.8	160, 174		
38b	165	4.8, 63d	150, 156	*Book of Elijah*	
43a	69				234, 243
63a	236	*Yoma*			
91b	236	3.2	239	*Book of Zerubbabel*	
93b	242				234, 243,
94a	161	MIDRASH RABBAH			292
96b–99a	237	*Genesis Rabbah*			
151b	236	33.3	236	*Chapters of the Messiah*	
		56.10	169		234
Šabbat		97	174		
21b	237	98.8	236	*Heikhalot Rabbati*	
118a	239	98.9	236		232
118b	239				
		Leviticus Rabbah		*Massekhet Hanukkah*	
Sukkah		29.9	169		237
51b	32				
52a	269	*Lamentations Rabbah*		*Megillat Antiochus*	
		Proem 2	241		237
Yoma		Proem 24	238		
19b	239	1.14.42	240	*Midrash Psalms*	
		1.16	174	21.1-2	174
		1.51	182	72.6	174

87.6	174	*Sipra* Behuqotai		Ambrosiaster	
93.3	174, 180	Lev 26	235	*Commentary on Galatians*	
104.5	174			5.24	204
127.1	241	*Sipre Deut.*		*Commentary on Romans*	
		306–41	237	3.31	204
Mishneh Torah		343	229	*Commentary on 1*	
Epistle to the Yemen 239				*Corinthians*	
Laws of Kings		ANCIENT CHRISTIAN		9.21	204
11–12	239	WRITINGS		*Questions on the Old and*	
Judges				*New Testaments*	
11.1	175	*1 Clement*		1.49	204
		50.3	200	2.51	204, 206
Mekhilta					
Shirah	237	*Acta Pauli et Antonini*		Aphrahat	
			190, 192	*Demonstrations*	
Pesiqta de Rab Kahana				I.4	178
16–22	237	*Acts of Sharbel*		II.6	177
18.6	240		178	IV.6	176
Supplement 6	231			IX.8	177, 178
		Ambrose		V.10	177
Pesiqta Rabbati		*De bono mortis*		V.14	177
2.5	237	48	207	XIII.46	177
5	237	*Commentary on Luke*		XIV.1	177
26	232	5.61	207	XIV.15	176
34	232	7.204-206	207	XIV.30	178
36–37	232	10.49	207	XIV.40	178
36	174, 232	*Commentary on the Psalms*		XIX.11	177
		1.47-48	207	XIX.9-10	177
Pirqe Rabbi Eliezer		1.54	207	XXII.5	178
3.5	174	7.17	207	XXIII.13	178
8.4	174	20.11	207	XXIII.16	176
11.3	174	21.8-9	207		
32.1	174	36.26	207	*Apocalypse of Peter*	
		39.17	207	2	162
Prayer of R. Simeon b.		118.3	207		
Yohai 174, 234		118.15-17	207	*Apocalypse of Pseudo-*	
		118.20.29	207		*Ephrem*
Prophecy and dream of		*Epistles*			295
Zerubbabel son of Shealtiel		13	207		
283		35	207	*Apocalypse of Pseudo-*	
		40	225		*Methodius*
Secrets of Rabbi Simeon bar		*Expositio Psalmi CXVIII*			181, 294,
Yohai		18.41	203		295
	234, 293,	*De fide ad Gratianum*			
	296	2	207	*Apocalypse of Shenute*	
		119	207		293, 295
Seder 'Olam Rabba		*De Isaac vel anima*			
	240	4.26	204, 206	Augustine	
		De Nabuthae historia		*Contra Iulianum*	
Sefer Zerubbabel		52	207	1.7.31	204
	294	*De obitu Theodosii*		*Contra litteras Petiliani*	
		29–32	207	2.239	204, 209
Signs of the Messiah		*De paenitentia*		*De civitate Dei*	
	234	1.22	207	16.38	204
				17.4	204
				17.6	204

20–22	210	Cyprian		Hymns on the Nativity	
20.6	210	Epistles		5.14	173
20.7	210	8	200	Hymns on Virginity	
20.10	204	9.2	200	6.6	178
20.30	210	51.18	200	Necrosima	
De Diversis Quaestionibus		Ad Fortunatum		67	178
LXXXIII		12–13	200	71	178
64.8	204, 209				
Enarrationes in Psalmos		De lapsis		Response to Hymns on the	
65.4 sermo 101.2	203	17	200	Unleavened Bread	
130 sermo 3.13	204, 209	Ad Quirinum testimonium		6	178
Enchiridion de fide, spe, et		adversus Judaeos			
	caritate	1.1-7	203	Epiphanius	
111–13	210	2.28	202	Panarion	
111.3	210	2.29	202	30.4-12	170
Contra Faustum		2.30	202	30.11.9-10	159
Manichaeum				66	287
12.44	203, 204, 208	Damasus I		Epistle of Barnabas	
15.9	204, 208	Epistles		3.6	192
Quaestiones in		9	204	4.3-5	192
Heptateuchum		Carmen		4.3	192
1.84	204	50.3	204	4.6b	192
In Evangelium Johannis		Daniel of Salah		6.8-19	192
tractatus		Commentary on the Psalms		6.15	192
7.13	203, 204, 209		180	7.9	192
				12.9	192
7.23	204	Didache		15.4	192
15.27	204, 209	11.3-10	286	16.3-4	192
15.28	204	12.1-12	286	16.4	192
15.29	204	16.3	286	16.5	192
19.16	210				
19.18	210	Dionysius of Alexandria		Eucherius	
40.4	210	On the promises		Instructiones	
			278	2.1	204
Book of Steps					
VI.2	178	Doctrina Iacobi nuper		Eusebius	
		baptizati		De martyribus Palaestinae	
Bardaisan		I.5	175	8.1	170
Book of the Laws of the		I.19	289		
	Countries	III.8	295	Historia ecclesiastica	
	171	III.9	175	1.13	171
		IV.3	175	2.23.3-19	166
Clement of Alexandria		V.1-2	175	3.11-12	166
Paedagogus		V.4-5	175	3.12	154
3.12	193	V.16	175	3.19-20	154
Eclogae propheticae		V.6	175	3.23.25	122
	193			3.32	154
		Edessene Apocalyptical		4.1.2	190
Commodianus		Fragment	294	4.2.1-5	189
Carmen apologeticum				4.6.2-4	158, 163
1041–59	212	Ephrem		4.6.2	156
Instructiones		Commentary on Exodus 1		4.6.3	225
1.45	212	2.2-3	173	4.22.1-7	167
2.35	212			6.14.2-4	122
				7.24-25	277

Index of Ancient Sources

7.24.1-25.7	193
7.24.4	194
7.24.6	193, 195
7.24.8–25.27	194
7.24.9	194
20.1-6	166
20.32	166

Faustinus Luciferianus
De Trinitate

39	204

Festal Hymnaries
Fenqitho

II, 41a	182
II, 234a	181
II, 238a	181
II, 253b	181
II, 465b	181
III, 84a	181
III, 202b	182
III, 293b	182
III, 385b	181

Hudra

I, 558	181
I, 559	181
I, 646	182

Gaudentius
Commentary on Isaiah

18.17	203

Tractate

17.5	203

Gregory of Elvira
Tractatus

12.31	204

Hilary of Poitiers
Commentary on Matthew

10.16	211
21.2	211
25.3	210
25.8	210, 211
26.1	211
26.2	210
27.4	211
33.2	210

Commentary on the Psalms

1.15-18	211
9.4	211
55.7	211
68.31	211
118.5	211
118.11	211
148.8	211

De Trinitate

11.19	204
11.36-49	211

Hippolytus
Commentary on Daniel

2.18.4	199
4.10.2-3	203
4.11	203
4.11.3	203
4.18.6	203
4.32.5-7	203
4.37	203
4.39.4-5	203
4.39.7	203
4.55	203

De Christo et Antichristo

	203

Ignatius
To the Magnesians

4.4	155

Irenaeus
Adversus Haereses

1.21.3	204
1.26.2	286
5.25-30	290
5.31-36	203
5.35.1-2	212
5.35.1	203
5.36.2	203

Jerome
Apology

II.25	256

Commentariorum in Abdiam liber

2.3	204

Commentariorum in Aggaeum liber

2.21-24	207

Commentariorum in Amos libri III

2.4-6	208
2.7	208

Commentariorum in Danielem

2.7.9a-10	208
4.12.1-3	208

Commentariorum in Ecclesiasten

12.13-14	208

Commentariorum in Epistulam ad Galatas libri III

3.6.5	208

Commentariorum in Isaiam libri XVIII

6.10	208
8.2	208
8.19	208
8.28	208
8.42	204
12.21	204
17.23	208
18.27	208
18.29	208

Commentariorum in Malachiam liber

3.1	204
3.17-18	208
4.5-6	204

Commentariorum in Matthaeum libri IV

2.12.36	208
2.20.23	208
4.24.27	207

Commentariorum in Nahum liber

1.1	208
1.3	207

Commentariorum in Sophonium libri III

1.10	208
2.3-4	208
3.1-7	208

Commentariorum in Zachariam libri III

1.2	204
3.6-7	207
3.11-14	208
3.12	204, 208
3.14	204, 207

Epistulae

21.11	207
65.13	204
108.13	204
125.1	204

De nominibus hebraicis

66.17	204

Tractatus in Psalmos

1	208

John Chrysostom
Adversus Judaeos

1.3	221

John of Damascus
De Haeresibus
60–61   295

Justin Martyr
Apologia I
31–36   156
31   191
31.6   162
32   164
32.3-4   201
32.12   164
47   158
54.5   201
Dialogus cum Tryphone
2.6   163
8.4   79
11.4   201
16.2   158
32.6–33.2   161
34   161
36   161
40.2   158
52   201
55–62   165
61.2   124
61.6   144
67.1   161
69.1   286
83.1-4   161
85   161
86.3   175
88.8   144
92.2   158
106.4   248
120.3-6   201
120.3-4   247
122.6   144

Lactantius
Institutes
4.7.4-8   204, 205
4.7.7   204
4.13.9   204
7.14-27   205
7.19.5   205
7.20.1   205
7.20.5   205
7.21.5-8   205
7.24.3   205
7.24.6   205
7.24.7-15   205
7.24.15   205
7.26.1   206
7.26.5-6   206

Letter to John the Stylite
295

Martyrdom of Barsamya
179

Martyrdom of Habbib
179

Martydom of Cyriacus
179

Maximinus
Dissertatio contra Ambrosium
301r, l.12   204

Maximus Confessor
Letter 14   295

Narsai
Homilies
17   179
21   179
30   179
33   179

Nepos
Against the Allegorists
24.4   193
Refutation of the Allegorists
278

Nicetas of Remesiana
Explanatio Symboli
3   204

Novella of Theodosius
225

Optatus
4.7.3   204
4.7.5   204

Oracle of Baalbek
283

Orientius
Commonitorium
2.347-92   212

Origen
Cels.
1.28   196
1.32   196
1.56   193
2.29   193
3.1   83
7.9   286
Homiliae in Leviticum
5.8   159
De principiis
2.11.2   193

Orosius
Histories
7.6.16-17   199

Passio Perpetuae
11–12   200

Procopius
Secret History
8.13   279
12.19-32   279

Prosper Aquitanus
Expositio psalmorum
104.12-15   204
Liber sententiarum
346   204

Prudentius
Liber Cathemerinon
9.106-14   212
11.101-16   212
Liber Peristephanon
4.9-60   212
10.16   204

Pseudo-Clement
Homilies
1.18.1–19.8   286
1.19   287
2.5.10   287
2.15.4   286
2.17.4   286
3.17.25   286
Recognitions
1.45.3   176

Rufinus
Commentarius in symbolum apostolorum
6   204

Second Treatise of the Great Seth   287

Shepherd of Hermas
Mandate
11.7-8, 11   286

Index of Ancient Sources

Similitude
5.3.3 200
9.24.4 200

Vision
3.1.9–2.3 200
29 200

Socrates
Historiae ecclesiasticae
7.38 276

Sulpicius Severus
Vita martini
24 199

Syriac Apocalypse of Daniel
29–30 180

Teaching of Addai the Apostle
 171, 174, 178

Tertullian
Apologeticus
3.5 204, 205
Ad nationes
1.3 204, 205
Adversus Praxean
21 203
28 204

Trophies of Damascus
 295

CLASSICAL AND HELLENISTIC WRITINGS

Aristotle
Poetics
2.6, 1451b11 71

Rhetoric
3.5.1 (1407a 19) 17

Aurelius Victor
De Caesaribus
42.11 275

Cassius Dio
58.32 189, 190
69.12.1 155
73(72).24.1-2 222

Cicero
De legibus
1.1.4 54
2.22.55-7 57
2.56 58
2.22.68 57
3.10-23-15.34 49

De natura deorum
1.44 55
3.5 55

Codex Theodosianus
16.8.9 225
16.8.12 225
16.8.20-21 225
16.8.25 225
16.8.25-26 225

Critias
Sisyphus
Fragment 25 49

Dio
58.32 190

Dionysius of Halicarnassus
2.34 53
2.60.5-7 55
2.76.5 57, 58
2.76.6 58

Ennius
Annales
72–91 53

Livy
1.7.1 53
1.16.5-8 50
1.19.4-5 49
1.19.5 55
1.34 54
40.29.3-14 59

Ovid
Fasti
3.273-76 57
Metamorphoses
15.487-551 57

Persius
5.179-84 32

Plato
Respublica
3, 389b-c 49
3, 414b-c 49
5, 473d 47
6, 487e 47
6, 499b 47
6, 501e 47

Leges
4, 711d 47
4, 711e 46
4, 712a 47
4, 713e 47
Phaedrus
260C 183

Pliny the Elder
Naturalis historia
13.84-86 58

Pliny the Younger
Epistles
10.96-97 134
10.96 155
96.5-7 135
97.2 135

Plutarch
Caesar
57–61 51
67.4 51
Comparatio Lycurgi et Numae
1.1-7 49
De fortuna Romanorum
9, 321A-322B 47
9, 321F-322A 56
9, 322A-C 45
Numa
1.4 48
2.1-3 47, 57
2.1-2 48
2.3 48, 50
2.4–3.1 48
2.5 48
3.2-3 48
3.4-7 48
3.4 48
3.5 48
3.6 49
3.7 49
4.1-8 49
4.1-2 47
4.1 49
4.2 49
4.3 49
4.4-8 49
4.8 49

5.1-15	49	21.4–22.1	57	Strabo	
5.1	47	21.4	57	*Geography*	
5.2-5	49	22.1-4	57	16.2.40	20
5.5	49	22.2	58		
6.1	47, 51	22.3-4	58	Suetonius	
6.2-3	51	22.4-5	58	*Divus Augustus*	
6.3	51	22.4	55, 58	95	53
6.4	51	22.5	57	*Vespasianus*	
7	52	*Romulus*		4.5	152
7.1-3	55	9.4-5	53	5.6	152
7.1	53, 56	16.4-8	55	*Claudius*	
7.2	53	16.5-6	53	25.4	199
7.3	53	16.8	53		
8–20	55	23.2-4	48	Tacitus	
8.1	54	26.1-2	53	*Annales*	
8.2-6	49	26.2	54	5.9	70
8.6	58	27.3–29.7	57	15.44	155
15.1	55	27.3-4	57		
15.2-6	55	27.3	56	*Historiae*	
15.2	55	27.5	57	5.2	34
15.3-6	56	28.1-3	50	5.13.2	152
15.6	56				
19–20	45	Polybius		OTHER ANCIENT	
19.6	46	6.53.1–54.1	57	SOURCES	
20.2	46	6.56.7	49	*London Papyri*	
20.3-6	46			912	191
20.7	46	*Scriptores Historiae*			
20.8	47	*Augustae Hadrianus*		*The Potter's Oracle*	
21.1-3	57	14.2	155		184-5
21.1-2	49				

INDEX OF AUTHORS

Abegg, M. G.   24, 79
Aberbach, L.   268
Achtemeier, P. J.   131–2
Adamson, J. B.   124
Ådna, J.   266–7
Aerts, W. J.   175
Aescoly, A. Z.   227
Alexander, P. J.   243, 279
Alexander, P. S.   157, 159, 161, 168, 174–5, 232–5, 237, 240, 243, 273, 280
Alexandre, M.   249
Alföldi, A.   53
Allison, D. C.   72
Altheim, F.   49
Altmann, A.   169
Ameling, W.   18
Anderson, P. N.   102
Applebaum, S.   190
Arce, J.   275
Arjomand, S. A.   243
Arnal, W. E.   71
Ashton, J.   98–9, 102
Atkinson, K. R.   31, 40
Attridge, H. W.   128
Auffarth, C.   198
Aune, D.   110, 136–42, 144
Ausloos, H.   249
Avi-Yonah, M.   243

Bacher, W.   168
Badilita, C.   199, 279
Badrosian, R.   293
Baer, Y. F.   168
Balch, D.   134
Bammel, E.   65, 69–70
Barclay, J. M. G.   186, 188
Bardy, G.   168, 295
Barker, M.   137
Barnard, L. W.   171
Barnes, T. D.   189
Baron, S. W.   275–6
Barrett, C. K.   70, 92, 94, 97, 116, 127, 129
Bartlett, J. R.   20

Barton, J.   109
Bauckham, R.   76, 98, 125–6, 133, 138–45, 156, 160, 162, 167, 202
Bauer, W.   171
Beaton, R.   85
Beavis, M. A.   76
Becker, A. H.   243
Bedjan, P.   179–80
Beker, J. C.   119
Belayche, N.   44
Bellinger, W. H.   132
Berger, K.   241, 243
Berthélemy, D.   255
Bertram, G.   202
Best, E.   133
Bichler, R.   17
Bickerman, E.   50
Bietenhard, H.   159, 168
Bilde, P.   33
Biller, G.   198
Billerbeck, P.   169, 174
Blanc, C.   204
Bloedhorn, H.   216–19
Blowers, P. M.   168
Böcher, O.   202
Bockmuehl, M.   25, 37, 65, 68–9, 71
Bogaert, P.   231–3
Bonhoeffer, D.   76
Borelli, D.   275
Borg, Marcus J.   74–5
Bornkamm, G.   113–14
Bousset, W.   251–2
Boyarin, D.   100
Brandon, S. G. F.   65
Brandt, O.   221–2
Braude, W.   231
Bredin, M.   140–1, 143
Brock, S. P.   172–3, 176, 181, 265
Brockington, L. H.   124
Brooke, G. J.   26, 79, 137, 150, 168
Brown, R.   84, 87–9, 92, 106
Brox, N.   132
Buber, M.   240–1, 286
Buchanan, G. W.   228, 234

Buchheit, V.   57
Büchler, A.   159
Buitenwerf, R.   184–5
Bultmann, R.   91, 131–3
Burger, C.   86
Burkert, W.   58
Burkitt, F. C.   171
Butcher, K.   218

Caird, G. B.   143
Cameron, A.   259, 290–2
Camery-Hoggatt, J.   83–4
Cancik, H.   44
Carleton Paget, J.   155, 192, 278, 285
Carmi, T.   231
Carmichael, J.   65
Carnegie, D. R.   142
Carrell, P. R.   138–40, 143–4
Carson, D. A.   14
Carter, W.   134
Cathcart, K. J.   263
Chancey, M. A.   72
Charles, R. H.   264
Charlesworth, J. H.   40, 109, 122, 132
Chester, A.   126, 185, 189, 200, 213, 263, 268
Chilton, B.   263
Christ, K.   51
Cohen, G. D.   240
Cohen, S. J. D.   151, 158, 227
Cohn, N. R. C.   200
Collins, John J.   6, 16–18, 23–4, 30, 35, 40–1, 43, 81, 100–1, 109, 136, 150, 164, 184–8.
Colpe, C.   202, 289
Conzelmann, H.   110
Cook, M.   286, 291
Corley, K. E.   134
Cotton, H. M.   151
Court, J.   136
Cox, C. E.   245
Cranfield, C. E. B   266
Crone, P.   286, 291
Crossan, J. D.   73, 117
Cullmann, O.   66
Cureton, W.   179

Dagron, G.   175, 277, 292, 295
Dahl, N. A.   80, 110–11, 113, 119
Daley, B.   198, 203, 211–12, 277–8
Dalman, G.   270
Dalton, W. J.   133
Dan, J.   283, 292
Darmo, T.   181
Davids, P. H.   124–5

Day, J.   115
De Boor, C.   292, 295
de Jonge, M.   16, 23, 98–100, 102, 109–12, 119, 140, 144
de Lange, N. R. M.   159, 167–8, 193, 244, 276, 280–1
de Savignac, J.   186
de Ste. Croix, G. E. M.   134
Dehandschutter, B.   140
Deines, R.   69
Delitzsch, F.   97
Deproost, P. A.   259
Deroche, V.   175, 194, 198, 277, 292–4
Desroche, H.   200
Dibelius, M.   124
Dierse, U.   198
DiTommaso, L.   175
Doble, P.   125, 132
Dodd, C. H.   97, 104
Dogniez, C.   249
Dorival, G.   245, 247, 254
Doutreleau, L.   286
Drijvers, H. J. W.   171
Droysen, J. G.   17
Duff, T.   45
Dulaey, M.   288
Duling, D. C.   86
Dunn, James D. G.   111, 118–19, 141
Dürr, L.   4
Durst, M.   201, 210–11

Edersheim, A.   78
Eger, H.   210
Eisenman, R. H.   65
Eisler, R.   65, 70
Eliav, Y. Z.   158
Elliott, J. H.   130–1, 133–4
Elsner, J.   217–18
Epstein, I.   165
Erder, Y.   232
Eskola, T.   111, 202
Estin, C.   258
Evans, C.   16, 26, 79, 81, 245
Evans, R. J.   71
Even-Shmuel, Y.   232–3, 283

Farmer, W. R.   132
Farrer, A.   73
Feldmeier, R.   130
Ferrua, A.   224
Fiedrowicz, M.   202
Field, F.   258
Fine, S.   219–20, 242
Fiocchi Nicolai, V.   221, 224
Fischer, B.   256

Index of Authors

Fishbane, M. A.   14
Fishwick, D.   51
Fitzmyer, J. A.   xvii, 16, 89, 91–2, 128, 141
Fleischer, E.   175
Flusin, B.   293
Foerster, G.   34
Fonrobert, C. E.   166
Fortna, R. T.   98
Fossum, J. E.   124
Fowler, R.   84
Frank, D.   232
Frankfurter, D.   184–5, 187, 190–1, 193–4, 197
Fredriksen, P.   110
Frend, W. H. C.   134
Freyne, S.   37, 42, 67, 72, 153
Friedländer, I.   296
Friedmann, Y.   288
Friesen, S. J.   137, 144
Frost, S. B.   6
Fuks, A.   190
Funk, R. W.   73

Gabriel, C.   260
Gaddis, M.   225
Gafni, I. M.   158
Gager, J. G.   110, 150
García M. F.   22–3, 81–2
Gaston, L.   110
Gathercole, S.   89
Gatz, B.   45
Geiger, J.   275
Gelston, A.   272
Gera, D.   18
Gesche, H.   51
Gese, H.   5–6, 8
Gibbs, J. M.   86
Gillingham, S. E.   245
Giovannini, A.   134
Glaser, K.   45, 49
Goehring, J. E.   191
Golb, N.   21
Goldberg, A.   174, 232
Goldman, J   215
Goldstein, J. A.   30, 220
Goodacre, M.   73
Goodblatt, D. M.   236
Goodenough, E. R.   186, 216–20
Goodman, M.   39, 151, 153–4, 160, 190
Goodspeed, E. J.   162
Goranson, S.   170
Gordon, R. P.   182, 263, 269–72
Goulder, M.   73
Grabar, O.   220, 292
Graf, F.   49

Green, W. S.   151, 183
Greeven, H.   124
Gregory, A.   95
Gressmann, H.   3–5
Griffith, T.   106–7
Grillmeier, A.   200, 202, 213
Gruen, E. S.   19, 33, 185
Grundmann, W.   110–11, 119
Gryson, R.   259–60
Guthrie, D.   142
Gutmann, J.   217, 220
Gzella, H.   246, 250

Haas, C.   192
Habas-Rubin, E.   167
Haber, S.   129
Habermehl, P.   202
Hachlili, R.   215–18, 220
Hadas-Lebel, M.   281
Hagner, D.   65
Hahn, A. and G. Ludwig   201–2
Hamacher, E.   8
Hanson, J.   38, 66, 153
Hardin, J. K.   68
Harl, M.   247, 249
Harnack, A. von   201–2
Hart, T.   143
Hays, R.   113–14, 140
Hecht, R. D.   186–7
Heid, S.   290
Heinemann, J.   161, 279
Hemer, C. J.   137
Hengel, M.   16–17, 37, 39, 66–9, 72–3, 110–12, 118–19, 128, 153, 184, 188, 190–1
Hennecke, E.   162
Henze, M.   180
Hertling, L.   224
Hill, C. E.   201–2, 290
Himmelfarb, M.   121, 234, 283, 292
Hitzl, K.   44
Holum, K. G.   159
Hooker, M.   83, 132
Horbury, W.   3–8, 11–14, 16, 20, 23, 28, 32–3, 44, 68, 70, 77, 89, 90, 98, 100, 102, 104–5, 107–9, 115, 117, 121–2, 128, 127–8, 139–40, 142, 144, 149, 154–5, 158, 160, 164, 175, 177, 183–4, 186–93, 198–9, 231, 246–7, 249, 253, 264, 273–4, 281, 285–6
Horovitz, S.   267
Horowitz, E. S.   276

Horrell, D. G.   66, 131, 133
Horsley, R. A.   37–9, 66–8, 72–4, 117, 122, 153
Hossfeld, F.-L.   10
Hoyland, R. G.   291, 293, 295–6
Hughes, K. L.   199
Hurst, D.   129
Hurtado, L. W.   114, 127–8, 136, 138–9, 142, 145
Hvalvik, R.   192

Idel, M.   228, 234
Irsai, O.   166, 276, 296

Jacobs, M.   160, 169
Jansma, T.   177
Japhet, S.   6, 12
Jenkins, R. G.   176
Jeremias, J.   75
Johnson, A. R.   4
Johnson, L. T.   123–5
Jörns, K.-P.   143
Joyce, P. M.   109
Juel, D. H.   83
Jülicher, A.   123

Kaegi, W. E.   291
Kaplony, A.   293
Kapstein, I. J.   231
Karrer, M.   54–5, 112–13
Käsemann, E.   130
Kasher, R.   269
Kellermann, U.   11
Kerkeslager, A.   196
Kerner, J.   213
Kessler, E.   169
Kessler, H.   216, 218, 220
Kessler, J.   7
Kim, S.   121
Kimelman, R. R.   167–8, 228
Kingsbury, J. D.   86
Kinzig, W.   165, 201, 212, 275
Kippenberg, H. G.   44
Kirschbaum, E.   224
Kittel, G.   253
Klausner, J.   4, 15, 28, 227–8
Klein, M. L.   264–5, 269, 271
Klijn, A. F. J.   327
Kobelski, P. J.   128
Koch, E.   202
Koch, G. A.   159
Koch, K.   5, 267
Koep, L.   202
Kokkinos, N.   31
Kortekaas, G. A. A.   175
Koschaker, P.   7

Kötting, B.   211
Kraeling, C. H.   218–20
Kramer, W.   110–11, 113, 118–20
Kroll, J. H.   225
Kutsch, E.   54

Laceranza, G.   275
Lahey, L.   165
Lane, W. L.   128
Lash, E.   279
Latte, K.   49
Lawlor, H. J.   163, 166
Laws, S.   123–4
Lehnart, A.   213
Lemmelijn, B.   249
Lenowitz, H.   241
Levenson, D.   275
Levey, S. H.   43, 174, 230, 263–4, 266, 270
Lévi, I.   283, 292, 294
Levine, L. I.   17, 34, 167, 217, 222, 225, 280
Levit-Tawil, D.   217
Lewis, B.   175, 179, 231, 234, 295
Lieberman, S.   170
Lieu, J.   104, 155
Lilius, H.   60
Lindars, B.   127–8
Liverani, P.   58
Loader, W. R. G.   99, 102
Loffreda, S.   225
Lohfink, G.   202
Lorein, G. W.   199
Luger, Y.   280
Luneau, A.   211
Lust, J.   245, 247–9, 253–5, 260–1
Luz, U.   80, 86

Maccoby, H.   65, 69
MacRae, G. W.   111
Madec, G.   203
Magness, J.   22
Mango, C. A.   276, 292, 295
Manson, T. W.   127
Markschies, C.   201–2
Marmorstein, A.   168, 294
Marshall, I. H.   118
Martin, R. A.   126, 248
Mason, R.   3, 7
Mason, S. N.   33, 137
Massebieau, L.   123
Massyngberde F. J.   140
Maynard-Reid, P. U.   126
Mazzaferri, F. D.   138
McCasland   112–13
McGing, B. C.   30–1

McGinn, B. 279
McGrath, J. F. 101
McHugh, M. P. 206
McKnight, S. 69
McNamara, M. 264
Meadors, E. P. 80
Meeks, W. A. 101, 103–5
Meiggs, R. 221
Mélèze-Modrzejewski 187, 190–2
Mendels, D. 20, 32, 36–7, 42
Mendelssohn, S. 286
Merz, A. 65, 69
Meshorer, Y. 32, 156
Mettinger, T. N. D. 54
Mildenberg, L. 156
Millar, F. 160, 217–18
Mingana, A. 179
Mirsky, M. 283
Möhring, H. 294
Moloney, F. 103, 105
Momigliano, A. 18, 45, 186
Mommsen, T. 54
Monsengwo-Pasinya, L. 247, 255
Moore, G. F. 227
Mor, M. 275
Morrison, C. E. 271–2
Mottahedeh, P. E. 156
Moule, C. F. D. 119
Mowinckel, S. 4–5, 29
Moxnes, H. 66
Munnich, O. 249
Musurillo, H. A. 190
Myers, C. 66

Nash, E. 46
Nestori, A. 223
Neugebauer, F. 119
Neusner, J. 43, 80, 109, 150, 161, 168, 227
Newman 121
Newman, H. I. 201
Neyrey, C. 104
Nickelsburg, G. W. E. 31, 41–2, 149, 250, 252
Niebuhr, K. W. 113
Nock, A. D. 58
Nogalski, J. 9
Noy, D. 216–19, 225

O'Connell, J. P. 207
O'Donovan, O. 137
Oakes, P. 117
Oakman, D. 66
Oegema, G. S. 16, 109, 184, 187, 189, 195, 245
Olster, D. 243

Osswald, E. 286
Oulton, J. E. L. 163
Oz, A. 15

Painter, J. 98–101
Palmer, A. 294
Paltiel, E. 29
Patai, R. 227
Paul, S. 286
Pavia, C. 217
Pearson, B. A. 191
Pease, A. S. 55
Penella, R. J. 275
Pérez F. M. 174, 176
Pergola, P. 223–4
Perrin, B. 45
Pietersma, A. 245, 261
Pigulevskaya, N. V. 179
Pines, S. 289
Pöhlmann, H.-G. 202
Polliack, M. 232
Posnanski, A. 177
Préaux, C. 17
Price, S. R. F. 137
Price, J. T. 153
Pritz, R. A. 165, 170
Prostmeier, F. R. 192
Pucci B. Z. M 189

Quell, G. 286

Raban, A. 159
Rabello, A. M. 276
Rabin, C. 267, 294
Rahlfs, A. 255, 258
Rajak, T. 33, 157
Ravitzky, A. 239, 241
Reed, J. L. 117, 243
Reeves, J. C. 234, 243–4
Reif, S. C. 279
Reimarus, H. S. 65, 70
Reinink, G. J. 165, 175, 294
Renov, I. 219
Rensberger, D. K. 105
Reumann, J. 125
Reuter, A. 198
Revel-Neher, E. 217
Rhoads, D. M. 36
Richardson, P. 31–3
Riedo-Emmenegger, C. 69
Riedweg, C. 58
Riley, W. 12–13
Rilliet, F. 177
Robin, C. J. 286, 291
Robinson, J. A. T. 94, 97
Rocca, S. 33

Roller, D. W. 34
Ropes, J. H. 123
Rösel, M. 248
Rosen, K. 59
Rousseau, A. 286
Rowe, C. K. 95
Rowland, C. 111, 117, 119, 137
Rubin, B. 279
Runesson, A. 221
Rutgers, L. V. 223

Sabar, S. 216
Sahas, D. I. 285
Salvesen, A. 176, 184, 255
Sanders, E. P. 132
Sänger, D. 113
Scardigli, B. 45
Schäfer, P. 155–6, 160, 174, 227–232, 275
Schalit, A. 32
Schaper, J. 7, 8, 10, 12, 245–6, 249–53
Schart, A. 9
Schendel, E. 202, 211
Schnelle, U. 102, 106, 110–11, 119
Schniedewind, W. M. 13
Schoeps, H. J. 287
Scholem, G. G. 4, 7–8, 150, 227–8, 239–41
Schreiber, S. 119–20, 174
Schreiner, T. R. 114
Schröder, W. A. 57
Schürer, E. 19–20, 80, 154, 204, 228
Schüssler F. E. 145
Schutter, W. L. 131
Schwarte, K.-H. 198, 211
Schwartz, D. 71
Schwartz, S. 160
Schwegler, A. 45
Schwering, W. 203, 205
Scott, J.. C. 68, 74, 122–3, 126–7, 134–5, 292, 295
Seeligmann, I. L. 246, 253
Segal, A. F. 121, 159, 169, 202
Segundo, J. L. 66
Sehlmeyer, M. 53
Seland, T. 130
Siber, H. 54
Simon, R. 289
Simonetti, M. 193–4, 278
Skarsaune, O. 163–6, 169, 176, 191
Slingerland, H. D. 199
Smith, M. 11
Smolar, L. 268
Sokoloff, M. 174
Sonne, I. 220
Sorek, S. 225

Sperber, A. 269
Speyer, W. 59–60
Spilsbury, P. 117, 137
Spitta, F. 123
Spurling, H. 283
Staerk, W. 4
Stählin, G. 116
Stanton, G. N. 40, 70, 80, 82, 86, 89, 91, 94
Stanton, V. H. 78–9
Starr, J. 289, 291
Stegemann, H. 16, 198
Stegemann, E. 107
Steinby, E. M. 46, 58
Stemberger, G. 170, 275–6, 292
Stern, E. 7
Stern, D. 283
Stone, M. A. 42, 213
Strack, H. L. 169, 174
Strauss, M. L. 87, 88, 94
Strauß, H. 200
Strecker, G. 107, 202
Stroumsa, G. 285, 288–9, 291
Stuckenbruck, L. T. 139
Stuhlmacher, P. 113, 118
Swartz, M. D. 231
Sweet, J. P. M. 70, 136, 138, 140
Syrén, R. 265, 271

Tardieu, M. 287
Taylor, J. 69
Tcherikover, V. 190
Telfer, W. 167
ter Haar R. B. 171
Theissen, G. 38, 65–9, 73
Thomas, L. A. R. 179
Thompson, M. 118
Thompson, L. L. 136–7
Thornton, T. C. G. 170
Thyen, H. 100, 103–4
Tigchelaar, E. J. C. 23, 81–2
Torrey, C. C. 110
Torstorici, E. 46
Towner, P. 118
Toynbee, J. M. C. 57
Tuckett, C. M. 80, 95, 128

Ulrich, E. 246
Urbach, E. E. 168, 227

van Bekkum, W. J. 277, 282
van der Kooij, A. 249, 253
van der Woude, A. S. 26
van Egmond, R. 84
van Ess, J. 296
van Henten, J. W. 18, 20, 30

Index of Authors

van Unnik, W. C.   97
VanderKam, J. C.   22, 132
Vanni, U.   137, 142, 144
Vermes, G.   169, 247
Verseput, D.   86
Vianès-Abou S. L.   201, 290
Viellefond, J. R.   167
Vogels, H.-J.   202
Vogler, W.   65
Volz, P.   251–2
von Rad, G.   286
Vööbus, A.   177

Wallace, D. B.   124
Wanke, G.   6, 8
Warthon, A.   292
Waschke, E.-J.   54
Wasserstrom, S. M.   296
Wedderburn, A. J. M.   118
Weinberger, L. J.   231, 280, 282
Weinstock, S.   51
Weiser, A.   202
Weiss, Z..   225
Weitzman, M.   172, 271–2
Weitzmann, K.   218, 220
Wenham, D.   118
Wertheimer, S. A.   233
Wessely, C.   176

Wevers, J. W.   247–8, 257
Wharton, A. J.   218–20, 225
Wilckens, U.   103, 108
Wilken, R. L.   277–8, 290
Willi, A.   59
Williams, R.   67, 71
Williams, T. F.   249
Williamson, H. G. M.   9, 12, 14
Windisch, H.   131–2
Wink, W.   66
Wintermute, O. S.   194
Wischnitzer, R.   220
Wlosok, A.   51
Wolff, H. W.   7
Wolfson, H. A.   186
Wright, N. T.   74–5, 111, 113–4, 116–8

Yahalom, J.   174, 231, 280, 283
Yarbro C. A.   35, 136, 143
Yoder, J. H.   66

Zakovitch, Y.   14
Zanker, P.   34
Zeller, D.   113
Zenger, E.   10
Zetterholm, M.   221
Ziegler, K.   45, 47, 254–5, 260
Zimmermann, J.   20, 22–4, 27, 40–1

INDEX OF SUBJECTS

Aaron 23–4, 26–7, 30, 128, 216, 286
angel(s) 16, 22–3, 27, 49, 54, 87, 93, 115–16, 121, 127, 133, 138–9, 144, 173, 180–2, 194, 203, 205–7, 224, 233, 279, 282–3
Antichrist 27, 107, 188, 194–5, 199, 203, 205–7, 210, 212, 230, 277–9, 281, 283, 285, 288, 290–1, 294–5
apostles 52, 55, 65, 68–9, 92, 202, 207
Aramaic texts 216
  Peshitta 172–3, 175, 177, 257, 265, 270–3
  Qumran texts 13, 15, 21–8, 30, 35, 40–1, 76, 78–9, 81–2, 84, 87–8, 91–2, 111, 115, 128, 133, 137, 142, 150–1, 262, 269, 271
  targums 43, 115, 164, 169, 172–4, 176–7, 180, 182, 184, 227, 229–31, 234, 240, 242–3, 246, 249, 252, 262–73, 282
art (*see also* Dura-Europas) 215–26

Bar Kokhba (Cocheba, Kosiba, Koziba) 39, 76, 150, 156, 158, 160–4, 167, 169, 174, 191, 198, 225, 241–3, 256, 270

canon (of Scripture) 127, 131, 216, 278
chiliasm/eschatological utopia 25, 27, 35, 41–2, 145–6, 183, 188–9, 193–7, 200–2, 205–7, 210–12, 239, 278, 290
Christology (*see also* son of man; titles of Christ) 78–96, 97–108, 109–21, 123–5, 127–9, 131–3, 139–46, 168, 173–6, 180, 192, 210–13, 245, 256, 258, 261, 263–4, 272
church 60, 71, 77, 95–6, 112, 119, 129, 131, 133, 137, 139–40, 142, 145, 155, 157, 166–8, 178, 181–2, 193, 198, 200, 206, 208–10, 213, 215, 218, 221, 225, 255–6, 258, 263, 265, 276–8
council 22
covenant 12, 21–2, 25, 67, 110, 129, 220, 271
creation 41, 96, 127, 132, 140–1, 144, 146, 164, 179, 182, 194, 210, 235, 251, 277, 282
cult
  of Christ 100, 115, 155, 209
  Jewish 12–13, 18, 32, 41, 112, 128–9, 131–2, 142, 173, 208, 209, 217, 219, 223
  ruler 33, 44–5, 47, 60–1, 89, 105–6, 114–17, 136–7, 144, 251

Davidic messiah 5–8, 13, 23–8, 33, 35, 37, 40, 42, 54, 77, 79–80, 82, 85–96, 111–12, 116, 145, 154, 156, 161, 164, 167–8, 176, 181, 201, 228–9, 230, 232–3, 236, 239, 245, 248, 263–6, 269, 271, 276, 280, 282–3
Davidic monarchy 5–6, 8, 12–3, 20–1, 30–1, 33, 40, 47, 229, 257
Dura-Europas 215–21, 224–5

elders (Christian) 125
eschatology 3, 8–9, 14, 16, 20, 22, 24, 26–8, 29, 41–3, 44, 66–8, 72–7, 80, 87, 92, 99, 107, 111, 115, 118–22, 124–5, 129, 133, 141–4, 149–50, 169, 180–7, 192–7, 204–8, 210–14, 230, 232–40, 243, 245, 248–9, 251, 254, 258, 265, 267–71, 273, 276–9, 282–3, 285, 288–91, 293–6
Essenes 21–2

Gnosticism 133, 192–3, 204, 228, 287
docetism 102, 106–7, 296
Greek text of Scripture 171
  LXX 6, 33, 40, 78, 93, 115, 128, 140, 164, 184, 190, 204, 245–261, 265, 268
  Aquila 204–5, 249, 255–61, 268
  Symmachus 255–61
  Theodotion 256, 259–60, 268

Hannukkah 19, 237
heavenly/pre-existent messiah 3, 42, 77, 89, 106, 111, 127, 132, 164, 180, 183, 188–9, 194, 200, 207, 211–14, 228, 230,

233, 251, 263–4
Heikhalot 227, 232–4, 242–3
high priest 16, 18, 20, 22,
    26–8, 30–1, 40, 67, 69,
    83, 106, 128–9, 142,
    145, 173, 175, 182,
    198, 203, 205, 212–13,
    240, 242, 245, 255,
    267–8, 270–1
human messiah 128–9, 183,
    203, 211–14, 228, 248,
    262–63

ingathering of the Jews 43,
    186, 228, 236–8, 267,
    270, 273, 280, 282–3

Jesus 15, 38, 43, 47, 49–52,
    54, 56, 60–1, 65–77,
    78–96, 97–108,
    109–21, 122–35,
    136–46, 154, 159, 162,
    165–9, 175–6, 181,
    191–4, 198–203,
    205–14, 218, 223–4,
    248, 254, 257, 259,
    266, 278–9, 287, 290
Jerusalem
    heavenly 200, 203, 233
    new 119, 142, 145,
        188–9, 210–11
judgement 20, 23–4, 38,
    40–2, 73, 111, 119,
    135, 142, 145, 182,
    185, 188, 199–203,
    205–8, 210–13, 230,
    239, 266, 278–80

king (messianic) 3–9, 11–14,
    24, 27, 32–3, 37, 39,
    52, 54, 79, 81–91,
    93–4, 96, 105–6, 109,
    115–16, 122, 128, 141,
    143–6, 170, 172–8,
    180–5, 198–202,
    204–5, 208, 210–14,
    220, 228, 246, 248,
    250–2, 254–5, 258,
    265, 271–3
Kingdom of God 27, 41,
    51–2, 68, 75, 80, 87,
    104, 111, 114–15, 118,
    143–4, 177, 202–3,
    210–11, 245, 281

Law (Torah) 24, 26–28, 87,
    98, 120, 124, 129, 161,
    164, 168–9, 185–6,
    196, 206, 216, 220–3,
    230–1, 235, 237–9,
    231, 249–50, 267, 273,
    280–1
liturgy 137, 176, 180–2, 204,
    231, 233, 237, 249,
    274, 279–81, 283

martyrs 68, 134–6, 141, 143,
    145–6, 154, 162, 179,
    202, 212, 221, 267
Melchizedek 23, 27, 82, 128
Merkabah mystics 111
Messiah
    priestly *see* high priest
    royal *see* (messianic)
        king
messianic hope 4, 7–9,
    11–14, 22–8, 29, 33,
    36–7, 42–4, 70, 75, 80,
    92, 109–10, 113,
    120–1, 149–51, 153–4,
    185, 192, 231, 274–84,
    296
messianism
    in biblical interpretation
        3–14, 22–8, 40–4, 77,
        78–96, 97–108,
        109–21, 122–35,
        136–46, 156, 160–1,
        163, 168–9, 174–80,
        182, 184, 186–9,
        192–5, 201–14, 220,
        230, 232, 235, 240,
        242, 245–61, 262–73,
        277–9, 281
    in social context 9–11,
        16–21, 28, 29–39, 43,
        149–57, 158–61, 241–4
    'theory of catastrophe'
        8, 239
'messianological vacuum' 6,
    13
miracles 45, 55–7, 72, 74,
    77, 81–2, 86, 98, 102,
    104, 218, 223, 228,
    253, 287
monotheism 100, 107–8,
    142, 144, 146, 179
Moses 11, 22, 98–9, 101,
    128, 140, 184, 186,
    216, 223–4, 258, 265,
    267, 276, 286–7

patriarchs
    biblical 84, 93, 111,
        128, 165, 169, 176,
        209, 216–17, 219,
        221–4, 249, 252, 257,
        267, 282, 286–7
    rabbinic 159–60, 170,
        236
Paul 55, 69, 74, 77, 82, 89,
    92–5, 102, 109–21,
    122, 126, 129–30, 132,
    134, 155, 179, 206,
    224, 265–6, 286
Peter 50, 68, 83, 91–93, 95,
    116–17, 122, 136, 130,
    131–4, 179, 208,
    224–5, 286
Pharisees 30, 36, 66, 69, 74
Piyyutim 227, 231–2, 234,
    243, 280–1, 283
prayer 13, 21, 44, 53, 56, 75,
    91, 113, 125, 174, 176,
    190, 225, 228–32, 234,
    242, 251, 269, 273,
    280, 282
prince 23–7, 32, 52, 82, 156,
    159–60, 168–9, 206,
    248, 253, 259, 271, 282
privileges (national Jewish)
    170, 196
prophecy 4–9, 11, 20, 23–8,
    38, 40–3, 53–4, 56, 68,
    70, 75–6, 81–2, 85–8,
    90–1, 98–9, 119, 131,
    138, 141–6, 151–4,
    161, 175, 177, 180,
    182–3, 185–9, 192–4,
    200–2, 205–14, 220,
    230, 232–5, 240, 252,
    254, 256, 269–73,
    278–9, 282–3, 285–96

Qumran community 21, 28,
    133

rabbinic messianism 8, 151,
    160, 168–9, 182,
    227–44
resistance 6, 65–77, 183, 273
    to Jesus/Gospel 55, 82,
        85, 90, 96
    political/military 5, 28,
        35–6, 43, 65–6, 69, 71,
        73–5, 77, 195–6, 273
    socio-economic 66–7,
        71, 77, 126

Index of Subjects

spiritual 74–5, 77, 130, 273
toward the world 126, 130, 134–5

resurrection 48, 52, 55, 59–60, 75, 77, 81, 91–4, 111, 114, 117, 119–20, 124–5, 133, 140–1, 145–6, 169, 179, 193, 202–3, 205–7, 210–13, 229, 232, 235, 281, 283
revolts 17–19, 21, 28–9, 36–43, 67, 104, 150–1, 153, 155, 160, 162, 186–92, 195–6, 198, 219, 241–3, 256, 262, 275

sacrifice 19, 30, 32, 47, 53–6, 128–9, 131–3, 135, 137, 142–5, 169, 173, 208, 216–17, 219, 221–4, 240, 281, 283
Sadducees 36, 69, 74
saints 117, 136–7, 142, 146, 188, 192, 194, 203, 211–12, 277
Samaritans 103, 105, 159, 206, 209, 243, 248
sanctuary 23, 34, 152, 154, 161, 175, 190, 267, 281
Sanhedrin 104, 276
son of man 23, 42, 66, 75–7, 100–2, 132, 199, 208, 213, 263
Spirit (the) 23, 49, 54, 81, 84, 87, 91–4, 100, 120, 137–8, 173, 211, 235–6, 282
suffering 25, 48, 50, 56, 77, 83–4, 92, 94, 96, 107, 119–21, 124–5, 130–4, 140, 143, 145–6, 162, 170, 210, 224, 249, 254, 260, 266, 270
'superhuman' messiah *see* heavenly messiah
symbol 32, 126, 138, 156, 173, 176, 178, 188, 192, 215–16, 220–4, 226, 246, 255, 257, 260, 270, 277, 292
synagogue
 buildings 91–4, 98–101, 103, 116, 159, 215, 217–22, 225–6, 228, 230–1, 238, 242, 274, 279–81, 293
 personified 101, 107–8

tabernacle 30, 173, 180, 223, 276
Teacher of righteousness 26, 76
Temple 12, 19–21, 23, 26, 31, 32–5, 39, 53, 74, 76, 90, 149, 152–4, 156, 161, 186, 188–90, 200–1, 209, 216, 218–20, 222–3, 225, 228–9, 231, 236, 240–4, 267–8, 275, 280, 282–3, 285, 290–3, 295–6
theocentrism 13, 281
theocracy 5, 13, 20, 27, 30, 35, 38–9, 52, 66, 82, 128
titles of the messiah/ of Christ 7, 24–5, 27–8, 33, 47–8, 54, 78–96, 97, 100–3, 105–6, 110–17, 123–4, 127, 138–45, 171–82, 186, 202, 204–6, 209, 246–52, 254, 260, 271–2, 294

war (eschatological) 25, 28, 41–2, 141, 143, 149–50, 187, 188–9, 205–6, 228, 230, 232, 234, 240, 269, 273, 278, 283, 289
wisdom 45–9, 57, 60, 80, 101, 125, 127, 132, 168, 186, 286

Zealot 37–8, 65–7, 71, 153–4, 188, 196, 238, 243
Zion 5, 8–9, 23, 39, 85, 106, 149, 179–80, 211, 228, 231–2, 236, 238–40, 242, 244, 250, 280, 282–3